Southern Literary Studies
Fred Hobson, Editor

SOUTHERN ABERRATIONS

Writers of the American South and the Problems of Regionalism

RICHARD GRAY

Louisiana State University Press   *Baton Rouge*   MM

Copyright © 2000 by Louisiana State University Press
All rights reserved
Manufactured in the United States of America
First printing

09   08   07   06   05   04   03   02   01   00
5   4   3   2   1

Designer: Michele Myatt Quinn
Typeface: Sabon
Typesetter: Coghill Composition Co., Inc.
Printer: Thomson-Shore, Inc.

Library of Congress Cataloging-in-Publication Data

Gray, Richard J.
    Southern aberrations : writers of the American South and
the problems of regionalism / Richard Gray.
        p.   cm. — (Southern literary studies)
    Includes bibliographical references and index.
    ISBN 0-8071-2552-0 (alk. paper) —
    ISBN 0-8071-2602-0 (pbk. : alk. paper)
    1. American literature—Southern States—History and
criticism.   2. Southern States—Intellectual life.   3.
Southern States—In literature.   4. Regionalism in
literature.   5. Canon (Literature).   I. Title.   II. Series.
    PS261.G687   2000
    810.9′75—dc21   99-059583

To Sheona

CONTENTS

PREFACE

All relationships with place are difficult, but some are more difficult than others. My aim has been to explore the difficulties. Concentrating on writers who, for very different reasons, have found their involvement with the American South particularly problematical, I have tried to explore the idea of regionalism. Asking myself the question of just what it means to belong to a place, a region, and, more specifically, what it implies for certain Americans to call themselves Southern, I have also attempted to examine some of the conflicting—and conflicted—notions of the South that have evolved over the past two centuries. In the process, I hope I have found something useful, different, and even provocative to say about the individual writers I look at—and, in particular, where they have stood or still do stand in relation to their homes and histories. At the same time, I hope I have managed to think again about the American South, and perhaps persuade others to think again too, by looking at it through the writings of those who have viewed it aslant.

The first chapter of this book concerns a writer who liked to call himself a Virginian even though he was not born in the South. Edgar Allan Poe was inclined to talk about his connections with the region in a distinctly slippery way. Believing, evidently, that he had to fashion his life as well as his art, he played many parts in the course of just over forty years, but the part to which he was most fiercely attached was that of Southern gentleman. My aim in discussing Poe has been to show how the writer's awkward relationship with the South helps explain some of the stranger tendencies of his work: the stress on difference, the hauteur, the plagiarism, the covert but hysterical racism. And Poe, like other writers I look at, is I think unique and symptomatic—his own utterly unrepeatable person as a writer but also someone whose poetry and prose betrays many of the instabilities that occur when a culture perceives itself as marginalized. A similar interest in the aberrations of an individual and a culture led me to look at Ellen Glasgow, the writer who is a focus—but, in this case, not the only one—of the next chapter. The difficulties of Glasgow's relationship with her home place issued, I believe, from a constellation of factors that made her experiences and work painfully personal and also revelatory in a more general way: traumatic change, the complex of social forces and sentiment I have called the matter of Virginia—and, not least, Glasgow's own status as a Southern woman of the privileged order, with all the subtle tensions of class and gender that implies. Some of these things she shared with Poe, some not; the end result, anyway, was to make her own encounters with the South as uneasy and even prickly as his.

In the third chapter of this book, I have looked at another form Southern aberration from a supposed cultural norm, or series of norms, has taken. What interests me here is how *a* South, or, to be more exact, one or two fairly specific versions of regional identity, were argued as *the* South for a while. The Nashville Agrarians, and those who succeeded them in the critical wars, fought against what they saw as the cultural hegemony of the North. And they fought so successfully on their own postage stamp of soil that they established their own form of hegemony. Southern writings of the tenor and tradition they approved of assumed canonical status. Other writing in the South was deemed to fail as *Southern literature* (with full weight given to both words, both terms on the badge of honor). It was, and to an extent still is, marginalized; shifted at least two places from the mainstream of culture, it was seen as aberrant, on the edges of a regional tradition that was itself located on the edge—a proud aberration from the strange gods of Americanism and modernism. I have tried to look at how and why this making of a regional canon came about. And since my main aim has been always to come back to individual works of the imagination, I have focused on two writers, in particular: two very different, equally and passionately conservative spokesmen who helped to foreground the agenda at work here, Andrew Nelson Lytle and Stark Young. My intention is not to expose; that would be futile and off the point, because writers like Lytle and Young made little secret of what they were trying to do, and what they were trying to defend demands our attention and, at least some of it, our respect and sympathy. It is to understand, and to understand above all the ironies implicit in this episode of cultural mythmaking: this is the strange story of writers who established their legitimacy, their centrality on the regional stage, by making the most of their peripheral position on the national one—only to find themselves nevertheless separated from the communities for which they claimed to be making their stand. Lytle, for instance, embraced a form of populist conservatism that led him to celebrate Native Americans as the true conservatives and to reject not only mainstream American notions of success but the paternalist, plantation model of the South because, as he saw it, both were fatally progressive and disruptive. Stark Young, in turn, dwelt on the theatricality of the plantation model and the patriarchal ideal and, in doing so, inadvertently called into question the relationship between the ideology and the history of his—or, for that matter, any—region.

The two chapters following this one deal with some of the writers who have been marginalized by the making of a Southern canon—at best, patronized and, at worst, dismissed as aberrations from an (aberrant) tradition. Between the two world wars, a considerable number of writers in the South devoted themselves to an imaginative recovery of the poorer people of the South. Most of the people they wrote about lived in the rural areas, nearly all were white; many of the best of the writers themselves were women. The writer with whom I begin and end the discussion of versions of the Southern poor in Chapter 4, Erskine Caldwell, is only the best known of them; and it may be symptomatic of how they have all been pushed to the regional margins that even he has enjoyed only a dubious reputation—a fame bordering sometimes on notoriety. My aim in this chapter is to explore these writers in the hope of discovering what they can tell us about class and gender relationships, and the struggle for power, in the region. More simply, it is to help bring into view a body of writing that, for reasons I try to explain, has suffered neglect. Much the same goes for the writers I talk about in the fifth chapter of this book: men and women who wrote about the Southern mountain areas and their inhabitants between the two world wars and beyond. The Southern highlands are, of course, a more obviously localized and marginal area; they have their own special history, a part of but more clearly apart from the larger historical narratives of the South. But they too and their inhabitants deserve the title of Southern as much or little as any place or person has done; and accounts of and fictions about them offer further, and to

my mind fascinating, variations on the themes of regionalism and difference. Along with the versions of poor folk discussed in the fourth chapter, they help to pluralize our idea of a regional culture and to see
Southern mythmaking as a process, a developing series of discrete stories.
For these reasons—and, as I hope to show, for others—attention needs
to be paid to these tales of hinterland and highland, poor rural people
and mountain folk, as a special and especially powerful branch of Southern literature; and, in the fourth and fifth chapters, I have attempted to
pay it.

The two final chapters bring things up to the present and to some new
difficulties: those experienced by contemporary Southern writers, as they
struggle to cope with a series of changes that have tended to call the
whole idea of regionalism, and the notion of a separate South, into question. I have tried to look at those changes, and their implications, in
detail. But here, as elsewhere in this book, my focus first and last has
been on writers and texts: the imagining of the South in very personal
terms. That personal imagining becomes, finally, my own. In a concluding note, I have attempted to sum up what I see as some of the main
issues at work here. Perhaps I should add that I have not tried to pull
everything together. That, in my view, would be both undesirable as an
aim and impossible as an accomplishment, since my emphasis throughout this book is on variance and pluralism: how a culture resists, continually defines itself against other cultures, and is made up of resistances,
conflicting interests, and internal differences. I have, however, tried to
make a contribution to what I see as the still developing story of the
South—and, along with that, to offer a few notes toward a definition of
regionalism.

Perhaps I should make a couple of final, further points about the title
of this book and my aim in writing it, although these are themes to which
I will periodically return. When I first mentioned the title to some of my
Southern friends, the response of several of them was the wry observation
that all Southerners are aberrant—coupled with the point that perhaps
"Southern aberration" was no more aberrant than, say, New England
eccentricity. That, in a way, is my point. My concern is with two kinds
of "aberration": the supposed "aberration" of the South, and in particular its literature, from national or international norms and the equally
supposed "aberration" of certain kinds of Southern writers and writing
from a regional mainstream. My argument, quite simply, is that *aberration* is a fundamentally slippery term because it is contextually, recipro-

cally defined. It is a function of discourse rather than a matter of fact; the "norm" or "center" is positioned and defined as being whatever the "aberration" or "margin" is not, and vice versa, in a complex dialectic of reinforcement. And it is according to this dialectic that the South can be and has been defined from a national (or other) "norm"—and that certain kinds of Southern writing, in turn, have been constructed as "aberrant," while others are construed as occupying the regional center. In making this argument, I have attempted to review the business of what I eventually come to call "Southern self-fashioning." This reflects my own long interest in the *construction* of the South—its reinvention through memory, say, through writing, talking, and telling about it. I have also tried to shift the critical paradigms a little, by discussing and attempting to rehabilitate neglected writers and areas of writing, by pluralizing the notion of Southern culture—and, of course, by looking in Chapter 3 at the initial making of a Southern literary mainstream or center from which those neglected writers were seen (if they were seen at all) to deviate. I said earlier that my aim in Chapter 3 was not to castigate writers like the Agrarians and New Critics, and an earlier generation of critics of Southern literature, for what they were trying to do in constructing a Southern canon, since that would be futile and pointless. I ought to add now, just in case it is not clear, that it would also be profoundly ahistorical. What I am trying to do is to appreciate, by historically situating, why and how this making of a canonical tradition came about—to honor it (since, after all, we owe those earlier writers and critics a profound debt) and also to place it. This also, I think, helps me to place my own approach. Every generation makes its own literary history, a making that involves the mapping of debts to and differences from earlier generations; and that is what—as a member of the present generation of critics of Southern writing—I aim to do here. The past is not the present, nor should it be, but, as every reader of Southern literature knows, the past is always there, helping to form our beliefs and judgments. And the best way to deal with its formative influence is to figure it: to know and respect the shaping minds of an earlier generation—and to know them, first and fundamentally (and despite the critical continuities), as different and historically specific people of their own time rather than ours.

I have accumulated many debts during the preparation of this book. Many people have helped me toward whatever understanding I have of the South, literature, and the problem of regionalism. A few of them have also seen drafts of some or all the chapters. They include Tony Badger,

Bob Brinkmeyer, Herbie Butterfield, Dan Carter, Jim Cobb, Susan Donaldson, Richard Godden, Cherry Good, Jan Gretlund, Lothar Honnighausen, Anne Goodwyn Jones, Richard H. King, Carter Martin, Michael O'Brien, Noel Polk, Peter Nicolaisen, Diane Roberts, Hans Skei, Tony Tanner, Helen Taylor, Tjebbe Westendorp, Charles Wilson, Bertram Wyatt-Brown, and Waldemar Zacharasiewicz. Sincere thanks are due to them, and to Fred Hobson both as a guide to the South and a supportive editor. They are also due to Trudie Calvert for being a meticulous copy editor, to Owen Robinson for compiling the index, and John Easterly and the editorial team at Louisiana State University Press for a rare combination of informal friendliness and scrupulous efficiency. I am indebted to the British Academy and the Humanities Research Board for providing support in the form of a research grant and then later a research award, and to the universities of Bonn, Edinburgh, Keele, Nottingham, Odense, Oxford, and South Carolina for allowing me to try out some of my ideas on impressively informed and constructively critical audiences. Above all, and as usual, I owe a huge debt to my family. My older daughter, Catharine, and my older son, Ben, I want to thank for keeping me interested in new writing and new ideas. My younger children, Jessica and Jack, I want to thank for the sheer delight of their constant company. Finally, to my wife, Sheona, for her warmth, kindness, understanding, and support, I owe a debt of enormous gratitude. She, and my children, have reminded me that there are things more important than books, but also that books help us realize their importance.

Richard Gray
Wivenhoe

SOUTHERN ABERRATIONS

1

"I am a Virginian"

Edgar Allan Poe and the South

Talking about regionalism once, the critic Raymond Williams raised the question of the cultural assumptions that, as he saw it, lay behind the term. The word *region,* he pointed out, was usually applied to an area that was judged to exist somehow on the fringes; *regional* and *regionalist,* in turn, were applied by "us," the members of a dominant cultural group, to "them"—some unfortunate lesser breed or area that was interesting precisely because it was not at the center of things. "The life and people of certain favoured regions are seen as essentially general," Williams pointed out, "even perhaps normal, while the life and people of certain other regions are, well, regional."[1] If Williams was right in arguing that regionalism must be seen in this way, as a product and expression, however apparently innocent, of centralized cultural dominance—and there is, surely, more than a grain of truth in what he said—then to say that a body of *writing* is "regional" can be viewed in similar terms: as a way, that is, of defining such writing as aberrant, a deviation from the way the dominant culture has chosen to define the norm. It is to place it, however instinctively or even benignly, in a special kind of cultural ghetto: if only because a "regional" literature is one that is defined, in the first instance, in terms of its difference, its separation from

1. Raymond Williams was, of course, consistently and passionately interested in this issue. However, the two books where it seems to me he explores the literary dimensions of the issue most fully and provocatively (and from which the quotations used here are taken) are *The English Novel: From Dickens to Lawrence* (London, 1970) and *The Country and the City* (London, 1973).

the national canon. A "regional" literature is one that has been assigned a peripheral status, banished to the edges of literary history. The measure of its "regional" status is the extent of its deviation from the national norm—a norm which, by a curious but common irony, its deviations may actually have helped to determine. The "central" or "mainstream" culture defines and maintains its centrality through a measured series of contrasts and comparisons with its "regional" counterpart; it is whatever the "regional culture" is not, just as it is not whatever the "regional" culture is. The circularities here are obvious: the cultural "norm" helps to define the "regional" while the "regional" helps to define the "norm" in a process that could be variously described as reciprocal, or tautological. Obviously circular and potentially redundant as this process is, however, as a matter of cultural practice it occurs whenever one group seeks to draw its borders by deciding what lies outside them and is consequently "other." That is, it happens all the time. Even within the relatively small world of American literary history, there are many examples of those often unspoken assumptions of a cultural "center" basic to the language of regionalism: that tendency to accept some texts as somehow determining national identity and others as somehow aberrant or peripheral, odd or abnormal or strange. But perhaps that tendency has found strongest expression, and that language its loudest voice, in the acceptance of Southern writing as distinctively regional: an acceptance that characterizes many writers from the South themselves as they struggle with the sense of being "other," writing somewhere of and from the margins.

This sense of writing somewhere on the periphery shadows, for instance, the work of someone who was not even born in the South but chose nevertheless to perceive himself in Southern terms. Edgar Allan Poe was not a literary regionalist in the sense that many later writers from the South were to become; he was profoundly uninterested in local color, or in giving any of his work an obviously local habitation and a name. He was, though, obsessed by his connections with things Southern and habitually talked about them, or felt moved by them; and he talked about those connections, more often than not, in a distinctively slippery way. The very self-consciousness and awkwardness of Poe's attachment to the South, in fact, begins to unravel some of the difficulties involved in calling a writer "regional"; even more than is usually the case, the regional identity was, for him, an act of will, a strategy of naming. "I am a Virginian," Poe wrote in a letter in 1841—then adding, "At least, I call myself one, for I have resided all my life, until within the last few years, in Richmond."[2] Any account of Poe's "Southern" status has to start, surely, with this: that Poe often thought of himself as a Southerner. Believing, evidently, that he had to invent his life as well as his art, he played many parts in the course of just over forty years: but the part to which he was most fiercely and consistently attached was that of Southern gentleman. There was some basis in personal experience for the pursuit of this particular role. Poe had, after all, been raised in considerable comfort in Richmond, Virginia, in a household with slaves; he had been educated there, for a while, and then briefly at the University of Virginia. And this at least partly Southern education had been supplemented by a period of attendance at West Point: in the sense that, as more than one historian has noted, the military tradition has always been strong in the South—quite apart from any other reason, because it tends to reinforce Southerners' obsession with the concept of honor.[3] Admittedly, the dubious privilege of being waited on by African American slaves was something

2. *The Letters of Edgar Allan Poe* edited by John Ward Ostrom, 2 vols. (Cambridge, Mass., 1948), I, 170. To Frederick W. Thomas, June–July 1841. The question of Poe's "Southernness" has been a matter of considerable debate. Two commentaries that emphasize the paucity of direct references to the South in the prose and fiction are J. V. Ridgely, *Nineteenth-Century Southern Literature* (Lexington, Ky., 1980); and Edward Rans and Andrew Hook, "The Old South," in *Introduction to American Studies* edited by Malcolm Bradbury and Howard Temperley (London, 1981). On the other hand, arguments for a Southern dimension to Poe's work are to be found in Marshall McLuhan, "Edgar Allan Poe," *Sewanee Review*, LII (1944), 24–33, and "The Southern Quality," *Sewanee Review*, LV (1947), 56–65; Jay B. Hubbell, *The South in American Literature 1607–1900* (Durham, N.C., 1954); Harry Levin, *The Power of Blackness: Hawthorne, Poe, Melville* (New York, 1958); and Joan Dayan, "Amorous Bondage: Poe, Ladies, and Slaves" and David Leverenz, "Poe and Gentry Virginia," in *The American Face of Edgar Allan Poe* edited by Shawn Rosenheim and Stephen Rachman (Baltimore, Md., 1995). As G. R. Thompson puts it: "Poe is the antebellum South's one original writer, and he is the one writer whose Southernness is suspect." "Edgar Allan Poe and the Writers of the Old South," in *Columbia Literary History of the United States,* edited by Emory Elliott (New York, 1988), 264.

3. See, e.g., John Hope Franklin, *The Militant South* (Cambridge, Mass., 1956); David Donald, "The Southerner as Fighting Man," in *The Southerner as American* edited by Charles G. Sellers (Chapel Hill, N.C., 1960); and J. Sherwood Williams et al., "Southern Subculture and Urban Pistol Owners," in *Perspectives on the American South: Volume 2* edited by Merle Black and John Shelton Reed (New York, 1984). On the role of gentleman, Julian Symons has observed: "Among the many parts he was to play in life, that of Southern gentleman was the earliest and the one to which he adhered most consistently." *The Tell-Tale Heart: The Life and Works of Edgar Allan Poe* (London, 1978), 15. See also Arthur H. Quinn, *Edgar Allan Poe: A Critical Biography* (New York, 1941), 204, 249; David Sinclair, *Edgar Allan Poe* (London, 1977), 56; Kenneth Silverman, *Edgar Allan Poe: Mournful and Never-Ending Remembrance* (New York, 1991), 30, 123, 332.

Poe was to grow unfamiliar with in his adult years, when his connections with the Southern ruling class became (to say the least) tenuous; and his Southern education was scrappy and incomplete. But like Mark Twain, Poe seems to have been profoundly affected by those early years spent amid a conservative, slaveholding community; and, unlike Twain, he clung to its conservatism, and many of its prejudices, even after he had become, to all intents and purposes, an exile, an outsider. This is perhaps most poignantly illustrated in his letters: where Poe tries to play the part of being Southern aristocrat while soliciting financial assistance, or complaining about his treatment at the hands of those with wealth and power. In 1827, for instance, he wrote this to his foster-father John Allan: "You suffer me to be subjected to the whims and caprice, not only of your white family, but the complete authority of the blacks—these grievances I could not submit to; and I am gone."[4] The touchy pride, the angry sense of offenses to personal honor, the racial bigotry (it is clearly the submission to "the complete authority of the blacks" that rankles most): all these are part of a persona that Poe constructs for himself in his correspondence—as a face-saving device, it may be, a way of preserving self-respect, and even as a prop to identity, a way of convincing himself and others that he is somebody and does have substantial presence.

This attempt to construct a Southern identity for himself takes many forms in Poe's correspondence. There is, for instance, his insistent adoption of the philosophical conservatism and resistance to the idea of Progress that found little widespread support in nineteenth-century America outside of the Southern patriarchal tradition. "I have no faith in human perfectibility," he wrote to James Russell Lowell in 1844, "I think that human exertion will have no appreciable effect upon humanity. Man is now only more active—not more happy—nor more wise, than he was 6000 years ago."[5] On a more practical level, there are his unremitting but, in the end, unsuccessful attempts to establish a Southern magazine that might rival the products of Boston and New York: to be published in the South, written largely by Southerners, and enjoyed by Southern gentlemen. This was one way, as he saw it, of challenging the hegemony of the North. Another was to give a public dimension to his role of aristocrat, to offer it to his readers as an alternative version of the American character: a rival possibility to the roles of democratic Yankee, rumina-

4. *Letters,* I, 8. To John Allan, 19 March 1827.
5. *Letters,* I, 256. To James Russell Lowell, 2 July 1844.

tive New Englander, or Boston Brahmin. This he did, most noticeably, in his essays and reviews, where again and again we find him playing the part of indolent but intelligent aristocrat, the dandy who—in conspicuous contrast to the earnest theocrats and frantic scribblers to the North—wears his learning easily, like an expensive suit of clothes. "During a rainy afternoon, not long ago," begins one contribution to the *Democratic Review*, "being in a mood too listless for continuous study, I sought relief from *ennui* in dipping here and there, at random, among the volumes of my library—no very large one, certainly, but sufficiently miscellaneous; and, I flatter myself, not a little *recherché*"[6] A library just like that of Poe's aristocratic heroes, in fact; and as if to prove just how *recherché* it is, Poe scatters his writing with (frequently inaccurate) references to obscure or difficult texts. Not only that, like his disciple Baudelaire, he seems sometimes only too eager to shock his more bourgeois readers or, at least, to dislodge their complacency, their innate American belief in the unchallengeable nature of democracy. "The sense of high birth is a moral force," he declares in one piece, "whose value the democrats, albeit compact of mathematics, are never in condition to calculate. '*Pour savoir ce qu'est Dieu*,' says the Baron de Bielfeld, '*il faut être Dieu même.*' "[7]

Of course, it could be argued that the role of Southern dandy sat uneasily on a man who was not born in the South, never really belonged to the Southern patriarchy, and attempted to earn his living as an editor and writer. There is some truth to this. Quite apart from anything else, the part of professional writer that Poe either chose or was forced to adopt ran directly contrary to the Southern belief that literature was the prerogative of the gifted amateur; like William Gilmore Simms—who complained once that being an intellectual in the South was about as rewarding as "drawing water in a sieve"—he discovered that there was an inherent and sad contradiction in his desire to become a Southern aristocratic man of letters. It needs to be pointed out, however, that if Poe simply played the part of gentleman, then so do most (and perhaps all) of those commonly described as gentlemen; as J. M. Huizinga has argued, an aristocratic culture is one in which people *imitate* some idea of aristocracy, some "illusion of heroic being, full of dignity and honour,

---

6. "Marginalia," *Democratic Review*, November 1844, in *The Complete Works of Edgar Allan Poe* edited by James A. Harrison (1902; New York 1979 edition), XVI, 3.

7. Ibid., XVI, 13.

of wisdom and, at all events, of courtesy."[8] And to this it needs to be added that if Poe's Southern patriarchal status was primarily a product of his imagination, a matter of knowing rather more than being, then so was that of, say, the so-called First Families of Virginia or that of the supreme fictional embodiment of Southern aristocratic ambition, the protagonist of William Faulkner's *Absalom, Absalom!,* Thomas Sutpen. The point is not an idle or perverse one. The fact is that the Old South invented itself, in the way that perhaps all patriarchal cultures do, by trying to interpret and regulate life according to some idealized version of the past. This is why so much recent historiography has concerned itself with the *idea* of the South, thinking in and about the Southern states: because the "Old South," or to be more accurate "the aristocratic Old South," was and is primarily a concept, a convenient but by no means always appropriate mythology, a device for mediating and structuring experience.[9] The South, observed one Southern writer, John Donald Wade, is "one of the really great abstractions of our race"[10]—a remark that, in its casual elision of "race" as species and "race" as (white) ethnic group, reveals far more than Wade probably intended. And Poe was perhaps never more of a Southerner than when he was imitating one: applying himself assiduously to the role of Virginia dandy, even when much of the historical evidence was against him.

Just as important as the particular persona Poe tried to construct for himself in his private and public writings—that is, as far as the problem of his "Southerness" is concerned—is the position that this self-appointed, self-anointed aristocrat chose to adopt in the literary battles of his day. Much of the time, and especially while struggling—unsuccessfully—to found a magazine, Poe chose to act as an intellectual flag-bearer for the region. "It is high time that the literary South took its own interests into its own charge," he insisted while editing the *Southern Literary Messenger,* and then followed this up a few months later by announcing boldly, "we are embarking in the cause of *Southern* Litera-

---

8. J. M. Huizinga, *The Waning of the Middle Ages* (New York, 1954), 39. See also Drew Gilpin Faust, *A Sacred Circle: The Dilemma of the Intellectual in the Old South, 1840–1860* (Philadelphia, 1977), 148.

9. See, e.g, Michael O'Brien, *The Idea of the American South: 1920–1941* (Baltimore, Md., 1979); Fred Hobson, *Tell About the South: The Southern Rage to Explain* (Baton Rouge, La., 1983); Jack Temple Kirby, *Media-Made Dixie: The South in the American Imagination* (1979; Athens, Ga., 1986 revised edition).

10. Cited in O'Brien, *Idea of the American South,* 215.

ture and (with perfect amity to all sections) wish to claim especially as a friend and co-operator, every *Southern* Journal."[11] There were certain specific reasons why Poe adopted this stance: fear of "being ridden to death by New-England," resentment of what he saw as some New Englanders' attempts to persuade the world that "there is *no such thing* as Southern literature," and perhaps the rather more calculated belief that controversy would help him make a name for himself—just as it had helped make a name for those Scottish reviewers who had attacked Leigh Hunt and his circle. But whatever the particular reasons, there is little doubt that this stance made him a formative influence as far as the ideas of a recognizably "Southern" literature and "Southern" culture are concerned. He lost no opportunity of pouring vitriol on New England—and Boston in particular, which he labeled "Frogpondium." "We like Boston," he insisted with irony that was heavy to the point of being elephantine, "We were born there—and perhaps it is just as well not to mention that we are heartily ashamed of the fact. The Bostonians are very well in their way. Their hotels are bad. Their pumpkin pies are delicious. Their poetry is not so good. . . . But with all these good qualities the Bostonians have no soul. . . . The Bostonians are well-bred—as *very* dull persons very generally are."[12] And along with these aristocratic sneers at bourgeois notions of correct behavior went a not entirely unself-interested defense of Southern writers, who, Poe claimed, had never received proper recognition largely because they *were* Southern. "Had he been even a Yankee," he declared of William Gilmore Simms, "His genius would have been rendered *immediately* manifest to his countrymen, but unhappily (*perhaps*) he was a southerner, and united the southern pride—the southern dislike to the making of bargains—with the southern supineness and general want of tact in all matters relating to the making of money."[13]

It does not take a great deal of ingenuity to see that Poe's championing

11. *Southern Literary Messenger,* II (June 1836), 460. Cited in Sidney P. Moss, *Poe's Literary Battles: The Critic in the Context of His Literary Milieu* (Durham, N.C., 1963), 52–53. See also 33.

12. *Broadway Journal,* 1 November 1843, in *Complete Works,* XIV, 11. See also Michael Allen, *Poe and the British Magazine Tradition* (New York, 1969), 51; review of *A Fable for Critics, Southern Literary Messenger,* March 1849, in *Complete Works,* XIV, 172.

13. Review of *The Wigwam and the Cabin, Godey's Lady Book,* January 1846, in *Complete Works,* XIV, 95.

of the Southern cause was getting him into difficulties here. It was all very well to adopt the pose of indolent dandy: but that sat uneasily with his insistence that the South could establish its intellectual independence only if it shook off its "long-indulged literary supineness"[14] and acted with vigor, thoroughness, and enthusiasm. Aristocratic carelessness was something that he could simultaneously praise and criticize, admire and lament, as the rather ambiguous tone of the passage just quoted indicates. In this, he was not alone: the very same blend of affection and irritation is to be found in the work of many Southern writers of the period— including John Pendleton Kennedy and William Gilmore Simms. In novels like Kennedy's *Swallow Barn* (1832) and Simms's *The Sword and the Distaff* (1853), the Southerner and, in particular, the Southern planter, was simultaneously cherished for his easy habits, his generosity, and candor, and challenged for his want of energy, calculation, and ambition; the aristocratic idea was celebrated and then, in the very next moment, treated with profound misgivings. The Old South's own uneasy relationship with the rest of the nation largely accounts for this. Placed in the position of an aberrant minority, forced to recognize that theirs was an old and shrinking economy set amid a young and growing nation, challenged on every front—morally, intellectually, racially, and politically— Southerners felt themselves compelled to defend their position and yet at the same time explain why they were in decline, to stick by the choices they had apparently made while trying to work out why those choices had not enabled them to prosper. Even those committed most fiercely to the pose of feudal aristocrat could not entirely suppress the hope that the Southern economy and Southern society might be revitalized. Even those who, like Poe, insisted that they had, quite simply, been born out of their due time into a contemptibly bourgeois culture could not wholly resist the idea of cultural renewal. And from this, surely, spring the contradictions at the heart of so much Southern writing of the time, its strange mixture of defiance and depression—as well as, more locally, the uneasy, equivocal tone that characterizes so much of Poe's own flag-waving for the South.

---

14. Review of *Georgia Scenes*, *Southern Literary Messenger*, March, 1836, in *Complete Works*, VIII, 259. For some of the more general issues mentioned here, see, e.g., Charles Sydnor, *The Development of Southern Sectionalism, 1819–1848*, Vol. V (1948) in *The History of the South* edited by Wendell Holmes Stephenson and E. Merton Coulter, 11 vols. (Baton Rouge, La., 1947–95).

A word of caution needs to be entered here about this sometimes fre-
netic flag-waving. Most of Poe's propaganda for the South coincided
with the earlier part of his career; and, even then, he often claimed that
he was attacking "Frogpondium" in the name of places other than the
South, simply challenging the cultural hegemony of New England rather
than speaking in the voice of the embryonic regionalist. After he moved
to New York, he even presented himself as a literary nationalist, eager to
promote the idea of a genuinely American literature. This word of caution, however, needs itself to be treated with caution. Poe's claims, in
some of his earlier essays, to be speaking for the West as well as the South
ring decidedly hollow, when set against his insistence elsewhere that he
was embracing the cause of a specifically Southern literature. And they
ring more hollowly still when it is remembered how very little interest
Poe took, not only in the landscapes but also in the imagery of the frontier. In his poetry, there is only the exotic allegory of "Eldorado," in
which the western explorer becomes "a gallant knight," and the western
lands are drained of all local atmosphere as well as all local color; and in
his prose, there is little more than the equally exotic and, in addition,
abortive and unpublished "Journal of Julius Rodman." Even his claim
that he was an Americanist, made after he had arrived in New York, is,
as Perry Miller suggested, highly suspect.[15] It seems likely, in fact, that he
made this claim only so as to guarantee the support of Evert Duycinck:
an important consideration for any young man trying to establish himself
in one of the few cities in nineteenth-century America where it was possible to earn a living as a writer. This is not to discount such claims entirely;
after all, it could be argued that "Poe the nationalist" and "Poe the friend
of the West" were no more the products of artifice, personal invention,
than "Poe the Southern gentleman" was. But it is to suggest that they
were less central to Poe's life, less symptomatic of his deepest impulses.
His roles of spokesman for the South, and Southern dandy, were adopted
early and then held fast to through most of his career. His desire to speak
from and for the region clearly issued from the pressures of his own background, the urgencies of his own being. This surely makes such roles and
desires rather more crucial, as a key to what often seems the mystery of
Poe, than attachments and allegiances that, whatever their interest, were
initially the result of calculation, a wish to flatter others and so help him
make his way in the world.

15. Perry Miller, *The Raven and the Whale: The War of Words and Wits in the Era of
Poe and Melville* (New York, 1956), 116, 268.

When anyone mentions Poe, however, it is not the editorial work or the reviewing that first springs to mind for most people. It is, of course, the poetry and, perhaps even more, Poe's fiction. Whether there is anything peculiarly Southern about Poe's poems, anything that attaches them to their creator's search for a regional habitation and a name, remains a subject of especially fierce debate. A few critics, at least, have suggested that there is. Killis Campbell, for instance, argues that Poe's "scrupulous avoidance of the didactic"[16] is a mark of his regionalism, setting him at odds with the moralists of New England; while Edmund Stedman traces the sometimes excessive musicality of his poems back to the Southern love of rhetoric, words chosen for their melody or melodramatic resonance rather than their meaning. Much more interestingly, David Leverenz deploys some of the ideas of Pierre Bourdieu to forge a connection between Poe's pursuit of a Southern version of what Bourdieu terms "postaristocratic" society and Poe's own preference for textuality and cultural play. In a postaristocratic society, Bourdieu argues, "cultural capital" secures and intimates the highest social status. Aesthetic taste or skill "rigorously distinguishes the different classes" by dividing the naïve from the sophisticated; while aesthetic detachment bestows distinction, "a distant, self-assured relation to the world." "The *petit bourgeois* do not know how to play the game of culture as game," Bourdieu provocatively suggests. "They take culture too seriously to go in for bluff and imposture or even for the distance and casualness which show true familiarity." Confusing cultural capital with the simple accumulation of information, they "cannot suspect the irresponsible self-assurance, the insolent off-handedness and even the hidden dishonesty presupposed by the merest page of an inspired essay on philosophy, art or literature." As self-made men, entrepreneurs and fashioners of their material identity, "they cannot have the familiar relation to culture which authorises the liberties and audacities of those who are linked to it by birth."[17]

This elides, Leverenz points out, with the role of the *flâneur* that Poe

16. Killis Campbell, *The Mind of Poe, and Other Studies* (1933; New York, 1962 edition), 115. Campbell also cites Edmund Stedman's argument mentioned here. See also Leverenz, "Poe and Gentry Virginia," 219–21.

17. Pierre Bourdieu, *Distinction: A Social Criticism of the Judgement of Taste* translated by Richard Nice (Cambridge, Mass., 1984), 330–31. See also 40, 56. For a fascinating, and somewhat different, reading of Poe's relations with the bourgeoisie, see Jonathan Elmer, *Reading at the Social Limit: Affect, Mass Culture, and Edgar Allan Poe* (Stanford, Calif., 1995).

liked to play in his literary journalism, his elegant posturing ("being in a mood too listless for continuous study, I sought relief from *ennui* . . ."), and his tendency to sprinkle (frequently spurious) high-culture allusions over his work like so much stardust. Perhaps even more to the point here, it also helps to locate the casual vitriol of Poe's attacks on his contemporaries (as the British cliché has it, "a gentleman is someone who is never *unintentionally* rude"), his flirtation with the vulgar in both his essays and his stories (as a kind of literary equivalent of slumming), and that pervasive slipperiness of tone that makes it difficult for readers to accommodate what is being said to conventional—Bourdieu might say, petit bourgeois—distinctions between the serious and the playful. The pleasure in aesthetic detachment, Bourdieu suggests, stems from "refined games for refined players."[18] And that phrase might stand as an epigraph to much of Poe's work, in prose and in verse. To this extent, there is surely a connection between the poetry, Poe's regional self-identification, and the curious forms of marginality, cultural exile, and dislocation sought by those whom Bourdieu identifies as of postaristocratic status. It is not simply that, in some of his poems, Poe adopts the Byronic pose or skates over the thin ice of borrowings from Byron. Nor is it just that his dislike of utilitarianism, functionalism of form and content, sets him at odds with what he saw as the pedants and poetasters to the North—and, more generally, with a national culture preoccupied with "use." These things matter, as far as the vexed question of Poe's "Southernness" is concerned. So does the sometimes excessive musicality of his poetic work: we have only to remember Ralph Waldo Emerson's contemptuous dismissal of Poe as "the jingle-man" to realize just how far a taste for verbal play set him apart from the high seriousness of at least some New England writers. They matter less, however, than the subterranean thread that links the politics and aesthetics of a man for whom, evidently, the ideal poem was one in which the words efface themselves, disappear as they are read: leaving only a feeling of significant absence, "no-thing."

It is important to get this connection right—especially as far as the poetry is concerned, since that poetry seems to inhabit such an exclusive, apolitical, and even airless environment. Biographers have clearly demonstrated how Poe would vacillate between the contradictory demands imposed by the role of gentleman: a courtly charmer with the ladies, a fastidious dilettante in some of his reviews and essays, and a bold verbal

18. Bourdieu, *Distinction*, 499.

fencer springing to the defense of Southern honor in others, ever prone to fits of haughtiness or heroic drinking. It is equally possible, surely, to link the vacillations here to two contradictions fundamental to the culture Poe tried so eagerly to embrace: the culture, that is, of early nineteenth-century Virginia. The First Families of Virginia as they eventually became known—that is, those people who formed the ruling class by the end of the seventeenth century—were almost certainly not aristocratic by origin, or, if there were aristocrats among them, they were very few. They were, as one historian writing in the early eighteenth century suggested, "of low Circumstances . . . such as were willing to seek their Fortunes in a Foreign Country"[19]—especially during the first years of colonization. Nevertheless, they tried quite deliberately to assume the prerogatives and manners of an aristocracy. To be more exact, they tried to accommodate themselves to a deeply ambivalent model of aristocracy, derived from England—which, as another historian, writing in 1724, caustically observed, "they esteem their home:"[20] a model that was an awkward and potentially disabling compound of gracious feudal aristocrat and bluff country squire. The ambivalences ran deep; and they were compounded by the fact that, by the time Poe was writing, the Virginia "aristocracy" occupied the position of a conscious and declining minority in a young and growing nation. The political importance of Virginia was reduced by the fact that emigrants to America usually moved into the West or East rather than the South, and by the fact that many Virginians themselves emigrated westward. At the same time, its economic status was badly damaged by the impoverishment of its soil—partly the result of improvident farming methods—by the growth of competition from the younger agricultural areas, and by the loss of special treatment in the markets of England. "A new order of things is come," John Randolph of Roanoke (a man who confessed "an hereditary attachment to the state of Virginia") declared gloomily in 1827: "The old gentry are gone and the *nouveaux riches,* where they have the inclination, do not know how to live. . . . Poverty stalking the land. . . . We hug our lousy cloaks around us, take another 'chaw of tobacker,' float the room with nastiness, or ruin the grate and fireplace, where they happen not to be nasty, and try conclu-

19. Robert Beverley II, *The History and Present State of Virginia* (London, 1722), 247. See also Silverman, *Poe,* 30, 123, 332.

20. Hugh Jones, *The Present State of Virginia* (1724; London, 1865 edition), 43.

sions upon constitutional points."[21] So if Poe was attempting to imitate anything, it was a model of behavior that, besides being profoundly flawed, was coming to seem decidedly anomalous. Besides that, it was one that Fredric Jameson would term a simulacrum: that is, a copy of something for which, in the culture in question, the original never existed. Like several of his own fictional heroes, in short, in declaring "I am a Virginian" Poe found himself trapped in the search for a phantom—a confused and confusing figure that disappeared even as he pursued it. He was, in short, Bourdieu's "postaristocrat" with a vengeance.

Which returns us to the poetry: perhaps here, more than anywhere, Poe's attempts to accumulate "cultural capital" are clear. Using the play of textuality to announce his status, he invokes a world of aristocratic ease and contemplation where refined players can play refined—because quite literally meaningless—games. "It is the desire of the moth for the star," Poe says famously of the poetic impulse in his essay, "The Poetic Principle," "Inspired by an ecstatic prescience of the glories beyond the grave, we struggle, by multiform combinations among the things and thoughts of Time, to attain a portion of that Loveliness whose very elements, perhaps, appertain to eternity alone."[22] In the "circumscribed

21. Letter to Dr. Brockenbough, 1827. Cited in William Cabell Bruce, *John Randolph of Roanoke, 1773–1833,* 2 vols. (New York, 1922), II, 5. See also Letter to Key, Sept. 7, 1818, ibid., II, 221. On Randolph's crucial contribution to the debates of the time, see Alison G. Freehling, *Drift Towards Dissolution: The Virginia Slavery Debates of 1831–1832* (Baton Rouge, La., 1982). On the economic and political developments sketched here, see Thomas P. Abernethy, *The South in the New Nation, 1789–1819* (1961), vol. VI of *History of the South* edited by Stephenson and Coulter; Clement Eaton, *A History of the Old South* (London, 1949) and *The Growth of Southern Civilisation* (London, 1961); Lewis C. Gray, *History of Agriculture in the United States to 1860,* 2 vols. (Washington, D.C., 1933); Sydnor, *The Development of Southern Sectionalism;* and Francis B. Simkins and Charles P. Roland, *A History of the South* (New York, 1972).

22. The poems, essays, and tales of Poe are available in many different editions. These include the *Complete Works* edited by Harrison (already cited); *Collected Works of Edgar Allan Poe* edited by Thomas Ollive Mabbott, 3 vols. (Cambridge, Mass., 1969–78); *The Annotated Tales of Edgar Allan Poe* edited by Stephen Peithman (New York, 1981); *Edgar Allan Poe: Essays and Reviews* edited by G. R. Thompson and *Edgar Allan Poe: Poetry and Tales* edited by Patrick Quinn (both New York, 1984). Given the general availability of most of the poems, essays, and tales cited here, in different popular paperback editions, my policy will be to cite line, paragraph, or (in the case of *Arthur Gordon Pym*) chapter. The exceptions to this policy will be those few cases in which a cited text is not usually available in such editions. The passage quoted here is from "The Poetic Principle," para. 12.

Eden" of the poem, the poet—and the reader privileged enough to share his linguistic pleasures—can indulge in those feelings of separation from the crowd, supremacy over the material, the "irresponsible self-assurance, the insolent off-handedness" (to recall Bourdieu) that are all the special prerogatives of the culturally privileged. This is not exactly the same kind of "circumscribed Eden" as William Byrd of Westover was dreaming of when he talked in the 1720s of sitting "securely under . . . vines and fig trees" with "a library, a garden, a grove, and a purling stream" as "the innocent scenes that divert our leisure." Nor is it quite the idyll of aristocratic leisure that Poe invoked via his preferred persona in literary reviews—or, for that matter, that John Randolph was commemorating and celebrating in this passage from a letter written in 1814: "Before the Revolution, the lower country of Virginia . . . was inhabited by a race of planters of English descent, who dwelt on their principal estates on the borders of . . . noble streams. The proprietors were generally well educated. . . . Their habitations spacious and costly, in every instance displayed taste and elegance. They were seats of hospitality. The possessors were gentlemen—better bred men were not to be found in the British dominions."[23] Nevertheless, all these imaginary landscapes bear the lineaments of the same desire: to fashion a riposte to the imperatives of the marketplace, to forge an antetype to the bourgeois standards of hurry, acquisition, and accumulation. "O! Nothing earthly," begins one of Poe's earliest poems, "Al Aaraaf." That captures his originating impulse as a poet, just as "The Poetic Principle" describes it in more elaborate and discursive terms. The originating impulse, however, is one that alludes to—is, in fact, conditioned by—the world of mass production from which Poe claims to abstract himself. Perhaps Poe was never more the Virginia gentleman than in the apparent abstractions of his poetry: where, struggling to establish his aesthetic mastery, he disclosed his marginality, and, insisting on transcendence and meditative release, he inadvertently revealed his likeness to both Bourdieu's model of the "post-aristocrat" and to the arguments for the defense, the case for patriarchy and feudal power in the Old Dominion.

23. Letter to J. Quincy, 12 March 1814. Cited in Russell Kirk, *John Randolph of Roanoke: A Study in Conservative Thought* (Chicago, 1951), 189. See also William Byrd of Westover, Letter to Mrs. Armiger, undated, *The London Diary, and Other Writings* edited by Louis B. Wright and Marion Tinling (New York, 1958), 38. On Byrd's uneasy, equivocal attitude toward his life in Virginia, see Kenneth A. Lockridge, *The Diary, and Life, of William Byrd II of Virginia, 1674–1744* (Chapel Hill, N.C., 1987).

The situation is, if anything, even more complicated as far as Poe's fiction is concerned, because the terms in which images of threatened and marginalized aristocracy form and inform the text are significantly multiplied. Here, as in the poetry, aesthetic separation is pursued as a mark of distinction. What Bourdieu calls "a distant, self-assured relation to the world" is, as we shall see, one of the evident targets of a story like "The Fall of the House of Usher"; in the process, the narrative rehearses the cultural moment it attempts to reject. But there are other ways, too, in which the South appears in Poe's tales: not as a convenient setting (he is as sublimely indifferent to the specifics of the Southern landscape in his tales as he is in his poetry) nor as the object of direct analysis (outside his openly journalistic work, he was rarely a commentator or even "a man talking to men" in the democratic, Wordsworthian sense) but as something else—a formative influence, an ancestral voice so deeply submerged in the text that only its distant echo can be heard, and the author himself often hardly seems to realize that it is there. From his tendency to displace unease about female "dirt" and black "danger" via stereotypes of purity and smiling passivity, through his scarcely articulable (and so covertly articulated) prophecies of revolt, to his dream figures of aristocratic (and, inevitably, masculine) charisma and control: through all this, Poe tapped many of the secret fears and guilts of his region. "The *return of the repressed,*" Herbert Marcuse has suggested, "makes up the tabooed and subterranean history of civilisation"[24]; and, in many of his tales, Poe appears to be acting as a teller of exactly this kind of history for the South— being "Southern," we might say, despite himself.

Not that the Southern dimension is always that repressed in Poe's stories. On the contrary, he sometimes openly declares the frame of beliefs, the ideology that lies at the back of nearly everything he wrote. Unsurprisingly, those beliefs are conservative: a sense of evil, a distrust of "meddling" and change, a preoccupation with the past, a rejection of the ideas of perfectibility and progress, a hatred of abstractions, and a belief in hierarchy. "Some Words with a Mummy" illustrates the way in which Poe sometimes brings these ideas into the foreground of his stories. In this tale, he employs the pretext and persona of an Egyptian mummy, reawakened after several thousand years, as a way of using the example of the past to act as a corrective to the present. "We sent for a copy of a book called the 'Dial,' " begins one, typical passage,

---

24. Herbert Marcuse, *Eros and Civilization: A Philosophical Inquiry into Freud* (1955; Boston, 1966 edition), xiv–xv.

and read out of it a chapter or two about something which is not very clear, but which the Bostonians call the Great Movement or Progress.

The Count [the mummy] said that Great Movements were awfully common things in his day, and as for Progress, it was at one time quite a nuisance, but it never progressed.[25]

As this brief passage suggests, Poe's approach to these issues is not especially subtle. And the ideas he articulates in stories like "Some Words with a Mummy"—or similar excursions into social and political comment, such as "The Colloquy of Monos and Una" or "Mellonta Tauta"—are not particularly striking or profound. They are, in fact, little more than the standard Southern argument of the time, used in defense of the region's economic and political position and, more specifically, in support of slavery. "I am satisfied with the existing laws," declared William Gilmore Simms in a book entitled *The Pro-Slavery Argument* (published, inevitably, in the South, in 1852) "until the gradual and naturally formed convictions of the community . . . shall call for their improvement." Writing in 1854, another self-appointed spokesman for the South, George Fitzhugh, agreed with him. The "abstract propositions . . . of . . . a Locke, a Jefferson," like the ideas of progress and equality, were the products of an era when "the human mind became presumptuous and undertook to form governments upon exact philosophical principles, just as men make clocks, or watches, or mills"; they represented nothing more, Fitzhugh added not without relish, than an "ignis fatuus," the airy "speculations of closet philosophers."[26] Commonplace as they are, however, these ideas Poe gave vent to occasionally reveal just how wedded he was to the Southern argument: in nineteenth-century America, at least, any wholesale dismissal of the Whig interpretation of history was very unusual—that is, outside of the slave states. Not only that: it was precisely these "political" ideas that supplied the cornerstones of Poe's writing, in the sense that Poe's "philosophy," as expressed in *Eureka* and enacted in his

25. *The Complete Tales and Poems of Edgar Allan Poe* (Harmondsworth, Middx., 1982), 546. All references to the generally less accessible tales will be to this (relatively) easily available edition.

26. George Fitzhugh, *Cannibals All!; or, Slaves Without Masters* (1857; Cambridge, Mass., 1960 edition), 187. See also 142, 175, 205; William Gilmore Simms, "The Morals of Slavery," in *The Pro-Slavery Argument: As Maintained by the Most Distinguished Writers of the Southern States* (Charleston, S.C., 1852), 233.

tales, is merely his "political" argument moved to another level. Characteristically, what Poe did, when it came to talking about the fundamentals of existence, knowledge, and belief, was to take the social and political idiom he shared with Simms, Fitzhugh, and others of the Southern persuasion and give it another dimension, a different slant.

Running through most apologies for the Old South and its peculiar institution, for instance, is a fierce insistence on human imperfection. "To say that there is evil in any institution," argues Chancellor Harper in the opening essay in *The Pro-Slavery Argument,* "is only to say that it is human." Defenders of the region before the Civil War embraced the idea of sin with an enthusiasm that bordered on the morbid. And while a devout reading of the Old Testament might have had something to do with this, there was another, more polemical motive: things should be left alone, the argument went, because nothing is perfect and meddling would only make them worse. Men and women were born "in a state of the most helpless dependence on others . . . to subjection . . . to sin and ignorance." They were not born free, nor were they born equal either: that "much lauded but nowhere accredited dogma of Mr Jefferson" was dismissed as "new-fangled philosophy," "the effusion of [a] young and ardent mind . . . which riper years might have corrected." In the name of the feudal, patriarchal version of Old Southern society—and, more specifically, in defense of an economic system founded on slavery—the Declaration of Independence, the contractual notion of society, the laissez-faire economy, the ideas of being born free, equal, and perfectible were all jettisoned. And evil was proposed as the determining factor of existence. The degree to which Poe himself participated directly in the proslavery argument is still a matter of controversy: the key text here is an 1836 review in the *Southern Literary Messenger* of two works defending the peculiar institution, the authorship of which continues to be disputed. If Poe did review James Kirke Paulding's *Slavery in the United States* and William Drayton's *South Vindicated from the Treason and Fanaticism of the Northern Abolitionists* (and the more convincing case, at the moment, belongs with those who claim he did), then, clearly, he was a public advocate of the polemical uses of evil, since it is the defense based on the idea of human imperfection that, among others, is cited by the reviewer and then given the stamp of approval. Even if Poe was not the author here, however, the fact remains that elsewhere he fell back on this idea when he was trying to articulate his "political" beliefs. And *Eureka* stands or falls by the notion that all created life is evil, because it involves fragmentation, the emanation of the imperfect Many from the perfect One. "My general proposition, then, is this," Poe declares at the beginning of his "Book of Truths," "In the Original Unity of the First Thing lies the Secondary Cause of All Things, with the Germ of their Inevitable Annihilation."[27] "In this view, and in this view alone," he explains later on in *Eureka*, "we comprehend the riddles of Divine Injustice—of Inexorable Fate. In this view alone the existence of Evil becomes Intelligible."[28] There are other issues at stake here, of course, other motives for Poe's commitment to a metaphysics of annihilation: among them, perhaps, his vague sense that this would be the ultimate form of aesthetic disengagement. The universe, according to this programe, would become the perfect poem: its material structures melting into the invisibility of "absolutely infinite space." But the material, historical, and above all *regional* base of all this can scarcely be ignored.

The irony here, of course, is that Poe himself showed a deep distaste for any material base—and for any instrument deployed to measure and understand it. The further irony is that in this distaste for rational speculation, logical thought, and scientific measurement, Poe was also betraying his Southernness. Here, for example, is Senator James Henry Hammond from South Carolina defending the South and attacking the North in *The Pro-Slavery Argument*:

> The primitive and patriarchal, which may also be called the sacred and natural system, in which the labourer is under the personal control of a fellow-being endowed with the sentiments and sympathies of humanity, exists among us. It has almost everywhere been superseded by the modern, artificial money power system, in which man—his thews and sinews, his hopes and affections, his very being, are all subjected to the dominion of capital—a monster without a heart—cold, stern, arithmetical—sticking to the bond—

27. *Complete Tales and Poems*, 211. See also "Preface"; Chancellor Harper, "Harper on Slavery," in *Pro-Slavery Argument*, 9 (see also 6, 7, 52); James Henry Hammond, "Hammond's Letter on Slavery," in *Pro-Slavery Argument*, 110; *Annals of Congress* (16th Cong., 1st sess.), 269, (6th Cong., 1st sess.), 230. The review of the two apologies for slavery mentioned here is to be found in the *Complete Works*, VIII, 265–75. Scholars did not question Poe's authorship of this review until 1941, when William D. Hull argued that it was written by Beverley Tucker. However, Bernard Rosenthal argues powerfully—and, in my opinion, convincingly—for Poe as the author: see, "Poe, Slavery, and the *Southern Literary Messenger*: A Reexamination," *Poe Studies*, VII, no. 2, 29–38.

28. *Complete Tales and Poems*, 308.

taking ever "the pound of flesh"—working up human life with engines, and retailing it out by weight and measure.[29]

It is worth bearing arguments like this in mind whenever we come across Poe fetishising intuition and memory, inveighing against rationalism or "physical philosophy" and those oracles of a "higher morality" contemptuously dismissed as "thinkers-that-they-think." Sometimes Poe openly attacked what he called "the small coterie of abolitionists, transcendentalists and fanatics in general" or "the frantic spirit of generalisation" that he felt stalked the land. Sometimes, it is more a matter of sensing the resistance to the "cold, stern, arithmetical" that surges like a tidal wave through his work. But always the connection between what Poe thought and felt as a self-appointed Southerner and what he wrote as a "philosopher-poet," a teller of tales and what he called a "Truth-Teller," is there. To understand Poe's work, in short, and the habits of thought that shape (not least) his fiction, we need to reread him in terms of regional debate.

The terms in which the rereading of the fiction might occur are, some of them, obvious. Although—as several commentators have observed— Poe makes few direct references to slavery and African Americans in his tales, when he does so he reproduces the familiar racist stereotypes. A character called "Toby," for example, in "The Journal of Julius Rodman," is said to have "all the peculiar features of his race: the swollen lips, large white protruding eyes, flat nose, long ears, double head, pot-belly, and bow legs."[30] The few descriptions like this in Poe's fiction match the account of "the peculiar character . . . of the negro" in that 1836 review of two apologias for the Old South, where we are told by the reviewer that some enigmatic power "works essential changes in the different races of animals" and must somehow be the agency that has "blackened the negro's skin and crisped his hair into wool." More telling than this, however—because it drives right to the heart of darkness in his work—is the way Poe is inclined to adopt a familiar Southern strategy of

29. Hammond, "Letters on Slavery," 162–63. Poe clearly felt that the virulence of his attacks was what Virginians wanted: this was, after all, what he told the first magazine publisher who employed him (see Silverman, *Poe*, 101). Some Southerners, however, believed that such attacks lacked what they saw as Southern tact and courtesy (see Louis D. Rubin, *The Edge of the Swamp: A Study in the Literature and Society of the Old South* [Baton Rouge, La., 1989], 131).

30. "The Journal of Julius Rodman," in *Complete Works*, IV, 84. See also VIII, 270–71.

associating visions of evil with versions of the black race. White Southerners, and white Southern writers in particular, have always tended to
associate feelings of fear and guilt, the sense of Nemesis or Original Sin,
with African Americans and what William Faulkner called "the old
shame" of slavery; Faulkner himself is only the most famous example.
And in something like his portrait of the island of Tsalal and the Tsalalians, at the end of *The Narrative of Arthur Gordon Pym,* Poe is only
pushing that tendency to extremes and giving it a peculiarly—but by no
means uniquely—sardonic twist: so that the Tslalalians become even
more blatantly racist caricatures, grotesque exaggerations of an already
exaggerated image.

The Tsalalians are, in fact, an absurdist extension of the "nigger minstrel" figure: that stereotype of childlike devotion that inhabits virtually
every plantation novel and that the author of the 1836 review in the
Southern Literary Messenger had in mind when he referred to "loyal
devotion on the part of the slave," "the master's reciprocal feeling of
parental attachment to his humble dependent," and "the language of affectionate appropriation" that identifies love with ownership. "That is
an easy transition," the reviewer declares, "by which he who is taught to
call the little negro 'his,' in this sense and *because he loves him,* shall love
him *because he is his.*"[31] The Tsalalians, as they are initially presented
in *Arthur Gordon Pym,* correspond to this figure that elides notions of
subjection and affection. They are, we are told, utterly black (they even
have black teeth!), with "thick and long woolly hair" and "thick and
clumsy" lips. Like the "darky" of plantation romance, they clap their
hands and slap their sides when they are amused; they keep hogs and
their favorite food is a species of fowl. The rub is that, as it turns out,
they are also deceitful and thieving, cruel and yet cowardly. Almost from
their first meeting with the white protagonist of the story, they inspire in
him feelings of distrust, uncertainty, and even paranoia; and these feelings prove an accurate symptom of a repressed reality when, finally, they
turn on Pym, attempting to kill him. Like "Hop-Frog" the dwarf in the
story of that name, they rebel against their alleged superiors, so confirming that they were smiling villains all the time, whose affability was just
a disguise for burning hatred. In this way, Poe ends up transforming all
the features of "the little negro," which he and the proslavery writers

31. *Complete Works,* VIII, 271–72. See also *The Narrative of Arthur Gordon Pym,*
chapter 19.

invented to reassure themselves, into something threatening and sinister. He not only turns the comforting stereotype on its head. He supplies a—necessarily indirect and certainly unconscious—articulation of the fear that created the stereotype in the first place. That fear was, of course, the greatest of all fears among Southern whites—that the slaves whom they liked to claim were the "children" in their "family" would one day take their vengeance on their "fathers"—and the other, more privileged members of this "primitive and patriarchal" system: in short, that they would rise and destroy the "family." It is not perhaps entirely coincidental, after all, that *Arthur Gordon Pym* was written just six years after Nat Turner led his slave insurrection in Southampton County, seventy miles south of Richmond in Poe's adoptive state of Virginia.

But perhaps the key text here, as far as the convolutions of Poe's adoption of a Southern identity is concerned, is not *Arthur Gordon Pym* but "The Fall of the House of Usher," a tale in which the controlling images, and the dominant structure of feeling, can all be traced back to the author's childhood home. Admittedly, the literal setting of "Usher" is not the South; it is a vaguely anonymous territory of a kind familiar to readers of gothic narratives. Imaginatively, however, it *is* the South: a glamorous and yet disastrous place that is indistinguishable in its figurative details from the world conjured up in the work of William Faulkner, Allen Tate, Robert Penn Warren, and William Styron. The driving force in the tale, of course, is Roderick Usher. To say that he is an idealized portrait of Poe himself—with his thin lips, enormous brow, nose "of delicate Hebrew model," and so on—is only to make the first and most obvious point. Beyond that, he is a blueprint for the central protagonist of Southern fiction: a figure whom W. R. Taylor christened "the Southern Hamlet" and whose avatars include Quentin Compson, Horace Benbow, and, in that most popular of all Southern books *Gone with the Wind,* Ashley Wilkes.[32] Neurotic, imaginative, introverted, obsessed with the past, he is a clear expression of aristocratic alienation, the young noble or dandy born out of his due time. More to the point, he is an incisive because utterly personal and particular figure for the South's sense of its own distinctiveness: its separation, as white Southerners saw it and sometimes still try to see it, from the bourgeois, utilitarian norms of the

---

32. See chapter 4 of William R. Taylor, *Cavalier and Yankee: The Old South and American National Character* (London, 1963). See also "The Fall of the House of Usher," para. 8.

nation, its impotence and apparently irreversible decline. Like so many Southern heroes, in fact, the reasons for his superiority are also the source of his weakness; he can achieve, at best, a moral or imaginative victory— literally, historically he must experience defeat. Observing Roderick Usher, the comment of John Randolph of Roanoke as he noted the diminishing economic and political importance of his beloved state of Virginia does not seem entirely inappropriate. "There is something in fallen greatness," Randolph mournfully reflected, "to enlist the passions and feelings of men even against their reason." It was also Randolph—who might even have been one of the models for Roderick Usher—who marked this passage from one of Macaulay's *Essays* for special attention: "It is difficult to conceive any situation more painful than that of a great man condemned to watch the lingering agony of an exhausted country . . . to see the signs of vitality disappear one by one, till nothing is left but coldness, darkness, and corruption."[33] Randolph was clearly thinking of Virginia when he scratched his pen alongside this; for us reading it, it is difficult not to recall the scene that greets the narrator when he arrives at what he calls "the melancholy House of Usher."

The other emblem of "fallen greatness" in this "very ancient family," Madeline Usher, seems to belong to this world even less than her brother does. She is an ethereal creature, a fleeting presence of a kind familiar to readers of Poe, more like a spirit or a statue than a woman, with pale skin, large eyes, and dressed in white. There are, no doubt, personal reasons why she is portrayed in this way (to do with Poe's loss of his mother) and broader "philosophical" ones too (to do with Madeline's role as an arbiter between this world and the next): but there is no denying that there are also historical ones. The locus classicus here is W. J. Cash's *The Mind of the South*, in which Cash became neither the first nor the last to suggest that Southern white women of the privileged classes have customarily been associated with "the very notion" of the region. The cult, Cash pointed out, rested on a clear division of roles. Black women were assigned the sexual function: that is, they became those with whom the

---

33. Letter to Dr. Brockenbough, 9 February 1829. Cited in Bruce, *John Randolph*, II, 364–65. See also I, 282; Letter to George Hay, 6 January 1806, Southern Historical Collection, University of North Carolina, Chapel Hill; *Annals of Congress* (17th Cong., 1st sess.), 903; "Usher," para. 1. Randolph was a delicate, sensitive, and well-educated man who insisted, "I am an aristocrat. I love liberty, I hate equality" (Kirk, *Randolph of Roanoke*, 21). The suggestion that he was one of the models for Roderick Usher is made, among others, by Leverenz, "Poe and Gentry Virginia," 213.

sexual dimension of experience was habitually and mythically associated. And this made it possible to transform the bulk of white women into creatures of angelic perfection, stainless expressions of the ideal, whose sexuality was minimized even if it was acknowledged. The white woman, Cash declared in a characteristically flamboyant passage, became "the South's Palladium . . . —the shield-bearing Athena gleaming whitely in the clouds, the standard for its rallying, the mystic symbol in the face of the foe. She was the lily-pure maid of Astolat. . . . And—she was the pitiful Mother of God. . . . There was hardly a sermon that did not begin and end with tributes in her honour."[34] Any threat to the fabric of Southern society, real or assumed, could as a result be interpreted as an indecent assault on her. So what Cash christened "the rape complex" was born: the paranoid belief that any black man who did not demonstrate complete subjection was after white women. The idealized figure of white womanhood became a totem—which, in an odd way, is just what it is for Roderick Usher. Madeline Usher becomes the site of Roderick's obsessions. He identifies her with everything that he feels he once possessed but has now lost: a sense of wholeness and identity, feelings of being and meaning. She is the mirror in which, so he believes, he can see what he is or might be; she enacts for him his sense of self—just as the more generalized figure of white womanhood came, eventually, to dramatize Southern self-consciousness.

The problem with any mythology that a culture organizes to explain and justify its practices is that, because it has been generated by awareness of those practices, it still bears their shape in however ghostly a fashion. Notable in Poe's few representations of African Americans, where he vacillates between rehearsing plantation stereotypes and forcing them to implode, this tendency not just to *re*press the impulses shadowing a legend but sometimes covertly to *con*fess them is even more notice-

---

34. W. J. Cash, *The Mind of the South* (1941; New York, 1967 edition), 89. This is an enormous topic with a growing field of scholarly material attached to it. On the condition of women in the Old South, among the books I have found most useful are Catherine Clinton, *The Plantation Mistress* (New York, 1982); Elizabeth Fox-Genovese, *Within the Plantation Household: Black and White Women of the Old South* (Chapel Hill, N.C., 1988); Ann Firor Scott, *The Southern Lady: From Pedestal to Politics* (Chicago, 1970). On literary representations, useful sources include Minrose C. Gwin, *Black and White Women of the Old South: The Peculiar Sisterhood in American Literature* (Knoxville, Tenn., 1985); Diane Roberts, *The Myth of Aunt Jemima* (London, 1995); Kathryn Seidel, *The Southern Belle in the American Novel* (Tampa, Fla., 1985).

able in Poe's peculiarly Southern ways with white women characters. Certainly, Poe was not above playing the regional game with women of color: the sly reference, in *Arthur Gordon Pym,* to the fact that "the women especially" among the Tsalalians "were most obliging in every respect" is proof enough of that. But it was in his portraits of white females of the privileged classes, like Madeline Usher, that the game was played with real enthusiasm. Two aspects of these women require special mention here. The first is obvious and frequently remarked on: these women are bodiless—quite literally so, of course, when, as they frequently are, they are dead—reminding us of those legendary times Mr. Compson recalls in Faulkner's *Absalom, Absalom!* "when ladies did not walk but floated." The second is just as obsessively there, even though it has received significantly less comment: they are marked by blood. Madeline Usher becomes typical of these women when, on her last appearance in the tale as she emerges living from her tomb, she is described in these terms: "there *did* stand the lofty and enshrouded figure of the Lady Madeline of Usher. There was blood upon her white robes, and the evidence of some bitter struggle upon every portion of her emaciated frame."[35] In "Ligeia," the return of the shadowy threatening spirit of the narrator's dead wife, Ligeia, is signaled by the fall of "three drops of a brilliant and ruby coloured fluid" into the new wife's goblet. In "The Assignation," the "pallor of the marble countenance . . . the marble bosom, the very purity of the marble feet" of the Marchese Aphrodite is "suddenly flushed over with a tide of ungovernable crimson." "Blood was its Avatar and its seal—the redness and the horror of the blood," we are told of the "Red Death" in "The Masque of the Red Death." And what that "seal" signifies, when it colors the "marble" bodies and the "white" robes of Poe's female characters, is not just death or disease, but the other half of the Southern story of white women: the part repressed, that is, when women are transformed into "ladies," drained of blood and all intimations of corporeal or sexual life, dressed in white and placed on a pedestal.

It is worth teasing out the duality of Poe's representations of white females just a little further. Julia Kristeva has described femininity as "that which is marginalized by the patriarchal symbolic order."[36] Women

---

35. "Usher," para. 39. See also "Ligeia," para. 16; "The Assignation," para. 7; "The Masque of the Red Death," para. 1; *Arthur Gordon Pym,* chapter 19.

36. Julia Kristeva, "Il n'y â pas de maitre à langage," *Nouvelle revue de psychoanalyse,* XX (Autumn), 135 (my translation). See also *Revolution in the Poetic Language* (New York, 1984); Mary Douglas, "Couvade and Menstruation," in *Implicit Meanings* (London,

are placed on the margins or borderlines of the culture, Kristeva argues, and there assume the shifting, disconcerting properties of all boundaries: neither outside nor inside, neither precisely known nor unknown. More to the point, they acquire an ambivalent character, simply because they *are* both within and without, on the edges of the male order. To the extent that they are within the order, shielding it from an imagined chaos, they can be seen as precious guardians of the law; to the extent that they are outside, however, in contact with that chaos, they can be seen as creatures of turbulence and darkness—not preventing chaos but partaking of it, even encouraging it to come again. The peculiarly Southern variation on all this is to translate white women into "marble" guardians or totems and to leave black women to take care of chaos. In turn, Poe's special contribution was largely to ignore women of color—apart from the occasional barbed remark about sexual laxity—and to reserve the ambivalences of borderlines purely for white women. His white female characters, like Madeline Usher, have all the insubstantiality that any self-respecting Southern white male of the period might have expected. But at crucial moments, they prove themselves unclean, the blood breaks through; and, as the anthropologist Mary Douglas has remarked— talking about male strategies for dealing with pregnancy and menstruation—"to express female uncleanness is to express female inferiority." It is not obviously menstrual blood that stains the white robes and marble skin of Poe's heroines at crucial moments. But it is a blood that reminds us that they are, finally, of the earth, earthly; and so it surely carries these connotations with it, along with many others. "All margins are dangerous," Douglas observes. Poe's heroines recollect that danger, as they dramatize the obsession with what Faulkner—rehearsing the male fear of, and fascination with, female blood—was to call "womanfilth." In doing so, they hauntingly retrace a pattern outlined by his African American characters: in a moment, the reassuring mask imposed by the master is ripped away to expose not so much a reality as another mask fashioned by fear and the will to power.

Madeline Usher is not just any white woman, of course. She is Roder-

---

1975), 62, and *Purity and Danger: An Analysis of the Concepts of Pollution and Taboo* (1966; London, 1984 edition), 40, 121. Terms like "womanfilth" are dramatically interrogated in William Faulkner, *Light in August* (New York, 1932). For analyses of male fear of female "fluidity," and in particular of menstrual flow, see also Luce Irigiray, "La mécanique des fluides," in *Ce sexe qui n'en pas un* (Paris, 1977); Jane Gallop, *The Daughter's Seduction* (Ithaca, N.Y., 1982).

ick's sister. Not only that, she is a strangely absent presence, like so many female characters in Southern fiction: Caddy Compson, say, in *The Sound and the Fury* or Peyton Loftis in *Lie Down in Darkness*. As for absence: it is not too difficult to see that, here as elsewhere in Poe's work, a primal drama is being acted out. Nor is it too hard, really, to appreciate that, in Poe's case, that drama is colored by two things: the fact that he was male and his wish to be a Southerner. The primal drama is the one Jacques Lacan famously described in which the child begins in union with the mother but then, as he or she realizes its split from the mother's body (the trauma of the "primal gap"), loses this plenitude or wholeness.[37] Narrative then becomes an attempt to catch up retrospectively on this traumatic split, to tell the story again and again in language that both reveals and conceals the fracture. The peculiarly male spin that Poe gives to this tale of repetition compulsion takes a dual form. Return, the rehearsal of old stories and the recovery of old names and places, is an indelible feature of his narrative and poetic personae: as, like sleepwalkers, they obey what the narrator of "Usher" calls "a very singular summons" out of the past—in search of a some-thing, invariably and ineffably female, that is also a no-thing. They are driven by a sense of loss on a quest along a chain of signifiers, supplements for that loss, toward a union that is coextensive with dissolution. Repetition, in turn, the compulsion to revisit the same subjects, replayed again and again in a variety of disguises, is a determining characteristic of Poe's *texts*. A tale like "Usher"—or, for that matter, a poem like "To Helen" or "The Raven"— seems to chase after an elusive, ever-vanishing object, the sign of which is a woman whose name (Madeline or Helen or Lenore or whatever) is always at the center of the narrative, but who is represented within it only in marginalized and shadowy or slippery form—as an obscure object of desire.

A male spin to the drama, and also a Southern one: a sense of loss may not be unique to the South but it seems, at times, as if Southerners are trying gamely to take out the American patent. The note of exile sounds like a melancholy bell through Southern writing: with every other text from the region appearing to play variations on the refrain from "The Raven," "Nevermore." "We that are banish't from those polite

---

37. Jacques Lacan, "The Mirror Stage as Formative of the Function of the I as Revealed in Psychoanalytic Experience," in *Ecrits: A Selection* translated by Alan Sheridan (London, 1977), 1–7.

pleasures" of the mother country, William Byrd of Westover mournfully reflected in colonial Virginia, "take up with rural entertainments." Byrd might often have felt such entertainments were pretty cold comfort, as he looked back with longing to England. A century later, however, John Randolph of Roanoke was gazing at the time when Byrd was writing with an equally fierce sense of deprivation: as he saw it, "the old Virginia planter," "lively and hospitable," capable of "rational and manly piety," was the appropriate subject of elegy. Less than fifty years after that, in turn, near the end of the nineteenth century, such writers as John Esten Cooke and Thomas Nelson Page were turning *their* eyes toward the "high times" before the Civil War when, according to them, "peace and plenty reigned over a smiling land." Perhaps, Page himself admitted once, this fondly remembered world was a "vague region" situated "partly in one of the old Southern states and partly in the yet vaguer land of Memory,"[38] but the dual location only made it all the more spellbinding. Not for the first or last time in Southern writing, the active *inventions* of the memorialist were celebrated. The old country, colonial Virginia, the "old days before the war": the object of affection might vary, but the impulse remained the same—to conjure up a vanished world of aristocratic ease and mourn its passing. And the peculiar situation that characterizes so many Southern narratives, of a male protagonist obsessed with a woman who is simultaneously "there" (in the sense that she dominates his thoughts and vision) and "not there" (in that she is hardly present physically, if at all), is tied like an umbilical cord to that impulse. The undertow of emotion in a story like "Usher," after all, is toward a female figure and a past that are all the more cherishable because they are elusive. In the process, that story line offers us a subtle correspondence, an echo of the feeling that everything that made life worthwhile, once upon a time, has somehow and irrevocably gone with the wind.

And then there is the fact that Madeline Usher is Roderick's sister: very close to him and uncomfortably close to death. "He admitted," observes the narrator of Usher, "that much of the peculiar gloom which thus afflicted him could be traced . . . to the severe and long-continued

---

38. Thomas Nelson Page, Preface to *Red Rock: A Chronicle of Reconstruction* (London, 1898). See also William Byrd of Westover, *London Diary,* 37–38; John Randolph of Roanoke, Letter to his niece, Christmas Day 1828. Cited in Bruce, *John Randolph,* II, 5; Francis Hopkinson Smith, *Colonel Carter of Cartersville* (London, 1891), 61; Thomas Nelson Page, *On Newfound River* (London, 1891), 2.

illness—indeed to the evidently approaching dissolution—of a tenderly beloved sister—his sole companion for long years—his last and only relative on earth. 'Her decease,' he said, with a bitterness I can never forget, 'would leave him (him the hopeless and the frail) the last of the ancient race of the Ushers.' "[39] "Sex and death," declares the narrator in William Faulkner's first novel, "the front door and the back door. How indissolubly they are united in us!" The dissolution of *le petit mort* into *le mort* is as much a constant in Southern writing as the elision of sexual desire and family feeling. Roderick Usher seems, in fact, to be as much in love with "Little Sister Death" as is that most autobiographical of Faulkner's characters Quentin Compson—who, of course, becomes haunted by that phrase in *The Sound and the Fury*. There are several probable reasons for the peculiarly intense linking of sex, death, and the family in many Southern texts. One is obvious: if miscegenation was the repressed myth of the South, then so was its consequence in the possibility of incestuous relationships. "The same law which forbids consanguineous amalgamation," declared Henry Hughes in the proslavery tract *Treatise on Sociology* (published in 1854), "forbids ethnical amalgamation." "Both are incestuous," Hughes added. "Amalgamation is incest." Although Hughes would hardly be likely to admit it, both laws were often broken in the Old South; and the first, it might be, as a direct consequence of the second. Interracial sexual encounters were a source of acute anxiety, not least because they might either involve or lead to incestuous ones; thanks to some earlier breaching of the "law" against "ethnical amalgamation," a white might well end up sleeping with a black relative. "I think I heard," wrote the wife of an early governor of Alabama of a notoriously promiscuous planter, "that his *child* and his *grandchild* have one mother?" She was by no means the only person to sense that a series of grotesque and inverted relationships were secreted beneath the Southern idyll of the family: representing a dual transgression—or, as that governor's wife put it, a "sin" or "the leprosy of the earth" that "nothing save the blood of the cross cleanses from it."[40] There is never a hint of miscegenation in "Usher"—it perhaps goes without saying—because the racial question is no more to the foreground here than any particulars of

39. "Usher," para. 13. See also William Faulkner, *Soldier's Pay* (New York, 1926), 111.

40. Fox-Genovese, *Within the Plantation Household*, 9. See also Henry Hughes, *Treatise on Sociology* (Philadelphia, 1854), 31.

the Southern landscape are—any local color, for instance, or stories about "the little negro." But it is surely not stretching a point to suggest that, since Poe grew up in a culture whose secret history connected the breaking of sexual taboos to the old shame of slavery and to the possibility of a collective doom or punishment, the suspicion of incest, linked to a sense of nemesis, would have a particularly compulsive hold on his imagination.

Closer to the surface details of the text, however, are two other reasons for the linking of sexuality and sisterhood in the South. One is a matter of (probable) fact: intense family feelings, especially between white brother and white sister, seem to have been a significant feature of life in the region before the Civil War. "The close association of brother and sister," the historian Bertram Wyatt-Brown has argued, "may have stemmed from the general character of isolated family-bound plantation life" and from "the deep antinomies" inherent in the patriarchal family structure. "The intensity of the brother-sister relation," Wyatt-Brown concludes, was "an island of comfort in a sea of misapprehension and dread of dependency upon mother's love and father's good favor, both often withheld." A second reason was not so much a matter of fact as of collective myth, the cultural fantasy that Southerners wove out of their historical experience. "The Southern family romance," Richard H. King has observed, "was the South's dream." "The region was conceived of as a vast metaphorical family, hierarchically organized and organically linked by (pseudo-)ties of blood."[41] A fantasy like this set up erotic tensions and generational conflicts; and, in particular, it turned every potential relationship between men and women into a version of sibling intimacy. In the terms of this collective myth, every young white woman became a "sister," a member of the clan, whose purity and honor had to be protected. From this springs the *generalized* force of the racist question, "Would you let your sister marry one?" And from this, too, stems the (not always successful) attempt to dissociate the "Southern belle"—as well as the "Southern plantation mistress"—from sexuality, and to assign the sexual function, mythically, to black women. For if this were not done, then the threat of incest inherent in the Southern family romance would be more or less unavoidable.

41. Richard H. King, *A Southern Renaissance: The Cultural Awakening of the American South, 1930–1955* (New York, 1980), 26–27. See also Bertram Wyatt-Brown, *Southern Honor: Ethics and Behavior in the Old South* (New York, 1982), 251–52.

So in one sense what stories like "Usher" do is develop and dramatize the intensity of certain relationships common in the life of the Old South and turn the metaphorical incest latent in the Southern family romance into something literal, occupying the foreground. "Every culture lives inside its own dream," Lewis Mumford pointed out.[42] Knowingly or not, Poe seems to be rehearsing a key element in the dream dreamed by the South before the Civil War, as he unravels the intimate relationship between a white brother and sister that achieves its fulfillment in death. The conclusion of "Usher," in which, "with a low moaning cry," Madeline falls "heavily inward upon the person of her brother" and bears him "to the floor a corpse" is, in these terms, a consummation devoutly to be wished since it intimates a dissolution of the self into its mirror image that is simultaneously sexual and corporeal. Regression and transgression are, in effect, combined in an act that replicates, on a deeply personal level, those impulses toward withdrawal and separation that characterize the region Poe embraced. In Freudian theory, incest is closely linked with the desire to retreat to the womb. So it does not take a great leap of the imagination to see how it can act as a paradigm and symptom of the tendency to resist change and growth—the pressures visited on any group by history—and to yearn—as, say, John Randolph did—for the recovery of some Golden Age. Incest is also linked to narcissism, since it implies a longing to be united with oneself, or at least one's own mirror image, to come apart from the world and be separate. And as an increasingly closed society, preoccupied with idealized self-images, particularly of its own past, the Old South certainly leaned toward narcissism, receding from the rest of the nation—first in intellectual and imaginative terms, and then politically. On this level, Roderick Usher is rather more successful than many Southern heroes. Sealing himself off within his fantasies, his self-centered image of perfection, he does finally unite with his own reflection and, at the moment he does so, the sound and the fury of the phenomenal world simply disappear.[43]

The third dominant figure in "Usher" is, of course, the house itself: a characteristically bizarre version of those mansions, intended to look old even when they were new, that Southern planters built as monuments to

---

42. Cited in King, *Southern Renaissance*, 26.

43. In this connection, see Robert D. Jacobs, "Faulkner's Tragedy of Isolation," in *Southern Renascence* edited by Louis D. Rubin and Robert D. Jacobs (Baltimore, Md., 1955), 174.

their own ambitions. Perhaps nothing more grandiloquently expressed the aristocratic pretensions of the Old South than these structures, often more facade than substance (wood, for example, was painted to look like marble); and Poe simply takes these dream palaces and makes them dreamier still—the House of Usher actually seems, not only decaying, but substanceless. The house is, in fact, as much mind as matter; inextricably attached to the nightmarish visions and haunted consciousness of its owner, it eventually dissolves with him into aboriginal nothingness. And it is, too, as much of a mirror as Madeline Usher is: a reflection of the obsessions, not only of Roderick himself, but of its imaginative creator, the author of the tale. As Poe has the narrator observe, "Usher" is "a quaint and equivocal appellation"[44] in that it refers to both the house and the family. But it is so in another sense as well—in that it has become a convenient, shorthand way of referring to the story, and so serves to remind us just how intimately connected house and tale are. Both Poe and his hero, after all, create their own imagined worlds—the one in "Usher" the tale, the other in "Usher" the house—into which the reader as well as the narrator is drawn. And the structure of the narrator's journey, from daylight reality, further inward toward even darker, more subterranean levels: that corresponds exactly to our own experience as readers as we plunge further into "Usher" the fiction. Roderick Usher uses his craft and his cunning to transform his guests' minds and expectations, just as Poe does with his imaginative guests; in their admittedly different ways, both seem intent on what Rimbaud was later to call "un . . . raisonné *dérèglement de tous le sens.*"[45] And at the moment of revelation—when the truth of the solipsistic vision is revealed—both "Usher" the house and "Usher" the tale disintegrate, disappear, leaving the narrator and reader alone with their own personal thoughts and surmises. In short, "The Fall of the House of Usher" is indelibly self-reflexive and hermetically sealed. Every feature of the tale refers us back to the actual process of production, by its author, and re-production, by us, its readers; Poe/Usher proceed to accumulate "cultural capital" by negotiating "a distant, self-assured relation to the world" and invite the readers, as far as we can, to share in that currency. In this sense, too, Poe's story

44. "Usher," para. 3. On the architecture of the period, see Richard B. Davis, *Intellectual Life in Jefferson's Virginia* (Chapel Hill, N.C., 1964), 205–52.

45. Rimbaud, Letter to Paul Demeny, 15 May 1871, *Oeuvres* (Paris, 1960), 346. See also William Faulkner, *Mosquitoes* (New York, 1927), 209.

stands at the beginning of a long line of Southern narratives, the determining features of which include a compelling inwardness, a stifling sense
of claustrophobia, a scarcely concealed hysteria, and the habit of looking
backward, not only for comfort but the means of salvation. "A book is
. . . the dark twin of a man," observes a character in one of Faulkner's
earliest novels: here, in "Usher," the "book" also seems the dark twin of
a culture.

When Poe died, in 1849, he left behind an uncompleted essay, called "A
Reviewer Reviewed." In it, the supposed author of this piece, one "Walter G. Bowen," adopts as he says Poe's "own apparently frank mode of
reviewing," and he then accuses his subject on "the great *point* which
Mr. Poe has become notorious for making . . . that of *plagiarism*."[46]
Several relatively trivial instances of unacknowledged borrowing on
Poe's part are offered. Then, just as more potentially damning examples
of what is called *"wilful and deliberate literary theft"* are promised, the
manuscript breaks off; Poe never completes the case against himself. Plagiarism was a constant preoccupation of Poe the critic. As anyone who
has read his commentaries on Longfellow or Hawthorne will know, he
accused many authors, often unjustly, of literary theft, often claiming
himself as the victim. It was also a not infrequent habit of Poe the writer.
A borrowing from Disraeli, perhaps, to demonstrate knowledge of the
recondite, or straight theft from Coleridge to develop his aesthetic theories: what one commentator has called a "mania for plagiarism" runs
like a secret stream of knowledge through his work. So it seems oddly
appropriate that one of the last pieces on which he worked should involve Poe, in fictional disguise, accusing himself: declaring that the supposedly plagiarized writer and stern critic of plagiarism was himself a
plagiarizer—promising that the accusation will be fully "accompanied *by
the proof*" but then, just as the crucial evidence is about to be submitted—and, in the manner of so many other of Poe's fictional narrators—
stopping short, denying any conclusion or resolution. "A Reviewer
Reviewed" reveals not only the centrality of plagiarism to what one critic

---

46. *Collected Works,* III, 1377–87. See also Daniel Hoffman, *Poe, Poe, Poe, Poe, Poe,
Poe, Poe* (Garden City, N.Y., 1972), 100–102. On Poe's habit of plagiarism, see, in particular, Stephen Rachman, " 'Es Lasst Sich Nicht Schreiben,' " in *American Face of Poe* edited
by Rosenheim and Rachman. Rachman discusses in fascinating detail the centrality of plagiarism to the social construction of Poe's literary style.

has called "the peculiar social construction of his literary style" but the typically self-conscious, and even histrionic, nature of Poe's particular habits of plagiarizing. Poe clearly knew what he was doing; and, in the manner of the plagiarist who apparently wants to be caught, he teases the reader into knowing it too. There are several possible explanations for Poe's "purloinings." They include his fondness for trickery and detection, his tendency to see art as a kind of conjuring trick performed by "the literary *histrio,*" and, not least, the fact that writing for money often tempts the writer into illicit shortcuts. One crucial reason, though, surely stems from Poe's adopted regional identity. To be more exact, it has to do with the anxiety of influence suffered by anyone—and, in particular, any writer—who believes that life is elsewhere, in some more favored, more central or mainstream place.

The critic Richard Slotkin has described one version of this anxiety, experienced by the early Puritan emigrants from England. In regard to the homeland they had deserted, Slotkin has argued, these emigrants were placed in a position that finds a fairly recent parallel in the position of American draft resisters who chose to emigrate to Canada during the Vietnam War. The American Puritans had opted out of an accelerating crisis. They had left voluntarily, despite exhortations to remain. To create their City on the Hill, they had "been compelled to breach and violate the ties of blood, custom, and affection that bound them to England." The continuing criticism directed at them by the English Puritans and royal magistrates further irritated their anxiety about the break. To the Puritans in England, in effect, "they were men fleeing from the task of rebuilding the church in England," while to the crown they were "political separatists, seeking to escape from the requirements of civil law and duty." In response, the early Americans, Slotkin goes on, experienced a psychological necessity to practice remembered English ways, oppose Indian savagery, and in every way disprove the charge that they had deserted European civilization for American barbarism. Yet they also felt compelled to justify their project in itself as unique and uniquely ordained. The American Puritan, Sacvan Bercovitch has suggested, "had to prove the Old World a *second* Babylon; otherwise, his readers might consider it (along with America) to be part of the universal spiritual Babylon." So, at one moment, the Puritan would affirm his Englishness by opposition to the Indian; at the next, he would link English and Indian and place himself in lonely opposition to both. These uncertainties of feeling and ideology, Slotkin contends, resulted in a colonial rhetoric notable for its instability: a mixture of, on the one hand, pride and defiance, and, on the other, insecurity, defensiveness, and deference. Colonial rhetoric, as Slotkin has put it, was marked by "a tendency towards polemic and apology," with the colonist simultaneously arguing "the firmness and stability of his European character and (paradoxically) the superiority of his new American land and mode of life to all things European."[47]

The instabilities of position and language that Slotkin and Bercovitch perceive among the early Americans find a curious correspondence in the uneasy rhetoric of Poe—and, more generally, in the sometimes belligerent, sometimes defensive arguments from the South. In this sense, at least, Southern writing has often assumed the qualities of a "colonial rhetoric": faced with the cultural dominance of the two Englands, old and new, writers like Poe seem compelled to reject and to imitate, to defy and copy, to assert difference while openly or covertly accepting many of the literary terms dictated to them. Which brings us back to plagiarism: Poe insisted on his Southernness again and again, and was proud to christen himself a Virginian. Inseparable from this pride, and the defiance of "Frogpondium," however, was a sense of uncertainty, even deference, that found its issue in regular acts of literary misappropriation. His tendency to steal from the works of notable European and American writers, in other words, was only the most extreme and embarrassing symptom of a secret sense of cultural marginality: the fear or suspicion that the place to which he had chosen to attach himself did, ultimately, exist on the periphery. To filch from "mainstream" writers became a convenient and covert means of making himself a part of the "mainstream"; further, to accuse such writers of filching from *him* (quite apart from appealing to Poe's taste for perversity and risk) offered another strategy for making him seem and feel less "marginal." Either way, he came closer to the center that he elsewhere claimed to despise; he could compensate for, at almost the same time as reveling in, his "deviance." Poe is a special case to the extent that his Southern identity was an act of will rather than birth: but it is surely unnecessary to invoke Allen Tate's famous description of him, as "our cousin, Mr. Poe," to note the signs of kinship with later, less contentiously Southern writers. Like Poe, many Southern writers are caught up in the disjunctions of thought and language that issue

47. Richard Slotkin, *Regeneration Through Violence: The Mythology of the American Frontier, 1600–1860* (Middletown, Conn., 1973), 40, 121. See also Sacvan Bercovitch, *The Puritan Origins of the American Self* (New York, 1975), 113.

from their acceptance or pursuit of a regional identity. They insist on the special, or even unique, character of their particular culture, its blessedly aberrant status, while bearing witness to the angry, irritable feeling that their claims to respect, and to the attention of their contemporaries and posterity, are diminished to the extent of their distance from the dominant culture. With one voice, they place themselves in proud isolation, asserting the distinctiveness of their place and its history. But, with another voice, they express the uneasy suspicion that their cultural inferiority can be measured by the degree of their separation from what is seen as the site of literary power. "The crucial problem from the perspective of political struggle," Hayden White observed, "is not whose story is the best or truest but who has the *power* to make his story stick as the one that others will choose to live by or in."[48] To this extent, Southern writers have usually lived by or in a story written by others, making assumptions that are by no means inevitable or natural about the centrality of a particular culture; and Poe is more like one of his own heroes than even he could ever have imagined—caught up in a narrative of which he was, and is, as much the subject as the author.

48. Hayden White, "Getting Out of History," *Diacritics,* XII (1982), 13.

2

"To escape from the provincial"

Ellen Glasgow, the Matter of Virginia, and the Story of the South

Ellen Glasgow was reluctant to think of herself as a Southern writer. She wanted, she declared, "to escape . . . from the provincial to the universal;" and her subject was human nature in the South, not the Southern nature. Like Poe, however, she was happy to claim the role of Virginian. "I am a Virginian," she once declared, "in every drop of my blood and pulse of my heart." And, unlike Poe, that claim was relatively easy to defend. She was, after all, born in the heart of the former Confederacy: in a large house in Richmond, Virginia—the town where she was to spend most of her life. Born only eight years after the end of the Civil War, she was also brought up in a family that seemed to contain within it some of the major tensions of those postwar years. Glasgow's mother, Anne Jane Gholson Glasgow, came from a family of jurists claiming descent from the early English settlers of Virginia. "Everything in me, mental or physical, I owe to my mother,"[1] Glasgow later insisted. Certainly, the daughter learned from her mother about ancestral pride, the burden of the past and tradition—and, not least, about the sad story of decline. By the time Ellen Glasgow was born, in fact, Anne Glasgow had had seven other children. She was to go on to have a total of ten, with an eleventh stillborn. Pregnancy and child rearing, the burden of the Civil

---

1. *The Woman Within* (New York, 1954), 16. See also 85, 87; "The Dynamic Past," *The Reviewer* (15 March 1921), 73–80; *The Letters of Ellen Glasgow* edited by Blair Rouse (New York, 1958), 116 (To Daniel Longwell [Spring 1932]), 257 (To Van Wyck Brooks, 4 October 1939), 329 (To Signe Toksvig, 14 August 1945); *A Certain Measure: An Interpretation of Prose Fiction* (New York, 1943), 90.

War and Reconstruction, the curious fate of trying to be a Southern lady—which meant, among other things, to deny substantial parts of her own self: this malign mixture had made of this proud descendant of a first family, not only "the perfect flower of Southern culture," "a perfect flower of the Tidewater" as her adoring daughter saw her, but someone "worn . . . to a beautiful shadow." A ghost in a way, in Ellen Glasgow's eyes Anne Glasgow was someone who had simultaneously lived too much and too little: too much in terms of the burdens she had had to carry, too little in terms of her own personal needs. The father could not have been more different. In her more charitable moments, Ellen Glasgow described Francis Thomas Glasgow as "stalwart, unbending, rock-ribbed with Calvinism." As a successful businessman, who operated the Tredegar Iron Works in Richmond from 1849 to 1912, he was a living embodiment of all those forces in the postwar South that were steadily transforming its economic and social structures. As a figure, in the eyes of his daughter, "more patriarchal than paternal," who combined unbending authority and devotion to a God who "savored the strong smoke of blood and sacrifice" with numerous sexual intrigues—often with the black servants of the house—he was something else as well: an emblem of male power, mainly malevolent. Of a very different family strain from his wife—"a descendant of Scottish Calvinists," as Ellen Glasgow put it—Francis Thomas Glasgow had all the energy and all the authority that came from having history on his side, and from being a man in a world run by men.

"I had the misfortune . . . to inherit a long conflict of types," Glasgow admitted. The conflict is so fundamental, in fact, that it seems almost too pat, too neat. The female emblem of the Old South and the male emblem of the New South, the romance of the past and the reality of the present, the fluid, yielding (and, in this instance, fading) "feminine" and the rigid, authoritative "masculine": antinomies like these were caught in Ellen Glasgow's own personal family romance. Not only that, true to her habit of analyzing and articulating the hidden determinants of character, Glasgow even drew attention to the opposites that constituted her inheritance; in effect, she tried to explain herself as fully as she usually tried to explain her fictional characters. "It is possible that from that union of opposites, I derived a perpetual conflict of types,"[2] she helpfully sug-

---

2. *Woman Within*, 16. See also *Letters of Ellen Glasgow*, 329 (To Signe Toksvig, 14 August 1945). On the biography of Glasgow, and in particular her relationship with her

gested in her autobiography *The Woman Within*. Which is true, up to a point: among other things, this would help to explain why nearly all commentary on Glasgow's fiction revolves around the question of which "type" the author gravitated toward—in other words, what was the measure of her intimacy with or distance from the forces represented by, respectively, her mother and her father. What Glasgow's self-analyses tend to leave out of account, however, are elements in herself that for whatever reason she wanted to deny or suppress and, beyond this, her double-edged relationship with the related inheritances of her family and her region. This is not simply a matter of something pointed out by Glasgow's biographers: that, while Glasgow claimed she "inherited nothing" from her father "except the color of my eyes and a share in a trust fund," she in fact showed the same determination to succeed, the same "vein of iron" and pursuit of authority (in this case, the authority of authorship) that she deprecated in him. Nor is it simply the case that on something like, say, the issue of her Southernness she would contradict herself: wanting to be "universal" rather than "provincial," she nevertheless (as we shall see) constantly situated and defined herself in regional as well as local terms. It is more than that. Glasgow was born into related crises of family and locality; she was the inheritor of a deeply conflicted literary tradition; and, as a female member of an upper-middle-class family, she was to face most of her life a peculiar—but, of course, by no means

---

father, see Marjorie R. Kaufman, "Ellen Glasgow," in *Notable American Women* edited by Edward T. James, 3 vols. (Cambridge, Mass., 1971), I; E. Stanley Godbold Jr., *Ellen Glasgow and the Woman Within* (New York, 1972); Monique P. Frazee, "Ellen Glasgow as Feminist," in *Ellen Glasgow: Centennial Essays* edited by M. Thomas Inge (Charlottesville, Va., 1976); Anne Goodwyn Jones, *Tomorrow Is Another Day: The Woman Writer in the South, 1835–1936* (Baton Rouge, La., 1981); Marcelle Thiébaux, *Ellen Glasgow* (New York, 1982). Many of these commentators also discuss the issue of how Glasgow's relationship to one or other or both of her parents affected her work. This is, of course, related to the question of the degree of ironic control that Glasgow achieved over her material. For two powerful arguments in favour of such control, see C. Hugh Holman, *Three Modes of Modern Southern Fiction: Ellen Glasgow, William Faulkner, Thomas Wolfe* (Athens, Ga., 1966), and Julius Rowan Raper, *From the Sunken Garden: The Fiction of Ellen Glasgow, 1916–1945* (Baton Rouge, La., 1980). For two equally powerful arguments against, see Louis D. Rubin, *No Place on Earth: Ellen Glasgow, James Branch Cabell, and Richmond-in-Virginia* (Austin, Texas, 1959), and Daniel J. Singal, *The War Within: From Victorian to Modernist Thought in the South, 1919–1945* (Chapel Hill, N.C., 1982). The phrase "vein of iron" is used with approval in more than half of Glasgow's novels, and of course supplies the title of the novel she published in 1935; it was also—as, for example, Thiébaux points out (*Ellen Glasgow*, 12)—a quality she attributed to her Calvinist father.

unusual—mixture of disadvantage and privilege. Ellen Glasgow sensed most of this and acutely analyzed some of it: but she was no more complete in her understanding of herself than anyone else. Her fiction is a compelling hybrid, because it not only diagnoses historical tensions but also because it offers symptoms of those tensions too; it tells us, better than even Glasgow herself knew, what it was like to live in a place of difficulty at a time of change.

Just five years before Glasgow was born, a British visitor observed of Richmond that "the devastating effects of war" were "still to be traced, not only on the houses and buildings, but on that which is of infinitely more importance—the minds of men." Other visitors agreed. Those of a more melodramatic turn of mind and more sweeping habits of language referred to "a dead civilisation and a broken-down system" or claimed to have seen "enough woe and want and ruin and ravage to satisfy the most insatiate heart," "enough of sore humiliation and bitter overthrow to appease the desire of the most vengeful spirit." Others preferred the moving anecdote, the telling detail. "I heard of one gentleman," declared a traveler who visited Virginia just after the Civil War, "who before the war had been unable to spend the whole of his large income, being now a porter in a dry goods store; and of another, who formerly had possessed everything which riches could supply, dying in such penury that his family had to beg of their friends contributions for his funeral."[3] Whatever the size of the canvas, however, contemporary observers painted a bleak

---

3. Foster B. Zincke, *Last Winter in the United States* (London, 1868), 97. See also George Rose, *The Great Country; or, Impressions of America* (London, 1868), 147; Sidney Andrews, *The South Since the War: As Shown by Fourteen Weeks of Travel and Observation in Georgia and the Carolinas* (Boston, 1866), 1; Edward King, *The Southern States of North America* (London, 1875), 451; Sir John Henry Kennaway, *On Sherman's Track; or, The South After the War* (London, 1867), 178–79; Virginius Dabney, *Virginia, the New Dominion* (Garden City, N.Y., 1971), 405, 406. On the developments sketched here, see Comer Vann Woodward, *The Origins of the New South, 1877–1913* (1951), vol. XI of *A History of the South* edited by Wendell Holmes Stephenson and E. Merton Coulter, 13 vols. (1947–95); J. S. Ezell, *The South Since 1865* (New York, 1963); Thomas D. Clark and Henry W. Grady, *The South Since Appomatox* (New York, 1967). For discussions of some of the issues raised here, see Paul M. Gaston, *The New South Creed: A Study in Southern Mythmaking* (New York, 1970); Bruce Clayton, *The Savage Ideal: Intolerance and Intellectual Leadership in the South, 1890–1914* (Baltimore, Md., 1972); Lucinda H. MacKethan, *The Dream of Arcady: Place and Time in Southern Literature* (Baton Rouge, La., 1980); Wayne Mixon, *Southern Writers and the New South Movement, 1865–1919* (Chapel Hill, N.C., 1980).

picture of a town in which "there was hardly a house which had not suffered more or less." With the decline of the old plantation and the old elites, however, came the rise of the new: people who, with the help of outside capital, began to transform the economic and social structures of the state. By 1880, investment was flowing into Virginia: "often welcomed," as one historian has put it, "with open arms and loud hosannahs" by "impecunious local citizens." Millions were poured into the coal mines of southwest Virginia; the trains of the Norfolk and Western Railroad carried the coal to the growing port of Norfolk; and northern capital both extended the Chesapeake and Ohio Railroad to the town of Newport News and enabled the building of coal and freight piers there. One telling symptom of the change from rural to urban was a change of name: the small town of Big Lick had ambitions to be a big town, and its civic leaders demonstrated their seriousness by renaming their home place Roanoke. Very quickly—in fact, within the space of five or six years—Roanoke became the state's newest metropolis. This change from a rustic title to something with more aristocratic and imposing connotations was an accompaniment of growth, of course, rather than a cause of it. But it was and is something else as well: which is to say, an illustration of how, in the postbellum South, the New and Old frequently found a means of accommodation. Virginians who benefited from the changed conditions, like Southerners generally, lost no time once they had acquired wealth in adopting the trappings of aristocratic privilege: a big house, preferably with columns, an estate, good china, silverware suitably engraved with perhaps a coat of arms, and servants. A planter from the antebellum era could, and sometimes did, make money too and then use that money to resurrect past glory: perhaps to buy back, perhaps to restore or replicate the land and with it the status he had lost. Not only that, after the "Bourbon" reaction, nouveaux riches and the old rich newly restored to good fortune could and certainly did secure power by an adept use of the patriarchal image: it was so much easier to elect a man, after all, if he possessed a name redolent of times past, had the air of feudal privilege, and called himself "Colonel." In short, new money might be transforming the material bases of Virginian and Southern society; but—especially after the era of Reconstruction, when Republicans were driven back north and the former slaves were driven back down—the old order kept its grip on the imagination of state and region. Glasgow was born into a situation in which style frequently acted as a mask for substance: where, in effect, the material and verbal economies were in direct conflict.

The situation was further complicated by the peculiar position of Richmond in all this. Certainly, Richmond participated in the economic growth of the state to an extent. There were men like Francis Thomas Glasgow—who had, it should be said, inherited the iron works over which he presided—ready to seize opportunity and to demonstrate what his daughter called "iron will" in the process. But that participation could hardly conceal and scarcely mitigated the fact of long-term decline. The once-great Confederate capital, its commerce eroded by the railroad and by the large ships that could not navigate the James River, was becoming a shrine. In Hollywood Cemetery, not that far from the Glasgow home, citizens unveiled a statue of the Confederate war hero General J. E. B. Stuart that seemed to say it all: "Dead, yet Alive," the inscription read, "Mortal, yet Immortal." It was one of Glasgow's aims as a novelist, she said, "to interpret . . . the prolonged effects of the social transition" of the Civil War and its aftermath "upon ordinary lives," which was a difficult enough task in itself. The task was rendered all the more difficult, however, by her local situation. The hard facts of postbellum Virginian and Southern culture were more at odds with the mythology that it used to explain and defend itself than they are in most cultures: more at odds than they have been, even, at other times in the history of state and region. That was one thing. But to this was added the problem of Richmond: a place that had been not just a center but *the* center of the Confederacy, now reduced to being a sideshow in the big show of regional revival, and compelled as a result to resurrect and rename its ghosts. James Branch Cabell, another novelist living in postbellum Richmond, claimed to have known Glasgow "more thoroughly and more comprehendingly . . . than did any other human being during the last twenty years of her living"; he also claimed that he gave Glasgow the idea that her novels, taken together, offered "a portrayal of all social and economic Virginia since the War between the States." Both claims are arguable. What Cabell could have claimed with justice, however, is that he knew intimately the masks with which both he and Ellen Glasgow were confronted in their hometown. On public occasions, Cabell said, the inhabitants of the town spoke of "a paradise in which they had lived once upon a time, and in which there had been no imperfection, but only beauty and chivalry and contentment." Even for a child, however, this posed difficulties: "because," as Cabell put it, "you lived in Richmond;

and Richmond was not like Camelot. Richmond was a modern city, with sidewalks and plumbing and gas light and horse cars. . . . Damsels in green kirtles and fire-breathing dragons and champions in bright armour did not go up and down the streets of Richmond, but only some hacks and surreys, and oxcarts hauling tobacco."[4] Even more than in most places in the state, Cabell said and Glasgow sensed, people were "creating . . . in the same instant that they lamented the Old South's extinction, an Old South which had died proudly at Appomattox without ever having been smirched by the wear and tear of existence." So if Glasgow became more interested even than most other Southern writers in people (as she herself put it) "unaware of the changes about them, clinging with passionate fidelity to the empty ceremonial forms of tradition," it is hardly surprising. Those forms, and the conflicts they generated, were felt everywhere in postwar Virginia and the South: but they were felt with an intensity unusual even in that state and region on the streets where she and Cabell lived.

Something else that Glasgow experienced with peculiar intensity was her own version of the Southern family romance. Glasgow tried to resolve the warring tendencies that were present in her family as much as they were in her region by claiming that, as a novelist, she had finally achieved a cunning synthesis. "I was never a pure romancer any more than I was a pure realist," she declared. She was, rather, a "verist" who recognized that "the whole truth must embrace the interior world as well as external appearances." The claim was one way of signifying that she

---

4. James Branch Cabell, "Almost Touching the Confederacy," in *Let Me Lie: Being in the Main an Ethnological Account of the Remarkable Commonwealth of Virginia and the Making of Its History* (New York, 1947), 145, 147, 148–49, 153–54. See also *As I Remember It: Some Epilogues in Recollection* (New York, 1955), 217; review in *Nation,* CXX (May 6, 1925), 521; *Woman Within,* 193; *Certain Measure,* 29; David R. Goldfield, "The City as Southern History: The Past and the Promise of Tomorrow," in *The Future South: A Historical Perspective for the Twenty-First Century* edited by Joe P. Dunn and Howard L. Preston (Urbana, Ill., 1991), 23. There has been extensive discussion of whether Cabell, as he claimed, gave Glasgow the idea of using her novels to present a recent social history of Virginia or whether this was Glasgow's intention at the outset of her career: see *Certain Measure,* 4; Cabell, "Speaks with Candor of a Great Lady," in *As I Remember It,* 217–33; Daniel W. Patterson, "Ellen Glasgow's Plan for a Social History of Virginia," *Modern Fiction Studies,* V (Winter 1959–60), 353–60; Oliver L. Steele, "Ellen Glasgow, Social History, and the 'Virginia Edition,' " *Modern Fiction Studies,* VII (Summer 1961), 173–76; Howard Mumford Jones, "The Earliest Novels," *Ellen Glasgow* edited by Inge, 67–68; Barbro Ekman, *The End of a Legend: Ellen Glasgow's History of Southern Women* (Uppsala, 1971), 9–13.

had come to terms with the law of the father by reconciling it with the shadowy imperatives of the lost figure of the mother. On a more strictly material level, it was also a way of suggesting that she had resolved the problem of a "realistic" New South cloaking itself in the "romantic" splendors of the Old South by taking and resolving the best of what New and Old had to offer. Looking in detail at what Glasgow actually did in her novels and said in her nonfictional prose, however, what emerges is not so much resolution as contradiction. The law of the father is simultaneously resisted and embraced, the maternal presence is quietly mocked but also adored; the one constant is a sense of the utter difficulty, in fact the impossibility, of reconciliation, synthesis—or, in simple, human terms a constant relationship, a stable family, a happy marriage. In *Life and Gabriella,* for example, subtitled "The Story of a Woman's Courage," the proto-feminist heroine is eventually swept off her feet by a conventionally virile man. "I'll come with you now—anywhere—toward the future," Gabriella breathlessly declares at the end of the novel. After years of struggle—in which, we are advised, Gabriella Carr has passed from "The Age of Faith" to "The Age of Knowledge"—the woman who was evidently meant to embody (to use Glasgow's own words) "a revolt from the pretence of being . . . a struggle for the liberation of personality" consigns herself and her fate into the hands of a man "able to command her respect by the sheer force of his character." "He was rough, off-hand, careless," Gabriella reflects shortly before surrendering to him, "she could imagine that he might become almost brutal if he were crossed in his purpose."[5] He is, in fact, a man not unlike Francis Thomas Glasgow; and, in this moment of capitulation, what Glasgow once called "womanhood so free, so active, so conquering" seems to be yielding to male authority in a double sense. Not only the heroine seems to be conceding the truer, stronger "vein of iron" to patriarchal authority, in short; Glasgow—the woman, the daughter, and the novelist—seems to be as well.

"A little too much has been made . . . of Ellen Glasgow's revolt against the lofty traditions of the Old South," James Branch Cabell argued, adding that Glasgow "has fallen in with that formalized and amiably luxurious manner of living to which, virtually, she was born."[6] On the personal

5. *Life and Gabriella: The Story of a Woman's Courage* (New York, 1916), 468. See also 480, 529; *Certain Measure,* 27–28; Jones, *Tomorrow Is Another Day,* 235.

6. Cabell, "Miss Glasgow of Virginia," *Let Me Lie,* 250. See also Jones, *Tomorrow Is Another Day,* 234–5. The man with whom Glasgow had the most enduring relationship during her adult years was Henry W. Anderson. Marjorie Kinnan Rawlings interviewed Anderson in 1953 as part of a plan for a biography of Glasgow. This and other interviews

level, Glasgow might have poured scorn on the "feminine ideal" that her own mother embodied—"the belief," for instance, "that the worship of a dissolute husband is an exalted occupation for an immortal soul." But that scorn did not prevent her from worshiping her mother and modeling her own life on hers. As her biographers have pointed out, even the little touches were telling here: she wore more than the usual amount of makeup to emphasize her femininity, she entertained after the fashion and tradition of the good Southern hostess, when she died her room turned out to be arranged exactly like her mother's. The man with whom she had the deepest, most enduring relationship during her adult life was of the firm opinion that, as he put it, "women are happier where the dominance of the man in the relationship is recognized," a creed that clearly informed the life of Glasgow's father and mother—to the obvious advantage of one and disadvantage of the other—and one that Glasgow was evidently willing to go along with some of the time. On the level of the fiction, in turn, there is the evidence of the novel in which the presence of Glasgow's mother is most clearly felt, *Virginia,* published three years before *Life and Gabriella,* in 1913. *Virginia* was intended, Glasgow said, as a "candid portrait of a lady" of a kind that had by then become "almost as extinct as the dodo." More needs to be said later about this account of a heroine who conforms to "the feminine ideal of the ages," and who clearly recalls for her creator the worn, self-denying figure of Anne Glasgow. For the moment, it is simply worth pointing out that the novel has a history reflecting Glasgow's own profound uncertainty about the central character and all she represents in terms of "the old feudal order" and its "consecrated doctrine" of female purity and passivity. Glasgow initially intended, she later admitted, to deal ironically with the Southern lady, but as she went on she discovered that her "irony grew fainter, while it yielded to sympathetic compassion." Her preliminary notes for *Virginia,* in fact, reveal that the book began as a contrast between a fading Southern belle and a rising industrialist—a contrast encapsulating "the transition from an aristocracy to a commercial civilization." It then, in a second outline, focused on the effect of the "unselfishness" of the heroine on her husband's character. Finally, it became much more of a tragedy: a critical, yet fundamentally sympathetic and even admiring investigation of the pastoral idealism that shaped the

conducted by her have been published in E. E. MacDonald, "A Retrospective: Henry Anderson and Marjorie Kinnan Rawlings," *Ellen Glasgow Newsletter,* XII (March 1980), 4–16.

character of the Southern lady. There is still irony in the final, published account of Virginia Pendleton: but there is, even more clearly, a quiet but by no means understated adoration of her stoic virtue—of what is called, toward the end of the narrative, her capacity "to suffer and to renounce with dignity, not with heroics." "One comes to feel," Louis D. Rubin has observed, "that it may well be the times, and not Virginia, that are out of joint,"[7] a point underscored by any reading of Glasgow's preface to the novel, written years later, where she draws attention to the contrast it offers between the "pure selflessness" of her heroine and the ruthless "self-interest" of the world she inhabits. To this extent, Glasgow's feelings about her mother, and all she came to embody for her daughter, seem just as conflicted as her feelings about the authoritative, "more patriarchal than paternal" figure of her father. So, for that matter, do her feelings about the evolutionary pattern, the social and psychic upheavals registered in this particular version of the family romance.

"I could not separate Virginia from her background," Glasgow declared of her heroine, "because she was an integral part of it, and it shared her validity." Which brings us to another level of conflict: stemming from Glasgow's uncertain relationship with the literary history of state and region. At first sight, that relationship might seem fairly straightforward. After all, Glasgow herself famously declared that what the South needed was "blood and irony." "Blood it needed," she went on, "because southern culture had strained too far away from its roots in the earth; it had grown thin and pale; it was satisfied to exist on borrowed ideas, to copy instead of create. And irony is an indispensable ingredient of the critical vision; it is the safest antidote to sentimental decay."[8] Added to that, Glasgow made no secret of her belief that, if she herself was not providing *all* that the South needed in this direction, she was nevertheless making her own substantial contribution. She could be scathing about the literary tradition she had inherited. Before the Civil War, she suggested, a conspiracy had been at work in the region to suppress a genuine literature. The Southern church "was charitable toward almost every weakness except the dangerous practice of thinking"; the code of easy living, hospitality, and "generous manners exacted that the

7. Rubin, *No Place on Earth,* 24. See also *Certain Measure,* 77, 78, 79; Oliver Steele, "Ellen Glasgow's *Virginia*: Preliminary Notes," *Studies in Bibliography,* XXVII (1974), 265–89; Notebook no. 2, Ellen Glasgow Papers, Alderman Library, University of Virginia.

8. *Certain Measure,* 28. See also 82.

artist should be more gregarious than solitary"; and the closed society created by the slavery controversy discouraged free thought and vital habits of imagination. After the war, in turn, "pursued by the dark furies of Reconstruction, the mind of the South was afflicted with a bitter nostalgia. From this homesickness for the past there flowered, as luxuriantly as fireweed in burned places, a mournful literature of commemoration."[9] Hating this "attitude of evasive idealism" and "moribund convention," Glasgow would, she insisted "revolt against the formal, the false, the affected, the sentimental, and the pretentious in Southern writing."

Every writer has to erect a tradition of a kind against which to test their ideas and inspiration; and Glasgow was not deviating either from that necessity of invention—nor, for that matter, departing entirely from the literal facts of her literary inheritance. The trouble was and is that, although she was telling something of the truth here, she was not telling the whole truth. Even on her own terms, her relationship to the literary transformations she both anticipated and celebrated was more convoluted and problematical than she cared to admit. For one thing, while she might mock the "sentimental infirmity" of Southern novelists of the old school, she was just as disparaging about what she termed the "patriotic materialism" of those who sought to reject the sentimental tradition. She had no patience with the writers of the region who came immediately after her, or with what she called the "half-wits, and whole idiots, and nymphomaniacs, and paranoiacs, and rake-hells in general, that populate the modern literary South."[10] More to the point, perhaps, in attacking the "uniform concrete surface" of modern life and the "mediocrity" of "Americanism" that she felt the New South had embraced, she began to sound rather like someone suffering from a "sentimental infirmity" herself. "The Americanism so prevalent in the South today," she complained, "belong[s] to that major variety which, by reducing life to a level of comfortable mediocrity, has contributed more than a name to the novel of protest"; it meant a "decrease in that art of living, which excels in the amiable aspects of charm"; and, without such arts, she felt, "a new class" rises "to the surface if not to the top." "It is this menace," Glasgow added, "not only to freedom of thought but to beauty and pleasure and picturesque living that is forcing the intelligence and the aesthetic emotions of the South into revolt."[11] At moments such as this, it is difficult

9. Ibid., 138. See also 136, 137, 139.
10. Ibid., 69. See also 139, 144.
11. Ibid., 148. See also 145, 147.

to disentangle Glasgow from the "evasive idealism" she elsewhere deprecated: "beauty and pleasure and picturesque living" is, quite clearly, a
phrase any self-respecting plantation novelist would have been proud of,
as they bathed their canvas in moonlight and magnolias. The story Glasgow told about the literary tradition of the South, and her relationship
with it, did not fit together—or, if it did, it was not in the way she evidently intended. What it revealed was not a seamless progress, a personal
odyssey from sentimental romance to stern realism, but something more
confused and interesting: a habit of vacillation, with the author never
really sure where, if anywhere, to take her stand.

That the story told more perhaps than the author had intended was
one thing. That it was, in any event, just that, a story, was another. It
does not take a great deal of ingenuity to see that, in her account of
Southern writing and her place in it, Glasgow was turning material fact
into myth: not denying the truth, exactly, but selecting, shaping, reor-
ganizing so as to create an enabling fiction, a usable past. The contrast
between a genteel, sentimental, but picturesque old style of literature and
a new style notable for its vein of iron(y), its toughness and "patriotic
materialism"—not to speak of its allegiance to the "uniform concrete
surface" of things: that, after all, is largely the story of Tidewater mother
and Scottish Calvinist father translated into aesthetic terms. The conflict
Glasgow outlines in her brief literary history of the region is of a recognizable, personal kind; and so too is its major, intended narrative
thrust—the tale of progress that she clearly intended it to tell. Some of
the most interesting and persuasive readings of Glasgow's work have emphasized her debt to the evolutionary theories of contemporary sci-
ence—it is not insignificant that in her first published novel, *The
Descendant,* she compares her characters to atoms, invokes "the old savage type, beaten out by civilization," and describes personal conflict with
reference to biological necessity, class conflict, and social progress. True
to a progressivist understanding of history—in this case, literary history—what Glasgow did, effectively, in her account of "the novel in the
South" and her part in it was suppress those parts of the past and present
that suggested continuity and foreground those that implied change. Like
the hero in a naturalist novel, Glasgow the novelist, as Glasgow the es-
sayist depicted her, was someone who built the new upon the ruins of the
old: whose relationship with the past could be described mainly in terms
of difference, struggle, and advancement. Glasgow *was* different, certainly, from the novelists of state and region who preceded her. She *did*

struggle to inject blood and irony into her writing. And she *did* advance the boundaries of fiction as far as concerns some of the issues she confronted: most notably, there were the two issues that she herself recognized as central to her work—what she called "the rise of the workingman in the South" and what her friend and neighbor Cabell termed (when trying to summarize her writing) her "complete natural history of the Southern gentlewoman."[12] What all this leaves out of account, however, are the ties that bind her to her predecessors, making her less definitively an icon of aesthetic progress than she liked to imagine. Above all, what it omits, or fails to take full cognizance of, is how the strange mixture of irony and evasion, satire and romance that characterizes her fiction—her resistance to the determining myths of the region and a kind of surrendering to them too—is anticipated in many of the novels she dismissed: some of them written in the very state she made both her home and subject.

One of the earliest and most notable plantation novels, *Swallow Barn,* for example, has a history or background that curiously anticipates the way that Glasgow came to write *Virginia* and subtly altered her attitude to her chosen subject both before and after publication. Published in 1832, *Swallow Barn* is set in Virginia in the early part of the nineteenth century. To an extent, it is not so much a novel as a set of sketches: written from the viewpoint of a northern relative, Mark Littleton, who is visiting Swallow Barn, the James River estate of the Hazard family, now transferred through marriage to a gentleman named Frank Meriwether. There is a plot, of a kind: but much of the narrative is concerned with offering the reader a detailed account of life and manners in rural Virginia. The author of this book, John Pendleton Kennedy, was not born in rural Virginia himself but in the city of Baltimore, Maryland, although he was descended on his mother's side from an old Virginian family. And, when he began writing, his intention was to adopt a fairly mocking, satirical approach toward his subject. A surviving early draft of the first chapter makes this abundantly clear. In this initial draft, the

12. *Woman Within,* 180–81; James Branch Cabell, "Two Sides of the Shielded," *New York Herald-Tribune Books* (April 20, 1930), sec. 11, 6. See also *The Descendant* (New York, 1897), 77. For a persuasive account of the impact of evolutionary thought on Glasgow's work, see Julius Rowan Raper, *Without Shelter: The Early Career of Ellen Glasgow* (Baton Rouge, La., 1971). For accounts that develop Cabell's summary description of Glasgow's work, see Ekman, *End of a Legend,* and Elizabeth Jane Harrison, *Female Pastoral: Women Writers Re-Visioning the American South* (Knoxville, Tenn., 1991), 17–42.

visitor is not a relative but a complete outsider; and throughout the extant fragment, *this* observer supplies a remorselessly ironic contrast between the pomposity and pretensions of the plantation owner—here called Frank Oldstock—and the poverty, even degradation of the estate—here blessed with the comic name Hoppergallop House. In the final, published version of the novel, there is still irony. Frank Meriwether, for instance, is quietly mocked for his belief that "the magistracy of Virginia is the staunchest pillar supporting the fabric of the Constitution"[13] as well as for the autocratic control he tries to exert over the opinions of his neighbors—considered "wholesome" only if they echo his own. A similar note of wry, dispassionate irony is discernible in, say, the treatment of a young female character, Bel Tracey. The daughter of a neighbor, Bel is said to have "her head . . . full of fancies" so that "she almost persuades herself that this is the fourteenth century"; in the name of such fancies, she even drags an unfortunate slave from retirement to play the part of "minstrel," in "livery" which is really a suit of broadcloth, and tries to train a singularly uncooperative hawk in the role of "falcon"—when it escapes, the narrator observes, it looks "a tawdry image of a coxcomb." The chapter headings often act as a measure of the gap the narrator discovers between romantic pretense and simple reality: a chapter titled "A Joust at Utterance," for example, actually describes in mock-heroic style a fistfight between Frank's son Ned and the village braggart at a crossroads store. And some minor characters seem to be there purely and simply for the purposes of satire. So, through the character of one Singleton Oglethorpe Swansdown Kennedy delivers a trenchant critique of Southern romanticism. A "man of pretensions," Swansdown "has the renown of a poet and a philosopher," we are told, "having some years ago published a volume of fugitive rhymes." In fact, he is nothing more than a poseur and a philanderer, deploying the same "multitude of pretty sayings" in the almost simultaneous pursuit of two different ladies.

And yet the irony is not sustained; mocking affection gradually yields

---

13. John Pendleton Kennedy, *Swallow Barn; or, A Sojourn in the Old Dominion* (1832), 32–33. See also 25, 86, 123, 358. All page references are to the New York, 1872, uniform edition, unless otherwise stated. On the life and work of Kennedy, see Charles H. Bohner, *John Pendleton Kennedy: Gentleman from Baltimore* (Baltimore, Md., 1961), and Joseph V. Ridgely, *John Pendleton Kennedy* (New York, 1966). Also of considerable use here are William S. Osborne, Introduction to the New York, 1962, reprint of *Swallow Barn* and Ritchie Devon Watson Jr., *The Cavalier in Virginia Fiction* (Baton Rouge, La., 1985), 80–102. For the surviving early draft, see 1962 edition of *Swallow Barn,* xlvi–lv.

to real affection, even admiration; at times, criticism is replaced by apology or celebration as the gap between "feudal" pose and simple reality disappears. For instance, in the chapter that gently satirizes Frank Meriwether for his air of "oracular" wisdom—and his white neighbors of the lower classes for paying due homage to the oracle—there is also an entirely idealized account of the genealogy of the ruling classes and an idyllic portrait of life among the gentry. "Gentlemen of good name and condition" constituted "the early population" of the Old Dominion, we are informed, and "brought within her confines a solid fund of responsibility and wealth." In the course of time, "this race of men grew vigorous" in the "genial atmosphere" of Virginia; the "cloudless skies" of the state "quickened and enlivened their temper"; and "in two centuries" the "sober and thinking Englishman" was "matured" into "that spirited, imaginative being who now inhabits the lowlands of this state." "The gentlemen of Virginia," the narrator explains, "are surrounded by their bondsmen and dependants; and the customary intercourse of society familiarizes their mind to the relations of high and low degree. They frequently meet in the interchange of large and thriftless hospitality. . . . Their halls are large, and their boards ample; and surrounding the great family hearth . . . the congregated household and the numerous retainers, a social winter party in Virginia affords a tolerable picture of feudal munificence."[14] In keeping with this portrait of feudal order and benevolent patriarchy, slavery is seen as an unfortunate burden on the white slave owner: "theoretically and morally wrong," perhaps, but in practice "a great duty," a charitable institution in the shelter of which the slaves enjoy "mild and beneficent guardianship, adapted to the actual state of their intellectual feebleness." Kennedy may have begun his account of life on the old plantation with the aim of gentle mockery; he may even have offered, some frequently sustained, comments on the provincialism and parochialism of Virginian life. By the end of the narrative, however, Littleton the narrator has almost become an apologist for the plantation system. "Ever since I have been at Swallow Barn," he reflects, ". . . I only want a thousand acres of good land, an old manor-house, on a pleasant site, a hundred negroes, a large library, a host of friends . . . a house full of pretty, intelligent, and docile children, with some few et ceteras not worth mentioning."

The pattern of resemblance between Glasgow's evolving attitude

14. Kennedy, *Swallow Barn*, 71. See also 70, 311, 453, 455–56.

toward her Virginia and Kennedy's feelings about *his* goes further still. Like Glasgow, Kennedy wrote a preface for his novel some time after the original date of publication—in his case, exactly twenty years later. In this, as in Glasgow's preface for *Virginia*, the sense of ironic distance was still further diminished. "*Swallow Barn* exhibits a picture of country life as it existed in the first quarter of the present century," Kennedy explained in his 1852 preface,

> Between that period and the present day, time and what is called "progress" have made many innovations therein. The Old Dominion is losing somewhat of . . . the mellow, bland and sunny luxuriance of old society—its good fellowship, its hearty and constitutional "companionableness" . . . that overflowing hospitality which knew no ebb. . . . An observer cannot fail to note that the manners of our country have been tending towards a uniformity which is visibly effacing all local differences . . . the whole surface of society is exhibiting the traces of a process by which it is likely to be rubbed down . . . to one level, and varnished with the same gloss.[15]

"The past presents a mellow landscape to my vision," Kennedy admitted in one of his essays, "rich with the hues of distance. . . . The present is a foreground less inviting, with . . . sharp lines and garish colours wanting harmony." It is noticeable how, in *Swallow Barn*, the portrait of John Smith—the navigator and writer whose life was so closely interwoven with the history of colonial Virginia—is even more admiring and sympathetic than the presentation of Frank Meriwether. Smith is, in fact, painted in still more glowing terms than that anonymous "race of men" who are said to constitute the "early population" of the state. "The sturdy and courteous cavalier who is so preeminently entitled to be styled the True Knight of the Old Dominion," Smith is favorably compared to "Bayard, Gaston de Foix . . . or any other of the mirrors of knighthood whose exploits have found a historian." Now distance lends further enchantment to the time of the Meriwethers too: if still not quite true knights, people like the master of Swallow Barn are part of a landscape rendered mellower, gentler, and more amiable by the passing of time.

15. "A Word in Advance to the Reader" (1852 and all subsequent editions). See also "Baltimore Long Ago," in *At Home and Abroad: A Series of Essays* (New York, 1872), 167; *Swallow Barn*, 499–500.

Like Glasgow, Kennedy even made subtle changes to the text in the later edition so as to soften any note of criticism. In the Virginia Edition of *Virginia,* for instance, published in 1938, a remark lamenting Virginia Pendleton's capacity for confusing truth and illusion, reality and romantic code ("if only she had seen for once the thing as it was, not as it ought to have been") is replaced by this comment, which does not put the blame for Virginia's unhappy marriage so much on the heroine herself: "Once he [Virginia's husband] had made one of that small band of fighters, who fight not for advantage but for the truth; now he stood in that middle place with the safe majority who are 'neither for God nor for His enemies.' Life had done this to him—life and Virginia."[16] Similarly, Kennedy altered the tone of the later edition of *Swallow Barn* so as to make it considerably less playful. Kennedy had written to his friend William Gilmore Simms in 1851 that a new edition of his 1832 novel might be timely, because of "the mawkish sentimentality which has been so busy of late inventing sympathy for the pretended oppression of the negroes." *Swallow Barn,* Kennedy explained, had revealed "a true picture of the amiable and happy relations" between master and slave in the South; and, significantly, it was on the chapter dealing with the slaves, "The Quarter," that he spent the most time and made the most substantial alterations and additions.

The point of all this is not, of course, that Glasgow was directly indebted to a writer like Kennedy—let alone, that she shared his less than critical attitude toward the slaveholding South. It is simply that both were part of a tradition that had deeply conflicted views of the Virginia gentry. More to the point, their common involvement in that tradition (at quite different historical moments, obviously) led to a strikingly similar process of vacillation: between ironic distance and gradually emerging sympathy, satirical intention and nostalgic result, initial motive and developing complication. Glasgow's history of writing in state and region and her place in it is much too neat, much too pat, just as her (related) story of the Glasgow family romance is; things in both the history and her story are much more mixed and confused than she tended to allow. That applies not only to versions of the gentry but also visions of the "plain man": there are curious, if often labyrinthine, connections between some of Kennedy's work and some of Glasgow's on this score too.

16. *Virginia* (Virginia Edition, 1938), 311. Cf. 404 of the original edition. See also Osborne, Introduction to 1962 edition of *Swallow Barn,* xl–xli.

Some three years after the initial appearance of *Swallow Barn*, Kennedy produced another novel, *Horse-Shoe Robinson*. The character whose name supplies the title here is like a rough first draft for one of Glasgow's heroic workingmen. "Nature had carved out, in his person, an athlete whom the sculptors might have studied to improve the Hercules," the narrator declares of Horse-Shoe: "Every lineament of his body indicated strength. His stature was above six feet; his limbs sinewy and remarkable for their symmetry. . . . His was one of those iron forms that might be imagined almost bullet-proof. With all these advantages of person, there was a radiant, broad, good nature upon his face; and the glance of a large, clear, blue eye told of . . . shrewd, homely wisdom."[17] The portrait of Kennedy's rough-hewn hero anticipates something like, say, Glasgow's description of Nicholas Burr in *The Voice of the People*. Burr, a plain man who rises to become governor of Virginia, is "tall and broad of chest, with shoulders which suggested the athlete rather than the student." "Among the men surrounding him his powerful figure towered like a giant's," we are told: "There was a splendid vigor in his thick-set frame and in the swinging stride of his hardy limbs. His face—the square-jawed, large-featured face of a philosopher or a farmer—possessed . . . a certain eccentric power. Rugged, gray, alert-eyed as it was, large-browed and overhung by his waving red hair—it was a face . . . not to be ignored."[18]

It is not just the physical and psychological features of these two yeoman heroes that resemble each other, however, it is the eventual place allocated to them by their authors within the moral economy of the novel. Strictly speaking, they are the heroes: the two titles, in their different ways, register this (since Burr is, of course, "the voice of the people"). Certainly, both dominate the narrative: Robinson through his heroism in war, Burr through his heroism in that arena of war by other means called politics. However, both are rather unceremoniously shuffled off, finally denied full title to the role of hero. At the end of *Horse-Shoe Robinson*, the story of Robinson himself is simply dropped. Another male character, from the gentry, is permitted to take center stage: Arthur Butler, whose "whole being," we have been informed, "denoted gentle breeding." Butler receives all the prizes customarily allocated to the hero in romantic

17. John Pendleton Kennedy, *Horse-Shoe Robinson: A Tale of the Tory Ascendancy* (1835; uniform edition, New York, 1872), 15.
18. *The Voice of the People* (New York, 1913), 185. See also 122, 303.

narratives: the heroine, elevation of status (to the rank of colonel), and the honor of a brief, concluding summary of his later life. Kennedy evidently cannot bring himself to give these prizes to his lower-class hero: Robinson gets most of the plot but none of the plot's rewards. In similar fashion, Burr is dispatched at the end of *The Voice of the People*: in his case, much more brutally, at the hands of a mob. The stage is again left to the gentleman: a member of one of the first families, named Dudley, whose "past began with the first Dudley who swung a lance in Merry England." Dudley goes on to enjoy his own elevation of status after Burr's death, by being elected governor. He has also earlier won the hand of the woman for whom he and Burr both struggled, Eugenia Battle. Status and power, the honor of the conclusion, the hand of the lady: all the rewards of the romantic plot are again given to the gentleman, while the plain man is sidelined. There is, certainly, irony in the motive attributed to Eugenia for choosing Dudley. Clan loyalty, the narrator informs us, finally wins out: "Battle breeding" has emerged "more invincible than the Battle virtue." The reader is left wondering, however, whether—as in the case of Kennedy's novel—it is more than just the clan loyalty, the "breeding," of the character that is at stake here. There is a sense, in both *Horse-Shoe Robinson* and *The Voice of the People* that it is the clan loyalty of the *author* that finally determines the direction of the plot and the character on whom the heroic garlands are bestowed. Julius Raper has argued that it is difficult to decide whether Burr's failure to win Eugenia "results entirely from psychological and social forces portrayed in the novel or is caused in part by a residual class arrogance in Miss Glasgow herself."[19] In both books, in effect, the plain man can only be allowed so much in the way of honor and attention; he has, in the end, to be shown his proper place.

Cabell called Glasgow "a Virginia gentlewoman"; and, he added, "she wrote and thought like a Virginia gentlewoman—which is to say, with more than a little romance and sentimentality about her."[20] That may be so. But "romance and sentimentality" are hardly the monopoly of the

19. Raper, *Without Shelter*, 142. See also *Voice of the People*, 13–14, 303; Kennedy, *Horse-Shoe Robinson*, 14. Allen Tate said of Glasgow: "she is an incredible old snob who would not receive in her house a 'man of the people' (as she would put it)." (*The Literary Correspondence of Donald Davidson and Allen Tate* edited by John T. Fain and Thomas D. Young [Athens, Ga., 1974], 243. To Davidson, 12 December 1929.) Cruel though this remark is, it is surely not without a grain of truth.

20. Cabell cited in Rubin, *No Place on Earth*, 11.

gentlewoman, Virginian or otherwise. More to the point here, the confusions of thought and feeling that often lurk in her novels have as much to do with the literary and intellectual situation into which Glasgow was born as they do with any attachment the writer may have had to the role of Southern lady. The mixed bag of irony and romantic sentiment, democratic flag-waving and aristocratic hauteur that characterizes books like *Virginia* and *The Voice of the People* was not something that she shared simply with other members of polite female society in Richmond. Neither was it a structure of feeling that she had in common just with Kennedy. As the local and regional crisis grew—immediately before, during, and after the Civil War—confusion of feeling became, even more than usual, *the* Southern way: as Southerners were torn, more fiercely than ever, between conflicting models of rural virtue, self-analysis, and self-defense, the recognition that there might be something wrong or at least weak about their way of doing things and the belief that, after all was said and done, that way was superior and grievously threatened. Glasgow was tied to this literary ancestry more than she knew, or at least more than she was willing to acknowledge; a series of tangled threads tied her to the conflicting ideologies at work in the writing of the South—and, in particular, the fiction of her home state. Two writers and two books bring this out—two examples among many of the way Southern fiction, and Virginian fiction especially, was riven by the crises of the times: one from just before the war and one from just after.

The earlier writer, John Esten Cooke, was actually a cousin of John Pendleton Kennedy; born in 1830, in Winchester, Virginia, he moved with his family to Richmond when he was ten. There he divided his time between writing and the practice of law before serving in the Civil War—for a while, under J. E. B. Stuart. He produced work both before and after the war—along with fiction, there were biographies of Generals Jackson and Lee—but his most popular novel appeared in 1854. Entitled *The Virginia Comedians,* it was set, as so much of his fictional work was, in what steadily was coming to seem the good old days: the period before the Revolutionary War that John Randolph of Roanoke, among many others, saw and celebrated as the local, state equivalent of a golden age. However, Cooke's aims, as he explained them in a letter to the writer and publisher (and former enemy of Poe) Rufus Griswold, were far from nostalgic or celebratory. *The Virginia Comedians* was, Cooke told Griswold, "profoundly democratic and American—the aristocracy, whom I don't like, getting the worst of it"; and to begin with the gentry in the novel, while not exactly "getting the worst of it," do come in for satirical scrutiny. The reader is quickly introduced to a character called Champ Effingham, recently returned from Europe, who seems in fact the living embodiment of the effete. Constantly yawning, complaining of weariness, reclining in elegant and languorous poses, here he is upon his first entrance into the novel: "His head is covered with a long flowing peruke, heavy with powder, and the drop curls hang down on his cheeks ambrosially; his cheeks are delicately rouged. . . . At breast, a cloud of lace reposes on the rich embroidery of his figured satin waistcoat. . . . Add velvet garters . . . —a little muff of leopard-skin reposing near at hand upon a chair—not omitting a snuff-box peeping from the pocket, and Mr. Champ Effingham . . . is before you."[21] Reinforcing the consistently ironic way in which Cooke describes Effingham, there are satirically conceived episodes in which the gentry reveal their snobbery and prejudice ("*Educate* the lower classes!" fumes Champ's father, "*Educate* my indentured servant . . . and have the knave talking to me of the 'rights of men,' and all the wretched stuff . . . of Utopian castlebuilders"); and, on more than one occasion, a direct assault is made on what is called "the wrong, oppression, and haughty and unchristian pride of rank, and birth, and wealth." These criticisms of "the old feudal system" are sometimes placed in the mouth of Patrick Henry, who makes a few brief appearances; more often than not, however, they are voiced by the alternative hero of this story, Charlie Waters. As his name implies, Charlie is a plain man—the son of a fisherman, in fact. He is also the spokesman for democratic sentiment and a rugged embodiment of the yeoman virtues. "By nature . . . a thinker" and of "well-known goodness and nobility of character," Charlie strikes the reader—and, for that matter, Patrick Henry himself—as a thoroughly worthy voice of the people: "his tone was so firm and proud," we are told, "his eye so clear . . . —his attitude so erect and noble." In short, if Champ Effingham seems to embody "the old

---

21. John Esten Cooke, *The Virginia Comedians; or, Old Days in the Old Dominion*, 2 vols. (New York, 1854), I, 17–18. See also 34, 92, 136, 183–84, 319. The contrast between "the old world and the new" occurs when Champ Effingham and a man in a red cloak (Patrick Henry) happen to be staying in the same tavern and is, in the first instance, a contrast between these two characters. On a broader canvas, however, it clearly applies to the comparisons drawn between Effingham and Waters. See also Jay B. Hubbell, *The South in American Literature, 1607–1900* (Durham, N.C., 1954), 511. For a detailed account of Cooke's life and career, see John Owen Beaty, *John Esten Cooke, Virginian* (New York, 1922).

world," then Charlie represents "the new"; past and future appear to meet and conflict in the contrast between them. The outcome of that conflict is evidently anticipated when the two men become rivals for the hand of the same woman, Beatrice Hallam. Champ pursues her; she prefers the natural aristocrat, Charlie; Champ then abducts her, severely wounding Charlie in the process; to avoid repercussions from this act of violence, Champ then has to flee the country. "The middle ages is past," Champ's father warns him as he advises his son to leave, "we cannot drop the portcullis, and from our castle bid defiance to all foes." The old ways are no longer viable; the gentry, having proved themselves to be not only weak but also violent, must yield to the new forces of democratic idealism. The message seems clear, as the first volume of the novel ends with Champ vanquished and banished while Charlie and Beatrice embark on domestic bliss in their "neat and cheerful and homelike" cottage.

And yet . . . scattered through volume one of *The Virginia Comedians* are glowing, nostalgic vignettes, idyllic moments snatched from the life of the old colonial gentry. "See this group of young country gentlemen," one such episode begins, "followers of the fox, with their ruddy faces and laughing voices. . . . Or pause a moment near that group of dignified gentlemen, with . . . lordly brows and clear bright eyes. . . . Hear them converse calmly, simply, like giants knowing their strength; how slow and clear and courteous their tones."[22] The rhetorical gesture of asking us to pause a while over such scenes reinforces the sense that we are being invited to gaze at a portrait of lost heroism: to watch the golden moment as it passes, and to shed a quiet tear over its passing. That rhetoric, and the frequency of such scenes recalling old forgotten things and battles long ago, only increase in the second volume: "Where are they now," begins an episode in volume two of the novel describing a day at the races, "those stalwart cavaliers and lovely dames who filled that time with so much light, and merriment, and joyous laughter? . . . They have gone away to the other world; their lips are dumb." The sense that Cooke's feelings about the gentry are considerably more riven than he cared to admit to Griswold is confirmed by the curious turn the story now takes. Champ Effingham returns home chastened and subdued, "his whole air and carriage . . . much more calm and collected." He is spiritually a changed man, although socially still a gentleman; and, in this reformed and refined state, he courts Clare Lee (whose surname is perhaps

22. Cooke, *Virginia Comedians*, I, 262. See also II, 30, 108, 128, 129, 148, 175, 279.

enough to suggest her own aristocratic status). His courtship of Clare confirms the impression the reader now has of him: that he is a bold but humble cavalier, willing to surrender to this ideal object of all his noblest affections. Cooke even helpfully supplies an explanation for Champ's previous behavior. Clare was his "ideal" in youth, Champ explains—"all my world was full of you," he says, "I dreamed and sang and thought of you alone." He was led astray by his infatuation with Beatrice. Now he has recovered his true love and with it—as in all the best courtship plots—his true character. In effect, Champ has taken over the romantic action. Charlie Waters, meanwhile, has been sent offstage: he has moved to the mountains in the western part of the state with Beatrice. To an extent, his role as sturdy voice of the people is filled by Captain Ralph Waters, Charlie's brother, who feels "no inferiority in the presence of any one" and is naturally "cognizant of the rules of good breeding." And Cooke even tries to tie his gentleman and newly announced plain man together by the simplest of plot devices: Ralph ends up marrying Henrietta Lee, Clare's older sister. However, the strategy of binding Champ and Ralph together within the extended family of the Lees hardly begins to compensate for the way Charlie Waters has been banished and Champ restored to the role and rewards of hero. Still more, confusion is worse confounded when Cooke has Charlie return at the end of the novel, now a widower, and join forces with Patrick Henry as Henry declares "the Revolution is begun!" By now, it is impossible to view the imminent Revolution with unmixed feelings: because it will mean the end of those glorious days of "stalwart cavaliers" and "lovely dames." In a way, Cooke has even made the upheaval Henry and Waters announce seem implausible, or to be more exact at odds with the logic of events: since the thrust of the narrative, in volume two, has been toward recovery and restitution of the old rather than the success through revolution of the new.

Cooke was able to swing between radically different emblems of local virtue—and, in particular, to slip from irony to nostalgia to a muted kind of triumphalism in his representation of the Virginia gentry—because *his* confusions were part of the confusions of the times. Repeatedly, visitors to the South just before the Civil War remarked on what one of them called a "singular contrast" between what Southerners said or did at one moment and what they said or did the next. The gentleman "of good intelligence, family, education, and breeding" might be the object of veneration; equally, the sturdy yeoman might be celebrated as the emblem of the South—a man "putting forth the thew and sinew of a giant . . . his only present recompense the possession of rude independence." State and region might be seen in terms of embattled decline or vigorous defiance; there was constant slippage between a version of the past richer even with the hues of distance than a Poe or a John Pendleton Kennedy could imagine, and the vision of a possible future, bright with hope, in which the sons of the South threw off the yoke of the North. Sometimes, defensive nostalgia and defiant utopianism were deployed in support of each other. In a novel published in 1836, for instance, *The Partisan Leader,* the author Nathaniel Beverley Tucker anticipates the day when most of the South will secede from the Union, with the battle still on for the land and soul of Virginia. "Old Virginia would yet show itself," Tucker proudly proclaims toward the end of the book, "in the descendants of the men who had defied Cromwell, in the plenitude of his power, and cast off the yoke of George the Third, without waiting for the co-operation of the other colonies."[23] In such cases, the past is not torn away from the present and future; in *The Virginia Comedians,* of course, it is. Both novels are riven, however, by what was the emerging crisis of state and region before the Civil War: with Southerners called on to defend the indefensible in the shape of the peculiar institution, confronted by the twin challenges of a possibly restless slave population and certainly hostile outsiders, aware of decline (or what one observer called "non-progressiveness . . . decay and desolation") and also (with the economic and political growth of North and West) of growing impotence. It is small wonder, then, that the books of the time veer between conflicting models of the good society,

---

23. Nathaniel Beverley Tucker, *The Partisan Leader: A Tale of the Future* (1836; Richmond, Va., 1862 edition), 23. See also Joseph Glover Baldwin, *The Flush Times of Alabama and Mississippi* (New York, 1853), 79–80; Tyrone Power, *Impressions of America During the Years 1833, 1834, and 1835,* 2 vols. (London, 1836), II, 235–36; James S. Buckingham, *The Slave States of America,* 2 vols. (London, 1842), II, 8; Fredrika Bremer, *The Homes of the New World* translated by M. Howitt, 2 vols. (London, 1853), I, 282; Charles Mackay, *Life and Liberty in America,* 2 vols. (London, 1859), II, 37. For contemporary observations on the state of the South, see also William N. Blane, *An Excursion Through the United States and Canada* (London, 1824), 202–3; Sir Charles Lyell, *A Second Visit to the United States of America,* 2 vols. (London, 1845), II, 60, 63, 109. For a fuller discussion of some of the issues raised here, see Charles S. Sydnor, *The Development of Southern Sectionalism, 1819–1848* (1948), and Avery O. Craven, *The Growth of Southern Nationalism* (1953), vols. VI and VII of *History of the South* edited by Stephenson and Coulter; also Charles G. Sellers, "The Travail of Slavery," in *The Southerner as American* edited by C. G. Sellers (Chapel Hill, N.C., 1960); Eugene Genovese, *Roll, Jordan, Roll: The World the Slaves Made* (1974; New York, 1976 edition), 25–49.

with their authors evidently never quite sure if they are writing elegy or prophecy. It was not so much a habit of "evasive idealism" that writers like Cooke handed to their literary successors as the habit of division, as they slipped around looking for appropriate models for their society and a possible foothold in either hope or memory.

A writer like Cooke—or Kennedy—does not, however, bring out one significant aspect of the literary situation of Ellen Glasgow—the peculiar ways of writing her state and region that she inherited. That aspect is not entirely unrelated to the fact that, although both survived the Civil War (Kennedy died in 1870 and Cooke in 1886), they are usually associated with antebellum fiction. "The challenge of war," the historian Anne Firor Scott has explained, "called women almost at once into new kinds and new degrees of activities." During and after the Civil War, she goes on, "southern women were changing to meet the changed time." One way they changed was in their greater willingness to take up more public roles; and one role the challenge of which they showed more willingness to accept was that of writer. "Not only did a large number of women see themselves as literary artists," Scott points out, "but many women active in other fields . . . wrote poems and stories on the side." "What southern literature lacked in quality," she adds, "it made up in quantity."[24] Scott might have added that what such writing lacked in quality it also often made up for in sales: of the seventy-two best-selling historical novels published during the period 1895 to 1912, thirty-four were written by Southerners, and four of the seven that sold more than five hundred thousand copies came from the South. Sometimes, economic necessity helped to force the role of writer on a woman: after all, a whole generation of those who had traditionally been seen as the breadwinners had been wiped out between 1861 and 1865. Sometimes, as in the case of Glasgow, it did not. Either way, there was a ready market for anything the "new southern woman" might produce. "The world will not hear our story," a Georgia girl had complained in her diary just a few months after Lee surrendered at Appomattox. She was thinking about the version of the South being disseminated in what she called the "horrid newspapers" of

---

24. Anne Firor Scott, *The Southern Lady: From Pedestal to Politics, 1830–1930* (Chicago, 1970), 118. See also 81, 102, 106–84; Eliza Frances Andrews, *The War-Time Journal of a Georgia Girl, 1864–1865* (New York, 1938), 371. Entry for August 18, 1865; Jay Herbert Martin, *Harvests of Change: American Literature, 1865–1914* (Englewood Cliffs, N.J., 1967), 16–17.

the "Yankees." Within a short while, however, she had been proved wrong. The world *did,* evidently, want to hear the story of the South, particularly the Old South. Southerners wanted to hear it for a variety of reasons: ranging from affection for what seemed to be irretrievably dead and buried, to the belief that economic growth might engineer a resurrection. And a triumphant North was eager to hear that story too, in order to find out about the people they had defeated: perhaps wondering what had been lost or gained with victory, perhaps interested in what might have survived to be integrated into the new dispensation—or, more likely, both. The market was there, then, and so was the means of producing for that market. The *Southern Literary Messenger* closed down in 1864; and publishing virtually disappeared in the South. In the North, however, radically improved printing techniques resulted in the production of cheap books for a mass market; while the number of magazines increased sharply, from about two hundred in 1860 to over eighteen hundred in 1900. Most of the women who took advantage of the opportunity created by these revolutions in social and professional life, and in the marketplace, are now largely forgotten: only the most comprehensive of libraries is likely to contain once popular romances by, say, Frances Courtenay Baylor, Virginia Frazier Boyle, Constance Carey Harrison, or Amelie Rives. One such writer wrote stories of old times in the Old Dominion that sold in the hundreds of thousands in their day but is now remembered, if at all, mainly for her later, less successful attempts to deal with evolutionary, social, and philosophical issues: Mary Johnston, the daughter of a Confederate veteran and the niece of General Joseph E. Johnston, who was born in Virginia just three years before Glasgow.

Johnston published her first book, *Prisoners of Hope,* in 1898. It was apparently written to help out the family finances, which had suffered severely after the war. If this was indeed her aim, then she was eminently successful. Like the novel that almost immediately followed it, *To Have and to Hold,* it was a best-seller, achieving sales in five figures; the proceeds from the two books together enabled Johnston to travel widely before returning to Virginia—and, for a while, to Richmond. The critic Lawrence Nelson has suggested that there was a kind of "civil war" in Johnston, "between the countrywoman and the cosmopolite, the woman and the feminist, the Virginian and the Universalist"; and Anne Goodwyn Jones agrees, emphasizing the way Johnston was torn between "the visionary sense of a perfectible future" and "the tragic sense of a limited past." Johnston herself seems to have felt much the same. In 1905, for example, she wrote this in a letter to a friend: "The American is very like Hamlet's cloud and has as many shapes as the given returns of the last census. He has other haunts than those of Broadway. He dips his sop in the dish of all the philosophies, including his own. He will work out. He is not always blatant. See how patriotic I am! And yet—and yet—in spite of all reason and merely an ingrained and hereditary matter, Virginia (incidentally the entire South) is my country, and not the stars and stripes but the stars and bars is my flag."[25] The conflict wryly measured here, between the American and the Virginian or Southerner, runs in fact through all Johnston's work. In particular, there is a deep fissure, a split of opinion in *Prisoners of Hope* strikingly similar to the one running through *Swallow Barn* and *The Virginia Comedians*; it also produces a similar result—extraordinary narrative tensions, and plot convolutions the main aim of which seem to be to conceal that split and so get the author out of trouble. Johnston was to deal with the Civil War later, in *Cease Firing* and *The Long Roll*; this first novel is set (like *To Have and to Hold*) in colonial Virginia; nevertheless, there is "civil war" of a kind here too, as the author struggles to come to terms with divisions that are at once her own and a part of her place in history.

There is, certainly, an element of daring in *Prisoners of Hope,* suggesting that Johnston was at least initially willing to cast a cold, critical eye on the colonial gentry of Virginia. For the first time in Virginia fiction, an indentured servant, Godfrey Landless, is permitted the privilege of a major role in the action. Thanks in part to this, the rough dwelling places and the even rougher lives of slaves and indentured servants are given about equal time with the courtly splendor of the lives of the gentry. There are even plans for a slave revolt during the course of the book. Both the privileged and those whose labor enables such privilege are allowed a voice: at times, in effect, the characters seem to be not so much in contrast or conflict as in debate, as they rehearse the arguments for and against a feudal order. "We *are* a little bit of England set down here

25. Mary Johnston to Otto Kyllman, 1 February 1905, in Mary Johnston Papers (5967), Alderman Library, University of Virginia. See also Lawrence G. Nelson, "Mary Johnston and the Historic Imagination," in *Southern Writers: Appraisals in Our Time* edited by R. C. Simonini Jr. (Charlottesville, Va., 1964), 76, 89–90, 101; Jones, *Tomorrow Is Another Day,* 186. For other useful discussions of Johnston, see Edward C. Wagenknecht, "The World and Mary Johnston," *Sewanee Review,* XLIV (Spring 1936); "Mary Johnston," in *Notable American Women* edited by James; Watson, *Cavalier in Virginia Fiction,* 197–212.

in the wilderness," the aristocratic heroine of the novel, Patricia Verney, declares, "Why should we not clothe ourselves like gentlefolk as well as our kindred and our friends at home? And sure both England and Virginia have had enough of sad coloured raiment. Better go like a peacock than like a horrid Roundhead."[26] This clearly is the argument for the hierarchical social system of Old Virginia. Godfrey Landless, in turn, openly challenges that system. "Is it of choice, do you think," he asks rhetorically, "that men lie rotting in prison, in the noisome holds of ships, are bought and sold like oxen, are chained to the oar, to the tobacco field, are herded with the refuse of the earth, are obedient to the finger, to the whip? . . . What allegiance did we owe to them who had cast us out, or to them who bought us as they buy dumb cattle? As God lives, none!"[27] At moments like these, the characters appear to be competing for the sympathy of the reader; and Johnston herself is leaving her critical options open, permitting her own divisions of opinion something like free play.

Only something like free play, though: while Landless and other characters are allowed to interrogate a system that, in the words of one of them, leaves the worker "bowed and broken" before he or she is freed, that interrogation only goes so far. Landless, it turns out, is a gentleman who has had the misfortune to fall foul of the law. True, he is Puritan in his inclinations and, as such, opposed to the Cavaliers and their ladies who live off his labor. But he is not a zealot, like most of the other Puritans given a voice in the novel—people like one Win-Grace Porringer, for instance, whose narrowness of mind and violence of language are clearly designed to alienate the reader's sympathy: "I, Win-Grace Porringer, testify against the people of this land: against Prelatists, and Papists, Presbyterians and Independents, Baptists, Quakers, and heathen . . . princes, governors, and men in high places. . . . Cursed be they all! Surely they shall be as Sodom and Gomorrah, even to the breeding of salt-pits and a perpetual damnation!"[28] More to the point, the sense of the injustice of forced labor is not even extended to cover all indentured servants—let alone the slaves. Most of the indentured brought over from Newgate,

---

26. Mary Johnston, *Prisoners of Hope: A Tale of Colonial Virginia* (1898; London, 1899 edition), 3. See also Jay B. Hubbell, "Cavalier and Indentured Servant in Virginia Fiction," *South Atlantic Quarterly,* XXVI (1927), 35–36.

27. Johnston, *Prisoners of Hope,* 312.

28. Ibid., 55.

together with the slave of African origin, are portrayed as little better than animals and easily led into violence by an evil mulatto called Luiz Sebastian. The potential slave revolt clearly poses a problem for Johnston, as far as her own division of loyalties is concerned. So she quickly deals with that problem by aborting the revolt and introducing a rebellion of African slaves in league with discontented local Indians led by Luiz Sebastian; in the face of this new threat from forces that are quite clearly "other," beyond the boundaries of culture as far as the author is concerned, Cavalier and Puritan join in an alliance proposed by Landless, to defend the closed world of the old plantation. Admittedly, Johnston later flirts with danger again, by having Landless and Patricia Verney enjoy a brief idyll together in the woods after he has rescued her from Indian captivity. But it is no more than a flirtation. The liaison does not survive the brief respite from the pressures of history and social status provided by the forest: the novel ends with Cavalier lady restored to the comforts of her aristocratic home and culture, while Landless is left alone in the wilderness, presumably to die. By a series of maneuvers that seem simultaneously desperate and cunning, Johnston separates the gentlemen victims from those victims who have the misfortune to come from another class or race. She then ensures that Landless, who is the hero of *Prisoners of Hope* to the extent that he dominates both action and love plots, does not receive the usual due of the hero—recognition, status, the hand of the lady—because, quite simply, he carries too much baggage with him, too much in the way of dubious social status. It is a familiar pattern by now in Virginia fiction. The forces that threaten to disrupt the narrative, by calling into question the legitimacy of the old order, are eventually excluded: banished from the narrative and consigned to the wilderness of the "other"—that which can exist only outside the boundaries of culture. After resisting, for a while, the undertow of feeling that draws her toward the social system of the gentry, the author ends by surrendering to it; *this* "civil war" ends, not in compromise or resolution, but in what is more or less a victory for the "ingrained and hereditary" attachments of a Virginia lady.

Just seven years after *Prisoners of Hope* was published, Mary Johnston wrote in her diary, "Ellen and I talked books; Webster, Ford, Congreve, Swift, Steele, and Addison, Chapman's Homer, Dickens etc." She and Glasgow were, in fact, part of a network of mutual support among women writers that also included, at various times, Charlotte Perkins Gilman, Rebecca Harding Davis, and Marjorie Kinnan Rawlings. The bond between Glasgow and Johnston was particularly close. "I want you to know and feel how my love goes out to you," Glasgow wrote to Johnston. "It always seems to me that I should like to take you in my arms and shield you." In turn Johnston wrote to Glasgow, "I dreamed of you the other night. I was in a house over against your house . . . and I looked out of my window across to your window."[29] Glasgow liked to call Johnston "my fellow craftsman." "I feel that I should be as glad as possible to know you better," she wrote to her early on in their friendship. "Yes, I daresay we are different in many ways," she went on, "—it will be interesting, don't you think, to learn *how* different. And the main thing, perhaps we both have." A year after writing this, Glasgow was to make the point about the differences and yet fundamental connection between them by citing a Buddhist proverb: "There are many paths down into the valley, but when we come out upon the mountains we all see the self-same sun." Perhaps the most immediate and pressing element in this communality of feeling was the shared sense of the simple *need* for such communality among women. "It is seldom in modern fiction that a friendship between two women . . . has assumed a prominent place,"[30] Glasgow lamented in one of her essays: something she surely felt she had particular cause to lament because she herself had both felt the urgency and experienced the value of such friendship. "Women are coming to understand their interdependence," she declared in the same essay: an interdependence she knew, in particular, with Johnston in the earlier part of her career and, some time later, with a younger writer from Florida, Marjorie Kinnan Rawlings. What Glasgow and Johnston had in common went beyond this, however, beyond even their shared interest in women's rights and female suffrage. They were women from the wealthier levels of Virginia society. They were both writing at a time that was unusually encouraging as far as opportunities for white women in the South were concerned. They were, however, both also writing at a time that offered peculiar challenges to people from precisely their place in Southern society. So it is hardly surprising that, despite the differences Glasgow acknowledged, there was a lot that contributed to their sense of a common

29. Mary Johnston to Ellen Glasgow, 27 September 1929, in Glasgow Papers (5060). See also Mary Johnston's Diary, in Johnston Papers (3588); Ellen Glasgow to Mary Johnston, Thursday [January 1905], in Johnston Papers; Ellen Glasgow to Mary Johnston, 22 March 1904, in Johnston Papers.
30. *Certain Measure*, 245.

pursuit or project. There is a confluence of aims here, as well as shared tensions and irresolutions; here, in fact, even more than in the ties that bind her to Kennedy and Cooke, Glasgow betrays her connection to the matter of Virginia—and, beyond that, to the story of the South.

The ties that bind Glasgow's work to the work of other writers from Virginia, and particularly other women writers like Johnston, are perhaps at their most obvious in a book like *The Battle-Ground,* published four years after *Prisoners of Hope.* Glasgow carefully researched this novel, making her way through the files of Richmond newspapers during the war years and visiting old battle sites. She also claimed later that she had tried in this book "to portray the last stand in Virginia of the aristocratic tradition" in a necessarily critical spirit: to expose the lie of "men who embraced a cause as fervently as they would embrace a woman, men in whom the love of an abstract principle became, not a religion, but a romantic passion." The febrile intensity of the phrasing here, however, suggests the problem. Glasgow was more than half in love with the "romantic passion" that, she claimed, she set out to interrogate; and, in the process of interrogation, she was in any case hampered by her use of fictional forms that drew her toward the romance of the old plantation— and to the elegies penned to the fall of the South in the Civil War. Certainly, there is what George Dekker, in a subtle analysis of the book, has called "a subversive agenda" at work here at times: notably in such things as the portrait of the choleric Major Lightfoot ("Without slavery, where is our aristocracy, sir?"), and in Glasgow's account of the absurdly romantic notions that the young hero Dan Mountjoy and the woman he loves, Betty Ambler, have of warfare—and that Dan carries with him to the battlefield. One of the most striking and effective aspects of *The Battle-Ground* is, in fact, Glasgow's critical use of intertextuality. With Dan away at the war front, for instance, Betty pores over his favorite books in fond commemoration of him: "Among them was a copy of the 'Morte d'Arthur,' and as it fell open in her hand, she found a bit of her own blue ribbon between the faded leaves. . . . Behind her in the dim room Dan seemed to rise as suddenly as a ghost—and that high-flown chivalry of his, which delighted in sounding phrases as in heroic virtues, was loosened from the leaves of the old romance."[31] What Major Light-

---

31. *The Battle-Ground* (New York, 1902), 335–36. See also 98, 198; *Certain Measure,* 13; George Dekker, *The American Historical Romance* (Cambridge, 1987), 290; Thiébaux, *Ellen Glasgow,* 48.

foot calls "a taste for trash" is clearly being used to illuminate the South's retreat into unreality: a retreat that Dan himself comes to take the measure of when he encounters the grim reality of battle—as Glasgow knew, and indicates in the sometimes gruesome detail of her descriptions, some of the bloodiest fighting of the war took place in Virginia. The strategy of using text to comment on historical context is further developed as Glasgow describes how "a garbled version of 'Les Miserables' passed from regiment to regiment" in the Army of Northern Virginia: the irony of one of the great stories of revolutionary democracy becoming the staple reading matter of soldiers fighting to protect hierarchy and privilege is not lost, on either the author or the reader. The irony has been prepared for, in fact, by another episode of reading. Dan forms a close companionship with Pinetop, a huge mountaineer who, although not a slave owner, will defend Virginia. He is shocked to discover Pinetop one day studying his primer and struggling to decipher the word "rat." "For the first time in his life," we are told, Dan,

> was brought face to face with the tragedy of hopeless ignorance for an inquiring mind. . . . Until knowing Pinetop he had, in the lofty isolation of his class, regarded the plebeian in the light of an alien to the soil, not as a victim to the kindly society in which he himself had moved—a society produced by that free labour which had degraded the white workman to the level of a serf. . . . To men like Pinetop, slavery, stern or mild, could be but an equal menace, and yet these were the men who, when Virginia called, came from their little cabins in the mountains . . . and fought uncomplainingly until the end.[32]

At moments such as these, Glasgow deftly uses the trope of reading to launch a critique, not only of Southern romanticism (the kind of romanticism, that is, that led Mark Twain to blame Sir Walter Scott for the Civil War), but of the injustices visited on both black *and* white by slavery. Clearly, she has more than just one kind of false consciousness in her sights.

But if there is an element of false consciousness present in Pinetop's willingness to fight for a system that has menaced him, and reduced him to semiliteracy, there is also—as Glasgow presents him—a measure of

32. *Battle-Ground*, 442–43. See also 445; Mark Twain, *Life on the Mississippi* (1883; New York, 1961 edition), 266.

heroism, however absurd. "At the call to arms," the narrator intones, Pinetop "had come, with long strides, down from his bare little cabin in the Blue Ridge, bringing with him a flintlock musket, a corncob pipe, and a stockingful of Virginia tobacco." The homely touches, the reminders of his local habitation, meld with the stress—here and elsewhere in the narrative—on his folkloric hugeness of stature. Pinetop is seen as a simple giant, whose alignment with the Southern cause may be—from a commonsensical, rational point of view—naïve and illogical, even directly contrary to his own economic interests, but also seems—in its own humble way—bold, greathearted, and courageous, a function of his instinctively local loyalties. Not for the first or last time in a Southern narrative, what makes a character appear slightly absurd also makes him seem admirable: the heroism, such as it is, springs precisely from his simple refusal to act in his own best *practical* interests. This sympathy that Glasgow betrays for someone she may also be gently satirizing recurs in her portrait of many of the gentry. Governor Peyton Ambler "looking complacently over the fat lands upon which his fathers had sown and harvested for generations"[33] seems as comically self-satisfied but also as endearing and even estimable as Squire Allworthy in *Tom Jones*—or, for that matter, Frank Meriwether in *Swallow Barn*. And Dan Mountjoy, riding his horse Prince Rupert like "a cavalier fresh from the service of his lady or his king," appears as careless and reckless as any young plantation Hotspur out of antebellum romance—and, in his way, just as thrilling. When Glasgow *uses* intertextuality in this book, the usual result is critical, interrogative: the reader measures the mistake the character is making in terms of the gap between what that character is and what he or she is reading. But there is another kind of intertextuality here, which is a matter not so much of use as of being used: the romance of Virginia and the South steers Glasgow toward a gently idyllic portrait of old times and their unfortunate fall, almost despite herself.

Which is all by way of saying that there is rather too much romance of the old plantation in *The Battle-Ground* for it to be as critical of Southern traditions, and the "evasive idealism" of the Virginia gentry, as Glasgow evidently intended. At the core of the novel, for instance, is a familiar strategy of Southern romance: the juxtaposition of two Southern families, the one headed by the courtly Governor Peyton Ambler and the

---

33. *The Battle-Ground*, 45. See also 136–37. For a very different reading of this novel, see Harrison, *Female Pastoral*, 17–19.

other by the "kindly rollicking" Major Lightfoot, enabling the author to separate out the different strands—of genteel aristocrat and bluff country squire—that went to make up the image of the gentry, and to make them seem less contradictory. Governor Ambler is "a bland and generous gentleman," with "a classic face": upright, clear-sighted, he is rational enough to realize the dangers of secession—in fact, the narrator tells us, "he fought hard against" it—but "when it rushed on in spite of him, he knew where his duty guided him, and he followed it, as always, like a pleasure."[34] If he corresponds to the figure of the Virginia Cavalier that crops up repeatedly in apologias for the South, then Major Lightfoot is closer to the prototype of the Kentucky Colonel. Irascible, stubborn, but also generous and warmhearted, Lightfoot is presented with more of a critical edge than the Governor is: his grandson, Dan, for instance sees him as "a braggart and a bully" and leaves home after quarreling with him, not long before the outbreak of war. However, the fact that Glasgow gives her two families names that recollect the attributes of different kinds of horses is not accidental: the Major, like the Governor, has breeding—signaled, not least, by the "Roman nose" he has inherited from his wellborn English ancestors. His irascibility is inseparable from his courage and daring: like his grandson, he is "a dare-devil" who "in his day . . . matched any man in Virginia at cards or wine or women—to say nothing of horseflesh." In short, he is as much of a romantic figure as his equally aristocratic neighbor is: almost a Byronic hero grown older, who invariably proves he has the right stuff in a crisis. The first time his grandson sees him after a separation of twelve years is when the Major is lying dead on the battlefield: "now he [Dan] knew that at least he was not craven," the narrator tells us "—that he could take blows as he dealt them."

Set against these gently burnished emblems of the aristocratic male are appropriate types of female virtue. The "frail and gentle" wife of Governor Ambler with a profile like "delicate porcelain"—whose delicacy of appearance belies the fact that "of all the souls on the great plantation" she "alone had never rested from her labours"[35]—is a typical plantation

34. *Battle-Ground*, 427. See also 16, 20, 41, 80, 376.

35. Ibid., 25. See also 23, 69. Analysis of the typology of the Southern family and plantation has a long and honorable history. Among notable analyses of this typology are Francis Pendleton Gaines, *The Southern Plantation: A Study in the Development and Accuracy of a Tradition* (New York, 1924); William R. Taylor, *Cavalier and Yankee: The Old South and American National Character* (New York, 1961); Michael Kreyling, *Figures*

dame or mistress. Her daughters Betty and Virginia—as much a part of the traditions of the state as their names imply—are the familiar pairing of Southern belles, the one small, energetic, voluble, and lively and the other tall, graceful, and quiet. The contrast between the two young women may eventually be drawn from Shakespearean comedy (one thinks, for instance, of similar pairings of types of aristocratic female virtue in *A Midsummer Night's Dream, As You Like It,* and *Twelfth Night*): but the more immediate debt is to the South's own version of the pastoral, which renamed the conventional figures of Elizabethan idyll and relocated Arcadia below the Mason and Dixon line. As for the characters who are not fortunate enough to be of the gentry and/or white, they are left to hover on the margins of the story. Pinetop, for all the recognition of his oppression, is little more than a sentimental stereotype of rural virtue: he sobs as he recalls kissing the mane of Old Traveller, General Lee's horse, in childlike farewell to the patriarch of the Confederacy after the War. The future in this novel belongs, not to him, but to the reformed aristocrats, Dan and Betty, whom we leave at the end of the novel about to begin again—building the new upon the ruins of the old. The black characters, in turn, are given even shorter shrift; they earn absolutely no place in the narrative beyond the conventional. Typical here is a slave called Big Abel who accompanies his master, Dan Mountjoy, to battle and carries him wounded from the battlefield. After the war, he insists on continuing to labor for Dan on the old plantation—"Let yo' darky do a bit of work if he wants to," he declares. Glasgow clearly saw slavery as a transgression of natural law, just as she sensed the anomaly of poor white folk fighting to preserve their own oppression. But she could, apparently, no more incorporate African Americans within the human terms of her story than she could translate her occasional perceptions of poor white deprivation into a sustained, critical analysis of the

---

of the Hero in Southern Narrative (Baton Rouge, La., 1986); Robert O. Stephens, *The Family Saga in the South: Generations and Destinies* (Baton Rouge, La., 1995). Diane Roberts also has some extremely pertinent points to make about the stereotyping of women in Southern narratives in *Faulkner and Southern Womanhood* (Athens, Ga., 1994) and *The Myth of Aunt Jemima* (London, 1995). Also relevant here are Judith R. Berzon, *Neither White nor Black: The Mulatto Character in American Fiction* (New York, 1978); Minrose Gwin, *Black and White Women of the Old South: The Peculiar Sisterhood in American Literature* (Knoxville, Tenn., 1985); Kathryn Lee Seidel, *The Southern Belle in the American Novel* (Tampa, Fla., 1985); *Slavery and the Literary Imagination* edited by Deborah McDowell and Arnold Rampersad (Baltimore, Md., 1989).

old order and a coherent program for the new. In this novel, black and poor white are as steadily excluded from social and narrative economies as they are in earlier tales of Virginia; they remain, in effect, irredeemably "other."

Of course, *The Battle-Ground* is a relatively earlier work; and, even among the earlier novels, a case could be made for saying that Glasgow could be tougher, more rebarbative about the past and future story of the South than this. Just two years after her account of the Amblers and the Lightfoots, for example, she published *The Deliverance*; this, in many ways, offers a corrective to the romantic tradition of postwar Virginia. The fundamental plot device is, in its own fashion, as conventional as the device of two families adopted in *The Battle-Ground*. Postwar decline is signaled as it is in many romances of the time—*Red Rock* by Thomas Nelson Page, for instance, or "Ananias" by Joel Chandler Harris: the plantation has been taken over by a ruthless and less than scrupulous overseer, and the aristocratic former owners have been forced into much humbler lodgings. Other writers like Page and Nelson, however, emphasized the tragic plight of the fallen aristocrats—rendered all the more sympathetic by their evident nobility and innocence—and the rampant greed and meanness of spirit of the new owners. Glasgow clearly had no time for this variation on the contrast between Cavalier and Puritan, greathearted Southerner and penny-pinching Yankee. On the contrary, the power of the book stems precisely from the interrogation, and dismissal, of the "evasive idealism" responsible for contrasts of this kind—and for the consequent illusion of Southern innocence. Presiding over the family of fallen aristocrats, the Blakes, is the matriarchal figure of Mrs. Blake, a widow whose eyesight failed just before the end of the war. Literally blind, she is so in a deeper sense as well. Frightened that the truth will destroy her, her children have woven an elaborate tissue of lies to protect her ignorance. "She lived upon lies," we are told. "For her the Confederacy had never fallen, the quiet of her dreamland had been disturbed by no invading army. . . . It was as if she had fallen asleep with the great blow which had wrecked her body, and had dreamed on steadily throughout the years. Of real changes she was as ignorant as a newborn child."[36] In her preface to the 1929 edition of *The Deliverance*,

---

36. *The Deliverance* (New York, 1904), 74. See also 90, 203. See also *The Deliverance: A Romance of the Virginia Tobacco Fields* (New York, 1929 edition), vi. *Red Rock: A Chronicle of Reconstruction* was first published in 1898; "Ananias" appeared in *Balaam and His Master and Other Sketches and Stories*, first published in 1891.

Glasgow explained what was, in any event, fairly clear. The blind Mrs. Blake was, she said, an emblem of Virginia and the South, "unaware of the changes about them, clinging with passionate fidelity to the empty ceremonial forms of tradition." With mordant irony, Glasgow takes a conventional form of postwar Southern elegy (the ascendant overseer, the declining aristocrat) and a deeply traditional figure for Southern commemoration and memory (the Confederate widow) and turns them against themselves: the thrust is toward, not elegy, but a critique of the elegiac impulse. This is a valediction to the Old South, forbidding mourning.

Powerful though this resistance to the traditional consolations of postwar romance is, however, it offers a further romantic irony of its own. Glasgow ends, not by dismantling the tradition of the Virginia gentry but recuperating it, translating it into terms that might ensure its continuance. A common resolution in the romance of the New South was a marriage between old and new—which usually meant a union between Southern aristocrat and Northern entrepreneur: a marriage by which the survival of the plantation was assured, as the happy couple settled down to renew the soil, restore the mansion, and continue the family line. It was a translation into fictional terms of a common hope or fantasy of boosters of a new economic dispensation: that, as Thomas Nelson Page put it, "The New South is . . . only the Old South with Slavery gone and the fire of exaction on its back." What Glasgow does in *The Deliverance* is simply a variation on this nostalgic utopianism. The happy couple, in this case, are Christopher Blake and Maria Fletcher. Christopher, the son of the blind Confederate widow, has breeding, or what in this novel is termed "blood." He begins with the qualities both good and bad that are characteristic of the Blakes, and which are intimated in the moment when he recalls his "reckless" forebears: "big, blithe, mettlesome, they passed before him in a long comely line," the narrator explains, "flushed with the pleasant follies which had helped to sap the courage in their descendants' veins." Experience, however, toughens him: toil in the fields gives him "muscles hard as steel and a chest that rang sound as a bell," while suffering gives him a fresh tenacity of character. Maria in turn, the granddaughter of the former overseer, may start from a lowly social position: but, we are told, she has inherited the superior genes of her mother rather than the vulgarity of her father. Still more crucial, through education she is able to rise to the level of a lady. When another, minor character meets Maria near the end of the novel, he is struck by her delicacy and gentility of manner. "Was it possible, after all, he questioned, that out of the tragic wreck of . . . the old customs . . . there should spring creatures of even finer fibre than those who had gone before?"[37] The answer to this rhetorical question, if Maria is any guide, appears to be "yes." Maria reads to Christopher—among other books, the medieval *Quest of the Holy Grail*; intoxicated by her words, Christopher feels himself liberated "like a drawn sword" from the brutality of his previous existence and restored to his true "heritage"; they then move back together into the Blake mansion. It is a curious conclusion. This is not a glimpse of the vision Glasgow claimed as her own, of the "plain man" building "the . . . structure of the future." On the contrary, the rehabilitated aristocrat joins with a woman whose every gesture reveals the fineness of her genes and her assimilation of all the best practices of the gentry. Inspired by the chivalric ideals of the Holy Grail, they have earned their right to become the true inheritors of Blake Hall; there it seems likelier—given their individual natures, their location, and the sympathies that brought them together—that their renewed energy and commitment will revitalize the aristocratic legacy, rather than engineer some fresh and genuinely democratic alternative.

Which is, to some extent, to agree with those critics, like Louis D. Rubin and Hugh Holman, who suggest that Glasgow's strength lay, not in her imaginative formulation of a social program for the twentieth-century South ("the rise of the workingman"), but in her portrait of the old order and its failures. Here a caveat is required, though, or rather a series of caveats. Glasgow's strengths were surely more specific than this. She was adept at portraits of the weakness and folly of the old order: but her subtlety came into something like full play, usually, when it came to analyzing the numerous burdens that this order imposed on women of a certain kind: that is, relatively advantaged white women. And she was, on the whole, less sure-footed when it came to offering a vision of something genuinely new growing out of the destruction of the old—*unless* such a vision could be harnessed to the fate of women of a certain other kind: that is, relatively *dis*advantaged white women. The point about the

37. *Deliverance*, 413. See also 90, 203; *The Builders* (New York, 1919), 112; Thiébaux, *Ellen Glasgow*, 61; Theodore L. Gross, *Thomas Nelson Page* (New York, 1967), 102. Page also declared, "the New South is . . . simply the Old South with its energies directed into new lines" (Thomas Nelson Page, "The Old South," in *The Old South: Essays Social and Political* [1892; New York, 1900 edition], 5).

old order is registered by some of Glasgow's most accomplished novels, *Virginia* and the trilogy Glasgow christened "Novels of the City"—*The Romantic Comedians, They Stooped to Folly,* and *The Sheltered Life.* The power of *Virginia* has its source in something already intimated: deeply personal feelings of involvement with all the heroine represented that encouraged the author to gravitate away from irony and toward something very like admiration. Behind the sad figure of Virginia Pendleton hovers the shadowy figure of Anne Glasgow; further behind her still, surely, lurks Ellen Glasgow's own sense of those habits of feeling and behavior that linked her, for good or ill, to her mother. There is still a powerful vein of irony in the eventually published first edition of the book. Through the account of Virginia's schooling at Miss Priscilla Batte's Dinwiddie Academy for Young Ladies, for instance, Glasgow offers one among many illustrations of the social mechanisms employed to keep women down: with the further felicitous point that, very often as here, the *immediate* agent of oppression is a woman—acting, in a sense, on behalf of men. Miss Priscilla Batte, we are told, works from the belief that "the less a girl knew about life, the better prepared she would be to contend with it. . . . Learning was to be kept from her as rigorously as if it contained the germs of a contagious disease." And Virginia proves such a good pupil that, much later on in life, the limitations of her education can be summed up in one devastating observation from her husband, Oliver Treadwell. "As a wife, Virginia was perfect," Oliver comments to himself; "as a mental companion, she barely existed at all."[38] All this is beautifully judged and ironically pointed, as is Glasgow's portrait of the young ladies very like herself who surround Virginia, alerting us to the fact that what we are witnessing here is a social process and not just a personal one. Virginia, we understand, "would have endured martyrdom in support of the consecrated doctrine of her inferiority to man"; and there is no doubt that, in scoring points like this, the author is asking us to take the measure of her heroine in terms of that traditional icon of martyred sainthood, the Southern lady.

For all the irony at play here, the power and, to some degree, the problems of the story of Virginia stem from its pathos: the quiet suffer-

---

38. *Virginia,* 231. See also 11, 17, 20; Louis D. Rubin, "Two in Richmond: Ellen Glasgow and James Branch Cabell," in *South: Modern Southern Literature in Its Cultural Setting* edited by Louis D. Rubin and Robert D. Jacobs (Garden City, N.Y., 1961), 129; C. Hugh Holman, "The Comedies of Manners," in *Centennial Essays* edited by Inge, 128.

ing, the capacity for mute forbearance that seems to be the determining characteristic of the heroine. It is, of course, something she has learned, a function of her culture and her assigned place within it; it is, none the less for that, a quality in her that comes to seem positively heroic. Early on in the novel, Virginia is waiting patiently for her future husband at a dance. Suddenly, the glimmer of a thought, the flicker of an intuition passes through her head. "Was that a woman's life, after all?" she asks herself, "Never to be able to go out and fight for what one wanted! Always to sit at home and wait, without moving a foot or lifting a hand toward happiness! . . . Always to will in secret, always to hope in secret, always to triumph or to fail in secret."[39] Waiting becomes her life, quietly attending to others—and, in particular, male others—becomes her lot: the rhetorical movement here from question to declaration simply anticipates the lesson Virginia has learned by the end of the novel. In this, she is contrasted with others who do not wait: men, of course, like her husband ("All life was for men, and only a few radiant years of it were given to women"), more emancipated women of her own generation like her friend—and Oliver's cousin—Susan Treadwell ("Sue had never given herself—The invio[la]bility of her soul had preserved the freshness of her body"), and the younger generation—including Virginia's own children—who have grown up "full of the new spirit." The contrast is by no means weighted against the heroine, however. For instance, Glasgow shows her characteristic uncertainty toward the whole issue of female emancipation by suggesting that the "free woman" enjoys a freedom which, "like that of man," has been "built upon the strewn bodies of the weaker." "She was one with evolution," the narrator observes of the "free woman," "and with the resistless principle of change"; so the counterpoint to the oppression of Virginia becomes a figure as deeply ambiguous, in Glasgow's vision, as an embodiment of the New South like her father Francis Thomas Glasgow. Hovering just on the edges here, of the conflict not just between Pendleton and Treadwell, Virginia, and Oliver, but also between "lady" and "freewoman" is the author's own version of the Southern family romance. Necessarily, this pushes the author at times toward elegy and pathos ("her ideals were the ideals of another period"); it also invites the heroic touch. The sheltered rose, the beautiful

39. *Virginia*, 123. See also 300, 332, 442; Oliver Steele, "Ellen Glasgow's *Virginia*: Preliminary Notes," in *Studies in Bibliography: Papers of the Bibliographical Society of the University of Virginia* edited by Fredson Bowers, XXVII (Charlottesville, Va., 1974), 282.

bird in a gilded cage (both comparisons are used repeatedly): within the terms of the narrative of *Virginia,* and the romance of both state and author, Virginia Pendleton is certainly this. She is, however, something else as well: a figure whose triumph seems to issue from her quiet waiting, just as much as her tragedy.

This feeling of triumph comes out, as much as anywhere else, in the differences Glasgow sketches between Virginia and her daughters. They have the independence and mobility, as well as the eagerness "to test life, to examine facts,"[40] that she clearly lacks. However, by comparison to their mother they appear superficial, even cold; as Marcelle Thiébaux observes, what they are good at is "competently managing their lives— they seem to have very little depth of feeling because, while they test life, they hardly get to be tested themselves." Virginia has suffered, but it is precisely her sufferings that have enabled her triumph: a triumph, not in practical terms of course, but a triumph, in the traditional Southern manner, of *character.* Her martyrdom turns her into Mater Dolorosa, our Lady of Sorrows: an emblem of female patience with which Glasgow instinctively sympathizes much of the time—or, perhaps it would be more accurate to say, she quietly adores. There is a historical dimension to this almost masochistic belief in the efficacy of a stern social code, its power to build character and positively deepen emotion. A useful comparison could be made, for example, with another novel set in a traditional society at the turn of the century—and written by another woman who knew, intimately, the class and social codes she was talking about— *The Age of Innocence* by Edith Wharton. Newland Archer in *The Age of Innocence* is as much a slave to tradition as Virginia Pendleton is; he also sacrifices feeling to form; as one who waits quietly and denies himself, he too is very different from a younger generation that "take[s] it for granted that they're going to get whatever they want"—represented, in this book, by his son. And there is the same sense in Wharton's book as there is in Glasgow's: that repression just might render the emotional life more intense ("The thing one's so certain of in advance," Newland asks, "can it ever make one's heart beat as wildly?"), that an experience unrealized but imagined might be "more real" than one simply lived through, and that the denials practiced in a closed society breed the suffering

40. *Virginia,* 300. See also Thiébaux, *Ellen Glasgow,* 106; Edith Wharton, *The Age of Innocence* (1920; London, 1993 edition), 249, 254; Arthur Mizener, *Twelve Great American Novels* (London, 1967), 70.

which in the long run breeds character. Glasgow shared this historical moment with Wharton. Daughters of privilege, they both witnessed the breakdown of a very specifically local version of traditional society—a breakdown that, in particular, called into question customary female roles. They even responded to the challenge in analogous ways: a rigorous process of self-education in the "new thought" that left them both torn between the roles of "lady" and "free woman" (in Wharton's case, the paradox was caught in an unkind remark made of her by an acquaintance: "She has ordered her intellect somewhere, as we would order a piece of furniture, to measure"). So it is hardly surprising that there should be this shared tension in both their books: issuing in deeply conflicted feelings about the character and fate of the protagonist. If anything, however, those feelings are even more conflicted in *Virginia* than they are in *The Age of Innocence* because, after all, Glasgow was writing more directly and autobiographically. She was talking about a woman like her mother and not unlike herself; she was talking, too, in terms that subtly recollected the tensions lurking within both her family and her literary tradition. More than that, she was talking about a society which, in terms of its closure, ranked second to none—and the self-recognition of which was (and perhaps, still is) intimately linked to the radical misrecognition of women. Small wonder, then, that the terms in which Virginia Pendleton comes to us involve such a rich mixture of idioms—and that Virginia herself remains one of Glasgow's most haunting, and even puzzling, characters. While Glasgow was not exactly likely to declare, "Virginia Pendleton, *c'est moi*," there are enough links between the perceived fate of her heroine and her own situation, as woman and writer, to make the protagonist of *Virginia* interestingly problematic—and to give the portrait of her a memorable emotional resonance.

With the "Novels of the City," we appear to be in different territory. Glasgow later explained that, after she had completed *Barren Ground*, she felt the need for laughter. For three years, she explained, she had "steeped" her "mind in the sense of tragic life"; now "the comic spirit, always restless when it is confined, began struggling against the bars of its cage," craving "delicate laughter with ironic echoes." So she turned to writing a trilogy of manners—in effect, a comedy of manners in three volumes—located in Queenborough, "the distilled essence of all Virginia cities." Set during the first two decades of the twentieth century, the three separate novels were to expose, in a delicate but sharply ironic manner, the radical social transitions that accompanied the disintegration of "the familiar order." "Everywhere in the world outside" the secluded social order of these fictions, Glasgow declared,

> old cultures were breaking up, codes were loosening, morals were declining, and manners . . . were slipping away. A whole civilization was disintegrating . . . and violence alone was strong enough to satisfy a craving for the raw taste of life, for the sight and savour of blood, for the brutal ferocity of lust without love. In Queenborough, where lip-homage was still rendered to the code of beautiful behaviour, the long reverberations of violence were felt chiefly under the surface.[41]

Two things are remarkable about this account of the origins of these "Novels of the City." One is that the feverish terms in which the emergence of the new order is described suggest that Glasgow was less than cheerful about the transitions she was witnessing—significantly less so, in fact, than one would expect from a self-proclaimed disciple of evolutionary theory and the gospel of progress. The moral wilderness announced here ("raw taste of life," "brutal ferocity") hardly seems preferable to the social and moral enclosures her Queenborough characters inhabit, and their "code of beautiful behaviour"—however anachronistic. The other is that, as a matter of fact, this account is not quite right, not quite the whole truth: taking the three novels in the order in which they were written, the notion of a comedy of manners seems gradually less and less apposite. True, *The Romantic Comedians*—a book that Glasgow said "seemed to bubble out with effortless joy" as she wrote it—seems to fit this description. Its central character, Judge Gamaliel Bland, is a descendant of an ancient comic type, the *senex romans* or elderly lover, albeit a very specifically Southern one; and the structure of the novel resembles an elaborate, ritualistic dance in which the Judge—surrounded by women who fulfill various roles for him, wife, sister, daughter, mother—indefatigably pursues an elusive object of desire. The book published three years after this, *They Stooped to Folly,* may have been begun in similar vein: but, as Glasgow herself was to admit, it gradually unfolded "as a serious study, with ironic overtones . . . of contemporary society"—and of the male myth of the "fallen woman." By the time of *The Sheltered Life,* published four years after this, the tone had darkened still further. The social scene may be populated here by "happi-

41. *Certain Measure,* 221. See also 211, 213, 214.

ness-hunters" as it is in the earlier books. However, the protagonist, General Archbald, hovers between the pathetic and the tragic. "What had his whole life been but saving his own or some other person's appearances?"[42] he muses at one point. As someone who—thanks to his devout observation of the code of the Virginia gentleman—has never really lived, he resembles, say, John Marcher in Henry James's "The Beast in the Jungle." As an increasingly isolated and anomalous figure ("the civilized man in a world that is not civilized," as Glasgow described him once), consoling himself with the thought that "character may survive failure," he is similar to Major Buchan in Allen Tate's *The Fathers* or William Alexander Percy as he presents himself in *Lanterns on the Levee*. Either way, he is clearly not a figure out of social comedy: world-weary, defeated, but clinging to mannerliness and the belief that "fortitude may be the last to go," Archbald really belongs in the great tradition of Southern stoicism. "Because Stoicism thrives on adversity and virtually assumes an unkind world without," Fred Hobson has observed, ". . . it was well suited to the South."[43] General Robert E. Lee, among many other Southern gentlemen, was profoundly influenced by the *Meditations* of Marcus Aurelius; and many of the Virginia gentry in the novels of Thomas Nelson Page reveal the same influence. "How fine and noble that old man was," Page says of one such character in his 1903 novel *Gordon Keith,* "sitting unmoved amid the wreck not only of his life and fortunes, but of his world." In her third book in the Queenborough trilogy, Glasgow is moving toward another tale of the triumph of character over circumstance: with a central character sitting, with quiet dignity and forbearance, amid the wreckage of his life and the familiar world.

Certainly, the irony is tempered in *The Sheltered Life* far more emphatically than it is in the two earlier Queenborough novels. At the center of each story is an old Virginia gentleman—a judge, a lawyer, a general—belonging to the courtly world of an older South, whose age and historical situation both emphasize his obsolescence. Only in the third novel published does Glasgow clearly begin to gravitate toward a tribute to Southern manners, high-mindedness, and stoicism: to see that gentleman figure, in short, as potentially noble. Even in the earlier two books, how-

42. *The Sheltered Life* (New York, 1932), 25. See also 394; *Certain Measure,* 203, 204, 237; *Woman Within,* 276.

43. Fred Hobson, *Tell About the South: The Southern Rage to Explain* (Baton Rouge, La., 1983), 279. See also 279–80 for the quotation from *Gordon Keith.*

ever, there are moments when what Hugh Holman has called "the gently corrosive irony" of the trilogy starts to falter under the pressure of other, less critical, more sympathetic feelings. In *The Romantic Comedians,* for instance, there is an endearing element to Judge Galamiel Bland's inexhaustible optimism and romantic blindness to reality; even at the end of the novel, when he has been cuckolded and abandoned by a wife half his age, he is busy planning fresh erotic adventures—with the pretty young nurse sent to look after him! In this, he has the innocence of other Virginia gentlemen in other romances that made no secret of their sympathy for the type. In Francis Hopkinson Smith's 1891 novel *Colonel Carter of Cartersville* for instance, Colonel Carter—a "frank, generous, tender-hearted fellow . . . hospitable to the verge of beggary"—is positively celebrated for his impracticality and his tendency to respond to all claims on his time and purse with the simple declaration, "I am a Virginian, suh. Command me." And, in his simple but somehow endearing inability to keep a hold on material fact, or note discouraging evidence, the Judge is not very far removed from the Colonel. More important, the dreams of romantic love that compel Judge Galamiel Bland into error are given a genuinely lyrical quality. His dreams are full, we are told, of "the glimmering ivory shapes of nymphs, who danced on rose-white feet to the music of running water. In spirals and wreaths and garlands, faintly coloured like the earliest spring petals, they spun round him, whirling, drifting, flying in the wind. . . . Clusters of girls, curving, swaying, bending, advancing, retreating, and always they smiled as they retreated, into the iridescent mist of April."[44] Not all of this may appeal to contemporary taste, of course: but there is no doubt that it would strike a responsive chord in anyone brought up in the late Romantic tradition like Glasgow herself—or, for that matter, her fellow Southerner William Faulkner, whose early work is full of such evanescent visions of the female. At one point in the story, as the Judge watches his young wife spin around the dance floor, he catches sight of himself in a mirror. "It seemed to him that a caged eagle gazed back at him from his dark bright eyes," the

44. *The Romantic Comedians* (New York, 1926), 69–70. See also 260; Holman, "The Comedies of Manners," 128; Francis Hopkinson Smith, *Colonel Carter of Cartersville* (London, 1891), 4, 10. Smith was a Baltimorean by birth and a New Yorker by inclination. His book, very popular in the North, neatly illustrates the point made by Edmund Wilson that, after the Civil War, Northerners "took over the Southern myth and themselves began to revel in it" (*Patriotic Gore: Studies in the Literature of the American Civil War* [New York, 1962], 605).

narrator tells us "—a spirit restless, craving, eternally unsatisfied, yet with a wild comedy in its despair." It is a vital moment of self-revelation. It *is*, in a sense, corrosively ironical; in another sense, however, it endows the Judge with pathos and dignity—and even with a strangely romantic quality, as if a part of him might genuinely belong to a landscape of nymphs and "the iridescent mist of April."

Where the irony is much firmer, much more alert and biting, is in the handling of actual relations between men and women—or, to be exact, the innumerable ways in which, in a traditional society, men misrepresent and mistreat women; the satirical power of these books in effect stems from their precise, detailed, and in the main comic portrait of male misrecognition. "Now, it is the peculiar distinction of all woman myths," Glasgow wrote in her account of the writing of *They Stooped to Folly*, "that they were not only sanctioned but invented by man." That point is made again and again in the Queenborough trilogy: as the reader is presented with persuasive examples of different women whose lives and personalities have been repressed and distorted by the story of them a man wants to tell. The point is fundamentally a social one and is often more or less explicit. Here, for instance, is Virginius Littlepage in *They Stooped to Folly* meditating on the women in his life and the changes in sexual mores he has witnessed:

> If only women had been satisfied to remain protected, how much pleasanter the world, even the changing modern world, might be today! If only they had been satisfied to wait in patience, not to seek after happiness! For it seemed to him . . . that there could be nothing nobler in women than the beauty of long waiting and wifely forbearance . . . surely it was not too much to insist that the true feminine character had never flowered more perfectly than in the sheltered garden of Southern tradition.[45]

There is a delicate balance here between personal misunderstanding and the social mechanisms that have created it. Virginius Littlepage longs for the "wifely forbearance," the capacity "to wait in patience" that Virginia Pendleton has—and that both have been taught to see as the special gift of "the true feminine character." Virginius, Virginia: as their names indicate, both are indelibly attached to their home place and its traditions.

---

45. *They Stooped to Folly: A Comedy of Morals* (New York, 1929), 319. See also *Certain Measure*, 225; Jones, *Tomorrow Is Another Day*, 234.

And both, in their way, are innocents—since, as Glasgow pointed out once, man is not "a conscious tyrant but . . . a victim to the conditions of social evolution" just as woman is. Littlepage's misrecognition of women, Glasgow intimates, has a very specific social origin. It is of a recognizably local kind, nurtured by "the sheltered garden of Southern tradition"; and the implication, here and throughout the novel, is that the ironic conflicts contained in such an attitude have been as responsible for the collapse of an entire class as the more obviously material facts of invasion and economic ruin.

"You will note that almost always, after finishing any book by Ellen Glasgow," James Branch Cabell observed, "what remains in memory is the depiction of one or another woman whose life was controlled and trammeled and distorted, if not actually wrecked, by the amenities and the higher ideals of Southern civilization."[46] That is as true of the Queenborough trilogy as it is of any of Glasgow's other works: what lingers in the mind here is the complex fate of being a Southern woman, as that fate is registered in the lives of a whole host of female characters and the stories men construct about them. The old Virginia gentleman in each of these novels has several crucial functions to perform: as an agent or catalyst of action, an embodiment of the old world ("the conservative forces of society and the moral order" as Glasgow once termed it), and a contrasting measure of the new, as someone who mirrors social change through his own decline. But his importance is defined in terms of his relationship with, and interpretation of, the women around him; how we judge him, finally, rests on what he makes of his female friends, relatives, and acquaintances. His significance lies, ultimately, in what he sees—or, more usually, fails to see—in them; their significance lies, on the other hand, in what they are and in what they might be, or might have been. The judge, the lawyer, and the general are not only outnumbered—to the extent, that is, that they are surrounded by the women whose lives they try to control, often successfully; they are overshadowed in the sense that these three novels are less about them than about male mythologizing of women and about women's responses to male mythology.

The part played by the character of Victoria, Virginius Littlepage's wife, in *They Stooped to Folly* is instructive here. At first, Glasgow later explained, "I had meant to keep her in the background, to draw her,

---

46. James Branch Cabell cited in Jones, *Tomorrow Is Another Day*, 233. See also *Certain Measure*, 241.

somewhat sketchily and flippantly, as a tiresome good woman" who sacrifices herself for her husband. But, "as the book progressed," she added, "I found myself concentrating upon her, and to be trying, through her mind and heart, to explore the depths of the average woman of good will." "I found that she had, as actors say, 'stolen' a chief role," Glasgow concluded. Which is what, on a larger scale, the women characters do in these three novels as a group: they "steal" the stories away from the men who might appear to dominate them. Touchingly, at the end of her life Victoria tries to write a letter to the husband who, after many years of marriage, hardly knows her. "There is something I wish to say to you," she thinks—but then, "It isn't important, or if it is, I have forgotten";[47] and so she dies with the "something" unsaid. In the Old South, Glasgow proclaimed, "as elsewhere, expression belonged to the articulate, and the articulate was extremely satisfied with his own fortunate lot," while those with a "less enviable lot" such as women were left "dumb and sterile." In the Queenborough trilogy, however, the "dumb" like Victoria are given voice in the sense that their plight is fully articulated; the "something" that needs to be said, by them or for them, *is* said—the silence is broken, at least to the reader.

Glasgow had turned to the Queenborough trilogy, she said, "thirsting for laughter" after the evidently traumatic experience of writing *Barren Ground*. Traumatic but also emancipatory: *Barren Ground* "became for me . . . almost a vehicle of liberation," she declared. She had lived close to the dominating figure of the novel, Dorinda Oakley, for ten years; she then took three years to produce what she felt, when it was completed, was "the truest novel ever written." It was "torn out" of herself, Glasgow confessed—and it was not only a deeply confessional work, it was one of profound self-discovery: "I wrote *Barren Ground,* and immediately I knew I had found myself." What distinguishes this novel from many of Glasgow's other sagas of plain folk, their survival and triumph is, in fact, twofold. One, as these statements make clear, is its deeply personal nature: Dorinda Oakley is close to the author in a way and to an extent that, say, Nicolas Burr in *The Voice of the People* or Ben Starr the "plain man" of the title in *The Romance of a Plain Man* can never hope to be. As a result, Glasgow offers a depth, detail, and intimacy of portraiture in *Barren Ground* that is singularly lacking in her accounts of Burr and Starr—who are not so much plain men as plain stereotypes. The other

47. *They Stooped to Folly*, 184–85. See also *Certain Measure*, 135–36, 244.

distinguishing feature is perhaps related to this. Burr, as we have seen, is eventually denied the heroic role and removed from the scene. Something similar happens to Starr: at the close of the novel, he refuses the presidency of the railroad which he has always coveted in order to devote himself to his wife—whom he takes off to southern California. "The rise of the workingman" is abruptly aborted again, since the workingman gives up his public role and rewards and moves off the narrative and historical stage—apparently content with domestic obscurity. Dorinda Oakley does not have precisely the same social origins as Glasgow's plain men. She comes, we are told, from "good people"—as opposed, that is, to "good family"—occupying "the social strata midway between the lower gentility and the upper class of 'poor white.' "[48] In the distant past there are the "sturdy English yeomen" who settled the county where she is born; in the more recent past, there is a mother descended from stern Scotch-Irish, Calvinist farmers who marries "a member of the 'poor white' class" because he reminds her of John the Baptist. Those origins are quite sufficiently plain, however, to bear comparison with those of Burr and Starr; and, in this case, the protagonist not only survives and stays on the scene, she achieves what is quite clearly a triumph of character.

The nature of that triumph is intimated toward the end of *Barren Ground*, as Dorinda meditates on her losses and gains. Glasgow explained that she had decided, when she came to tell the story of Dorinda, that "for once, in Southern fiction, the betrayed woman would become the victor instead of the victim." And, as Dorinda contemplates her position, the sense of victory over circumstance—and even a measure of success—is evident in comments such as these: "The storm and the hagridden dreams of the night were over, and the land which she had forgotten was waiting to take her back into its heart. Endurance. Fortitude. The spirit of the land was flowing into her, and her own spirit, strengthened and refreshed, was flowing out again toward life. This was the permanent self, she knew. This was what remained to her after the years had

48. *Barren Ground* (New York, 1925), 5. See also 9; *Woman Within*, 243–44; *Letters of Ellen Glasgow*, 90 (To William H. F. Lamont, 9 February 1928), 118 (To Daniel Longwell, 12 July 1932), 341 (To Signe Toksvig, 4 February 1944); *Certain Measure*, 152–53, 155, 180. Thiébaux points out that Glasgow makes a crucial mistake in *The Romance of a Plain Man* (New York, 1909) by placing "the stolid cardboard Starr" at the center of the action (*Ellen Glasgow*, 93).

taken their bloom."[49] This triumph of Dorinda's has been variously read. It is, we are told, a resiting of Calvinist theology in secular terms ("The moral fibre that had stiffened the necks of the martyrs lay deeply embedded in her character if not in her opinions"); a feminist victory ("Since she had proved that she could farm as well as a man there was less need for her to endeavour to fascinate as a woman"); another version of Southern stoicism ("A deep-rooted religious instinct persuaded her . . . that dullness, not pleasure, was the fundamental law of morality"). There have been readings that interpret Dorinda as a classic case of repression and sublimation, as her "distaste for physical love" after an unhappy romantic liaison and a miscarriage leads her to devote herself to work. There have been others that claim to discern a determinately female pastoral in *Barren Ground,* founded on an erotic, creative, and fundamentally unexploitative relationship with the land: although it is difficult to see exactly how this fits in with Dorinda Oakley's "fierce sense of possession," her business acumen and enterprise—or, for that matter, her scientific farming methods and strict commitment to cash crops. Whatever else *Barren Ground* may mean or be, however, what a passage like the one just quoted makes clear is the author's own deep involvement in the inner and outer struggles of her protagonist. Dorinda Oakley is a farm woman experiencing a moment of intimate contact with nature, certainly; she is the daughter of farmers realizing that there too, in farming, is where she must make her stand. But she is also fundamentally like her creator—who said that, in order to write this story, she had to reach "far down into a past that was deeper and richer than conscious recollection"—in that she is someone in the process of realizing her true vocation and, with that, a proper place and identity.

"For the setting of this novel," Glasgow later explained, "I went far back into the past." The countryside of *Barren Ground* was as familiar to her, she added, "as if the landscape unrolled both without and within." The metaphor of interpenetration of human body and the body of the earth that Glasgow uses here of herself, just as she uses it of

49. *Barren Ground,* 524. See also 81, 202, 350, 387, 472; *Certain Measure,* 153, 160. For very different interpretations of *Barren Ground* see, for example, Monique Parent, *Ellen Glasgow Romancière* (Paris, 1962) (which investigates the feminist dimension of the novel); Ekman, *End of a Legend* (in which the autobiographical, vengeful, and repressive elements in the heroine are emphasized); Thiébaux, *Ellen Glasgow* (in which the Calvinist inheritance is given particular attention); Harrison, *Female Pastoral* (which discusses the book in terms of Glasgow's rewriting of the pastoral tradition).

Dorinda Oakley at the end of the novel, is only one measure among many of the intimate relationship between author and character here. Another, and surely more striking one, is suggested by the curious differences between the story of Dorinda and the stories of the women who surround her—including, especially, her mother. Early on in the novel, Dorinda is betrayed in love and left pregnant. She goes to New York, where she becomes delirious, passes out, and awakens in a hospital. There in the hospital, she meets a handy deus ex machina called Dr. Faraday, who, having put her back on her feet, provides her with employment, helps introduce her to scientific farming and "the biological interpretation of history," lends her money to go back and renew the family farm—and whose wife, into the bargain, supplies some handy addresses of possible customers for her farm produce. It is a new life and Dorinda has a new personality to fit that life: something to which we are oddly alerted by the nature of Dr. Faraday's strictly medical help. Dorinda suffers a miscarriage as the result of her accident: a convenient reversal of fortune, since it leaves Dorinda unburdened, free to pursue the vocation Glasgow has chosen for her. This, however, is only alluded to; it receives only passing, indirect mention and there is certainly no sense of emotional loss. What receives emphasis, on the contrary, is an operation on Dorinda's *head*: the first things she notices when she comes round in the hospital is that "she could not turn her head because it was bandaged and . . . she discovered that her hair had been cut away on one side."[50] A practical explanation is offered for this—she hurt her head when she passed out and fell, we are told—but the focus on the head injury and subsequent operation seems oddly superfluous, even beside the point: unless, that is, we read this as a moment of transformation of character and not just a turn of fate. Dorinda has changed; as she observes later of herself, "I suppose I'm different from other women." And this is the moment of change, if any single moment can be picked out: the point at which she begins to carve out a special story for herself.

That story, as Dorinda realizes, makes her different from other women: women such as her mother—who has been worn out caring for others, always putting other people in her family before herself. A worn, shadowy, self-sacrificial figure not unlike Virginia Pendleton, Mrs. Oakley dies the way she has always lived. She perjures herself for one of her sons, an act that her daughter regards "as sentimental rather than

50. *Barren Ground*, 215. See also 325, 461; *Certain Measure*, 154.

unselfish," and one that turns out to be one sacrifice too many for her exhausted body and spirit. "Her mother's shrunken figure" tells Dorinda that "the old woman must have paid a fearful price for her son's freedom"; and she quickly crumbles away—her preferred final companions her dogs "because they did not bother her with questions"—rambling on, just before she dies, of what she might have done had she not married Dorinda's father. "The woman in there has been dying for twenty years," observes the doctor who comes to call on her. And every choice Dorinda makes after her operation seems designed, among other things, to resist the example of her mother, and to deny that "evasive idealism" which leads Mrs. Oakley to live quietly, passively—and, in the end, for a lie. "The vein of iron in her nature would never bend," we are told of Dorinda, "would never break, would never disintegrate in the furnace of emotion." "She would never be broken while the vein of iron held in her soul." Dorinda, we soon find out, is done with the illusion of romantic love ("Oh, if the women who wanted love could only know the infinite relief of having love over!"); she is through with any feeling that might dominate her, ("she had lost beyond recall the gift of poignant emotion"); all she feels for her ex-lover is "disgust"; all she feels for her mother and father, when they die, is "a sense of pity rather than . . . grief." "You're hard, Dorinda, as hard as stone," she is told: to which she replies, with an "exultant" smile, "Yes, I am hard. I'm through with soft things." What that "hardness" enables her to achieve is measured whenever she turns to the land and her farm: to what she has *done* rather than what, like her mother, she has simply dreamed. "She had worked relentlessly through the years," she reflects, "but it was work that she had enjoyed, and above all it was work that had created anew the surroundings amid which she lived. . . . And there was more than hard work in her struggle there was unflagging enterprise as well. . . . Without . . . the courage to borrow money, she could never have made the farm even a moderate success. This had required not only perseverance but audacity as well."[51]

Dorinda is not like her mother, then, after her transformation. Nor is she like her father, a pathetically unsuccessful figure who looms in her memory "as a titanic image of the labourer who labours without hope." What she is like, in a sense what she has become, is suggested by Glas-

---

51. *Barren Ground*, 348. See also 170, 180, 308–9, 324, 325, 335, 338, 340, 342, 466.

gow's accounts of the liberating effect of the writing of *Barren Ground*—
and by a passage like this from Glasgow's portrait of *her* father:

> His virtues were more than Calvinistic; they were Roman. With
> complete integrity, and an abiding sense of responsibility, he gave
> his wife and children everything but the one thing they needed
> most, and that was love. Yet he was entirely unselfish, and in his
> long life . . . he never committed a pleasure . . . he held fast to
> property . . . I understand, now, that he must have suffered, beneath
> his stern fortitude. . . . At his death, many of the men who worked
> under him . . . came to express their . . . grief. . . . Over and over,
> they repeated: "He was always just."[52]

The source of the power of *Barren Ground* surely lies here: in the charged
family feelings that Glasgow brought to it, as she engaged in her own
struggle for vocation—feelings that, it is perhaps worth repeating, were
tangled up in Glasgow's case with the matter of Virginia and the story of
the South. The transformation Dorinda experiences is to some degree
one from old order to new; only to some degree, however, since she is as
much involved in the secularizing of the Calvinist spirit and conscience
as she is in turning agriculture into a business. Much more fully and
unambiguously than this, it is a change from what—in her own variation
on the narratives of state and region—Glasgow saw as the pliant, passive,
yielding figure of the mother to the stern, active, unbending figure of the
father: as Dorinda abandons the wasted, romantic, evasive model of Mrs.
Oakley and her kind, she discovers her own vein of iron. *Barren Ground*
has often been celebrated for its narrative drive and emotional intensity.
It has, almost equally often, been attacked for its "thwarted and twisted"
emotions, and for a "repressed and vindictive" heroine who appears to
excite far too much sympathy in her creator. These are, surely, different
sides of the same coin: in this, her most successful fictional account of
personal and social change, Glasgow and her heroine both gravitate from
what is perceived to be the "female" principle to what is seen as the
"male" one. To adopt the vocabulary, the series of assumptions only
partly hidden in the narrative, the two discover and affirm vocation—
and, in the process, "become men."

52. *Woman Within*, 15–16. See also *Barren Ground*, 300; Thiébaux, *Ellen Glasgow*,
125.

"I was a radical when everyone . . . was conservative, and now I am a conservative when other people appear to be radical," Glasgow wrote in *The Woman Within.* That is, at best, a half-truth. Glasgow was much more deeply conflicted than she cared to admit; the story of Virginia was, in its own way, just as conflicted; so was the story of the South—and particularly so at the time when Glasgow was, as she claimed, "a radical." Quite apart from anything else, Glasgow's curious if hardly unusual myopia about African Americans in even her most "progressive" texts makes for complication: in *Barren Ground,* for example, we are reminded several times about the "indolence" of "that immature but not ungenerous race." True, Dorinda Oakley enjoys the companionship of her African American maid, Fluvanna: but, quite apart from the condescension inherent in the relationship, the narrator cannot help noting how Fluvanna's "sunny sympathy" and "cheerful alacrity" enable Dorinda to overlook "an occasional slackening of industry."[53] Closer to the emotional bone, there is the point that the "male"/"female" opposition which informs the subterranean levels of Glasgow's accounts of progress inevitably created problems when it came to confronting issues like female emancipation. This does not significantly affect expressions of opinion. On the contrary, the question of the rights of women—and the related problem of the wrongs of men—receives powerful, unambiguous expression in many of the novels. Not the least felicitous element in Glasgow's work, in fact, is the series of shrewd older women, minor characters who embellish the narrative with observations like "The woman that waits on a man has a long wait ahead of her," or "it ain't the blows that wears a woman out, it's the mortal sameness." What it does affect, however—or, rather, complicate—is the development of character. In *Barren Ground,* as in *Virginia* and *Life and Gabriella,* attributes of personality tend to be gendered, with all that is passive, yielding, and regressive associated with the "female" and all that is active, authori-

---

53. *Barren Ground,* 469. See also 281; *Woman Within,* 42; William Faulkner, *Sanctuary* (1931; London, 1964 edition), 15. Elizabeth Schultz notes that Dorinda's attitude to Fluvanna is marred by "an inherited feeling of condescension" ("Out of the Woods and into the World: A Study of Interracial Friendships Between Women in American Novels," in *Conjuring: Black Women, Fiction, and Literary Tradition* edited by Marjorie Pryse and Hortense J. Spillers [Bloomington, Ind., 1985], 70–71). Examples of the shrewd older women who comment, in a habitually skeptical way, on relationships between men and women include Mag Twine in *The Ancient Law* (New York, 1908) and Betsey Bottom in *The Miller of Old Church* (New York, 1911).

tative, and progressive identified with the "male"; and *that,* almost invariably, complicates and problematizes accounts of both the "traditional" and the "new" or "free" woman. To this extent, Virginia Pendleton and Dorinda Oakley are sharers of the same secret: that, for Glasgow—to quote a later Southern writer for whom she had little time, William Faulkner—"Progress is 'he.' "

And Progress was something that came to seem less attractive to Ellen Glasgow as she grew older. To this extent, at least, she was right: she did grow more fiercely and unequivocally conservative in her later years—so following a familiar pattern among writers of her state and region. Two final works testify to this: *In This Our Life,* which appeared in 1941, and a short sequel, *Beyond Defeat,* which was not published until 1966, more than twenty years after her death. By the time they were written, the New South and the recognition of its character inherent in the literature of the Southern "renaissance" were both established facts. The First World War was one of several agents of economic and social transformation: accelerating changes that had been occurring, at different paces in different localities in the South, ever since Lee surrendered. If she wished to, Glasgow had only to look at the nearby port of Norfolk to witness an example of how things could alter—suddenly and almost without warning. In 1910, Norfolk had a population of less than seventy thousand people, most of whom were devoted to the exporting of agricultural produce and the importing of manufactured goods. It had been a reasonably prosperous place since not long after the Civil War. Within a few months after the outbreak of world war, however, it had become something else again: invaded by a hundred thousand newcomers, drawn by the demand for labor at the government naval stations and in the new industrial centers. According to almost contemporary reports, the town became "overnight the center of government activities involving the expenditure of millions and transforming its outlying districts into hives of industry crowded with naval workers. . . . Business of all kinds . . . expanded beyond facilities to handle it."[54] Norfolk was in some ways a special case, of course, being a seaport, and the process of change was never seamless—world war, for example, was followed by the almost inevitable postwar recession. But what was happening in Norfolk happened in

54. *Norfolk Virginian-Pilot,* 29 December 1918, cited in George B. Tindall, *The Emergence of the New South, 1913–1943* (1967), vol. X of *A History of the South* edited by Stephenson and Coulter. See also *Certain Measure,* 69.

many other Southern places too; the end of the First World War did not so much stop industrialization as slow it down; the decline of the old structures and the old elites not only continued but also gathered pace. Glasgow knew this. She could see it close at hand; she could also discern its impact on the writing of her region in what she called "the weird pages" of "the modern literary South." And, in their different ways, both of her last novels represent a reaction to all the changes in life and literature she saw around her; they were her way of coping, her strategies for dealing with a world that had come to seem increasingly strange. The strategies of the two are different, but each in its way is typical: typical, that is, of Glasgow herself, the place from which she came—and of many writers who try to deal with social transformation in a specifically localized setting.

In This Our Life offers the strategy of romance. At the center of the story is an older person like Glasgow herself, Asa Timberlake, a gentleman of the old school: who offers a largely negative judgment on his children, grandchildren—and also on contemporary life. His offspring, as Asa sees it, are eccentrics, deviations from the traditional norms, who demonstrate by their deviation the "general breaking-up in the pattern of life" to which they belong. They have lost touch with the controls normally placed on human behavior, with inherited codes and systems of belief, and they have nothing with which to fill the gap except their own random impulses. "Responsibility and integrity" have disappeared, as facts and standards of judgment; and all that remains to distinguish one person from another is "the superiority . . . a very wide margin of vested interests . . . can confer"—in other words, the cash nexus. "Nobody . . . had any patience, nowadays, with the graces of living," Asa laments. "Acceleration, not beauty, was the strange god of our modern worship." Lacking any code other than the fiscal, the younger generation Asa sees around him seems to lack whole and functioning personalities; and, lacking this, they tend to lack reality. Like the "unreal, unsubstantial houses" they inhabit, they offer little more than a series of appearances, empty gestures, and meaningless facades. Set in opposition to this new world, this New South that manages to be material without ever being real, is an old world that corresponds to the best that was ever thought and said about the Old South and the Old Dominion. Asa, like his creator, is an old person situated in a strange landscape which he hardly understands and certainly does not like. It seems appropriate to him, then, to turn to memories for relief and to judge the present in terms of an entirely romanticized past. Author and character turn back in this novel, without hesitation or ambiguity, to past times celebrated for their "elegance, grace, dignity, and beauty." The approved social model is an aristocratic one; and Asa's own father is taken as its paradigm, a man as accomplished as any figure dreamed up by earlier Virginia romancers. "In the old days," Asa observes, "his father had known the name and face of every man he employed. One and all, he and his men belonged to a single social unit, which . . . was held together by some vital bond of human relation. . . . There had been injustice . . . but one had dealt with flesh and blood, not with a list of printed names."⁵⁵ No apologist for what Glasgow had once disparagingly called the "old feudal order" could have put it better. The contrast sketched out here is between a social structure that supposedly expresses the personal values of "family feeling" and romantic love, and one that reduces all motives to the economic: the "human" and "vital" on the one hand and, on the other, the mechanical. We are not far from the vocabulary and the vision of the arguments for slavery, let alone early plantation romance. More to the point, the irony that played around the portraits of Virginia Pendleton or Virginius Little-page and *their* closed worlds has now more or less disappeared.

Irony is still further out of the picture in *Beyond Defeat*. "So many readers missed the point" of *In This Our Life*, Glasgow claimed, that she had to write something to correct the error—and to underline the fact that Asa Timberlake is "not a failure in life, but a man in whom character, not success, was an end in itself."⁵⁶ *Beyond Defeat* is not so much another Glasgow novel about the triumph of character, however, as a story that shows the compensatory uses of myth. It is autumn. Asa's errant daughter, Roy, returns home with a child, the result of a single night's liaison with a stranger. "She had lived and died and been born over again," we are told, and experienced a "resurrection of the body." Asa, meanwhile, has been restored to health by working on the farm, in the company of the woman he has always loved, Kate Oliver. He has the appearance of someone who has "been to the end of his life, and . . . come out somewhere else, in another beginning." He has "fought . . .

---

55. *In This Our Life* (New York, 1941), 13. See also 31, 32, 55, 111, 122, 218; *Virginia*, 55.

56. *Letters of Ellen Glasgow*, 304 (To Bessie Zaban Jones, 20 July 1942). All quotations in this paragraph are from *Beyond Defeat* edited by Luther Y. Gore (Charlottesville, Va., 1966).

through the dark forest," and is renewed; Kate, in turn, has always been a vital creature of the earth, "a part of the autumn," "her nature . . . rooted in some hidden identity with the land." Roy achieves reconciliation with her idealized father figure: "my deepest roots are in you, Daddy," she declares. She also renews her bond with a young idealist called Craig Fleming; and together she, Craig, and her child form a close relationship that is intimate without being erotic. Reunion, reconciliation, renewal: the moment is fleeting, since it occurs within "the changeless, perpetual, rhythm of time passing." But, while it lasts, it offers a kind of perfection: "This is peace," Roy thinks, "I have suffered enough. This is the end of strain and violence, and of wanting that is never satisfied." It also offers, it is hoped, "the living seeds of tomorrow," something that belongs "not with the buried past but with that endless becoming which was the unknown, and as yet unborn, future." What that peace entails, and what those seeds contain are clear enough: the perfect family, from which all strain, struggle, and tension have miraculously disappeared. The gracious, vigorous father, the benevolent, vital, earth mother, the sympathetic spouse, the beautiful child of singular origin, the marriage of true minds: all these figures are woven together for the benefit of the daughter who returns to rest and forgiveness. This is the family Glasgow herself never enjoyed; it is also the family romance as neither Virginia nor the South ever knew it. Created out of the pressures of family, state, and regional histories, it has struggled free of those histories, to inhabit its own special element of dream, fulfilled desire.

Glasgow herself was inclined to attribute the increasingly regressive strain of her last works to "the inevitable recoil from youth to age." She was also tempted to draw a sharp distinction between her "external life" of family, friendship, trust funds, and war and her "interior world . . . thickly woven of recollections." Both touches of self-analysis are as much the result of her habit of dualism as they are of accurate perception: youth/age, external/interior were two further sides of the discursive coin, two more mutually exclusive opposites to add to her already extensive lexicon when it came to explaining any character—including her own. In a way, these two were even less close to the truth than many others. The pull toward feudal romance or family mythology did not begin with her last two books, the undertow of nostalgia is always there in even the most "progressive" work; and the ebb and flow of sympathy that so much of her writing betrays is something deeply personal, certainly, but also a function of her place in history—which is to say, the literary and other histories of Virginia and the South. Her insecurity was less obvious than Poe's (a writer with whom, incidentally, she declared an affinity) but it was detectable in her nonetheless. It encouraged her to pursue theory, to construct plans and dualistic categories—and constantly, lengthily to explain. "I will become a great novelist or none at all,"[57] she wrote early on in her career; and that ambition set her at odds with the example of both her father and her mother: for whom the words "writing," "career," and "woman" were just about mutually exclusive. For once, perhaps, a (female) character in one of Glasgow's earliest novels reflects the opinion of both of the author's parents when she says, of women novelists who expect to be taken seriously: "It's as if they really pretended to know as much as a man." "When they publish books I suppose they expect men to read them," she goes on, "and that in itself is a kind of conceit." Glasgow certainly expected to be taken seriously. That meant coping with the problem, not only of being a woman, but of being a Southern woman in changing times. Small wonder, then, that she often felt inclined to resist the Southern label or to declare that, even while she was writing "a social history of Virginia from the decade before the Confederacy," she was certainly no provincial. She was, after all, trying to make her way in a world and secure her reputation on terms that required of her, as she saw it, constant vigilance, wariness, and defense. Her writing declares almost despite itself its author's status as a Southern woman—and, more particularly, a Virginia lady—and that is one major reason why it is so conflicted. It is also a reason why Glasgow's books— and what a later Southern writer, Allen Tate, rather testily referred to as their "mixed thesis . . . of old Southism and Progress"—are indelibly a part of her home place and its past. There is another, related reason for this connection, though, which is nicely caught in a personal anecdote in *The Woman Within,* about Glasgow's very first memories of writing. "In my seventh summer I became a writer," Glasgow recalls. "One summer day," she explains, she made "a new hymn—a hymn of my very own"— consisting of just five lines. " 'That's po'try,' my heart sang over and over, 'and I wrote it!' " The exultation, however, lasted only until she ventured

---

57. *Letters of Ellen Glasgow,* 25 (To Walter Hines Page, 22 November 1897). See also *Woman Within,* 42. The remark about women novelists occurs in *The Wheel of Life* (New York, 1906), a novel in which, Glasgow declared, "I was seeking . . . a way out of myself" (*Woman Within,* 193).

into her sister's room and overheard her sister reading her "precious verses" aloud to her guests with "kindly ridicule and amusement." "I fled," she recalls. "My skin felt naked and scorched, as if a flame had blown over it." "Was the sensitiveness I have always felt about my work," she asks by way of conclusion, "rooted in the sharp mortification of that awakening?"[58] Perhaps it was. Whether it was or not, however, it is clear that in this "sensitiveness" she was not alone. The fear of being misread was not unique to Glasgow—although clearly it was something deeply personal; on the contrary, it is something that many other writers from the South have felt, another sign of the fear that real life may be elsewhere, in another place or region—and the real writing that goes along with it. Other voices, other rooms calling into question the seriousness and centrality, or even the reality of your own voice—it is a poignant moment, recalled and rehearsed with scrupulous craft; it is also a revealing image, telling us more than even Glasgow is aware—or, at least, chooses to confess—about being a woman writer, and a Southern one.

58. *Woman Within,* 36–37. See also *Certain Measure,* 3; Tate, *Literary Correspondence of Davidson and Tate* edited by Fain and Young, 245 (To Davidson, 12 December 1929).

3

"The most powerful propaganda"

Stark Young, Andrew Nelson Lytle, the Agrarians, and the Making of the Southern Literary Canon

"With the war of 1914–1918," Allen Tate famously declared, "the South reentered the world—but gave a backward glance as it slipped over the border." "That backward glance," he went on, "gave us the Southern renascence, a literature conscious of the past in the present." Tate's declaration of the South's literary rebirth was published in 1945: but it had been anticipated in essays written by him, and other members of the Fugitive and Agrarian groups, over the previous two decades. Quite apart from providing academics with handy titles for their books and essays on modern Southern writing, that declaration proved a powerful, in fact determining, influence on the way that writing was read: the "Southern renascence" as Tate himself understood it was to become the prism through which the literature issuing from the region from the second decade to, say, the middle of the century was seen—by both the public and the critical eye. Tate, like the more astute of his fellow Fugitives and Agrarians, recognized the vital connection between history and narrative; he knew how much it mattered just whose story got told. After all, it was precisely the sense that others had control of the narrative which had helped push the Agrarians into print, and prompted Tate himself to declare in 1927—as he saw so many Northern, liberal commentators mocking what they saw as a benighted region—"I've attacked the South for the last time." Tate was offering a typically oblique advertisement for himself, as well as a fanfare for a certain kind of writing he at once typified and favored, when he talked about "a literature conscious of the past in the present." He was trying to rewrite *literary* history from a self-consciously reactive position just as much as, in his social and political essays, he was trying to reinvent the broader history of the West from a stance of equally self-conscious reaction: "whenever the demagogues cry 'Nous allons!,' " he wryly confided to his friend and fellow Fugitive Donald Davidson, "if the reply is 'Non! Nous retardons!' then you may be sure the reply indicates the right values."[1] And although Tate was particularly and fiercely knowing about this, it is not difficult to see that other Fugitives and Agrarians, as they metamorphosed into New Critics, were resiting the critical narrative in similar ways. Recent commentary on the New Criticism, particularly of the Southern variety, has been primarily concerned with locating a vein of ideological—and, more specifically, political—continuity between this phase of the career of Tate, Robert Penn Warren, John Crowe Ransom, and others and their earlier, aesthetic and agrarian manifestations. That continuity may well be there. Another way of reading these careers, however, suggests a kind of *discon-tinuity*. Tate and the others had moved on, we could say, acknowledging

1. *The Literary Correspondence of Donald Davidson and Allen Tate* edited by John Tyree Fain and Thomas D. Young (Athens, Ga., 1974), 191. To Donald Davidson, 1 March 1927. See also "The New Provincialism," in *Collected Essays* (New York, 1959), 545. The material on the Agrarians is extensive. Useful books, and books containing helpful discussions, include John M. Bradbury, *The Fugitives: A Critical Account* (Chapel Hill, N.C., 1958); Louise Cowan, *The Fugitive Group: A Literary History* (Baton Rouge, La., 1959); John L. Stewart, *The Burden of Time: The Fugitives and Agrarians* (Princeton, 1965); Alexander Karanikas, *Tillers of a Myth: Southern Agrarians as Social and Literary Critics* (Madison, Wis., 1966); Louis D. Rubin, *The Wary Fugitives: Four Poets and the South* (Baton Rouge, La., 1978); F. Garvin Davenport, *The Myth of Southern History: Historical Consciousness in Twentieth-Century Southern Literature* (Nashville, Tenn., 1980); Richard H. King, *A Southern Renaissance: The Cultural Awakening of the South, 1930–1955* (New York, 1980); William C. Havard and Walter Sullivan, eds., *A Band of Prophets: The Vanderbilt Agrarians After Fifty Years* (Baton Rouge, La., 1982); Daniel J. Singal, *The War Within: From Victorian to Modernist Thought in the South, 1919–1945* (Chapel Hill, N.C., 1982); Thomas D. Young, *Waking Their Neighbors Up: The Nashville Agrarians Rediscovered* (Athens, Ga., 1982). Perhaps the most comprehensive history of the Agrarians is Virginia Rock, "The Making and Meaning of *I'll Take My Stand*: A Study of Utopian Conservatism, 1929–1939" (University of Minnesota Ph.D. diss., 1961). Two recent studies that concentrate on the possible continuities between the different stages of the careers of the Fugitives, Agrarians, and New Critics are Mark Jancovich, *The Cultural Politics of the New Criticism* (Cambridge, 1992), and David Stenhouse, "The Literary Project of John Crowe Ransom" (University of Edinburgh Ph.D. diss., 1996). Two books by the author of the present volume also include discussions of the Agrarians: *The Literature of Memory: Modern Writers of the American South* (Baltimore, Md., 1977) and *Writing the South: Ideas of an American Region* (Cambridge, 1986).

their failure to change the world; however, they moved on to become critics whose critical principles offered the best possible context in which to understand and value their own work in poetry and fiction, past and present. They acted as cultural producers *and,* quite separately, as cultural commodifiers, supplying the ideal critical mediation for the sorts of stories, poems, and plays that they themselves had written and, in some cases, were continuing to write. The obliging reader, instructed by Tate about the "Southern renascence" and equipped by him with an understanding of what was determinately and valuably "Southern" ("conscious of the past in the present"), could then go on properly to appreciate works like *The Fathers* or "Ode to the Confederate Dead."

Just how calculated all this was it is difficult to say: not least, because some writers, like Tate, were more *openly* calculated than others, such as Ransom: more willing, that is, to admit that what they wanted to do was alter the narrative. Although (despite his Francophilia) Tate would have found little enough in common with Louis Althusser, he might well have found Althusser's idea of the "script" appealing: the notion of a model or map, that is, learned in and from a culture, according to which each member of that culture "reads" life, including his or her own. Tate wanted to rewrite that script for *his* culture. At its most grandiose, this involved a revision of Western history since the early modern period and perhaps even before that. At a much more modest level, it involved imposing a particular blueprint on the recent literary past of his region. The larger scheme failed, spectacularly. In terms of the more modest aims, however, Tate was part of a project that was even more successful than he might have hoped; since his version of Southern writing in the first half of this century is still with us today. He may not actually have created the canon of modern Southern literature, but he greatly assisted in its creation: by naming some names worthy of inclusion in any such canon and, even more crucial, by helping to formulate the critical principles, the basis on which the canon was erected. Just how greatly Tate and the other Agrarians assisted in this respect is suggested by one single event. Eight years after Tate's essay on "the Southern renascence" was published, a collection of essays appeared using that phrase for its title and subtitled *The Literature of the Modern South.* It was edited by Louis D. Rubin and Robert D. Jacobs; and in it the editors declared their belief that, as they put it, "the volume provides the first reasonably thorough treatment of the literature of the modern South." Twelve years after this, in 1965 on the occasion of the fifth printing of the book, the same editors expressed the same idea in a slightly different way. "What we did in 1953," they proudly declared, "was to publish the first attempt at an inclusive examination of the literature of the modern South." "Possibly a good bit of what was said in this book will now appear dated and, occasionally . . . even chauvinistic," they admitted. "But *Southern Renascence* was the first of the sort and some of its essays are of the kind that endure."[2] Writing more recently, Noel Polk has stated matters more baldly. "*Southern Renascence*," he pointed out, ". . . almost singlehandedly established 'Southern literature' as a legitimate academic field." Polk then makes a further, equally important point that somehow escapes the attention of the editors of this book: *Southern Renascence,* as he puts it, "helped to insure that Southern literature as defined by the Vanderbilt intellectual circle would dominate both academic and nonacademic discussions of the South." The *Southern Renascence* that Rubin and Jacobs and their contributors celebrated was, in short, Tate's "Southern renascence."

Even a cursory glance at the Table of Contents suggests how much the literary priorities of Tate, Ransom, and their literary accomplices are enshrined in this seminal 1953 volume. Two of the contributors, Andrew Nelson Lytle and Donald Davidson, also contributed to the 1930 Agrarian Symposium, *I'll Take My Stand.* There are essays on both of them and, among the other Agrarians, on Tate (who warrants two pieces), Robert Penn Warren (two essays again), Stark Young, and John Crowe Ransom. Merrill Moore, a contributor to *The Fugitive,* is accorded an essay. So is the New Critic and close associate of Warren, Cleanth Brooks. So is Tate's wife and co-worker in the fields of literary reaction, Caroline Gordon. So, too, is the deeply traditionalist John Peale Bishop: who once wrote, in a letter to Tate, "With us Western civilization ends." Among the other contributors are Richard M. Weaver, writing on "Aspects of the Southern Philosophy" and Walter Sullivan, whose subject is "Southern Novelists and the Civil War." Weaver was later to publish a book titled *The Southern Tradition At Bay* in which the Old South is

2. Louis D. Rubin and Robert D. Jacobs, "Preface to Fifth Printing" (1965), *Southern Renascence: The Literature of the Modern South* (1953; Baltimore, Md., 1965 edition), ix. See also "Preface," v; Louis Althusser, "Ideology and the State," in *Lenin and Philosophy, and Other Essays* translated by Ben Brewster (London, 1977); Noel Polk, "Faulkner and World War II," in *Remaking Dixie: The Impact of World War II on the American South* edited by Neil R. McMillen (Jackson, Miss., 1997), 133.

celebrated as *"the last non-materialist civilization in the Western world"*
and in which also "the system of slavery" is said, "like that of military
discipline," to have enforced "habits of health and regularity"—"when
it was suddenly removed," Weaver argues, "the hitherto unknown ills of
syphilis, consumption, and insanity made immediate appearance" among
the former slave population. In his essay for *Southern Renascence,*
Weaver writes in a similar key. Contrasting "the Southerner" with "the
dominant American type, which still may with reasonable accuracy be
called the Yankee," Weaver insists that the Southerner is an "authentically religious being" with a "discipline in tragedy"; "if the world continues its present drift toward tension and violence," Weaver concludes, "it
is probable that the characteristic Southern qualities will command an
increasing premium."[3] Walter Sullivan, in turn, was to publish *A Requiem for the Renascence* some twenty-three years after his essay for
Southern Renascence; in *Requiem,* Sullivan laments the loss of "traditional culture, as it was in the South" and "the new commitment to the
social and political clichés of our time." "I know of no contemporary
novel about the race problem which is likely to survive," he declares; and
reading this remark, written in 1976, it becomes easy to understand the
comment made by one reviewer, Tom McHaney, who said that the book
reminded him of one of those Japanese soldiers who has hidden somewhere in the South Pacific for thirty years, to emerge still fighting the
war. One would have to add, though, that the war Sullivan is fighting in
both 1953 essay and 1976 book took place, not in the 1940s, but in the
1860s. After all, in his essay for *Southern Renascence,* Sullivan quotes
with approval Tate's claim that the Civil War "must be understood as

3. Richard M. Weaver, "Aspects of the Southern Philosophy," in *Southern Renascence*
edited by Rubin and Jacobs, 14, 15, 29. See also *The Southern Tradition at Bay: A History
of Postbellum Thought* edited by George Core and M. E. Bradford (New Rochelle, N.Y.,
1968), 268, 391; *The Republic of Letters in America: The Correspondence of John Peale
Bishop and Allen Tate* edited by Thomas D. Young and John J. Hindle (Lexington, Ky.,
1981), 48. To Tate, 25 August 1931. The most useful discussions of Weaver are M. E.
Bradford, "The Agrarianism of Richard Weaver," *Modern Age,* XIV (Summer 1970),
249–56; George Core, "One View of the Castle: Richard Weaver and the Incarnate World
of the South," in *The Poetry of Community: Essays on the Southern Sensibility of History
and Literature* edited by Lewis P. Simpson (Athens, Ga., 1972); Fred Hobson, *Tell About
the South: The Southern Rage to Explain* (Baton Rouge, La., 1983), 323–35. The Foreword
to *The Southern Tradition at Bay* by Donald Davidson and the Preface by Bradford and
Core are also very helpful.

the climax of Southern culture, the last moment of order in a traditional society," and he concludes his discussion with these sonorous words:

> Whether or not we have been doing without God ever since the War, I cannot say with certainty. But even the spurious God, of whom Mr. Tate speaks, that deity fashioned by the sixteenth century merchants, must have been sufficient for a while. Because in the Old South the honor and pride were there, not as individual virtues in isolated men, but as part of the public consciousness, the moral basis on which the culture was constructed. This is the reason that the War has been used so often by so many Southern writers. . . . It is the only moment in American history when a completely developed national ethic was brought to a dramatic crisis.[4]

Southern Renascence is remarkable, though, not just for moments of regionalist piety such as this—which recollect the higher historical arguments of the Agrarians—but for acts of omission that also suggest how closely tied its essays are to the ideas of Tate and his intellectual associates. There are, in fact, two kinds of crucial omission in the book. The first kind is the more obvious. Looking at the Contents, it is clear that a place at table has been found for writers who can be assimilated to traditionalist, agrarian values, such as William Faulkner from one generation and Eudora Welty from another. There is also a place for those who can be seen to work within a determinately folk and predominantly rural tradition—as long as they are white—like Thomas Wolfe and Erskine Caldwell. And even though the Nashville/Vanderbilt circle is the presiding intellectual presence here, there is even room for those two eminent citizens of Richmond, Virginia, Ellen Glasgow and James Branch Cabell. No room is found, however, for any of the proletarian novelists. Among the younger generation, Carson McCullers (who had published

---

4. Walter Sullivan, "Southern Novelists and the Civil War," in *Southern Renascence* edited by Rubin and Jacobs, 125. See also 116; *A Requiem for the Renascence: The State of Fiction in the Modern South* (Athens, Ga., 1976), xix, xxi. Also Thomas L. Mchaney, review of *Requiem for the Renascence, Mississippi Quarterly*, XXX (1976–77), 185–88. Walter Sullivan is himself the author of some very fine traditionalist fiction, including *Sojourn of a Stranger* (New York, 1957): which invokes "the simple fact of the continuity of life, the single thread that is never cut but which goes on generation unto generation to the end of time. The simple truth that the future and the past are a part of the same passage" (234).

most of her major work by 1953), Truman Capote, and Tennessee Williams are ignored. James Agee is omitted, presumably because he was too liberal, as is Lillian Hellman, who had the misfortune to be both liberal and a woman. As for African American writers, there is simply no mention of either Richard Wright or Zora Neale Hurston, both of whom had enjoyed international fame by the time of the publication of this volume. Which leads, naturally, into the other kind of omission. There is little or no mention of the pressing social and historical issues of the day: issues which, it could be said, served to arouse interest in things Southern and so make a book like *Southern Renascence* seem timely. Just as the writers who merit a place in the volume are either deeply resistant to modern times, or else considered to be so, so the arguments and assumptions of nearly all the essays are deeply committed to Tate's "backward glance." *The* war here is the one with the North, not the one with Germany and Japan; the issue of civil rights, the race question that had after all led to the formation of the Dixiecrat Party only a few years before, the growing controversy over segregation in schools—all this is simply circumvented. "It was more than two decades ago that twelve Southerners published *I'll Take My Stand*," declares one of the editors of *Southern Renascence* (in an essay titled "Poe and the Agrarian Critics"). "In this volume the most cogent attack of our time upon technology and the doctrine of Progress was mustered."[5] That sets the tone for every reference to the Agrarian symposium that follows and for the book as a whole. Despite that "modern" in its subtitle, *Southern Renascence* shares with *I'll Take My Stand* a deep distrust of modern times, the longing for a lost rural and traditional order and a usually unstated racial exclusiveness. It is, for good and ill, a book that responds to contemporary trauma, regional, national, and international, by for the most part suppressing it. And it set the agenda for subsequent writing about the literature of the region.

Eight years after the initial publication of *Southern Renascence,* the two editors of that book produced another collection that was to prove almost equally influential—which is to say, determining in the formation of a Southern canon. The title of this book, *South: Modern Southern Literature in Its Cultural Setting,* implied a greater awareness of context; and, to a certain extent, this was true. This time, the editors permitted themselves the benefits of a reasonably lengthy Introduction in which

---

5. Robert D. Jacobs, "Poe and the Agrarian Critics," in *Southern Renascence* edited by Rubin and Jacobs, 35.

they could point to the social pressures that had helped turn attention South. "The present volume," they explained, "appears at a time when recent political and social developments have fixed worldwide attention upon the region south of the Potomac and Ohio rivers." "Readers all over the world," they added, "have naturally enough looked to the novelists and poets of the modern South for clues to the sometimes baffling behavior of its inhabitants." Entering into specifics, Rubin and Jacobs then went on to point out that, "though it is not with Supreme Court edicts and school referendums that writers are primarily concerned," nevertheless "so momentous an issue [*sic*] is bound to have its impact upon the artistic image that writers will create out of Southern life." "The 1954 decision of the Court only gave a kind of ultimate dimension to an issue that is almost as old as the region itself," the editors admitted: but "to speak of the South today is to speak of the Negro" and events like *Brown vs. the Board of Education* are a handy reminder that "the Negro's role in Southern life will continue to be for its writers what it has always been: a symbol of change." A symbol of change, only more so than ever: since "the former peasantry" that made life as it was lived in the traditional South possible "has now declined to continue performing its function" and "demands full rights and privileges of membership."[6] All this was very promising, suggesting a breakaway from the cultural agenda of *Southern Renascence* and *I'll Take My Stand*. The problem was that, as the Contents pages revealed, all the usual suspects had been rounded up: Warren, Ransom, Tate, Davidson, Lytle, Gordon, Faulkner, Welty, Glasgow, Cabell, Wolfe, Caldwell. True, there were a few additions: notably an essay on McCullers, a piece on Southern drama that included discussion of Williams and Hellman, and an account of Southern fiction in the 1950s that found room for brief consideration of (among others) Flannery O'Connor, Truman Capote, and William Styron. But there was still the familiar essay on "The Southern Temper" which praised the region for "the coincidence of a sense of the concrete, a sense of the elemental, a sense of the representative, and a sense of totality"—and declared, in passing, "these critics, sometimes called 'reactionary,' have done a considerable service to democracy." More to the

6. Louis D. Rubin and Robert D. Jacobs, "Introduction: Southern Writing and the Changing South," in *South: Modern Southern Literature in Its Cultural Setting* (Garden City, N.Y., 1961), 13–16. See also Robert B. Heilman, "The Southern Temper," in *South*, 48, 50.

point, there was no essay on proletarian writers or African American writers. In the Selected Checklist "For Further Reading" at the end of the volume, only one African American writer was given individual mention: Ralph Ellison. Space was found, however, for such notables as Hamilton Basso, John Peale Bishop, George Garrett, and Merrill Moore. Clearly, "the Negro" was important as a symbol of change in this collection, but not as a writer.

The difference between *Southern Renascence* and *South: Modern Southern Literature in Its Cultural Setting* is not, in fact, a matter of substance but of rhetoric. The turbulent events of the middle and late 1950s had made it impossible for the editors of and contributors to the later volume to continue simply to suppress and omit. The immediate cultural context is alluded to; the racial issue—and, more specifically, the fact that the traditional South depended for its existence on racial inequality and oppression—is brought into the orbit of attention; the ineluctable nature of modernism, the sheer inevitability of "the breaking up of that old, closed agrarian society and its replacement by a cosmopolitan, fluid industrial society"—this, too, is given preliminary acknowledgment. But when the contributors to the 1961 volume come to judgment, there is no essential change: the names remain the same because the fundamental critical principles remain the same. Traditionalism, literary reaction, the system of belief that activates *Southern Renascence* and, before that, *I'll Take My Stand* is declared anomalous, even morally dubious—and then deployed as the basic principle of selection and assessment; it is, in a sense, written out by the editors and then written into almost every literary judgment made in the book. Arguably, this paradox is never clearer than when the editors feel compelled to ask themselves the question, "What of the Southern writer who is a Negro?" The question is asked about halfway through the Introduction; and the fact that it is asked at all is a measure of the distance traveled between 1961 and 1953—let alone, 1930. Suppression and omission are no longer viable, it seems; what is required is a piece of verbal legerdemain. "The fact is," the editors declare, "that, until very recently, literary work by Southern Negroes has been of very little *literary* importance, though of considerably more *social* importance." "Only in our own day have Southern Negroes produced literary work that has made its appeal on aesthetic grounds," we are told, "rather than because it was written by a Negro or because of its particular subject matter."[7] The opposition on

---

7. Rubin and Jacobs, "Southern Writing and the Changing South," 18. See also 16.

which this argument is built—between the "literary" and the "social," the aesthetic and the historical/cultural—is pretty shaky in itself; besides, it leaves the reader wondering precisely what the function is of the "cultural setting" mentioned in the book's title. What is even more remarkable, however, is the way this argument is developed: through a brief discussion of *Native Son* by Richard Wright and *Invisible Man* by Ralph Ellison.

That *Native Son* was a "tremendous sensation" when it was first published in 1940 the editors readily acknowledge; however, they insist, "the novel is seldom read nowadays." The reason is very simple: "Wright's purpose was precisely that of social protest." So "passionate" were his views on the issue of civil rights, we are informed, that "artistic objectivity"—"by which is meant the subordination of the 'message' to the literary demands of the material"—was impossible for Wright. A remark made by Faulkner, that "the Negro writer" must "have equality in terms that he can get used to it and forget that he is a Negro while he's writing," is quoted approvingly. So is Faulkner's added comment, "You can't write sympathetically about a condition when it's constant outrage to you, you see." "The reader of Wright's autobiographical *Black Boy* can understand why he wrote as he did in *Native Son*,"[8] Rubin and Jacobs admit. Nevertheless, Wrights's inability or unwillingness to suppress his sense of race and racial outrage is cited as the ultimate reason for the failure of the novel. By an adroit twist of argument, the social and economic deprivations the writer suffered become the causes of his artistic failure: he could not help writing the way he did, about a system that had been a "constant outrage" to him, but the way he wrote meant that he could never write very well. By a further adroit twist of argument, a particular *kind* of ideology—the kind that informs *Native Son*—is dismissed because it is ideological, because it carries a "message." While another kind of ideology—the kind that informs *I'll Take My Stand, Southern Renascence,* and *South: Modern Southern Literature in Its Cultural Setting*—is equated with what the editors, elsewhere in their Introduction, call "the fullness of experience" and here term "artistic objectivity." To write as a traditionalist is evidently to write objectively about "flesh-and-blood Southerners" and to write something of aesthetic importance; while to write in a way that interrogates traditionalism is to fall victim to polemic and propaganda. "Social protest" has rendered *Native Son* negligible,

8. Ibid., 19.

apparently; and, as a general rule, it is this that has "impeded the Negro novelist."

The singular exception to this sad rule, the editors suggest, is Ralph Ellison: "it is with the publication of . . . *Invisible Man*," we are told, "that a Southern Negro novelist became a novelist who was a Southerner and a Negro." Disentangling this apparent tautology, what is evidently being said is that Ellison has succeeded where all others failed because "he draws heavily upon the Southern scene, but . . . does so without distorting the scene beyond artistic credibility." Like Wright, Ellison "went through a Marxist period": but, "unlike him, he emerged from it" and, after doing so shrugged off the bonds of a "narrow naturalism." The result is a novel that "transcends the immediate social and political implications and becomes a parable of the human quest for identity"; he has, it seems, shifted from the particular to the universal. The New Critical criteria at work here are clear enough: the reverence for the mythopoeic, the distrust of the social and political (which really means a distrust of particular *formulations* of the social and political), the belief in symbolism and transcendence of the historical. So is the evident need of the editors to find at least one African American novelist worthy of positive comment: there *is* a difference of rhetoric in this later volume, and that difference requires at least a gesture toward a greater inclusiveness. That *Invisible Man* stands alone, however, is perhaps the clearest and most remarkable point to emerge out of this brief discussion. The editors can find no literary antecedents for Ellison's novel; and they conclude their comments on it by saying, "since then Ellison has published no new novels; one waits to see whether he can go on from there"—so suggesting that it may have no successors, and certainly has none at the time of writing. *Invisible Man* becomes, in this context, a freak, an aberration: the exception that proves the rule. And the rule is a very simple one: anything that strays from the true path of literary traditionalism wanders into the wilderness of dogma, social protest, propaganda, and "message." That goes for any writer, African American or otherwise. To be a good Southern writer still means, in this volume, to be a writer of the kind Allen Tate both admired and was. Which is why the editors conclude their introductory remarks with the suggestion that the more recent writers covered in their book are perhaps not Southern at all: at least, not as Southern as Tate and his contemporaries were. "To the extent that the Southern novel has always presupposed a strong identification with a place, a participation in its life, a sense of intense involvement in a fixed, defined society," Rubin and Jacobs observe, then "the best work of the leading younger Southern writers is not in these respects 'Southern.' "[9] Only "an attitude toward language" and the "conception of man as a limited, dependent being" mark out some of the newer writers as being of as well as from the South. Otherwise, the great tradition is on the wane; the literature is becoming less and less "Southern" as it steadily becomes more "modern."

So, in a way, the title *South: Modern Southern Literature in Its Cultural Setting* could hardly be more misleading. In terms of the only partly hidden critical agenda of the volume, the phrase "modern Southern" is oxymoronic; while the worst thing a writer can do, evidently, is address his or her "cultural setting." "The historical sense, the idea of community-as-all, are nearly gone," the editors lament in the closing sentence of their Introduction, "and the protagonists of the recent Southern novel are moderns who live in a fluid, changing world." For all the gestures toward the immediate political situation, the introductory essay—like the collection it serves—is a commemoration of old, forgotten, far-off things and battles long ago; it is part of that great tradition of Southern elegy that it also exists to celebrate. Which is not at all to denigrate either the Introduction or the collection but simply to place them as documents of their time: they are not about "the South" or even "the literary South" at all but, rather, particular *kinds* of both. *South* is continuing the narrative of *Southern Renascence* and *I'll Take My Stand*: the premise of which, like that of all compelling narratives, is that it alone tells the objective truth whereas others have only an ax to grind, a point to make, a bias to serve. In this connection, something that Roland Barthes has said about the role and function of myth may be worth mentioning. "What the world supplies to myth," Barthes suggests, "is an historical reality, defined, even if this goes back quite a while, by the way in which men have produced or used it; and what myth gives in turn is a *natural* image of reality. . . . The world enters language as a dialectical relation between activities, between human actions; it comes out of myth as a harmonious display of essences."[10] "The very principle of myth," Barthes goes on, is that "it transforms history into nature." "And just as bourgeois ideology

9. Ibid., 24–25. See also 19–21.

10. Roland Barthes, *Mythologies* selected and translated by Annette Lavers (London, 1972), 142. See also 110; Rubin and Jacobs, "Southern Writing and the Changing South," 25.

is defined by the abandonment of the name 'bourgeois,' " he adds elsewhere, "myth is constituted by the loss of the historical quality of things; in it, things lose the memory that they once were made."[11] Those writers and critics who established "Southern literature" and "the Southern renascence" did not, of course, set out to make a myth; they set out to construct a version of the literary present and past that expressed their own critical priorities. But, in the sense that Barthes describes here, they were in effect mythmakers: because, in erecting a canon, they were—whether by instinct or calculation—defining terms like *literature, Southern, modern, objective,* and *aesthetic* according to their own ideology, their own cherished system of beliefs. They were, in short, turning "history" into "nature," interpreting their South and the kinds of writing and social values they preferred as, not just the most significant, but the real, the only essential ones.

What this all comes down to, finally, is not the fact but the acknowledgment of selection. *Southern Renascence* and *South* are important and seminal books. They are also selective, as any act of criticism must be: from the plurality of texts available, only a few can ever be taken for analysis and assessment. Where the difficulty occurs here is in the evident reluctance to admit selectivity as a guiding principle: the assumption, and in some instances the argument, that the essays collected together in the 1953 volume and then in the 1961 one are somehow inclusive—describing not *a* literary South but *the* literary South. Not unrelated to this is the belief implicit in both books that, in all genuine Southern writing, the relationship between text and cultural situation—while complex—is relatively unproblematic. The argument at this point tends to become circular. Authentic Southern literature is elided with traditionalism in both collections of essays. So any fiction, poem, or play that betrays an uneasy or interrogative relationship with traditionalist forms is to that extent seen as inauthentic—not genuinely literary or not properly Southern or both: it is inserted in some subliterary category, such as "social" or "protest" writing, and/or it is denied full right to a regional title, because it belongs to a "fluid" and so distinctively un-Southern world. What is remarkable about all this is not just that it leads to the exclusion of any kind of work the agenda of which cannot be seen to coincide, somewhere, with the social and cultural agenda of *I'll Take My Stand.* It also tends to the suppression of crucial elements in the work that do come

11. Barthes, *Mythologies,* 142. See also 129.

under scrutiny. For the work that does receive sympathetic attention is, for the most part, praised for supplying "objective" accounts of "the fullness of experience" and "flesh-and-blood Southerners,"[12] rather than for doing what it really does: which is offer powerful, and sometimes persuasive, demonstrations of commitment. It is celebrated in terms that ultimately assume a direct and detailed reflective relationship between text and context; the good book, in other words, is seen to hold an ample, unbiased mirror up to Southern society, past and present. This conveniently evades the point that, for good or ill, the writing favored in *Southern Renascence* and *South*—and in the plethora of books on Southern writing that have followed them—is as involved in the business of protest and polemic, and has as deep an ideological underpinning, as *Native Son* has. It is as concerned to follow a bias and trace out a particular map of the region—perhaps even to chase a specific diagnosis of social malaise through to its conclusion. Not only that, the pursuit of this aim has created problems for the authors of this work: problems that make *objective* seem the least appropriate word to describe either the individual text or the relationship it inscribes to the South—and, more specifically, to the South's feudal pretensions and traditionalist forms. The sheer contentiousness and difficulty of what the writers praised in *Southern Renascence* and *South* were trying to do is perhaps nowhere clearer than in the work of two people whose presence seemed central to the making of *I'll Take My Stand*, and to the literary tradition formulated by Rubin and Jacobs, but who now tend to be disregarded: Stark Young and Andrew Nelson Lytle.

The value of Young and Lytle in this context is that both wanted to make a case. Beginning with two quite distinct but equally backward-looking agendas, they sought to develop and defend that case in all their work. So, quite apart from the intrinsic interest both writers hold for us, their writings offer a handy prism for looking at the issues raised by the building of the Southern canon: the link between aesthetics, politics, art, and ideology that was there when the foundations of the canon were laid, the connection between making a fiction and making an argument, and the identification of particular versions of regional practices with the norm, the cultural center of the region. Deeply conservative, Young and Lytle were no different in fundamental intentions from other Agrarians (although how those intentions were to be carried out was, of course, a

---

12. Rubin and Jacobs, "Southern Writing and the Changing South," 14.

matter of radical disagreement among *all* Agrarians); they were, however, more open than most—with the obvious exception of Tate—when it came to acknowledging links between the aesthetic and the ideological. It is this openness, the sheer ferocity and candor of their conservatism that makes the denial of ideology or any programmatic aim seem especially odd and inappropriate in their case; it also highlights the cultural work involved in the articulation, the gradual shaping of a regional "great tradition." The patently open conservatism of Young and Lytle, together with the writings it engendered, discloses something else as well. For in arguing for the centrality of their particular paradigms of the South, both men ended up setting themselves at odds with their localities and the accompanying legends. Despite all their efforts, the center did not hold for them; their work plainly measures, as a result, the distance between their desire to speak for the South and the destiny they shared with the rest of the Agrarian movement—which was to speak, each of them, of one, distinctly awkward South among many. Writing in terms that were, in the clearest and often best sense, partial and opinionated, Young and Lytle can help us to register just how much any map the Agrarians drew of their region was a mental one—and how much, too, the literary history they all helped to initiate was a matter of inspired invention, verbal, and cultural performance.

At the time when the idea for *I'll Take My Stand* was being formulated, the presence of Stark Young in the Agrarian symposium was seen as vital. "As for Stark Young," Donald Davidson wrote to Allen Tate in 1929, "I think it would be extremely wise to have such a man as he is." Davidson did add a cautionary note, however: Young would make a valuable contribution, he confided, "if we can be sure he understands the full import of the affair and does not treat it simply as a literary or sentimental excursion." Davidson even ventured the suggestion that Young should be one of just six contributors to a possible symposium in praise of the traditional rural virtues of the South, along with Davidson himself, Tate, Ransom, Warren, and Lytle. In response, Tate shared Davidson's enthusiasm for the inclusion of Young but, if anything, was even more forthright, and sardonic, when it came to sounding a note of caution. The presence of an essay by Young would be fine, Tate suggested, provided he could be "prevented from including anecdotes about his grandmother."[13] The

---

13. Cited in Thomas D. Young, *Gentleman in a Dustcoat: A Biography of John Crowe Ransom* (Baton Rouge, La., 1976), 206. See also *Correspondence of Davidson and Tate*, 235–36. To Tate, 26 October 1929.

reasons for both the enthusiasm and the note of caution are not hard to fathom and were, in fact, related. Although born in Mississippi, with extensive connections among the old planter families, Young had long ceased to live in the South. Having taught at Amherst College, he had then earned a reputation as a drama critic for the *New Republic* and a translator of Chekhov. In exile, as it were, he had acquired a national reputation, which would help secure attention for any collection of essays, once it was published. There was a clear danger, however, that such exile would also make Young's essay more aberrant, less clearly aligned with whatever common aims the Agrarians might manage to formulate: distance—not to speak of Young's elite family connections—might lend more enchantment to his contribution than was good for it. In the event, the uneasiness felt by Davidson and Tate about Young's potential contribution proved to be well-founded. *I'll Take My Stand* hardly offers a coherent statement of a social program or a consistent ideology; nevertheless, Young's essay, "Not in Memoriam, but in Defense," is more aberrant, more peculiarly individualistic even than most. There is no economic or social program here; no system of value that could appropriately be called agrarian. There is no hope of deliberate reaction, a return to an earlier, traditionalist model of society. On the contrary, Young begins his essay by declaring, "if anything is clear, it is that we can never go back" because the "dead days are gone, and if by chance they should return, we should find them intolerable." Nor is there any evident interest in the practices and pieties of farming and the rural life. "In talking of Southern characteristics," Young loftily declares, "we are talking largely of . . . a life founded on land and ownership of slaves." "Of the other people living in the South of that epoch we know less," he adds, both "the people who worked their own farms with their own hands . . . a fine yeomanry," and "the so-called poor whites . . . more shiftless and less self-respecting."[14] The claim of ignorance on this score would have surprised many of the other contributors to *I'll Take My Stand*: as would Young's subsequent claim that it was neither "yeomanry" nor "poor whites" who had given Old Southern civilization "its peculiar stamp." "Our traditional characteristics derive from the landed class," he insisted. And those characteristics came down for him, in the end, to certain ineffable qualities of feeling: habits of noblesse oblige, courteous manners, and refined emotions, that he associated in their purest form

---

14. "Not in Memoriam, but in Defense," in *I'll Take My Stand: The South and the Agrarian Tradition* (1930; New York, 1962 edition), 336–37. See also 328.

with the Southern gentry of the past—but also claimed to find, in a tempered and diluted form, among the regional elite of his own time.

Distancing lends enchantment in two ways in Young's essay and in his work as a whole, in fact. There is, first and more obviously, distance of time. "Not in Memoriam, but in Defense" is, despite its title, easily the most unashamedly nostalgic of the contributions to *I'll Take My Stand*. What is called "the old life . . . the old practices . . . the old beliefs and standards" is recollected with reverence and affection. So are the "white columns and the great white moons of the magnolias" that inevitably populate his portrait of Old Southern life. So are the dramatis personae that give a human dimension to this portrait, and recall the more celebratory moments of the fiction of John Pendleton Kennedy or John Esten Cooke: the squire, say, with his sense of "responsibility for others," his "personal honor" and "habit of domination"—and, not least, his "gentlemanly acquaintance with the classics . . . , whiff of the poets, . . . respect for a polite degree of polish and cultivation, and . . . genuine taste for oratory." Young's very first novel, *Heaven Trees,* published four years before *I'll Take My Stand,* begins with the narrator declaring, "It all seems romance to me so far back in the fifties, like a gentle elegy of remembered things, never quite real almost." That could stand almost as an epigraph to his contribution to the Agrarian symposium. For that matter, it could serve as the refrain for his reminiscences of youth. "It does not matter at all if the reader of these pages should find he cannot keep straight various characters and stories that appear in them," is the frank way in which Young begins his fragment of autobiography. "The point is the quality represented here and there in one name or one story and another and the memory that remains of them."[15] Memory becomes the gentle medium in which everything is diffused, dissipated: so that what is left is not so much an idea, let alone a character or event, but an intangible atmosphere, an emotion so delicate that it cannot be pinned down to the particularities of time and place. We are back here with the kind of cultural capital in which Poe invested so heavily: a sensibility or sensitivity, an elusive quality of temperament that distinguishes the elite from the commonplace and enables those in the know to know each other. Aligned with this is a scarcely disguised contempt for those who cannot claim such capital. On the one hand, there is the patrician, "the South-

---

15. *The Pavilion: Of People and Times Remembered, of Stories and Places* (New York, 1951), 5. See also *Heaven Trees* (New York, 1926), 1; "Not in Memoriam, but in Defense," 338, 341, 342, 347, 349, 354, 358.

erner of good class, . . . a gentleman of honorable standards, pride, and formal conceptions." On the other hand, there is the variegated mob whose vulgarities help, by contrast, to secure patrician status: the "cobblers" and "small traders," the "arrivistes and paid performers," the "masses" demonstrating "peasant stolidity and middle-class confusion," "some self-made foreman in a shoe factory," "some Bowery child." "Our tradition of family involves the fact that so many of our families came from the British isles," Young triumphantly declares, ". . . and remained unmixed with other bloods." The racial and social exclusivity signaled here, however, seems less important to him than the exclusivity of temperament shadowed by the essay as a whole. What seems an aristocracy of birth is really, for Young, an aristocracy of feeling; the aristocrat he commemorates emerges in his true colors as the postaristocrat.

"Art's function is to extend life into dream," Young declared once, in a characteristic flourish, "since reality, for all its being close at hand, is beyond us." "For us," he added by way of explanation, "the actuality of real things has no solidity as compared to the reality of our illusions and the precision of our emotions." This is a recurrent note sounded in Young's writing: in his fiction, social comment, and critical essays and reviews. And it suggests the other kind of distancing that characterizes a piece like "Not in Memoriam, but in Defense" and all his other work: for all his celebration of "the land" as the substantial basis of Southern aristocracy, there is in fact very little sense of that land, a dear, particular, and concrete place in his accounts of aristocratic life. Place is subjected to a process of dissolution and diffusion too: what the reader is offered is not so much a sense of place (of the kind we find in, say, "Antique Harvesters" or *Delta Wedding*) but, rather, the feelings generated by place, the generalized emotions the land—and, preferably, the lost land— seems to inspire. "No matter where you are," Young declares in his essay for *I'll Take My Stand*, ". . . some old song suddenly heard again . . . or some fragrance remembered from a garden . . . brings tears to your eyes of its memory of some place." "I am not sure," he suggests, "that one of the deep mysteries, one of the great, as it were, natural beauties of the heart, does not lie in one's love for his own land. If there is a sadness, or old memory, added to this sense, it may become part of the substance on which the soul makes its tragic journey."[16] "Art is not art until it ceases

---

16. "Not in Memoriam, but in Defense," 345. See also 333; *Pavilion*, 28, 187; *The Flower in Drama: A Book of Papers on the Theatre* (New York, 1923), 16; *Glamour: Essays on the Art of the Theatre* (New York, 1925), 194–95; *Encaustics* (New York, 1926), 5–6.

to be life," Young argues in one of his critical essays. Equally, he appears to argue or assume that place is not truly place until it ceases to be there, concrete and earthy: what matters is not the labor it requires or the visible landscapes it offers but the complex of sentiments it generates. "It was based on gentle feeling," Young says of culture in the Old South in his memoir, "on a certain vainglory of polish and grandiloquence, and on the life of the affections." The basis of traditional life is, in effect, seen as emotional; those emotions might have been inspired by the land but they do not, in Young's view, seem to be indelibly attached to it—in fact, they seem to flourish in its absence, in the *memory* of the land. It is this that makes it possible for him to suggest, in his essay for the Agrarians, that he sees "much of the old life surviving" in the industrialized economy of the contemporary South, "the old practices that belong with the land, the old beliefs and standards"—and to argue that, while the regional economy will continue to change, the South can and must still "find its own use" for "this inheritance of ours." Young's position is, in fact, not only nonmaterialistic, it is vividly antimaterialistic, since he actively denies any necessary connection between material change and mental or moral alteration. To this extent, his position is decidedly more at odds with that of the other Agrarians than even Tate and Davidson might have feared. Most of the others admitted a vital connection between means of living and manner of life—although they might then have gone on to disagree about the details of both that means and manner. For all his celebration of the old plantation, however, Young saw it simply as the *occasion* for a way of life—or, to be more accurate, a habit of feeling—that did not seem to be entirely dependent upon it, that could indeed survive its passing. "In the natural world around us what survives . . . is form, idea," he suggests in one of his semiphilosophical excursions. "Why not likewise in the realm of human living and thought?" "Forms of living" are what matter for Young, finally, "forms of thought, in which our human life completes and expresses itself forever"; and these appear, in his view, to be tied only by accident or coincidence to particular social practices.

Which is perhaps why, in his nonfictional work at least, Young manages to discover a number of avenues of expression for the lover of fine gesture and even finer feeling, quite apart from the inheritance of the South. The "glamour" and "frank artifice" of certain styles of theater are constantly admired in his dramatic criticism, for instance: Henrik Ibsen is a particular bête noire here, because of what is seen as his positivism and scientism, while an actress like Eleanora Duse is praised for the "brilliance" of her costume and "formal style." "Ibsen's drama of 'The Lady from the Sea' has turns of psychology, biology," we are informed, "beginning stately . . . and winding up in a muddle of pseudo-scientific and moralistic explanations." "When Ibsen's Ellida comes on the stage," Young complains, ". . . a diagnosis is suggested"; whereas, "when Duse's Ellida came on the stage what we got was a poetic idea, a thing free and complete in our minds."[17] Another theater critic, Eric Bentley, has pointed out the connection between Young's "prejudices on the South" and "his love of ladies in fine array, of aristocratic gesture, of delicate sensation and splendid spectacle—of theatre, in fact." "If the Old South of southern romance is a golden age imposed upon the past" for Young, Bentley suggests, "the romance of the stage is a golden age imposed on the here and now." Which is true; all that needs to be added to Bentley's observation, really, is that, at times in his essays, Young finds similarly golden qualities in other phases of the "here and now": in "the old life and passionate soul of the Mediterranean," for instance, or the rituals of Roman Catholicism. Activating all such preferences, of course, is not just a positive taste for style but the same kind of horror of those "safe, stale things," equality and uniformity, that fired the writing of Poe or the arguments of the apologists for slavery. For Young, "realism" is the virus of "democracy" entering the body aesthetic, an act of leveling that leaves people without benefit of a code and consequently lost. "Realism," he explained in one of his critical essays, "having its truth in the actual surfaces of living," is fatally connected to "democracy," in which "the ass [is] as good as the rider." "Exactly as democracy has flattered . . . 'Everyman,' " Young suggests, "telling the merest imbecile that he has the right to judge his government's imperialistic problem . . . so too has the realistic theory flattered him. . . . No expertness of sense is asked of him; no fine hearing or sight; no culture in words . . . no tradition; no training in taste. There is no element present to put him in his place; everyone is equal. He has no ruling or dominating social idea to which he will subject the living material on the stage before him."[18] The function of the code

---

17. *Glamour*, 15. See also 43; *The Three Fountains* (New York, 1925), 27, 175; Eric Bentley, "An American Theatre Critic! (or the China in the Bull Shop)," *Kenyon Review* XII (Winter 1950), 145.

18. *The Theatre* (New York, 1958), 112–13. See also *The Twilight Saint* (New York, 1925), 11.

or style is to situate people within an order larger than themselves, Young would say, to give them the feeling of another, magical dimension—"a life larger than life" as he put it on one occasion ". . . / Invisible from all; whose lack alone / Is death." Equally, a less sympathetic observer might say that the function of style is to subjugate: to remind the mass of men and women of their proper "place" on the scale of sensibility—to point out to the average person that he or she is *merely* average.

This point about the average nature of the average person, and the consequent need for something to orient and control him, is one that is made more than once in Young's fiction. Here, the style recommended is a specifically Southern one; and the men recommending it are Southern gentlemen. "There is no code to follow any more," complains old Major Dandridge in Young's 1929 novel, *River House* (set in the New South). "There's only the individual case, you decide it for yourself." "That's all right, if you are an exceptional being," the Major points out. "But for most people a society depends on a code and without a code they are lost." The same idea is put even more bluntly by one of the major characters in Young's most successful work of fiction, *So Red the Rose,* published in 1935—which at one time almost rivaled *Gone with the Wind* in popularity. *So Red the Rose* is set before, during, and (for a few chapters) just after the Civil War, and it centers in traditional fashion on two families, one illustrating the courtly, squirearchical strain in the Southern gentry ("the Virginia gentleman" of earlier legend) and the other typifying more knightly, romantic qualities ("the Kentucky Colonel"): respectively the Bedfords (descended from Virginia and, eventually, England) and the McGehees (drawn from the outlawed McGregors of Scotland). It is the leader of the McGehees, Hugh, "a man of great refinement and restraint," who voices the argument for the code on this occasion. "This notion that you must judge everything for yourself," he complains, ". . . the only thing the matter with it is it requires brains. And where's the average man to get any brains? . . . If he's inspired, the result is inspired. If he's average, the result is average . . . the . . . idea of civilization will have been forgotten, and so you will have thousands of people thinking at random."[19] "Thousands of people thinking at random" is a

19. *So Red the Rose* (New York, 1935), 132. See also 396; *River House* (New York, 1929), 83. For an even more emphatic celebration of the traditional "code" see Young's play *The Colonnade* (New York, 1924), 24–25. One of the more intriguing aspects of the portrait Young draws of the Southern ruling class is his insistence that one symptom of the deterioration of that class is that it has had to defend its position and, as part of that

phrase that transforms the vision of democracy into a version of chaos. And there is no satirical intent here, any more than when Hugh McGehee later compares democracy unfavorably with slavery: "democracy, a good theory, a great human right," he thinks, "which works out none too well; slavery, a bad thing, a great human wrong, which works out none too badly." For it is precisely the argument from privilege—the argument issuing from the sense that certain people have finer sensibilities than others, and so should guide the tastes and tendencies of those less fortunate than themselves—which fuels both remarks. *So Red the Rose,* like all Young's work, is founded on the belief that there is such a thing as a cultural elite. More to the point, like all his fiction (and essays such as "Not in Memoriam, but in Defense"), it is also based on the conviction that such an elite was to be found once among the first families of the South—and is still to be found, at the time of his writing, among some of them.

In *Southern Renascence,* Walter Sullivan, while praising *So Red the Rose,* describes it as "a loose, sprawling sort of book," while Donald Davidson suggests that, "despite its large scope, numerousness of characters, and wealth of detail," it is "singularly compact." In an odd way, both have a point. Like all Young's fiction, *So Red the Rose* is not very strong on plot—there is no sense of a dominant narrative or even a dominant character or two to carry the action through. The story tends to wander from one location and one perspective to another; the controlling frame of the action is merely chronological and, within that frame, there is a mass of incidental detail. To that extent, the novel does seem to sprawl. For all that, however, there *is* a peculiar sense of constraint, an almost claustrophobic sense of control or containment to *So Red the Rose*—or, for that matter, to all Young's fiction—and it is created by two factors: the sense of typicality and the pursuit of a thesis. The reader is never less than aware that the characters are more representative than

---

defense, define itself. So Hugh McGehee complains about those Northerners who invade the South during Reconstruction: "these men haven't enough life behind them to match me. I mean by 'life' tradition, forefathers and a system of living. Don't laugh at me for a professor or a common editor: but these people make you want to explain things you'd always taken for granted. When you begin to explain things that you've always taken for granted, you've already begun to lose them" (*So Red the Rose,* 395–96). Implicitly, this offers a sly comment on the deliberate form of traditionalism that inspired books like *So Red the Rose* and essays like "Not in Memoriam, but in Defense." Young's art is so self-conscious, evidently, that it comments self-consciously on its own self-consciousness!

individual, belonging to a traditional regional typology; and that what this typology illustrates is what Sullivan himself rather disarmingly terms "Mr. Young's thesis." In short, a novel like *So Red the Rose* draws on the tradition of fictional arguments for the South to present its own fictional argument for Southern tradition. There is a set-piece quality to his tales and novels. The action often resolves itself into a series of picturesque tableaux, each with its own ritualistic significance: the jousting tournament (embodying the chivalry and gallantry of the Old South), the dinner at which "the table groaned" with the plentiful nature of the provision (reminding us of Old Southern hospitality and ceremony), the evening entertainments set amid "the great white blossoms of the magnolia" to the accompaniment of the musical voices of the slaves (reflecting the "gentle feeling" and "civilized style" of those who organize them). Even when the scene is set after the Civil War this ritualistic quality is sustained, only now the tableaux are intended to alert us to the random nature of modern life. There are still parties, for instance, in *The Torches Flare,* a novel set in twentieth-century New York and Mississippi. In this case, though, they are parties at which "you were neither an intimate nor a stranger" because nobody has either a past or a future; everyone is as little or as well known as everyone else in a world of "mere transients," where the "rambling egotism of talk" becomes the voice, the articulate form of "competition without social principles."[20]

"The portrait-painter of that day who visited Mississippi," observes the narrator in *Heaven Trees,* "painted clothing best of all . . . and becoming arrangement. . . . As to the likeness, it was not so certain." Whether or not Young knew he could have been describing his own aesthetic practice here it is impossible to tell: although there *is,* certainly, a knowing quality to his work—inseparable from his preference for self-conscious artifice—which suggests that he did. Either way, he might well have been describing it. His characters are, in fact, just as formalized and emblematic as the settings. The planters inhabiting his Old South, for example, are either gentlemen who read Lucretius and Sterne on the battle front or bold cavaliers, regional equivalents of "Sir Walter Scott's knights," unafraid of "the devil himself"; the white women are either

20. *The Torches Flare* (New York, 1928), 3, 26, 89. See also *Heaven Trees,* 35–36, 38, 150, 158; *So Red the Rose,* 11, 30–31, 54; Sullivan, "Southern Novelists and the Civil War," 120, 122; Donald Davidson, "Theme and Method in *So Red the Rose,*" in *Southern Renascence,* 264.

"gracious, warm" matriarchs, or belles whose "magical beauty" invites comparison with birds, butterflies, and nymphs. Within the constraints created by this typicality of characterization, the kinds of relationships that develop seem inevitable and strictly formalized. When the young plantation cavalier meets the plantation belle, for instance, in the kind of "warm, living, and abundant surroundings" and "boundless quietness" that typify nearly every antebellum setting, then not much else can follow but romantic love and a marriage that sustains the family lines. There is little place in these narratives for Southern white characters who come from outside the elite—except, occasionally, as portents of a dismal future ("poor whites," declares Hugh McGehee when the Civil War is over, ". . . now the world's changed, you give 'em time, they'll swamp us"). Young makes no bones about this, any more than he does in his essay for *I'll Take My Stand*: the poorer whites of the region simply do not interest him because, in terms of cultural presence and influence, they do not matter. "There was still a world of piney-woods whites," we are casually informed in *So Red the Rose*, "poor whites who owned no slaves," but "so far as plantation society went" they "might as well not have existed"; "the Bedford children had never seen any people of this sort, except on the roads and two or three times, some Saturday in Natchez."[21] What do

21. *So Red the Rose,* 8, 37. See also *Heaven Trees,* 10, 79, 127, 149, 213, 403. Examples of the plantation gentleman or squire in Young's fiction are "Uncle George" McGehee and Grandfather McGehee in *Heaven Trees* and the men of the Bedford family in *So Red the Rose*. Plantation cavaliers include Charles Boardman in *Heaven Trees* and the men of the McGehee family and Charles Taliaferro in *So Red the Rose*. Among the plantation matriarchs are "Aunt Martha" McGehee in *Heaven Trees* and Mrs. Bedford in *So Red the Rose;* and the plantation belles include Georgia McGehee and "cousin Virginia" in *Heaven Trees* and Vallette and Lucy McGehee in *So Red the Rose*. The general tenor of Young's portrait of the old plantation is registered by his description of Portobello, the home of the Bedfords in *So Red the Rose,* as "the product of romantic feeling and thought" (5), and by the constant references to "dream," "haze" and "vagueness" in his work. "My cousin Virginia was one of those people who are like some gentle glowing hour out of a day you remember," observes the narrator of *Heaven Trees,* "she defeated you like music; to write intelligently of her is hard. Her gray eyes rested on whatever she looked at clearly and with a caress, and her voice was so sweet and so gracious and tender with something so low and yet so bright in it" (180). The emphasis on eyes and voice, the associations with music and memory, above all the suggestion that this womanly paradigm of the Old South is a transcendent figure defying language and intelligence: all establish another connection with Poe's romantic typology of the region. That connection is all the closer because Virginia is a frail and doomed figure who receives particularly detailed attention during and just after her death. "The deathlessness and perfection" of her dead body, the narrator confides,

interest him, however, apart from the elite, are characters drawn from the traditionalist typology of the region who help him develop his thesis—and who represent two possible kinds of enemy, one from without and one from within: the Yankee and the African American.

With the African American characters the familiar stereotypes and comfortingly stereotypical situations recur, to complete the sense of a benevolent patriarchal order. Individually, there are reassuring figures like "Aunt Tildy," the "Mammy" to the Bedford children in *So Red the Rose* (each child, we are told, also has a "darkey" for a "playmate"), or Solomon Clay in *Heaven Trees,* bought by the patriarch of that novel, "Uncle George" McGehee, "because he was funny"—"he used to talk African for us sometimes, and laugh and laugh," the narrator fondly recalls, "just why we could not tell." "Solomon Clay's one talent," he adds, "apart from splitting Uncle George's sides to look at him, was for doing exactly what Uncle George told him." Complementing these individual emblems of puppylike devotion are generalized—and for the traditionalist reader, equally comforting—images of the slave population. In *Heaven Trees,* for instance, the slaves, simple, naïve, and helpless, are compared to "children" or "animals" who, nevertheless, are granted the privilege of humble domestic bliss ("Each cabin had its own little yard, with flower-beds . . . they were well sheltered and well cared for"). Similarly, in *So Red the Rose,* slaves share in the antebellum idyll in their own modest way: "plenty of people," one character observes, "let the darkies raise their own patches of Nankeen cotton for pocket money." Unsurprisingly, perhaps, given the way they are characterized, narrative events involving the slave population tend to resolve themselves into the prototypical, recalling the familiar situations of nineteenth-century Southern pastoral: the planter riding many miles to buy the children of one of his slaves, the white family visiting the quarters to minister to the sick or to bring Christmas greetings and gifts, the slaves unenthusiastic when offered their freedom. Character, event, everything to do with relations between slave and master is rendered in a softly romantic haze, every ritual

---

"touched in some form every mind among us, and it was we who seemed to stand like the dead about her there" (197). In this respect, too, it is clear that Young is following Poe's tendency to identify his ethereal heroines with the romantic, otherworldly, and ultimately doomed sanctuary of the South. For Young's further development of the typology of woman/sanctuary/South, see the discussion of the "invasion" of Montrose in *So Red the Rose* later on in this chapter.

of slave life tends to occur—as the narrator in *Heaven Trees* says of a
black baptismal ceremony—"like a dream." It is, however, a dream with
a deeply polemical basis, a particular argument to communicate—as this
passage, from the later chapters of *So Red the Rose* handily reminds us:

> the [Southern] people found it confusing when they heard that the
> slaves were freed because slavery was a sin and then recalled even
> such a trio [*sic*] of facts as that Mrs. Grant had her slave with her
> at Vicksburg; that Lincoln's announcement of the emancipation of
> slaves in seceding states as a part of his platform in December, 1862
> caused Ohio, New York and Pennsylvania (no state west of the
> Hudson . . . thought much of it) to fail to support him with the
> vote; that negroes in the states that had not seceded from the Union
> were still slaves; and that General Sherman had announced that
> loyal masters could recover their slaves who had fled to Union
> lines.[22]

As in earlier Southern romance, the representation of the African American as a happy although humble member of the plantation "family" is
closely aligned with two factors, two fundamentals of the traditionalist
argument clearly signaled here: fear of the repressed and fury about what
is seen as the duplicity of the opposing forces.

As for fear of the repressed: that comes out even more clearly in *So
Red the Rose* when, for a moment, the "children" threaten to take over
the family. In one particular chapter, Young describes the looting and
burning of Montrose, the McGehee family home, by black troops led by
a white officer. Agnes McGehee, Hugh's wife, tries to stop them. "She
could hear them tramping in the parlors and the rattle of their sabres and
spurs," we are told:

> She rushed in to her daughter. There they were. Lucy [the daughter]
> was in the bedroom and the negroes were tramping through the
> sitting-room, threatening, cursing.
>   "Get out!" Agnes ordered. "Get out of my house. Get out of my
> sight!"
>   A big black who seemed to be in command gave a guffaw, and
> the other negroes . . . followed. One of them came up to her and

22. *So Red the Rose,* 272–73. See also 34, 38; *Heaven Trees,* 35, 131, 13, 169, 274–75,
276.

with his open hand boxed her on the cheek. At once another negro put a pistol against her breast; she could smell his sweat. Then the big negro who had struck her said, "Don't shoot her, Mose, slap her. Slap the old slut." He broke into a stream of abuse.[23]

The destruction then continues: with "pictures on the walls . . . being slashed or cut down" and "black soldiers" "pouring turpentine over the library," smashing furniture "for kindling a fire" and "carrying out silks, objects, painted window-shades, damask curtains, linen, blankets and men's clothing." Donald Davidson, in discussing the novel in *Southern Renascence,* picked out this episode for special praise: it was, he claimed, "as 'objective' as, say, Hemingway's account, in *A Farewell to Arms,* of the Italian retreat from the Caporetto, but . . . far richer in its complex of meanings." A complex of meanings it may have; "objective" is, however, just about the last word to describe it, since what it signals is a fear that hardly dare speak its name. The black invaders invade and destroy the closed world of the plantation; in the process—just as in *The Narrative of Arthur Gordon Pym*—the mask of affability and deference is ripped off to be replaced by the signs of evil, treachery, and brutality. That much is obvious and fairly clearly stated. What is less obvious, but nevertheless clearly there, is the sexual threat that these invaders offer to the purity of elite white womanhood: to the plantation belle, as she hides in her bedroom, and, even more, to the plantation matriarch. Agnes McGehee can smell the sweat of one violator as he presses the—plainly phallic—pistol to her breast; one calls her slut, another treats her as such by slapping her across the face. The animal connection is still present, retained from the earlier mask of the "darkey," so is the grinning and laughter. Both, however, have shifted into another, and far more sinister key, assumed a far rawer, more dangerous edge. These are "animals," we are asked to believe, who are tearing up the definitively "human" culture of the plantation; they are smiling, but they are smiling villains. They are no longer the good "children" of the family, it seems, but rebellious upstarts: who, in crossing the threshold of Montrose, looting and burning the house, and (above all) assaulting and insulting white women, have forced themselves out of their assigned place and followed this up by committing ultimate acts of sacrilege.

23. *So Red the Rose,* 324–25. See also Davidson, "Theme and Method in *So Red the Rose,*" 274.

In his account of this episode, Davidson describes it as representing "the collapse of civilized society," which, of course, measures just how closely aligned are the critic's ideas of what constitutes civilization with those of the novelist he is discussing. He then points out that it is followed by a moment offering what he calls a "parody" of the black soldiers' "gross violation." In the middle of the looting, a small boy, one of the slaves of the household, steals something and begins to run. "What you got in yo' han', boy?" Bessie, a mulatto house slave asks him. "She . . . pried open his little black fingers," we learn, "which were clutching a red silk handkerchief." Hugh McGehee witnesses the episode, "watching the little negro's eyes, from which the tears ran down to make a worse smudge of a sooty face." "It eased him," the narrator explains, "to see the destruction and pillage reduced to this level. . . . 'Let him have it, Bessie,' he said."[24] For Davidson, this is a moment of tender satire: appropriately concluding, by counterpointing, a "powerful scene." But a more appropriate way of seeing it, surely, is as an act of reassurance. Young has exposed the fear that helped shape the comforting stereotype of the "darkey" in the first place; he now wants to reinsert that stereotype. The African American is reinscribed as a naïve, foolish, but fundamentally amiable child; the elite white character, although materially defeated, reasserts moral control with an act of patriarchal benevolence. The author is being "eased" here, as much as his character is, by putting the final emphasis on the sheer *childishness* of these "children": they may be dangerous, the implication is, but the danger can be contained—and has to be contained for their sake as well as the sake of others. This is an argument for subjugation that tiptoes up to a vision of chaos, random destruction, but then scurries back from it again. Montrose may be destroyed, the Old South may be gone: but style is still there—the traditionalist flourish of both author and character—to ensure that each person may be put in his proper place.

That subjugation is not that easy is suggested by the other element of danger in Young's narratives: the Yankee, who becomes the figure of the modern in his fictional accounts of the twentieth century—a character notable for his or her utter incoherence. "The health of a society, high or low," observes the narrator of *The Torches Flare,* "rests on the unity of its nature, and depends on the absence from it of hypocrisy, a confusion

24. *So Red the Rose,* 326. See also Davidson, "Theme and Method in *So Red the Rose,*" 274.

in desire and a culture that is false to it."[25] It is perhaps unfair to recall Walter Benjamin's remark that fascism aestheticizes politics, whereas communism politicizes aesthetics: for all the reactionary nature of his beliefs, Young is no fascist, and, besides, the political nature of his message can hardly be evaded, and should certainly never be minimized. Nevertheless, Benjamin's remark does help to foreground the degree of slippage that occurs between Young's aesthetic and social commentary. By his account, a lack of polish and symmetry is fatally disabling in a work of art—and in a society as well; it can cause cultural, as well as artistic, breakdown. And that lack is insisted on again and again in his stories: whenever Young ventures into a portrait of the Northern and/or modern. At its most obvious, the lack is shown at those moments when Young plays a variation on the Southern traditionalist theme of Yankee hypocrisy. In *Heaven Trees*, for instance, there is a seamstress from Iowa who attacks slavery but would like certain slaves shot because they are inefficient; in *So Red the Rose*, there is the businessman who insists that "what we philosophize and what we do in business are two separate things." On a more complicated level, that same lack is revealed by certain characters—again, invariably, Northern and/or modern—who are not so much hypocritical as dissociated; and, of these, easily the most telling—which is to say, the most revealing of Young's aesthetic motives and strategy—is the character of General William T. Sherman in *So Red the Rose*.

When General Sherman first appears in the novel, he has come to console Agnes and Hugh McGehee over the loss of their son Edward in battle. Although on opposing sides in the war, before the conflict Edward had been one of Sherman's pupils at the Louisiana Military Academy; and Sherman can share their grief because he himself has lost a son. Agnes and Hugh are perplexed by their visitor: both note "the air of cynical indifference . . . that showed despite the nervousness and the twitching about the mouth as he bowed, looking at them." He laughs "like a boy"; he paces up and down, talking of "a mad world"; his movements are jumpy and jerky and, occasionally, he blushes. "Could this man . . . be the Sherman with the looting, burning, and wreck behind him?" they wonder; while Hugh tells his wife, "Yes. He's good. I can't

25. *Torches Flare*, 346. See also *So Red the Rose*, 60, 386. Also Walter Benjamin, "The Work of Art in the Age of Mechanical Reproduction," in *Illuminations* translated by Harry Zohn (London, 1973), 235.

understand it." They are additionally puzzled because, for all his personal kindness, Sherman makes it clear that, in his opinion, the Southern planter class must be "replaced" by any means necessary. On the one hand, he seems discomfited by the evil opinion Southerners have of him; on the other, he sees that opinion as a useful instrument. "This conflict of policy had become a conflict in his own nature," Agnes thinks, "and . . . the story that was building up of him as a ruthless monster did at the same time both serve him and his purposes as a picture of war, and antagonize, grieve, and enrage him as a picture of himself."[26] Sherman is, in sum, a dissociated man: torn between thought and feeling, the public and the private, notions of the useful and ideas of the good. "Sherman is the Enemy," Davidson observes in his essay on Young in *Southern Renascence*, "a grand apotheosis and cataclysmic realization of the cult of divided personality." He is that, to an intense degree. He is, in fact, as ideologically conceived and didactically freighted a character as we are ever likely to encounter in fiction. He is like the embodiment of Force, say, in Naturalist stories or the human emblem of Capital in proletarian novels—or, for that matter, the state's attorney, Buckley, the embodiment of institutionalized white power in *Native Son*. The only difference between a figure like Sherman and Buckley is that, in *Native Son*, what we the readers see is what the protagonist Bigger Thomas sees: the extremity of the character could consequently be interpreted as a symptom of Bigger's fear, his entrapment by white power and white institutions, as well as a product of Wright's very clearly polemical intentions. Quite simply, Buckley may seem a seamless villain: but so he would to the eye of the story, which is the eye of someone over whom he now has the power of life and death—and over whom, before that, he and his kind exercised more or less absolute control. In *So Red the Rose*, by comparison, there is no such narrowing down to one eye, one perspective. There is, as Donald Davidson observes, a constant shifting of angle of vision, within "the impersonal current of the general narrative." "Evidently Stark Young wished to retain the breadth of perspective and richness of context af-

26. *So Red the Rose*, 304. See also 301, 302, 303. See also Davidson, "Theme and Method in *So Red the Rose*," 265, 271–72. Fundamentally, the portrait of Sherman rests on the traditional Southern rendering of the Yankee/modern as a product of a conflicted culture: the conflict being between, on the one hand, "New England Puritan old maid idealism" (*So Red the Rose*, 61) and, on the other, pragmatic individualism/laissez-faire materialism.

forded by the 'omniscient point of view,' " Davidson suggests "—that is, the method of classical narrative." The view, however, is not "omniscient" at all; masquerading as omniscience, it is a view closely identified with a position that sees Sherman precisely as the Enemy. The didactic purpose here, in fact, is more naked and uncomplicated than it is in *Native Son,* simply because there is no *avowedly* subjective element. The narrative vision presents itself as "objective" and authoritative; in the process, it only exposes its own didacticism, its fundamentally programmatic and polemical nature. The state's attorney is there in *Native Son* to make a point, and to dramatize the fear of the man through whose eyes we receive the story; General Sherman is there in *So Red the Rose* just to make a point.

That the romantic stories of Stark Young carry a heavily freighted message should really come as no surprise. That is, it should surprise no one familiar with the idea that any work springs out of the beliefs, and cultural situation, of its author. For that matter, it should come as no surprise either to anyone acquainted with the argumentative bases of Southern plantation fiction. What may surprise some, however, is the deeply autobiographical origins of these stories. As his memoir of youth and "of people and times remembered," *The Pavilion,* makes clear, Young drew from his own family records and reminiscences for his portrait of "old landed society, with its responsibilities and traditional heritage." "There was a certain fabulous character to some of my simple surroundings when I was growing up in Mississippi," Young confides in his memoir; and it is precisely this "fabulous" character, as he recollected it, that Young attempted to render in his fictional portraits of what he unabashedly terms, at one point, "the ruling class." Donald Davidson, in his account of Young for *Southern Renascence,* sees this autobiographical basis as proof positive that Young's fiction is scrupulously correct: that, in short, the "objective" truths of the stories are founded on "objective" facts. But the "fabulous" quality of Young's supposedly factual recollections—which are, in any event, shaped by his unconcealed adoration of the Southern "ruling class"—could surely lead to another conclusion. In his memories of people like his great-uncle Hugh McGehee, just as in his portraits of fictional characters like Hugh McGehee of Montrose, Young is remembering at a distance—a distance of place, that is, as well as time. He is writing as an exile: someone who has become, whether he likes it or not, part of the socially and sexually fluid ambience of the modern city. To simplify only a little: Mississippi and plantation culture is his past while he writes, while New York City and its theatrical world is his present. The stories circulating around Young's ancestors may well have been fabulous to begin with; in any event, like any memories they came loaded with their own cultural assumptions—pieties that lent them some of the qualities of fable. Whatever elements of fable they possessed, however, were added to almost beyond measure by the sense of difference and the enchantment that difference lent. In *The Torches Flare,* the plainly autobiographical hero Henry ("Hal") Boardman finds the "drifting" nature of existence in New York unsatisfactory and returns to his small Mississippi hometown, only to find that unsatisfactory too: "in these confused times of ours," he reflects, "there is little to choose between"[27] one place or another. By the end of the book, he is preparing to return to New York. He has made the discovery that supplies the imaginative motor for all Young's work and that Young had confessed on almost the last page of his very first novel: that the "generous, rich" land described by traditionalists is not a geographical place at all, it is instead a "country of the heart." It is a product of absence, engendering a sweetly romantic melancholy: loved, and perhaps understood, precisely *because* it is not there.

With Andrew Nelson Lytle, the presence of an autobiographical base to the work is, if anything, even more obvious than it is in the case of Stark Young. In fact, in what one commentator has called a virtual last testament, Lytle's most personal—and, in the event, last—major work was the saga of his own family, *A Wake for the Living: A Family Chronicle,* published in 1976. Reversing the usual process, by which—as Faulkner put it—the actual is transformed into the apocryphal, Lytle reconstructs here the historical bases of much of his previously published fiction. It is the story of the complex intertwinings of his mother's and his father's families, the Nelsons and the Lytles: people who, in their different ways, succeeded in "living in one physical place through successive generations." Lytle wrote the chronicle of his family, he told Allen Tate, as a way of "instructing the three girls," his daughters, "as to who they are": as the remark indicated, the past was and is the present for him—a function of being, a part of identity. And, in writing his account of a clan settled in middle Tennessee since the American Revolution, Lytle revealed again two dominating features of all his work: his belief in the

---

27. *Torches Flare,* 373. See also 3; *Heaven Trees,* 286; *Pavilion,* 100, 125; Davidson, "Theme and Method in *So Red the Rose,*" 275–76.

power of voice, the bardic tradition, and his equal belief in the power of family as the source of the real and the basis of culture. As for voice: Lytle was following a family tradition handed down to him by his father, said to be a "celebrated raconteur and repository of family lore"—and so expert that Lytle's friend Caroline Gordon suggested that there might be some storytelling artist buried in the Lytle family past with tale-telling gifts lurking "beneath the level of consciousness." At gatherings of his clan, Lytle once said, "There would always be one voice more capable . . . of dominating the conversation. . . . It was a kind of bardic voice." "The bard . . . collects the segments," he added. "In the end, in the way he fits the parts together, the one story will finally get told." Lytle is clearly the "bardic voice" here, in *A Wake for the Living*, telling "the one story" that hovers as an influence, a shadowy presence in all his work. And as for family: for Lytle, the family was and is—as he put it in one of his essays—"*the* institution of Southern life." Not only that, in his view, it clearly is or should be *the* institution of life anywhere; and so it is to the credit of the South—or, at least, the traditional South—to have acknowledged this in its cultural practices. In *A Wake for the Living,* in fact, Lytle begins his account of the past with a declaration of belief. "The sense of eternity," he declares, "gives a perspective on things and events which makes for a refreshing clarity"; and the family "by its habits and customs discovers the identity between the natural and supernatural, that mystery which becomes ceremony to people who make their living by the land and the sea."[28] In short, family is seen as the basis of the good—which is to say, stable—society and the substantial foundation of reality. It places the human being accurately in time by situating him or her in the perspective of eternity; in the process, it reveals itself to be of religious, or to be precise sacramental, significance.

What Lytle demonstrates in a book like *A Wake for the Living* is, in effect, an ancestor worship that goes way beyond that of his fellow

28. *A Wake for the Living: A Family Chronicle* (New York, 1975), 3. See also 105; "Foreword to *A Novel, A Novella, and Four Stories*" (New York, 1958), xviii (this essay is also to be found in *The Hero with the Private Parts* [Baton Rouge, La., 1966] and, retitled "The Subject of Southern Fiction," in *Southerners and Europeans: Essays in a Time of Disorder* [Baton Rouge, La., 1988]); *The Lytle-Tate Letters: The Correspondence of Andrew Lytle and Allen Tate* edited by Thomas D. Young and Elizabeth Sarcone (Jackson, Miss., 1987), 296. To Tate, 31 January 1960; Caroline Gordon to Andrew Lytle, 15 March 1943, cited in Mark Lucas, *The Southern Vision of Andrew Lytle* (Baton Rouge, La., 1986), xii, 136.

Agrarian, Stark Young; and this is by no means the only, or even the most significant, point of difference between them. There is a conservative ideology at work in all the writing of Lytle too: but it is a conservatism that goes off in quite another direction. That is clear enough from Lytle's contribution to *I'll Take My Stand*. The very title of Lytle's essay begins to measure the difference: instead of the sonorities of "Not in Memoriam, but in Defense," we have the blunt folk saying, "The Hind Tit." The title refers, Lytle explains in his essay, to the runt pig, the feeblest member of the litter, who is "squeezed and tricked out of the best places at the side" of the sow and "forced to take the little hind tit for nourishment." A folk metaphor for any exploited person or group, it becomes his favored way of defining the place of the countryman in the changing social structures of the South: but at least as important as this is its function in establishing the tone, a sense of belonging to the soil and the rural community that is vital to our conception of Lytle's chosen persona. The person at the center here, it is clear, is not Young's gentleman planter at all but the farmer, the tiller of his own land; and, as several passages make even clearer, far from simply arguing for the preservation of an attitude, a complex of feeling as Young does, Lytle is demanding action. With deliberate earthiness, Lytle calls on farmers to stick to the life they know and, into the bargain, commit themselves wherever necessary to turning back the political and cultural clock. "Do what we did after the war and the reconstruction," Lytle tells his Southern readers, "return to our looms, our handcrafts, our reproducing stock. Throw out the radio and take down the fiddle from the wall. Forsake the movies for play-parties and the square dances." As Louis D. Rubin, Jr., has suggested, there may well be an element of rhetorical exaggeration here: but there is also a fierce, burning conviction—caught not just in what Lytle says but how he says it, his calculated attempt to use the language of the character, the model of being he is celebrating. "As for those countrymen who have not gone so deeply into the money economy," Lytle asserts, "let them hold to their agrarian fragments and bind them together, for reconstructed fragments are better than a strange newness which does not belong. It is our own, and if we have to spit in the water-bucket to keep it our own, we had better do it."[29] A passage like this has a sting in its tail, underlining the writer's allegiances. His life, the

29. "The Hind Tit," in *I'll Take My Stand*, 245. See also 234; Rubin, *Wary Fugitives*, 268.

implication is, is the same as the farmers' life; his words, their words. Even his enemies turn out to be their enemies. For the people Lytle chooses to attack, and so locate the virtues of his country folk, are quite different from the ones chosen by Young. In Young's essay, the paradigm of modern life is the displaced entrepreneur and the rapacious business-man. In "The Hind Tit," however, the enemies of traditionalism are the idle and effeminate—those who do not work at all rather than those who work in a certain way. The effete poetaster or dilettante replaces the man of commerce as the satirical target, because he offers a far more effective contrast to the robust virtues of the poor farmer. He has the kind of lethargy and corrupt sophistication that can place Lytle's rustics in an appropriately flattering light. If he sounds, as a result, as much like Young's *hero* as his villain, that is because he has some of the qualities Young admires: leisureliness, for example, and a taste for the amenities of life. Virtues in "Not in Memoriam, but in Defense," they have now undergone a sea change. The populist context of "The Hind Tit" has transformed them into vices; and that in itself is a measure of the distance between these two men "conscious of the past in the present."

Unlike Young, too, Lytle tended to stay at home. After studying drama at Yale and acting briefly in New York, he returned to live on the family land near Nashville; for a while, he even had a stab at practicing what he preached by farming the land. That fact is less important, however, than the determining nature, the centrality of the *idea* of the good farmer to nearly everything Lytle produced. The family that shaped his imagina-tion, and haunted his arguments, was specifically a farming family: tak-ing its means of living and way of life from direct engagement with one small spot of earth. Something of this is registered, again, in that essay for *I'll Take My Stand*: with its beautifully modulated mapping of the country family's place in both time and space. "Before dawn the rooster and the farmer feel the tremendous silence, chilling and filling the gap between night and day," we are told. The farmer,

> gets up, makes the fires, and rings the rising bell. He could arouse the family with his voice, but it has been his custom to ring the bell; so every morning it sounds out, taking its place among the other bells of the neighborhood. . . . One or two of the girls set out with their milk-pails to the barn, where the cows have been kept over-night. There is a very elaborate process to go through with in milk-ing. First the cow must be fed to occupy her attention; next, the

milker kneels . . . the milking begins. There is always a variation to this ritual. . . . The left hand holds the pail, while the right does the work, or it may be the reverse. The hand hits the bag tenderly, grabs the teat, and then closes the fingers about it, not altogether but in echelon.[30]

Gradually, the reader is led through the times and stations of the farming day; accompanying this, there is a tender reading of the local geography, the dear, particular place in which these rituals are grounded—the house with its furniture "shiny from use, and its arms smooth from the polishing of flesh," the land and the surrounding, sustaining community. There is a touch of the British agrarian tradition in fiction here: it is difficult, for instance, to read Lytle's scrupulously detailed account of the "very elaborate process" of milking without thinking of similar scenes in *Tess of the D'Urbervilles*. There is also an echo of Thomas Jefferson's famous belief that "the small landowners are the most precious part of the land." What "The Hind Tit" only partially discloses, however, is something that is made perfectly clear by Lytle's arguments for the farming and family life elsewhere, in fact and fiction: which reveal just how different Lytle is, from either Thomas Jefferson or Thomas Hardy, in his understanding of the role of the simple farmer and his clan. For Jefferson, the plain farmer acted as a guarantor of social stability and natural rights; for Hardy, he called to mind not only the beauty but also the inequity of inherited ways. In Lytle's eyes, on the other hand, what mattered was the fundamentally conservative nature of farming as well as family life: the way it helped to act as a bulwark against change.

The special way in which Lytle understood the good farmer was inherent in his reading of history: which he outlined most clearly in his highly imaginative biography of the Confederate general Nathan Bedford Forrest and in a number of essays—many of them written for the conservative journal *American Review*. In these, Lytle argued that the self-reliant farmer could be identified with "the older Christian sense of order," because he represented everything that was "static, historical, cultural." His way of life made him a natural conservative, with a humble sense of

---

30. "Hind Tit," 219–20. See also 218; *The Papers of Thomas Jefferson* edited by Julian P. Boyd (Princeton, 1950–   ), VIII, 682. To James Madison, 28 October 1785. For further biographical details and helpful critical comment, see Thomas D. Young, *Tennessee Writers* (Knoxville, Tenn., 1981), 44ff.; Lucas, *Andrew Lytle;* Robert O. Stephens, *The Family Saga in the South: Generations and Destinies* (Baton Rouge, La., 1995), 92ff.

his own contingency and a clear understanding of the sacramental nature of life. The "good farmer," Lytle declared, "is faced constantly and immediately with a mysterious and powerful presence, which he may use but which he may never reduce entirely to his will and desires." He "knows of minor successes," he "remembers defeats": but "he is so involved in the tremendously complex ritual of the seasonal drama that he never thinks about idle or dangerous notions."[31] As an historical figure, the farmer "knew that equality and independence were two different things": "economic and political independence," he recognized, "did not mean that all men were equal," and he cherished the freedom granted to him by his landholdings while dismissing notions of equality and inequality as "entirely irrelevant." The gentleman planter, Lytle claimed, was quite different and deserved neither respect nor imitation. "The backwoodsman's fear of aristocratic Virginia . . . has a profound significance," said Lytle, locating what he saw as the determining conflict between farming and plantation culture way back in American—and, indeed, Western—history. "The Colonial gentleman, like his English counterpart, was the agent of those disrupting forces which had been at work since the sixteenth century," he went on. "The gradual disintegration of Feudalism . . . broke down by degrees the farms and the estates"; and the rich men of the colonial South "fashioned their ways after the English gentry of the eighteenth-century, and not after an earlier day when baron and yeoman met on freer ground." Those who dominated the economy of the prerevolutionary South became "vainglorious," they pursued capital; in the event, they helped to guarantee the reduction of "a union composite of spiritual and temporal parts to the predominance of material ends."

At first, Lytle argued, the New World of the colonial South was a refuge for "yeoman agrarian society" after its collapse in the Old: but then certain crucial events tended to discourage its growth and channel social development in another—and profoundly unfortunate—direction. In part, Thomas Jefferson was to blame here: because he combined a

31. "The Small Farm Secures the State," in *Who Owns America? A New Declaration of Independence* edited by Herbert Agar and Allen Tate (New York, 1936), 248. See also "Caroline Gordon and the Historic Image," in *Hero with the Private Parts*, 162; *Bedford Forrest and His Critter Company* (London, 1939), 10, 15; "The Backwoods Progression," *American Review*, I (September 1933), 411–12; "Foreword to *A Novel, A Novella, and Four Stories*," xx.

sound belief in the yeomanry with a political philosophy that was a destructive "abstraction." "He hoped to produce a stable farming society," Lytle observed; however, "much of Jefferson's special legislation—especially the abandonment of primogeniture and the separation of Church and state—contradicted his general idea and obstructed the establishment of the agrarian State." "The overdeveloped political instincts" of people like Jefferson and John Taylor of Caroline, Lytle declared, "misled them into believing . . . that the Constitution, a political contract could take the place of all those traditional institutions which make for an abundant and complete life"; "the Republican conservative let his principles be compromised by liberal abstractions." And worse was to come: as a political society, the South and its leaders then made two further mistakes—fatal as far as its own survival was concerned, and deeply distressing to any true agrarian. The first mistake occurred in time of peace. The "cotton snobs," committed to cash crops and profit rather than self-subsistence, were permitted ascendancy. As Lytle put it (switching tenses in a way that betrayed his sense of the contemporary relevance of the point he was making): "An agrarian economy was basing its culture on the pay of an industrial economy, which by its nature is hostile to it." "This," he added darkly, "is full of peril." The second mistake came with the Civil War. "The last of the Yeomanry . . . went to the war," Lytle declaimed in his biography of Forrest:

> He brought with him no fine candies, but a jug of molasses, a sack of corn, and his father's musket which, if outmoded, would knock a hole in a man.
>
> These young men were without medieval visions. They were going out to fight because they had heard the Yankees were coming down to tramp their fields and tear up their barns. They were the plain people, the freest people in the South, whom the cotton snobs referred to as the "pore white trash." And they were going away . . . to defend their particular way of life, although they would not have spoken of it in such flat terms.[32]

32. *Bedford Forrest*, 35–36. See also 16, 44, 71, 139, 373; "Backwoods Progression," 414–15; "John Taylor and the Political Economy of Agriculture," Part III, *American Review*, III (November 1934), 97–98; "Robert E. Lee," in *Hero with the Private Parts*, 238–39. Lytle's essay on Lee is remarkable for being one of the few post–Civil War attacks by a Southerner on a figure who has normally been the subject of veneration in the writing of the region. See Thomas L. Connelly, *The Marble Man: Robert E. Lee and His Image in American Society* (Baton Rouge, La., 1977). "Who cares about Lee?" Robert Penn Warren

These men, Lytle suggested, "made up the largest body" of the population in the South; the terrible mistake Jefferson Davis and his advisers made, however, was that "they chose to rest the foundations of the Confederacy on cotton and not on the plain people." In effect, Davis and his associates relied for victory on the wrong class. They put their trust in generals who were the "representatives in military of the cotton snobs," "West P'inters" who preferred abstract military theory and gentlemanly rules of engagement to the ruthless realities of war. Men of plain pioneer stock, like Forrest, with an instinctive understanding of fighting and a sense of the need to win, were simply passed over; and so "these butternut soldiers were to see their victories vanish at the hands of their commanders." The South went down to defeat because it was led by generals like Lee—a man "unwilling to demean his personal code to save the cause"—rather than men like Forrest—who knew that "war means fighting and fighting means killing." And defeat would have been followed by lasting devastation if Forrest had not, fortunately, had the opportunity and the will to form the Ku Klux Klan, "that society which made survival possible," and so help put an end to Reconstruction. Even after betrayal, the remnants of the yeomanry were still there, helping to defend the culture that had so often betrayed them.

It goes without saying, perhaps, that this reading of Southern history is different in almost every crucial respect from that enshrined in the novels of Stark Young. From the standpoint of Lytle's right-wing populism—at once revisionist, reactionary, and radical—the "ruling class" that Young celebrated is portrayed as actively destructive of traditionalism: an agent of progress and capital. In turn, the plain folk so airily dismissed in both Young's novels and essays ("it is not they who gave civilization its peculiar stamp," he says of them in *I'll Take My Stand*)

---

complained. "Now there's a man who's smooth as an egg. Turn him around, this primordial perfection: you see, he has no story" ("An Interview with Flannery O'Connor and Robert Penn Warren, held at the Vanderbilt Literary Symposium, 23 April 1959." Photocopy in the University of North Carolina Library, Chapel Hill). Similarly, John Peale Bishop warned Tate, when he was planning a biography of Lee, that "With Lee, you have a most difficult subject. There seems to be no drama, no conflict in the man." Tate's reply to this was, "You are right about the problem of Lee," and eventually he gave the project up (*Correspondence of Bishop and Tate* edited by Young and Hindle, 38 [To Tate, 24 June 1931], 64 [To Bishop, 19 October 1932]). It is one symptom of Lytle's radicalism that he *did* find a story to tell about Lee, and one that measured his distance from other Agrarians as well as other Southerners.

are placed at the cultural center, made the true keepers of the agrarian faith. Not only that, they are associated with many of the values normally attached to the gentry in the Southern argument: a sense of ceremony and ritual, a feeling for the traditionally sanctioned and sacramental, a commitment to a society that changes very little even if at all. And they are defended in terms that, in the context of the South at least, recall apologies for feudalism and the old plantation: the ineluctable nature of evil, the futility of idealism, the organic rather than contractual basis of all communal relationships. Of course, none of the assumptions or arguments Lytle deploys in support of the plain farmer and his family were utterly unknown to earlier keepers of the yeoman faith. Even Thomas Jefferson wanted social stability of a kind (although, unlike Lytle, he tended to associate stability with an orderly process of change rather than virtual stasis); even Ellen Glasgow, in her paeans to the plain folk, could acknowledge the possibility of failure (although, again unlike Lytle, she did not make a sense of evil a determining factor in her thought). The radical and revisionary nature of Lytle's thinking here is a matter of selection and emphasis, rather than absolute departure from precedent. It is, nevertheless, radical. For, by concentrating on the conservative qualities of what he calls "the livelihood farm," dissociating it from any elements of progressive thought and attaching it to traditional arguments against change, an emblem of rural life that, in so many other texts has been an embodiment of liberal principle is transformed into something quite the opposite: a representative not just of the status quo but of the status quo ante—or, as Lytle put it when he recalled the Agrarian project in the 1950s, of "a certain inheritance, a certain polity . . . whose history [is] as old as Christendom."[33]

It is in the fiction, however, that Lytle's radical revision of arguments for agrarian simplicity is at its clearest—and sometimes most startling. In his second novel, for example, *At the Moon's Inn*—and, for that matter, in the short story "Alchemy," published a year after the novel, in 1942—Lytle dramatizes a contrast familiar to any reader of fiction from the South: between the capitalist and the agrarian. The capitalists here are the Spanish Conquistadores and, in particular, their leader, Hernando de Soto. "The westward movement of the Europeans," Lytle argued in his essays, "beginning with Columbus, not only shattered the narrow physi-

33. "The Agrarians Today: A Symposium," *Shenandoah*, III (Summer 1952), 30. See also "Small Farm Secures the State," 240; "Not in Memoriam, but in Defense," 337.

cal boundaries of Christendom, but weakened it," by pursuing and promoting "the Faustian view" of experience, "relying entirely on material ends as the proper reward for action." And this is illustrated and developed in the portrait of de Soto: who begins by paying lip service to his priestly advisers but, when he is forced to choose, sets "his private will outside the guidance and discipline of the Church." In a scene central to the meaning of the story, de Soto is attending Mass after a battle when the priest suddenly halts the ceremony and orders him, by the authority of the Host, to leave Florida. De Soto refuses. "From here," as one of de Soto's more perceptive followers, called Tovar, observes, "it is only one further step to supplant God's will by man's will and call it divine."[34] This step de Soto effectively takes, by not only disobeying the order of the priest but also taking the Host from him; in doing so, he assumes the spiritual power for himself. Deifying his own will and conscience, he is an exotic version of the figure of the Yankee to be found in so many arguments for the South: like that figure, he places himself above the restrictions of the code—a traditional and communal system of principles—and pursues ambitions that are, at best, a confused mixture of the material and spiritual and, at worst, simply a form of hypocrisy. With his "fractured view" of reality, de Soto is as much the enemy here as General Sherman is in *So Red the Rose*—a divided, antitraditional, deeply isolated man—whose moral confusion is emblematized by his wearing of a crucifix that functions at once as a religious icon, a precious ornament, and a handy weapon. Only in his dying moments does he begin to see his mistake: when he confesses, to his followers, "The will is not enough." By then, however, it is too late.

Too late, that is, for de Soto, the Spaniards, and America: "The study of American history," Lytle insisted, "is . . . the record of those acts which have precipitated the sorry evils responsible for the chaos of modern society . . . it tells the triumph of senseless greed." And the tale of the triumph of greed begins here: in the story of men who jettison all customary sanctions in their pursuit of gain. To an extent, the customary sanctions, the settled order that de Soto and his men throw overboard, is that represented by the priest: the order of the Church, that is, and Christendom. Only to an extent, however: since the strongest part of the narrative focuses on de Soto's struggles, not with the culture he has left behind,

---

34. *At the Moon's Inn* (New York, 1941), 374. See also 397; "Foreword to *A Novel, A Novella, and Four Stories,*" xx.

but with the one he invades—the Native Americans who, within the terms of this version of American history, become the first agrarian victims of the forces of progress and capital. Like all agrarian heroes, the Native Americans in *At the Moon's Inn* enjoy an "absolute oneness" with their surroundings. "Their very stillness was motion," we are told, "the motion of the sap under the bark, their walking a kind of flowing, an unobtrusive extension, an integral part of the wilderness."[35] The Spanish, by comparison, seem to be constantly in an adversarial relationship with nature: de Soto is "like a mechanical man" driven by the motor of profit and, guided by him, most of his followers "pit their will" to work against their environment rather than with it—to conquer and to exploit. Just as "The Hind Tit" observes the times and stations of a typical farming day, so this novel reverently follows the rhythms, the chores, and the ceremonies of a farming year: while the Native Americans engage in a fertile, productive, and ultimately religious contact with the earth and "the four sacred seasons," the Spanish commit themselves to a hunt for gold that turns out to be literally, as well as spiritually, barren. In a way, there can be no communication between these two cultures; they simply do not understand each other, although they can certainly sense the innate conflict. "The crops are good and ready for harvest," one bewildered Spaniard reports of a conversation with an Indian, "but when I speak of a yellow metal, he pleads ignorance."

What is particularly remarkable about Lytle's portrait of Native American culture in this novel is the way it reveals, again, the profoundly conservative nature of his thinking—and, related to this, just how willing he was to attach many of the qualities usually associated with the gentry to his version of livelihood farming. Certainly, there is a quality of simplicity attributed to the locals that hardly suggests patrician values or an aristocratic way of life. "They had no gold," the Spaniards observe with constant amazement; they bring, to their invaders, "gifts of mulberries and plums, sable furs and the strong-smelling skins of the cat. Rich and welcome gifts, but not what the Governor wanted." And, allied to this simplicity, there is a sense of communality, sharing the fruits and benefits of the earth, that rehearses Lytle's populist distaste for aristocratic hauteur and his romantic recollections of earlier times when "baron and yeoman met on freer ground." "The Indians went freely about," we are told,

35. *At the Moon's Inn*, 133. See also 143, 195, 290, 374; "John Taylor and the Political Economy of Agriculture," Part I, *American Review*, III (September 1934), 432.

"and strangers would walk into a dwelling as if they were come to their own home with an 'I am come.' And the only reply, 'Good, you are come.' " The simplicity, the unassuming hospitality, and even democratic openness of the way of life Lytle describes is not, however, the whole story as far as style and manners are concerned. Like the plain folk in Lytle's version of more recent Southern history, the native folk in this novel are also notable for their sense of ceremony, the decorous forms of their behavior, the studied and stately manner in which even the most trivial task is performed. The contrast between what is called "the deliberate formality of Indian ways" and the "dangerous haste" of the Spanish is brought out, with particular emphasis, whenever there is a conference between the two sides. The Native Americans, we are told, conduct themselves with "grave and stately mien," their deportment before the invaders is "the perfection of irony and courtesy." "The Christians," on the other hand, "showed little patience during the long hours of talk. They shifted from place to place or walked away during the long pauses the Indians kept." They betray the same nervousness and discomposure—the same inability, John Crowe Ransom might say, to fathom and perform their natures—as General Sherman does in *So Red the Rose*. And in this respect, the Native Americans are just like Young's aristocrats. They observe the odd behavior of the Spanish "with indifference and a marked haughtiness." "At such times," the narrator explains—focusing the Native American reaction on their leader—"a red film clouded for an instant the cacique's eyes, but only by this did Aguacalaquan show his contempt for his enemies."[36]

The character who describes the coolly aristocratic behavior of the Indian leader here is de Soto's follower Tovar, who takes up the narration once the expedition to the New World has begun. Tovar is a useful instrument for Lytle, because he is a Spaniard who comes to value the Native American way of life: something that is signaled, among other ways, by his marrying into the local community. To this extent, *At the Moon's Inn* offers a variation on the conversion narrative: as in so many fictions that have a clear social or historical point to make, the reader is invited to share the experiences—and, in this case, the viewpoint—of someone who starts as a neutral, or even an enemy to the cause, but ends as an initiate, a disciple. Tovar leads the reader into the gradual discovery of this different way of life and, perhaps, into appreciation of and even identification

36. *At the Moon's Inn*, 225–26. See also 135, 272, 293, 296, 332.

with the difference. Certainly, Tovar has "become" a Native American in many ways before the end of the novel. He begins to see the destructive implications of the imperial quest of de Soto—and, by extension, the dangers of progress and capital. Gradually, the narrative eye defines the *Spanish* as the strangers, the alien culture operating according to laws that are, at the very least, open to question and, quite possibly, intolerable and indefensible—as this passage, describing the building of a fort in the wilderness, suggests: "The palisades, the soldiers' messes, and the cleared space around the town had changed the appearance of the world. It would have taken the Indians years . . . to have cleared away such a space. De Soto had done it in a week. That was a dangerous, hostile act, an act of magic. He smiled to himself. There he went thinking like an Indian again."[37] Like the Yankee progressive of so much traditionalist Southern thought, the Conquistadores are seamless capitalists, at war with the natural order of things; like the "cotton snobs" in Lytle's version of the regional past, they are also involved in an enterprise that is ultimately sacrilegious. The Native Americans map out the agrarian alternative: one that neatly brings together Lytle's love of simplicity and ceremony, his distrust of change and individual initiative, and his belief that communal, familial life on the land is blessed. Lytle's Spaniards are on the move, constantly; at once unnatural and uncultivated, they have no sense of their spatial or spiritual limitations. His Native Americans do have that sense, deeply, just as his plain white folk do; and it is this, above all, that gives them their oneness with nature as well as their cultivation, their ability to be at ease with themselves—and, above all, an almost preternatural stillness.

"In a healthy country society," Lytle once wrote in a letter to his friend and fellow Agrarian the historian Frank Owsley, "man finds himself in his right relation to nature." "The country is still a place where both work and play move at a leisurely pace," he added. "It is still, to a great extent, free from the rapid tempo of modern affairs." This hymn to country life, as the still center of an ever more rapidly turning world, could act as a gloss to many of Lytle's works, including "The Hind Tit," *At the Moon's Inn,* and *A Wake for the Living.* In fact, it serves as the preface to his first novel, *The Long Night*: where it helps to frame an extraordinary story. Briefly, that story concerns an act of revenge: a character called Pleasant McIvor attempts to avenge the death of his father, Cameron. Cameron was murdered by a conspiracy of slave stealers; and Pleasant sets out to dispose of about fifty men. Over the following years, as he lives in "the long night" of revenge, he kills many. The Civil War intervenes, however, forcing him to choose uncertainly between personal and public duty; and he slowly finds his fierce intent waning. Told initially by Pleasant's nephew, then by Pleasant himself, and finally by an anonymous third-person narrator, the story is really a sort of ballad or tall tale, the stuff of legend, as Lytle signals in his prefatory letter to Owsley. A country society, Lytle claims here, "largely lacks the artificial pleasures which the towns and even the villages now seek"; what it has, instead, is more than compensation, though—"stories, the tall tale . . . or the discussion of the idiosyncrasies and high deeds of some kinsman, now long dead."[38] It was from such a story, Lytle discloses, told by Owsley, that his novel derives; it is part of that "bardic" tradition he was later to celebrate in *A Wake for the Living*. From the voice of earlier men, this epic tale of vengeance has passed through Owsley to Lytle; within the frame of the narrative, it now passes back from a McIvor of one generation through the McIvor of another, and then on to a more impersonal, anonymous voice. That last voice, of course, is like the "bardic voice" of *A Wake for the Living*, which "collects the segments," pieces the family legend together; it is also like the voice of the community, the folk speech that speaks in the traditional ballad. In this way, through the actual medium of the narrative, Lytle is rehearsing and celebrating the culture that is also his subject. *The Long Night* is a novel that makes its case, not least, in and through its narration: its speech and the manner of story it tells.

The further dimensions of that story are spelled out in the account of the revenge motive and its gradual waning. Perhaps the crucial scene is the one in which, after the death of Cameron, the McIvor clan meet to discuss what they should do. One solution is the law: suggested by one of the younger "kin," William, "a quiet man and something of a scholar." His suggestion is quickly dismissed by the others. "The courts, sir," as one of the older and more respected members of the family, Armistead McIvor, puts it, "are for land litigations and the punishment of the state's criminals." The onus, it is generally agreed, is on the family to avenge what is fundamentally an offense against it; the law of the courts

38. Letter to Frank Owsley, August, 1936: Preface to *The Long Night* (New York, 1936). This letter can also be found in subsequent editions.

and contracts has no place here; this is a matter of "blood," imperfect people in an imperfect world responding to instinctive allegiances and what they instinctively know to be right. There is an anticipation here of the contrast Lytle draws in *At the Moon's Inn* between, on the one hand, the legalism and casual cruelty of the Spanish and, on the other, the Native Americans' strict sense of the appropriate levels of vengeance for a wrong done against one of their number: "to take hair" from the corpse of the wrongdoer is usually "enough," we are told in that later novel, but "when the insult [is] insupportable," then "only the severed body . . . will requite the injured party." And there is no doubt that, in both novels, whatever his views on the detailed maneuvers of the avenger, Lytle sees the revenge impulse as a sound one, precisely because it issues out of the right attachments—family and community—and an accurate appreciation of just what is feasible, given the flawed nature of humanity. "Son, I understand how you feel," says Armistead to William as he tries to console the young man for the rejection of his proposal to take the murderers to law: ". . . you're find that all we can do in this world is to be good neighbors, be kind to our inferiors, respect our betters, and let things go on like they ought to."[39] Seen from this perspective, vengeance seems to be, not so much an act disruptive of community as one that confirms it, because the code of vengeance issues out of those intimate "interrelationships of blood and kin" (to use Lytle's own phrase) that are seen as the essence of the communal.

What goes wrong in *The Long Night*, in fact, is put down not to the revenge motive but, rather, to change: altered circumstances that make the issue of allegiance suddenly problematic. The altered circumstances are, of course, those of war. To begin with, Pleasant still pursues revenge: he joins a unit with five of his father's murderers in it, lulls them into a false sense of security, and kills them. He then pretends to General Johnston, who interviews him, that the unit was attacked by the enemy, and that he only managed to drive his opponents off by pretending to be several men. Johnston's response to this story, "Always do your duty with as much intelligence," points to the dilemma in which Pleasant has found himself and only just begun to understand. Just what is his "duty" here? Is it to his family or to his community, the McIvors or the South? "Public duty, when your country is in peril," Armistead McIvor observes,

39. *Long Night*, 71. See also 33, 65; *At the Moon's Inn*, 221; "The Working Novelist and the Mythmaking Process," in *Hero with the Private Parts*, 179.

"comes before private." The face of Pleasant's mother, at the funeral of his brother, tells him the opposite: that to neglect revenge is to "let his father lie uneasy in his grave." And Pleasant never really resolves this dilemma. He simply vacillates: committing himself to his soldierly duties, neglecting his role as avenger—and then suddenly taking up that role again. The crisis comes when Pleasant momentarily pursues vengeance, leaving his comrade in war to do so: only to discover that "his will had snapped" and he cannot pull the trigger. "His private vengeance had been swallowed by something greater than his love for his father," the narrator observes, "—no, not greater, only more overpowering."[40] Worse still, when Pleasant returns to the field of combat, he discovers that his temporary desertion of his military duties has led to the death of his brother in arms. He has failed in both his public and his private duties. This is his personal tragedy, certainly: but there is no doubt at all that Lytle intends us to see this as, ultimately, a tragedy of the times. What is being illustrated here is the thesis, held in common by many of those who contributed to I'll Take My Stand, that in an ideal—which is to say, traditional and rural—society, there is no divorce between the public and the private, whereas in an untraditional one—or in circumstances leading to the breakdown of tradition—there inevitably is. As Lytle's friend and fellow Agrarian Allen Tate put it, in traditional society "the man as he appeared in public was the man, his public appearance was his moral life." "The traditional community," Tate declared, "is made up of men who . . . are making their living all the time and affirming their code all the time"; "the life of men and their livelihood approximate a unity in which to speak of one is to speak of the other." In an "untraditional society," however, separation becomes the sign of the times. The rural idyll is obliterated, and what is left is a landscape of fragmentation and waste: "means," as Tate put it, "are divorced from ends, action from sensibility, matter from mind, society from the individual, religion from moral agency, love from lust, communion from experience, and mankind in the community from men in the crowd. There is literally no end to this list of dissociations because there is no end, yet in sight, to the fragmenting of the western mind."[41] This is the traditionalist nightmare: the logi-

40. Long Night, 327. See also 199, 209, 316.

41. Allen Tate, "The Man of Letters in the Modern World," in The Forlorn Demon: Didactic and Critical Essays (London, 1953), 111. See also Stonewall Jackson: The Good Soldier (London, 1930), 12; "Liberalism and Tradition," in Reason in Madness (New York, 1941), 210–11. Lytle's remarks about the "last moment of equilibrium" are from "Note on a Traditional Sensibility," in Hero with the Private Parts, 173.

cal termination of what Lytle called those "disrupting forces" that had been at work for four centuries. And it is patently clear that the author of *The Long Night*—like the author of *The Fathers* and, in this case, also the author of *So Red the Rose*—sees those forces at work in the Civil War: destroying what Lytle called in one of his essays "the last moment of equilibrium" in Western history, "the last time a man could know who he was." Pleasant McIvor cannot know what his proper duty is, whether he should avenge his father or defend the South. He is a divided man, whose divisions mirror those of the emerging, triumphant culture; he is also an ignorant man, in the sense that—according to Lytle's definition of self-knowledge—not knowing where his true allegiances lie means that Pleasant cannot really know who he is.

The question of self-knowledge is fundamental to all Lytle's work, not just *The Long Night*; and, in all that work, the answer to that question is indelibly tied to issues of family and community—the human agent finding his or her place in the human world. In the novels, too, it is explored and dramatized in a peculiarly knowing way: Lytle was a careful, conscientious, and sophisticated critic in the New Critical mold who offered some fairly influential explications of his own work. With his third novel, for instance, *A Name for Evil*, published in 1947, Lytle made it quite clear that the book should be read as a critique of romanticism. The novel resulted, Lytle explained, from his reading Henry James's "The Turn of the Screw" again, and asking himself what would happen if adults rather than children were the main protagonists. From this bookish beginning, it then developed into a dramatic analysis of two men, Henry Brent and his ghostly ancestor Major Brent, who both believe they can deny time and the imperfections of human life in time. Many years before the narrative present, we are told, the Major left the crops on his plantation to rot: "It has reached perfection," he declared. "It can do no more." Now, in the narrative present, his descendant Henry wants to resurrect the past that the Major wished to inter: he is, as the novel puts it at one point, "the man with the strained neck, looking always back to Eden." In terms of what Lytle the critic called "the action proper" of the novel, Henry and his ghostly ancestor are antagonists: the one transfixed by a legendary past that he hopes to restore and replicate in the present, the other obsessed with a personal past that he hopes to keep untouched. But in terms of what Lytle called "the enveloping action," relating to the fundamental meaning of the story, the two are fatally alike. "The orderly life of individuals," we are told at one point in the novel, "depends on a balance between light and darkness. We perish only when the sun gets jammed at high noon or the moon glides forever at full."[42] And both Henry and the Major make the mistake of assuming they can stop time, jam the sun at high noon; their error, which leads eventually to the death of Henry's wife, Ellen, is that they cannot find a balance between light and darkness. Idealists, they never manage a name for evil.

All this is very effectively done, up to a point. The ambivalent relationship between Henry Brent and his ghostly ancestor is etched out with care. Lytle was a sufficiently subtle writer, and sufficiently subtle reader of James, to leave the question of the *reality* of Major Brent—the question, that is, of whether the Major is a "real" presence or a projection—open. The meaning of the story is underlined by the symbolism—dark and light, wilderness and garden, and so on. And, just in case any reader might be uncertain about that meaning, there is always the helpful comment to guide him or her in the right direction: "I am, I was, that most unhappy of hybrids, the false romantic," Henry Brent explains. "With will and deliberation, and this is the essence of the difference, the false romantic ignores the true nature of reality."[43] The trouble is that, as this quotation suggests, the narrative is just a little too helpful, just a little too self-explanatory. It pushes us, sometimes gently and sometimes in a rather more emphatic way, toward one particular reading. To an extent, this is true of all Lytle's fiction: for good or ill, it is fiercely committed and grows directly out of his understanding of history, the human community, and the family. The particular complicating factor here is that at certain points—when it comes, for instance, to reminding us that Henry and the Major are idealists who want to freeze time—the narrative wears its meaning on its sleeve, while at others it is disconcertingly vague. It fluctuates between shouting its meanings and mumbling them, or being troublingly mute. *A Name for Evil* "refuses to comment on Agrarianism and the South," argues Thomas Carter in his essay on Lytle in *South: Modern Southern Literature in Its Cultural Setting*, adding, "Henry

42. *A Name for Evil*, 214. *A Name for Evil* was first published in 1947. All references here are to the edition of the book in *A Novel, A Novella, and Four Stories* (New York, 1958). See also 212, 247; "Foreword to *A Novel, A Novella, and Four Stories*, xiv, xv.

43. *Name for Evil*, 182. See also "Foreword to *A Novel, A Novella, and Four Stories*," xxv; "The Forest of the South," in *Critique: Studies in Modern Fiction*, I (Winter 1956), 4; "Political Economy of Agriculture," Part I, 447; Thomas H. Carter, "Andrew Lytle," in *South* edited by Rubin and Jacobs, 295.

Brent is deranged, for whatever reason; he represents an extreme case. And he is a daft Agrarian. He meant literally to restore the past." This, quite apart from verging on self-contradiction (not an Agrarian / "daft Agrarian"), begs too many questions. And so does the story itself. In what ways, precisely, *do* the Agrarians differ from Henry Brent? After all, didn't Lytle and Young also want "literally to restore the past" ("Throw out the radio and take down the fiddle from the wall")? Weren't the contributors to *I'll Take My Stand,* in their different fashions, haunted by ghosts—the troubled memories of a region that seemed sometimes to resist and sometimes to reinforce their arguments? One possibility might be that Lytle's aim was to offer a critique of those agrarians, like the Jeffersonians, who advocated a return to agriculture in a "vacuum," without reference—as Lytle himself put it in one of his essays—to the "complex of institutions" on which it depends. But that possibility poses problems too. How is this particularity of critique achieved? How is the narrative focused in this way? And to what extent did people like Lytle or Young manage to fill this vacuum themselves, by meeting the need fully to situate their ideals of the rural life? In short, *A Name for Evil* is a story with a message, but the message is blurred. Not only that, the blurring is related to something basic to the traditionalist argument. Lytle, like other Southern traditionalists, claims that he is placing history at the center, assigning it a constitutive function; and in one sense he is, since he makes so much of the interplay between past, present, and future. But in another sense he is being no more historical than anyone else is who (to quote Barthes again) "transforms history into nature": because he is presenting his arguments, his particular version of a particular history, as a fundamentally accurate account of the essence of things. Despite the fact that traditionalist Southern thinking has been shaped by historical circumstances often peculiar to itself and has invariably changed in response to changing pressures, it assumes an air of permanence—an absolute quality, and an exemption from the very circumstances that shaped it. So, in *A Name for Evil,* the reader is presented with a paradox: a narrative insisting on the need to situate all human projects in history that remains vague about its own historical sources and situation. Inadvertently, the story exposes the irony at the heart of traditionalist thinking, its habit of transforming "history" into "nature" by claiming it is doing precisely the reverse. And it does so by offering us a fable that floats free of its historical anchorage, while making the case for anchors; it insists on seeing things in time and place while remaining, in these terms, peculiarly myopic.

"An idea *must* turn flesh before it is fiction,"[44] Lytle insisted: a remark that perhaps reveals more than its author knew—and, certainly, more than traditionalist critics seem to have noticed. After all, it gives priority, at least in the temporal sense, to the idea—which is assumed to be there, fully articulated, before the fiction is even begun. For a writer like Faulkner, who tended to claim that a novel started with an image, this would have been surprising, even contentious. It suggests, however, how very much aware Lytle was of the argumentative origins of his stories: how, for him, the practice of writing was not just an inescapably but also a self-consciously *ideological* one. Of course, Lytle would have disapproved strongly of that term, *ideological*, because of its supposedly scientific connotations—probably preferring instead to dwell on the biblical resonances of the idea/word made flesh. He would no doubt also have agreed with John Peale Bishop's contention—made in a letter to Allen Tate—that "communists" and liberals "wish to criticize life through ideas, while we must constantly criticize ideas through life": which repeats the sleight of hand, mentioned earlier, by which the traditionalist idea of life is equated with "life" itself, while its untraditionalist opposite is demoted to the status of a mere "idea." For all that, Lytle's work does deal in ideas more clearly than even most fiction does; and his best writing is his best, not in spite of the fact that it argues a position, but precisely because it does—and does it well. Nowhere is this clearer than in his fourth novel, *The Velvet Horn*, which many commentators account his finest: the strength and weakness of which issue directly from its status as a careful fleshing out of Lytle's ideas. That remark about the idea becoming flesh comes, in fact, from Lytle's own very detailed account of the making and meaning of *The Velvet Horn*, "The Working Novelist and the Mythmaking Process": here, more clearly than anywhere else in his writing, Lytle underlines his message—or perhaps it would be more accurate to say, his two messages—the two, quite separate ways in which Lytle tries to unravel for us the implications of living, both in time and (as he put it in *A Wake for the Living*) "in the sense of eternity."

The first message is the one that Lytle emphasizes in his essay on *The Velvet Horn*, and that most of those who have found time to discuss the

44. "Working Novelist and the Mythmaking Process," 180. See also *Wake for the Living*, 3; *Correspondence of Bishop and Tate* edited by Young and Hindle, 92. To Tate [14–23 December 1933].

novel have found dominating their attention. It is the message of human imperfection: the belief that, as Lytle puts it in "The Son of Man: He Will Prevail," "without knowledge of evil, and its place in the divine scheme, there is no life." The hero of *The Velvet Horn,* young Lucius Cree, is initiated into this knowledge in learning the history of his family: most of whom, he learns, when suddenly confronted with the responsibilities of adulthood, sought some kind of escape. One, for instance, sought sanctuary in an Edenic retreat, a world of primeval innocence, a pastoral womb entered by passing under a mountain through a cave concealed beneath a waterfall. Another sought refuge in a way familiar to any reader of "The Fall of the House of Usher" or, for that matter, *The Sound and the Fury*: that is, in an incestuous relationship with his sister—which, as Lytle helpfully explains in his essay on the novel, represents another form of "return to . . . prenatal . . . innocence and wholeness," "the refusal to engage in the cooperating opposites that make life." The singular exception to this family history of bad example is Lucius's "Uncle Jack" Cropleigh: whose positive function as a guide and model is suggested in a variety of ways. Jack Cropleigh "kept the home place" when other members of the family fled, we are told: a crucial yardstick for someone like Lytle who clearly believes in living as and where you are. Symbolically, he is associated with revival and resurrection: he works as a "water-witch" bringing life to the dry land and, at one point, he stumbles drunkenly into an open grave only to emerge unscathed—"Me and Lazarus, boys," he declares to the gravediggers who help him out. He is also, Lytle points out, "the spiritual hermaphrodite." Evidently containing within him connections with both sexes, he *does* engage with the cooperating opposites of life; so, like Tiresias in "The Waste Land," he can perform a prophetic function—as Lytle phrases it in his essay on the novel, "He alone could suffer the myth." Not only that, he alone can act as a guide to Lucius, as his nephew goes through his rite of initiation, and, in the end, confront Lucius with the choice between responsibility and retreat. Lucius discovers that a poor white girl, Ada Belle Rutter, has become pregnant by him; and, after resisting an initial impulse simply to deny all knowledge of her, he has to make a decision—the nature of which Jack Cropleigh carefully outlines. He can marry and flee west and become "nameless, an anonymous kind of fellow"[45] ("What the West

---

45. *The Velvet Horn* (New York, 1957), 332. See also 27, 213, 261, 359; "The Son of Man: He Will Prevail," in *Hero with the Private Parts,* 127; "Working Novelist and the Mythmaking Process," 184, 189.

means to you is a place to hide," Jack tells him). Or he can stay, accepting responsibility for what he has done and his place in his family and his community. Prompted by Jack, Lucius chooses to stay. In the process, it is clear, he is also acknowledging imperfection: or, as Jack puts it, Lucius is embracing his own, newly discovered "bastardy" (he is the product of an illicit, and also quite probably, incestuous relationship) and the "social bastardy" of his wife (who, unlike him, is not "of good family"). He has become, finally, an adult through his knowledge of evil and his and its place in the scheme of things.

In *South*, Thomas Carter describes *The Velvet Horn* as "Andrew Lytle's most impressive achievement to date . . . which he spent nine years in writing"; and as recently as 1985, the novel was hailed as "one of the major achievements of the Southern Renascence." Certainly, *The Velvet Horn* represents a definite stab at a big book, using the narrative form favored by the majority of traditionalist Southern writers of this century, symbolic naturalism. The problem is perhaps signaled by the fact that the most influential, and one of the most detailed, explications of the novel has been supplied by the author himself. With its elaborate freight of imagery and symbol, the narrative sometimes reads like a gift to the New Critic. The title itself is a symbol with multiple meanings: the velvety horn of the young buck, the phallic horn, the horn of plenty. Lytle refers to the horn as "the controlling image," but there are surely other contenders for this honor: among them, the myth of Eden, the Waste Land (there is a drought in "the failing season," at the beginning of the novel), the imagery associated with the womb. And, while the narrator is developing and emphasizing these images and symbols, there are many others besides: the West as retreat and refuge, the house that is little more than a facade revealing the "incompleteness within" of its owner, Lucius's literal trek up the mountains that is also a "climbing into entanglement with life." Lytle rarely misses an opportunity to signal meaning, to point the moral and adorn the tale; and, in this, is greatly assisted by the voice of Jack Cropleigh. The reader is constantly being alerted to a symbolic subtext that, in itself, is lurking only just beneath the surface; he or she is constantly being told, in effect, just how to read the novel. Some comments almost directly transcribe comments and arguments from Lytle's essays: Jack Cropleigh's "The naked man is the natural man. He's forbidden," for instance, recalls Lytle's own "The natural man is an abstraction." Others simply carry, in a fairly overt way, the whole weight of Lytle's thinking: "the bitter travail which is man's common lot," "that self-begetting, self-perpetuating wholeness before division which is knowledge, the bitter first fruit whose aftertaste set us slobbering wanderers in this world."[46] The point is not that comments of this kind are necessarily inappropriate but that they are too frequent and demand too much attention. Like the symbolism, they enforce one authoritative reading; it is the writerly equivalent of highlighting. What is more, it is distinctly at odds with where the real strength of the book lies: which is its rendering of the life and the community Lucius knows—and, in the end, comes to accept.

The Velvet Horn is set in the Cumberland hill country of Tennessee in the late nineteenth century: in other words, in the place that Lytle and his kinfolk made their home, and at a time that overlapped with the author's earliest memories. The life of that area of the South, east of the Mississippi and west of the mountains, Lytle confides in "The Working Novelist and the Mythmaking Process," "seemed to me to be what was left of the older and more civilized America, which as well retained the pattern of its European inheritance." Effectively, "the Civil War had destroyed that life," he explains, "but memory and habit, manners and mores are slow to die." As a boy, he says, he had witnessed the "ghostly presence" of this habit of life, "and yet the people which this presence inhabited were substantial enough." Such people, his neighbors and kin, "were alive in their entire being"; and "they seemed all the more alive because their culture was stricken." "The last active expression of this society seemed to fall somewhere between 1880 and 1910," Lytle suggests; "those decades seemed the effective turning point of the great revolution which was to diminish a Christian inheritance." After that, "the family was uprooted by destroying its attachment to place"; and by family, he points out, he means what he always does—"the large 'connections' " of "blood and kin" that "extended to the county lines and by sympathy overlapped the states."[47] In the best sense, as these comments indicate, *The Velvet Horn* is a book conceived out of attachment to mem-

---

46. *Velvet Horn*, 95. See also 19, 27, 34, 185; "Working Novelist and the Mythmaking Process," 185, 186; "Foreword to *A Novel, A Novella, and Four Stories*," xv; Carter, "Andrew Lytle," 295; M. E. Bradford, "The Passion of Craft," in *The History of Southern Literature* edited by Louis D. Rubin et al. (Baton Rouge, La., 1985), 382. The abundance of symbolism in *Velvet Horn* is noted with approval by Brewster Ghiselin, "Trial of Light," *Sewanee Review*, XLV (Winter 1957), 656–65. A similar verdict, that *Velvet Horn* is "Lytle's masterpiece," is offered by Young, *Tennessee Writers*, 51.

47. "Working Novelist and the Mythmaking Process," 178–79.

ory and community; it is fired into life by Lytle's burning conviction that what he knew as a boy, and what his ancestors knew before him, is the true knowledge that is life. Like "The Hind Tit" or *A Wake for the Living*, it presents us with country life in a way that makes that life seem both commonplace and profound: of the earth, earthy, and yet also of religious significance—an act of communion with both the dead and the living.

This sense of a complex network of communal relationships sustaining the individual is registered, early on in the novel, by the reactions of the local folk to the death of a neighbor. The response of one of them, the best cook in the village, is typical: "Bake this cake I will," she declares. "It's the least I can do. . . . There's little enough you can do . . . but I always say neighbors ought to be neighborly." Parties, funerals, weddings punctuate the narrative, reminding us of the deeper rhythms that act as a ground-bass to daily life, and of the rituals that bind the community together. "Hands clasped around the ring," the narrator observes of the dancers at a wedding, "the bodies arched and still . . . the floor boards quiver, giving and returning with one rhythm." And, to prevent things getting too portentous, the accounts of such moments are laced with jokes and gossip. "I note Sister Baskins still has her waistline," comments one local man "slyly" at a wake; "Shorely the preacher's done found it by now," responds his companion; "they burst into ribald merriment," adds the anonymous voice of the narrator, "but they made no sound." All the while, too, there is just as much feeling as there is in all Lytle's best writing for that daily life itself, the simplicity of its customs but also the seriousness of its ceremonies. No one quotation can properly capture this dimension of the story, because it depends for its impact on the slow accretion of detail. But perhaps the following gives some idea of how, in reading *The Velvet Horn,* we gradually accumulate a rich, intimate knowledge of country pleasure and labor: "In the next field two miniature farmhands were standing in wagon beds spreading manure. They lifted the forks with the same throw they would sow grain with, only a slower, heavier pause as the tines plunged into the rich heaped pile. Spring was always at a stress; yet all here went at a measured pace, as if there were no crisis."[48]

This is the message that works in *The Velvet Horn,* the one that does get across: the sense of a life lived on the livelihood farm as at once lively

48. *Velvet Horn,* 289. See also 173, 205, 267.

and stately, a matter of both personal crises generated by the present and communal rituals inherited from the past—and, in this sense, partaking of both time and eternity. As for the details of this message: the portrait of the world that Lucius Cree finally accepts as his own is no more literal or "objective" than, say, the account of Native American life in *At the Moon's Inn* is—or the dramatic rendering of the life of Bigger Thomas and his family in *Native Son*. The country community that we encounter in *The Velvet Horn* is one written into life by ideas. It lives on the page, precisely because it is the product of profound affection and equally profound conviction: Lytle's fundamental belief that what makes human experience vital and meaningful is what he learned from blood and kin and then tried to promote in, for instance, his essays for *I'll Take My Stand, American Review,* and *Who Owns America? A New Declaration of Independence*. Autobiography, the history of family, and the history of community were all part of "the one story" for Lytle, and that story mattered fiercely for him because it supplied the vital source, the wellspring for his arguments: the basis on which he erected the radical, reactionary case that characterizes all his work, whatever its formal or generic ties. *The Velvet Horn,* Lytle's last major novel, is different from *A Wake for the Living,* his last major work of any kind, if only because one reinvents history while the other claims simply to recollect it: one is written *from* the experience, of family and community, the other claims to be *about*. Through them both, though, sounds the voice of the author, animated by the lessons he had learned and the meanings he had to disclose. Books like these remind us, if reminder is needed, that Lytle, Young, Tate, and their colleagues were just as captivated by ideas as anyone else—and, in more local terms, just as committed to commenting on and, if possible, changing the course of events as any other writers of their time. They were necessarily ideological as any person in any culture is; they were also *consciously* ideological to the extent that they were committed to defending and promoting a cause. That cause led them in quite different directions, even within the pages of *I'll Take My Stand,* as the steadily diverging histories of Lytle and Young show. But the cause was clearly there for them; it enabled and shaped their writing. And it is still there for us, or should be, as we try to understand their work today.

Over thirty years after the publication of *Southern Renascence,* a book entitled *The History of Southern Literature* offered a crucial redress to the imbalances of that earlier volume. A major work of scholarship and criticism, *The History of Southern Literature* is essentially a collection of essays covering the period 1607–1982, each of them written by an expert and all of them adding up to a multidimensional, richly layered account of the literature of the Southern states. The Introduction by one of the editors—Louis D. Rubin, who was also one of the editors of *Southern Renascence* and *South*—is disarmingly modest. "Our choices will not satisfy everyone entirely," the reader is told, "but no choices would; perhaps no choices should." There is a recognition here of the necessarily selective nature of all scholarly judgment and critical comment: which is then combined with an acknowledgment that selection need not and should not mean willful bias. "Given the human limitations of our collective editorial wisdom," Rubin says, "and the practical limitations of space available, we believe that we have been thorough and reasonably objective." "Reasonably objective" is perhaps a less accurate phrase here than "necessarily pluralistic." One strength of this book is precisely that it acts from the assumption that there are multiple kinds of Southern writing—and have been ever since the early settlement of Virginia. Pluralistic, the fundamental approach is also, in the best sense, knowing: the editors historically situate themselves as men "born in the South of the 1910s and 1920s," growing up in the "1920s and 1930s" and graduate students "during the 1940s and 1950s." "They were born and grew up," Rubin explains, "in a South that was still economically impoverished, rurally dominated, in politics monolithically Democratic, and racially segregated." As their careers developed, however, they witnessed radical change, economic, social, and political; at the same time, they found themselves "roughly the contemporaries of what has been called the 'second generation' of the writers of the Renascence, who began writing their stories and poems in the 1940s and 1950s."[49] The communality of experience defined here does not significantly affect the choices made; on the contrary, *The History of Southern Literature* is the very reverse of consensual. Like all good literary histories produced over the last two or three decades, it eschews the totalizing or encyclopedic orientation of earlier scholarly projects of this kind in favor of polyphony—the inclusion, and sometimes the clash, of different perspectives and voices. Nevertheless, the fact that it is felt necessary to offer a brief sketch of the (remarkably similar) intellectual biographies of the editors suggests the length of the route traveled between *Southern Renascence* and *The His-*

49. Rubin, "Introduction," *History of Southern Literature*, 3–4.

tory of Southern Literature. Despite its rather monolithically sounding title ("the" rather than "a"), *The History of Southern Literature* is a powerful achievement, not only because of the editors' recognition of plurality (and willingness to act on that recognition), and not only because of the collective variety and individual specificity of the essays that go to make up the volume—but thanks to the willingness to accept the *possibility* of contingency. At the back of the volume, in other words, lies an acknowledgment that literary history may well have its own equivalent of the indeterminacy or uncertainty principle: according to which, what you see depends upon where you are.

There are still echoes of the old, overdetermined and overexclusive voice to be found at times in this book. In a bibliographical essay toward the end, for example, we are informed that Richard King's "sympathy for the liberal tradition" in *A Southern Renaissance* "makes a balanced treatment of the literature impossible"; Walter Sullivan, on the other hand, whose approach remains unlocated and undefined, is said to argue "in brilliant style" in books such as *A Requiem for the Renascence.* Here we are back to the old assumption that somehow traditionalism holds the monopoly on reality; coextensive with the real, it does not have to be placed; anything else, to the extent that it is a departure from this, has to be both placed and measured for its bias. This is a mercifully brief moment, however. Most of the essays, and *The History of Southern Literature* as a collective whole, draw their vitality from the premise that the only viable way of looking at literature, Southern or otherwise, is through a variety of windows. "One of the faults of the liberals and Communists," Allen Tate declared in a letter to John Peale Bishop, "is that their art has not gone beyond the most naïve propaganda." After talking it over and over, Tate explained, the Agrarians had come to another view: "that the most powerful propaganda that any social movement could have is a mature literature which is superior to propaganda."[50] Quite

---

50. *Correspondence of Bishop and Tate* edited by Young and Hindle, 78. To Bishop, 7 April 1933. See also, "Preface" to *Reason in Madness,* 19; "Literature as Knowledge," in *Reason in Madness,* 60; M. Thomas Inge, "Appendix A: The Study of Southern Literature," in *History of Southern Literature,* 595–96. It is perhaps worth reiterating here the point I made in the Introduction that, in their judgments, the contributors to and editors of *Southern Renascence* and *South* were very much people of their time: something illustrated by the fact that nearly every "enlightened" white Southerner of the period, including liberals such as Howard Odum and Ralph McGill (nearly every white Southerner, that is, short of Lillian Smith), was in broad agreement with them. My aim here is to situate these critical

how a literary work could be both "the most powerful propaganda" and "superior to propaganda" Tate did not then go on to say, beyond citing the formulation "a mature literature." But, in a way, he did not have to. The whole nature of the project on which he, and other Agrarians, were embarked started from the premise that a mature literature offered (as Tate put it once) "complete knowledge of man's experience"; and complete knowledge was what the traditionalist writer first saw and then transposed into the mythical order. So it was "propaganda" only in the sense that it propagated the truth, the "completeness . . . not of the experimental . . . but of the experienced order"; other "propaganda" was just that, propaganda, its "sense of the natural world . . . blunted by a too rigid system of ideas." The ground on which Tate and his brothers in literary arms took their stand was, to say the least, slippery; nevertheless, it became the base, the foundation on which the canon of modern Southern literature was erected. As *The History of Southern Literature* shows, however, that ground has shifted now—or, rather, the boundaries have been stretched, the estate of modern Southern literature has been vastly expanded. Taking the measure of these new bounds, we can see the kind of writing Tate both practiced and praised as no more mature, and no less committed, than other kinds of writing in the region. Tate, Young, Lytle, and their companions had a case to argue too. They argued it bravely; much of the time, they argued it fiercely; and, very often, they argued it well. They also argued it with the canny intuition that one way of making people sit up and take notice was to situate themselves at the center of things, regional and writerly—as *the* literary spokesmen for the South.

---

works historically, not to argue from hindsight that they could or should have been other than they were. Now that the critical perspectives and paradigms have shifted, we need to rethink the canon that these earlier critics helped establish (some of those critics are, as I have indicated, now actively helping to rethink it), but we need to respect their achievement as well as measure it.

4

"These are the unknown people"

Stories of the Rural Poor of the South Between the Two World Wars and Beyond

On 18 February 1935, the first of a series of four articles appeared in the *New York Post*. It was written by Erskine Caldwell; and the *Post* obligingly provided a brief prefatory note to the article explaining, for those who might not know, just who Caldwell was. Even the news that Caldwell had himself worked in various menial jobs—among them, those of "cotton seed shoveller in an oil mill, hod carrier on construction," cotton picker, and bottle washer—could not, however, have prepared the reader for the devastating account of the lower depths that followed. "For four years economic conditions in the South have been as acute as any in the United States," the piece began, "but in this fifth year of the depression conditions have never been as bad. In parts of Georgia human existence has reached its lowest depths. Children are seen deformed by nature and malnutrition, women in rags beg for pennies, and men are so hungry that they eat snakes and cow dung."[1] Caldwell continued with a harrowing mixture of statistics and scenes. In sections of his home state of Georgia, he explained, the system of sharecropping, oppressive as it had been, was "rapidly giving way to an even more vicious system of labor extraction" that reduced the former tenant or sharecropper to a day laborer—working eight, ten, twelve or sometimes fourteen hours, when he was needed, for no more than twenty-five or thirty-five cents a day. The cotton country, Caldwell reported, was becoming "a

---

1. *New York Post*, 18 February 1935, Sec. 1, 1, reprinted in *Critical Essays on Erskine Caldwell* edited by Scott MacDonald (Boston, 1981), 97. See also 98.

desolate land"; and "the American people of the cotton country, robbed of their means of livelihood by the downfall of systems of farming," were being "forced into the swamps, the stony acres, the waste land." "These are the unknown people of 1935," he declared, "the men, women, and children who hide their nakedness behind trees when a stranger wanders off the main-traveled roads." "Here are the deformed, starved, and diseased children born since 1929," he continued. "Here are the men who strip leaves off the trees, dig roots out of the earth, and snare whatever wild animal they can. These are the people who were forced off the tillable land, these are the women and children, the urban residents deny that exist. . . . There is hunger in their eyes as well as their bellies. They grasp for a word of hope. They plead for a word of advice."[2] The three articles that followed this powerfully rhetorical portrait of people inhabiting the interstices of American society continued in the same vein: economic detail was fired into life by the dramatic, and sometimes even melodramatic, vignette. In the fourth article, for instance, an analysis of the starvation diet of many Southern people—with its consequences in rickets, deformity, and anemia—was pointed up by portraits of individuals that bordered on the gothic: "on the floor" of one house, the reader was told, "before an open fire lay two babies, neither a year old, sucking the dry teats of a mongrel bitch."

Caldwell's articles were clearly intended to get a reaction: craftily mixing, as they did, the sociological and the literary ("waste land," "main-traveled roads") with the kind of eloquence he had perhaps learned from his preacher father—all informed by that eye for bizarre detail, the touch of nightmare, that has characterized so much writing from the South. And a reaction soon followed. "Erskine Caldwell, author of 'Tobacco Road' and 'God's Little Acre' is conducting a column for the sensational New York Evening Post," the *Augusta Chronicle* caustically reported, "a sensational sheet which is out Heroding Herod and beginning to make the yellow tabloids feel ashamed of their conservatism." The portrait of Georgia and the South offered in these articles was "grossly overdrawn," the *Chronicle* insisted. "Could such horrible conditions as Caldwell describes exist in any civilized community?" the paper asked. "What of the churches, of the Christian men and women? Are they so indifferent to

---

2. Ibid., 99. See also *New York Post*, 21 February 1935, Sec. 1, 20, reprinted in *Critical Essays on Caldwell* edited by MacDonald, 106; "Tenant Farmers," in *Some American People* (New York, 1935), 212, 213.

conditions around them that they would allow them to continue?" Nevertheless, an investigation was probably required to establish the truth or falsity of Caldwell's charges. "Certainly . . . there is poverty . . . among some of the wretched poor whites of our section," the *Chronicle* admitted, ". . . but we cannot believe that a condition exists anywhere in this section of the South such as Erskine Caldwell depicts in his sensational article"; and, once those charges were "proven not to be true let's tell the world about it, so that millions of people in this country may not believe that we are heartless heathens." The reaction of the *Chronicle* was clumsily expressed—the word *sensational,* for instance, is used like a refrain throughout the article—but, even in its clumsiness, it was typical. Many locals were apoplectic and almost incoherent with rage: one man complained that "Erskine Caldwell is one of those neurasthenic egomaniacs in the infliction of which upon mankind the Creator seems to have been guilty of unnecessary harshness to an erring world." Still, an investigation had to be set up, the feeling was, if only to prove that Caldwell was wrong. Jefferson County, Georgia, had been a particular focus of Caldwell's attention; and, as the chairman of that county's board of commissioners put it,

> The statements of Erskine Caldwell, I believe, are entirely unfounded.
> I will start an investigation through the county commission and make a detailed report of true conditions as they are in Jefferson county.[3]

Unsurprisingly, given the position from which they began, investigations of this kind came to the conclusion that, at most, there were a few, exceptional cases of the kind of extreme poverty that Caldwell described: exceptions proving the rule that things in general were not nearly as bad as the *New York Post* articles had suggested. The *Augusta Chronicle,* for example, after what it claimed were extensive inquiries and research, reported that there were "10 or 12 to 35" families in the three adjacent counties of Jefferson, Burke, and Richmond "in utter need of rehabilita-

---

3. *Augusta Chronicle,* 5 March 1935, 1, reprinted in *Critical Essays on Caldwell* edited by MacDonald, 110. See also 107–8 (*Augusta Chronicle,* 4 March 1935, p. 1); 115 (*Time,* XXV [25 March 1935], 8). That Caldwell was out to get a reaction is clear from his suggestion at the end of the first *Post* article that, if the poor could have their way, "it is not unlikely that they would petition the Federal Government to nationalize the State of Georgia" (*Critical Essays on Caldwell* edited by MacDonald, 99).

tion." The immediate solution for these "dull, stolid, stupid people, seemingly unaware of all their ills save hunger" was certainly support of some sort—as it was for "the unfortunate substratum of any region's population"—and "our study shows, relief work continues." In the longer term, however, the authors of the report declared, other remedies might prove better; there were other, more plausible strategies for dealing with these "victims of their own shiftlessness and ignorance." "The consensus," the *Chronicle* concluded, "seems to be that, in many instances, scientific sterilization would play a great role in removing from society its worst enemy, the dregs of itself." There were a few dissenting local voices here. Notable among these was Caldwell's own father, the Reverend I. S. Caldwell, who sent a message to *Time* magazine—after *Time* had reprinted one of the *Post* articles and received some vitriolic mail— declaring in bold capitals. "ERSKINE CALDWELL'S STORY TRUE . . . EFFORTS BEING TO COVER UP [*sic*] FACTS. NEWSPAPER PROPAGANDA IS BEING SENT IN EFFORT TO HIDE FACTS IN CASE."[4] The Reverend Caldwell, unlike his son, was clearly regarded with affection by the local community, even if that affection was mixed with the kind of condescension reserved for those regarded as hopeless idealists by their neighbors. He was invited to join the investigation conducted by the *Chronicle,* and seized the opportunity this gave him to show investigators the examples of extreme poverty he knew of in the area: it was he, in fact, who led the investigators to most of the extreme cases they admitted finding. Nevertheless, he did not seriously affect the conclusions local inquiries drew; and it is difficult to see how he could have, since those conclusions were more or less there, fully drawn, before inquiries began.

Seen in the context of what was happening elsewhere in the world, and what was to happen four years later, it is not just the conclusions themselves but also the language in which they are framed—and the assumptions implicit in that language—that are disconcerting in the extreme. There is a strange and disturbing mix here, ranging from the moralistic to the pseudo-scientific and taking in along the way the idiom of social engineering. The faces of the poor are "dumb and stolid," we are told, and "vacant of intelligent expression." "Generally, their mentality is extremely low"; "they are ignorant, shiftless and incapable"; and "they are, in the full meaning of the phrase, a burden on society." "We

4. *Time,* XXV (25 March 1935), 8, reprinted in *Critical Essays on Caldwell* edited by MacDonald, 116. See also 117–18, 119 (*Augusta Chronicle,* 10 March 1935, 1).

observed a group of people lacking in ambition," the investigators declared, "lacking in concern for the conventionalities of civilization and
lacking any connection with the world which comprises civilization." To
Erskine Caldwell's claim that poverty was a cancer in society and had to
be rooted out, the answer was simple, it was the poor people themselves
who were the cancer: "There is no use to be sentimental about the matter.
. . . These people are a cancer on society, a menace to themselves and the
state; and to perpetuate the condition only increases their number. There
should be a law to control the situation and a remedy to back up the
law."⁵ Admittedly, this comes from a letter to the *Augusta Chronicle*,
written by someone claiming to be a social worker: but the position of
the investigators, as announced in the editorial columns of the *Chronicle*,
was no different. "Living in squalor and primitive ignorance . . . breeders
of disease and imbecility," these people, the *Chronicle* declared, had "no
share in those higher aspirations which have glorified history three thousand years"; they were "shorn of almost every trace of moral responsibility" and were, "in truth . . . humanity's dregs." So "segregation and
sterilization" were urgent priorities. "A nation-wide program of rehabili-
tation," "with . . . closest of supervision," was required, immediately,
"for those not too far lost in degeneracy, together with sterilization of
the unfit and institutional care of the totally irresponsible" so as "to remove from our civilization one of its ugliest blots." The children of these
"human derelicts" would have to be taken away from them and, wherever necessary, made the subject of "a selective sterilization law": that,
along with the other measures, the *Chronicle* argued, was "the only possible hope" for "this hopeless class." "We may be approaching a time,"
an editorial dated 24 March 1935 declaimed, "when these people, the
flotsam and jetsam in the sea of human misery, may be taken care of until
they themselves pass out, with the knowledge that their progeny will be
sterilized and that their race will be extinguished with the next generation."⁶

This controversy continued, with Caldwell writing a further series of

5. *Augusta Chronicle*, 17 March 1935, 4, reprinted in *Critical Essays on Caldwell*
edited by MacDonald, 134. See also 122 (*Augusta Chronicle*, 11 March 1935, 1); 123
(*Augusta Chronicle*, 12 March 1935, 1); 128 (*Augusta Chronicle*, 14 March 1935, 1);
135–36 (*Augusta Chronicle*, 17 March 1935, 4).

6. *Augusta Chronicle*, 24 March 1935, Sec. 2, 16, reprinted in *Critical Essays on Caldwell* edited by MacDonald, 138.

articles for the *New York Post,* the *New Republic* wading in (surprisingly, perhaps, praising the *Chronicle* for "its courage"), and a senator from South Carolina claiming that the *Post* articles as a whole were "vicious propaganda and gross exaggeration." Two things were clear from the beginnings of this controversy, however, and were only confirmed by what happened later. Caldwell had used every weapon in his armory as a writer to make what he called "the unknown people" of the rural South known, both to his fellow Southerners and to other Americans. And his fellow Southerners had responded to his revelations, for the most part, with a comprehensive act of denial. For people like the editors and investigators of the *Chronicle,* and the doctors, social workers, and local administrators whose comments were reported in the newspaper's pages, "these people" did not exist; or, if they did, they existed outside of "civilization." They were irredeemably "other," marking the outer limits of the culture; and, if possible, that "otherness" had to be institutionalized, given the full strength of law. Segregated in fact as they already were, they had, while they continued to survive and breed, also to be segregated in principle. Certainly, this act of separation was not applied to all the rural poor. Investigators were often quick to insist that there were different kinds or classes of poverty. At one point, local investigators even tried to regulate this perception: to define the poor in terms of "three general classes," "tenant farmers or sharecroppers," "wage hands," and "derelicts," of which, they said, only the third class should be subjected to the full range of "corrective measures." With almost equal certainty, we can conclude that the Reverend Caldwell was wrong when he claimed the presence of a conspiracy "TO COVER UP FACTS" and deny the existence of these "unknown people." But that act of separation, and accompanying it the act of denial, remained as the fundamental, almost instinctive local reaction to disclosure. The people Caldwell had claimed to find—cut off, as he put it, "across creeks without bridges, fields without even so much as a cowpath,"[7]—were not there or not typical. If they did exist, they did so in a strange moral wilderness; they had no genuine *social* existence and, with luck and the proper legislation, they would soon cease to have *any* existence at all.

---

7. *New York Post,* 18 February 1935, Sec. 1, 1, reprinted in *Critical Essays on Caldwell* edited by MacDonald, 99. See also 119 (*Augusta Chronicle,* 10 March 1935, p. 1); 140 (*New Republic,* LXXXII [27 March 1935], 172–73); 148 (*New York Post,* 19 April 1935, p. 19).

As with the life, so with the literature: one of the more curious facts of literary history is the degree to which the act of denial that followed Caldwell's revelations was replicated in the story of Southern writing. In the same year as those revelations, for example, Donald Davidson contributed an essay "The Trend of Literature" to the anthology *Culture in the South,* in which he explained that he had decided to exclude all books dealing with poor whites because they betrayed habits of mind that were "not quite healthy." Writers who wrote about poor white people, Davidson opined, like those whose subject was "Negro life," were turning away from "southern life in its broader aspects." For Davidson, the choice was simple. The Southern writer could either observe "fidelity as an artist to his subject-matter" or he could surrender to "the social programs that emanate from the metropolis"; and, evidently, if he directed his attention to the poor, black or white, he was doing the latter. By an adroit, if not untypical or even intended, twist of irony, those who opted for writing about the rural poor were accused of yielding to the pressures of the city, and what Davidson dismissed as "the little Russians of the New Republic." "As a student of farm tenancy in the South," Davidson observed in a review of one of Caldwell's books, "Mr. Caldwell would make a splendid Curator of a Soviet Park of Recreation and Culture."[8] Seen in this light, to write of the "unknown people" of the Southern countryside was not to write as a Southerner; it was doubtful if it was even to write as an American. Davidson's position was an extreme one, or at least extremely stated. Still, his fellow Agrarians arrived, if rather more circuitously, at similar conclusions. For Robert Penn Warren, for instance, the "tragic contradiction" that confronted the Southern writer had its source in an absolute and necessary opposition between the regional and the political; while John Donald Wade and Cleanth Brooks both criticized novelists like Caldwell severely for what Brooks

---

8. Donald Davidson, "Erskine Caldwell's Picture Book," *Southern Review,* IV (1938–39), 18. See also "The Trend of Literature: A Partisan View," in *Culture in the South* edited by W. T. Couch (Chapel Hill, N.C., 1935), 185, 199, 204; Robert Penn Warren, "Some Recent Novels," *Southern Review,* I (1935–36), 624–33; John Donald Wade, "Sweet Are the Uses of Degeneracy," *Southern Review,* I (1935–36), 449–66; Cleanth Brooks, "What Deep South Literature Needs," *Saturday Review of Literature,* 19 September 1942, 8–9. Something that Wade says in his essay is perhaps worth quoting here: "His [Caldwell's] literary output would be more impressive if—a good Southerner still—he were not as plaintively anxious as he is to please the kind and class of people that he has come to be affiliated with—the detached, nervous, thrill-goaded metro-cosmopolitans of his own day" (466).

termed "propaganda for various causes with a resulting confusion of . . . attitude toward . . . material." Implicit in such strictures were the same values that steered Davidson toward the exclusion of such novelists from the hallowed precincts of Southern writing. To write of the poor was to write of the political and to write of the political was not to write as a regionalist. Just as Caldwell's "unknown people" were segregated, marched off into the ranks of the peripheral and atypical, so those who wrote of them were quietly dispatched to the regional margins. If the people themselves were not seen, strictly speaking, as part of Southern society, then the writers who took them as their subject were not seen as part of Southern literature. Both groups became hidden, absent presences in the local view, denied a determining or even significant status.

This exclusion from the regional canon has not, of course, continued with quite the same degree of intensity. There have been some powerful accounts of the writing Davidson casually dismissed. Nevertheless, the habit of segregating or, if not that, sidelining such writers has not entirely abated. As late as 1981, for instance, one critic could point out that Caldwell himself has been "the subject of less . . . critical discussion than . . . any American writer of comparable stature";[9] while, in *The History of Southern Literature* published in 1985, most writers who wrote about the rural poor between the wars are briefly considered under the heading "The Fiction of Social Commitment," as if somehow such commitment were their exclusive preserve and determining characteristic. What is more to the point, perhaps, is the fact that, whatever the critical situation now, this tendency toward denial of the literary value and the regional centrality of what they were doing was one of the conditions in which these writers generally had to write. They were faced with a local audience that, for the most part, regarded their work as failing on both aesthetic and regional grounds and, as such, hardly to be described as Southern literature. To make matters even more complicated, and arguably worse, they were also challenged by a reception from outside the South that was at once the opposite and the mirror of this local response. For those many critics of the period between the wars for whom writing was an agent of social change, literary accounts of rural poor folk *had* to

9. Scott MacDonald, "Introduction," *Critical Essays on Caldwell,* xi. See also James Mellard, "The Fiction of Social Commitment," in *The History of Southern Literature* edited by Louis D. Rubin et al. (Baton Rouge, La., 1985), 351–55. Mellard's essay is nevertheless an astute and incisive account of the writers surveyed.

be openly political and programmatic; and a common charge leveled at such writing from the South was it was not—or, at least, was not sufficiently so.

The reaction to Caldwell himself is a case in point here. For the reviewers in journals like *New Masses,* the complaint about Caldwell's work was that, as social and political commentary, it did not go far enough. "He lacks social understanding which is the life of revolutionary prose," the proletarian novelist Jack Conroy explained in one review; "he should go left," another commentator in *New Masses* recommended; while a third, also in *New Masses,* declared that "he must go into the higher sphere of dialectical development of characters placed in situations that clamor for treatment today." At the back of such advice were assumptions curiously similar to those of the Agrarian critics. Writing about the poor people of the South was *necessarily* political, the Agrarians either claimed or assumed. The critics on the metropolitan left merely turned this formal imperative into a moral or ideological one: writing about such poor people need not necessarily be political, they argued, but it should be. The writer had a social obligation, a duty to approach a subject like the Southern rural poor with the correct degree of "social awareness." As a citizen as well as a writer, an analyst of the current crisis as well as an inventor of narrative, he needed to write in such a way as to enable political understanding and implement social change. "His talent deserves a higher plane on which to function," one *New Masses* reviewer, Edwin Rolfe, observed of Caldwell in 1933,

a broader perception of the struggles of men than he has seen fit to reveal. He is surely aware of the class conflicts raging throughout the country and of the crisis in which not only American, but world capitalism find itself; his support of the Communist candidates in the last presidential election would indicate this. His logical development as a writer must begin to parallel his development as a social being; if it does not, the artificial cleavage will become increasingly apparent . . . as it is apparent in his achievement thus far, and destroy the vitality which mere technical proficiency in writing can never sustain by itself.[10]

10. Edwin Rolfe, "God's Little Acre," *New Masses,* VIII (February 1933), 26, reprinted in *Critical Essays on Caldwell* edited by MacDonald, 24. See also 25; 7 (Norman MacLeod, "A Hardboiled Idealist," *New Masses,* VII [July 1931], 18); 18 (Jack Conroy, "Passion and Pellagra," *New Masses,* VII [April 1932], 24–25).

Arguments like this put the *New Masses* critics and their kind at odds with their Agrarian contemporaries, as far as measuring where fictional portraits of the rural South went wrong. On one fundamental level, however, they reflected the same belief as the Agrarians: that there could only be one viable way of drawing such portraits. For the Agrarians, that way was anathema, for the urban critics of the left it was the ideal: but for both groups there was only one way. The pity of it, for the Agrarians, was that this way had to be followed—it somehow went with the territory—and, for leftist critics, that it ought to be but, on the whole, was not. Either way, the model for writing about the rural folk of the region was singular, prescriptive, unalterable; and, either way, that model was wrong. It did justice to neither the plurality nor the power of the books about such folk actually being produced then in the South. Using this monolithic model or blueprint, most critics of the time missed both what the writers of such books evidently felt they ought to do, and what they did. Like many critics since then as well, they seemed more or less blind to the sheer variety of writerly practice to be found among those attending to the "unknown people" of the South; for that matter, they also seemed blind to the variety, and frequent vigor, of the achievement.

Not that those writing about the poor folk of the Southern countryside did not engage openly in social and political debate. Many of them did. Some of them even attempted to formulate programs for change, the redemption of the land, and the revival of the farming system—although such programs rarely, if ever, resembled those plans for revolutionary alteration favored by the reviewers in *New Masses*. Among the more notable books that embrace the idea of reform of some kind are *In the Land of Cotton* (1923) and *Can't Get a Redbird* (1929) by Dorothy Scarborough, *The Golden Cocoon* (1924) by Ruth Cross, *Cotton* (1928) by Jack Bethea, *Cane Juice* (1933) by John E. Uhler, *The Share-Cropper* (1937) by Charlie May Simon, and three books by a son of sharecroppers, Harry H. Kroll, *The Cabin in the Cotton* (1932), *The Usurper* (1941), and *The Rider on the Bronze Horse* (1942).[11] Naturally, the loca-

11. Dorothy Scarborough, *In the Land of Cotton* (New York, 1923), *Can't Get a Redbird* (New York, 1929); Ruth Cross, *The Golden Cocoon* (New York, 1924); Jack Bethea, *Cotton* (New York, 1928); John E. Uhler, *Cane Juice* (New York, 1933); Charlie May Simon, *The Share-Cropper* (New York, 1937). In addition to the three novels by Harry H. Kroll mentioned here, *The Cabin in the Cotton* (New York, 1932), *The Usurper* (New York, 1941), and *The Rider on the Bronze Horse* (New York, 1942), his nonfictional book,

tions of these novels differs widely: Dorothy Scarborough, for instance, sets her action in Texas, Jack Bethea in Alabama, and Harry Kroll in Tennessee. There are also subtle and sometimes even radical differences of emphasis. Some books, for instance, like *Can't Get a Redbird, The Cabin in the Cotton, Cane Juice,* and *The Share-Cropper,* dispense with or at least marginalize romantic plot elements, concentrating almost exclusively on the drama of the land. Others, such as *In the Land of Cotton, Cotton, The Golden Cocoon,* and *The Usurper,* use those romantic elements to develop the social and political dimensions of the narrative: borrowing a device from post–Civil War romance, but giving it a decidedly modern twist, writers like Scarborough, Bethea, and Kroll all explore the problematic relations between the classes via romantic/sexual entanglements across class divisions, that are sometimes resolved in marriage (*Cotton*) and sometimes not (*In the Land of Cotton*). Always, there are vivid differences of plot and argument that can be registered only by a reading of an individual novel. Nevertheless, as with all writing, certain patterns emerge; and one way, perhaps, of weighing the burden of the preoccupations that these writers share, and measuring the quality of attention they bring to their subject, is to trace at least some of the patterns they have in common.

The reform of the land, for instance, is frequently associated with the redemptive figure of the returning son: who comes back to the home place, after learning that there are other ways, possibilities undreamed of by his father, that can bring new life to the decaying system. The protagonist in *The Cabin in the Cotton* is driven to his advocacy of change by the haunting image he retains in memory of his father, "a kindly bent

---

I Was A Share-Cropper (New York, 1936), is well worth citing in this context. For the sake of convenience, these individually very different writers are referred to as reformists although, needless to say, they were never a group. The critical literature on them and other writers dealing with the rural poor of the South is relatively slight. Easily the most useful discussion is Sylvia Jenkins Cook, *From Tobacco Road to Route 66: The Southern Poor White in Fiction* (Chapel Hill, N.C., 1976). Also helpful for accounts of texts or contexts or both are Daniel Aaron, *Writers on the Left: Episodes in American Literary Communism* (New York, 1961); John M. Bradbury, *Renaissance in the South: A Critical History of the Literature, 1920–1960* (Chapel Hill, N.C., 1967): James Gilbert, *Writers and Partisans: A History of Literary Radicalism in America* (New York, 1968); Shields McIlwaine, *The Southern Poor-White: From Lubberland to Tobacco Road* (Norman, Okla., 1939); *Proletarian Writers of the Thirties* edited by David Madden (Carbondale, Ill., 1968); Walter B. Rideout, *The Radical Novel in the United States, 1900–54: Some Interrelations of Literature and Society* (Cambridge, Mass., 1956).

man, throwing up endless cotton beds . . . endless rows behind a plantation mule" without ever achieving even solvency. Bill Bradley, in turn,
the main character in *The Share-Cropper,* takes the history of his father
as his warning: "year after year passed," Bradley recalls, "bringing only
hard work and no compensation. . . . Mrs. Bradley became more and
more querulous and complaining, and Bradley drifted, bit by bit, into the
humble, beaten man that he was, with only his religion to comfort him.
Both grew old before their time."[12] The role of the father is not always
to act simply as a warning. In *Cotton,* for example, the young protagonist
Larry Maynard stores in his memory a model of endurance against all
odds—the image of a father "who had fought on, knowing he was
beaten, and had not whimpered after the grind of poverty had robbed
him of hope." Still, the contrast between old and new generations remains fundamental and determining. Transplanting one of the most ancient myths to the South of their own times, these reformist writers show
us a land awaiting the return of its hero, the liberation of the dying land
and the dying figure of the father by the newly enlightened son.

Inevitably, perhaps, this figure of redemption and enlightenment tends
to be idealized. "He was a young giant in size," begins the description of
one such character, Johnny Carr in *Can't Get a Redbird,* "more than six
feet tall, weighing almost two hundred pounds, with the strength of an
ox. . . . His face, almost the color of bronze from the wind and sun, made
his gray eyes bluer than ever, and his shock of hair was like wheat-straw
yellow-brown in the sun."[13] There is very little to be said in favor of
portraits like this: except, perhaps, that they are a function of the mythic
dimension of these novels. Books like *Can't Get a Redbird, In the Land
of Cotton,* or *The Share-Cropper* are curious, and often potent, hybrids,
mixing social realism with the romantic and legendary. We do not object
to such idealized versions of the hero in earlier examples of reformist
pastoral; it may be that we should be not so quick to object in this case—
or, at least, to see this as one, less successful product of a fascinating
generic mix. Less problematic, anyway, are the moral qualities that most
of these writers give to their redemptive heroes, and the powerful terms
in which each protagonist expresses his desire for independence and
equality, his opposition to the system into which he was born and, above

12. Simon, *Share-Cropper,* 116. See also Kroll, *Cabin in the Cotton,* 67; Bethea, *Cotton,* 44. Also Scarborough, *In the Land of Cotton,* 8–9; *Can't Get a Redbird,* 21.
13. Scarborough, *Can't Get a Redbird,* 91. See also *In the Land of Cotton,* 215.

all, his fierce love/hate attachment to the land, "the rich, black soil" and the plants he "gives life to." Here, for instance, is Ben Wilson, the redemptive hero in *In the Land of Cotton,* explaining the sources of his knowledge, and his anger: "I know what it means to raise cotton. . . . I know what it means to get up before daylight, to plow in the winter cold, to plant in the spring, to chop cotton and poison bugs through the sizzling summer. I know what it means to work like a slave picking cotton, and drive your family before you into the field like so many niggers, to save the stuff before the weather ruins it."[14] Later on in the novel, Ben recollects his endless "succession of days spent between cotton rows," and thinks to himself, "life seemed a struggle like those with fabled dragons, the only difference being that he had heard of no rescuer who might free him." He has, he learns, to be his own rescuer, and the rescuer of others: by the end of the book, he is dead, but the plans he has formulated to help cotton farmers are to be carried on. In this version of the myth, the dragon is not yet slain but it promises to be, thanks to the knowledge and sacrifice of the hero.

The hero is one, though, who is not above using the phrase "like so many niggers": problems of class, caste, and prejudice collide with the more legendary and pastoral elements in these reformist novels. And, it has to be said, it is not always to the credit of the novelist that they do. Larry Maynard in *Cotton,* for instance, has detailed plans for the recovery of the farming system in his area but, he explains, he has a very specific scheme for the black farming laborers on his own land: "Every day I set the niggers a certain task they have to do before they take out the mule in the evening." "When you give a nigger something definite to shoot at," he adds, "he'll work."[15] The author appears to endorse the—at the very least—patronizing attitude to black laborers revealed here; there is the same implicit prejudice at work as when, later on in the narrative, Maynard defines the superiority of pedigreed cotton seed by declaring, "breeding tells whether it's in plants or people." What is remarkable about many of these novels, in fact, is that, while perhaps recording the racial discrimination and casually racist language that was a part of that place and time, their authors and protagonists do not often register the need for change and accommodation of racial practices: a need that is

14. Scarborough, *In the Land of Cotton,* 209. See also 260; Simon, *Share-Cropper,* 143. Also Kroll, *Usurper,* 220; Scarborough, *Can't Get a Redbird,* 64.

15. Bethea, *Cotton,* 89. See also 108; Simon, *Share-Cropper,* 196; Kroll, *Usurper,* 442.

there, not least, because the problems they depict cut right across the color line. Sometimes, as in *Cotton,* those practices appear to be defended or endorsed; sometimes, as in the novels of Scarborough or Ruth Cross, the plight of black farming people tends simply to be ignored. Occasionally, as in *The Share-Cropper,* a union of farmers, "negroes and whites together, forgetting for the time their race barriers," is anticipated for the golden future; at others, however, as in *The Usurper,* that future seems to be the exclusive preserve of what is called "the more virile poor whites." This is all by way of saying that the reformist impulses at the back of these stories are fundamentally populist: the haunting mixture of social polemic and romantic mythmaking should probably alert us to that. The history of Southern populism is a profoundly mixed one; it has included racist demagogues as well as racial reformers, all depending on just who "the people" were conceived to be. There is a similar slippage in the meaning of words like *the people,* similar debate about just who is to benefit from reform and just how much, in these novels; in this respect, at least, their authors seem "in" the history of their times but mostly unable to get "out" of it and take a longer view.

That the longer view is there in another sense is guaranteed by three elements commonly present in all these novels. The first is a perception of the present system of farming as oppressive to nearly all those it involves. In particular, this means that the two classes most commonly seen to be at odds with each other, the landowner and the tenant or day laborer, are both presented as victims, living in "a condition of peonage," the tenant or laborer to the landowner and the landlord to the banks and loan companies. Telling parallels are drawn between them. Commonly degraded by a degrading economic arrangement, the so-called "shiftlessness of the poorer farmers" is matched by the "indolence" of the landowner; while the poor farmer's attempts to filch something from the landlord find their reflection in the richer farmer's efforts to steal from the bank or factor. "When I reflect on the landlord's side, I can see easily enough how he justifies himself," observes Dan Morgan, the protagonist in *Cabin in the Cotton.* "He has to charge high rates and advances, and force collections, and maybe shave corners to get by." "Then I think about the tenant's side," Morgan adds. "He's either a poor white, or underprivileged black, fighting the earth for food, clothes, and shelter, barely living from year to year." "It was a chase in mad circles," he reflects later, "with cotton at its center . . . a vast business with no method or sense of business." "The system—that was it," Morgan concludes,

". . . It was as plain as the nose on your face."[16] The fundamental decency and victim status of all those involved in that system is either assumed or stated. In *In the Land of Cotton,* for example, Scarborough actually gets a tenant, a planter, and a lawyer together to analyze a situation from which, ultimately, nobody really profits and for which no particular group or interest is to blame. The farmer is partly to blame for not raising something besides a cash crop: but, then, "the landlord wants all cotton." The landlord is to blame, then: but "you go to the merchant, an' ask hire to run a year, an' he want to know how many acres o' cotton." Is the merchant to blame then? Hardly, since he has to protect his investment; and "you've got to recognize that the merchant takes more risk in" selling or lending to someone "with no financial standing."[17] Good liberals that they are, the reformist writers cannot countenance the possibility of fundamental class conflict, let alone ineradicable evil or malevolence. The system is wrong. It is to the advantage of no individual and no class, evidently, that it should stay wrong. So, in the long term—and perhaps even in the medium term—it can and should be changed without too much difficulty: which is to say, without too much resistance from any interest group, once people are taught to understand where their true interests lie.

The terms of this alteration in the system are there in the two other elements in these novels that enable a longer view, a clearer and more hopeful perspective. One of these relates to the question of the teaching of true interests. The redeemer hero is the figure who embodies the possibility of social change. Very often, like the protagonists of *Cotton, Cabin in the Cotton,* and *Cane Juice,* he is also supplied with enough in the way of education to express that possibility, to say what changes need to take place—and what changes are actually occurring. If he is not, then the hero is given the company of a more articulate analyst of society, its present state and possible future direction: someone who puts into words what the hero is trying to put into action. The lawyer who takes part in the three-way conversation in *Can't Get a Redbird* just mentioned performs this role, offering a national and even international perspective on the plantation system that is unavailable to the young protagonist. Similarly, a planter's daughter in *Cotton* is sharp and informed enough

16. Kroll, *Cabin in the Cotton,* 40–41, 227. See also Scarborough, *In the Land of Cotton,* 165, 167.

17. Scarborough, *In the Land of Cotton,* 164–65.

to see that her lover, Larry Maynard the hero, is doing something that involves "trying to make over the manner of living of a whole section of the country,"[18] in the process disclosing his redemptive role both to himself and to the reader as well as the path to possible redemption. It is moments like these in the novels of reform that come closest to supporting the claim made by Agrarian critics about the openly political agenda at work in stories about poor farming people—although, needless to say, the message of class reconciliation and social amelioration such moments offer would hardly invite the approval of far left critics, like those *New Masses* reviewers, either. In principle, though, it is surely a legitimate strategy: to open up the horizons of the story—particularly its range of social reference—in the way that, say, the lawyer Max does in *Native Son* by Richard Wright or the character of Nettie in Alice Walker's *The Color Purple*. It is also a common one, frequently favored by the Agrarian writers themselves: one thinks, for example, of the ruminative, generalizing narrators at the heart of *The Fathers* by Allen Tate and Robert Penn Warren's *All the King's Men* or the character of Jack Cropleigh in *The Velvet Horn*. Sometimes it works—as when, say, in *Can't Get a Redbird* the verbal debate is integrally related to personal and social conflict; sometimes it does not—as when, in *Cotton*, it seems an excrescence, hardly attached to the narrative action. But this, the matter of practice, hardly invalidates the principle. Characters in fiction, after all, have as much right to talk about social concerns as about sexual ones; in this respect, at least, they are like the rest of us.

The social concerns that do habitually engage the characters in reformist fiction are the third and final avenue by which the producers of this fiction pursue a longer view. It is, perhaps, unnecessary to rehearse here the full range of measures advocated to enable the transformation of "the system" and the revival of the dead land. They include, inevitably, crop diversification to encourage self-reliance among the farming population; collective bargaining to enhance the buying power of the sharecropper and the selling power of all those who work the land; industrial organization and scientific farming to promote efficiency on both small and large farms; and the use of government financing to facilitate the division of large plantations into small, self-sufficient holdings. What lingers in the mind after any reading of these novels is not so much this, though, their account of the mechanics, the specifics of possible change,

18. Bethea, *Cotton*, 103.

as their simple articulation of hope. Drawing on a noble American tradition, the reformist writers at their best combine diagnosis with possible remedy—a full look at the worst with a passionate search for a way to the better. Two of the most interesting of these novels show clearly this telling mixture of naturalistic detail and hopeful mythmaking: one from the 1920s, *Can't Get a Redbird,* and one, *The Share-Cropper,* from the 1930s. At the beginning, and for the most of the duration of both novels, the emphasis is on the sheer grind of farming work, and the cycle of poverty to which the existing system seems to condemn the poor farmer. Here, for instance, is the young hero of *Can't Get a Redbird* struggling with the annual task of plowing the exhausted fields: "The root of last year's cotton stalks, the grass, the weeds, the heavy clods made the ground hard to work, so that holding the plow straight and steady was a terrible task. But Johnny gritted his teeth. . . . The worst thing was getting the plow turned round at the end of the furrow. Lifting, straining struggling, mind and muscle tortured, he would all but despair, and then finally manage it."[19] Portraits like this, at the very least, offer a useful corrective to the idyllic accounts of farm life favored by the Agrarians: it is perhaps worth recalling that several of the reformist writers, like Scarborough herself, came from farming families. Those portraits supply the framework, the context in which the need for reform is articulated; and, while the degree of reform realized in the narrative present naturally varies from one novel to the next, no novel does more than lay the groundwork for change, the possible foundations on which a change in the system might be built.

Can't Get a Redbird goes further here. The hero manages to redeem his own land, thanks to the use of scientific farming methods and diversification; he organizes a local farm bureau; and he even manages to send his son to agricultural college. But cotton prices collapse; the son dies; the redeemer hero has to start all over again to alter not only the local but the national and international system. "I have to see this job go through," he says: the job being, quite simply, to change things. The note

---

19. Scarborough, *Can't Get a Redbird,* 50–51. See also Simon, *Share-Cropper,* 58; Gordon, *Golden Cocoon,* 6–7. For details of the measures advocated, as outlined here, see, e.g., Bethea, *Cotton,* 13–14, 17, 45, 61, 88; Kroll, *Cabin in the Cotton,* 292, *Usurper,* 240–41, 342, *Rider on the Bronze Horse,* 151–52, 206; Scarborough, *Can't Get a Redbird,* 113, 281, 311, 379, *In the Land of Cotton,* 164, 339–41, 363; Simon, *Share-Cropper,* 190; Uhler, *Cane Juice, passim.*

of renewed hope on which Scarborough's book ends is played in a different key in *The Share-Cropper*. Here, the hero Bill Bradley finds himself thwarted at every turn. His attempts to form a union among sharecroppers, for example, and then to organize a strike for better conditions, meet with disaster. The strikers are arrested as vagrants, and made to work on the plantations as convict labor; while Bill and his family are driven from their home, owned by one of the planters, and have to seek shelter on nearby swampland along with others rendered homeless. What saves Bill, however, and makes this a reformist novel, is his indomitable nature. Here, and throughout the narrative, he refuses to accept defeat; he continues to believe in his plans and the necessity—indeed, the inevitability—of change. "Somehow . . . he felt that his own young ones could have a better life than he or Donie [his wife] or their parents had," Bill reflects at the end of the novel,

> There would come a change, he knew, though he might not live to see it himself, and it would be possible, somehow, for them to have land of their own. Land that would not be taken away for mortgages and debts. Or if they were renters, there'd be good houses to live in, schools to send their children to, and a church to worship in. They'd pay a fair price for their goods. . . . And they would be protected against cheating bosses, so they'd know just where they stood at the end of the year. It would have to be an honest system, one that would not drag them down to where they could never rise up. . . .
>
> Bill smiled and he reached out his hand for Donie's. They were still able to dream and make plans for the future.[20]

Passages like this would have met with the approval of neither the Agrarian nor the *New Masses* critics: to the first group they would have seemed too "political" while the second would have thought them not "political" enough—which is to say, lacking in scientific analysis and "the higher sphere of dialectical development." It is important to register, however, just how grounded such passages are in two powerful traditions: naturalism and prophecy. Reformist writers like Scarborough and

---

20. Simon, *Share-Cropper*, 246. See also Scarborough, *Can't Get a Redbird*, 390; *The Republic of Letters in America: The Correspondence of John Peale Bishop and Allen Tate* edited by Thomas D. Young and John J. Hindle (Louisville, Ky., 1981), 77. To Bishop, 7 April 1933.

Simon were careful to base their stories in an understanding of the harsh realities of country life: drawing, sometimes instinctively and sometimes consciously, on the traditions of American realism, they invited their readers to leave the "main-traveled roads" and contemplate the grim, hidden facts of rural poverty. But they also wanted to do more than this. So, tapping another vein of American writing, they offered tentative versions of the pastoral: visions of a world made possible when men and women stop despairing and start dreaming. They were writing at a time when radical change of some sort seemed not only possible but inevitable: Allen Tate was only one among many Southerners then who anticipated what he called "the destruction of the middle class-capitalist [*sic*] hegemony." And they were writing in a way that was intended, like Caldwell's articles for the *New York Post,* to provoke emotion but not paralyze thought: to expose the cancer of rural poverty *and* prescribe viable remedies. Certainly, their work mixes genres in a manner that is often surprising and sometimes clumsy, and it is not immune to the prejudices of its time. But that is to argue partly from hindsight. For good or ill, the reformist novels are embedded in the conflicts of the period; they are part of the struggle they articulate; if we exclude them from our attention, or try to minimize their importance, then we are losing sight of a fascinating moment in literary and social history—and our map of Southern writing becomes, at best, a very partial one.

The redemption that novelists like Scarborough and Simon sought, and occasionally found, was of a specifically social kind: the task of the redeemer hero, as they and he saw it, was to change the system, alter the mechanisms at work in rural life. Another group of writers, however, imagined a very different sort of redemptive process: one by which the protagonist proved *imaginatively* superior to a situation that he or she was unable to alter—or, if not that, then at the very least equal to the challenges, the dreadful routine, the traps and humiliations their life offered. At the most positive and hopeful end of this equation, what was imagined was a kind of transcendence, even spiritual transformation of material circumstance. The hero or heroine might be imprisoned in body but the mind was liberated, somehow untainted by its conditions; and with the aid of the liberated imagination, even the most oppressed might be capable of, not only survival, but moral victory—the triumph of the spirit. Clearly, this was a message that might well appeal to readers caught in analogous circumstances. Equally clearly, it might appear less threatening to anyone with an interest in the continuation of the existing system. Be that as it may, what is particularly interesting is that the authors of these novels were nearly all white women and black men. Among the most notable novels of this kind by white women are *Return Not Again* (1938) by Annette Heard, *Something More Than Earth* (1940) by Helen Norris, and, above all, the fiction of Elizabeth Madox Roberts, notably *The Time of Man* (1936). The relevant books by African American males, in turn, include *Inchin' Along* (1932) by Welbourn Kelley, *Ollie Miss* (1935) by George Henderson and a later book, *A Good Man* (1952) by Jefferson Young.[21] Of course, it is difficult to say just when spiritual transcendence shades off into stoic endurance: other books that might be associated with this tendency are those in which the central and usually female rural character achieves a curious form of triumph, spiritual justification, in personal disaster, even death. They include *Mrs. Haney* (1933) by Foxhall Daingerfield, *Patterns of Wolfpen* (1934) by Harlan Hatcher, and *Rachel's Children* (1938) by Harriett Hassell. With some of the very best of these novels, however, it is quite clearly the relatively cold comfort of spiritual equanimity that is at stake, acquiescence in rather than transcendence of the prisonhouse of farm routine and the farming system. Here, the most impressive names are again female: Marjorie Kinnan Rawlings, author of—among other books— *South Moon Under* (1933), *Golden Apples* (1935), *The Yearling* (1938) and, later, *Jacob's Ladder* (1950), and Edith Summers Kelley, whose book simply entitled *Weeds* (1924)[22] is an eloquent testament to the drudgery and the stoicism of the South's "unknown people." From spiritual liberation to the wintry gift of a stout heart, a stoic spirit: the war between mind and material circumstance offers a series of variations here, shading off one into another, that can only be crudely measured by

21. Welbourn Kelley, *Inchin' Along* (New York, 1932); George Henderson, *Ollie Miss* (New York, 1935); Elizabeth Madox Roberts, *The Time of Man* (New York, 1936); Annette Heard, *Return Not Again* (New York, 1938); Helen Norris, *Something More Than Earth* (Boston, 1940); Jefferson Young, *A Good Man* (New York, 1952).

22. Edith Summers Kelley, *Weeds* (New York, 1924); Foxhall Daingerfield, *Mrs. Haney* (New York, 1933); Marjorie Kinnan Rawlings, *South Moon Under* (New York, 1933), *Golden Apples* (New York, 1935), *The Yearling* (New York, 1938), *Jacob's Ladder* (Coral Gables, Fla., 1950); Harlan Hatcher, *Patterns of Wolfpen* (New York, 1934); Harriett Hassall, *Rachel's Children* (New York, 1938). Perhaps it should be emphasized that terms such as *transcendence* or *endurance* are merely a matter of critical convenience. These writers were no more a formal group than the reformists were.

these distinctions. Nevertheless, the distinctions are there. The different kinds of little victories still available to poor farming folk—in a system seen as, if capable of change, capable of it only for the worse—can be marked out, in particular, by the differences between Elizabeth Madox Roberts, Marjorie Kinnan Rawlings, and Edith Summers Kelley—and, even more particularly, by the different fates of their heroines, Ellen Chesser (*The Time of Man*), Piety Lantry (*South Moon Under*), and Judy Pippinger (*Weeds*).

All the novels of Elizabeth Madox Roberts reveal her to be, if not Agrarian, then at least an agrarian: not associated with the Nashville group and profoundly uninterested in cultural politics, she nevertheless betrays an abiding belief in the land and its cultivation. At its least plausible, this belief is dramatized in terms of a recurrent rhythm of return and recovery. The protagonist of her 1928 novel, *Jingling in the Wind,* leaves the city and its "human turmoil" ruled by "Breed . . . capitalist, philanthropist . . . instigator of events, promoter"; and, together with his true love, he is then reborn in familiar pastoral surroundings and a simple life close to nature. Similarly, the female characters at the center of three of her other novels, Theodosia Bell in *My Heart and My Flesh* (1927), Jocelle Drake in *He Sent Forth a Raven* (1935), and Dena James in *Black Is My Truelove's Hair* (1938), all achieve moral redemption when they escape from the urban world and find a separate peace in the country. There, amid "abundance of fields and pastures," they enjoy an idyll in which "days pass . . . flowing without monotony" and their bodies surrender to the rhythms of the farming seasons. "Jocelle's thought was sweetened by a will to leave armies and treaties and international blunderings and predictions of after-war disasters," we are told in *He Sent Forth a Raven,* "and to make here," in the Southern countryside, "an order, a peace, through her own person set to rights, and to make comfort and pleasure for the other one," her lover. The problem with these narratives is that protagonists like Jocelle Drake do not so much engage with the contradictions that make up their lives; they simply acknowledge them as a preliminary to evading them. And so does their creator, when she tries to elaborate on the blissful life her characters discover as a result of their flight: the rural world that acts as a sanctuary and a balm to hurt minds here is, more or less, defined by the motives of wish fulfillment that brought it into being. At its worst, this simply means that this world is idealized to the point that it hardly appears to belong to history, let alone the history of the South. With its quaint folkways and picturesque characters, it may be set *in* the twentieth century but it is in no sense *of* it: this is a community of people "new with the beginning of the earth," the reader is told in *My Heart and My Flesh,* "beyond the reach of truism . . . the dew of new-birth on every saying . . . free of all but the bare statement of themselves as standing out before time, before running duration."[23] At its best, however, there is a curiously magic, mythic quality even to Roberts's most unabashedly lyrical celebrations of life on the small farm. As Jocelle Drake looks after the chickens, for instance, she finds herself healed by the rhythms of the work. And the sheer intensity of focus Roberts brings to her descriptions of that work, the specificity and detail, makes the ideas of escape and recovery—at least, for a moment—plausible:

> The chickens . . . were strangely gentle creatures, bred in abundance and security. . . . If Jocelle leaned over their drinking pans or feeding bins, they would flutter to her shoulders and away, so that they were a continual flowing spray that drifted over her, their small pink feet tapping lightly on her hands or leaping over her arm. . . . Jocelle fed them and sensed their eagerness to have the food, their creeping into little hutches as dark began to fall, their identical purrings of twilight fear and assurance.[24]

Jocelle is saved here through the minute particulars of country life, and the replication and resolution of her own dilemmas in the odd, touching behavior of the creatures she cares for. For a moment, the pattern of "fear and assurance," panic and retreat that motivates these books finds its release in an entirely appropriate way, because the enchantment and rescue here issue directly from labor: which is to say, from a close engagement—on the part of both character and author—with the daily work, the routine of the farm.

A quotation that recurs in Roberts's work is taken from the eigh-

---

23. Elizabeth Madox Roberts, *My Heart and My Flesh* (New York, 1927), 265. See also *Jingling in the Wind* (New York, 1928), 201; *He Sent Forth a Raven* (New York, 1935), 177, 199; *Black Is My Truelove's Hair* (New York, 1938), 75–76, 78.

24. Roberts, *He Sent Forth a Raven,* 190–91. For a discussion of how Roberts's own ancestry arguably supplied her with "a stable, rooted agrarian heritage," see Harry M. Campbell and Ruel E. Foster, *Elizabeth Madox Roberts: American Novelist* (Norman, Okla., 1956), 6 and *passim.* Roberts was one of the few novelists discussed in this chapter regarded with some respect by the Agrarians, who tended to read (and, in my view, misread) her as a traditionalist.

teenth-century idealist philosopher Bishop Berkeley: "All those bodies that compose the mighty frame of the world have not any substance without a mind. They take being through being perceived or known." That, perhaps, alerts us to the vein of thought, the belief animating all Roberts's portraits of rural life. And the power ascribed to human consciousness by Berkeley, the idea that knowing is prior to and prescriptive of being, is particularly worth bearing in mind when reading her two finest novels: *The Great Meadow* (1930) and, even more, *The Time of Man*. In a sense, *The Great Meadow* is a historical novel; it is set in the early nineteenth century and deals with the settlement of Kentucky. Only in a sense, however: what it is really about is an act of creation, of the kind figured by Berkeley. The characters, notably the heroine Diony Hall and her father Thomas, conduct an errand into the wilderness; there they build a world and an identity for themselves, they bring an agrarian civilization into being. The themes of destiny and knowledge supply the lifeblood of the narrative. "The Author of Nature has point-blank made a promise land," declares Thomas Hall, "A place fitted to nurture a fine race, a land of promise." "I, Diony Hall," the heroine reflects to herself, "subtracting herself from the diffuse life" around her, "I, Diony . . . I am one, myself." Traveling with her family to "a sort of Eden," "a land that calls for . . . a brave race," Diony finally discovers a world commensurate with her capacity for wonder. Where she and her family determine to settle, she has, the narrator discloses, "a sudden overwhelming sense of this place as of a place she had known before, feeling that she had been here before, that these events were the duplicate of some former happening." Here, Roberts is unraveling the nostalgic utopianism that lies at the center of the American pastoral, and not just the Southern versions: Diony's mind is looking both before and after for a world adequate to its needs. And it is this *conscious* deployment of myth, this stress on the belief that the world is ushered into birth by mental as well as physical labor, that saves *The Great Meadow* from simple romantic triumphalism—even in passages like this one, describing the society Diony and her companions start to build: "They marched forward, taking a new world for themselves, possessing themselves of it by the power of their courage, their order, and their endurance. . . . Fields turned up by the plow . . . sheep . . . turned in on the hillside to . . . glean a fine rich eatage for themselves . . . stone walls . . . setting bounds to the land, making contentment and limitations for the mind to ease itself upon . . . this man's farm beside that man's, all contained now . . . and shared."[25] Moments like these in *The Great Meadow* are resonant with the need to give life to thought; they expose that belief in the possible intersection between mind and matter, pastoral dream and rural routine that supplies the deep structure of all Roberts's work. If there is a weakness here, and there surely is one, it is in the absence of tension: the "promise land" of the novel is rather like the dream of Adam in *Paradise Lost*—the protagonist awakes, and then finds it true.

What is missing from *The Great Meadow* is what, in its presence, makes Roberts's finest novel, *The Time of Man*, so spellbinding and plausible: the sense of a constant *struggle* between fact and desire, earth and spirit, out of which redemption grows. Ellen Chesser is one of Caldwell's "unknown people," born to a tenant family whose life of wandering and "a-walken" from one small patch of hired land to another is described in all its harsh details. Nothing is spared or excluded from the report. The cabins she lives in are ramshackle; the land she cultivates is barren; and the work she has to do, every day, has little enough to do with the pastoral dreams of the Agrarians. Describing how she came to write the book, Roberts said, "I began to think of the wandering tenant farmer of our regions as offering a symbol for an Odyssey of Man as wanderer buffeted about by the fates and the weathers." Reading it, though, what is first likely to strike anyone is, not the allegory but the drudgery, the plain facts of rural poverty. This is a novel that matches *Barren Ground* or *Weeds* in its brutal evocation of what it is like to be a woman forced to work a land that seems actively hostile to human intervention. This, for instance, is Ellen in the fields hoeing: "The near way of the clods, as she knew them, as she leaned over them, were a strength to destroy her strength. There, present, the heaviness of the clods pulled at her arms and the field seemed to reach very far before it stopped at the pool by the quarry. . . . She felt the weight of the grass as she tore it away, and now and then a blow so sharp that it made her flanks ache was needed to turn the soil."[26] Things are not improved by marriage. She and her husband

25. Elizabeth Madox Roberts, *The Great Meadow* (New York, 1930), 168. See also 3, 5, 10, 105, 173. Bishop Berkeley is quoted on pages 198–99 of this novel and, at the beginning of the story, Thomas Hall, Diony's father, is described reading Berkeley's work (6). For the impact of Berkeley's ideas on Roberts, see Campbell and Foster, *Roberts*, 80. For an account of *The Great Meadow* that views it as a historical narrative, see George Dekker, *The American Historical Romance* (Cambridge, 1987), 283–38.

26. Roberts, *Time of Man*, 248. See also 349; Earl H. Rovit, *Herald to Chaos: The Novels of Elizabeth Madox Roberts* (Louisville, Ky., 1960), 9.

still have to work land owned by other people. In fact, Ellen's recognition of the fundamental bleakness of her life only sharpens the older she grows. "It mattered much less . . . now what country she lived in," Ellen observes to herself after what seems endless wandering, ". . . or whether there was a tree in the yard or a spring or a well. . . . A year on Robinson's place, a year on McKnight's, it was all one."

Whatever that last observation may seem to suggest, though, *The Time of Man* is much more than a tough account of life among the poor—and something other than a celebration of rural stoicism. There is a constant tension in the novel between its documentary level, which tells us of what is, and what might be called the level of dream or desire, which intimates to us just what might be. Roberts's strategy for realising this other level is quite simple: she makes us share in the consciousness of Ellen Chesser and her imagining of "some better country" where her mental and material needs might be met. The reader is invited to witness the act of the mind: the continuing, never quite completed process by which the consciousness attempts to build an ideal, a possibility out of the ruins of the actual. At the very least, this generates narrative conflict and a mood of stubborn optimism in the protagonist. *The Time of Man* bears witness to a constant fight between human thought and the poor, dull, stale reality to which that thought seeks to give meaning. "It had seemed forever that she had traveled up and down roads," Ellen Chesser reflects, "having no claim upon the fields but that which was snatched in passing." It also offers us a heroine who not only never gives up but also never gives up hoping and dreaming. Even at the close of the story, Ellen continues to believe "dreamily" that she "could take what there was out of the hard soil and out of the stones and she would have, in the end, something from the clattering rocks." And she is heartened to see the growth of similar beliefs in her son: "his want startled her with its determination and its reach," we are told, "coming upon her as something she knew already, had always known, now enhanced and magnified, unappeased."[27] To this extent, the dream of a better life is perceived as something that exists apart from reality—that acts as a means of transcendence. It is more than this, however; it is also an agent of transformation. What Ellen Chesser manages is not just to survive life, nor even just to rise above it, but to change it. If there is one thing that makes *The Time of Man* different from, on the one hand, a reformist novel like *The Share-*

27. Roberts, *Time of Man,* 374. See also 262, 368, 382.

Cropper and, on the other, a paean to stoicism such as *Barren Ground* or *Weeds* it is the sense that its central character can use her idea of the good life actively to improve her condition; somehow, thanks to the sheer energy of her needing and thinking, she can achieve real moments of redemption.

It is important to get this right. Roberts is not subscribing here to the kind of unambiguous idealism that would deny the pressure of the actual; nor is she falling back on those rhythms of return and recovery that characterize several of her other novels. She is simply imputing as much power to mind as to matter in the creation of the real; she is permitting the idea of the good land, and good labor upon it, to act as a tool of hope and technique of renewal. The facts in the case of Ellen Chesser are disappointing and drab, there is no doubt about that but, even at their drabbest, Ellen manages to give those facts a further resonance, a richer dimension. The agrarian dream—the dream, that is, of a world in which each moment of farm life becomes meaningful—not only enables the heroine to keep on going, it also furnishes the simplest of her routines with a quality of ritual. It breathes life, and the sense of an almost sacramental significance, into even the most ordinary and everyday of tasks:

> She would take the turkey bread in her hand and go, bonnetless, up the gentle hill across the pasture at sundown, calling the hens as she went. She was keenly aware of the ceremony and aware of her figure rising out of the fluttering birds, of all moving together about her. She would hear the mules crunching their fodder as she went past the first barn, and she would hear the swish of falling hay, the thud of a mule hoof on a board, a man's voice ordering or whistling a tune.[28]

This is different from those moments of rescue to be found in, say, *He Sent Forth a Raven* when Jocelle Drake finds security and assurance in the warm, womblike sanctuary of the farm: not least, because Roberts makes no secret of the fact that Ellen Chesser, unlike Jocelle, is constantly "buffeted about by the fates and the weather." The squalid experiences of the tenant farmer are not denied here, far from it. But those experi-

---

28. Ibid., 374. See also 9, 79. The inner focus of the narration is discussed in F. Lamar Janney, "Elizabeth Madox Roberts," *Sewanee Review*, XLV (1937), 388–410. See also Frederick P. W. McDowell, *Elizabeth Madox Roberts* (New York, 1968). Cook takes a rather different view of the book (*From Tobacco Road to Route 66*, 23–24).

ences are made to engage with another, deeper idea of the rural life; the possibility of redemption is entertained and now and then, as this passage shows, that possibility seems to become actual. Ellen can retain hope of somewhere where she and her kind really do enjoy some dignity; more to the point, she can use that hope to relieve her circumstances, informing them with a significance they would not otherwise have. " 'The time of man,' as a saying, fell over and over in Ellen's mind," we learn. Quietly meditating on that phrase, she imagines "the strange men that lived here before our men, a strange race doing things in strange ways, and other men before them, and before again"; and she hears, so she fancies, the "strange feet walking on a hillside for some purpose she could never think." That sense of the strange *in* the familiar, informing and even altering it, is perhaps the true source of the book's vitality. The story of Ellen Chesser is one that makes us see things aslant: from an angle that allows for the determinations of the world but also permits sight of the desires of the mind—and finds, in those desires, an odd chance of salvation.

Compared with Roberts, most other writers who find moral strength among poor farming folk do so in a much more muted key; courage, hope, desire—every positive, creative impulse has to struggle, in their work, against all the odds. This is true even of those books that deal with the black farmer. Resilience, endurance, indomitable optimism—the features usually associated with African Americans in traditionalist Southern fiction—are all qualities of the major characters in *Inchin' Along, Ollie Miss,* and *A Good Man.* But at least as much emphasis falls on the viciousness of a system that makes these qualities a necessary defense, a bulwark against despair. In these circumstances, optimism becomes a protective device to prevent corrosion of the spirit; it is part of the armory of survival rather than a possible agent for change. *Inchin' Along,* for instance, is an ironic success story about a determined, patient, ferociously hardworking black farmer called Dink Britt who, at the beginning of the book, has come within sight of his cherished goal of independence. After years of struggle, he has been able to buy sixty acres of land from a white farmer—sold to him only because the farmer believes that Britt will be helpless by himself and that he will be able to buy the land back later at a much lower price. "He was gazing reverently at an empire constructed by his own hands," the narrator observes of Britt on almost the first page of the novel, "an empire which was both a reality and a dimly fierce dream—an empire which was a tiny two-room cabin."

"During the last ten years," we are told, Dink "had lived with but a single purpose: he would not remain a sharecropper." Now he has a chance to fulfill that purpose; and the terms in which we are told of this hover between the vernacular detail of documentary and the suggestive possibilities of dream in a way that recalls similar moments in *The Time of Man*. The difference here, and it is a crucial one, is that Britt has then to cope with problems and traumas that never trouble the likes of Ellen Chesser. In the course of the narrative, he is faced of course with the familiar struggle against nature and the marketplace. There are floods, blinding heat, the boll weevil; and the merchants and millers charge him exorbitant prices that he has, of necessity, to accept. In addition to all this, however, he has to suffer other forms of humiliation that are specifically racial in origin. As one white character comments, "As far as niggers in this part of the country are concerned, there's never been such a thing as the Civil War";[29] and, as if to prove the truth of that statement, Britt's white neighbors force him to help build the local school, even though it is only for whites, in lieu of paying unfairly assessed taxes, and allow him to buy only land that nobody else wants—needless to say, at an absurdly inflated price. One of his neighbors even rapes his wife, who has a child as a result; once again, Britt finds there is nothing he can do about it, by way of redress or reprisal. All he can do is face the facts and survive them. In this sense, and this sense only, Britt's position significantly improves as his life goes on: he comes properly to understand his situation, he arrives at something like political consciousness.

Understanding occurs after an auction of land sold for taxes, described toward the end of the book. The white buyers conspire to carve up nearly all the land at a cheap price. All that is left for Britt is some poor land that they do not want—for which, inevitably, he has to pay far more than it is worth. It has happened before to him, but this time the experience, and the accumulation of other moments of victimization and humiliation that have preceded it, are enough to grant him his own small epiphany. "For the first time he became fully aware of the overpowering odds that his color had placed against him," the narrator comments, ". . . the white men had nothing against him . . . they were simply disregarding him. . . . He was only an animal."[30] That last comment measures the distance be-

29. Kelley, *Inchin' Along*, 35. See also 2, 8.
30. Ibid., 161. See also Tony Tanner, *City of Words: American Fiction, 1950–1970* (London, 1971), 51.

tween a figure like Dink Britt and someone such as Ellen Chesser, as far as the drama of moral survival is concerned. Britt survives; in his own modest way, he even prospers. But the survival is hedged around by the ironies of race; and the leap of consciousness the protagonist makes enables transcendence only to the degree that he is able to stand outside his condition sufficiently to understand it. There is no real sense of transformation or redemption here; still less is there any chance of altering that condition once it is known. What Britt has gained in understanding, however, is at once very little and very much. It is very little to the extent that such understanding can be used neither as a tool of material change nor as a technique of imaginative renewal: neither the ways of Scarborough's heroines nor those of Roberts's are yet open to him. It is very much, though, in the sense that he now can take the measure of his own oppression, mark the limits of the prison to which the white man has consigned him. And to the degree that he can do this, he can begin to gauge just what and who he is. For an African American farmer—and, for that matter, any African American—this is a not inconsiderable achievement. After all, as the eminent African American novelist, Ralph Ellison, observed, "The nature of our society is such that we are prevented from knowing who we are." By the end of *Inchin' Along*, Dink Britt has come close to knowing who he is, by seeing clearly just what mechanisms white society deploys to stall or prevent such knowledge. Recognizing white misrecognition of him ("He was only an animal"), his neighbors,' denial of him as a human subject, he has begun the painful task of learning and perhaps even declaring his own subjectivity, his own human identity. In that way, at least, he has realized a kind of mastery over his condition; he is not simply a victim.

"From dawn to dusk, man and beast had to sweat, plowing and hoeing" begins a passage in *Ollie Miss* by George Henderson: "When the plow was caught up, plow hands took over a hoe. Mules went to pasture and man and woman had to sweat alone. From sun to sun, from Monday morning to Saturday noon. Saturday afternoons they went to ball games and picnics. Saturday nights they went to frolics. And on Sundays there was church. They had to go to church. They couldn't sweat and sin the week long for nothing."[31] A passage like this reminds us of the point where the life of the poor farmer—and fiction recapturing that life—crosses the color line. Henderson is writing about black farming life, of

---

31. Henderson, *Ollie Miss*, 110.

course, but it could just as easily be white. The rhythms of the week evoked here apply just as much, for instance, in the work of Marjorie Kinnan Rawlings, although her subjects are the white "crackers" of the piney woods, swamps, and scrub country. There is a deeply agrarian feeling in Rawlings's work, too, that invites a comparison with Elizabeth Madox Roberts. In her novel *Golden Apples,* for example, we are offered the story of people who discover purpose and friendship in working with the earth. "Nothing was more important than growth," one character in the book reflects. And later on, as another character contemplates a successful harvest, a burgeoning orange grove, he offers this quiet hymn to life on the land: "A man was a puny thing, frightened and lonely; transitory and unimportant. When he blended himself with whatever was greater than he, he found peace. He shared the importance of growth and continuity. When a man shaped growth to his ends, he put his hand on the secret core of creation, and in the shaping was a moment's mastery, and in the mastery was his dignity."[32] Nevertheless, even these reflections underline the distance, the difference between Rawlings and Roberts. For Rawlings, there is no question of the heroic consciousness transforming nature. Man, or woman, for her, is "a puny thing," comparable to the creatures of the undergrowth, the snails, coons, and squirrels; and, as the protagonist of one of Rawlings's short stories observes quite simply, "Every man was at the mercy of the winds of chance. . . . Life was the enemy." This is the lesson that Jody Baxter in *The Yearling* has to learn. He grows up by discovering that, as his father puts it, "life goes back on you." "Life knocks a man down," Jody's father confides to him, "and he gits up and it knocks him down agin. I've been uneasy all my life." With the discovery, he ceases to be a "yearling" and enters into his patrimony: which is no more and no less than the simple struggle to survive.

What Jody learns, apart from the fact of struggle, though, is registered in that comment of his father—and in the model, the example of sheer perseverance that both of his parents offer him. "It's pure impudence to complain," declares the narrator of one of Rawlings's tales, ". . . we got

32. Rawlings, *Golden Apples,* 351. See also 74; "The Enemy," in *When the Whippoorwill* (New York, 1940), 174; *Yearling,* 426. For some sensitive contemporary observations on this aspect of Rawlings's work, see Howard Baker, "Grand Tour of Fiction," *Southern Review,* IV (1938), 810–12; Otis Ferguson, "Spring Fiction," *New Republic,* XCIV (27 April 1938), 370–71; Helen McAfee, "The Yearling," *Yale Review,* XXVII (1938), x.

no right to holler against such things as getting old and dying." And that typically laconic statement of rural stoicism is echoed in a later novel, *Jacob's Ladder*, where the heroine says simply, "I don't belong to be skeert." Life may be like Jacob's ladder in the song: "If you try to climb, yor boun' to fall." But the important thing is to get up, not be scared, and try to climb again. In the struggle, most of Rawlings's characters even find a strange kind of satisfaction. This comes out, with particular force, in Rawling's second novel, *South Moon Under*. Toward the end of the book, a dance is held to celebrate the gathering of the harvest; and the narrative spotlight falls here, as it has done for much of the action, on the women, old and young. We see these women through the eyes of one of them, the heroine Piety Lantry; and what she observes is the sheer intractability, the toughness of both their lives and their natures. "Age marked these women early," Piety remarks to herself. "The young girls were inclined to be plump and buxom. . . . Life pared them down in a hurry. . . . Almost without exception the older women were stripped and gaunt and meager, as though they had walked on foot a long sandy way."[33] "But if the road had been hard," Piety then reflects,

> it was also pleasant. If a living was uncertain, and the sustaining of breath precarious, why, existence took on an added value and a greater sweetness. The tissues of life were food and danger. These were the warp and woof, and all else was an incidental pattern. . . . Love and lust, hate and friendship . . . even birthing and dying, were thin gray and scarlet threads across the sunbrowned, thick and sturdy stuff that was life itself.[34]

In a move typical of a Rawlings character, Piety Lantry graduates here from observing stoicism to embodying it, expressing it in the harsh, homely terms that come naturally to her. In a mix that is equally typical, the sweet and the bitter in life are given just about equal due. All else beside "food and danger," evidently, is incidental to existence; even what are commonly thought to be the elementals of life—namely, birth, love, and death—are pronounced less central, less significant than the rough fact of struggle. Yet that fact itself is said to generate its own stern forms of satisfaction, even pleasure. This is not precisely cold pastoral, although the comforts of country life are pared almost to the bone.

33. Rawlings, *South Moon Under*, 305. See also "Cocks Must Crow," in *When the Whippoorwill*, 251; *Jacob's Ladder*, 63, 106.
34. Rawlings, *South Moon Under*, 305.

"Planting, growth, and harvest," Piety's husband laments to himself at one point, "planting, growth, and harvest. . . . If there were not cows to fight there was drought; if not drought, insects, incessant rain, or mildew." As *South Moon Under* shows, however, it is not just "life" in general or the inexorable routines of farm life that define the struggle. It is the inequities of a system growing even more inequitable with change. At the beginning of the book, a small farming community that up until then has been secure in its isolation finds itself no longer isolated, after a lumbering company cuts down much of the surrounding forest and the state legislature builds roads through the clearings. Police suddenly appear to enforce laws against illicitly distilled liquor and trapping outside of certain seasons. Both laws are seen as an outrage by people like Piety and her family, since they deny them a useful, and sometimes indispensable, source of food and income. "I've killed me hun'erds of deer in my time," says one old man, a neighbor, "and with my age upon me, the law says I got no right to take me a leetle piece o' venison to fill my pore ol' guts." Previously marginalized and ignored, the Lantry folk and their kind suddenly find themselves and their way of life challenged by the law. To their own bewilderment, they then find themselves, many of them, pronounced lawbreakers. During the course of the narrative, in fact, both Piety's father and her son are forced by hardship to resort to moonshining; falling foul of the law, and driven to violence, each of them in turn has to become a fugitive. The system creates new areas of criminality, turning the unknown into the known, wanted and hunted; and Rawlings underlines this point by dwelling on one instance of the conflict between old customs and new (or newly enforced) laws in particular—a clash as ancient as pastoral itself, between commons and enclosures. The tourists who suddenly appear, thanks to the new roads, complain about livestock wandering on or near the highways. Responding to this, the state legislature passes a law requiring the enclosure of pasture land. At first, farmers like the Lantrys continue open pasturage by "tacit consent," because almost none of them can afford to build miles of fences. Then a newcomer begins to confiscate "strayed" cattle, "intruding violently on the community agreement." The locals respond with their own, customary forms of rough justice, by giving him a whipping. He, in turn, responds by taking them to the courts. "The folk were aghast," we are told. "Insult had been added to injury. They had given the law no trouble in their history. They had settled their own disputes themselves."[35] The case is dismissed for

35. Ibid., 260. See also 31, 233, 255–56; Louis Althusser, "Ideology and the State," in *Lenin and Philosophy, and Other Essays* translated by Ben Brewster (London, 1977), 169.

lack of evidence; nevertheless, the message is clear—a system that, up until then, has largely excluded them now wishes to control them. "A subjected being," Louis Althusser has argued, ". . . is . . . stripped of all freedom except that of freely accepting his submission"; society recognizes him only to the extent of requiring of him a fixed, definite, and subject(ed) status. Unlike Althusser, Rawlings is no Marxist: but it is clear that what she is describing in *South Moon Under* is precisely this kind of subjection, the transformation of (as Althusser puts it) "individuals into subjects," an act of socialization that is essentially an act of subjugation. Life may be an enemy for Rawlings's poor folk, but so too is a system that seems designed to deny them and the value of their social practices—and takes them in only to keep them down.

Faced with these different forms of struggle, a figure like Piety Lantry certainly seems "a puny thing." "A man's life was not his own," her husband reflects, ". . . He moved like a cedar chip on the breast of the river; like a chicken feather lifted by the high wind." And as Piety's father watches her turning the beds for sweet potatoes, that generalization assumes a moving particularity: her life in the fields, and even her body, seem not to be hers, either to own or control. "She drove a pony-like white horse and small plow," he sees: "The plow handles pulled at her armpits, so that her shoulders jerked at every roughness and her bare feet flew up behind her. She held the plow steadily . . . the plow-point caught a root and bucked. The girl plunged forward in a somersault . . . in a moment she was on her feet. He could see her brush the dirt from her face with her arm and take up the plow-line again."[36] This is very different from the way Ellen Chesser transforms task into ceremony. There is no heroic transfiguration here, quite the opposite: a small creature, literally and figuratively, Piety seems to be dwarfed and mastered by the plow and the earth, the burden of her work and the circumference of her days. Nor is there any sense of a solitary, brooding, and creative consciousness either. Instead, this lonely figure in the field is dissolved into fragments and a random series of gestures: her shoulders jerk, her feet fly up, her body turns in a somersault. In an act almost of humiliation—and, certainly, one confirming her subjection—the land even trips her up. But then, apparently without pause or complaint, she picks herself up and she starts again. "Life knocks a man down and he gits up and it knocks him down agin." Piety's gesture is a perfect example of the not entirely cold comfort available to her and her kind. She may be "boun' to fall,"

36. Rawlings, *South Moon Under*, 32. See also 42, 54.

perhaps, but she can still rise again—and again; and in the sheer rhythm of rising and falling and rising she can maybe find something "pleasant," because earned and real. "Piety . . . felt a sharp pleasure in the details of the precarious thing that was existence," we learn. ". . . The tug of the plow was good, and the sight of the cane and corn sprouting green above the earth . . . all the small creatures that crossed her path were good to watch." Drawn, as we are at times, into her mind, we can share Piety Lantry's "sharp pleasure," even while, at others, we take the more distanced measure of her pain; and we can begin to unravel the tangled threads of her life. Like Rawlings's other poor farming folk, her story is not one of victory, material or mental, but neither is it one simply of defeat borne bravely or grim acquiescence in the inevitable. What it tells us is that no battle is entirely lost or won. Even the most subjected can continue to fight, and find a strange kind of joy—or what Piety's husband calls a "secret triumph"—in the fight; even the smallest creatures, the dispossessed, can stand up to the forces that beat against them with a willpower, a quiet passion that makes the struggle sweet.

The sweetness of the struggle is, however, hardly something that Judy Pippinger, the heroine of *Weeds* by Edith Summers Kelley, ever encounters. As Sylvia Jenkins Cook has commented, "*Weeds* offers no systems of social reform or metaphysical consolation" for the poor whites of Kentucky it describes. What it prescribes instead, through the story of its central character, is a kind of numb acceptance of conditions that seem to be at once a part of life and the product of a particular social system. Indeed, if there is a weakness in this extraordinarily powerful novel, it stems from Kelley's unwillingness or inability to distinguish between the facts of life and the processes of history. The sufferings of Judy, her family, and her kind are clearly contingent in part upon her class position and the market economics to which, as tobacco farmers, they are particularly vulnerable. Judy, however, never distinguishes between these kinds of suffering and others to which her friend and neighbor Uncle Jabez Moorhouse is referring when he declares, "the earth's a mean and stingy stepmother."[37] Neither does the narrative point of view, which identifies with

37. Kelley, *Weeds*, 201. See also Cook, *From Tobacco Road to Route 66*, 22. Also Margaret J. Hagood, *Mothers of the South: Portraiture of the White Tenant Farm Women* (Chapel Hill, N.C., 1939). Kelley was not born in the South; however, *Weeds* remains one of the seminal fictional treatments of the Southern rural poor between the two world wars, and no account of this subject can afford to minimize its importance, let alone ignore it.

the heroine with an intensity that tends to inhibit analysis: in this context, the fluctuations of the tobacco market and the inequities of the Southern farming system come to seem almost as "natural" and inevitable as flood or drought. They are the way things are, the burden of the narrative is, and, as such, simply have to be borne. This elision between life and the social system, the conditions prescribed by the seasons or weather and those dictated by a particular history and certain economic arrangements, is not, of course, unique to *Weeds*. It is endemic in writing about poor whites, and as such was a constant source of aggravation to people like the reviewers of *New Masses*; for that matter, it occurs in *The Time of Man* and *South Moon Under*. Nevertheless, it is particularly marked in *Weeds* because Judy Pippinger and, by implication Kelley herself, evidently believe with a passion that life simply *is*—and that the beginning and end of wisdom lies in accepting this unalterable fact. The slippery definition of "life" that *Weeds,* in fact, shares with many other books about rural poverty in the South consequently looms larger; it is more openly there, almost inviting the reader to call it into question.

Problematical though the notion of "life" in *Weeds* may be, the story of Judy Pippinger is one of the most powerful accounts of the particulars of poor white existence. The conceptual frame of the book may be uncertain, even flawed—certainly, any *New Masses* critic would find it profoundly unsatisfactory—but within that frame a drama is enacted that, in the blank despair of its detail, seems to anticipate the documentary photography of ten years later, as well as recall—and bear comparison with—the very finest of earlier antipastoral literature. The fundamental rhythms of the book are familiar, perhaps, from other versions of the antipastoral. To begin with, Judy is a high-spirited young woman with abundant energy and a deep attachment to nature. She and her family live in a small, three-room shanty "standing upon forty-seven acres of heavy clay land which Aunt Annie Pippinger had inherited from her father." This little Kentucky landholding is described with the kind of eye for minute particulars that recalls Andrew Nelson Lytle's loving portraits of the small farm in his novels and *I'll Take My Stand*. The only difference, and it is a crucial, determining one, is the sense of poverty and enclosure that plays like a somber bass note throughout the description. "The back dooryard was beaten bare . . . by the playing feet of children," we are told, "the dumping of endless tubs of soapsuds and pans of dishwater." Beyond this bare spot, "a fringe of mustard, ragweed, and burdock reached the picket fence"; and "a stone's throw beyond the picket fence stood a barn . . . in need of repairs these many years." "This was the center of the universe for the Pippinger children," the narrator goes on. "A radius of some eight or ten miles about the farm formed their entire world." Within this tiny circle "was Clapton, the source of groceries, candy and Christmas toys, as were also the homes of the various grandparents, aunts, uncles, and cousins with whom they visited."[38]

Kelley is careful not to paint too bleak a portrait in these opening pages. There is a feeling for family and community here and an affectionate notation of the customs of country life: the visiting, the days of festivity, the family dinners and dances. "There was no sin greater than the sin of being stingy with your time, your food, or your work," the narrator explains. "To intimate by word, deed, or look that visitors were not welcome was unthinkable in the social circle in which Bill's family and their kin moved." Bill Pippinger, Judy's father, shows this to a fault: "He was prompt with neighborly assistance. . . . He had never been known to refuse a neighbor the loan of anything that he owned." The neighborliness, the generosity, the hospitality are all there among this small circle of tobacco farmers, just as they are in more idyllic accounts of life on the land. But, even here, Kelley points out the dreadful constriction and the deprivation that makes these people old before their time. At one dance, for example, the "old folks" who join in the dancing prove not to be old in the usual sense at all. They are people in their forties and even thirties who have been worn down by their lives. "It was a scarecrow array of bent limbs, sunken chests, twisted contortions, and jagged angularities," the narrator reveals, "that formed the circle for the old folks' dance. Grotesque in their deformities, these men and women who should have been in the full flower of their lives, were already classed among the aged."[39] One of this group "old . . . in body and spirit," under the influence of the alcohol he has been drinking to give him the energy to dance, collapses— then gets up and breaks into futile boasting. "I tell ye, I'm a baar in the woods," he shouts. "I don't take no sass from nobody . . . I tell you I'm a baar in the woods." His boasts are a bizarre parody of the rhetoric of the old frontier, just as, in a way, the "old folks" and their dance are a nightmare version of a familiar moment in American pastoral. What was once an expression of backwoods confidence has become something quite different: sheer bluster—a mask for despair and a sense of worth-

38. Kelley, Weeds, 8. See also 6–7.
39. Ibid., 91. See also 3, 9, 92.

lessness that really only exposes the feelings it is meant to conceal. The story at this stage is not all darkness. On these and similar occasions there is still a feeling of intimacy, burdens shared, and casual conversations about both the problems and pleasures of life. Nevertheless, the determining attitude here remains caustic, ironic. Even during these moments of sociability, we are being reminded of the gap between what other books tell us and what is, in fact, the case.

"The men loafed in the barnyard," the narrator comments during the description of one visit, "the children played . . . the women cooked and washed dishes . . . and talked about the price of calico, the raising of chickens." Observations like these—and they run through the book— help carry the burden of one particular message in *Weeds*: although life is hard for everyone on the small tobacco farm, it is especially hard on the women. Bill Pippinger is an attractive figure, but he is also a little feckless. "It was none of his doing," he claims, "if the weeds grew so fast that they overtopped the corn." Tasks such as the mending of fences, the hauling of manure, and cutting the brush to allow the pasture grass to grow: "these things preyed more or less on Bill's mind, but he did not allow them to annoy him too constantly." Judy's mother, on the other hand, has to carry the constant burden of five children, housework, farmwork. Worn down by this, she dies even younger than most, before Judy is grown up and married. The men drink to escape from the poverty of their condition; the women, denied even the cold comfort of alcohol, find refuge at the few times they are not working, only in the thought or talk of some other life. None of this worries Judy at first, however. She delights in nature and "all the small life that fluttered . . . and hopped and crawled about the farm." Certainly, there are intimations of the cruel necessities at the back of her existence, waiting to make themselves known. All her attempts to keep animals meet with disaster: "mud turtles brought from the swampy lands . . . always died. Butterflies imprisoned in an old, rusty bird cage . . . always died" and, "it seemed to Judy at such times . . . that . . . she was foredoomed to failure." A similar moment of disillusionment occurs when she sees her pet kitten crunch a minnow mercilessly. "From that day," we are told, "she learned to take for granted certain laws of nature which at first had seemed distressingly harsh and cruel." For all such lessons in failure and the iron laws of survival, however, Judy remains at this point a free spirit: a part of nature, as she feels it in its abundance and ripe amorality. This feeling becomes particularly powerful when she meets the man, Jerry Blackford, whom she eventually marries. "It was a speedy, simple, natural court-ing," we learn, "like the coming together of two young wild things in the woods." Judy is remarkably frank and simple in her attitudes towards sexuality and her own physical needs, and so is Kelley. In passages that seem to recall *Tess of the D'Urbervilles,* say, and even *The Rainbow,* the warm sensuality of the opening stages of Judy's relationship with Jerry is identified with "warm, still sunny days . . . without a break" and the rich, lazy life of the earth during the summer. "In the mornings when Judith stepped out into the yard," one such passage begins, "the grass was covered with flimsy gossamer webs encrusted with dewdrops, each one a rainbow in the sun. The beds of geraniums and the bunch of scarlet sage along the stone wall seemed to grow each day a richer red. . . . They were very silent, these mornings. No bird spilled music in the sunshine."[40]

Quiet delight in the life of the body, and the body of nature, even continues for a while after Judith and Jerry are married. Almost inevita-bly, it seems, Jerry becomes a tenant farmer raising tobacco; and all their first summer together "in spite of the toil in the field, Judith was joyous and radiant." Kelley subtly interleaves the story of the newlyweds here with the story of the cultivation of tobacco; setting, topping, hoeing, har-vesting, and the stripping of the crop for the market are all described in some detail, in terms of the daily lives of her central characters. And just as subtle are the terms in which the author slowly gathers the shades of the prisonhouse around her heroine. To the earlier intimations of disas-ter—the poor folk old before their time, the trials of the women, the dark side of nature, and so on—is added what is perhaps the most powerful and memorable theme running through the novel: repetition, the inexo-rable nature of work and the monotony of life for the poor. The endless-ness of summer days devoted to the discovery of sex and love is one thing; the endless work demanded by the farm and that "mean and stingy stepmother," the earth, quite another; and Judith begins to learn the dif-ference. Slowly, the one rhythm of repetition shades into the other. Qui-etly, the theme is introduced at first: "each day was exactly like the one before it," one apparently innocuous passage informs us, ". . . she found herself continually longing for something new."[41] The images of circular-ity that recur throughout the narrative—the family circle, the "radius" of the farm and neighborhood, the circle formed at the dance—all play

40. Ibid., 76. See also 4, 10, 16, 17–18, 21, 102.
41. Ibid., 160. See also 124.

into the repetitive rhythms; within the circle, Judith comes to seem, and feel, more and more enclosed. And the feeling of enclosure, entrapment even, becomes overwhelming as failure turns into the law of her life: one year crop failure, the next a radical fall in the price of tobacco. The imperatives of the weather and the marketplace appear to collude in driving the heroine down; and, here as elsewhere, Kelley makes no real distinction between them. For Judy, and evidently for her creator, they are just different aspects of that force, that necessity which is making her home, as she sees it, "her prison."

It is, it seems, as it always was, worse for the women; it is at this stage in the narrative, in fact, when Judy Pippinger fully recognizes the numbing reality of her life, that she also realizes the additional, back-breaking burden of being a housekeeper, a wife and mother. When crops fail, the men simply have nothing to do except lounge "on the shady sides of each other's barns, whittling aimlessly at bits of stick, chewing straws and tobacco." Their situation may be desperate, but the situation of women like Judith is more desperate still since, for them, "there was no such thing as change nor anything even vaguely resembling a holiday season":

> Families must be fed after some fashion or other and dishes washed three times a day, three hundred and sixty-five days a year. Babies must be fed and washed and dressed. . . . The endless wrangles among older children must be arbitrated. . . . Fires must be lighted and kept going as long as needed for cooking . . . Cows must be milked and cream skimmed and butter churned. Hens must be fed and eggs gathered and the filth shoveled out of henhouses. Diapers must be washed . . . and all the other articles that go to make up a farm woman's family wash. Floors must be swept and scrubbed and stoves cleaned and a never ending war waged against the constant encroaches of dust, grease, stable manure, flies, spiders, rats, mice, ants, and all the other breeders of filth that are continually at work in country households.[42]

All these labors, Judith now knows, "with the occasional variation of Sunday visiting, made up the life of the women, a life that was virtually the same every day of the year." They are also her lot now, her meager portion in life. Her husband may try to delude himself with the belief

42. Ibid., 195. See also 191, 197, 228.

that, as he puts it, "things'll come out all right, so long as we have each other," but she knows that is a lie. Faced with the truth, she alters—growing, in her turn, old before her time. "The buoyancy and effervescence of youth were gone," we learn. "It was as if the life spirit in the still young body had grown tired. She rarely sang any more, and was not often heard to laugh."

The vision of a farm woman's lot that gradually overpowers Judith Pippinger is a grim one; and it derives at least some of its potency from a characteristic inversion of the pastoral tradition. Here, as elsewhere in *Weeds,* Kelley invokes the pieties of other, more idyllic portraits of rural life only to mock and reverse them. In the accounts of, say, the local color writers rural life is cherished precisely because of its simplicity and rhythms of repetition. Set in contrast with the fraught, complex life of the city, life in the country is seen to devote itself to the daily round, the common task, the simple dictates of the seasons, and the narrow circumference of farm and village—and to be all the better, that much closer to perfection, because of all this. In *Weeds,* however, all the qualities the local color writers held dear are seen, as it were, through a glass darkly. Simplicity is interpreted as an effect of poverty and a cause of monotony. These people's lives are "simple," the message is, because they cannot afford anything beyond the basic—sometimes, they cannot afford even that; and the minimalist nature of their way of living means that variety, change, escape—any of the standard human ways of finding relief from routine—are never really there for them. "The occasional variation of Sunday visiting" is all that rescues them from the narrow confines of their home place and a life marooned in repetition; and that is not enough. For the women especially, the daily round is a treadmill and the common task only too common because it remains "virtually the same every day of the year." This is antipastoral with a vengeance; and, toward the end of the novel, Judith has become so desperate that she embarks on an affair with an evangelist preacher. In its own way, though, this too becomes part of the ironic fabric of the book. The country woman and the preacher: it is a story as old as folklore itself. The difference here, though, is that again the familiar theme is given a twist. The affair ends in boredom; it turns out to be, not so much a way of escape for Judith from her prison, as part of the prisonhouse itself. "She had grown into the habit of looking forward to the end of the day," the reader learns. "Its approach meant that the waking hours of dismal tasks and constant frets would soon be over, that the whines and wants and wrangles, the scraping of chairs, the tramping of muddy shoes, the whole meaningless turmoil would come to an end, and for a little while there would be peace."[43]

"For a little while there would be peace": it is meager consolation, perhaps, but by the close of the novel it is just about all Judith Pippinger has. Her sense of identification with the lovely particular things of nature takes on a new dimension now, and a far more somber one. Looking at the turkeys on her farm, for instance, "wrapped in the glowing twilight," she feels herself "like those humbler creatures an outgrowth of the soil, its life her life even as theirs." Stoically, grimly, she thinks: "Quiet, peace and calm, these things belonged to them." These same things, she considers, "in less measure her own life had to offer. These things at last she was ready to accept." The peace and quiet of the earth, sleep, and eventually death: this is all, apparently, that Judith now wants and—which is much the same in her eyes—feels able to have. Heroic transformation of her circumstances has never been an option for her. Now, it is clear, struggle, sweet or otherwise, is no real choice either. "She had realized the uselessness of struggle," the narrator explains: "Like a dog tied by a strong chain, what had she to gain by continually pulling at the leash? What hope was there in rebellion for her and hers? The boys would grow up to bury their youth in the fields as Jerry had done. Little Annie [her daughter] would be in the years to come . . . a harassed mother like herself. . . . She had grown timid . . . since the days of her forthright girlhood. Peace was better than struggle, peace and decent acquiescence before the thing which had to be."[44] Given the burden of the narrative, with its endless circularities and repetitions, and the gradual spiraling down of Judith's own life into "a sad, dead level of unrelieved monotony," it would be wrong to call this "new spirit" a choice on her part. Judith simply takes the only option available to her: numbness, resignation, the small crumbs of dignity that can be gathered from accepting necessity—in other words, from reminding oneself that things irretrievably are as they are. The trials of living must continue to be faced, Judith realizes. "She would go on for her allotted time bearing and nursing babies"; and, "when her time of child bearing was over she would go back to the field, like the other women." Eventually, "she would be too old to work in the fields," and would then "sit all day in the kitchen in the

43. Ibid., 327–28.
44. Ibid., 370. See also 328, 331, 332, 333.

winter and on the porch in the summer shelling peas or stripping the corn from the cob." And for the duration she will, she hopes, find "a measure of mutual comfort" in sharing with Jerry "the joint burden of their lives." Punctuating this will be the moments of peace supplied by sleep, a resigned heart, and a sense of kinship with the "humbler creatures"; completing it—and devoutly to be wished, according to the logic of this new spirit—will be the more lasting peace of death.

The ending of *Weeds* is dark, even desperate. What makes it different, however, from other novels that detail the apparently inexorable repetition of the farming life and the trap of rural poverty is Kelley's intensity of focus on the spirit, the consciousness of her heroine. Narrated in the third person, this is nevertheless clearly Judith's own story; more to the point, it is a story that we, the readers share. What the book arguably lacks in terms of social analysis, in fact, is more than made up for by its trenchant lyricism—thanks to which, we participate in the changing moods of the heroine. Judith's altering but always intense relationship with nature, the sensuality of her youth and the stoicism of her maturity, her sexual ardor and her spiritual despair: these are all things that we come to know in an intimate way, just as we know equally intimately the dreadful, paralyzing sameness of her adult years, and the process by which she comes to learn about the iron law, the necessity that governs her life. True, Kelley's ironic use of pastoral, and her naturalist eye for detail, also require us to see such experiences in more general terms—to interpret Judith's gradual disillusionment, and its causes, as deeply personal but also emblematic, representative. But it is Judith Pippinger, what she sees and feels, that we are likely to remember from this book; for the duration of *Weeds,* in effect, *her* life becomes *our* life—which is what, after all, makes the novel such an immensely affecting experience. What this means, in turn, is that, although bleak, the conclusion of *Weeds* is not as bleak as it might have been—and, indeed, as many, similar novels of the period are—thanks to the bedrock value of the heroine's stoicism, her grim but determined acquiescence in what is and what has to be—an acquiescence which, like all her other moods, we share. Those contemporary reviewers who saw the end of the book as an affirmation of love and family, and a triumph of the will,[45] were surely wrong; it is far too harsh to be read in these terms. Still, their odd reading of the book contains one small grain of truth. The heroine, and her creator, have asked them-

45. See Cook, *From Tobacco Road to Route 66,* 23.

selves what to make of a diminished thing; their answer is not a prescription for happiness but it does allow for peace. It commands respect and permits a measure of self-respect. The case for life in the last pages of *Weeds* is a minimalist one, certainly, but it *is* there; the spirit, shriveled though it is, survives.

The presence of positive energies in *Weeds,* however minimal, becomes clearer in comparison with a group of writers of this period who chart similar patterns of repetition and enclosure, but offer no mental consolation for material suffering. For them, the deadly routines of Southern tenant farming numb the spirit as well as the body; this is a prison, it seems, from which there is no way out—no loophole for the soul, not even the residual dignity to be gained from a grim acceptance of the inevitable. Their protagonists may struggle to improve their condition, but they invariably fail either to achieve or to maintain independence; if there is any change possible at all, it seems, it is only for the worse. Among the books that map this geography of white rural despair are *This Body, the Earth* (1936) by Paul Green, *Stubborn Roots* (1936) by Elma Godchaux, *Land Without Moses* (1938) by Charles C. Munz, *Boot-Heel Doctor* (1941) by Fannie Cook, and *First, the Fields* (1941) by Charles Wood; and among those that chart, in a similar spirit, the very particular forms of destitution suffered by the African American farmer are *Sweet Man* (1930) by Gilmore Millen, *Deep Dark River* (1935) by Robert Rylee, and two later books, *A Wind Is Rising* (1946) by William Russell and *High John the Conqueror* (1948) by John W. Wilson.[46] Impotence is the mark of the farmer in these novels and, in particular, the novels about the white farmer. In *This Body, the Earth,* for example, the chain gang

46. Gilmore Millen, *Sweet Man* (New York, 1930); Robert Rylee, *Deep Dark River* (New York, 1935); Paul Green, *This Body, the Earth* (New York, 1936); Elma Godchaux, *Stubborn Roots* (New York, 1936); Charles C. Munz, *Land Without Moses* (New York, 1938); Fannie Cook, *Boot-Heel Doctor* (New York, 1941); Charles Wood, *First, the Fields* (Chapel Hill, N.C., 1941); William Russell, *A Wind Is Rising* (New York, 1946); John W. Wilson, *High John the Conqueror* (New York, 1946). Other fiction of what will here be called the new slavery includes another remarkable novel by Paul Green, *The Laughing Pioneer* (New York, 1932). Presented through the eyes of a crippled poor-white boy—who, by virtue of his disability, has been permitted the time to read and write—this story combines a powerfully pessimistic account of a world where "men plow from sun to sun and where women and children stagger under loads too heavy for their strength" (15) with the kind of picaresque narrative of adventure more usually found in Southern fiction of the nineteenth century.

"with its broken, rotted lives" becomes an emblem of the bondage to which the tenant farmer appears doomed; *Stubborn Roots* ends with the protagonist deciding "you couldn't win . . . you couldn't struggle"; while *First, the Fields* has the hero eventually reflecting that "like the negroes he was concerned with nothing more than making a hand-to-mouth living"—"he had no purpose beyond that," he thinks, "and every minute of his day cried what a bare purpose that was." "Some faculties of feeling he had lost altogether," he realizes: but even that, the ability to realize one's own degradation, seems to be denied the central character of *Land Without Moses,* called Kirby Moten. Kirby has witnessed the lifelong humiliation of his father, Tamp Moten: from which Tamp finds relief in only two things—kicking "hell out of the dog" or, on occasion, beating his wife and children, and dreaming of a better land across the county line. Kirby promises himself that things will be different for him, but they turn out, inevitably, not to be. By the end of the narrative, having escaped across the county line only briefly—but long enough to discover that "hit ain't so much different a land as Pa thought"—he finds himself enslaved to the same landlord as his father once was, and exactly the same system. The final scene, in fact, is one of utter abjection. Advising Kirby to "settle down and behave himself," the landlord lets his young tenant off a portion of his debt. "Tears of thankfulness" well in Kirby's eyes; "I reckon hit's because you got such a kind heart," he declares in gratitude to the man who once exploited his father and now exploits him. The landlord then gives him some advice about work and breeding. Spring and summer "ain't no time to have a baby," he tells Kirby, when the women are wanted in the fields; "I have to watch out for that," the landlord goes on, "same as I do for breedin my cows." Autumn and winter are the right times for replenishing stock, including the human one. "Now ain't that the way to do it?" "Yes, sir," says Kirby in response to this patently rhetorical question. "I reckon you're a mighty smart planter." "Get your hoe, boy," the landlord adds—obviously tiring of giving his tenant the benefit of his wisdom—"and get to work." Kirby's response is simple and provides the final words of the book: "Yes sir, Mr. Longneik, I'm gittin'."[47]

It is not difficult to see here, in the last moments of *Land Without Moses,* a grim parody of plantation romance: the grotesque figure of

___

47. Munz, *Land Without Moses,* 368–70. See also Green, *This Body, the Earth,* 413; Godchaux, *Stubborn Roots,* 403; Wood, *First, the Fields,* 277.

Kirby Moten, shuffling off to work having listened to his master's voice dispense wisdom, recalls the complaisant "darky" of Southern pastoral—just as the comparison with animals, and the language of fawning obedience ("Yes sir . . . I'm gittin' "), clearly do. Some of these books offer a barely more intelligent encounter with questions of race than the conventional plantation novel does: that comment of the protagonist in *First, the Fields* that he has become "like the negroes" is meant to make us feel sorry for *him*—and regret that he has declined so "low"—rather than to reflect, critically, on the fate of the people with whom he compares himself. Some of them, however, capture both the community of suffering that should draw black and white farming folk together and the absurd, mind-forged manacles of racial consciousness that make this something less than a probability. The image of the chain gang, or Kirby Moten dancing obedience to the landlord, tells one side of this story: as the protagonist in *This Body, the Earth* observes, "everywhere it was the same, the landlord, the niggers and the poor whites . . . the leaking, rotten tenant houses . . . gouging despair, and the waiting darkness of the grave." The intricate social habits, and the deeply scored prejudices of the white tenants, tell quite another. Tamp Moten is outraged when a family of black tenant farmers moves into a neighboring cabin. "Hit ain't right to ask me to work an' live right next to them stinkin niggers," he complains. Similarly, his son Kirby is posed with a peculiar social problem when, as a young man, he goes to a local black man, Keet Riffle, to learn how to count, to read, and to write. Keet begins to teach him not only about these particular subjects but about the social necessity of education. "Mistah Kirby, there are a thousand sharecroppers in the cotton country, and there's no end to the things they ought to learn," Keet tells his pupil, "but the first thing they ought to learn is that two plus two equals four, not eight or five." "If a man doesn't know two plus two equals four, he's a slave," he explains, "and if a man does know . . . he's on his way to being free."[48] Nevertheless, as that "Mistah Kirby" alerts us, things are never that simple for either the teacher or the pupil. Kirby, in particular, is vexed by the problem of how to address the man instructing him. He persuades himself, however, that he can call him "professor" since "it was not like calling Keet 'Mister,' but more like calling a preacher 'Reverend,' and everybody did that." The episode captures, in

48. Munz, *Land Without Moses*, 79. See also 45, 72; Green, *This Body, the Earth*, 413.

a slyly comic way, the absurd social practices to which the racial codes of that time and place subject those living on both sides of the line, the vocabulary of fear and division. To be more precise, it exposes the contradiction at the heart of the relationship between white and black rural poor: similarly enslaved, the determining condition of their life and language is, not that common slavery at all, but notions of caste difference and social deference. Kirby Moten is willing to learn from an African American, but he is unwilling to grant him full human status; his attitude toward his black neighbors is, in fact, not that different from his father's—and while it remains so, the implication is, the freedom that Keet Riffle talks about seems no more substantial than the dream of a better life in a neighbouring county.

If Kirby Moten in *Land Without Moses* finds himself reenacting the downtrodden life of his father in the end, then Alvin Barnes, the central character in *This Body, the Earth,* eventually finds himself reenacting his own life. Paul Green's novel begins with a sweeping description of people on the road—not, as in mainstream American writing, out of hope or a sense of adventure but as a result of simple economic necessity:

> When the end of the year comes around, the roads that run crisscross over the great plain are dotted with wagons and steer-carts and rattly Ford trucks of sharecroppers on the move. And the loads they carry are the same—a few chickens or geese in a crate, a bed or two and an old stove, a battered bureau, a washstand, a few quilts . . . a stool, a bench, and a rocking-chair. On the front of the load sit the lean, haggard husband and his silent wife, and behind them any number of ever-present children from three to ten, most often ten. For this last chattel is at a premium among landlords, for cotton-picking and the nimble-fingered duties of tobacco-raising.[49]

This is the documentary mode at its best: combining a panoramic sweep with a meticulous noting of small, significant particulars, cutting between the contours of the visible world and the personal compulsions, the social forces that give those contours life and color. The eye of the camera offers us a long shot of a whole countryside on the move, glides in for a closer view of people and possessions, and quietly explains the law that supplies the motor for this strange annual ritual. The commitment is there already in the sardonic reference to children as a "chattel," held at a premium

49. Green, *This Body, the Earth,* 4. See also 440.

among those who own the land; once again, we are back with the vision
of tenant farming as the New South equivalent of slavery. And the cool
despair that charges this vision runs through the narrative that follows,
as we are introduced to what is obviously only one possible story among
many: that of the Barnes family and, in particular, the father, Alvin. The
story is a tangled one but its fundamental rhythms are simple. Alvin, a
sharecropper and the son of a sharecropper, wants to own his own land;
for a short while he succeeds, to the extent of farming land bought with
money borrowed from the bank; eventually, though, he loses crop, land,
and money and finds himself on the road again. He is back where he
began. So is the book. A passage toward the end of *This Body, the Earth*
in fact repeats almost word for word that haunting account of annual
migration with which it opened. "The end of the year had come round,
and the roads . . . were dotted again with wagons, steer-carts, and rattly
Ford trucks of tenants on the move," it begins, "And the loads they carried were the same." All that remains for Alvin, as he sees his end repeat
his beginning, is to give up and die; the family then move on again, with
Alvin's oldest son taking up the reins, ready to take his turn at experiencing the cycle of poverty.

What makes the story of Alvin Barnes or Kirby Moten different from
that of Judy Pippinger perhaps needs underlining. There is no hope in
Judy's story, but it is not exactly hopeless because of the sense of internal
resistance, the presence within her of what Ellen Glasgow would have
called a vein of iron. Resistance, however, seems impossible in books
like *This Body, the Earth* and *Land Without Moses*—or, for that matter,
Stubborn Roots and *First, the Fields*. The system of "big fish eat little
fish," as it is called in *This Body, the Earth* seems inexorable; its laws
somehow unalterable; its processes apparently calculated to crush the
spirit as well as the body. Like the reformists, these writers regard nobody
as genuinely profiting from the system; unlike them, though, they see
everyone, every level caught in the chain, trapped in rhythms of repetition
and revenge. Within this chain, the "Goddam' slavedrivin' bankers"
pressure landlords into operating their holdings "like places of business"
concerned with "profits, power, and . . . exploitation." "Sweated by the
big men further north," the landlord turns to the tenants and sharecroppers and day laborers and "sweats them grievously." The poor farmer,
in turn, pursues his own forms of revenge and reenactment: the white
farmer steals from and humiliates the black, the man of the house beats
the women and children. Every form of oppression becomes a mirror of

another form: even the killing of the occasional, rebellious tenant farmer by the landlords finds its reflection, in these stories, in the spasmodic lynching of an "uppity nigger" by the poor white folk. Every moment carries with it the burden of other previous moments just like it. "The life that Alvin and [his wife] Ivy Barnes lived in the few succeeding years" after their failure to improve their condition, we are told, "would have appeared to any casual observer as typical of that great tobacco-farming class. . . . One year the crop would be rather good and the price satisfactory. And then they'd be able to buy a few things for the house . . . and a few clothes. The next year the weather would be bad, the crop would be short, and finally both the furniture and the clothes would wear out before another year came around. And so it went on."[50] "And so it went on": the feeling of weary inevitability expressed here measures the limits of possibility for the Barnes family and their kind. Their life is inscribed as "typical," and that typicality casts its shadow over the future as well as the past and present. Within the constraints of this typology, and the inexorable temporal and economic cycles that accompany it, no one, it seems, is innocent—and no one can find release or relief. They end up, like it or not, conforming to type.

This, perhaps, is the problem with the documentary mode or the naturalist vision, when both are divorced—as they tend to be, in these novels—from any close analysis of the potential for change. The social system under inspection, and the processes of living it prescribes, come to seem as immutable and ineluctable as the seasons. The reformists anticipate and even sometimes begin to engineer social change in their stories. They are capable, like any of the writers dealing with the plight of the poor farmer, of confusing the system with the seasons: but they offer, however clumsily, enough understanding of the engine, the forces driving that system, to open up the possibility of altering things—given hope, luck, and the right tools. Less materialist in their approach, those writers—like Roberts, Rawlings, and even Kelley—who seek some kind of chance of redemption for their rural protagonists drive inward, searching for a resource that might liberate or at least supply a prop, a stay against confusion; and the actual direction of their search—their bias toward inwardness, the life of the consciousness—greatly assists them in finding what they seek. Emphasizing subjectivity, in short, they usually end by finding consolation, however small, in the subjective. With writers like

50. Ibid., 412–13. See also 47, 413, 428.

Green and Munz, though, the cycles of oppression are remorseless. Their protagonists may try to alter their condition, but the fierce emphasis of these novelists on the objective, material surfaces of life—together with the imagery of imprisonment, and the circular pattern, that characterize these stories—suggest how futile, and ultimately meaningless, such efforts are. The present mirrors the past in these narratives, and the future will undoubtedly reflect its past, in turn; the son fights to be different but ends up imitating his father—or, rather, *being* the father, playing exactly the same subjected role. The same dour rhythms of repetition run through the books of this kind that deal with the plight of the black farmer. "The pattern of waking and working and sleeping, repeated on every plantation, was so standard," we learn in the first pages of *A Wind Is Rising* by William Russell, that the protagonist "learned with surprise," on his first trip outside his home state of Mississippi, "that it was not the pattern of the entire world."[51] Two elements, however, give an extra inflection to the tale, in these particular versions of what might be called the drama of the new slavery. One is the tendency to see the economic predator as, in addition, a sexual predator; and the other is the habit of linking the sense of dispossession to the feeling of being actively possessed by those—invariably white—people who are in control. The tie that binds the old slavery to the new would, after all, be especially strong in the case of African Americans; and so it is not perhaps surprising to find the notion of bondage, and the cycle of enforced poverty, being given—in these stories of poor farmers who happen also to be black—a greater resonance, a further twist.

In *Deep Dark River* by Robert Rylee, for example, we are introduced to a serious, patient African American called Moses who goes to work on the Mississippi plantation of the Rutherford family as a sharecropper. The difference between the two generations of the Rutherfords living in the plantation house is clearly meant to signal an economic change taking place in the region as a whole, from paternalism to a less diluted form of capitalism. Lon Rutherford, the nominal owner, is a planter of the old school, who manages to convince himself that he is a kind of "father" to the croppers—people who are, to all intents and purposes, still owned by him. Lon is old and senile, however, and power has fallen into the hands of his sons, Orvil and Lonnie. Together with the plantation manager, Mr. Birney, they try to operate the plantation according to business princi-

51. Russell, *Wind Is Rising*, 12.

ples—with plenty of cheating on the side. "At the commissary Mr. Birney presented bewildering statements of advances," we are told, "and explained volubly and with overwhelming rhetoric why the left-overs in cash were so appallingly small. The negroes scratched their heads and, pocketing their small earnings, trudged off."[52] Not content with economic exploitation, Birney also exploits the tenants and sharecroppers sexually. In particular, he forces himself on Moses's wife. When Moses finds out, he puts an end to things: but he feels, and indeed is, powerless to do anything more about it. He is not in control of any part of his life. He, his house, and his family can, it seems, be invaded and possessed at any time. The point is made succinctly in another of these novels, *High John the Conqueror* by John W. Wilson, when the central character, a young black tenant farmer called Cleveland Webster, discovers that *his* wife, Ruby Lee, has been the object of similar sexual advances from his landlord. "He worked and he lived," Cleveland reflects, "but the crops he raised could not be counted his. . . . Nothing was his own . . . not even Ruby Lee." In the face of such dispossession, several responses are possible. One is resistance: Moses resists, fights back, and ends up in prison. Another is flight: the protagonists of both *Sweet Man* by Gilmore Millen and *A Wind Is Rising* escape northward. And a third possibility is capitulation: Cleveland Webster is last seen walking along a dusty road near to the land where he works as a day laborer, followed by a telling emblem of his own subjection—an abandoned dog, its "head low and tongue panting, hanging and dripping." None of these solutions, it is clear, approaches being satisfactory; they simply confirm the omnipotence of the system. "Mississippi law was written . . . to preserve the status quo," we are told in *A Wind Is Rising*; and that law, in Mississippi and elsewhere in the rural South, seems designed to keep the black farmer down and out.

"You had to take a lot of things on faith," the black protagonist of *A Wind Is Rising* tells himself. "If Seabury King [the landlord] said something was so, that was the way it had to be. No way of checking up on him. No reason to, either, because no matter what you found out you had to go on pretending to believe."[53] As in *Deep Dark River*, a difference of generations in the ruling class becomes here the measure of historical

---

52. Rylee, *Deep Dark River*, 89. See also 165; Wilson, *High John the Conqueror*, 139; Russell, *Wind Is Rising*, 252–53.

53. Russell, *Wind Is Rising*, 13. See also 12, 39, 259.

difference. Seabury King distributes small presents to "his" sharecroppers at Christmas in the time-honored manner of the master of the old plantation, whereas his son is an emblem of the new farming world of "fuel oil and banks, efficiency and bleak selfishness." In neither *A Wind Is Rising* nor any of these other books, however, is there any trace of nostalgia for the old system: old Lon Rutherford, it is disclosed, used to force himself on his black sharecroppers' wives, and a small Christmas gift marks the limits of Seabury King's paternalism—he will not, for instance, come to the aid of any of his sharecroppers who fall sick or lack food. "You felt like you was living between high walls," observes the black hero of *A Wind Is Rising*; and, while the writing on those walls may change, they have evidently always been there. There is, perhaps, a certain remorselessness about these novels of the new black slavery. Certainly, in retrospect there is a powerful—but, at the very least, problematical—emphasis on the male gaze, the male perspective: according to which, for example, possession of land and possession of a woman, and the dispossession of both, tend to be equated. But that is part of their claustrophobic intensity: the reader is caught with the male protagonist within the confines of his cell—a cell that, in the final analysis, is not even his; and everything is dictated by the imperatives of his own drastically limited experience of life. Ironically, the limits of the protagonist's experience and vision are ones he cannot alter even if he wants to. The white landowners are firmly opposed to the black sharecroppers acquiring an education, we are informed in *A Wind Is Rising,* because "the very first thing they [the sharecroppers] would want to read would be the ledgers where their accounts were kept." And those limits, small as they are, are constantly being violated: the whites claim the power, it seems, to invade land and body, on the premise or assumption that the black farmer does not even have a right to his own life. The one element that survives all this, evidently, is consciousness: the poor rural black has to "go on pretending to believe," but that pretense is a measure of the fact that he is not entirely owned. To know the misery of their condition and the reality of a life that is not their own, to guess at or suspect the gap between what is so and what the white man says is so and the consequent need for disguise: this is the small allotment of understanding permitted the protagonists of these novels. It is less than the heroine of *Weeds* is allowed; it is less, even, than Dink Britt in *Inchin' Along* manages, since there is little sense here of taking the full measure of white misrecognition, its motives and the social mechanisms that sustain it. It is, though, something more than the abject protagonist of a book like *Land Without Moses* (with his "tears of thankfulness" for the "kind heart" of his landlord) can finally muster; and it does, at least, leave open the dim possibility of change. In his book *The Fire Next Time,* James Baldwin refers us to an African American who was "defeated long before he died because, at the bottom of his heart, he really believed what white people said about him."[54] Unlike the man Baldwin describes, the black farming folk in these novels of the new slavery do *not* believe what white people say about them, even if they have to pretend that they do. It is a small thing, it is in fact the only thing they genuinely have, but—as a present resource and a faint source of hope for the future—it is, at the very least, there.

In the novels of the new slavery, black or white, there remains a belief in the residual worth of the human subject called the poor farmer. That belief is significantly stronger in books about the enslavement of the black tenant farmer: but the weary pathos that characterizes the end of *This Body, the Earth,* and the angrily comic spirit in which the closing pages of *Land Without Moses* were clearly written, indicate that the writers of these books too felt real sympathy for the downtrodden creatures they described. The pathos, the anger, the bleak comedy are there in books like these because, hopeless though writers like Green or Munz take the situation to be, they still want to make a distinction between fundamental value and false currency: the humanity and potential dignity of people such as Alvin Barnes and Kirby Moten—and the denial of that humanity and the crushing of that dignity by the system, as it grinds remorselessly on. Quite simply, social change has not brought about total character change in these novels: even if, in *Land Without Moses,* the chances of that happening seem to be entertained at the end. In other narratives of this time, however, the one kind of alteration *has* led to the other; a material transformation has been followed by a mental one; poor white farmers have metamorphosed into "shiftless white peckerwoods, always on the move." Significantly, many of these narratives were written during and after the period when the Roosevelt administration and the WPA opened up the possibility of new kinds of work and some forms, at least, of welfare. More significantly still, perhaps, the majority of them are set in small towns and are concerned, explicitly or otherwise, with

54. James Baldwin, "My Dungeon Shook," in *The Fire Next Time* (New York, 1963), 13.

the exodus from the farm. Whatever their social origins or implications, though, what marks them all is a relentlessly comic portrait of what one of these books, *Cross on the Moon* (1946) by John Hewlett, calls "coarse, white trash"[55] and the pseudo-culture they have fashioned in the decaying countryside and small town—a portrait that, in many of its details, recalls the southwestern humorists of the nineteenth century, or the kind of grotesque, brutal "comedy" that Poe always seemed to enjoy. These books of the new humorists—to use a convenient shorthand for a necessarily complicated phenomenon—include *Boss Man* (1939) by Louis Cochran, *God Rides a Gale* (1940) by James R. Peery, *Fire in Summer* (1942) by Robert Ramsey, *The Fingers of Night* (1946) by Hubert Creekmore, and *Joshua Beene and God* (1946) by Jewel Gibson. For that matter, they also include the work of John Faulkner, older brother of William: one of whose novels, *Dollar Cotton* (1943), charts the slide into that degeneracy which the other one, *Men Working* (1941)[56] portrays at cruelly comic length.

"He was lean, bony; his shoulders forward," the narrator of *God Rides a Gale* observes of one of the main poor white characters, called Fate Bollis. "His face was small, bewhiskered in gray and black, distorted and wrinkled with long years of pain and miserly expended toil. His chin, masticating with jerky rhythm upon a cud which might have been to-bacco . . . was streaked with brown stain."[57] This is an inhabitant of William Byrd of Westover's Lubberland or Mark Twain's Bricksville transplanted into the twentieth century: one of many "products of shift-lessness, ignorance, disease, carelessness about mating and superstition" observed with a mercilessly detached eye. The central consciousness in *God Rides a Gale* is an educated man, a country doctor, battling against

55. John Hewlett, *Cross on the Moon* (New York, 1946), 190.

56. Louis Cochran, *Boss Man* (Boise, Ida., 1939); James R. Peery, *God Rides a Gale* (New York, 1940); John Faulkner, *Men Working* (New York, 1941), *Dollar Cotton* (New York, 1943); Robert Ramsey, *Fire in Summer* (New York, 1942); Hubert Creekmore, *The Fingers of Night* (New York, 1946); Jewel Gibson, *Joshua Beene and God* (New York, 1946). The new humorists were not formally a group, of course. For further discussion of the southwestern humorists of the nineteenth century, see Walter Blair, *Native American Humor, 1800–1900* (New York, 1937), *Horse Sense in American Humor* (New York, 1942); Kenneth Lynn, *Mark Twain and Southwestern Humor* (Boston, 1959); Constance Rourke, *American Humor: A Study of the National Character* (New York, 1931).

57. Peery, *God Rides a Gale*, 11–12. See also Hewlett, *Cross on the Moon*, 16, 93, 181; Gibson, *Joshua Beene and God*, 185; Creekmore, *Fingers of Night*, 106.

the bigotry of his surroundings. This is typical, if by no means invariable. The central character of *Cross on the Moon,* for instance, a young man named Johnny Bean, learns to detest the "raw fundamentalism" of his small Georgia town—including a father who beats him and neighbors who organize a lynching—at the knee of the local doctor: who explains to Johnny, and by extension to us, about "these narrer hidebound people in leetle Southern towns"—and teaches him the necessity of leaving what he calls "Dixie's land of Genesis and Original Sin." What characters like these disclose is what is nevertheless there, if implicit, in all these novels: like Byrd or the southwestern humorists, the narrators have little connection and even less sympathy with their subjects. This is the land of Southern grotesque: where, as in *Joshua Beene and God,* a preacher can compose psalms in his own honor ("Praise ye the name of Joshua Beene, greatest of all the prophets") or, as in *The Fingers of the Night,* a man can persecute his children in the name of his own primitive beliefs. "It's all filth and scum and slime that men and women do in bed," the man—called Maben Ellard—tells one of his daughters, "the rot of life, and marryin is the trick the devil uses to get you to do it."

In some of these books, there is a conservative direction to the argument. In *God Rides a Gale,* for example, what is called "the congenital indigence" of Fate Bollis is squarely blamed on welfare programs and the relief food that Fate uses as a form of currency, to buy himself beer. Similarly, in *Fire in Summer,* a poor white character called Spence Lovell is only too eager to go to town to live off handouts. In others, the perspective is more that of a privileged, enlightened liberal. So, in both *Joshua Beene and God* and *Cross on the Moon,* the impetus is more toward establishing a link between, on the one hand, the violence of poor white culture and, on the other, the false consciousness generated by religion and the racial divide. "Ah've presided at as many lynchin's as anybody heahabouts," announces the "Chairman" of a lynching party in *Cross on the Moon.* "Ah intends to do mah duty's long as th'Almighty'll permit me to live." The "Chairman," the narrator explains, "grew up, in keeping with all of his kind, in active contempt of the Negro, his economic revival, and the one element in all the world over whom he could boast superiority and demonstrate it to the vast satisfaction of his pride by violence of the boot, the rope, the Smith and Wesson, and the lash."[58] It would be wrong, though, to place too much emphasis on the difference

58. Hewlett, *Cross on the Moon,* 195. See also Peery, *God Rides a Gale,* 60.

in political leanings in particular narratives. What matters here, much more, is the distaste all these books share for the people they describe. "They might not have money enough to buy good clothes," observes the local doctor in *God Rides a Gale* of the poor white women in the area, "but they managed to get money enough to pay for a permanent. And cheap lipstick, powder and rouge that they put on their faces without half washing their necks."[59] These narratives are punctuated by scenes of violence—frequently, lynchings—and revival scenes that turn into thinly disguised orgies; and their fundamental rhythms are dictated by the shift-lessness and acute apathy of the poor white populace, what seems from this coolly distanced perspective to be an infinite capacity for "leanen 'n' dreamen." There is no sense of a specifically poor white culture here, built around the agricultural year and rural traditions. On the contrary, these poor white folk seem to have little in terms of material goods and even less as far as social and spiritual resources are concerned; and, when they act together, it is not as a community but as a mob.

"Mobs were sometimes ruthless," Joshua Beene reflects in the novel named after him and his divine assistant, "but mobs were invariably right." This "rightness" consists, of course, in obeying the dictates of people like "Uncle Joshua" himself or a similar charlatan in *God Rides a Gale* called Newt Carter. Joshua Beene runs everything in town. Re-garding himself as a "prophet," favored by a God whom he tends to treat as a junior partner ("the Lord could learn a trick or two from me if He would," he declares), he is revered almost as much as he reveres himself by the poor white folk of the area—who believe he can raise the dead, make rain, and strike down the living. "He had trampled unrelentingly the scorpions of wickedness and heresy," we are told; and, to ensure that he retains power, he has always either occupied the important local of-fices or filled them with his placemen. Authoritarian as he is, though, he had, the narrator confides, "never interfered with Negro mobbings . . . because he considered that you had to hang a Negro every once in a while as a warning." That same special blend of religion and racism is at work in Newt Carter, a poor white "scrawny from head to toe" who turns himself from a quack medicine merchant into a preacher, using, as the basis of his self-education, just three books: the Bible, a Sears Roe-buck catalog, and "One Thousand and One Ways to Make Money."

59. Peery, *God Rides a Gale,* 106. See also Gibson, *Joshua Beene and God,* 56; Coch-ran, *Boss Man,* 66.

Reluctantly, Newt is willing to agree that "a part of heaven would be occupied by niggers"; however, he consoles himself and his congregation with the belief that what will be reserved for them is "not the best part." Set against demagogues like Newt and Joshua are defeated figures of enlightenment: the local doctors in *God Rides a Gale* and *Cross on the Moon,* who can do little more than lament the bigotry of their neighbors and sew them up when they hurt each other, or, say, the school principal in *Joshua Beene and God,* an African American called Adrian J. Hendrix. Hendrix, we are told, "had thrown himself wholeheartedly into the education of the community," and "striven undauntedly throughout the years to break down racial and religious prejudice through enlightenment." But, he comes to realize, "all his hopes and plans and dreams had been thwarted" by Joshua Beene. Beene finally gets rid of him "and his ideas about changing the South"—replacing him with someone who, like most of the local white population, takes for granted the belief "that Uncle Josh's word was law."[60] Hendrix and his kind must remain prophets without honor in their own backcountry. The honored prophets are, invariably, those who, as the local doctor bitterly remarks in *God Rides a Gale,* stick to "preying on the superstitious and the ignorant."

In effect, all these new humorists are like the old southwestern ones to the extent that they betray a deep distrust of, as well as a profound distaste for, poor white folk. They are not populists, like the reformist writers. On the contrary, whether they are on the right or left of the political spectrum—or, for that matter, somewhere in between—they are remarkable for their elitism. Enlightenment, as these novelists see it, would issue from the privileged, educated few assuming responsibility for the direction of society. Darkness has come from the corruption of democracy: the old, stable social order has broken up, the implication is, to be replaced by a kind of socially legitimized anarchy run by demagogues responding to the worst instincts of the people. The old southwestern humorists were clearly frightened by the disappearance of a more secure order, with its habits of deference and respect; and their tales rehearsed that fear; in different ways, they tried to use comedy to contain and control what was for them an unknown world—a frontier territory characterized, as one of them put it, by "vulgarity—ignorance—. . . unmitigated rowdyism . . . bullying insolence" and "swindling . . . raised to the dignity

---

60. Gibson, *Joshua Beene and God,* 83, 88. See also 4, 37–38, 45, 223; Peery, *God Rides a Gale,* 30, 32, 50, 207.

of the fine arts."[61] Control is less on the agenda with these new humorists. All that is available to the enlightened, according to books like *Cross on the Moon* or *God Rides a Gale,* is departure or detachment: those who cannot bear the violence and bigotry can either flee it, or seek shelter in a kind of mocking aloofness. But there is the same impulse, as with the earlier humorists, to transform a perceived social anarchy into comic spectacle, and so achieve an *emotional* containment. There is the same need to deal with the rough beast of a changing society and altering folkways by finding release in laughter; to mock something is, after all, one way to make it feel like a little less of a threat.

One writer who clearly betrays those feelings of unease and instability that lurk behind many of these stories is John Faulkner, whose two novels chart the loss of a rural Eden and its bizarre consequences. The later book, *Dollar Cotton,* is concerned with loss, the disappearance of the old agricultural order; and, in fact, the title with its ironic linking of cash and crop alerts the reader to the book's message. The central character, a poor Mississippi hill farmer named Otis Town, first prospers from a rise in cotton prices and land values and then sees all his prosperity vanish when both the cotton and land markets collapse. A journey to Wall Street, made with his usual stoic patience to protest against the seizure of all his property by the banks that loaned him money, gives him a chance to express his creator's own agrarian values. "You fellers don't know what it's wuth to grow things," Otis declares to any bankers who will listen, "You . . . never put no seed in the ground and saw it come through a plant." However, the only practical result it has is to heap physical injury on top of material: he suffers partial paralysis of the limbs, brought about by exhaustion and his acute sense of frustration. Disasters pile up remorselessly on the Town family. Otis's white son is found guilty of a "murder" that is really a road accident. His black son is wrongfully accused of raping a white woman and killed by a lynch mob. And for every disaster, Faulkner suggests, there is one cause—agricultural crisis—to the extent that both the jury who convict the white man, and the mob who

---

61. Joseph Glover Baldwin, *The Flush Times of Alabama and Mississippi: A Series of Sketches* (New York, 1853), 88–89. I have not embarked on any detailed account of the southwestern humorists of the nineteenth century here, partly because it is not directly relevant to the discussion and partly because I have already considered those earlier humorists at some length in two previous books, *The Literature of Memory: Modern Writers of the American South* (Baltimore, Md., 1977) and *Writing the South: Ideas of an American Region* (Cambridge, 1986).

lynch the black man, are made up of farmers frustrated to the point of madness—and intent on venting their rage on anyone who comes within their power. The final blow falls in this tragedy of economic fate when Otis returns home, paralyzed but still driven by a "rock-like" determination to (as he puts it) "git me another crop started," only to find that he has neither the land nor the money needed to make a beginning. The portrait of him, as he learns this, completes the dissolution of a human being into a human nullity: "his eyes held steadily," we are told, "but the thoughts, the determination, the plans drained out from behind them, and they were now two shallow grey pools. . . . There was not even desperation in them, nor surprise, nor anger, nor regret. With the emptying of steady purpose, from them, there was nothing left."[62] With the loss of the land comes the loss of the man; Otis is now a moral and emotional void.

The state of emptiness in which Otis Town is left at the end of *Dollar Cotton* is the subject of John Faulkner's earlier novel, *Men Working*. In place of economic tragedy, here we have the kind of grotesque comedy that characterizes the new humorists; again, however, there is an ironic intention in the title. The characters in this book have moved to town where, if they work at all, they work on welfare projects; and for Faulkner, evidently, that is no work at all. Real work, according to the more or less explicit agenda of this story, is work on the land, and that has disappeared. An almost elegiac passage that occurs early on in the story makes that clear:

> The good land lay idle beneath the sun. The pale green stripes of growing corn and cotton and sorghum . . . had become solid green mats of weeds and grass. The mules stood idle in their pastures for there were no longer people to work the good land. The plows stood unused at the end of rows and the weeds grew taller and taller . . . the fields became smaller and smaller. Grass grew over the furrows, covering the wheel tracks, and the ditches choked with weeds and filled and overflowed. And the fields lay idle beneath the sun. For the people were moving to town.[63]

Among those people who have moved to town are the Taylor family, who have already reached the bottom, the moral pit to which Otis Town is

---

62. Faulkner, *Dollar Cotton*, 304. See also 230–31, 302, 303.
63. Faulkner, *Men Working*, 63. See also 160, 176, 200, 300.

descending at the end of *Dollar Cotton*. The Taylors are freaks, grotesques: dispossessed poor white farmers whose dispossession, according
to their creator, has deprived them of dignity and even humanity. The
father is typical. Living on welfare, he is only too happy to squander the
money he obtains from this source on tobacco, alcohol, and a series of
steadily larger radio sets rather than on food, rent, or the medical help
that his crippled children desperately need. When he has to work, forced
to do so by the welfare authorities, he does as little as possible on the
grounds that he "just cain't try much any more." And when he is at
home, as he is most of the time, he soon turns the house given to him by
the welfare people into a slum—greatly assisted in this by his slovenly
family. His pose at the end of the narrative is typical. Undeterred by the
recent death of his mentally disabled son, and the abandonment by her
husband of his sick and pregnant daughter, he waits in what the narrator
calls "complacent unendeavor" for his next welfare check, rapt in his
dreams of the new radio tubes he will buy with it. Seen purely in terms
of externals, and with a coldly comic eye, Taylor is the antithesis of those
happy farmers that constituted Jefferson's chosen people. Self-reliance
has been supplanted by a culture of dependence; energy and industry
have disappeared, replaced by apathy; in place of thrift, sobriety, and
integrity there is only waste, slovenliness, and deceit. *Men Working* certainly reveals the distaste for the rural poor that characterizes the books
of the new humorists, and the sense of loss that fuels their comedy. What
it also does, though, in its own deeply conservative way is show the uses
of humor to these writers. Here in the portrait of the Taylor family, as
elsewhere, the comic becomes a means of containment for feelings about
the disaster of the new poor white life. For John Faulkner and those
writers like him, neither reform nor any sort of redemption seems to be
available; culture has spiraled down into anarchy. The only way of chain-
ing the rough beast of populism, evidently, is to turn it from a beast into
a freak: to laugh it out of existence or, if that is impossible, at least out
of mind.

The notable exception to all this, as far as the uses of humor are concerned, is that writer who tried to bring "the unknown people of 1935"
to the attention of the readers of the *New York Post*, Erskine Caldwell.
Generally, critics have had a hard time with Caldwell—and Caldwell has
had a hard time with them. Some simply dismiss him. "The mirror which
Caldwell says he holds up to human nature," complains Louise Gossett,

"reflects not a representative selection of mankind but a private chamber of horrors." John Bradbury agrees: "Caldwell's characters never come across . . . as people," he observes, "but only as absurdly amusing or grotesquely fascinating examples of a new subhuman species." Others are more sympathetic, but plainly puzzled or even confused. As early as 1933, Carl Van Doren suggested that Caldwell was to some extent "impenetrable." And eleven years later, Malcolm Cowley was memorably to formulate a reason why so many commentators have found impenetrability in apparently so clear a writer. "Erskine Caldwell is two writers, both good of their kind," Cowley declared, a "sociologist" and a creator of "impossible fancies and wild humor." Only occasionally, in a short story, is there an "almost perfect union" of "the social doctrines of the first" with "the exuberance of the second"; generally, however, and without exception in the novels, the "two Caldwells" "seem to be working at cross purposes." This has been a common complaint among those who find, at least, something interesting in Caldwell's work. Very broadly, one might say that those with a bias toward the kind of criticism typified by the Agrarians have marked with approval the local humor in Caldwell's work, and deprecated any tendency toward social commentary. By contrast, those *New Masses* and other leftist commentators who have treated the work seriously have admired Caldwell's social concern but felt uncomfortable about what one *New Masses* critic called "the decadent possibilities latent" in "the humor of his treatment." What such critics have in common is an assumption that the comic and the social reformist elements in Caldwell's fiction are at best counterproductive and at worst mutually exclusive: to deploy both is consequently to invite chaos and confusion. There is even some of this, the sense that the work is odd, lopsided, and even conflicted among critics of Caldwell's work who clearly move in a much more positive direction. "Caldwell's novels suffer from a multiplicity of meanings which are incompatible with each other," W. M. Frohock comments, adding that "when we take everything into consideration we are likely to feel that, in spite of Caldwell's ambiguity, he is greater than we know." Sylvia Jenkins Cook, perhaps the finest of Caldwell's critics, is more forthright. The work, she suggests, shuffles between what Caldwell himself called "antics and motivations"—"comic and irrational behavior," as Cook terms it—and "the rational and deterministic origins behind people's conduct." "There can never be a fixed balance between the explicable and the inexplicable," she argues; and, as they vacillate between "different kinds of causality and the possibility of no cause at all,"[64] Caldwell's books map the uncertain territory we all occupy, the instabilities that mark and mar all our lives.

"I think regional writing is much more important than trying to be universal . . . or trying to write the great American novel,"[65] Caldwell confided to an interviewer; and perhaps one way of appreciating his finest accounts of the rural poor—in some of the stories, that is, *Tobacco Road* (1932), and *God's Little Acre* (1933)—is to see the "antics and motivations" that Cook so astutely observes in a specifically regionalist way: which is to say, in relation to other writers from the South writing about similar times, people, and places. The comic dimension is powerfully there in his work, linking him with other Southern humorists old and new. So is the reformist element, the willingness to seek practicable solutions to social problems that connects him with novelists such as Scarborough and Simon. But so, too, is that sense of spiritual hunger, emotional need that makes a comparison with someone like Edith Summers Kelley seem appropriate, or that feeling for the indefatigable optimism of the rural poor that brings to mind Marjorie Kinnan Rawlings. For that matter, so also is that understanding of the dreadful, numbing treadmill of oppressive work, and the stale routines of the workless, that are to be found in the fiction of the new slavery, by writers both white and black. This is not to say that Caldwell was necessarily aware himself of these different fictional portraits of the "unknown people," still less that he was influenced by them. Some of them, in any case, preceded his best work, published in the 1930s, and some followed after. It is, however, to suggest that, as in his *New York Post* articles but on a far larger canvas, Caldwell was seeking two things: attention and explanation. He was asking his readers to attend to the lives of his subjects, to make the unknown known; and he was pursuing that elusive object of human

64. Sylvia Jenkins Cook, *Erskine Caldwell and the Fiction of Poverty* (Baton Rouge, La., 1991), 116. For the other comments on Caldwell quoted here, see Louise Y. Gossett, *Violence in Recent Southern Fiction* (Durham, N.C., 1965), 25; Bradbury, *Renaissance in the South,* 101; Carl Van Doren, "Made in America: Erskine Caldwell," *Nation,* CXXXVII (18 October 1933), 443–44; Malcolm Cowley, "The Two Erskine Caldwells," *New Republic,* III (6 November 1944), 599–600; Rolfe, "God's Little Acre," 24; W. M. Frohock, "Erskine Caldwell: Sentimental Gentleman from Georgia," *Southwest Review,* XXXI (1946), 358.

65. Richard B. Sale, "An Interview in Florida with Erskine Caldwell," *Studies in the Novel,* III (1971), 331.

thought and effort, some reason for what he saw. In this project, he was no different from those others in his region who attended to the rural poor of the time. The only difference, really, was that he placed explanation at the center of his agenda. He sought to understand the reason why there seemed to be such a stupid gap between what people want and what they get—and, in particular, between what the dispossessed of his time and place wanted and what they got; he wanted to know why things were so. Other writers wanted to know too. For them, however, the answer was less central or less problematical; in the event, it also tended to be a singular rather than a multiple one. Caldwell was not confused—at least, in his best work he was not—he was unpacking a complicated and potentially confusing problem and using necessarily different strategies to do so, aligning him with different kinds of approach, different sorts of writers. In the process, he created characters that, more even than most, are at once freaks and seekers, animals and dreamers.

"He still could not understand why he had nothing, and never would have anything," Caldwell comments on Jeeter Lester toward the end of *Tobacco Road,* "and there was no one who knew and who could tell him. It was the unsolved mystery of life." Jeeter tries to explain the mystery to himself, or anyone willing to listen: but what he says always turns out to be not so much a solution as a symptom of the problem. "My children all blame me," he tells his son-in-law Lov,

> because God sees fit to make me poverty-ridden. They and Ma is all the time cussing me because we ain't got nothing to eat. I ain't had nothing to do with it. It ain't my fault that Captain John shut down on giving us rations and snuff. It's his fault, Lov. I worked all my life for Captain John. I worked harder than any of his niggers in the fields; then the first thing I knowed, he . . . say he can't be letting me be getting no more rations and snuff at the store. After that he sells all the mules and goes up to Augusta to live. I can't make no money, because there ain't nobody wanting work done. Nobody is taking on share-croppers, neither. Ain't no kind of work I can find to do for hire. I cain't even raise me a crop of my own.[66]

A speech like the one from which these remarks are taken is a useful example of how comedy and social concern are interwoven in Caldwell's

66. Erskine Caldwell, *Tobacco Road* (1932; London, 1948 edition), 22. See also 172; MacDonald, "Introduction," xxiii; Kenneth Burke, "Caldwell, Maker of Grotesques," in *Critical Essays on Caldwell,* 171.

work—and then interlaced with that sense of the grotesque mystery, the hidden dimensions of life, which Kenneth Burke was probably thinking of when he called Caldwell a surrealist. Jeeter is clearly trying to shuffle away from blame here. On one level, his speech is a masterpiece of evasion, self-exoneration: on a par with, say, some of Pap Finn's more self-aggrandizing statements in *Huckleberry Finn,* or Anse Bundren's wonderfully irresponsible defenses of his own lack of responsibility in William Faulkner's *As I Lay Dying* (a book, incidentally, that Caldwell called "superb"). Inseparable from this, however, is a quest for someone or something to shift the blame to. Jeeter comes up with several possible culprits: God, his former landlord Captain John, and a system that apparently denies the sharecropper, the tenant farmer, or even the day laborer work. He does not stay with any of these culprits for long, slipping between them with a strange (but characteristic) mixture of desperation and bravado; and part of the comedy here comes from this slippage, this abrupt shifting between different targets. Targets they are, however, not scapegoats. Through Jeeter's comic litany of self-exculpation, Caldwell is setting up a series of different possibilities—and preparing us (this speech comes in an early chapter) for a narrative that shows how power circulates in different arenas, some of them controllable by human or social agency and some of them perhaps not. When *Jeeter* alludes to God and the part He has played in making him "poverty-ridden," he is either falling back unawares on a common tendency to confuse system and season—what is susceptible to immediate human intervention, in other words, and what is less so; or he is cannily playing on that confusion so as to avoid all blame; more probably, he is doing something that wobbles between the two. In bringing God into the frame, along with Captain John and the system, *Caldwell,* however, Jeeter's creator, is doing something more interesting. He is situating the condition of Jeeter and his kind in terms that compel us to recognize need as a problem requiring a plurality of solutions. He is also asking us to attend to that condition as one that invites wonder as well as pity, a sense of awe along with feelings of rage—as we see that the forces traditionally associated with the idea of God, and the human desire for the divine, have as much a part to play in the story of the "poverty-ridden" as the longing for "rations and snuff."

"When the winter goes, and when it gets to be time to burn off broomsedge in the fields," Jeeter declares only a few sentences after the remarks just quoted, "I sort of want to cry." "It's in my blood—burning broomsedge and plowing in the ground this time of year," he explains, ". . . The land has got a powerful hold on me." Want is the fundamental condition of Jeeter's life; it prescribes his experience and his character. What is true for him is true for those around him. The first five chapters of *Tobacco Road*, after all, consist of a danse macabre of wanting, in which Jeeter Lester uses his daughter Ellie May to distract his son-in-law Lov in order to steal a bag of turnips from him. Here, hunger for food and for flesh play against each other. Shaped by their compulsions, characters like Ellie May are need given (barely) human form, grotesque vessels of longing: "Ellie May got down from the pine stump and sat on the ground. She moved closer and closer to Lov, sliding herself over the hard white sand. . . . 'Ellie May's acting like your old hound used to when she got the itch,' Dude said to Jeeter. 'Look at her scrape her bottom on the sand. That old hound used to make the same kind of sound Ellie May's making too. It sounds just like a little pig squealing, don't it?'"[67] If this is a drama of wanting, however, it is also a drama of watching. Dude is watching Ellie itch after Lov, as this passage makes only too clear. Jeeter watches. So do three black passersby at the gate to the Lester farm. And, as they watch, they all comment: all invite us to share with them, as it were, the role of a self-conscious audience, who can draw inferences, explanations for what they are seeing. Jeeter, for instance, once he has grabbed the turnips from Lov, pauses midway in his flight with his booty, to comment on their possible quality and the relationship between this and his own social condition. "Has these turnips got them damn-blasted green-gutted worms in them, Lov?" he inquires. "By God and by Jesus, if they're wormy, I don't know what I'm going to do about it. I been so sick of eating wormy turnips, I declare I almost lost my religion. It's a shame for God to let them damn-blasted green-gutted worms bore into my turnips. Us poor people always gets the worse end of all deals, it looks like to me."[68] Wanting, watching—and witnessing: what these

67. Caldwell, *Tobacco Road*, 24–25. See also 23. Caldwell's debt to southwestern humor was noted as early as 1933 by Van Doren, "Made in America," 444. The specific borrowings from the humorists are perhaps at their most obvious in *Georgia Boy* (New York, 1943), in which the boy of the title describes the antics of his "old man" and, in the process, draws the portrait of an entertaining, impoverished rascal not unlike George Washington Harris's Sut Lovingood (*Sut Lovingood: Yarns Spun by a "Natural Born Durn'd Fool"* [New York, 1867]). But it is in *Tobacco Road, God's Little Acre*, and perhaps *Tragic Ground* (New York, 1944), that the deeper purposes, as well as the surface structure, of southwestern humor come closest to being recovered.

68. Caldwell, *Tobacco Road*, 39. See also 176; *God's Little Acre* (1933; New York, 1961 edition), 170.

characters do, along with revealing and observing need is testify to causes. This is just as true of those who comment on the death of Jeeter and his wife, Ada, at the end of the novel ("Jeeter is better off now than he was. . . . He was near about starved to death half the time."), as it is of Ty Ty Walden in *God's Little Acre* whenever he observes the beauty or lovemaking of his daughters ("Did you ever see such a sight? . . . Now ain't that something?"). Death or love, labor or leisure, poverty and appetite: Caldwell's characters share a need to search for an understanding of the forces that drive them and their kind—to see, know, and explain, as well as to experience.

This is all by way of saying that the brutal comedy is not subverted by the social commentary or the more surreal, dreamlike elements of Caldwell's best stories. Each of these levels of the narrative plays off and into the others. The comedy situates the actions of the Lesters and the Waldens as spectacle, something that compels our—as well as the characters'—wondering attention. The commentary then places the comic spectacle for us. We, and they, are brought to look and then maybe begin to understand. Sometimes, as in that speech where Jeeter Lester looks around for someone to blame, the understanding is on shifting, slippery ground that alerts the reader, at least, to just how hard it is—though not impossible—to know human need and its reasons. At other times, some fragment of commentary supplies a shaft of insight. This is at its most obvious in, say, chapter 7 of *Tobacco Road,* where the narrator assumes an openly pedagogical role so as to alert us to the material causes of poverty among people like the Lesters. "Jeeter could never think of his land and goods as anything but a man-made calamity," the narrative voice informs us, before going on to explain that "an intelligent employment of his land, stocks, and implements would have enabled Jeeter, and scores of others . . . to raise crops for food and crops to be sold at a profit. Co-operative and corporate farming would have saved them all."[69] This is Caldwell at his most reformist. Awkward and openly didactic as it may sound, though, it works in context because that context is one that deploys comic exaggeration and distancing, and the habitual practices of

---

69. Caldwell, *Tobacco Road,* 65–66. See also 177; *God's Little Acre,* 108. Some of Caldwell's stories make clear the close relationship between the bizarre behavior and the acute poverty of his characters. See, e.g., "Daughter," in *The Complete Stories of Erskine Caldwell* (New York, 1953), 237, 239; "The Growing Season," in *Complete Stories,* 258–61.

watching and bearing witness, to make us examine these people as *cases*, freakish instances of a common condition. Constantly, almost compulsively, characters will turn aside from the absurdity of their situation so as to place it, for them and for us, to make a step toward understanding. Whether it is Lov after the death of Jeeter explaining "that was all he wanted in this life—growing cotton was better than anything else to him," or Will Thompson in *God's Little Acre* pointing out that cotton brokers are called that "because they keep the farmers broke all the time," these people seem to see themselves as odd, remarkable, worth a comment or attempt at explanation; they step back to join us in gazing in wonder at their strange ways, and the even stranger reasons for them.

As they step back in this way, something else that is extraordinary often occurs. Characters like Ty Ty Walden or Jeeter Lester, drawn into confiding and explaining, are also drawn closer to us, the readers. The narrative slips quietly and subtly from distance into a kind of intimacy. Bizarre though these people are, peculiar as their situation is, we are compelled to acknowledge compulsions, forces in them that suggest both their status as human subjects and their connections with, their *likeness* to us. "There was a mean trick played on us somewhere," Ty Ty Walden explains,

> —God put us in the bodies of animals and tried to make us act like people. That was the beginning of trouble. If He had made us like we are, and not called us people, the last one of us would know how to live. A man can't live, feeling himself from the inside, and listening to what the preachers say. He can't do both, but he can do one or the other. . . . A man has got God in him from the start, and when he is made to live like a preacher says to live, there's going to be trouble.[70]

This, like Ty Ty's hymns to sexuality—or, for that matter, Jeeter Lester's lyrical celebrations of the land ("The Lord made the land, and He put me here to raise crops on it")—suddenly sets up a circuit of feeling, a current of empathy between character and reader. We are forced to acknowledge, not just the very particular material conditions that dictate these people's lives, but the simple fact that, for all their freakishness, these *are* at bottom people, the terms of whose emotional and sensual lives are, after all, not that different from our own. Part of what we are

---

70. Caldwell, *God's Little Acre*, 299. See also *Tobacco Road*, 115.

asked to watch and witness, in other words, is our connection as human agents with these characters who, at first sight, might seem to have nothing to do with us. The narrative enforces an act of sympathy, and humility, as we learn that, freakish though they are, they have feelings and conflicts similar to our own.

It is worth emphasizing what Caldwell is doing here. He is not falling prey to confusion or vacillating between "the two [or more] Caldwells"; he is creating meaning out of the collision between different narrative approaches. The reader is drawn out and in, compelled both to observe the spectacle and to share; and all this is part of one project—to make us know what, up until then, has been the unknown. The clarity of Caldwell's prose, the apparently unpremeditated flow of his narratives, Caldwell's own avowed skepticism about "style" and his claim that "story . . . has to build itself as it goes": all this perhaps blinds us to the *writerly* nature of his work—to the way, that is, that, in his best books, different layers of the story play off of one another. The reader is invited on to the literary equivalent of a switchback ride—not to daze and confuse us but to prevent us from settling into complacency, the assumption that we already understand these people. And the switchback continues right up to the end. Certainly, both *God's Little Acre* and *Tobacco Road* close on a dreadful sense of circularity, the numbing repetitions of life, that recalls the novels of the new slavery: at the end of *God's Little Acre* Ty Ty returns to his familiar work of digging for gold, while *Tobacco Road* concludes with the son taking on the role of the dead father (" 'I reckon I'll get me a mule somewhere and some seed-cotton . . . and grow me a crop of cotton this year,' Dude said"). There is also a sense, however, of resilience, indefatigable optimism. Jeeter never gives up hope of raising a crop in spite of all the evidence to the contrary and, once gone, his son carries that hope on for him; similarly, Ty Ty never loses his belief that, if he cannot survive on what he puts into the ground, he may well prosper on what he gets out of it and goes back to digging for gold. Beliefs like these may, on the face of it, add to our sense of the absurdity, the grotesque innocence of such characters; it is less easy to deploy ideas of stoicism or phrases like "vein of iron" when describing them because the terms in which they express their refusal to surrender are so comic, so freakishly at odds with the facts. But it is difficult, on the other hand, simply to dismiss them out of hand or to see their continued faith in things as *merely* a matter for laughter. Ty Ty Walden bending over his shovel at the end of *God's Little Acre,* wondering how soon his son "would come back to help him dig," is not Judy Pippinger accepting "peace and decent acquiescence before the thing which had to be," or Piety Lantry finding pleasure in struggle. Nor, for that matter, is Dude Lester at the close of *Tobacco Road* absurdly speculating that "Maybe I could grow me a bale to the acre, like Pa was always talking about doing."[71] But neither are Dude and Ty Ty cowed into submission like Kirby Moten or Alvin Barnes, or simply comic witnesses to their own degradation in the manner of Fate Bollis or the Taylor family in *Men Working*. Caldwell has left them precisely poised between defeat and survival, freakishness and faith; it is a mark of their absurdity, and of a kind of dignity, that life has defeated them but they will not lie down. Engaging with different narrative strategies, we the readers find ourselves similarly poised between feelings of strangeness and kinship, the temptation to laugh and another inclination, to sympathize or even admire—we are drawn, in short, into the full possibilities of knowing.

Just how rich those possibilities can be is something measured by another dimension of these novels that moves us into the territory of silence and dream. This is a territory inhabited primarily, although not exclusively, by Caldwell's women. In *Tobacco Road,* the women characters are mostly quiet or even mute. At the beginning of the novel, Lov has come to speak to Jester about his wife—and Jester's daughter—Pearl who, we learn, "would not talk . . . would not say a word." She has "never talked," apparently. Only her mother, Ada, was able to converse with her before she married Lov, and once upon a time Ada was just like that, just as mute herself. Ada, the narrator confides, "had begun to talk voluntarily only during the past ten years"; before that, "Jeeter had had the same trouble with her that Lov was now having with Pearl." In turn, Pearl's sister and her grandmother are still like that: Ellie May is a mute witness to her own desperate sexual needs and, as for Mother Lester, "even when she was hungry or sick, no word had passed her lips." Of all the female characters in this book, only the preacher "Sister Bessie" Rice is given to talking almost as much as the men; the rest are quiet, almost silent witnesses to the spectacle—or, as in that opening scene where Ellie May drags herself toward Lov, they *are* the—equally silent—spectacle, the mute object of watching themselves. Things are different with the women in *God's Little Acre,* in a way. Rosamund, Darling Jill, and Gris-

71. Caldwell, *Tobacco Road,* 180. See also *God's Little Acre,* 303; MacDonald, "Introduction," xx.

elda all talk. What is emphasized about them, however, is not their talking but their status outside the parameters of language: the physical beauty about which Ty Ty is continually rhapsodizing, and their evidently inborn, mostly unstated knowledge of what Ty Ty calls "the secret of living." Male voyeurism runs through the book, and so does male hunger for the female. "They're that pretty," Ty Ty declares of his daughter-in-law's "rising beauties," "it makes me feel sometimes like getting right down on my hands and knees like these old hound dogs you see chasing after a flowing bitch. You just ache to get down and lick something." Oral and visual satisfaction are pursued as Ty Ty or Will Thompson or even Pluto Swint or the albino Dave gaze longingly at one or other of the three women, as they seek to slake a need that, as Ty Ty acknowledges, can never be slaked: "when you seen them once, that's only the start," he admits, ". . . every time you see them it makes you feel just a little bit more like that old hound dog I was talking about."[72] What is more, these elusive objects of desire seem to know intuitively what Ty Ty has to learn painfully and talk constantly about. "When you sit down by yourself and feel what's in you, that's the real way to live. It's feeling"; "the girls seemed to realize," he observes, "but the boys did not," they seem to understand about "the God inside of the body." Which is why, perhaps, the "girls" can act as quiet witnesses to the momentary presence of that God in the "boys" around them. When, for instance, Will Thompson declares, "I'm Will Thompson. I'm as strong as God Almighty," and then—in an extraordinarily surreal scene—tears off Griselda's clothes "quickly, eagerly, minutely," before making passionate love to her, all three main women characters respond in understanding silence. Darling Jill is excited ("Never before had she felt so completely aroused"); his wife, Rosamund, is a model of composure ("There was an expression of sereneness on Rosamund's face that was beautiful to behold"); Griselda herself looks up at Will "as if he were a precious idol come to life." All three of them seem to sense that Will is responding to the imperatives of "the real way to live"; all three seem to know his power.

And power is the heart of the matter here, in this landscape of silence and dream. The mills where Will works are at a standstill, due to a lockout; Will and other workers long to turn on the power—as if that act in

---

72. Caldwell, *God's Little Acre,* 128–29. See also 128, 221, 222, 225, 227, 261, 262, 269, 271; *Tobacco Road,* 10, 179.

itself will appease their hunger and give them back the sense of being in control they have lost. The need for each of them is to become what Ty Ty Walden calls "a real man" by feeling "the God inside of a body"; that need expresses itself in craving for the land, craving for the aural and visual satisfactions promised by woman, and, not least, craving for those forces that drive the engine of a modern society—money and energy. One critic, Lawrence Kubie, has astutely observed that *God's Little Acre* is "a story in symbolic language of the struggle of a group of men to win some fantastic kind of sustenance out of the body of the earth, the body of factories, and the bodies of women."[73] Stripped of economic power, the males of this novel feel their bodies have been assaulted too. They feel impotent and incomplete—it is noticeable that, in both *Tobacco Road* and *God's Little Acre,* watching sex appears to take priority over having it—and they pursue lost potency by grabbing feverishly for the modern coinage of power—gold in Ty Ty's case, of course, and in Will Thompson's, electricity. Fundamental to their experience is material need, but that need is then articulated *and experienced* as a mental, emotional, and sensual one. It is a matter of feeling and flesh: which is why social and sexual longing become coextensive in all Caldwell's best fiction, and especially in *God's Little Acre.* This surely is the explanation for one of the most haunting moments in the story of Ty Ty Walden and Will Thompson, when Will has a waking dream, a vision of women working in the mills. In other mills in other towns, he reflects, the women some time ago took over the work "because girls never rebelled against the harder work, the stretching-out, the longer hours, or the cutting of pay"; while they worked, the men "stood in the streets looking, but helpless." "When evening came," he continues in reverie, "the doors were flung open and the girls ran out screaming with laughter. When they reached the street, they ran back to the ivy-colored walls [of the mill] and pressed their bodies against it and touched it with their lips. The men who had been standing idly before it all day long came and dragged them home and beat them unmercifully for their infidelity."[74] This strange, surreal vision clearly connects social to sexual power: the women are "possessed" by the mill in every sense. And the impotence felt by the men is just as comprehensive. Deprived of "their" women, excluded from the magic circle

73. Lawrence Kubie, " 'God's Little Acre:' An Analysis," in *Critical Essays on Caldwell* edited by MacDonald, 163.
74. Caldwell, *God's Little Acre,* 98–99. See also 272.

of the workforce, they can only look helplessly on, and then find release for their frustration in violence. Mapped out here is the knowledge of what engenders need and drives hunger: the sense, or rather the conviction, haunting these men that they have been dispossessed of their bodies, deprived of themselves.

Animating this vision, of course, are the needs of the man who experiences it, Will Thompson. Like so many of Caldwell's characters, and especially his male ones, he is an animal and a dreamer: promiscuous, a heavy drinker, often brutal in language and actions, he is also driven by the appetite for something else, something to complete himself and confirm his status. He is, in a way, like one of Elizabeth Madox Roberts's idealists seen in a distorting mirror, a broken glass that highlights the freakish aspects of his character and the perverse behavior forced upon him by circumstance. The moment in *God's Little Acre* when he tries to realize his dream is like all such moments in Caldwell's better fiction. It exposes his illusions cruelly, but also confirms the sheer ferocity of his commitment; it unravels his mistakes as it underlines his need. The beginnings of this episode have been alluded to already. Enraged by the decision of the union to arbitrate, and so prepare the way for surrender, he becomes determined to realize his obsession and turn the power back on in the mill. "We can run the damn mill," he declares. "We can run it better than anyone else." With his mind now made up, he feels a fresh surge of energy rush through his body. "I'm Will Thompson," he announces, "I'm as strong as God Almighty Himself now, and I can show you how strong I am." "Just wait till tomorrow morning," he explains, ". . . I'm going up to that [mill] door and rip it to pieces like it was a window shade." There is, however, no need for the women to wait until the next morning to bear witness to this strength. They feel it already; and they can see it as he rips Griselda's clothes to pieces as a prelude to possessing her as he has always wanted to. "We're going to start spinning and weaving again tomorrow," he tells Griselda, "but tonight I'm going to tear that cloth on you till it looks like lint out of a gin." As an omen and imitation of what he is going to do tomorrow when he rips the mill door to pieces, Will's ripping apart of Griselda's dress links two kinds of violence, the social and the sexual, and confirms Will's growing sense of himself as a "real man." It is also, as Will himself suggests, an act of deconstruction, de-creation. Will's sense of himself depends in part on the work he has done, has recently been stopped from doing, but now hopes to do again. "I'm a loomweaver," he tells Griselda proudly, "I've woven cloth all my life, making every kind of fabric in God's world. Now I'm going to tear all that to pieces so small nobody will ever know what they were. They'll look like lint when I get through. . . . We're going to start spinning and weaving again tomorrow, but tonight I'm going to tear that cloth on you till it looks like lint out of a gin."[75] It is as if the surge of energy that has seized him compels him to go back to beginnings—to assert his power over the raw materials of his life by tearing down the present fabric of his life and then building something from that—a new work, a new body.

What follows the next day, when Will and the other workers briefly seize the mill, is at once an act of affirmation and a defeat. Will, asserting his will to power (the punning on his name is clumsy, but clearly intentional), turns the electricity back on and now tears *his* clothes, his shirt, to pieces before setting down to work with the other men. The linking of social and sexual energy is obvious enough: all the men tear their shirts off and throw them out of the windows before beginning work, while the "wild-eyed Valley girls with erect breasts" stand outside watching and bearing witness—"behind the mill windows," the narrator observes, "they would look like morning glories." For a moment, there is the scent of victory and potency recovered. But the guards in the mill then drive the men out; Will is killed and the power is, once again, turned off. The whole episode is a haunting mixture of naturalism and surreal fantasy: a mix caught, say, in that moment when the shirts torn off by the men, and thrown out of the windows, sail down through the air to lie "knee deep on the green" outside the mill, where "the three company sheep so fat had grazed for eighteen months."[76] It is typical of the finest moments in this novel, and *Tobacco Road,* in that it allows different narrative strategies to collide so as to help the reader understand fully the problems of loss and need. Will and his brothers in arms prove themselves to be "real men" to the extent that they momentarily try to take charge and, in the process, feel a rush of social and sexual energy. Their actions, issuing out of their earlier, comprehensive sense of their own impotence, confirm the point made by the book as a whole that poverty is something felt, first and last, in and by the body. The men experience material loss as a loss of control over their own flesh as well as their spirit; quite simply, to be poverty-ridden determines their consciousness of their bodies, their

75. Ibid., 224. See also 217, 221.
76. Ibid., 243. See also 241.

selves. Reversing the equation, they seek to grab back power, electricity, and the electric charge of sexuality, as if it were simply there for the asking and taking—as if, to put it simply, that power can be recovered in a quick rush of sexual excitement. The strength of a novel like *God's Little Acre* is that it shows just how complex is the algebra of need. Caldwell reveals how need circulates everywhere, in every direction; it is like a cancer eating into every area of the body and bodily consciousness. He shows how men cease to see themselves as men, how people lose a sense of dignity, and even a sense of identity, as they struggle to close the gap between having and wanting; and he also shows how the simple habit of wanting makes them something more than freaks—in their own way, as conflicted as ourselves. Seeking to unpack this subject in all its complexity, he attacks it from different angles: the reformist collides with the humorist in his work, naturalism mixes with the surreal, the social is experienced as the sexual. He does not, however, confuse these different angles or approaches. What we experience in *Tobacco Road* and *God's Little Acre* is, as it were, a plurality of equations, not a muddling of them; Caldwell uses many routes to his subject here but he does not mistake one for another. Nothing perhaps illustrates this better than the story of Will Thompson. Will is workless; Will feels debilitated, deprived of power in every respect. Caldwell clearly links lack of labor to other lacks here, as his character fights against his sense of a loss of manhood. What Caldwell certainly does not do, though, is what Will does: think that the whole process can just be rolled back, with recovery of manhood leading to a restoration of power and a return to work—that somehow repossession of the body means also repossession of the body politic. "I'm Will Thompson . . . strong as God Almighty": in the context of the novel as a whole, we can see both triumph and disaster, affirmation and error in that phrase. And the fact that we can is, surely, one measure of Caldwell's achievement; at his best, we feel, he *has* explained what it is and feels to be poor.

Just a year after Erskine Caldwell published his articles in the *New York Post*, the writer James Agee and the photographer Walker Evans accepted a commission from *Fortune* magazine to write a series of articles on the rural poor of the South. The two men spent about six weeks in Alabama, largely with three families; and, although the articles and photographs that came out of this were rejected by *Fortune*, they were eventually published, revised, and expanded, in the form of a book, *Let Us Now Praise*

Famous Men, in 1941. The book, a documentary, was typical of its time in many ways. Documentary did not spring suddenly into life in the 1930s, but it did assume a peculiar centrality as writers struggled to make known—and perhaps make sense of—the lives of the dispossessed. In the same year in which Agee and Evans stayed in Alabama, in fact, Caldwell and his wife, the photographer Margaret Bourke-White, traveled around the South. Out of *their* journey, too, came a book, *You Have Seen Their Faces,* published in 1937 and intended, as Caldwell later put it, "to show that the fiction I was writing was authentically based on contemporary life in the South."[77] What was different about *Let Us Now Praise Famous Men,* though, was its passionate self-reflexiveness; it is alive with Agee's sense of the difficulty, and maybe the impossibility, of his project. "This is a *book* only by necessity," he explains in the Preface. "More seriously, it is an effort in human actuality." "If I could do it, I'd do no writing at all here," he says elsewhere. "It would be photographs; the rest would be fragments of cloth, bits of cotton, lumps of earth, records of speech." "It is important that you should so far as possible forget that this is a book," Agee insists; "words cannot embody; they can only describe"; and, in trying to capture "the cruel radiance of what is," he finds himself, he claims, not only subdued to the element he works in but imprisoned by it. "All I want to do is tell this as exactly and clearly as I can and get the damned thing done with," he declares with exasperation; the problem is, the more he continues the more he becomes aware of the enormity of his task, the burden of properly knowing and telling.

This, the sheer intensity of focus on the tough job of understanding and writing a life is what makes *Let Us Now Praise Famous Men* unique; no other book about the lives of the rural poor in the South between the wars makes anything like so much of its own problematical status. To say that, however, is not to deny that those writers who turned to fiction to make those unknown lives known assumed that there was an immediate, single path to knowledge. They may not have protested the troublesome nature of their task as much as Agee, but that did not mean they

77. Caldwell, *Call It Experience: The Years of Learning How to Write* (New York, 1951), 163. See also James Agee and Walker Evans, *Let Us Now Praise Famous Men* (1941; London, 1965 edition), xv, 11, 12, 215, 219. For some discussion of documentary books like *Let Us Now Praise Famous Men* and *You Have Seen Their Faces* (New York, 1937), see Richard H. Pells, *Radical Visions and American Dreams: Culture and Social Thought in the Depression Years* (New York, 1973); William Stott, *Documentary Expression in Thirties America* (New York, 1973).

found the task an easy one or the way to handle it straightforward and obvious. One measure of that is the sheer range of their work, the many different ways in which these novelists attended to the poor and struggled to make their readers attend too. The quality of their novels is certainly variable. So too, however, is the nature of their approaches; as a result, terms like "social commitment" or "humor" cannot begin to chart all the territory they cover. And another gauge or measure of this is the poise, the care many individual novelists bring to their characters, making it clear that they see them as at once special and typical, the victims of very particularized forms of oppression and human agents very much like ourselves. "The nominal subject" of *Let Us Now Praise Famous Men,* Agee suggested "is North American cotton tenantry." "Actually," he added, "the effort is to recognize the stature of a portion of unimagined existence, and to contrive techniques proper to its recording, communication, analysis, and defense. More essentially, this is an independent inquiry into certain normal predicaments of human divinity."[78] Not all the writers who wrote about the poor country folk of the South during this period shared this aim with Agee. Arguably, though, the best of them did. They recorded what was specifically there in their locality, even while they linked it to other kinds of life, personal and social; they examined the conflicts peculiar to their characters and the agricultural system of the South, but did so along lines that enabled their readers to relate those conflicts to other systems, and other forms of consciousness. "Human divinity" may be a term that hardly seems to fit in some cases, because of the anger or leaden despair, the reforming zeal or humor, or the strange mixture of all these that fuels many of these stories. But some notion very close to this does drive many of these writers and, in the last analysis determine their agenda: as they struggle to make us aware of how their concerns connect with ours—how what they say humanly matters, in terms of what is and also what might be.

78. Agee and Evans, *Let Us Now Praise Famous Men,* xiv.

5

"Our contemporary ancestors"

Versions of the Mountain Folk (and Some River Folk)
Between the Two World Wars and Beyond

"The aristocrat of the mountains, living in quiet dignity and splendid isolation in the most primitive of wilderness homesteads . . . the aristocrat of the ridges is the lineal descendant of the pioneer families . . . and he cherishes the traditions of his clan. He resents the intrusions of the outlander who would peddle him clothes and religion. . . . The pure-stock mountain man may be poor in material goods, but he does not therefore welcome crude charity; he still considers a donkey of his own better than a horse of another's."[1] This small hymn to the virtues of

1. Maristan Chapman, "The Mountain Man," *Century Magazine* (February 1929), 507. See also 506, 508, 509. The authors of "The Mountain Man" were typical of commentators on this subject, not least, in their combination of apparent scientific precision and a fairly cavalier, romantic attitude toward matters of genealogy. The division of mountain folk into three supposedly sociological "types" was characteristic. So, too, was the confident assertion that the descent of the mountain folk was to be clearly traced from one dominant and vigorous strain, although opinion here was divided between those who, like Chapman, opted for "the Anglo-Saxon" and those who preferred to invoke a Scottish Highland or Scotch-Irish ancestry. For other examples of the division into "types," see John C. Campbell, *The Southern Highlander and His Homeland* (New York, 1921); Arthur W. Spaulding, *The Hills of Ca'liny* (Washington, D.C., 1921); S. T. Wilson, *The Southern Mountaineer* (New York, 1916). Among those who emphasize the Anglo-Saxon strain are Margaret W. Morley, *The Carolina Mountains* (Boston, 1913); Mandel Sherman and Thomas R. Henry, *The Hollow Folk* (New York, 1933); W. R. Thomas, *Life Among the Hills and Mountains of Kentucky* (Louisville, Ky., 1926). Those who favor the Scottish Highland heritage theory include William G. Frost, "The Southern Mountaineer," *American Monthly Review of Reviews*, XXI (March 1900), 303–11; W. H. Haney, *The Mountain People of Kentucky* (Cincinnati, 1906); J. P. McLean, *Scotch Highlanders in America*

mountain life and character is taken from an essay in *Century Magazine* published in February 1929. Called simply "The Mountain Man," the essay offers an unqualified and unambiguous celebration of its subject. The author, one Maristan Chapman, admitted that there might be different kinds of folk living in the Southern Appalachians. "In the quiet upland valleys of the Cumberlands," the reader was told, "are found pleasant farmsteads, good living conditions," and "a measure of community life," whereas in "the Plateau Belt . . . there has been much wasteful mining" and "in those desolate places that are left a few families of hand-to-mouth wastrels live . . . further pauperized by well-meaning if mistaken welfare workers." Nevertheless, while admitting that there might be no such thing as a "typical mountaineer," Chapman devoted most attention to—and bestowed utter devotion upon—the people of the high ridges. "The mountains here stand up sharply, in proud forested heights," Chapman declared, "with rich valleys hidden between." Here, in this idyllic remoteness, the mountain man cherished freedom ("freedom is his first insistence") and practiced "native decency." "He is a gentleman," the reader was informed; "there is a tough and sinewy forthrightness about the southern highlander that is part of his heritage." A natural aristocrat, "he is not put out by the jeers of those who count themselves his intellectual superiors"; and "if he holds a belief it is because it is his belief, and he means to defend his property." He was also, for the most part, an Anglo-Saxon—because, Chapman helpfully explained, "it is characteristic of that race to survive climatic difficulties and to refuse absorption into other races." In any event, "along with his directness and virility, the Anglo-Saxon has . . . the power of assimilation." So, even where mixing of a kind had occurred, he had taken "weaker racial strains to himself without apparently suffering any thinning down or dilution." Whatever mingling might have taken place among "the . . . races that first inhabited the mountains" had resulted in the triumph of the superior specimen: "the dominant Saxon, who remains to-day fair-haired and blue-eyed and very much himself."

"The Mountain Man" was followed a month after its publication by

---

(Cleveland, 1900). And among the many who focus on the Scotch-Irish theme are Horace Kephart, *Our Southern Highlanders: A Narrative of Adventure in the Southern Appalachians and a Study of Life Among the Mountaineers* (New York, 1922); James W. Raine, *The Land of Saddlebags: A Study of the Mountain People of Appalachia* (New York, 1924); Samuel H. Thompson, *The Highlanders of the South* (New York, 1910).

another article in *Century Magazine* entitled "American Speech as Practised in the Southern Highlands." This second essay revealed the original source of the fascination of mountain folk for Maristan Chapman— which was, as it turned out, a pseudonym for a husband and wife working together. "These people . . . speak a cultured backwoods tongue all their own," the reader learned, a true "Saxon tongue" and living relic of an earlier, purer form of speech. "We are now witnessing its period of decay," Chapman went on, but it still might "enrich our national speech"; "its gracious courtesy requires too much circumlocution for our daily use, but it may modify in some degree our extremes of 'pep,' 'snap,' or 'jazz.' "[2] The theme was one that was taken up, with a vengeance, in the fiction that the same husband-and-wife team published under the same name. *The Happy Mountain,* for instance, published in 1928 is awash with carefully cultivated archaisms and dialect, while a young mountain hero in *The Weather Tree,* which appeared four years later, declares that he will not dilute his speech to cater to strangers—on the contrary, he says, "I'll speak to the outlander with the proud tongue of my own race." This originating interest in speech anchored the hymn to the mountain man in something very basic and quite specific: the words of the Southern highlander *were* his world, the contention was. His way of life was caught and explained in the still living tissue of his language; and what that language disclosed was a story of survival against the odds. With a curious mixture of populist hope and antiquarian nostalgia that they were neither the first nor the last to exploit, the team that called themselves Maristan Chapman celebrated what they called "a speech, a philosophy of life, and a culture that stopped in the eighteenth century" when the mountain folk first came to the mountains. They commemorated its survival over the passage of time; they lamented its passing with the invasion of the highlands by the exploiters, industrialists, folklorists, and educators, and the migration of many highlanders to the lumber camps, mills, mining towns, and factories; and they expressed a belief in the possibility, at least, of recovery and recuperation—the absorption,

2. Maristan Chapman, "American Speech as Practised in the Southern Highlands," *Century Magazine* (March 1929), 623. See also 617; *The Weather Tree* (New York, 1932), 40; "Mountain Man," 509. Also *The Happy Mountain* (New York, 1928), 5, 14–15. For other examples of the interest in the curiosities of mountain speech and custom, see Caroline Gardner, *Clever Country: Kentucky Mountain Trails* (New York, 1931); Wayman Hogue, *Back Yonder* (New York, 1932).

that is, of some of the mountain speech and spirit into the national mainstream. "The direct speech" of the highlander "is never rudeness," the reader was told, "he never need apologize for his words or deeds, because he says and does what he believes to be right"; and "the spirit is uncompromisingly individualistic." "Whatever befall the mountain people today," "The Mountain Man" concludes, "the stuff of the stock is indestructible; the spirit will animate the race. If the people are scattered and taken up into the body of the nation, so much the better for the nation, for it is a gallant and generous spirit."[3] An emblem both of past pastoral perfection and possible regeneration in a more urban future, the Southern highlander was a figure calculated to appeal. Marginal he might seem, but his very marginality was the secret of his success—thanks to it, the argument was, the figure of the Anglo-Saxon pioneer had survived, just, into the present. More to the point, any hero like this, drawing his strength from his rural apartness, was likely to have particular resonance for a region that had built its identity on being similarly apart and different.

The resonance of the figure of the mountain man—and, sometimes, the mountain woman—for the regional imagination goes back to a period well before those two articles appeared in *Century Magazine*. The story of the Southern mountains, especially during the nineteenth century, could in fact be summed up as "like the South, only more so": what captivated those who searched out and celebrated the figure of the mountaineer was precisely his status, as they saw it, as a heroic paradigm, an example in small and in extremis of the best that was ever thought and said about the South. Even if we look at the beginnings of the story of the mountain folk, we can find a sort of heightened typicality in their acute isolation—they tended to go one better than all their neighbors in the region even in their simple, initial ability to cut themselves off from the rest of the world. Like other Southerners, the mountain people were isolated from the dominant historical tendencies of the nineteenth century; their society, once established (mostly in the early days of the Republic), seemed more or less immune to the industrial revolution and urban drift. They seemed to carry that isolation much further than other Southerners did, however, so that even the few symptoms of change that

3. Chapman, "Mountain Man," 509–10. For further examples of this belief in the redemptive possibilities of the mountain folk, see H. J. Ford, *The Scotch-Irish in America* (Princeton, 1915); Samuel Tyndale Wilson, *The Southern Mountaineers* (New York, 1914).

did appear in other parts of the region—like improved methods of transport and communication—hardly impinged on their lives at all. For more than a hundred years they lived in a historical vacuum, largely unaffected by events occurring elsewhere, like some outpost of empire that had been colonized and then simply forgotten. People living in the last decades of the nineteenth century sang the same ballads as their ancestors had sung, and used the same primitive methods of farming and bartering. Of course, the inaccessibility of the highland areas had something to do with this strange situation, but the sheer indifference of the "outlanders" (as mountain folk liked to call their neighbors) also played a part. The highlands were relatively barren ground, and there was little interest in them for most people while the lands to the West were still to be opened up. So they remained an undiscovered country inhabited by a race who, apparently out of weakness or stubbornness or both, preferred what they found there to the more fertile and more contested soil of other areas.[4]

Then, in the last few years of the nineteenth century, the "outlanders" slowly began to take notice. The West had been appropriated, the possibility of coal mining and timber farming in the highlands was being explored and, as symptoms of the changing attitude, a number of travelers and anthropologists made the long trek into the Southern highlands, to bring back reports of the people and way of life they found there. For some of these observers, it was like rediscovering the past. Here, they claimed, were the good old days of rural simplicity perfectly preserved, in a setting that might have been designed by a utopian pastoralist. William G. Frost was typical of these observers when he referred to the mountain folk, in an article for *Atlantic Monthly* published in 1899, as "our contemporary ancestors" and, as such, demonstrating virtues—indelibly attached in the regional and national imagination to those who labor in the earth—that the rest of society seemed to have lost. The phrase, "our contemporary ancestors," was taken up by, among others, the popular novelist John Fox Jr., who has a character in his 1908 story

---

4. For some detailed discussions of this period see, e.g., Edward L. Ayers, *The Promise of the New South: Life After Reconstruction* (New York, 1992); George Brown Tindall, *The Emergence of the New South, 1913–1945* (1967), vol. X of *A History of the South* edited by Wendell Holmes Stephenson and E. Merton Coulter (13 vols.; Baton Rouge, La., 1947–95); Comer Vann Woodward, *The Origins of the New South, 1877–1913* (1951), vol. IX of *History of the South* edited by Stephenson and Coulter. The bibliographies of these books offer a wealth of material on the Southern mountain people of this period, as does the *Appalachian Journal*.

The Trail of the Lonesome Pine refer to highlanders in precisely these terms. "Within the two days' gallop of a thoroughbred," a heroine of an earlier Fox story, *The Kentuckian,* observes, "were people living like pioneers, singing folk songs centuries old, talking the speech of Chaucer, and loving, hating, fighting and dying like the clans of Scotland."[5] As Frost and Fox illustrate, some of these accounts of highland life claimed to be fact, while others confessed themselves as fiction based on fact. All of them, however, were characterized by the need to locate a regional ideal in the newly discovered territory. By the time those articles by Maristan Chapman appeared, the legend of the mountain people was at its height. Here, for example, is a paean to the highlander and his way of life taken from a book published in 1921:

> The Highlander is the true American, and the type of American usually seized upon as representative of all Highlanders is the early pioneer type. The pioneer is, indeed, still to be recognized in many of his mountain descendants—tall, lean, clear-eyed, self-reliant, never taken by surprise, and of great endurance. . . .
>
> We have, then, in the Southern Highlander an American, a rural dweller of the agricultural class, and a mountaineer who is still more or less of a pioneer. His dominant trait is independence raised to the nth power.[6]

"By their very isolation," another observer of the mountain people claimed, "they have preserved much that is best in America." That was a common theme. "In the recesses of the Appalachian Mountains," readers were assured, ". . . fundamental elements of the American character are found today in stark simplicity," offering a "rich deposit of Americanism," the "unspoiled heritage of the American people." There might be some, implicit disagreement about just how old this "old-fashioned" culture of the highlands was. Some talked of a people "still living in the eighteenth century"; others preferred to invoke "Shakespeare's America" or "the language of the 'Canterbury Tales' "; still others maintained that the mountain people had kept "alive and fresh in memory the unwritten song, the speech, the tradition of their Anglo-Saxon and Anglo-Celtic

---

5. John Fox Jr., *The Kentuckian* (New York, 1897), 67. See also *The Trail of the Lonesome Pine* (New York, 1908), 97; William G. Fox, "Our Contemporary Ancestors in the Southern Mountains," *Atlantic Monthly,* LXXXII (March 1899), 311–19.

6. Campbell, *Southern Highlander and His Homeland,* 72, 91.

ancestors." "We have with us today," declared one excited traveler and observer in 1922, "in flesh and blood, the Indian-fighter of our colonial border—aye, back of him, the half-wild clansman of elder Britain. . . . Here, in great part, is spoken today the language of Piers the Plough-man."[7] Despite such disagreements about precisely which past was being preserved in the mountains, however, the consensus was still there. The mountain man was a "frontiersman." For that matter, there was "some-thing magnificent" both in the men and the women. Together, they be-trayed all the best tendencies of the "pioneer-farmer." "Patience, endurance, and resignation are written in the close-set mouths" of the mountain folk, these observers declared; "life has been one long, hard, cruel war against elemental powers" and out of this had grown an abid-ing love of the soil and "the most outright independence to be won on earth." "Man is close to the soil here," one female traveler commented in 1913. "He loves the land"; along with that, man and woman had learned, as another observer put it, "rugged independence" and a fierce "regard for personal honor."[8] The ferocity of this individualism did not, evidently, prevent the mountain folk—and, in particular, the mountain men—from showing the same "clan loyalty" as their pioneer ancestors. They were ready to fight for their own as well as themselves; and they were, according to most of these commentators, "never laggard in de-fense of their country." This, the fighting spirit of the highlander, was a favorite theme; and it perhaps never received more piquant expression than on the occasion when the World War I leader Sir Douglas Haig was brought in to provide the appropriate approving comment. Talking of the 30th Division of the U.S. Army, composed largely of men from the mountains of Tennessee, Haig was quoted as crediting these men for the first break in the supposedly impregnable Hindenburg Line and then add-ing this gloss: "Ninety per cent of the men were pure Anglo-Saxon. No division is so truly American. . . . Tall, lean, and corn-fed. . . . Silent

7. Kephart, *Our Southern Highlanders*, 285. See also Jean Thomas, *Blue Ridge Coun-try* (New York, 1942), 3; Raine, *Land of Saddlebags*, 62; Vance Randolph, *The Ozarks: An American Survival of Primitive Society* (New York, 1931), 41; Alberta P. Hannum, "The Mountain People," in *The Great Smokies and the Blue Ridge: The Story of the South-ern Appalachians* edited by Roderick Peattie (New York, 1943), 85; Morley, *Carolina Mountains*, 171.

8. Morley, *Carolina Mountains*, 35; W. D. Weatherford, *Pioneers of Destiny* (Bir-mingham, Ala., 1955), 64, 67. See also Campbell, *Southern Highlander and His Homeland*, 93, 140; Kephart, *Our Southern Highlanders*, 339, 380, 387.

and polite men, used to solitudes, thinking definitely and simply in old-fashioned terms of life and death, they were touched with the crusade spirit from their very origin . . . more intensely than dwellers in the cities."[9] Clearly, the belief in the simple virtues as well as the racial purity of the mountain folk was not confined just to those who traveled there, or lived nearby.

Comments like those of Haig suggest, perhaps, just how closely the figure of the mountain man in these supposedly factual accounts could be accommodated, not only to the Jeffersonian/Agrarian idea of the happy farmer, but also to the national blueprint for the American Adam. Taciturn and yet also "leisurely and friendly," with "an economy of words that does not betoken a scarcity of ideas," the highlander was depicted in these reports as a kind of Christian noble savage—with his very Christianity, "part mysticism, part fatalism," suggesting the quiet strength and rough poetry of his character. "The mountaineer is very old-fashioned," one commentator insisted, "so old-fashioned that he values native shrewdness above what he calls 'book-larnin;' so old-fashioned that he thinks his neighbors as good as himself, and himself as good as his neighbors, irrespective of who has the biggest corn-field; and so old-fashioned that he believes progress to be a menace against his personal freedom."[10] Another commentator revealed even more frankly the vein of nostalgic utopianism he was tapping in his report on the mountain folk. Southern highlanders, he declared, were "the last remnant of the undefiled"; "in these mountains," he added, "is the original stuff of which America was made"; and Americans would do well to learn what they could from "this distinctively American race." Self-sufficient but also hospitable and loyal, simple but also wise, undemonstrative and taciturn but also deeply attached to certain pieties and people: the mountain man offered access to the past, according to these accounts, and a possible beacon for the future. The mountain woman played a subsidiary role in all these narratives—as, for that matter, she does in the myths they recollect; the image

9. North Callahan, *Smoky Mountain Country* (New York, 1952), 104. See also Levi W. Powell, *Who Are These Mountain People?* (New York, 1966), 27.

10. Morley, *Carolina Mountains*, 145–46. See also Edwin E. White, *Highland Heritage: The Southern Mountains and the Nation* (New York, 1937), 23; Ford, *Scotch-Irish in America*, 573; Campbell, *Southern Highlander and His Homeland*, 140; Powell, *Who Are These Mountain People?*, 26–27; Arthur W. Spaulding, *The Men of the Mountains: The Story of the Southern Mountaineer and His Kin of the Piedmont* (Nashville, Tenn., 1915), 44.

of her "watching, waiting, enduring, succouring," though, complemented the figure of her man, fearing only God and loving nothing more
than the land, and filled out the sense, or rather the conviction, spelled
out again and again by observers that this world hidden in the folds of
the Appalachians and Ozarks represented a return to an earlier, simpler,
and purer America.

The point about all this is not, of course, that it was absolutely and
positively wrong: even the articles written under the name of Maristan
Chapman had some valid, valuable comments to offer on mountain life
and language. What these commentators had to say about the life of the
Southern highlands contained elements of fact; the problem was that the
portrait as a whole was selective to the point of simplification, and even
distortion. Highlanders did, certainly, preserve many facets of an older
way of life, ranging from the songs they sang and the ring dances they
enjoyed to some more primitive beliefs that helped locate them "just a
step and a jump from the Middle Ages";[11] and these supplied some reason for a connection between them and the heroes and heroines of agrarian myth. To make the connection while hardly qualifying it, however
(which was what most of these observers did), was to ignore, or at least
minimize, the radical difficulties of mountain existence that went along
with its pleasures—the things that made a comparison with rural ideals
problematical. The mountain people had, after all, been *forced* into the
mountains in the first place. Like the backwoodsmen discovered by the
Southwestern humorists of the nineteenth century, they had been deprived of the rich tillage of the seaboard and delta country, and the land
to which they had retreated was in many ways a last resort. This was not
exactly the perfect location for a rediscovery of what Jefferson had called
"the chosen people of God"; in a way, with its barren ground and the
root attitude of defensiveness shown (often with justification) by its inhabitants, it was more a paradigm of rural poverty—an example of the
hardships issuing from an unequal distribution of the land and other resources—than it was a subject ready for mythologizing. Anyone who did
not take this aspect of mountain life into account, and try to come to
terms with it, lay themselves open to the charge of romanticism, or just
simple daydreaming.

11. Charles C. Givens, *The Devil Takes a Hill-Town* (New York, 1939), 30. The interest in what were considered to be the superstitious beliefs and practices of mountain people
can be seen in, e.g., Muriel E. Sheppard, *Cabins in the Laurel* (Chapel Hill, N.C., 1935);
Thomas, *Blue Ridge Country*.

The charge became all the more appropriate, and forceful, as time passed and the mythologizing got well under way. For a special irony here was the one alluded to already: people like Frost and later the husband-and-wife team of Maristan Chapman, whatever else they might have been, were the heralds of change. They represented different stages in an invasion that was to end by destroying such few claims as the mountaineer ever had to identification with the good farmer of legend. The "outlander" came in to observe the "old, common, native"[12] customs, and, by the mere act of coming in, tore down the barriers that had helped preserve those customs. The highlander's contact with the outside world, which had been minimal for over a century, was being renewed at the very moment when highland life was being celebrated for its habits born of isolation. The vacuum in which the old dispensation had been preserved had been punctured; a breach had been made and through it, along with the folklorists, anthropologists, linguists, and other observers, poured every kind of feasible business investment. Mines and factories were opened up, cities were built, and a tourist industry gradually developed. Mountain folk could be tempted into work that paid an apparently steady wage—especially if they found themselves dispossessed of the land they had thought their own—while people from outside could come in their thousands to look at the communities they were helping to destroy. It is a familiar story, especially in these days of international investment and mass tourism but it is not, for that or any other reason, a less striking or less significant one.

Some of that story *was* told by the commentators on mountain life writing in the earlier part of this century. Even Maristan Chapman, as we have seen, admitted that mountain life and mountain idioms were "now," in the 1920s, in a "period of decay"; and others were more forthright. One observer, writing in 1926, lamented what he called "the superimposition of twentieth-century industrialism upon a community of self-sufficient households" in the Southern highlands; another, twelve years later, complained that "the twentieth century is pushing back further into

12. Thomas Wolfe, *The Web and the Rock* (New York, 1939), 30. I have not explored the issue of Wolfe's own relationship with the Southern Appalachians here, partly because I want to examine the achievement of other, mostly neglected writers from the mountains, partly because that relationship was peculiarly problematical (so problematical, in fact, that many critics would resist seeing him in these terms), and not least because I have already attempted to explore this whole question in *The Literature of Memory: Modern Writers of the American South* (Baltimore, Md., 1977), 133–49.

the mountains each year." On the whole, the amateurs and specialists who traveled into the Appalachians or Ozarks were not reluctant to concede that, as one of them put it in 1921, "commercialism has discovered the mountains." Some even went further: as a book published in 1933 admitted, "in the second decade of the twentieth century the balance between the old and the new way of life began to be upset" with the arrival of a "machine age in the hills."[13] With a few exceptions, however, these concessions to the fact of change did not go very deep or last very long. What commentators from Frost to Chapman and beyond found spellbinding, and dwelt upon, was the recollection of older, agrarian pieties; in many cases, what also haunted their imaginations was the possibility of recuperation, the recovery of some "kernel"—which is to say, the substance or essence of "the true American"—by others outside the highland regions. To this extent, their anthropological exercises, amateur or professional, were an act of narrativity, imaginative creation: they were engaged in making, reinventing what they saw. They were creating an idea of the mountain folk that was fired into life as much by notions of the marginal (and its uses) and ideals of the pastoral (in their regional/ national forms) as by anything that could be called experience or evidence. An eminent historian of the Southern Appalachians, writing in 1962, summed up the changes occurring in mountain life in the early twentieth century by saying this: "The growth and improvement of public education . . . rural electrification . . . mass communication . . . improved roads . . . all contributed to the weakening of traditional values. . . . It was a period of novel experience, new opportunities . . . and after it was all over there would be no complete return to the old ways."[14] With the change of a "way of life," the historian observes, has

13. Malcolm Ross, *Machine Age in the Hills* (New York, 1933), 53. See also Thomas, *Life Among the Hills and Mountains of Kentucky*, 8; Elizabeth S. Bowman, *Land of High Horizons* (Kingsport, Tenn., 1938), 22; Kephart, *Our Southern Highlanders*, 454. For other powerful accounts of economic and social transformation in the Southern highlands between the two world wars, see, e.g., J. Wesley Hatcher, "Appalachian America," in *Culture in the South* edited by William T. Couch (Chapel Hill, N.C., 1934); M. T. Matthews, *Experience Worlds of Mountain People: Institutional Efficiency in Appalachian Village and Hinterland Communities* (New York, 1937); Jennings J. Rhyne, *Some Southern Cotton Mill Workers and Their Villages* (Chapel Hill, N.C., 1930).

14. Thomas R. Ford, "The Passing of Provincialism," in *The Southern Appalachian Region: A Survey* edited by Thomas R. Ford (Lexington, Ky., 1962), 30–31. See also 34; W. D. Weatherford and Wilma Dykeman, "Literature Since 1900," in *Southern Appalachian Region: A Survey* edited by Ford, 260–61.

come a profound alteration of the entire experience world of the mountaineer; gradually, in "their beliefs, their fears, and their aspirations,"
mountain people have grown to be "not radically different from . . . most
other Americans." This was an outcome that those earlier observers of
highland life were reluctant to admit; memory and desire were mixed
almost equally in their accounts, as they recollected the virtues of their
"contemporary ancestors." In this context, another comment made by
some other fairly recent commentators on highland life acquires additional point and poignancy. "Almost totally overwhelmed, in many parts
of the [Appalachian] region," they argue, the traditional arts and way of
life of the highlands "may well find their last refuge between the covers
of a few books."

Those "few books" are, in fact, many. Quite apart from the literary
excursions of travelers and observers, they include works that declare
themselves to be fiction. The people of the Southern highlands were, in
fact, the subject of a rich vein of stories that built upon the sense of their
being special and separate. Sometimes admitting the pressure of change
and sometimes not, these stories—written in the first half of this century
and, for the most part, between the two world wars or just after—are
remarkable for the way they illustrate how a sense of pastoral possibility
began to focus on the mountains just at the moment when all residual
elements of pastoral were disappearing there. There had been earlier fictional attempts to record and celebrate the special qualities of mountain
life, of course; and there were, during this period, a few attempts to claim
that "simple country people still exist" in other backwaters of Southern
life. And the novelists who turned their attention to the Southern mountains need perhaps to be seen in the context of these earlier writings about
the highlander, and contemporary accounts of rural nobility surviving on
the margins—as well, that is, as in terms of the crisis mountain life was
facing at the time and the often highly imaginative reports of travelers
and professional observers. To take the earlier writings first: the first notable appearance of the Southern mountaineer is as a minor character in
antebellum romances like *The Valley of Shenandoah* (1826) by George
Tucker, *Guy Rivers* (1834) by William Gilmore Simms, and *George Balcombe* (1836) by Nathaniel Beverley Tucker. Although a marginal figure,
he is distinctly drawn. George Tucker calls *his* mountain character a
"worthy" and "free-spoken man;" Nathaniel Beverley Tucker describes
his as a "trusty henchman" of the hero and in another novel, *The Partisan Leader* (1836), introduces a similarly "sturdy mountaineer" to the

ranks of his secondary figures. Another writer of the time, John Lewis, in a romance entitled *Young Kate* (1844), also opts for the phrase "trusty henchman"[15] to sum up *his* highland character: a man who, in the manner of his kind, offers the gentlemanly heroes of the story what he calls an "eddication" in frontier ways—showing them the trail through the highland wilderness, and teaching them how to use a tomahawk and a knife. Distinctly drawn, the mountain man was—as all these details suggest—already granted the standard characteristics of the simple yeoman type: qualities that disqualified him from the status of hero—that was preserved for his wealthier lowland neighbors—but also made him an embodiment of the best possibilities of democratic pastoral. Those possibilities were taken up, and then developed, by other writers writing just before or after the Civil War, notably John Esten Cooke and Sidney Lanier. In Cooke's *Leatherstocking and Silk* (1854), for example, an old mountain man, living in a rough and ready cabin (a reminder, we are told, of his "picturesque past") is made to represent the simplicity of pioneer existence in distinct contrast to the elaborate artificialities of village life ten miles away. Similarly, in Lanier's novel, *Tiger-Lilies* (1867), a minor character called Cain Smallin is described as a "tall, raw-boned,

---

15. John Lewis, *Young Kate* (New York, 1844), 1. See also 63; George Tucker, *The Valley of Shenandoah* (New York, 1824), 49; Nathaniel Beverley Tucker, *George Balcombe* (New York, 1836), 193. In *Guy Rivers* (New York, 1834) by William Gilmore Simms and *The Counterfeiters* (New York, 1834) by Thomas Singularity, the mountain characters possess similar qualities. In *The Counterfeiters,* for instance, mountaineers are described as "obliging, generous, hospitable, and faithful to friends." If occasionally they break the law, we are told, it is as a result of drinking and recklessness and not because of "corrupted hearts" (145). Their few vices as well as their many virtues are, in effect, a product of their simplicity, social dependence, and marginal status. Some of the most useful information concerning the Southern mountaineers remains unpublished or relatively difficult to obtain. It includes Louise C. Boger, *The Southern Mountaineer: A Bibliography* (Morgantown, W.Va., 1964); Carvel Collins, "Nineteenth-Century Fiction of the Southern Appalachians," *Bulletin of Bibliography,* XVII (1943), 186–90, 251–57 and "The Literary Tradition of the Southern Mountaineer, 1824–1900" (Ph.D. diss., University of Chicago, 1944); Thomas D. Edward, "A Critical Study of the Literature Portraying the Mountain Folk of Eastern Kentucky and Tennessee" (M.A. thesis, University of Southern California, 1939); Everett E. Edwards, "References to the Mountaineers of the Southern Appalachians," United States Department of Agriculture Bibliographical Contributions No. 28 (Washington, D.C., 1935); Isabella D. Harris, "The Southern Mountaineer in American Fiction, 1824–1910" (Ph.D. diss., Duke University, 1948); Ruth F. Lewis, "The Southern Mountaineer in Fiction" (M.A. thesis, University of Virginia, 1929); John A. McLeod, "The Southern Highlands in Prose Fiction" (M.A. thesis, University of North Carolina at Chapel Hill, 1930).

muscular mountaineer"; and the reader is invited to admire him, not only for his strength and simplicity, but also for his proud and sensitive nature. Admiration was one thing, though, imaginative sympathy or an acknowledgment of subjectivity something else again. In one novel of the time, *Our Cousin Veronica* (1855) by M. C. W. Latimer, "mountain men . . . looking as wild as untamed colts" suddenly erupt on to the scene: that registers the sense of strangeness, part respectful and part fearful, that lies behind many of these portraits. In another novel, Cooke's *The Virginia Bohemians* (1880), an old moonshiner, having outwitted the local sheriff, invites him to "come agin," adding with glee, "we poor mounting people like to meet with strangers. . . . If I hear anything of them moonshiners I might drop you a word."[16] That registers the other side of the same equation. Caged in dialect, the mountain character becomes a white variation on the theme of Brer Rabbit—an outsider whose native intelligence enables him to outwit his supposedly more knowledgeable neighbors, but an outsider, a stranger nevertheless. There is no room for such characters, serious or comic, at the center of the narrative; on the contrary, their strength and interest for their creators derive precisely from the fact that they *are* peripheral.

The further chapters to this tale of the Southern highlander in earlier fiction are supplied by two witnesses to the beginning of the end of highland isolation, Mary Noailles Murfree and a writer mentioned earlier, John Fox Jr. For both of them, writing at the turn of the century, mountaineers were "our contemporary ancestors." What appealed to each, though, as far as the specifics of this past recollected in the present were concerned, was interestingly and influentially different. For Murfree, it was what she saw as the breathtaking scenery and simple home surroundings of mountain life, the idiosyncratic, antique language of the mountaineer, and the homely customs, and odd, illogical beliefs of mountain society. The general approach was lively, interested, and inquisitive; the mountain folk were now granted detailed attention. The sense of strangeness, distance, and diminishment was hardly reduced, however, not least because Murfree was unable mostly to see her highland characters as anything other than picturesque specimens: "placed" by their

16. John Esten Cooke, *The Virginia Bohemians* (New York, 1880), 101. See also *Leatherstocking and Silk; or, Hunter John Myers and His Times* (New York, 1854), 160; Sidney Lanier, *Tiger-Lilies* (New York, 1867), 6; M. C. W. Latimer, *Our Cousin Veronica* (New York, 1855), 277.

quaint forms of speech (which Murfree played with to excess), notable for their curious indifference to the landscapes about them, marked by their ignorance of the world outside, their superstition, and their utter dislike of change. The tone was respectful, at times: we are told, for instance, in Murfree's *In the Tennessee Mountains,* of "a hospitality that meets a stranger on the threshold of every hut, presses upon him, ungrudgingly, its best." On other occasions, it was rather more patronizing: in the same volume, Murfree describes for us a dance at which the "awkward young mountaineers clogged heavily . . . with the stolid-looking, lack-lustre maids of the hill." Consistently, though, the mountain folk emerged as emblems, pictures from an exhibition of rustic curios. Even the female characters, to whom Murfree paid more attention than any of her predecessors, corresponded for good or ill with a familiar typology: the weary but defiant women in *In the Tennessee Mountains* who neither expect nor receive sympathy for their trials, the romantic heroines of other books and stories with eyes like "limpid mountain streams," hair like "skeins of sunshine," and, invariably, "an exquisitely fair complexion."[17] The approach was not precisely that of either the literary tourist or the antiquarian, but there was enough of the voyeurism of the one and the specialist curiosity of the other to short-circuit any sustained current of sympathy between author/narrator and reader. As one critic has observed of Murfree's stories, "our most profound interest is not in *why* the characters do what they do; they act as they do because they *are* the kind of people they are." The narrative works only to the extent that the reader is fascinated by the sheer strangeness of the mountain characters and convinced that they are, in human terms, utterly aberrant.

Different kinds of narrative are deployed in the—once equally popular—stories of John Fox Jr.: the encounter, and sometimes the romance, between highlander and lowlander, tales of feuding, moonshining, and violence. Fox is, if anything, even more willing than Murfree is to emphasize the ancient, unsullied character of the mountain blood line and language. In one of his stories, for instance, Fox has his hero conclude that

17. Mary Noailles Murfree, *The Juggler* (New York, 1897), 69; *In the Clouds* (New York, 1886), 100; *His Vanished Star* (Boston, 1894), 8–9. See also *In the Tennessee Mountains* (New York, 1884), 139, 227; Thomas Daniel Young, *Tennessee Writers* (Knoxville, Tenn., 1981), 15. Also Edd W. Parks, *Charles Egbert Craddock* (Chapel Hill, N.C., 1941); Richard Cary, *Mary Noailles Murfree* (New York, 1967) ("Charles Egbert Craddock" was the pseudonym of Mary Noailles Murfree).

his mountain sweetheart belongs to "a race whose descent . . . was un-mixed English; upon whose lips lingered words and forms of speech that Shakespeare had heard and used."[18] If anything, though, he is even less willing than Murfree to challenge the unwritten rule that, being a primi-tive, pioneer type, the mountaineer cannot assume the subjectivity and status of the hero figure. Pretty mountain women are educated by their lowland lovers before undergoing a miraculous transformation in lan-guage, manner, and dress that makes them appropriate brides. Simple mountain men are suddenly discovered to have aristocratic ancestors be-fore they can be considered worthy of marriage to the ladies of the low-land. Despite all his talk of the racial purity and antiquity of the mountain people, in fact, Fox does not release his mountain characters from the margins of the narrative in anything other than the most literal sense. And where the magic wand of the author is not transforming them into acceptable, marriageable types, it is their backwardness, and an idio-syncrasy bred of isolation, that compel narrative attention. Very often, Fox's fictional highlanders recollect the poor white folk described by the Southwestern humorists. Violent and comic, they rally their debtors to their side in a feud (in "A Cumberland Vendetta") or sign a truce, an agreement to stop feuding for a while, in order to negotiate a land deal or elect a Republican to office (in *The Heart of the Hills*). Viewed with a mixture of amusement, curiosity, and wonder, these highland characters are not even allowed the chance of a sentimental education. As long as they remain *mountain* people—and are not, that is, the subjects of some strange process of social transformation—they are assigned a subject(ed) status. They are not permitted, any more than the "trusty henchman" of earlier Southern fiction was, to claim the due rewards of the guarantor of seriousness in a fiction: centrality, subjectivity, the chance to give the story the sense of an ending.

If the Southern highlander and his homeland came gradually to attract the interest of those searching out their contemporary ancestors, then so too did the inhabitants of another neglected corner of the region—the people of the river. The literature on this particular margin of Southern society is certainly less extensive than that on the mountains and moun-taineers, but it bears witness to a shared impulse. Like those who began to observe and write in detail about the Appalachians and Ozarks from

18. John Fox Jr., *A Cumberland Vendetta and Other Stories* (New York, 1896), 8. See also 118; *The Heart of the Hills* (New York, 1913), 33.

the early years of this century on, the celebrants of river life were searching out a place in the present that somehow preserved some of the rural practices and pieties of the past—and, perhaps, offered a moral resource for the future. "There is a last frontier in America," one observer writing in 1938 declared, "where men still live with their fishing lines and rifles in almost as primitive a fashion as the pioneers who set out for the West a hundred and fifty years ago. This frontier extends along the Mississippi River and its tributaries."[19] There were several correspondences between this, in the main reverential, account of river life and the emerging literature of the mountain folk. "The river contains a rich treasury of American folkways," one writer declaimed; and "the Mississippi fisherman is a rebel against mechanization and regimentation, as were the pioneers he so closely resembles." Strong, "trusty" (a constantly used epithet in this writing too), independent, taciturn, and stoical, he was, it was argued, just as suspicious of outsiders as the mountain people were, but happy to form "a close-knit fraternity" with those of his kind. The river man lived "quietly, happily, much as his ancestors lived a hundred years ago." In turn, "the women . . . like their husbands, remind the observer of the pioneer folk"; "patiently they go about their household duties," the reader learned, "they are as self-reliant as the men." Often, the suggestion was that the correspondence between river and mountain folk was rather more than that, being a matter of blood ties and common descent. The river folk were "closely related to the poorer natives of the Southern mountains," the reader was told; many of them were also people who had actually come down from the mountains, seduced by "the lure of the cities," and then, rebelling against "the thundering of machines and the punching of time clocks," had "drifted down the river to freedom." As with the broader portrait of river life and character, there was an element of truth to this tracing of a common family tree or continuity of experience, but there was also a measure of imaginative reinvention issuing out of need. The people who fished the river and tilled the river's acreage, who worked as loggers and lived in the shanties were as marginalized

19. Ben Lucien Burman, *Big River to Cross: Mississippi Life Today* (New York, 1938), 65. See also 28, 70, 82; *Children of Noah: Glimpses of Unknown America* (New York, 1951), xii, 22, 23, 30, 31–32; Harnett T. Kane, *Deep Delta Country* (New York, 1944), xviii, 264–66. For accounts of Mississippi river life that, on the contrary, emphasize social transformation and change, see, e.g., Hodding Carter, *Lower Mississippi* (New York, 1942); Lyle Saxon, *Father Mississippi* (New York, 1927).

and deprived as the mountain folk, perhaps even more so; they certainly corresponded less to traditional images of pastoral virtue or the conventional agrarian ideal. "It is a lazy life," the reader was informed, "there is much time to talk"; what might have been added, but was not, was that life on the river was also a desperately poor one.

In short, the writing about life on the river that emerged in the first half of this century betrays many of the same tendencies as contemporary accounts of the mountains. There is the same inclination to see the human subject in Adamic terms (in this case, the American Adams created by Mark Twain come to mind), the same apparent need to see things with a carefully, radically selective eye—so that, for instance, lack of gainful employment becomes "lazying," an opportunity to chat, and poverty and deprivation are translated into "simplicity." There is also the same impulse to treat that subject not so much as a subject as an exhibit, odd, idiosyncratic, notable for his curious speech and even more curious behavior—a source of fascination precisely because of his strangeness, his deviation from what both writer and reader assume to be the norm. This is particularly the case with writing about the river folk that admits to being fiction—rather, that is, than laying claim to the status of documentary, history, or anthropology. The relevant books here include *Mississippi* (1929), *Steamboat Round the Bend* (1936), *Blow for a Landing* (1938), and *Rooster Crows for Day* (1945) all by Ben Lucien Burman, *Lightwood* (1939) and *River Rogue* (1942) by Brainard Cheney, *Swamp Water* (1941) by Vereen Bell, and *River Song* (1945) by Harry Hamilton.[20] The standard narrative practice in novels like these is similar to that of an earlier local colorist like Murfree: plot is kept to a minimum so as to focus our wondering gaze on the special character and eccentric social practices of the world described. Some of these books, like *Swamp Water* and *River Song,* have in fact no overriding plot at all. In the novels of Burman and Cheney there is more overall plotting, but it is of the most minimal kind: *Mississippi, Rooster Crows for Day,* and *River Rogue,* for instance, all employ the same basic narrative pattern of growing up in an isolated river community and/or leaving it for a while

20. Ben Lucien Burman, *Mississippi* (New York, 1929), *Steamboat Round the Bend* (Boston, 1936), *Blow for a Landing* (New York, 1938), and *Rooster Crows for Day* (New York, 1945); Brainard Cheney, *Lightwood* (New York, 1939) and *River Rogue* (New York, 1942); Vereen Bell, *Swamp Water* (Boston, 1941); Harry Hamilton, *River Song* (New York, 1945).

only to realize its value and return. What a loose structure like this enables, of course, is precisely what it does in the stories of Murfree. The narrator can spend his time drawing our attention to his gallery of unusual characters, and the peculiarly isolated, anachronistic world they inhabit. "There were rumors of European war . . . but . . . people were not interested in such things," Hamilton explains in *River Song* (set among a shanty-boat community on a place called "Island 21"), "they seldom saw a newspaper and they never heard a radio, as no electricity was brought over to the Island."[21] In this fictional world, and ones like it, significant crisis—like change—does not occur, it seems; wars, along with plots, belong to a world elsewhere.

"I ain't scared of nothing that's a-living," the central character in *Swamp Water* boasts, "no man ner varmints in this world." That sets the tone for most of the male protagonists of these books: they know what they believe, and they are ready to fight to defend it. The emphasis here is where it is in the early mountain novels, on certain values construed as male and connected with the frontier. This is perhaps one reason why there is so much attention given to the sheer, masculine stature of major characters. Dr. John Pearly, the protagonist in *Steamboat Round the Bend*, has, we are told, "a dignity almost patriarchal"; while a character called Bud True in *River Rogue* is said to be so big that he is "like two men poured into one." The emphasis is all the more noticeable because the relationships that matter in these stories tend to be those between men; and what one man usually learns from another, beside the habit of intimacy, is the ultimate necessity of force. Brainard Cheney is typical in this respect. His *Lightwood*, for instance, is concerned with the attempts of river families to prevent a Yankee timber company getting their farms—theirs in the sense that, while they have no legal title to the land, they have lived on it for many years. The central relationships in the book are between, on the one hand, Micajah Corn and, on the other, Micajah's father and Micajah's son, Jethro. And it is through Micajah, in particular, that both the reader and Jethro learn about the importance of fighting to defend your corner—and doing what you believe to be right, even if the law tells you to the contrary. "Pa said, by God, what did he want with papers," explains Jethro, "there wasn't anybody going to move on his land." If "the law of Georgia" won't help them, we learn, then "the law of the shotgun" will. "A man's got to take care of his own," Micajah

21. Hamilton, *River Song*, 18–19.

discloses. "I've found the best way is to keep yore gun cocked and ready to shoot."[22]

The habit of self-help, carried if necessary to the point of violence, is one that the young protagonist of Cheney's *River Rogue* also learns as he grows up, like Jethro Corn, on a Georgia river. And in this case, the process of learning this and other ways of the river folk supplies the sole sustained narrative thread. The hero, called Ratliff, learns how to be a river man, not from his father but a father figure, leaves the river for a while but then comes back to his earlier home and allegiances—and that is the end of the story. Ratliff is taught to recognize no rules but his own. He fights whenever his honor is challenged: for instance, when someone questions a story he tells about wrestling an alligator—and when someone else suggests he has "nigger" blood in him. He also shows his sense of honor when the woman of the man who has acted as his mentor starts to make sexual advances. "I don't pay a debt by foolin' a fellow's bed," he declares "—even if he is fool enough to keep a woman like you in it."[23] The loyalties on this river world are raw, white, and male. If African Americans appear in these books, it is in terms of the threat of mixed blood or in casual, contemptuous references to "the niggers who drifted for the big Yankee sawmillers." Female characters, on the whole, are given more attention and more respect—except, that is, when they cross the line and threaten male honor. One river woman, for example, "clad in faded dress and sunbonnet," is said to have "all the dignity of a figure from the Bible"; another, the mother of the protagonist in *Blow for a Landing*, seems as she feeds the chickens "merely another feathered creature, a hen, or a variety of blue-bird." As that last remark suggests, however, they are not treated with the same seriousness as their male counterparts, nor granted anything like equivalent significance. The real bonding takes place, for the most part, between men; and male characters tend to monopolize even the nurturing and teaching roles. The "last frontier" of the river described in these novels seems as reluctant to negotiate heterosexual romance and sexuality as the old frontier of legend was; women, and even more blacks, are consigned to the margins of this marginal world. Perhaps nowhere, in fact, do these stories of the river betray

22. Cheney, *Lightwood*, 115. See also 31, 45–46; *River Rogue*, 52; Bell, *Swamp Water*, 16; Burman, *Steamboat Round the Bend*, 4.

23. Cheney, *River Rogue*, 186. See also 69, 77, 84; *Lightwood*, 9; Burman, *Children of Noah*, 22, 38; *Blow for a Landing*, 14; *Mississippi*, 13.

their mythical origins, and the needs that fired them into life, more than in this. The Mississippi of Burman, the Georgia waterways of Cheney, the Georgia swamplands and the river islands portrayed by Bell and Hamilton: all are alike in their distance, not only from what one of these writers calls "the mechanized America of today," but also from related conflicts of race and gender. These are territories mapped out of the need to find somewhere, some place apart where the pressure of otherness does not exist, and the landscape is an extension of self ("Sometimes you seem to me you was kind of part of the river, pappy," the hero of *Mississippi* is told). "Railways were all right," Micajah Corn in *Lightwood* reflects, "but the river had always been there and always would be there"; and it is this sense of the river as an abiding resource, and a sanctuary for beset manhood, that tends to animate all these novels.

"It is a vast kingdom . . . where life has changed little with the passing of the years," observes the narrator of one of these books about river folk. "Whatever changes may have come upon the towns . . . the river remains basically as it was in the olden days." "A old river and a old country's all wore out, like a old man," comments a character in another book by the same author. "It's with a young river like the Mississippi and a new country like America that you learn things."[24] The paradox is a familiar one. The river is simultaneously old and new, because it speaks the speech of an aboriginal, agrarian America; through its vital connection with "the olden days," it recollects a lost innocence, a primitive social purity and perhaps even offers the possibility of cultural renewal. Precisely the same paradox feeds into the mountain fiction of the same period, between the two world wars and just after. What is remarkable here, though, in this fiction about highland folk, is the variety of forms that paradox of an old/new culture then assumes. The fiction about river people written at broadly the same time tends to follow a certain simple pattern, to repeat the basic rhythms of American pastoral. So, for that matter—for all their occasional acknowledgments of cultural change and social disintegration—do many of the contemporary accounts of visitors to the mountains and observers of highland life. Earlier fiction about the Southern mountain folk, in turn, has a habit of playing on the marginal nature of its subject: whether as "trusty henchman" to the hero, picturesque mountain girl or moonshiner, the strangeness of the highland character—or, rather, the revelation of that strangeness—becomes an end in

24. Burman, *Big River to Cross*, 22–23; *Rooster Crows for Day*, 302.

itself. Similar impulses are at work in mountain fiction from the 1920s to the early 1950s. It is difficult to imagine, in any event, how any writing about the Southern highlands during this period could evade the temptations of pastoral, or the feelings of difference and distance generated by this culture that seemed both antique and fresh—as well as subject to sudden, radical change. The point is not that the many writers of this fiction suppressed these impulses but, rather, that they channeled them in a variety of often intriguing ways. They approached the subject of the Southern highlands with a range of conflicting expectations; their perceptions of what was happening at the time, and the possible consequences, were extraordinarily diverse—granted that most of them admitted the fundamental fact of change. They deployed all manner of narrative strategies to search out and develop those perceptions and, necessarily, those strategies, the forms and structures they used, refracted and reshaped what they were trying to see and say. In short, this is a body of work notable for its quality of *difference,* its capacity to play changes on the story of the mountains and even surprise. If there are common threads here, sometimes, they are woven into different patterns; if, at some level, the old story of the happy farmer is being told here again, it is being told in a variety of voices.

One set or series of voices echoes an earlier novelist like Mary Noailles Murfree or John Fox Jr. to the extent that crossing the border between highland and lowland becomes the subject as well as the premise of the story. The plot devices are simple ones. The protagonist leaves his or her mountain home for the low country, learns to value what was left behind, and then returns from cultural exile. Alternatively, a lowland protagonist enters the high country, usually to educate or exploit, only to learn to value what they aimed to change. Either way, the trope of passage, journeying from one way of life and means of living to another, allows the novelist to measure the gap between highland and modern cultures and to consider the possibility, at least, of bridging it. This trope or device animates—among other fiction of the period—*The Quare Woman* (1923) and *The Glass Window* (1925) by Lucy Furman, *Flight to the Hills* (1926) by Charles Buck, *The Mountainy Singer* (1928) by Harry H. Kroll, *The Happy Mountain* and *The Weather Tree* by Maristan Chapman, *Some Trust in Chariots* (1930) by Fiswoode Tarleton, *Mountain Path* (1936) by Harriette S. Arnow, *Lonesome Valley* (1949) by Henry Hornsby, *The Enduring Hills* (1950) by Janice Giles, *The Singing Hills* (1951) by Lillian Craig, and *The Long Way Through* (1959) by James

Ballard.[25] It is at perhaps its simplest and most elemental in the two novels by Chapman, alluded to earlier. In *The Happy Mountain,* the story concerns a young man who leaves the hills to visit the city; in *The Weather Tree,* two "outlanders," a young man and woman, journey to the mountains to observe and bring "civilization" to the people there. Both, however, are centered in the fictional highland community of Glen Hazard, and both are preoccupied with challenging accepted notions of the civilized.

Of the two books, *The Happy Mountain* is the less successful. Describing the departure and return of a hillman called Waits Lowe, it is almost remorseless in its cataloging of lowland vice and highland virtue. "The world's full of wonders," Waits declares, ". . . and I aim to view some of 'em." What he finds, however, when his "wandering thoughts" lead him first into the lowland farm areas and then into the city, is not "wonders" but a loss of identity and communality. People do not look him in the eye, much less speak to him or offer him food or shelter; in town, "crowds broke around him," we are told, "like a rock in mid-stream." The farms he encounters are "more like mill-factories," he observes, with "monstrous machinery to tend and gather the crop," while the farmer spends his time "in an office-place with books." The city is even worse, with no sanctuary, no place to pause or reflect. "Street-car bells were clanging and streams of folk were running across the roads like black

25. Lucy Furman, *The Quare Woman: A Story of the Kentucky Mountains* (Boston, 1923) and *The Glass Window: A Story of the Quare Woman* (Boston, 1925); Charles Buck, *Flight to the Hills* (New York, 1926); Harry H. Kroll, *The Mountainy Singer* (New York, 1928); Chapman, *Happy Mountain* and *Weather Tree;* Fiswoode Tarleton, *Some Trust in Chariots* (New York, 1930); Harriette S. Arnow, *Mountain Path* (New York, 1936); Henry Hornsby, *Lonesome Valley* (New York, 1949); Janice Giles, *The Enduring Hills* (Philadelphia, 1950); Lillian Craig, *The Singing Hills* (New York, 1951); James Ballard, *The Long Way Through* (Boston, 1958). In these novels of passing or crossing the border, the trope of crossing might be fruitfully compared with "the chronotope of threshold" that Mikhail Bakhtin describes in "Forms of Time and of the Chronotope in the Novel" (*The Dialogic Imagination* translated by Caryl Emerson and Michael Holquist [Austin, Tex., 1981], 248). Bakhtin describes this as "the chronotope of *crisis* and *break* in life," which may be "combined with the motif of encounter." The comparison is useful, not least, because Bahktin emphasizes the coincidence of the personal and social in such crises and encounters, and the fact that this chronotope may coexist in the same narrative with others. Similarly, in mountain stories of crisis or passing, the notions of a personal encounter and a social or historical one are inextricably connected; and the trope or idea of crossing can coexist with others, such as change. In other words, the categories outlined in this chapter (such as crossing, or invasion and exodus) are by no means mutually exclusive.

water"; "fresh automobiles . . . came spitting down the long streets," we are told; there is noise, annulling thought, everywhere. Even the possible cultural resources of the outlander prove a disappointment. Visiting a library, Waits is overwhelmed by the sheer number of volumes there ("he felt himself washed out of the wide front door—waves of books pushing him forth"), until he explains to himself that "books ain't a thing but words, hard words." "Books ain't a thing but words crowded together, same as city folks is," he thinks. "Words is pretty things. But they don't matter . . . in the middle of the bigness of life"—or, for that matter, by comparison with "the soft lilting sounds of life to be drawn when he needed" from the fiddle he always carries with him. In the face of a culture of surfeit and information, in effect, Waits makes his own choice in favor of his "one corner of the earth": where learning comes, not from the written word, but from actual cultural practice—and where everyone is a producer as well as a consumer of the "sounds" by which "the bigness of life" is mediated. It remains unclear whether the authors of *The Happy Mountain* are aware of the ironies at work here. The written word is, after all, being used to celebrate an oral/aural culture; this is a calculated, and sometimes sentimental, defense of a community that is valued, above all, for its uncalculated, unsentimental acceptance of what is called, early on in the story, "life's roughness." Whether it is or not, however, the novel ends where it began: in Glen Hazard, with Waits concluding, "happen all the things I set out to find was overcoming as books, I'm best in my home-place."[26] He has come home to his people, who accept him and their own way of living without question; and since he went away, apparently, nothing has changed.

The subtlety of *The Weather Tree*, by comparison, stems from the fact that it acknowledges the alterations wrought by time, economic intervention, and social engineering—and, at the same time, admits that the kind of return to the old, instinctive practices that Waits Lowe eventually favors is, to say the least, very difficult. The story begins with the arrival in Glen Hazard of Lynn Clayton, a young townsman with plans as he puts it "to build a new community here and to found a business" which will bring, he hopes, "money, education, progress into this backwoods place." He is joined there by Lida Grant, a university student who, aside from providing Lynn with financial help, aims to write a sociology paper: "I've got statistics on food and clothing, and the schools," she explains

26. Chapman, *Happy Mountain*, 218. See also 6, 16, 19, 181, 195, 209, 302.

not long after she arrives there, "and how many people live in each house." There is a quiet plurality of perspective from the beginning. The mountain folk are seen on their own terms—thanks to the observations and comments of characters like the young local woman, Thelma Lane, who is attracted to Lynn Clayton—but they are also seen as Clayton himself tends to see them. They are "tall and sturdy folk, friendly to the hills," we learn, with their own quiet customs and assurance; and they are also, as Clayton observes, "poor and downgone" to the extent that they have to fight the earth for a living. There is no doubt whose side the authors are on, any more than there is in *The Happy Mountain*. Even Clayton, we are told, begins to learn "the lesson of silence" from the people he wanted to teach; "no longer did he talk quick and sharp like a rifle firing, but could wait and think about things in peace" just as the hillfolk, "the home-grown, lanky men of slow minds and even slower speech," already do. The difference here is that they are not reluctant to admit the material poverty of the mountain community, even while warmly commemorating its rituals—the deprivation that makes Clayton's plans, at the very least, understandable. The mountain folk may not want the wealth Clayton promises ("All your talk is things, and money, and noise," Thelma Lane contemptuously tells him); they may be alternately amused and annoyed by the meddling advice of outlanders ("Thing that makes me just leaping mad," says one local, "is the folks they send spying to tell us what's amiss"). It is clear, though, that they are poor. This is no pastoral idyll. On the contrary, if anyone indulges in dreams of an arcadian community it is Clayton. "I can't help planning ahead," he confesses, "I visualize . . . a lovely village here, perhaps an industrial school. . . . We'll revive the old trades of spinning and weaving."[27] His plan, in fact, involves not just marrying the new to the old but using the one to revive the other: the wealth generated by his new business practices will fund a return to the customary forms.

For a while, *The Weather Tree* flirts with the possibility of marriage in another sense as well. Romance grows between Thelma Lane and Lynn Clayton, opening up the prospect of a union that both symbolizes and seals the connecting of old and new, highland and lowland, a traditional culture and the wealth that ensures its revival. But the possibility is entertained only to ram the message home more clearly: Clayton's plans are not only absurd and anomalous, turning culture into a commodity ("you

27. Chapman, *Weather Tree*, 235. See also 52, 64, 68, 77, 92, 121, 159, 214, 235.

and Mist' Clayton wish life ready-made like store-boughten," one local tells Lida Grant), they are also doomed to fail. By the close of the narrative, the business venture has collapsed, the romance between highlander and outlander has faded, and the two outlanders have already departed. The dream of what Clayton calls "a model village" never materializes. All that is left at the end is the rather less dreamlike village of Glen Hazard with its vanishing past and uncertain future. To this extent, *The Weather Tree* is less about the crossing of boundaries than the impossibility of ever doing so. There is a comedy of errors played out throughout the novel, issuing from a failure of understanding or communication between the two cultures. "There was a woman person come snooping around the store one day," recalls a villager, "claimed she'd been paid to come and count how much we ate. Who'd been paying to learn that? Claimed we'd ought to eat other than we do, but failed of saying where we'd get it."[28] There is also a more somber story unraveling at the same time of a culture that is vanishing under the twin pressures of assessment and alteration. The inherent conflict between the customary and the calculated was one well understood by the Nashville Agrarians. Allen Tate was not the only one among them to observe that "the Southerner" who wished to retain or recover traditional forms (the essence of which is their "irrational," instinctive nature) using "rational" (which is to say, self-conscious, deliberate, and political) means was placed in a deeply conflicted position—or, as Tate himself put it, "faced with a paradox." The paradox is one that a well-intentioned outlander like Lynn Clayton cannot resolve; it is one among several reasons why his project fails, disastrously. And, *The Weather Tree* intimates, it is a paradox likely to press home more and more on the mountaineers themselves, as they are subjected to the analysis and the advice of outside observers. The victims of gradual, irreversible social change and economic disruption, the villagers of Glen Hazard are also transformed into cultural specimens by people like Clayton, Lida Grant, the "woman person" who "come snooping"— or, for that matter, the husband-and-wife team of amateur linguists

---

28. Ibid, 64. See also 129, 252. "How may the Southerner take hold of his Tradition?" Allen Tate asks in "Remarks on the Southern Religion" and then answers, "by violence." "The Southerner is faced with a paradox," Tate argues: "He must use an instrument, which is political, and so unrealistic and pretentious that he cannot believe in it, to re-establish a private, self-contained, and essentially spiritual life" (*I'll Take My Stand: The South and the Agrarian Tradition* [1930; New York, 1962 edition], 174–75).

known as Maristan Chapman. In the final analysis, *The Weather Tree* offers an even more devastating dissection of "words" and "books"— that is, commodified knowledge—than even its predecessor does, because it suggests that the self-consciousness—the sense of being watched, measured, and recorded—being visited on mountain folk has its part to play in the process of cultural disintegration. Glen Hazard will survive, perhaps, only as a museum exhibit, a heritage park—or in novels like this one.

In some other novels of the time based on the trope of crossing the novelist seems to be less aware of the curiously paradoxical nature of his position, as a symptom of those changes helping to ensure the obsolescence of the very culture being celebrated. In *The Mountainy Singer,* for example, Harry Harrison Kroll devotes as much time and attention to the folklore and folk songs of the highlands as Maristan Chapman—and, before that, Mary Noailles Murfree—do to its distinctive patterns of speech. Around a thin narrative thread of departure and return, Kroll weaves an elaborate portrait of a society that expresses and understands itself in terms of stories and ballads "brought over the seas from Scotland three hundred years before"—and with a history no doubt going back beyond that "to the misty days of the Vikings." The hero, Dan Hubbard, leaves this society for a while to get a schooling but returns, eventually, and finds himself appreciating its forms and customs all the more. "It seemed to Danny," we are told, ". . . that his love for his own people . . . their customs, their songs, their folk-speech, constituted a culture far superior to anything which so many of his unthinking teachers undertook to ram down his throat." "That's what most of the teachers called 'education,' " Dan reflects, "a few words like 'hit' (for 'it') and what to do with your knife when you ate." There is a different, deeper kind of education available in the hills, he learns; and the lesson is learned, in particular, at social gatherings back in his home place. At one party, for instance, he listens to the assembled guests singing the old ballads, and it comes to him that "their songs . . . were their very souls." At another, he has a similar epiphany as he watches his neighbors dancing:

> The music, the mathematical beat-beat of heavy feet, the swaying bodies, the set, grave faces of the dancers so intent upon their pleasure that they made a labor of it, the sheer poetry of rhythmic motion—all of it merged into a tender hypnotism. . . . Danny looked at the silent, set faces of the dancers. . . . It came to him how close

his people lived to the soil. They were made of the clay of the fields, the stone of the hills, the brown fibers of the oaken logs of the four walls within which they danced.[29]

It does not occur to Danny, nor to his creator, that it is precisely this capacity to observe and reflect on mountain culture that sets him apart from "his people." They are what they are, of the earth, earthy; and do what they do as a matter of habit, the customary practices of their culture. Danny, by contrast, has to make an educated choice, based on a comparative analysis of highland and lowland societies. In his own way, he is as much of a folklorist—as much in the business, that is, of recording folk practices for a literate, outland audience—as Kroll is; indeed, that is his primary function, as far as the hidden agenda of the novel is concerned. At the end of *The Mountainy Singer*, Dan marries his childhood sweetheart, a typical way of sealing the return to traditional mountain culture in these novels. Dan and his new wife "would sing at gatherings among the neighbors and kinfolks up the mountains and down the hollows," we are informed, ". . . then in the spring he would put in a crop." There is little sense here that, perhaps, you can't go home again—that, once you have turned inherited practices into information, you cannot simply reverse the process.

The same belief, that you can somehow step into the same cultural stream twice, seems to animate another, quieter, sadder novel, *Lonesome Valley* by Henry Hornsby. Brought up by an uncle and aunt, after his unwed mother is sent into exile, the hero, Johnny Barnes, knows only the condition of "lonesomeness and stillness." Unlike Kroll or Chapman, Hornsby places the main emphasis on the isolation of mountain life, breeding an ethic of independence and an emotional hunger for companionship. Johnny dreams of a world elsewhere in the city of Richmond, "the people . . . meeting, laughing and talking." "People didn't get lonesome in a place like Richmond," he tells himself, "not with a crowd around all the time." And his dreams of human congregation and community, which offer some refuge from the echoing emptiness of the hills, drive him down into the lowlands: where he discovers a loneliness in the city worse than anything he had ever known before. "Wasn't it lonesome

29. Kroll, *Mountainy Singer*, 298. See also 22, 192, 195–96, 234, 309. A teacher during his adult years, at Lincoln Memorial University and then the University of Tennessee at Martin, Kroll taught two other writers interested in life in the Southern highlands, James Still and Jesse Stuart.

everywhere?" he asks himself. "Was being lonesome up in the holler any worse than being lonesome some place else?" At least, it occurs to him, "one of the nice things about living up in the holler was that a body didn't expect anything much. A body expected lonesomeness, and when it came to him he didn't take it too hard." On one level, the return here is, not to culture and community, but to an acceptance of isolation, accompanied by the mournful reflection that "no place was good enough to keep a body from wanting a better place"; and on this level, of personal dream and unrealizable desire, the narrative denial of change is both moving and plausible. What makes that denial more problematical, however, is the suggestion that the quality of lonesomeness is more palatable and less strained in the hills, not just because the lonely peaks and valleys are a fit accompaniment to a lonely soul, but thanks to something else more mysteriously positive. "People didn't act and talk one way and feel another," Johnny thinks of hill folk before he leaves Richmond. "They were honest people." "Back here, life was simple," he is convinced after he has gone back home. "People worked at what they needed to do and didn't have to worry whether they were doing the right thing, because they always knew. People went to bed early and got a good night's sleep. . . . If they had questions, the questions could be answered by a full belly and a night's sleep and a neighbor to talk to the next day."[30] This is pretty cold pastoral, but it is pastoral nonetheless: the notion of a life "so simple . . . so quiet and peaceful" (as the narrative puts it elsewhere) that the human burden of apartness and anxiety is lightened—at times, perhaps, even lifted. Like many other mountain novelists—and despite his recognition of the bleak lonesomeness of "lonesome valley"—Hornsby cannot entirely resist the impulse toward rest and closure. The protagonist returns to a world that has somehow managed not to change at all; he even, in the manner of such protagonists, marries his childhood sweetheart from the hills and takes up the rhythms and satisfactions of an old way of life ("the corn was something he had made, and he felt so proud of what he had done he could have cried"). "He had come back to where he had started from," the reader is told; and there is no sense that either Johnny Baker, or the place he started from, has altered in the least. To this extent, *Lonesome Valley* answers a common need—common, that is, among accounts of highland life written at this time—to find the past alive in the mountain present. In the quiet byways of the

30. Hornsby, *Lonesome Valley*, 267. See also 32, 107–8, 249, 331, 384.

hills, apparently, the fact of loneliness is sweetened by the continuance of the familiar pieties. Whatever else might be said, about the sadder dimensions of their lives, the hill folk of this novel possess many of the features of the primitive, pioneer type; above all, they are simple, honest, caught up in the time-honored rhythms of the earth—and not drowning in their own subjectivity.

The curious thing about those mountain novels of crossing, passing over borders, that are also novels of change is that this sense of the presentness of the past is just as strong as it is in, say, *Lonesome Valley* and *The Mountainy Singer.* It is just that, in this case, the past is alive as a resource—a source of possible salvation for a social system in crisis. The narrative premise in *Some Trust in Chariots* by Fiswoode Tarleton, *The Quare Woman,* and its sequel *The Glass Window* by Lucy Furman, is fundamentally the same: a process of mutual education offers promise for the future. The outlander, in both cases a woman, comes into the mountains; she encounters suspicion and hostility, while in turn betraying her own ignorance of highland life. Eventually, though, an accommodation is reached which suggests both change and continuity. Outland society, it is suggested, will learn from highland culture, just as the highlander will learn at schools established in the first instance by the outlander; out of this process, or synthesis, will eventually emerge an enlightened highland culture, and an educated highlander, both of them offering a beacon of hope—and not just to those living in the hills. "A better day is dawning now," a young, educated mountain man declares at the end of *The Glass Window,* ". . . I have great faith in our people. When they wake, they will be like Samson . . . there must be education first." Here, and in *Some Trust in Chariots,* there is an almost mystical belief in the manifest destiny of the—suitably educated—pioneer hill man. "We mountain people, shut away here for so long," declares the same young mountaineer in *The Glass Window,* ". . . have been better able to keep the faith of our fathers." "Who knows but that some day plain rugged men like us may again be needed to make the nation safe," he asks rhetorically, "—that we have been shut away here for so long for some divine purpose?"[31] If this sounds like a strange mixture of optimism and nostalgia, politics and prophecy, then so too does the speech with which the Tarleton novel ends. The speech is given, appropriately enough, at a school prize-giving, by a lawyer named Cliff Bett, who has

31. Furman, *Glass Window,* 35–37. See also 198.

helped the schoolteacher from the lowland spread the good word about education. And it shows in a succinct way how, in these novels, a belief in the moral power and potential of mountain life is mixed with a bleaker view of its material dimension. "The lowlands get everything and the highlands nothing," he complains. "Such scattered schools as we have are inadequate." "No roads. No telegraph. No newspapers," he goes on. "All we hear and know are the tired sounds of mountain struggling." But then comes the commemoration of old, pioneer heroism and the celebration of its possible metamorphosis into newer forms. "The tenacity, courage, physical strength and high spirit" that Bett claims to see among the pupils at the prize-giving show, he suggests, the "persistence of blood" through their fathers who walked "twenty miles over the hills for cartridges or provisions and then twenty miles back, to the revolution, back to the first settlers." "It is small wonder," the lawyer argues, "that these boys and girls, with that determination and courage in their blood, cannot be thwarted in their desire for learning. Life has always been hard in these hills." Rather handily for the rhetoric, although implausibly in any other terms, the most important of "these boys and girls" is called Daniel Boone. Daniel has been persuaded by his teacher to run as a congressional candidate for his district, and this allows Bett one final flourish. "The hills need a leader," he intones, ". . . A man named Daniel Boone led our ancestors through the wilderness to freedom. Another man named Daniel Boone . . . will lead us to another freedom."[32] So the bridge between heroic past and an equally heroic future is completed; the circle is closed, with only the brute materialities of the present excluded.

At their best, these novels describing a positive, creative crossing of borders play with the different perspectives on mountain life in a way that is, at once, quietly humorous and deeply serious. The view held by at least some of the teachers brought in from the lowlands, in *Some Trust in Chariots,* that hill people are "a degenerated race . . . slow witted and slow of action" is set off against, not only the unassuming dignity of mountain customs, but also the quick-witted fun the highlanders have at the expense of their visitors. "Subtle meanings flashed from eye to eye" of a highland class, we learn, as one teacher—sublimely unaware of the "pantomime developed into an art" that is going on around him— indulges himself in a lecture about the backwardness of the highland mind. Another teacher is more perceptive. "Sometimes I fear that we

32. Tarleton, *Some Trust in Chariots,* 303–4. See also 288–89.

outsiders, we lowlanders, just flatter ourselves that we understand the highlander," she confesses. "I feel that these mountain people . . . resent us strongly . . . they are 'as eagles looking down on us, the lowland breed.' "[33] The collision between the two cultures is a productive as well as a comic one, though—at least, that is what these novelists would have us believe. The teacher learns from the pupil—about, say, mountain dialect in *Some Trust in Chariots,* or mountain traditions "passed down through the centuries by word of mouth" in *The Quare Woman.* In turn, the pupils acquire from the teacher all the skills needed to energize mountain society, and enable it to meet the challenge of the new. After they settled in their "rugged, penned-in land," one hill man explains in *The Quare Woman,* the hill folk "was . . . shut in for uppards of a hundred year . . . never bettering their condition—you might say, worsening it." Now the opportunity is there to "send the youngens out to school, or to fetch larning into them."[34] True to the gospel of progressive enlightenment that informs these stories and others like them (such as the trilogy by Hubert Skidmore, *River Rising* [1939], *Hill Doctor* [1940], and *Hill Lawyer* [1942]), education is seen as the key. Education of the lowlander by the highlander will restore some of the pioneer virtues, the promise of early America, to the emergent culture; in turn, education of the highlander by the lowlander will help turn a stagnant culture into a vital, developing one. This belief in a process of mutual instruction is what gives these books a curious, naïve nobility; nevertheless, it also points to a crucial weakness. There is little sense of the economic bases of this crossing of cultures; the workplace that is the dramatic site of crossing here is the schoolroom, rather than the mine, the mill, or the factory. Education occurs in a strange vacuum, more or less exempt from the pressures of the material. To see this as dangerously partial is not, by any means, to argue for education as an instrument of economic policy. It is simply to say that, in the highlands, the teacher crossed over with the industrialist, the mine or mill owner; in these novels, however, the teacher is a lone figure who brings in the new world virtually all by herself.

33. Ibid., 19. See also 40, 41.

34. Furman, *Quare Woman,* 53. See also 124. Apart from his progressive trilogy, *River Rising* (New York, 1939), *Hill Doctor* (New York, 1940), and *Hill Lawyer* (New York, 1942), Hubert Skidmore also wrote novels that record an evidently endless cycle of highland poverty and oppression: *I Will Lift Up Mine Eyes* (Garden City, 1936) and *Heaven Came So Near* (Garden City, 1938).

Easily the most memorable of these novels of crossing, however, is another one that places a teacher at the center of the narrative: *Mountain Path* by Harriette S. Arnow. The story line, as with most of this fiction, is simple. A young woman called Louisa Sheridan comes to Canebrake, a small settlement in the Appalachian Mountains in Kentucky, to teach and so finance her studies at the university. Such plot as there is revolves around her growing knowledge of mountain ways and a simmering feud between the Bucks, the family with which she stays, and the Barnetts—a feud that occasionally boils over into violence. The plot is less important, though, than the placing of both the main character and her situation. In a preface written for the 1963 edition of the novel, Arnow makes it clear that it is based on her own experience as a teacher of a world she "first saw in the summer of 1926." Louisa Sheridan is not, of course, Harriette S. Arnow even at one or two removes, but this basis in personal recollection is perhaps why everything is filtered through her eyes and is the subject of her meditations: this is a novel of initiation to the extent that the protagonist undergoes a mental and moral alteration, which we witness and even share, as she quietly balances the good and bad of mountain life. Like most good novels of initiation, *Mountain Path* is also concerned with social, as well as personal, change; the world that Louisa enters is altering even while she perceives it. Arnow makes this clear in her 1963 introduction. "Life in the hills was on the whole worse than it had been for decades," she observes of the period between the wars when the novel is set: "The big timber was gone, the oil, and the soil washed from the hillsides and ridge tops; game was scarce. There was little left but scrub timber, worn out soil, and people—many people, for though there had always been emigration from the hills the Great Migration had not yet begun."[35] "Self-sufficient as the average, hard-working hill family was," Arnow adds, "it could not live entirely without 'cash money.'" The trouble was, she explains, "all the sources of petty cash open to families such as my own" in the lowlands, like "the sale of eggs and poultry, dairy products, vegetables, the shipping of cream" were unavailable to "the roadless, marketless hill community." In turn, "industry was non-existent" in the hills; "saw and stave mills had long since gone with the timber"; even the moonshiner was finding things difficult

---

35. Harriette S. Arnow, "Introduction" to *Mountain Path* (1936; Berea, Ky., 1963 edition). All subsequent references are to this edition.

because "by the late twenties he was being hunted down with unusual bitterness."

In her introduction to *Mountain Path,* Arnow makes the additional point that the mountain world she encountered in 1926, and that Louisa Sheridan takes us into, has now "more completely vanished than ancient Greece and Rome." The need for work and cash was "already destroying the world I saw when I taught my first school," she says; and with "the Great Migration that began with World War II and continues still," it has become more irredeemably lost even than "Pompeii under the ashes," since "it cannot be excavated and re-created." This sense that, by the early 1960s, "a combination of war and technology" had "destroyed a system of life" adds a further touch of pathos to anyone reading the book now. What is perhaps more to the point, though, is that the feeling of a social system under pressure, a world slipping away, is already there in the novel itself. Louisa is altering, as she learns to appreciate the pleasures and pains of highland culture, but that culture is altering too—and vanishing, not so slowly. The alteration that Louisa herself undergoes does not involve a simple surrender to the charms of life in the hills. On the contrary, what is remarkable about this book is the degree to which Arnow, through the vision and voice of Louisa, stresses the earthy, mundane qualities of this life, its strains, harshness, and the toughness required of those who live it. There is no lavatory in the house where Louisa stays, the family use the garden; the hogs rub their backs against the schoolhouse and have to be chased away; the fleas from the hogs often infest the schoolhouse. The poor soil and rough weather are constant enemies. "In Cal Valley," where Canebrake is situated, Louisa reflects, "men hunted in the rain, got wood in the rain, and went to church in the rain," and "they never complained." "Louisa often thought," the reader learns, that the mountain folk "gloried in their ability to withstand rain and wind and snow"; what she grows to admire in them, gradually, is their "reservoir of primitive strength and calmness," a quiet stoicism that enables them to deal with all their trials and tribulations, and even construct a decent life in the face of them. These people are not the "pure-blooded Anglo-Saxon" of legend, Louisa tells herself, in fact "she doubted if there was a pure-blooded anything in her school" or outside of it. They are, however, something subtler and better. What that something is, is caught in her observation of Corie, the matriarch of the Buck household—who, we discover, "without being a pessimist . . . expected the worst of all possible combinations in all things and as a result was eternally grateful for some little thing."[36]

Corie Buck is important to the education of Louisa Sheridan because she encapsulates all that Louisa learns, about mountain strength and steadiness of purpose, the simple dignity of mountain customs, and a knowledge of "important things about living" that belies "the . . . illiteracy exceeded only by . . . poverty" that is the apparent lot of Canebrake folk. "Corie might be nothing more than a long brown bare-footed woman in an ill-made cotton dress," we are told, "but she had a natural dignity and reserve that Louisa, accustomed only to the dignity that comes of heroic corseting or much learning or money, respected too much to attempt to violate." Louisa learns subtle lessons in manners from Corie, who "might guilelessly ask her how much a dress had cost or where she had got her shoes" but would never inquire "into the cause of her father's death" or want to know "if she belonged to a church or what her politics were." "Civilized people back at school" in the lowlands, by contrast, "were never impolite enough to ask the price of a garment, but they did want to know things that Corie thought were none of her business." So the lesson in manners shades into a lesson in morals; this difference of assumption about what can and cannot be asked, what should or should not be spoken, Louisa infers, "all came from a difference in . . . sense of values." "Who valued the right things," Louisa wonders, and slowly comes to decide that the respect for fundamental privacy, the individuality and concern for the individuality of others that determine Corie's conduct, represent the right system of values, a moral code that is somehow closer to the truth. A lesson in manners and morals, what Corie Buck also offers her young guest is a lesson in knowledge, understanding. Corie is illiterate but, Louisa discovers, she "could read people as she read weather signs at sunset or in a cow's teats"; the young schoolteacher "learned things from Corie that she had never found in books"—"not information," precisely, but a more instinctual and customary perception of life and sense of how to cope with it. As she

36. Ibid., 215. See also 53, 104, 209. Glenda Hobbs, in fact, sees *Mountain Path* as a parodic version of the traditional mountain narrative of crossing in which an educated outsider learns about what really matters from a highland community ("Starting Out in the Thirties: Harriette Arnow's Literary Genesis," in *Literature at the Barricades: The American Writer in the 1930s* edited by Ralph Bogardus and Fred Hobson [University, Ala., 1982], 151).

watches the older woman, Louisa learns, for instance, about "gratefulness and thankfulness for all things: dry wood, rain when the spring was low, cold snaps that cured up colds and made a spell for killing hogs, sunshiny days."[37] Comparing herself with Corie Buck, Louisa "wanted to wreck the mould of her universe," the reader is told, "and make of herself a person, an individual with a place in the world of her choosing." "She could do that by staying here" in Canebrake, she believes, "marrying maybe" so as to put down roots. There is, after all, a suitable partner available, a young man called Chris Bledsoe who is staying in the Buck household, hiding out from the Barnett clan. "What would it be like," she asks herself, "living with Chris?"

The terms in which Louisa Sheridan begins to contemplate marriage are worth considering carefully. This is not the standard romance between lowlander and highlander. Louisa is certainly attracted to the man in question. She is, however, even more attracted to the idea of imitating Corie Blake, almost becoming her. Louisa wants to "be a woman and bear children," we are told, "and learn the things that Corie knew"; she wants to make herself into a mountain woman. She has already, she feels, gone some way along the path of reinventing herself. "It was not," she decides, "that her ambition was dying, it was only that the thing she desired seemed less desirable." University, lowland learning, and culture have lost their attraction; "she liked to do the things she had been doing here—too well." Observing Corie, sharing her life with her, the young schoolteacher tells herself, "the things that woman had felt" and she has come to cherish "she would never know" any more if she were "to escape it all by being civilized and going away."[38] If there is a true romance here, then, it is the romance between two women, the admiration and affection bordering on worship that lowland woman feels for her highland counterpart. *Mountain Path* is remarkable, although by no means unique among highland novels of the period, in that, unlike its predecessors in the tradition of mountain fiction, it places female experience at the center. The woman learns from the woman; the differences between highland and lowland cultures, some of them subtle and some of them more obvious, are measured mainly—although not, of course, exclusively—in terms of female possibility, the different roles and paths available to people like Louisa Sheridan, Corie Blake—or, for that matter, Harriette S. Arnow.

37. Arnow, *Mountain Path*, 214–15. See also 97, 213–14, 238–39.
38. Ibid., 286. See also 282–83, 367–68.

If Louisa thinks that she herself has a real choice here, though—as opposed, that is, to the chance to discriminate between what she has been and what she has learned—she is sadly mistaken. The small community of Canebrake is altering, breaking up even while she observes it. She herself, she recognizes, is an agent of change. The mountain people, in turn, "sent their children to school because they wanted to, and not because of a state law they never heard of"; they sense that a different kind of learning is needed by the next generation, as the old customary community yields to a culture in which illiteracy is a synonym for ignorance. The children learn; and are then tempted to leave the "worn-out soil," a "poverty of environment that in turn impoverished the family," for the promises, however deceptive, of the world outside. The illusion Louisa cherishes, that she can re-create herself as a mountain woman, another Corie Blake, is exposed as just that—an illusion. In practical terms, the door on that scheme—or, rather, dream—is shut tight when, at the end of the novel, Chris Bledsoe is killed. In response to his death, Louisa collapses in shock, feeling a terrible numbness in "her fingers and a little of her brain." "The rest of her would die," she feels. "It was dead already."[39] It is the death of a hope; it is also the death of another identity, another possible role she has tried to assume. She can love Corie Blake, having learned to appreciate what she and her kind are and how they live, but she cannot *be* her; nor, for that matter, can the children of Corie and her neighbors, the young people who have been Louisa's pupils. They, the children, are becoming just as irrevocably a part of a different culture as their teacher is; staying or, more likely, going in the future, whether leaving the mountains or remaining to watch them alter—either way, they will find the old ways will be beyond reach for them too. *Mountain Path* is a novel of visiting, the crossing of borders, but it is also a novel about the impossibility of the visitor being anything more than that, because she or he carries the germ of change into an already changing community. Passing into the small, strange world of Canebrake, Louisa may be learning things about herself and her surroundings that she never knew before but, like her creator, Harriette Arnow, she must take what she learns elsewhere—to another place or time, where it becomes a cherished memory, a subtle influence on behavior, and perhaps even the subject of a book.

"Who can excavate a fiddle tune," Arnow asks at the end of her intro-

39. Ibid., 374. See also 124.

duction to *Mountain Path,* "the coolness of a cave now choked with the water of Lake Cumberland, or the creakings and sighings of an old log house?"[40] The answer, as she surely must have known, was a novelist like herself. The commemorative strain is heard intermittently throughout the story of Louisa Sheridan; for that matter, it sounds with even more resonance in those novels of the mountains that play on the legendary, the strange, or magical qualities of highland life. This playing with legend is perhaps at its most obvious in those narratives that exploit the local history of the mountains, or dwell on the contribution the highlander has made to the history of region or nation. There are many narratives of this kind, ranging from popular romances to stories with more serious pretensions; still, despite their number, one of the more remarkable aspects of these more historically focused narratives is just how selective they are, as far as subject is concerned, the periods that seize and circumscribe attention. Not entirely, but certainly for the most part, these stories circle around three defining moments in the Southern past: the days of early pioneering, the War of Independence, and the period just before the invasion of the outlander and exploitation of mineral resources in the hills. In the process, they disclose in their variously subtle or naïve ways some other, interesting parts of the agenda of those who told the tale of the "aristocrat of the mountains," they measure the degree to which their story of the highland past was motivated more than usual—which is to say, more even than most stories about the past in the highlands or elsewhere are—by the needs, the pressures, and the concerns of the present.

As far as novels of pioneering in the mountains are concerned, the agenda at work is hardly a hidden one. The simplest way of demonstrating the frontier virtues of mountain life, after all, is to concentrate on the period when the Southern mountains literally were a frontier. Celebrating the moment when the primitive, pioneer ethic of the highlander was supposedly fired into being—or, as one of these stories puts it, "carved out of the wilderness"—becomes an act of commemoration, a way of imaginatively preserving the highland past. It also becomes, in these novels, a gesture of continuity—which is to say, a means of suggesting that this past could—and perhaps already does—feed into the bloodstream of the present. One of these books, *The Scotswoman* (1954) by Inglis Fletcher, makes this idea of moral continuation clear from the start, in its dedication. "To the Highlanders," the dedication reads, "bold and

40. Arnow, "Introduction" to *Mountain Path.*

valiant, whose inherent love of freedom, courage and integrity, have contributed much to the strong character of this country." "This country" presumably means here the United States, but a reader of these books of early pioneer days might be forgiven for assuming that it signifies two other countries entirely: Scotland and the mountain country where the early Scots emigrants of this fiction settle. These two places, after all, constitute most of the literal terrain of books like *Long Hunt* (1930) by James Boyd, *Free Forester* (1935) by Horatio Colony, *The Dark Stranger* (1940) by Constance W. Dodge, *By Reason of Strength* (1943) by Gerald W. Johnson, *The Far-Off Land* (1944) by Rebecca Caudill, and *There is a Season* (1957) by Alice R. Colver, as well as *The Scotswoman*.[41] The same two areas also tend to circumscribe these books' mental maps, their moral and emotional terms of reference. Not only that, the two are closely linked together; the imaginative tie that binds Scottish and Southern highlands together in these pioneer novels is a powerful one, a matter simultaneously of blood, soil, and politics. In *The Scotswoman,* the narrator even goes so far as to suggest that the early emigrants to the Southern mountains set out there to preserve old Scottish ways. " 'Tis just this vice we're caught in," a character—in fact, the husband of the heroine—complains as he contemplates leaving for America, "all of us, of the old pressing against the new. The old chiefs dying off, and the new ones bringing English ideas from the universities. The land wearing out and forcing us into trade. There's just no room for us Old Scots here any more . . . we're used to living in traditions of our own, while our world has got so old and small we have to live close with others and accept new strange ways."[42] There is only one solution, he tells his wife, to set off for the New World; "there with all the good land," he believes, "a man can live his own life." And a woman too: his wife, the eponymous Scotswoman, also senses that her "politics . . . rooted in her sense of injustice to individual persons"—an injustice perpetrated by English and lowland

---

41. James Boyd, *Long Hunt* (New York, 1930); Horatio Colony, *Free Forester* (Boston, 1935); Constance Dodge, *The Dark Stranger* (Philadelphia, 1940); Gerald W. Johnson, *By Reason of Strength* (New York, 1943); Rebecca Caudill, *The Far-Off Land* (New York, 1944); Inglis Fletcher, *The Scotswoman* (New York, 1954); Alice R. Colver, *There Is a Season* (New York, 1957). The phrase "carved out of the wilderness" comes from *There Is a Season* (120), although in these novels of mountain pioneering it is also something of a commonplace.

42. Fletcher, *Scotswoman,* 41. See also 51.

establishments on their neighbors in the highlands—will be able to flourish there, in the mountains of North Carolina.

The Scotswoman even goes as far as to suggest that the mountain *character,* along with the mountain love of liberty, was forged by the Scottish tradition. Among those who accompany the Scotswoman and her husband across the Atlantic and into the hills are two cousins, who are clearly meant to constitute the two major strains of mountain difference—in the old country and, consequently, the new. "In David," we are told, "the strong Scots love of caber-throwing, of warfare and of good farming asserted itself; he loved action and the present." "In Dougald," by contrast, "the Scots reticence was combined with the love of skirling pipe-music, the commemoration of . . . past deeds." Not all pioneer novels push things to these extremes; most of them focus, though, on the same strange mix of martial courage and mysticism. Many of them, too, make this brew all the headier by suggesting that these early emigrants came down out of the Scottish hills, and then up into the Southern ones, after the defeat of Prince Charles Edward—bringing with them little but their "passion for the land," their fierce love of personal freedom, and their memories of home and clan. "Keep the counsel of your own heart," the heroine of *The Far-Off Land,* Ketty Petrie, tells herself again and again, "To change a thing . . . a body has to step aside from the crowd." What she brings with her to her new mountain home is little; it is, however, more than the hero of *The Dark Stranger,* Lachlan MacLean, can manage—all he has to accompany him, the reader learns, is a bronze statuette, "of all the pride and tradition of that fallen house, this was the sole remaining symbol." "It was a noble land which her children's children would inherit," the heroine of *By Reason of Strength* reflects, "—not Scotland, to be sure . . . but in its way a noble land." Linking dreams of past nobility to visions of possibility—often through the matriarchal figure of the heroine—these stories argue for the "aristocrat of the mountains" in a way that is more or less literal. They offer the reader, not just the natural aristocrats of other mountain novels, but aristocrats of the more conventional, lineal kind—aristocrats in exile, many of them, like their true king and leader, Bonnie Prince Charlie. In turn, these noble exiles are seen as the founders of another series of dynasties, generations of men and women with perhaps more of the true aristocratic hauteur about them than their lowland neighbors, and certainly more claims to a special, different genealogy. Part of this is pure daydreaming, romantic confusion about the nature of mountain difference, translating cultural distinctiveness into a difference of blood. And part of it suggests a different, more millennial vision—daydreaming of a more prophetic, and more dangerous, kind. One novel puts that daydreaming in the baldest, most brutal possible way. "These Southern mountain people are a great people," the novel explains, "stowed away by providence for a time of need. . . . When we come to think of our country as a whole, with its ever increasing foreign population; with the riffraff of every nation pouring in upon us daily by the thousands, then it would seem that these pure blooded Americans are the hope of America."[43]

Few, if any, of the novelists of mountain pioneering would argue for the future in quite so crude and openly provocative a fashion. Still, the burden of what they *do* argue—with its emphasis on lineal purity and continuity—pushes the reader in this direction. If there is an agenda for the past and future here, and there surely is, it is determined by exactly that abhorrence of the foreign, the strange, and mixing with things strange, that is ascribed here to mountain culture itself. The romance of the defeat of feudal Scotland by bourgeois England shades off, in these novels, into the romance of the defeated Southern highlander; the disinherited clan chieftain translates into the dispossessed aristocrat of the Appalachians. There is a feeling for the purity and privacy of mountain life that suggests, not just commemoration of a primitive nobility now gone with the wind, but a sense of its redemptive qualities: the suspicion, and perhaps even the hope, that the pure blood line of the mountains can *still* cleanse and irrigate. As a reading of the past this is—it goes without saying—disablingly selective. Not only those with a taste for caber-throwing or skirling pipe music made the long trek into the hills. And as a sounding of the present and possible future it has a slightly eccentric, even sinister quality, as any *exclusive* focus on ethnicity surely does. To say that the Scottish tradition was and is a crucial cultural determinant for the Southern highlands is not controversial; to suggest, however, that it was and is more or less the only significant one clearly is. Many of these novels of mountain pioneering lean toward the idea that the cul-

43. Eloise B. Ebbs, *Carolina Mountain Breezes* (Asheville, N.C., 1929), 207. See also Fletcher, *Scotswoman*, 18; Colony, *Free Forester*, 3; Caudill, *Far-Off Land*, 113, 227; Johnson, *By Reason of Strength*, 146. The book by Ebbs is not a narrative of mountain pioneering; it shares with those narratives, however—and states more baldly than most of them do—the potent mixture of ethnic exclusiveness and millennial vision that tended to shape their reinventions of the past.

tural baggage brought over from Scotland defines both the memorable past of the Southern hill folk and the hopeful future of the hills and elsewhere. And, in doing so, they perform a peculiar kind of cultural work, they set up an unusually treacherous relation with the hard facts of mountain history—of the sort that the critic Philip Fisher surely had in mind when he proposed the notion of "privileged settings." "Every history," Fisher observed, "has, in addition to its actual sites, a small list of privileged settings."[44] These privileged settings, he explains, "are not at all the places where key events have taken place." On the contrary, they are "ideal and simplified vanishing points toward which lines of sight and projects of every kind converge." From such vanishing points, "the many approximate or bungled states of affairs draw order and position," since "whatever actually appears within society can be interpreted as some variant, some anticipation or ruin" of a privileged setting such as the wilderness, the virgin land, or the little house on the prairie. Arguably, the mountains have acted in this way, as a privileged setting, for the imaginations of many Southerners: a place where the hard facts of social change and the problems of mixing with otherness are not only rendered tolerable but also neatly resolved. Certainly, they perform this cultural work in many of those novels concerned, specifically, with the *past* of the Southern hills. Here, the fluid exchanges that emigration and settlement, conflict and alteration brought about are translated into a fixed pattern of figures and acts—around which, it seems possible, argument and daydreaming, policy and in some cases prophecy can occur.

This is just as true of those mountain novels centered on the American Revolution; and here, even the choice of historical setting tells part of the story. There are relatively few hill narratives that take as their sole or central subject the Civil War, almost certainly because the relationship of highland society to that later conflict was ambiguous and—from a Southern viewpoint, at least—problematic. The "privileged setting" of the War of Independence, on the other hand, allows the writer to celebrate mountain patriotism in both a national and local sense; the mixed, conflicted character of hill culture—particularly as far as relations with slave society and the lowland plantations were concerned—can be circumvented. The notion that the Southern highlander could find conflict between those two terms, of being a Southerner *and* a highlander, is evidently unimagin-

44. Philip Fisher, *Hard Facts: Setting and Form in the American Novel* (New York, 1987), 9.

able and so, for the most part, is left as just that—unimagined; and lines of sight converge, instead, on a place, an imaginative site where the hill man can make his stand as a true defender of the regional faith—as well as, of course, a defender of his own local culture and the belief systems attaching to it. Novels of the Revolutionary War in the mountains include *Drums* (1925) by James Boyd, *Rogue's March* (1949) by Maristan Chapman, *The Ragged Ones* (1951) by Burke Davis, *Slow Dies the Thunder* (1956) by Helen T. Miller, *Tall in the Sight of God* (1958) by Robert A. Bowen, and *The Carolinians* (1959) by Jane Barry.[45] For that matter, some of the novels of mountain pioneering, such as *The Dark Stranger* by Constance Dodge or *There Is a Season* by Alice Colver, carry their heroic stories forward to the days of revolution and political independence. What all these narratives have in common is measured by these two brief passages, the first from *Drums* describing how the mountain troops of the Revolution appeared, the second from *Rogue's March* explaining who they were and what they fought for:

> They trudged with a firm, stout step, the marching step of veterans. Like their gait, their faces were dogged and stolid . . . caps of wool and muskrat and beaver, old cocked hats, guns of all makes and sizes . . . above . . . all the rest, the frontier rifle. . . . The legs below the hunting-shirts were clad in . . . deerskin leggings and moccasins, in the broadcloth breeches and spun-yarn stockings of a farmer's Sunday best.

> They were fighting for their own right to stand on the face of the earth. They did not even fight for "home and loved ones" in the abstract. For each man there was his own home, up a particular cove, behind a special mountain, and in it, his woman, his children.[46]

45. James Boyd, *Drums* (New York, 1925); Maristan Chapman, *Rogue's March* (New York, 1949); Burke Davis, *The Ragged Ones* (New York, 1951); Helen T. Miller, *Slow Dies the Thunder* (Indianapolis, 1955); Robert A. Bowen, *Tall in the Sight of God* (Winston-Salem, N.C., 1958); Jane Barry, *The Carolinians* (New York, 1959). These novels of the Revolution in the Southern highlands share their preoccupation with this theme with other, more journalistic or literal accounts of life in the mountains: see, e.g., Campbell, *Southern Highlander and His Homeland,* 31; Thomas, *Blue Ridge Country,* 31; Weatherford, *Pioneers of Destiny,* 15–16.

46. Boyd, *Drums,* 5; Chapman, *Rogue's March,* 101. See also Barry, *Carolinians,* 19, 140; Boyd, *Drums,* 473.

As the narrator in *The Carolinians* observes, these "tall men in buckskin with their long rifles" were engaged in a "fight for survival"—a fight determined by their "love of the land," and springing out of "the human roots which had taken hold here," in their mountain homes, over the years. This was "a people believing sincerely," the reader is told, "that the Great Jehovah belonged to New Englanders and had no place in their slower-paced, more tolerant mode of living." They were defending attachments, loyalties that were specifically local and regional. "They were not profound political philosophers," we learn in *Drums*, "those solitary hillside people, but what thoughts they had were clear and straight"; and "the British would never own that country while there was a pine-tree standing and a man or woman to fire from its cover."

Ranged against this army of rugged individualists—"ragged ones," as they are called in the novel of that name, "with hardly a uniform among them"—is a monstrous regiment of British and Tories that combines oppressive power with privilege. The antirevolutionary forces were "a monstrous toy," the reader is informed in *Drums;* its leaders were men "reared in indolence, pampered by tutors," *The Ragged Ones* explains; the men they led simply accepted orders without question, marching "in unison . . . their column . . . a unit," and fighting always according to what are termed in *Rogue's March* "accepted modes of combat and warfare." "Nobody who's anybody is with the rebels," a Tory sympathizer in *The Ragged Ones* sniffs, ". . . ah, that dirty ragtag rabble . . . not one ever had two shillings to rub together." Contempt is often accompanied by bewilderment, however. "These riflemen are as picturesque as they are unexpected," observes a British general in *Rogue's March,* "They have no civilized equipment . . . no tents to protect them at night, and are indifferent to the weather, which has been excessively inclement"; "from their rough countenances and common speech," he adds, "I should judge them a numerous army of nobodies."[47] Occasionally, in these novels, this contrast between, on the one hand, populism and local patriotism and, on the other, power and privilege, is given an additional, Southern shading. In *The Ragged Ones,* for instance, one character is described as "a man bred to become a Tory, if any were" because he is "heir to one of the great green estates of Maryland" and "tended by slaves." This is a comparatively rare touch, though. What these novels of the Revolution in the mountains do, for the most part, is establish their

47. Chapman, *Rogue's March,* 324. See also 315; Davis, *Ragged Ones,* 47, 56.

heroes as simultaneously mountain populists and Southern patriots: happy farmers who, we are told in *Rogue's March,* "left their crops to be harvested by their womenfolk" while they set off to defend their farms—if necessary, to the death.

The line of convergence here is with earlier Southern narratives of Revolutionary heroism, like *The Partisan Leader,* that celebrate the martial virtues of the hill man; only now that hill man is not just a "trusty henchman" of the hero, he is the hero himself. For that matter, it is also with earlier Southern narratives of the Civil War—as this passage, from a long description of the Confederate forces in a book called *With Saber and Scalpel: The Autobiography of a Soldier and Surgeon* (1914) shows only too clearly:

> The vast majority were uneducated, many could not read or write; but they were a class far from being ignorant. . . . Their homes were of logs, some hewn . . . and some so primitive that the bark was left on . . . their lives were simple, and in general they were obedient to law. They were, however . . . quick to resent an affront. . . . They dressed with extreme simplicity . . . they raised everything they ate, except sugar and coffee . . . their wants were few and easily supplied. . . . Their convention was that freemen had the inherent right to do as they pleased, and as freemen they would stay in the Union or secede.[48]

"I don't favor of 'having' to do anything," the hero of *Rogue's March,* Lantry Ward, declares; "mountain man. Very troublesome breed," a Tory character observes of him, "Set authority at nought." Plainly, Lantry is

48. James A. Wyeth, *With Sabre and Scalpel: The Autobiography of a Soldier and Surgeon* (New York, 1914), xiv–xvi. See also Chapman, *Rogue's March,* 17, 158; General J. B. Gordon, *Reminiscences of the Civil War* (New York, 1904), 18, 217–18, 381; William R. Taylor, *Cavalier and Yankee: The Old South and American National Character* (London, 1963), 287–89. The other narratives of the Civil War mentioned here are George C. Eggleston, *A Rebel's Recollections* (New York, 1878); James Dinkins, *Personal Recollections and Experiences in the Confederate Army* (Cincinnati, 1897); Randolph H. McKim, *A Soldier's Recollections: Leaves from the Diary of a Young Confederate* (London, 1910). For another example of the link forged in these narratives between the Revolutionary War and the Civil War, see McKim, *Soldier's Recollections,* 160. On William Gilmore Simms's attempt to forge an imaginative connection between the Revolutionary War and sectional conflict in books like *The Partisan: A Tale of Revolution* (2 vols.; New York, 1835) and *The Forayers; or, The Raid of the Dog-Days* (New York, 1855), see my own discussion in *Writing the South: Ideas of an American Region* (Cambridge, 1986), 47–55.

cut of the same cloth as the Southern troops described in *With Sabre and Scalpel* and other narratives of the Confederacy—troops who, we are told, "were not disposed to obey anybody except for good and sufficient reason given" and joined battle driven only by "the God-implanted instinct which impels a man to defend his own hearthstone." But, equally plainly, the conflict in which Lantry and his kind are involved is another conflict, and in another imaginary country, entirely. Nor is any attempt made, in *Rogue's March* or any of these other mountain novels set during the Revolution, to link the earlier conflict to the later one. Narratives of the Civil War, with titles like *A Rebel's Recollections* (1878), *Personal Recollections and Experiences in the Confederate Army* (1897), and *A Soldier's Recollections: Leaves from the Diary of a Young Confederate* (1910), all forged a connection between Confederate troops and their "heroic sires" of the American Revolution. In fact, the connection in these narratives between the two wars, and in particular between the two armies fighting for home and freedom, became something of a commonplace. For that matter, even a novelist writing *before* the Civil War might try to suggest a link between sectional and Revolutionary conflict: in books such as *The Partisan* (1835) and *The Forayers* (1855), William Gilmore Simms makes little attempt to conceal the connection he is making between his story set during the War of Independence and his hidden agenda of furthering the independence of the South ("I have long since regarded the separation [of North and South] as a now inevitable necessity," he wrote in 1850). Simms's Tories, after all, have all the ferocious materialism and futile idealism of the stereotypical Yankee, while his patriots are Southern gentlemen and yeomen. No such correspondence is made or even hinted at in these novels of the Revolution in the hills, however. That Revolution is portrayed as a conflict sui generis, the typology of which has a significance beyond itself only to the extent that it supplies a checklist of mountain values—and tends, in particular, to foreground the courage, the soldierly qualities of the mountain man. As a special, privileged setting, it enables unconflicted celebration of the Southern highlander's role in the Southern past; it allows the writer to insert the mountain man in history, while springing him free of the contradictions that any life—and, particularly, a life lived on the margins—usually carries with it. In short, it offers a perfect, miniature illustration of the strategy by which a culture can accommodate difficult facts and make them tolerable—not least, by allowing the unsayable to remain unsaid.

What is left unsaid in those novels that deal with the hills just before the outland invasion is perhaps less obvious; nevertheless, there is a similar narrowing of focus. And what that narrowing entails is suggested by this passage from one novel of more recent mountain history, *Their Ancient Grudge* (1946) by Harry H. Kroll: "Anderson Hatfield . . . was . . . still a warlike figure. He was a heavy man . . . ; his forked black beard, streaming behind him as he rode, gave him a Mosaic aspect. . . . He wore high black boots, and he toted his Winchester as a cavalryman carries a carbine. Grim, hard, a little theatrical, he was the picture of a warrior."[49] *Their Ancient Grudge* draws its material from an actual, epic feud between two mountain families, the Hatfields and the McCoys; and, in doing so, it leans heavily on the image of the hill people as primitivist heroes, men and women as tough as the land that shaped them and as unrelenting as the lives and weather they endure. Anderson Hatfield, the patriarchal head of the Hatfield clan, is a figure out of the pages of the Old Testament, a little larger than life, a man whose measured and dramatic gestures turn his every waking moment into ceremony. In this, he is no different from the heroes and heroines of all the novels of this kind, which focus on the ritualized violence of earlier mountain life: among them, another novel by Kroll, *The Smouldering Fire* (1955), as well as *Moonshine* (1926) by John F. Oertel, *Devil's Brigade* (1930) by John L. Spivak, *Our Bed Is Green* (1934) by Clyde Wilson, *Roseanna McCoy* (1947) by Alberta P. Hannum, and *Hill Man* (1954) by John Garth.[50] These books are populated by grim, determined men and equally grim, enduring women, whose lives are ruled by the stern laws of blood and kin. Implicitly, they set the hard ways of the old days in the hills—and the rough stoicism those ways engendered—against the mired complexities and soft character of modern life—which is to say, the times in which the books were written. Reading a novel like *Their Ancient Grudge*, we may perhaps be reminded of what W. B. Yeats said about his own work

49. Harry H. Kroll, *Their Ancient Grudge* (New York, 1946), 2.

50. John F. Oertel, *Moonshine* (Macon, Ga., 1926); John L. Spivak, *Devil's Brigade: The Story of the Hatfield-McCoy Feud* (New York, 1930); Clyde Wilson, *Our Bed Is Green* (New York, 1934); Harry H. Kroll, *Ancient Grudge* and *The Smouldering Fire* (New York, 1955); Alberta P. Hannum, *Roseanna McCoy* (New York, 1947); John Garth, *Hill Man* (New York, 1954). See also W. B. Yeats, *Autobiographies* (London, 1956), 274. Another connection between Yeats's project and these novels of more recent mountain history is, of course, their frequently conscious mythologizing of the past and, indeed, their active interest, many of them, in the mythologizing process.

in his *Autobiographies.* "As I look backward upon my own writing," Yeats observed, "I take pleasure alone in those verses where it seems to me I have found something hard and cold, some articulation of the Image which is all the opposite of all that I am in my daily life, and all my country is." This is not to say, of course, that Kroll and the others set out deliberately to construct the mountain character as a kind of Yeatsian Anti-Self. There is, however, the sense in all these novels that what the hills once had—deliberation, discipline, an epic kind of dignity—is all that modern culture has lost.

"If it was a hard and narrow life in lack of money," the narrator of *Their Ancient Grudge* observes of old mountain culture, "in other ways it was abundant enough." What that abundance consisted in, we learn, was the reward for fighting one's own corner, relying on self and clan: "plenty of meat and bread," "clothes . . . from the weaving and spinning of the womenfolk," "their own wheat . . . carried . . . to the mill along with their corn to be ground into flour and meal." This is not Arcadia, though, nor even a variation on the Agrarian notion of the good farmer. The common emphasis on feuding and breaking of the *written* law, and more generally on the dour but dramatic side of mountain life, should perhaps alert us to that. The men and women of these novels are a haunting mixture of the elemental and the theatrical: like the elements in their harsh simplicity and lack of sentiment, and unlike them to the extent that their elemental natures are learned. "When men fought," Roseanna McCoy reflects in *Their Ancient Grudge,* "it was like storms and fires. The women, like the little creatures, were the ones that suffered." "The womenfolk endured it," we are told elsewhere in the novel, "as they stoically accepted everything else in this man-made world of the wild mountains." The mountain world of these books is "man-made" in a dual sense. It is the work of culture. It is also clearly the work of a harshly *masculine* culture for which the defense of pride and power is crucial; consequently, it imposes a particular burden on women, who are called on even more than usual to serve and to suffer. "It was so natural that no woman ever rebelled against giving herself to her man when he desired her," the reader learns in *Their Ancient Grudge,* "she had her babies in season and out; she worked in the kitchen and labored in the fields; and sometimes she willingly fought with him when the call came to shoot and kill." This theme of the burden of women borne stoically is common in all kinds of mountain novels—and, for that matter, in all kinds of Southern stories—between the wars. In books like *Their Ancient Grudge,* however, it is not definitive, determining; it is, rather, one thread in a pattern woven out of a fundamental sympathy for "masculine" values. "If it could be made to seem a sordid existence," the narrator of Kroll's novel explains, having detailed how the hill women could suffer, "it also had its stalwart side and its grandeur. Few of the hill men philandered. They defended their homes with a fierce integrity. If their women were violated the men went forth to avenge them. As best they could, they provided a home for their families. They did it by common labor, by farming, by timbering, making whiskey. Nobody worried about book learning, for it was so rarely needed it became a social grace and almost an affectation."[51] Plainly, the priorities at work here in the hidden agenda of the narrative are "man-made" too. The men are forceful, even violent, the women suffer as a result: but, according to the terms of this agenda, the men redeem themselves by performing the fundamental male duty of defending "their" homes and "their" women from other men—if necessary, by force. In this hard, cold, and fundamentally patriarchal world, action and performance take precedence over sentiment and reflection; the men may be cruel at times, but that cruelty is seen as a function of their elemental simplicity and primitive energy—as such, while not necessarily condoned, it is certainly extenuated and "explained." What these novels of the recent mountain past describe, in short, is a sanctuary for male and modernist anxiety: a privileged setting where, even if female suffering is acknowledged, it is so finally as the price that must be paid for a culture of power and theatrical "grandeur."

Their Ancient Grudge ends with a narrative touch that is typical of these stories. One of the Hatfield clan, who goes by the name of Cotton Top, is hanged for the murder of one of the McCoys. It is a public hanging and, as Cotton Top stands on the scaffold, he declares, "I want to sing this hyar gathering my ballad, which contains my last will and testament of faith." In this ballad, we learn, "Cotton Top told of his childhood at his mother's knee. Then his first cigarette. Then his first drink." He also describes how "he was led astray by a wicked woman . . . shot craps, played cards . . . ran with wild companions," and how he arrived at the final chapter of his story—"at last murder and now his doom." The story comes with a moral. "He wanted all within sound of his voice never to take the first cigarette," we are told, "the first drink of the Demon Rum." "While in jail," Cotton Top reveals, "God had put His

51. Kroll, *Ancient Grudge,* 51–52. See also 76.

hands upon him"; as a result, "he had repented his sins, made his peace with God."[52] As a whole, the episode provides an appropriate finale for a novel that clearly aims for some of the cold passion, the steely theatricality of traditional tales and folk song—where notions of sin and salvation certainly have a place but not the finer feelings associated with, say, the sentimental novel, or the subtler thought processes to be found in modernist narratives. "There is a relation between discipline and the theatrical sense," Yeats argued in *Autobiographies.* "If we cannot imagine ourselves as different from what we are and assume that second self, we cannot impose a discipline upon ourselves, though we may accept one from others. Active virtue as distinguished from the passive acceptance of a current code is therefore theatrical, consciously dramatic, the wearing of a mask. It is the condition of arduous full life."[53] The "arduous full life" is exactly what the characters of these novels of the recent past are seen to be living, especially the male ones, as they struggle to imitate and perform an idea of active, individual discipline. Anse Hatfield toting his Winchester, Cotton Top Hatfield singing on the scaffold: both are grimly determined and powerfully theatrical men, for whom virtue, proper conduct is a matter at once of ethics and aesthetics—something that demands both strenuous moral commitment and a strong sense of style. In this "man-made" world, it is the fixed and firmly theatrical that does the true work of culture; the impulsive, errant fluencies of sentiment are to be controlled, dominated, turned into some kind of art. If we want a convenient paradigm for novels such as *Their Ancient Grudge* it is surely this, the song on the scaffold, with its intimations of aestheticizing violence, resisting fear, and ritualizing pain. Casting a cold eye on life and death, these books and the hill folk they describe rarely relax and never surrender to sentiment; for them the truth of life consists, precisely if unconsciously, in fiction, the wearing of a mask.

Their Ancient Grudge, The Smouldering Fire, Roseanna McCoy, Hill Man, and other books like them could perhaps be described as primitivist. Certainly, the description fits to the extent that all these narratives celebrate and sometimes seek to imitate the primitive grandeur, at once simple and theatrical, of traditional mountain culture. Primitivism is, though, a notoriously slippery word, loaded with a freight of different meanings; and there are other novels of mountain life in which quite

---

52. Ibid., 323–24.
53. Yeats, *Autobiographies,* 469.

different equations are at work—primitive = savage, primitive = natural and, perhaps most interesting of all, primitive = mysterious. Among those novels that identify hill culture as one of primitive, aboriginal savagery, an additional dimension is at work, in that the relationship with time in them is fluid and indeterminate, sometimes to the point of appearing to resist assignment to any particular day or date. One of them, *Heathen Valley* (1962) by Romulus Linney is set in 1898 but that hardly seems to matter since it describes a people who, we are told, belong to some ahistorical "pagan land." In another, *Dossie Bell Is Dead* (1939), the author Jack Boone is at pains to tell the reader, in a Foreword, that, although his story is set in the past, "the primitive conditions described . . . still hold to a great extent."[54] And in two other books written by the same author, John Fort, *Stone Daugherty* (1929) and *God in a Straw Pen* (1931), the reader is quickly alerted to the fact that the narrative is functioning primarily on a mythical, subliminal, and even antihistorical level. *Stone Daugherty,* Fort insists in a Preface more than once, is "not a historical novel." That denial would serve equally for *God in a Straw Pen,* which centers on a religious revival figured as a moment of orgiastic release—surrender to a much darker, wilder god than the one who is supposed to be the object of worship. For that matter, it would cover both *Heathen Valley,* about the doomed attempt of a missionary to convert a lost upland valley to his faith, or *Dossie Bell Is Dead,* a book with a tangled plot of sex, betrayal, and violence involving people who couple or kill each other without thinking or even feeling very much about it. "Emotionless" is a word that recurs in *Dossie Bell Is Dead,* to describe its mountain characters; "benastied" occurs even more frequently in *Heathen Valley* for the same purpose. Both terms measure the distance between *these* hill people and common notions of human motive, sense, and sensibility; they are outside of history, it seems, because they are icons, emblems of aboriginal impulse—a force that drives them, irresistibly and almost never for the good.

The narrative spine of *Heathen Valley* is a journey of a kind common

54. Jack Boone, "Foreword" to *Dossie Bell Is Dead* (New York, 1939), vi. See also Romulus Linney, *Heathen Valley* (New York, 1962), 57; John Fort, Preface to *Stone Daugherty* (New York, 1929). Also John Fort, *God in a Straw Pen* (New York, 1931), 129. Stories that tap the equation "Southern highlands = primitive = savage" have continued to be popular: note, for instance, the success of James Dickey's novel *Deliverance* (New York, 1970).

to many novels compelled to explore the heart of darkness: the protagonist travels inward—in this case, into "a high, upland valley, boxed in by
vicious spurs and ridges"—and, as he does so, finds himself confronted
and eventually conquered by a world that challenges all his notions of
the civilized. The protagonist, an Episcopalian bishop, is haunted by the
tales of a botanist he meets, who tells him of an "isolated and desolate
and romantic" spot in the North Carolina mountains. There, in that
spot, the botanist reveals, live a people,

> forsaken and isolated, slipping back into savagery as the memories
> of the eastern seaboard . . . of towns and houses and churches and
> meetings left them. A people the botanist vividly characterized as
> haunted by hallucinations and night spirits, obsessed by lunacy and
> death, hungry and violent, celebrating their passions and fears in
> wild, amoral sprees, wandering barefoot with ancient homemade
> long rifles . . . and speaking a curt, blunt language, occasionally
> obscured by forgotten words unknown to him. They killed and they
> starved . . . they lived like goats and monkeys . . . inbreeding, not
> only close kin but direct descendants, father and daughter, mother
> and son.[55]

The bishop is driven to make the long, difficult journey into the mountains by what he hears, in particular, about the superstitions and wild
religious rituals of these strange and desolate souls. "At Christmas unspeakable riots took place," he learns. "It was the last, sad remembrance
of their religion . . . and . . . they celebrated the nativity with loathsome
imagery." And as he makes that journey and then tries to convert "the
forsaken mountain pagans" he finds there, the singular power of his story
stems directly from the way his bewildered vision of things is imposed
upon us. "The ancient, virgin forest, somber, drenched in summer rain
. . . closed arms" on the bishop and his traveling companion, we are told.
The mists that hover in the valley seem "incredible, foreign . . . fantastic
dancers, amorphous, unworldly"; they dissolve the concrete lineaments
of their surroundings—and challenge the fixities and definites of their
faith. In this lost world, the travelers find themselves disoriented by a
people who do not know the difference between the biblical Bethlehem
and Bethlehem, Pennsylvania, who believe in charms and spells and confuse the notion of the devil with some vague memory of the king of En-

55. Linney, *Heathen Valley*, 47. See also 46, 58, 63, 277.

gland. For a while, the bishop struggles along with others to alter the material conditions and the spirit of the place. Eventually, though, he and they withdraw defeated. The mountain folk "fall back into their slovenly ways"; and the man who would have changed their strange, surreal legends is himself absorbed into them, becomes part of the fabric of their superstition and savagery. "The Bishop passed into myth," the narrator discloses, ". . . he was the black Bishop . . . and already they were frightening their children with tales of his devil's order . . . another demon populated their long nights."

Like the creatures the bishop meets in "heathen valley," many of the hill people in these novels appear to live outside of all law, religious or civil; the quality of independence celebrated in so much other writing about the Southern highlands is translated here into a stubborn and dangerous form of selfishness. "I hain't got no time for no law," insists a character nicknamed "the Iron Squire" in *Dossie Bell Is Dead.* "I says if a man does what he figgers is right, hit's right. Hit's right for him and wy should he be worryin' whether hit's right for anybody else." Acting on this belief, the Squire beats his pregnant daughter to get the name of the father of her child out of her. Similarly, in the name of "what he figgers is right," another character casually kills two men he overhears talking in disparaging terms about himself and his deceased wife; while the Squire's daughter shows herself to be of a like mind with her father, by killing the man she wanted to marry when he rejects her. The lives of all these hill people are nasty, brutish, and chaotic. They act on simple impulse, driven by personal desire, will, and pride. Religion is something unknown or unwanted by many of them—"I haint wantin' to inherit no kingdom of God," "the Iron Squire" explains, "I got enough to do here on earth lookin' after my bottom farm";[56] and if it is practiced at all, it acts merely as another expression of anarchy, a means of orgiastic release. Explaining why he is off to a big revival meeting, for example, a character called Jed McConnel in *God in a Straw Pen* says simply, "The only reason I'm a-goin is to do some wrastlin' with the women folks . . . I'm aimin' to get a belly full o' religion and women afore it's over." Like all these characters, of course, Jed speaks only for himself; nevertheless, the central scene of revival in this novel makes it clear that, for all these mountain folk, worship is just another way of loosing their fundamental, inner disorder upon the world. "Women leaped to the tops of logs,

<hr/>

56. Boone, *Dossie Bell Is Dead,* 115. See also 116.

shrieked and screamed," the narrative reveals, ". . . reaching their hands upward with a tremulous jerking movement, fingers wide apart and shrieking as if invisible power flowed downward through them." Some of the men, in turn, "fell to the earth on their hands and knees and barked like dogs, frothing and foaming at the mouth in delirium." Women and men come together, finally, as the assembled company, caught "like leaves in a gale of wind" runs "screaming out into the woods." "Low laughter of a woman from behind a dark screen of laurel bushes" is heard, we are told, as the narrator ends the orgy by taking us back to that mountain man who earlier disclosed just why *he* was going to the meeting, "You're tearing the dress, offen me, Jed."[57]

In his monumental study of Orientalism, Edward Said has identified the way the Occidental imagination has positioned the Orient as "an 'object' of study, stamped with otherness—as all that is different, whether it be 'subject' or 'object.' " "The Orient is *watched*," Said explains, ". . . the European, whose sensibility tours the Orient, is a watcher, never involved, always detached, always ready for new examples of what the *Description de l'Egypte* called 'bizarre jouissance.' "[58] Endowed with "a constitutive otherness," an "essentialist character" that excludes even the possibility of historical change, "the Orient becomes a living tableau of queerness"; and, inevitably, the "queer" then helps to define the "normal" just as the "normal" served to determine the "queer" in what Said calls "a rather complex dialectic of reinforcement." Said underlines the link between discourse and policy here. The " 'object' of study will be, as is customary, passive, non-participating," he argues, ". . . non-autonomous, non-sovereign with regard to itself," it will be acted upon rather than acting. So "a typology . . . which makes the studied 'object' another being with regard to whom the studying subject is transcendent" becomes, in effect, a function of the "will to govern." There are several fairly obvious ways in which this practice of watching, the fashioning of an essential otherness, can be read into Southern writing. As far as the larger problem of the South is concerned, there is clearly a connection between the forms of domination Said identifies and the habit of positioning Southern literature and culture as definitively *regional*. According to these terms, the positioning of the South as

---

57. Fort, *God in a Straw Pen,* 214. See also 28, 183–84.

58. Edward Said, *Orientalism* (London, 1978), 96. All quotations here are from pages 92–100, concluding the first section of the book, "The Scope of Orientalism."

"other," we could say, is a means not merely of denying it serious status but also of exercising forms of control—or, as Said puts it, "a . . . style for dominating, restructuring, and having authority over" it. It is not necessary, after all, to adopt a conspiratorial notion of history in order to see how a discourse that defined the South as "other"—and, into the bargain, inactive and unsovereign—would enable policies that, for good or ill, ignored its interests. On a more particularistic level, the model Said proposes is useful when looking at "difference" *within* the culture of the South as well as at the broader notion of Southern "difference." The positioning of African Americans as "other," and the importance of that positioning as an expression of a specifically white Southern will to power, is perhaps obvious. A discourse that defines black Southerners as "customary, passive . . . non-autonomous, non-sovereign" objects clearly enables—and even supplies an ideological justification for—white domination of them; practices of "watching" quickly translate here into policy. Less obvious, perhaps, but especially to the point here is the positioning of mountain culture as "other," "a living tableau of queerness" to use Said's phrase. Books like *Heathen Valley, Dossie Bell Is Dead,* and *God in a Straw Pen* take the reader into some exotic, ahistorical world the bizarre nature of which springs precisely from its difference: difference, that is, from the normative values of the watching outlander—which is to say, both the narrator and the reader.

It is important, in this context, to distinguish between different kinds of strangeness as far as portraits of mountain life are concerned. After all, a sense of strangeness or otherness could hardly be excluded from any account of a society that, by any definition, was marginalized and—for a while, at least—separated from the general pace of cultural development. The books that gravitate toward primitivism go further than this, however. In their necessarily individual ways, they present the hill people and their world as definitively, constitutively "other," their otherness determined by the watching eye, the normative view of the narrator. These people are separated off from history, not just in the sense that they do not share the same series of historical changes at the same time as their lowland neighbors, but in a more essentialist way: because, for good or ill (or both), they exist apart from the forces operating in the field of historical evolution. As such, they are not quite as human as "we," the narrator and readers are; blessedly free of modernist anxiety or damnably pagan and anarchic, they are without subjectivity; they are, in a word, exotics, the strangeness of whose lives is something that is both defined by, and helps to define, the "norm"—which is to say, "our" own experience. This holds just as true for the characters in those books for whom the equation primitive = natural or primitive = mysterious is the one that matters. Here, too, writers draw on what seems to be an almost bottomless reservoir of strangeness. Those novels that explore the "natural" character of mountain life are, on the whole, the less interesting because the strangeness, the exotic differences rehearsed here are more familiar and predictable, the staple idiom of pastoral literature. Living close to the body of the earth, feeling the pulse of the seasons, bowing to the compulsions of nature: traditional pastoralist themes like this, and the narrative rhythms they inspire, are played out in all these books— among them, *Mountain Born* (1930) by Emmett Gowen, *Sharon* (1931) and *Hawk in the Wind* (1938) by Helen T. Miller, *Shadows Slant North* (1937) by Mary Bledsoe, *The Hills Step Lightly* (1941) by Alberta P. Hannum—and two later works by one of those commentators who suggested that the old ways of the hills might "well find their last refuge between the covers of a few books," Wilma Dykeman, *The Tall Woman* (1962) and *The Far Family* (1966).[59] For that matter, those themes and rhythms are at work locally in a passage like the following. It comes from *Mountain Born,* but it could just as easily be found in countless other forms of the pastoral—outside the mountains, or outside the South: "Round and round Fate brogued behind the plow, plowing and feeling the beat and rhythm of the plow. . . . There was a rhythm in the toilsome quivering of the big rump muscles of the team, in the creaking of the single-trees, in the soft thudding of the earth as it turned up slickly on the share and curved in a running brown wave."[60]

If there are special variations on the pastoral in these novels praising the "natural" quality of mountain life, they take two forms: both of them issuing out of the inclination all these novelists share to associate the bodies of their hill folk with the body of the earth. One variation follows

---

59. Emmett Gowen, *Mountain Born* (Indianapolis, 1930); Helen T. Miller, *Sharon* (Philadelphia, 1931) and *Hawk in the Wind* (New York, 1938); Mary Bledsoe, *Shadows Slant North* (Boston, 1937); Alberta P. Hannum, *The Hills Step Lightly* (New York, 1941); Wilma Dykeman, *The Tall Woman* (New York, 1962) and *The Far Family* (New York, 1966). Among the writers who explore the equation "Southern highlands = primitive = natural," Dykeman is not the only one to have contributed to collections of essays on mountain life and culture: see, e.g., the essay by Alberta P. Hannum, "The Mountain People," in *Great Smokies and Blue Ridge* edited by Peattie.

60. Gowen, *Mountain Born*, 12–13.

on from that portrait of Fate Shannon, the hero of *Mountain Born,* plowing the land. It is, quite simply, to foreground the primacy of physical sensation, the immersion of these mountain characters in the material substances of themselves and their surroundings. This is not merely a matter of comparison between the human and the natural, although that certainly plays its part: Fate's body, for instance, is compared to "a sapling just getting big enough to be called a tree," while his lover and eventual wife, Nearne Fields, is said to be "like a flower, with a white stem and a yellow blossom." Connections like these are important—not least, because of the sheer specificity of the comparison (not just any sapling, but one at a particular point in its growth, not just any flower but one with close correspondences of coloring). They are, though, less vital to the *physicality* of a narrative like this than that emphasis on the interpenetration of the human and the natural, communality of experience rather than simple correspondence, that is there in the portrait of everything someone like Fate or Nearne does, be it at work or play. Dancing, Fate "gave himself over to the sound" of the fiddle, we are told, "his body swaying like a willow in a musical wind." Fighting, he "knew the wild joy of feeling his fists crash against flesh and bone." Drinking, Fate's brother Dave "aimed to feel the warm fumes" of the alcohol "spread from his stomach outward. He aimed for it to get him a joyful wildness, like that of a storm raging in the mountains." It is, perhaps not surprisingly, when two human bodies join with each other that this feeling of joining with the earth reaches a peak of intensity among these mountain characters. What is more surprising is how the earth itself becomes bathed in erotic feeling. One hill man in *Mountain Born* dreams of "the mountain, the spring and the two elongated hills turn[ing] into a vast-sized woman, lying on her back, with the hills as outstretched legs." Another, we are told, "lay on his back, sensually conscious of the pressure of his weight against the earth;" then "he rubbed one outstretched hand through the dew-wet grass, caressing it with a strange voluptuousness."[61] Usually, these erotic fantasies are linked to an eventual human subject: the man who sees the mountain landscape as an outstretched woman, for instance, is dreaming of the spot where he saw an actual woman bathing naked. That, however, is part of the point. The circuit of sensual feeling runs unbroken from one body to the next, into the earth and then out of it again. This is an imagined land where the boundaries between the

---

61. Ibid., 121, 172. See also 11, 23, 77, 107.

human and the natural, men and animals, women and landscape, are slippery and amorphous, shifting to the point of invisibility.

In *Mountain Born,* the connection between the bodies of men, women, and earth occurs in the realm of the senses; it is charged with a feeling for the vibrant, sensual beauty of the hills. In other novels for which the primitive = natural equation matters, though, what tends to be foregrounded is the sublime, the cold, harsh splendor of highland landscape and character. More to the point, this sublimity that translates into human terms as stubborn pride and dour grandeur is a quality that is specifically attributed here to women—and women living, for the most part, alone in an emotional sense, if not quite literally. The novels by Helen Miller, Mary Bledsoe, Alberta Hannum, and Wilma Dykeman all place a woman at the center, and a woman for whom—as Dykeman observes of her protagonist in *The Tall Woman*—life's "softness had almost disappeared behind a thin set line of determination." These are heroines who bear comparison with the central female figures in *Barren Ground* or *Weeds:* the only, but determining, difference being that identification with the mountain earth enables them not only to survive but also to triumph. It is an identification that is, at once, emotional, imaginative, and physical. Ivy Thurston, the strong woman in *The Far Family,* "felt the links of a long chain reaching backward and forward" on the family farm, the reader is told, "the farm was a world of its own part mountain, part valley, both wild and tame." The same combination of controlled strength and primitive energy she finds in her surroundings impels her—as it does Lydia McQueen the "tall woman" in the book of that name—to work "from before sun till after dark," "until the muscles in her arms were hard and her skin was tough and brown." There is a touch of the formulaic in these stories. The description of the heroine of *Hawk in the Wind,* for instance, could stand for all these strong highland women: she was, we learn, "a tall, strong woman with power in every inch of her tallness, in her steady grey eyes, her proud nose . . . an iron-colored woman, with a purposeful face."[62] The men die, depart, or just linger on the margins while these women, invariably, survive thanks to an obstinacy, an indomitability that is clearly associated with—in fact, derived directly from—the hills; these women endure, we are led to believe, because they are *from* and *of* their surroundings—subdued to the

62. Miller, *Hawk in the Wind,* 2. See also Dykeman, *Tall Woman,* 15, 40, 101; *Far Family,* 120.

elements in which they work. In distinct contrast to *Mountain Born,* it is not the circuit of feeling running from human body to human body via the earth that counts but, rather, the connection of one female body to another one conceived of purely in female terms. These women get their satisfaction, as well as their strength, not so much from men or even other women as from their "mother earth" in the mountains; they learn from those mountains, too, their habits of isolation and survival. "There's something beyond even love," says Lydia McQueen trying to explain what her hills have taught her, "for a woman as well as a man. A body's personhood." It is a bleak ethic. It is, however, one that helps explain the simple power of these narratives—which, in many ways, re-call Elizabeth Jane Harrison's definition of "female pastoral." Eschewing or marginalizing the "courtship plot," these stories focus on the land as what Harrison terms "an enabling force for the woman protagonist." The mountain heroine here enjoys an interaction with the mountains which—as Harrison puts it when referring to female pastoral generally—"changes from passive association to active cultivation or identifica-tion";[63] in the process, she earns the right to the two epithets that recur constantly to describe her home place and now describe her. She is "tall," along with the hills, and, with the hills also, she is "enduring."

"Embedded within the literature written by women about the Appala-chian mountains," Carole Ganim has argued, "is . . . a paradigm of the female union between the concreteness of the physical world and the psychological, moral, and political expression of this earth-based exis-tence." That may be true for some of the fiction written by women about the mountains, Appalachian or elsewhere; it is not, however, universally the case. It hardly applies, for instance, to one woman writer who set her remarkable stories in the hills of Tennessee, Mildred Haun. For her, highland life, far from being earth-based, concrete, and natural was the very opposite of that; in her stories it is, quite literally, the supernatural—the shifting, shadowy, and fundamentally extraordinary—quality of that life that appeals to the imagination; identifying highland places and char-acter with primitive mystery, she represents the extraordinary character of her subject as just that, extraordinary—which is to say, beyond con-ventional *modern* notions of what constitutes the human and real. In this respect, her two books, *The Hawk's Done Gone* (1941) and a larger

---

63. Elizabeth Jane Harrison, *Female Pastoral: Women Writers Re-Visioning the Ameri-can South* (Knoxville, Tenn., 1991), 11. See also Dykeman, *Tall Woman,* 16.

collection published after her death, *The Hawk's Done Gone and Other Stories* (1968), bear comparison with other narratives that foreground the magical or marvelous: most notably, *Bloody Ground: A Cycle of the Southern Hills* (1929) by Fiswoode Tarleton and *Little Squire Jim* (1949) and *Julia Gwynn* (1952) by Robert K. Marshall.[64] All these books measure hill life in terms of its eccentricity, its deviation from realist definitions of the "natural," or positivist notions of the truth. The landscape, as it is represented here, assists in this flight from normalcy into the fantasy, the surrealism of folk tale or fairy tale. These mountain characters inhabit an amorphous, deeply unsettling territory where, as the narrator of *Little Squire Jim,* puts it, "a cloud might sit on a man's front step and mist his windows before slipping quietly out over the yard, leaving far below a great blue valley," or where "the January snows might fall on violets in bloom."[65] In this odd world, the familiar signposts disappear and the customary rules and dividing lines quickly melt away. Using the classic strategy of the gothic artist, these writers immerse us in a world with its own bizarre logic, where the aberrant is made to appear the norm. In the process, the rough magic of *this* version of mountain life acts subversively, to call into question conventional notions of what is usual, humanly plausible, and what is not. Ideas of the normal and the marginal are folded in on each other as the reader is denied the possibility of stable ground, a firm basis for deciding what exactly happens in the story, how it happens and why.

The destabilizing techniques practiced by these writers are partly a matter of language. In *Bloody Ground,* for instance, a peculiarly laconic, rhythmic, and repetitive style defamiliarizes everything, turning every event into a kind of frozen tableau. Men leaving town at night and preparing for a fight, for instance, become—under the pressure of this style—participants in some mysterious, hieratic ritual, whose every ges-

64. Fiswoode Tarleton, *Bloody Ground: A Cycle of the Southern Hills* (New York, 1929); Mildred Haun, *The Hawk's Done Gone* (New York, 1940) and *The Hawk's Done Gone and Other Stories* (Nashville, Tenn., 1968); Robert K. Marshall, *Little Squire Jim* (New York, 1949) and *Julia Gwynn: An American Gothic Tale* (New York, 1952). See also Carole Ganim, "Herself: Woman and Place in Appalachian Literature," *Appalachian Journal,* XIII (Spring 1986), 258. It is possible to see these stories in which the equation "Southern highlands = primitive = mysterious" is at work as offering variations on the gothic: that is, if we are willing to accept the idea of gothic as a generic field rather than a specific genre (see, e.g., Fred Botting, *Gothic* [London, 1996], 2–15).

65. Marshall, *Little Squire Jim,* 17.

ture is invested with weight and significance—so much so, that it is as if we were witnessing this recovered moment and their strange but purposive movements in deliberate, slow motion:

> Gabe Morgan is taking the lead with his brother Dave. Walt and Tod Clay are right behind them. The Clay boys are carrying teapots; Walt is carrying a trumpet. Fallon walks by the side of Rackteen. Nobody speaks. . . . After a while, Gabe Morgan leaves the road and crawls under another fence. The others follow. A cow rises to her feet . . . moves away. . . . A white mule turns her head slowly and looks at them. Dave Morgan lights the wicks in the teapots and places them in a circle around the pasture. Nobody speaks. Things move mechanically, silently, weirdly as in a dream.[66]

Both *Bloody Ground* and *Little Squire Jim* make much of the storytelling and songmaking traditions of the mountains. "History recorded in song!" observes the narrator in *Bloody Ground,* "Where dark as well as uplifting deeds find records. . . . A page from Chaucer in every stark hill." "Their speech still held . . . echoes of Celtic lore," we are told of the people in *Little Squire Jim,* "the woes of Barby Allen and the tragic jealousy of the 'Two Sisters' over one man were sung to them in their cradles." Spoken of in terms that recollect the grave idioms of folk speech, these characters use the same starkly poetic forms of tale-telling themselves. Not only that, they seem to inhabit a world of tall tale and ballad as well as sing of one. A character like Gabe Morgan, for instance, settles disputes about belief through trial by combat—for that is the purpose of the fight being prepared in the passage just quoted—while Little Squire Jim, in the novel of that name, rides through the hills every night on his horse—looking, as he does so, "like to nothin born on land or sea."

Just why Little Squire Jim chooses to spend his nights in the way he does, or why Gabe Morton relies on ritualized violence to settle matters of belief, remains a mystery. Narratives like these resist the familiar explanations of naturalist fiction. Nor do these characters tend to seek explanations for themselves. Little Squire Jim's neighbors, for example, are content to see him as a phantom, a portent, something that just *is.* He "became something in their hearts and imaginations," we are told; "a glimpse of him bent low over the red stallion . . . or the sound of his passing in the night . . . and the hoof marks left clear in the soft loam . . .

---

66. Tarleton, *Bloody Ground,* 91–92. See also 70; Marshall, *Little Squire Jim,* 18, 34.

—these were enough to set their hearts beating."[67] Certainly, these neighbors are willing to take his shadowy presence as a sign, a warning perhaps to mend errant ways; with equal certainty, for many of the women among them he exercises a seductive fascination. They never search behind the sign, however, or care to examine or explain the vocabulary of their belief. Nor do the women he seduces and abandons ever understand the source of his attraction: it is just there, as enigmatic as it is erotic, like a natural magnetic field—or, for that matter, like the pull of the dark stranger in old tales and ballads. There is the clear danger here of melodrama, or the kind of gothic fantasy that thrives on the strangeness of a strange culture—and on finding something sinister and threatening in the simple fact that such a culture is hidden, lurking somewhere on the margins. What mostly saves stories like these from that danger, however, is their immersion in the speech and narrative styles of the people they describe: men and women for whom mystery is a part of nature, a natural function of life. In this small, strange imagined space of the mountains, men perform odd rituals while a cow moves by or a white mule turns its head and watches them; people interpret themselves and their neighbors in terms of signs and signatures that are at once mundane and magic, concrete and tangible—like a hoof mark clearly imprinted in the soft earth. This is a world of *natural* mystery, where spells are to be discovered in the trees, streams, and rocks, and the artefacts of everyday life evidently possess a supernatural power. Just as the stories traverse the gap between fact and fantasy, nature and magic, so do the characters as they struggle to read the signs around them; narrative and narrative subject alike are guided by the belief that the ordinary world opens up almost unlimited access to enchantment and occult meaning.

Of none of these stories is this, perhaps, truer than the ones by Mildren Haun: which, as one commentator, Herschel Gower, observed, work precisely because their "complex . . . rendering of romantic fantasy and realism" is "always within hearing distance of the folk tradition."[68] The tales told in *The Hawk's Done Gone* tell of witchcraft, incest, miscegenation, and infanticide. They also tell of constant supernatural intervention in the natural world. When a witch dies, we learn from these stories, her cow gives bloody milk; the cry of an owl is an omen of death; a dove singing on a house roof signifies a death within a year; burning

67. Marshall, *Little Squire Jim*, 58–59.
68. Herschel Gower, "Introduction" to *Hawk's Done Gone and Other Stories*, x.

sassafras roots ensures a tragedy in the family; a marriage consummated while red haw bushes are in bloom will inevitably end in disaster. Several times, spirits return from the dead in a Haun tale, to assist or advise their loved ones; one character talks to God through a bluebird; another speaks to her dead mother, learning that it takes ninety-one days to travel from earth to heaven. All these tales and others derive their power from Haun's understanding of her hill community, the easy commerce that seems to exist there between, on the one hand, the simple, physical facts of mountain life and, on the other, the metaphysical world—that place from which hidden spirits send their messages, writing their signatures on even the smallest elements. And, despite their constant stress on the aberrant and magical, they draw their plausibility, as documents of genuinely human meaning, from the pull of mountain speech, their devoted attention to the act of telling. All the stories in *The Hawk's Done Gone,* for instance, are told by a woman at the center of the close-knit community she describes: Mary Darthula White Kanipe, a "Granny-woman" for three generations and the most respected person in the county. Haun had once planned to become a "granny-woman" herself in the Hoot Owl District of Cocke County, Tennessee, where she was born—that is, a woman who traditionally attended to the sick, to women at childbirth, and at the laying out of the dead. She was, however, diverted while at Vanderbilt University into a study of the folklore of her home place, under the supervision of the Nashville Agrarian Donald Davidson. The two things, her initial impetus to become a participant in her community and her later desire to tell of that community, then came together in her creation of Mary Kanipe. "I've been Granny-woman to every youngon born in this district for nigh sixty years now," Kanipe informs us in the Prologue to *The Hawk's Done Gone.* "I've tied the navel cords of all the saints and sinners that have seen their first daylight in Hoot Owl District. They all have bellies about alike. There's not much difference."[69] Kanipe has had a colorful and often difficult life in her own right, the reader discovers. The mother of an illegitimate child, she has been married for forty years to someone who has no love for her, and who, in the story that gives the volume its title, takes pleasure in selling off all her possessions cheap—as a sign, it seems, of both his contempt for and his power over her. More to the point, as far as her role as narrator is concerned, she knows more than anyone else in Hoot Owl District about the equally colorful and sometimes even more difficult lives of her neighbors. She is

69. Haun, "Prologue," to *Hawk's Done Gone,* 12.

a witness for the hill community. Her knowledge as a "Granny-woman" supplies the material of these stories; her voice gives that material its drive and rhythm. What is more, by drawing us into her act of telling, she makes us, the readers, act as witnesses too; listening to the tales of a woman who is, by all accounts, both a kind of witch and a midwife, a maker of charms and spells and a doctor, we are plunged with her into a living stream of tradition that seems at once mythic and homely—a world of localized enchantment, grounded mystery.

Just how magic is woven into the everyday lives of Haun's hill folk is suggested by a story like "The Pit of Death." Here, in this story, we learn that Joe White, the narrator's illegitimate son, is regarded with fear and dislike by most of the community because he is a Melungeon, a frontier people probably descended from a mixture of races. Only one local woman, Tiny Brock, is attracted to him; and, when Tiny is forbidden to see him, she and Joe begin meeting in the woods. Apart from the secrecy they offer, the woods seem the right place to meet because they are Joe's true home. He is a trapper with unusual gifts; some local people believe he has even found a way to set traps in a cave between his house and the Brock house. "A few folks thought Joe knowed some paths through that cave," Mary Kanipe recollects. "They allowed there were all sorts of animals in there but nobody had ever been able to get further back into it than five or six yards," she explains. "They allowed Joe might have found a path through it . . . I don't know. He did sometimes grin mighty big when he heard folks talk about that cave." Eventually, Tiny becomes pregnant and when she is about to give birth Joe goes to collect and bring her back to his mother for the delivery. He never returns. Perhaps he has been killed by his stepfather, who, Mary recalls, followed Joe out of the house carrying a gun and on his return "looked sneaking—more sneaking than a sheep-killing dog." All she knows is what she witnessed nine days later, when she went to the Brock house to assist Tiny. Coming home early in the morning after the baby was born, Mary confesses that she "feared to pass that cave." "When I got close to it, I felt like wooly bugs were crawling all over me," she remembers. "It was so quiet I could have heard a feather drop. I tried to run past. My legs wouldn't work. Something made me stop—right in front of the cave." What she heard next, she says, was "chains rattling" in the cave, "animals hollering. And a man's voice—Joe's voice. I knowed it was his voice. And I was sure."[70]

70. Haun, "The Pit of Death," in *Hawk's Done Gone*, 43. See also 35, 40; William Shakespeare, *Hamlet*, Act I, v, line 66, Act II, ii, lines 255–56.

What she was "sure" of remains undisclosed; nevertheless, the intimations are that she is now "sure" of Joe's violent death, her husband's responsibility for it, and the telling of the murder by its victim. The story works perfectly well, of course, as a study of suspicion breeding projection; here and elsewhere Haun draws ambiguity from the use of her "Granny-woman" as witness and narrator. But it works equally well as a study of the fluid boundaries that exist in this version of hill culture between the natural and the supernatural, the cave as a local landmark and as a site of local legend—or, for that matter, between life and death, fact and belief, knowing and understanding. One epigraph for many of these stories might well be that memorable and frequently quoted testament to indeterminacy, narrative or otherwise, in *Hamlet,* "there is nothing either good or bad, but thinking makes it so." What Mary Kanipe believes she sees and hears is not necessarily what she does see and hear. But there is another famous observation from the same play that might make a more suitable epigraph here, because it challenges rational positions more directly and exclusively: there may, after all, be "more things in heaven and earth . . . / Than are dreamt of" in our "philosophy." What Mary believes may, after all, be closer to the truth than we think.

Whether Mary Kanipe is right or wrong about what she "knowed" and how, though, one thing is certain. There is absolutely nothing she can do about it. Haun's stories describe a community in which women can have strange powers—to put "a sure witch sign" on someone they disapprove of, for instance—but where they remain, in the last analysis, powerless. Mary is by no means unique in being at once a person of skill, respect, and influence and someone at the mercy of a man who can do what he likes, it seems, with her property, her loved ones, and her. A common symptom in these stories of this slippage into victim status is incest; whatever position or reputation female characters may have in the community, many of them seem to be at the mercy of their kin in the most literal, brutal sense. In a story called "The New Jerusalem," for example, the women prepare a young girl called Effena Kanipe for her wedding night. "The womenfolks pulled off her last piece of clothes," we are told. "She stood there limp as a hot cabbage leaf and let them put the gown on her. It was the first gown Effena had ever had. She made it herself."[71] Then, "Donna Fawver raised Effena's arms up, and somebody else slipped the gown over her head. All together they lifted her up and

71. Haun, "The New Jerusalem," in *Hawk's Done Gone,* 83. See also 84, 86.

laid her over on the far side of the bed—on the side next to the wall."
Having prepared Effena, and after ringing a cowbell to announce she is
ready, they withdraw. The new husband, Murf Owens, then arrives. His
wife, though, shrinks from him—not, it turns out, because of shyness but
out of shame. "I'm not pyore," she confesses, and so she believes not
worthy to be a bride. Effena is not "pyore," she tells Murf, because she
has been sexually assaulted by her half-brother. Her husband is willing
to "forgive" what was, after all, not her fault; Effena's half-brother, however, is by no means ready to give up what he has possessed, and now
feels he owns. He kills Murf and, even though Effena is carrying Murf's
child, he then continues to assault her. She cannot escape the trap of her
family, it seems; there is no way out for her, because she is both powerless
and ashamed. Her mental imprisonment is doubly oppressive, since her
half-brother believes that she is his and, acting on that, has made her
believe that *she* is in the wrong—that she is not "pyore," and so has lost
her value as a woman and wife. This is a new twist to the story of the
mountain woman; and it shows how deeply Haun was convinced of the
conflicted status of her sex in traditional hill culture. The women in these
stories draw whatever strength they possess, not so much from the concreteness of the natural world as from the vitality of custom; their belief
in themselves flows from their tapping into the wellsprings of magic and
ritual. Their powerlessness, however, issues from the same source. Whatever women like Mary or Effena Kanipe know, whatever strength they
enjoy, is profoundly vitiated by the belief bred into them by kin and community that their magic does not yield mastery. The final, acknowledged
source of authority here remains male; power, all the signs of kin and
tradition tell them, belongs to the man—even that little of it ceded, for a
while, to a woman.

The irony of this position was never more subtly sketched out than in
one of Haun's stories published after her death. Called "The Look," the
story is told by a young woman, the only female child in a large family
who discloses in a quietly stoical and laconic style just how brutally she
has been treated by her mother and brothers. The opening statement of
the story is particularly cryptic. "She didn't say e'er a word as she was
dying, Ma didn't," the young woman observes. "She just looked at me,
like a cat looking at a bird, setting its eye on it, making it set still where
it is. And I come back home." Thanks to that "look," she has decided to
stay at home after her mother dies. "I couldn't a-handily been blamed if
I hadn't," she admits, ". . . if I had stayed away and let the boys shift for

themselves. But after that look that last morning I could do nothing else but come."[72] She could have hardly been blamed if she had stayed away, we learn, because her brothers have constantly abused her, selling her property for their own gain, taking her wages after making her do outside work, beating and humiliating her; one brother has also sexually assaulted her since she was twelve. But whenever she has been mistreated, her mother has always defended and excused her brothers. Now, although the young woman would prefer to live elsewhere—with a widowed cousin, who plainly loves and respects her—that last "look" from her mother compels her to come back and, quite probably, suffer still more abuse. Gradually, the reason both for her mother's defense of the abusive behavior of her sons, and that "look," are unraveled by the narrator. The young woman was, she feels, "unwanted" by her father, while her mother had constantly told her "she didn't want a girl youngon"—"I reckon she meant it," she adds. Why she meant it, the narrator understands from a conversation with her cousin, stems from the belief that a "witch woman" loses "their power with men folks when a girl youngon is born to them." Her mother was a witch, and giving birth to the narrator meant that she lost her magical power over men. Not over women, however: that last "look," the young woman believes, has placed her under her mother's spell. She is bewitched or—what is the same thing for her—firmly believes she is. Her story ends, really, where it began: the young narrator has to give up her place of sanctuary for precisely the same reason as she has submitted to the abuse of her brothers over the years. She has no will, no power that she can call her own.

Like most of Haun's stories, "The Look" can be read in at least two ways, as a study in enchantment or as a psychological study in subjection. The mother's "look," after all, can be read as a witch's stare or as a gaze that reduces the human subject to subjected status. The two are not, of course, mutually exclusive; and either way the ironies of the story remain fundamentally the same. The women here are at odds to the extent that it is the mother's "look"—and all that "look" implies—that strips her daughter of defenses. As the young woman sees it, her mother denies her what above all determines subjectivity: the capacity to choose and then both articulate and enact that choice. It does not take a particularly intensive reading of the story, however, to see that—despite the coldness and

72. Haun, "The Look," in *Hawk's Done Gone and Other Stories,* 101. See also 105, 107.

even hatred that exists between them—mother and daughter are also ironically alike in their ultimate powerlessness. They may be at odds, divided, but the crucial division exists elsewhere—between the men, who hold all the important cards, and the women who have to live somehow with what they are dealt. This is true in a practical sense: it is the men here who do what they want with bodies and properties, while the women either suffer or make excuses. And it is true also of the belief systems at work here, informing cultural practice. The mother believes that such power as she has over men is not just diluted but drained away by the birth of a female child. She resents her daughter as both a cause and a sign of impotence, the occasion and the mirror of that part of herself which is feminine and consequently weak. What is more, the daughter believes that too; she is a victim, finally, because she thinks she is and deserves to be. The fact that it is the daughter, the victim who tells us the tale, only adds to our sense that her manacles are mind-forged in a double sense: a function of beliefs that she and the other women of her mountain community share, fiercely and devoutly, with their men. Like her, the women of Haun's stories may be strong but their strength consists, finally, in dealing with a world they never made and a culture, a way of life over which they have little control. Even for the evidently powerful witch women of the Hoot Owl District, this, the fact of fundamental impotence, remains true. Enchantment, mystery may be their special preserve but, their conviction is, the men remain the source of authority here as well. Mary Darthula White Kanipe or the mother in "The Look" may have magical abilities but, it seems, those abilities require a male stamp or signature of authenticity; even in the world of magic, it seems, power is ultimately gendered.

"There's something to dreams and tokens," declares a mountain character called Peg in *Hie to the Hunters* (1950) by Jesse Stuart. "I believe everybody gits the warnin' before the real thing comes along." Peg, we learn, "is the seventh child of a seventh child"; and so, like Haun's witch women, is reckoned to have special, magical powers. He can, one friend and neighbor comments, "blow three times in a baby's mouth and cure the thrash. He can raise knockin' sperets"; "Peg has heard the rattlin' of chains in dark places," the friend adds, "and he's seen lights come on and go off all over these hills."[73] Jesse Stuart came from a poor highland

73. Jesse Stuart, *Hie to the Hunters* (New York, 1950), 215, 219. The other works by Stuart cited here are *Man with a Bull-Tongue Plow* (New York, 1934); *Head o' W-Hollow*

background similar to that of Haun—in his case, the highlands of Kentucky; and he also received encouragement to write about his home place from Donald Davidson. There the similarity ends, however. Stuart was a far more prolific writer than Haun. Besides novels, his output includes poetry (such as *Man with a Bull-Tongue Plow* [1934]), collections of short stories (including *Head o' W-Hollow* [1936], *Men of the Mountains* [1941], *Ploughshare in Heaven* [1956] and *Save Every Lamb* [1964]), and extensive autobiographical writings dealing with his family (*Beyond Dark Hills: A Personal Story* [1938]), his father (*God's Oddling* [1960]) as well as his own experiences as a child of the hills and then later a teacher and a writer (*The Thread That Runs So True* [1950], *The Year of My Rebirth* [1956]). More to the point, Stuart was obsessed both with what he saw as the uniquely agrarian character of mountain life and the disappearance of that life under the steamroller of change. His work is crowded with hymns to the highland earth and character. "All my strength goes back into the land," admits the hero of one of his novels, *Trees of Heaven* (1940), "the land is all." "We are the blood of the hill people, we have always been hill people," declares another man in one of Stuart's short stories, "the hills have become a part of us, in our brain and the dirt of the hills is the clay of us." That "always" is a cry of desperation, however, torn out of a sense of crisis. All Stuart's work is framed by his feeling that, as he put it in 1964, "my world has changed since I was a boy. No one digs all his livelihood from the soil here any more." "My once wonderful world has changed," he lamented, "into a world that gives me great unhappiness."[74]

Not surprisingly, perhaps, given this sense of disconnection from a "wonderful" childhood world, many of Stuart's portraits of the traditional hill culture of Kentucky—both those that are fictional, and the ones that claim to be unvarnished fact—are little more than excursions into a kind of rough pastoral. The author's father, Mick, in particular, is translated in memory into "an uneducated poet of the earth" who "liked

---

(New York, 1936); *Beyond Dark Hills: A Personal Story* (New York, 1938); *Men of the Mountains* (New York, 1941); *The Thread That Runs So True* (New York, 1950); *The Year of My Rebirth* (New York, 1956); *Ploughshare in Heaven* (New York, 1956); *God's Oddling: The Story of Mick Stuart, My Father* (New York, 1960); *Save Every Lamb* (New York, 1964). A useful selection of his work is to be found in *A Jesse Stuart Reader: Stories and Poems Selected and Introduced by Jesse Stuart* (New York, 1963).

74. Stuart, "Introduction" to *Save Every Lamb*, 9–10. See also *Trees of Heaven* (New York, 1940), 55; "This Is the Place," in *Men of the Mountains*, 316.

to watch things grow" and "didn't have to go away to find beauty" because "he found it everywhere around him." Mick Stuart seems to hover behind the natural poets and mountain patriarchs that crop up constantly in his son's work: the old man in *The Good Spirit of Laurel Ridge* (1953), for instance, who claims that "there are still pockets of earth left as God made 'em. Fruits, nuts, and wild game as they have been in the beginnin'," then adds that Laurel Ridge where he has a small farm "is one of those places." Where Stuart departs from the pastoral, however, is at those moments when the crudity and violence of hill life compel his attention: most notably, in *Taps for Private Tussie* (1943), in which a large hill family called the Tussies spend the GI insurance money of one of their kin as quickly and wildly as possible—only to discover that he is not, in fact, dead. The comedy here is broad, even grotesque. The Tussie family, all forty-five of them, are known locally as "a breed of cats." The opening portrait of the head of the household, Grandpa Tussie, focuses on the stream of tobacco juice running down his white beard "that he would catch with his tongue and pull . . . back into his mouth and spit . . . out again." When Grandpa and the other Tussies go to get "relief grub," we are told, they often "get tanked on rotgut and fussed with one another. Sometimes they tried to fight." And, when the Tussie clan rent a big house with the insurance money—which they then proceed to devastate—young Sid Tussie, the narrator, is spellbound by the sight of an indoor toilet. "I wondered what we'd do for something to laugh at on moonless nights when one of us used to take a lantern and go," he explains. "We'd even watch Grandpa and Grandma"; "Grandpa . . . would keep it lit all the way," he adds, ". . . it pleased him to hear us laugh at him from the schoolhouse. . . . But Grandma always got mad. She'd call us a lot of fool names . . . that I had never heard before."[75] The references to GI insurance, relief food, and indoor plumbing are the clues here. Often—although by no means always—when Stuart turns his attention to hill life just before or just after the Second World War, the pastoral elements melt away. What takes their place is a type of broad comedy that bears comparison with Caldwell: not least, because it casts a cold eye on social change. The difference with Caldwell, though—and it is a crucial one—is that the comedy is not informed by any redemptive social message; the story here is much simpler. Change has turned the sturdy

75. Stuart, *Taps for Private Tussie* (New York, 1943), 74. See also 11, 40, 41, 56; *The Good Spirit of Laurel Ridge* (New York, 1953), 74; *God's Oddling*, 38–39.

mountain man into a rough beast, it seems; and comedy becomes a means of defusing any anxiety the author—and, by implication, the reader— may feel about that beast. The humor is not, as it is in Caldwell's fiction, a tool for understanding and maybe altering social mechanisms; it acts merely as a temporary means of emotional release. In this respect, *Taps for Private Tussie* belongs with several books of the period that attempt to deal humorously with mountain life and its contemporary alterations: among them, *The Doctor's Pills Are Stardust* (1938) and *The Devil Takes a Hill Town* (1939) by Charles C. Givens, *The Potters o' Skunk Hollow* (1946) by Ivan Blair Anthony, *Jackson Mahaffey* (1951) by Fred Ross, and *Mountain Mating* (1954) by Marian Parker.[76] In all these books, comedy has a cathartic and not a corrective function; it is there just as an escape valve for disquiet.

Several times in *Taps for Private Tussie*, Sid the narrator and some of his relatives visit town to collect relief. This is how they prefer to find a means to live, apparently—that is, until the GI insurance money comes along; certainly, they would rather do this than try, somehow, to make a living. "I'd seen people come and ask Grandpa to work," Sid confides, "but he'd always tell them that he was down in his back." The bad back does not prevent Grandpa from dancing or walking to town once a week to take the "relief grub" home. But it provides a convenient excuse for him to do what he likes best: "he'd send me to the woods to find sticks for kindlin," Sid recalls, ". . . while he lay under the shade of the hickory trees and picked his banjer." On the trips to town, Sid sees many men and women who, to all appearances, seem exactly the same as the Tussies. And, on the way back home Sid observes "many we passed staggerin on the turnpike with full sacks of relief grub over their shoulders"; "many of the men," he adds, ". . . had sold their fresh eggs for less than the grocery stores sold them and they'd brought beer or rotgut. They could get rotgut anyplace on relief day."[77] The premise of the comedy lies here, in the perceived corruption of mountain folk by the welfare agencies and money markets of the lowlands. Each of the Tussies retains one or two of the traditional hill talents or values. Grandpa Tussie, for

76. Charles C. Givens, *The Doctor's Pills Are Stardust* (New York, 1938) and *The Devil Takes a Hill Town* (New York, 1939), Ivan Blair Anthony, *The Potters o' Skunk Hollow* (Boston, 1946); Fred Ross, *Jackson Mahaffey* (Boston, 1951); Marian Parker, *Mountain Mating* (New York, 1954).

77. Stuart, *Taps for Private Tussie*, 56. See also 31, 32, 182, 248.

instance, has an abiding love of the land: with $300 of the insurance money left over after most of the rest has been frittered away, he buys a small plot and "as he spoke of ownin land," his grandson recollects, "he was happier than I had ever seen him." Sid's Uncle Mott, in turn, is knowledgeable about hunting and trapping, while his Uncle George has a talent for music and folk song—"his magic fiddle," we are told, "had played his way into the hearts of many women." These residual virtues cannot, however, hide the fact that the Tussies have been demoralized by change. In this respect, the easy money that comes to them from the GI insurance scheme acts as a comic paradigm of the similarly easy money to be had from the relief agencies, marketing their products or selling their labor rather than working for themselves. There is no sympathy here for the panaceas of either the welfare liberal or the business capitalist; nor is there any belief in the possibility of turning back the tide of social change or altering its direction. All that remains, in comedy like this, is the momentary translation of rage and regret into laughter: the Tussies may seem freakish to us—and, indeed, to some of their neighbors—but, the message is, they are only an exaggeration, an extreme but accurate caricature of what will soon be all that is left of life in the hills.

"The Valley had gone soft—charity soft," reflects "Brother Wally," the principal narrator in *The Devil Takes a Hill Town*, ". . . half the town . . . was on relief. The whole section had changed. Not only in its philosophy and morals but in its entire complexion." The narrative premise of this novel is more bizarre than that of *Taps for Private Tussie*: God and the Devil, in the form of a "Mr. Peebles" and a "Mr. Hooker," visit a small mountain town called Lees. Nevertheless, what lies behind it and similar comic novels set in the highlands are exactly the same anxieties as those that inform the tale Sid Tussie tells. "I'm down here in the hills, jis' watchin' to see what'd happen when they started to drive *mountain* men out of their homes," declares Mr. Peebles. "I had hoped to see a scrap what *was* a fight." "But no; no fight," he complains, ". . . I'm afraid these hill fo'ks don't love their homes as much as I hoped . . . they ain't no more hun'erd-per-cent Amer'cans left."[78] The "devil" that takes the hill town is, in fact, both Mr. Hooker and a malign combination of businessmen, developers, government welfare workers, and dam builders who, between them, ensure what is called, at one point in the novel, "the end of an epoch." "Lees wasn't a southern town any more," Mr. Peebles

78. Givens, *Devil Takes a Hill Town*, 142–43. See also 66, 67, 285.

concludes, "it wasn't a hill town any longer"; and, in the emerging battle between urban capital and urban labor, "both sides is wrong" because both sides have collaborated in the loss of Eden. "The Garden of Eden was in the hills," Mr. Peebles mournfully reflects as he watches the antics of the mountain folk selling their homes and their labor. He then withdraws back to heaven, only to find that the Glory Road is being worked on by the WPA! The bizarre conclusion completes the metamorphosis of pastoral dream into urban nightmare; even the hills of heaven, it seems, are defenseless against the invasion of the outlander. The comic fall witnessed by the people of Lees, along with the Tussie family, is also a Fall in another sense, from the grace of pure being and the glory and innocence of the original garden. With Eden gone from the hills, and relief workers busy repaving even the road to salvation, it is not difficult to see the death of hope—all possibility of deliverance, social or otherwise— lurking at the back of this humor.

It is remarkable, in fact, just how sadly or sardonically these comic novels end. *Mountain Mating,* for example, which is an odd mixture of comedy and fantasy—freakish hill characters and the equally strange hill gods that preside over them—finishes with the prospect of cultural obliteration. The locals talk of the government making a compulsory purchase of all their land in order to turn it into a national park. There is some feeble talk of resistance followed by the acknowledgment that, if they have not gone already, "the young folk will hafta migrate sooner or later." The legends of the mountains will disappear, evidently, the magical and mysterious will be supplanted by the bland; still worse, mountain culture will become a small part of the heritage industry. *Jackson Mahaffey* has a more caustic conclusion. The character who gives the book its title is an amiable and generally harmless rogue who describes himself as "sort of a farmer, more of a miller, a landowner, and a sportsman." "I raised just enough to feed myself and my stock," he says. "I got my spending money by being a careful poker player, lucky at dice, and by owning good game roosters at times."[79] As such, he is a spiritual descen-

---

79. Ross, *Jackson Mahaffey,* 23, 75. See also Parker, *Mountain Mating,* 273. Also Johnson Jones Hooper, *Some Adventures of Captain Simon Suggs, Late of the Tallapoosa Volunteers* (1845; Philadelphia, 1857); George Washington Harris, *Sut Lovingood: Yarns Spun by a "Nat'ral Born Durn'd Fool"* (New York, 1867). On the possible functions of Southwestern humor—many of which make them worth comparing with the mountain humorists discussed here—see, e.g., Walter Blair, *Native American Humor, 1800–1900* (New York, 1937) and *Horse Sense in American Humor* (Chicago, 1942); Kenneth S.

dant of all those tricksters who inhabit the work of the old Southwestern humorists, like the protagonists of *Some Adventures of Captain Simon Suggs* (1845) and *Sut Lovingood: Yarns Spun by a "Nat'ral Born Durn'd Fool"* (1867). Unlike most of them, however, he rises to a degree of power, and not only financial. By the end of the novel, through a mixture of bribery and outrageous cheating, he has won a seat on the state senate. His shenanigans seem a little more sinister now, his cheerful amorality a little more dangerous because he has jumped on the bandwagon of change and become a beneficiary of the new age in the hills. Only a *little* more sinister and dangerous, though: Jackson Mahaffey's tricks for gaining money and office are so obviously tricky, so much the work of a comic scoundrel, that they are likely to amuse us rather than alarm us. They are likely, really, to allay fear about social change rather than provoke or exacerbate it, because the scoundrel at the center of that change is such a lovable, *familiar* kind of scoundrel. And that is precisely the point, the function of his tricks and japes—just as it is of the freakishness of the Tussies or the bizarre, fantastic comedy of books like *The Devil Takes a Hill Town*. The humor acts as a palliative here, with the strange new ways turned into comic routines, the agents of social transformation playing the traditional role of the trickster, and their subjects transformed into scamps and freaks. One way of dealing with the inevitable and intolerable, after all, is to laugh at it; in these books, the draining away of the old life of the mountains and the eruption of the new become, quite literally, a joke.

Among the most powerful mountain novels of this period, however, are those for which the machine age in the hills is no laughing matter. Change, radical and irrevocable, is admitted at the level of labor, the productive life of the mountains; the task the authors of these novels then set themselves is that of discovering, and then disclosing, just how change has impacted on other habits of living in the highlands, the entire material fabric of the culture. Invasion and exodus are the shared assumptions here. Not only that, they shape the narrative pattern; they are the common structural principle of novels as otherwise different as *Teeftallow* (1926) and *Bright Metal* (1928) by T. S. Stribling, *At Top of Tobin* (1926) by Stanley Olmsted, *Angel* (1926) by Du Bose Heyward, *Homeplace* (1929) by Maristan Chapman, *This Day and Time* (1930) by Anne

Lynne, *Mark Twain and Southwestern Humor* (Boston, 1959); Constance Rourke, *American Humor: A Study of the National Character* (New York, 1931).

W. Armstrong, *Call Home the Heart* (1932) by Fielding Burke (alias Olive Dargan), *To Make My Bread* (1932) by Grace Lumpkin, *River of Earth* (1940) by James Still, *Wind Before Rain* (1942) by John D. Weaver, *Darker Grows the Valley* (1947) by Harry H. Kroll, *Everywhere I Roam* (1949) and *The Four Lives of Mundy Tolliver* (1953) by Ben Lucien Burman, *Hunter's Horn* (1949) and *The Dollmaker* (1954) by Harriette S. Arnow, *The Pike* (1954) by May D. Hoss and *A Death in the Family* (1957) by James Agee.[80] All these books start from, and explore, the fact of the irruption of factories and market forces into the once secluded Southern highlands—and the slow erosion of the old habits of work and ways of living, as the highlanders find themselves uprooted. "Looks like everybody is goen away," observes a mountain character in *Hunter's Horn;* and the road by which "everybody" goes out and the new society comes in becomes one of the more pervasive structuring images in these stories. "Below Big Gully Hill a great wound lay along the side of the slope," reveals the narrator in *Homeplace,* "dripping red clay like blood on the green scrub, and in the end of the gash was a huddling of busy roadmen, like maggots gnawing. . . . Now the

80. T. S. Stribling, *Teeftallow* (New York, 1926) and *Bright Metal* (New York, 1928); Stanley Olmsted, *At Top of Tobin* (New York, 1926); Du Bose Heyward, *Angel* (New York, 1926); Maristan Chapman, *Homeplace* (New York, 1929); Anne W. Armstrong, *This Day and Time* (New York, 1930); Fielding Burke (Olive Tilford Dargan), *Call Home the Heart* (New York, 1932); Grace Lumpkin, *To Make My Bread* (New York, 1932); James Still, *River of Earth* (New York, 1940); John D. Weaver, *Wind Before Rain* (New York, 1942); Harry H. Kroll, *Darker Grows the Valley* (New York, 1947); Ben Lucien Burman, *Everywhere I Roam* (Garden City, 1949) and *The Four Lives of Mundy Tolliver* (New York, 1953); Harriette S. Arnow, *Hunter's Horn* (New York, 1949) and *The Dollmaker* (New York, 1954); May D. Hoss, *The Pike* (New York, 1954); James Agee, *A Death in the Family* (New York, 1957). The fact that the categories outlined in this chapter are by no means mutually exclusive is suggested, perhaps, by the recurrence of certain familiar names here among these novelists of invasion and exodus—writers whose imaginative excursions into mountain life clearly encouraged them to use different but overlapping narrative strategies, like Arnow, Chapman, and Kroll. In her "Introduction" to *Mountain Path,* Arnow even argues for a close link between that book, *Hunter's Horn,* and *The Dollmaker.* Different as they are, she suggests, they nevertheless dramatize related stages in the growth of communication between the Southern highlands and the outside world and in the consequent transformation of highland life and character. Arnow began, she explains, with the account of a "roadless, marketless hill community" in *Mountain Path,* moved on to "a hill community near the end of a graveled road" in *Hunter's Horn* and then, in *The Dollmaker,* started her story "where the graveled road led onto the highway." To this extent, all three books—whatever their differences of narrative strategy—could be seen as part of one long and sustained chronicle of invasion and exodus.

misted sunlight was made ugly by the shrieking of the great steam-shovel that bit nearer to the old farm with every scoop of its hungry mouth . . . the rattling scoop spit the mouthfuls of hillside down the lower slope, while each fresh bite bled drops of earth. It ate the last safety betwixt Glen Hazard and the outside."[81] The highway that pierces the final barrier between highland and outland supplies the title for *The Pike;* while "the drone of the bulldozers and steam rollers" building it provides a steady, sinister accompaniment to the narrative action—a bass note reminding the characters, as one of them puts it, of "the modern kind of life we all got now." In turn, the main character in *Hunter's Horn,* watching "a graveled road" being laid down "close to the edge of the farm," reflects that now "the world was close in his face." "The road . . . would be a handy thing to take things out," he tells himself, "but what could take out could bring in— . . . strangers to see his run-down farm and ragged children." This is an image and ideology of the road quite distinct from the ones to be found in the traditions of Walt Whitman, say, or Jack Kerouac. Roads here are not the roads to freedom; on the contrary, they are conceived of as freedom's enemy, because they puncture the vacuum in which the aboriginal, pioneer liberty of the hill people was supposedly preserved. With the loss of solitude and the familiar forms of labor also goes the loss, apparently, of a kind of innocence; even before they experience dispossession and displacement, the hill folk in these novels fall into an acute, embarrassing self-consciousness—they begin to see and perhaps even judge themselves by outland standards, according to which they are underprivileged, "ragged," and "run-down."

Exodus closely follows on invasion. At the beginning of *The Four Lives of Mundy Tolliver,* the central character is first seen trying to hitch a lift. "His eyes seemed to search the horizon," the narrator declares, "as one of his shepherd forebears might have searched the Scottish peaks for a straying lamb." The only real stray now, though, is Mundy Tolliver himself. "Forever moving yon and back," complains a character in *River of Earth,* "setting down nowhere for good and all, searching for God knows what"; and she speaks, not only for herself or a character like

---

81. Chapman, *Homeplace,* 36–37. See also Arnow, *Hunter's Horn,* 297, 343; Hoss, *Pike,* 5, 293. Another illustration of the point just made in note 80, about different but overlapping strategies, is supplied here by the passage quoted from *Homeplace.* Observing the devastation wrought by the "busy roadmen" is Waits Lowe, the main character in *Happy Mountain.* "The wide open road's close on us," he comments (36).

Mundy Tolliver, but for all the displaced, wandering mountaineers in these stories—as one of them puts it, in the appropriately titled *Everywhere I Roam*, "Something's happened. Everybody's moved away." "Their forebears had come into the valley with hope in their eyes," a character in *Darker Grows the Valley* tells himself; now, "they were going out with bitter acquiescence"—forced out by industrialists and developers, along the roads those developers had built. Several of these books suggest a connection, a correspondence with earlier clearances. In *Wind Before Rain*, for example, the elderly grandfather of the central character tells his grandson about the oppression suffered by his family in "the old country." "He told the boy of broken families," we learn, ". . . He told of high-handed lairds grabbing the best land . . . of the men who stumbled into Glasgow, hoping to work the new machines . . . starving in the grimy, bustling city quicker than starving at home." The grandfather also tells "of pastures turned into forest, stocked for English sportsmen who came . . . shooting the game like butchers. . . . He told how the skirling, blood-warming airs of the pipes faded out of the Highlands." For the grandson, the correspondence is obvious, as he sees the factories "skin th' hills," as he puts it, and witnesses the gradual subjection of his neighbors: "living on comp'ny land . . . prayin in comp'ny church . . . sayin yessir when th' comp'ny men go by, jumpin when th' comp'ny whistle blows, gittin' up an' eatin, goin home an' sleepin when th' comp'ny says its time to."[82] He and his kind, he recognizes, are part of a long story of dispossession and subjection—a story that includes their Scottish ancestors. They are suffering under the simple but apparently irreversible law that is summed up in a song that recurs, as a kind of refrain, in *Everywhere I Roam*: "Little bee makes the honey / But the big bee takes the comb. / Little man fights the battles / But the big man stays at home." They are the victims of a history that is at once particular to them and part of a recurring conflict—between "big man" and "little man," those who run the machine and those who are run by it.

With most of these novels, however, it is not social analysis that matters. As far as diagnoses of the crisis in mountain society are concerned, most of them hardly venture beyond the suggestion that—to quote from *Everywhere I Roam*—there "ain't no place for a little man no more" and

82. Weaver, *Wind Before Rain*, 196–97, 256. See also Burman, *Four Lives of Mundy Tolliver*, 5; *Everywhere I Roam*, 254, 277; Still, *River of Earth*, 51; Kroll, *Darker Grows the Valley*, 398.

so the "little man might as well be dead." Some of these books even subscribe to a weary fatalism that actively undermines such analysis. *At Top of Tobin,* for instance, opens with a funeral and litters its account of the passing of the old hill culture with graveyard imagery and portraits of "mourners with their nerve-racking wails at funeral services of week-day noontides." In this narrative, material dispossession and mortal decay are linked and seen as equally inevitable; the social changes outlined here are translated, in an odd way, into a *natural* event—and so as about as susceptible to rational inquiry or active revision as the fall of a leaf, or the decay of the flesh. Few other narratives of mountain displacement push things as far as this; nevertheless, what powers them, for the most part, is the need simply to record the passing of a culture rather than diagnose the reasons for its passing. The process of recording is, in any event, a vivid and wrenching one. In *The Pike,* for instance, the removal of the family home, to make way for the highway, is registered in terms that make it act as a catalyst for the shock of the new, the sheer pain attendant on the experience of cultural invasion and uprooting. "On the manjack, his house, the small square white frame . . . suddenly heaved," the hero Hugh Clabo observes. ". . . On the green rye grass appeared slowly the naked, red clay square heaped with the junk of thirty years, where she had stood. The gradual exposure of the square infertile island of human residues appalled Hugh as if indecent. . . . The house vibrated lifelessly, like a dead body."[83] Again, there is the sense of not only killing a culture but also shaming it beforehand: the house is exposed in an almost obscene fashion, before the place and roots that gave it life are finally torn away. One consequence of the invasion of the road in this story is precisely the same as in *Hunter's Horn:* to bring the germ of self-consciousness, the sense of exposure, into mountain society and so accelerate the process of destruction. There is a bitter historical irony here, since several of these novels make the point that the hills were first settled by men and women who—among the many reasons for leaving the lowlands—wanted to find a place where they could live free of the daily humiliations visited on them in a more complex, hierarchical society. "All the trade of the piedmont and tidewater was in the hands of Scotch merchants who came in shoals to get rich and grasp power," the narrator of *Darker Grows the Valley* declares, talking about colonial

83. Hoss, *Pike,* 215. See also Burman, *Everywhere I Roam,* 277; Olmsted, *At Top of Tobin,* 328; Kroll, *Darker Grows the Valley,* 11.

times, ". . . The poor man was looked down on, snubbed, excluded from all social intercourse" and so went off "to find hope in the wilderness" of the hills—and, with hope, a measure of self-respect. Now, centuries later, those with control of the markets have followed the poor man into the hills and, while taking his land and means of living from him, have again made him feel watched and inferior. Like their homes torn up at the roots to make way for highways, the hill folk here are subjected to an almost "indecent" exposure of their poverty as well as their powerlessness; along with their privacy, they are robbed of their pride.

Occasionally, these novels of mountain displacement tend toward a nightmarish vision of the new order: a landscape dominated by ravaged farmlands and dark satanic mills. As the protagonist of *Everywhere I Roam* sets off in search of some place where the idyll of the hills survives, for instance, he leaves behind him an urban wasteland dominated by "the monstrous smoking structure" of a factory, "ugly walls of slag from which steam was still rising," "pines . . . seared and blackened, their branches hidden under a thick layer of dust," and "ant-like workers, scurrying about as though devotees at the altars of some fiery gods." This might be the Kentucky mountains, the reader infers; then again, it might just as well be Hell. More common, though, and subtler are those stories that register contemporary hill society as mixed, plural, still in touch with the old forms of living while gravitating steadily and ineluctably toward the new. Partly, this is perceived as a matter of the difference between generations. Grandparents in these stories connect to the past, to memories of the old way of life and traditions in the hills: the grandfather in *Wind Before Rain*, who tells the protagonist about the sufferings of his Scottish ancestors, or the grandmother in *River of Earth*, who lives by the hill laws of blood and vengeance, stoutly declaring, "I allus said, times come when a feller's got to fight. Come that time let him strike hard." Sons and daughters, in turn, generally search out the future. In both *Hunter's Horn* and *This Day and Time*, for example, the young people are seduced by the lure of the city. "They . . . had turned against the land as soon as they were old enough to go away," we learn of the young men and women in *Hunter's Horn*. "He wouldn't stay . . . forever working on his father's farm," one young man in *Hunter's Horn* declares; while a young woman in *This Day and Time* announces that the last thing she wishes to do is stay at home and become a farmer's wife— "I hain't studyin' nothin about marryin'," she insists. In between these generations are the men and women caught squarely in the conflict between past and future, unable either to live according to the old cultural patterns or reconcile themselves to the new. The central character in *Hunter's Horn,* for example, is a farmer but only thanks to the extra money he has earned as a coal miner: "he didn't like to work in the mines," the narrator confides, "but the pay was good." Similarly, the central and this time female character in *This Day and Time,* Ivy Ingoldsby, works in a series of mind-numbing jobs in factories before returning to the farm—only to find that she can support herself and her family only if she also works as a cook and a cleaner. The days of self-subsistence are now gone, she soon realizes. What is more, she is confronted even in the hills with a younger generation whose aims and imaginations identify them as children of the city—for whom what matter are the products of mass culture, the cars, goods, and makeup they can buy once they put their labor out for hire. " 'Times is changin',' Ivy murmured . . . Fords, victrolas, lipsticks. Everything was changing."[84] These young folk cannot connect with memory, any more than Ivy can; unlike Ivy, however, they hardly seem to care.

The plural character of modern hill society is one thing, however, the generation gap quite another—even though many of these novels may use generational differences to highlight plurality, the divisions within a social group brought about by change. Cultural tension, instability in these novels is a function not merely of age but of the language all the hill characters use, the lives they all lead—grandparents and grandchildren as well as those caught in the middle. All these hill folk, for instance, take the assault of the new idioms, a vocabulary that defines them and the words they use as marginal, beyond the bounds of proper society and speech. As Gertie Nevels, the main character in *The Dollmaker,* moves to town, for instance, the voices that she hears make her feel that she is

---

84. Armstrong, *This Day and Time,* 83. See also 75; Burman, *Everywhere I Roam,* 8; Still, *River of Earth,* 120; Arnow, *Hunter's Horn,* 3, 25, 36. The characters caught between past and future, the "middle generation" who very often occupy center stage in these narratives, recall the figure that tends to be the protagonist in what Georg Lukacs has called "the classical form of the historical novel." It is the task of such a figure, Lukacs argues, "to bring the extremes whose struggle fills the novel, whose clash expresses artistically a great crisis in society into contact with one another. Through the plot, at whose centre stands this hero, a neutral ground is sought and found upon which the extreme, opposing social forces can be brought into a human relationship with one another" (Georg Lukacs, *The Historical Novel* translated by Hannah Mitchell and Stanley Mitchell [1962; London, 1969 edition], 36).

in a foreign land—or, if not that exactly, then in a land where she is an unwelcome and unregarded stranger; "once again," we are told, "she heard, in the cheap, broken-into pieces language, the word 'hillbilly' "—and the word tells her how peripheral, how small and insignificant she is here. Words heard then feed into words spoken. One hill character in *Darker Grows the Valley,* called Love Clinch, goes to work for the Tennessee Valley Authority as a "population readjustment representative," reasoning that she will be able to help her own people move from their valley, soon to be flooded, more efficiently and with more tact than anyone from the outside world. It soon turns out, however, that she is wrong: not least, because she becomes immersed in an "alien" language—the coinage of bureaucracy and the marketplace—that changes her and the entire way she sees things. "No longer were there such words as home hollow, moving out, home hunting, heartbreaking, tears, grief," we learn. "Instead, 'clients relocated.' As a 'population readjustment agent' she would call Clinch Valley the 'flowage area.' "[85] Less extreme, but no less telling, are Ivy Ingoldsby in *This Day and Time,* who is constantly trying to correct her "dialect" speech at the behest of her son, or Hugh Clabo in *The Pike,* who notices how the idiom of his friends and neighbors is altering under the pressure of invasion and, in particular, the mixed accents of tourists, "the guitar-strong Middle West, the blubber-lipped Deep South, the Oxford-like Carolina coast, the clipped East talk." Along the new highways of communication come new tongues, all of which contribute to the voice of urban culture—and the sum of which reduces mountain speech to the status of "dialect" and the speakers of that speech to "hillbillies."

"Going through the front room," the narrator observes of Hugh Clabo as he returns to his highland home, "he turned down the radio volume slightly. . . . He went into the kitchen. . . . A grease-spattered 'Snuffy Smith' strip was scotch-taped up behind the new Athensville Utilities electric stove over the pagoda wallpaper. Next to that, propped slanting on a split Presto log to drip down the pipe, stood the blue-enameled icebox, with an open cellophane pack of pork rinds and a dime potato pie and a pot of African violets on the top."[86] This is a more affluent setting than is perhaps usual in the mountain novel, which may

85. Kroll, *Darker Grows the Valley,* 318. See also Arnow, *Dollmaker,* 143; Armstrong, *This Day and Time,* 201; Hoss, *Pike,* 73.

86. Hoss, *Pike,* 4–5. See also 163.

in part be because it is set after the Second World War. Among the novels of mountain displacement written over the whole of this period—which is to say, between the middle of the 1920s and the middle of the 1950s—it is, however, typical in the way it records the erosion of the sights and signs of the old life, and the steady emergence of the new. The hill folk in this fiction live in a world that is recognizably urban and modern: a world of rapid communication, chain stores and convenience foods, cartoon strips and picture shows. If at some times these people sing folk ballads, at many others they prefer pop songs heard on the radio. If they cook the old meals, they cook them now on the electric stove; they can buy the food they need, instead of producing it for themselves, and then store it in the icebox. And if they go to a revival, they are more than likely to encounter there a preacher who spreads his message with the help of microphones, loudspeakers, and "pink, mimeographed handbills," and travels from town to town in a large car. This is a culture of material change, leading to radical poverty for some folk and relative, limited affluence for a few others; it is also conflicted, a culture of crisis. What is more, some of the best novels of dispossession and departure—which are, as it happens, among the best mountain novels of any kind—take this material change, and the conflict and crisis it engenders, as their subject, and then examine the possible mental and moral consequences—the direction in which the nonmaterial culture of the hill folk is likely to go. They look at changing ways of making a living in the Southern highlands, and immediately around them; and they investigate how, exactly, those changes have affected the way of life, the emotional and ideological impact of invasion and exodus. Needless to say, the results of these investigations are as mixed as the mountain culture they investigate; they are also as many and varied as the individual texts and writers involved, and as different from each other as the different *particular* moments at which those texts were written. Still, one register of the different structures of judgment at work here, in this dramatic examination of mountain exile, is offered by three novels that take three quite different routes into their subject. Remarkable in themselves, as individual stories, the three together are representative in the sense that they measure the range of cultural work these novels perform, the shared opinions and obsessions that exist within this plurality of belief. In order of publication, the three are *To Make My Bread* by Grace Lumpkin, *The Dollmaker* by Harriette S. Arnow, and *A Death in the Family* by James Agee.

To Make My Bread has been described by one critic, Walter Rideout, as "local color fiction performed with a radical purpose."[87] There is an element of truth to this, although the description does not quite do justice to the power of Lumpkin's portrait of a mountain community disrupted by change. Nor does it catch just how much the novel is fired into life by the writer's sense of both the conflicts and the connections between the old culture and the new—as her characters struggle to come to terms with ways of life that are not only oppressive but unfamiliar, and move hesitantly toward different forms of belief. Centered on a mountain family called the McClures, *To Make My Bread* is one of several novels of the time that use the historical circumstances of a strike of cotton mill workers in Gastonia, North Carolina, to explore social conflict and cultural transformation. The strike, a bitter and violent one, took place in 1929 and became a focus for national attention, pitting the local establishment against workers, many of them newly arrived from the hills, and the media and forces of law and order against Communist Party organizers from the North. It was the source or basis of, among other books, *Strike!* (1930) by Mary Heaton Vorse, *Call Home the Heart* by Fielding Burke, *Gathering Storm* (1932) by Myra Page, *Beyond Desire* (1932) by Sherwood Anderson, and *The Shadow Before* (1934) by William Rollins Jr.[88] What *To Make My Bread* has in common, in particular, with *Call*

87. Walter B. Rideout, *The Radical Novel in the United States, 1900–1954* (Cambridge, Mass., 1956), 174. Rideout was talking about *To Make My Bread* and the novels by Fielding Burke (Olive Tilford Dargan) and Myra Page cited in note 88.

88. Mary Heaton Vorse, *Strike!* (New York, 1930); Fielding Burke (Olive Tilford Dargan), *Call Home the Heart;* Myra Page, *Gathering Storm: A Story of the Black Belt* (New York, 1932); Sherwood Anderson, *Beyond Desire* (New York, 1932); William Rollins Jr., *The Shadow Before* (New York, 1934). While basing his narrative on the events of the Gastonia strike, Rollins changes the setting to a textile town on the East Coast with a substantial immigrant population. The review mentioned here is A. B. Magil, *"To Make My Bread,"* New Masses, VIII–IX (February 1933), 19–20. For the details of the Gastonia strike, see Liston Pope, *Millhands and Preachers: A Study of Gastonia* (New Haven, Conn., 1942). For the contemporary debate over the direction radical and proletarian literature should take, see Daniel Aaron, *Writers on the Left: Episodes in American Literary Communism* (New York, 1961), 158; Alfred Kazin, *On Native Grounds: An Interpretation of Modern American Prose Literature* (New York, 1942), 409–10; Howard Zinn, "A Comparison of the Militant Left of the Thirties and Sixties," in *The Thirties: A Reconsideration in the Light of the American Political Tradition* edited by Morton J. Frisch and Martin Diamond (Dekalb, Ill., 1968), 27–43. This analysis of Lumpkin's novel is developed out of Rideout's point about radical writing in the 1930s. "What happened," he says, "was the adaptation of a radical ideology to what might be called the inherited literary conscious-

Home the Heart and *Gathering Storm* is an emphasis on the experience of mountain *women*, as they struggle to reconcile their traditional status as matriarchal keepers of the house with the new demands made on them by an oppressive system of wage labor and the poverty and deprivation attendant upon it. The conflicted role of the hill woman in the emergent culture of town and factory offered Lumpkin, just as it did Burke and Page (or, for that matter, novelists who did not draw their inspiration from the Gastonia strike, like Anne W. Armstrong and Harriette S. Arnow), the chance to measure social alterations as alterations of consciousness—to register a material change as, in addition, an ideological one. To this extent, there was a telling link between what the author of *To Make My Bread* was doing and what she was dramatizing. Both Lumpkin and her women characters were caught in the crossfire between old and new, and trying to make sense of it. For Lumpkin's women, this meant struggling to meet the challenge of an altered world while not entirely forfeiting traditional beliefs; for Lumpkin herself, it meant finding some way of achieving a rapprochement between inherited literary forms and a radical agenda. Just how successful either was is a matter for debate: the *New Masses* reviewer, for instance, thought that there was too little class consciousness in either the characters or the narrative approach, too much rural portraiture and romantic pity, and not nearly enough revolutionary fervor. The novel is remarkable, however, precisely because Lumpkin does not take the easy way out, by either jettisoning the old ways or ignoring the new ones; the novelist tries, in terms of both creative practice and imaginative analysis, to see even violent social transformation, and the pain and sense of promise it engenders, as a product of necessity—part of a vital, evolutionary pattern.

To Make My Bread begins in the mountains. The McClure family are living on a small farm that belonged to the husband of Emma McClure. Emma, a widow, lives with her father, "Grandpap," and her children, among them a son named John and a daughter, Bonnie; and the family scrape a living from farming, hunting, and brewing moonshine. Mostly, they depend on credit from the local store. Lumpkin is particularly adept here in sketching out the peculiar impact of religion on the hill folk. The

---

ness" (*Radical Novel in the United States*, 207). For a more sardonic judgment on novelistic interest in the Gastonia strike and the radical writing of the period generally, see Leslie Fiedler, "The Two Memories: Reflections on Writers and Writing in the Thirties," in *Proletarian Writers of the Thirties* edited by David Madden (Carbondale, Ill., 1968), 13–15.

attitude of people like the McClures to the admonitions of the local Baptist preacher is one of wary belief. When the preacher condemns music and dancing, for example, Grandpap, a skillful fiddle player, marches out of the church in protest, and the entire McClure clan follow him. Nevertheless, the McClures then feel that they must make a "sacrifice" to God, just in case, as they put it, "Grandpap's made the Lord mad." Religious events, like baptizing day, in any case supply moments of sociability and community: they are, as the narrator puts it, "an occasion for neighbors and kin who had not seen each other for a year or more to meet. People came from miles around."[89] And, at such moments, the cathartic rituals of the Baptist church, with their emphasis on both suffering and release, offer a handy insight into mountain character. Normally stolid and stoic people like the McClures are carried away on a tide of feeling, singing songs about immersion "In the blood, in the blood of the Lamb," while their half-naked children are plunged into the chill mountain streams. That, Lumpkin intimates here and later, is the fundamental rhythm of feeling and personality in the hills: pious endurance punctuated by startling moments of release like baptism day. Contemporary observers of the Gastonia strike, and especially those from outside the area, were sometimes baffled by the strikers' vacillation between apathy and violence, mute acceptance of their lot and then sudden eruptions of political awareness and action. Already, in her sketch of hill religion, Lumpkin is disclosing a possible reason for what outsiders seemed to find so strange; in this sense, she suggests, the striking mill workers from the hills were translating into political terms an emotional language they had first learned from their religion.

The other aspects of life in the hills that receive special emphasis in *To Make My Bread* are scarcity and the sufferings of women. There is a communal life here, at church gatherings, dances, or the local store, but whenever "food became scarce," we are told, then "neighbors kept away from neighbors as if they were afraid or ashamed to show each other their misery." Emma McClure is described as "a strong woman," but at such times her strength is sorely tested, as she struggles to make meals without much food to make them with or is forced to "tell the others the last potato had been eaten." On occasion, there is a primeval quality to

---

89. Lumpkin, *To Make My Bread*, 55. See also 49, 61. On the strikers' vacillation between apathy and violence, see Sylvia Jenkins Cook, *From Tobacco Road to Route 66: The Southern Poor White in Fiction* (Chapel Hill, N.C., 1976), 90.

her troubles and pain. As she gives birth to a child, for example, Grand-pap bending over her bed is compared to "a man bending over a slaugh-tering," while "Emma's last cries were those of a pig with the knife at its throat." So when strangers arrive talking about a "promised land" in the mill towns, she is torn between confused skepticism and a kind of desper-ate faith, the belief that there must be some kind of deliverance beckoning somewhere. "Hit's hard t' know what to believe and what not, these days. Everything's changin' so," she says, but then begins to dream of working in the mills as, quite probably, "a very neighborly arrange-ment." Maybe, she tells herself, it will be pleasant working in a "quiet" factory "at a leisurely pace" in the company of others—"as if neighbors had gathered to sit around and talk at a quilting . . . bright shining dollars would pour into her lap." "With the money," she fancies, "she would buy new clothes for the young ones, and books for school, a fiddle for Grandpa, and perhaps for herself a new waist or a scarf for her head."[90] In effect, her wandering imagination transforms the mills into both a refuge from mountain scarcity and a place where the old pieties of moun-tain life may be conveniently resurrected. For her, the pastoral dream of quiet surroundings, gentle labor, good company, and a modest suffi-ciency is relocated in the town.

The process by which Lumpkin strips Emma and her family of all their illusions about the new methods of labor is a detailed and, in many ways, a familiar one. The mill village, far from supplying release and neighbor-liness, offers only imprisonment and anonymity. "The rows of houses . . . were silent as if all the people had deserted their homes," Emma observes. "Only smoke coming from some of the chimneys showed that life was going on inside." Grandpap is humiliated by being told he is too old to be given a job ("Grandpap is changed if he can stand that kind of talk," Emma reflects); and Bonnie, treated as a unit in the cotton mill, begins to think of herself "as Bonnie Thirteen instead of Bonnie McClure." The achievement of the novel does not really lie here, though, in its material portrait of life in the mill town, stark and powerful though that portrait is, but elsewhere—in the carefully graduated account of the different re-sponses among the hill folk to the new forms of labor and affliction. Some, like Grandpap McClure, just give up and try to retreat into the past. At first, the retreat is a purely emotional one. Grandpap attends a Confederate rally, for instance, at which the main speaker is one of the

90. Lumpkin, *To Make My Bread*, 140. See also 13, 28, 29, 136, 137.

owners of the mill, who sings the praises of what he calls "Race Domination." "The Creator in his wisdom made the Caucasian race of finer clay than he made any of the colored people," the mill owner declaims, adding to his all-white audience, "here in the mills . . . you have made a New South, a South . . . of smooth-running factories . . . where you possess peaceful homes, and the freedom to work."[91] There is an ironic echo of Emma McClure's dream of a promised land here. An even deeper irony, however, lies in the cultural work a speech like this is performing. Old habits of division are serving the purposes of new kinds of subjection. Although Grandpap does not realize it, and the speaker would certainly not acknowledge it, the Confederate flag is being waved over the factories to legitimize them and the oppressive system they require—to give them a peculiarly Southern stamp of approval.

Eventually, the purely emotional withdrawal from the present afforded by occasions like a Confederate rally is not enough for Grandpap. He goes back to the hills, in what turns out to be an unsuccessful attempt to live off the land. His daughter is attracted to this herself: "sometimes," we learn, "Emma talked of going back." Most of the time, however, she is caught as most of her generation are in these novels of exodus between bewilderment, anger, and resignation. "There's no use getting mad," she tells herself. "Hit's the way the Lord made things to be." "I get that way sometimes," she adds, "mad at something I don't know what. Then I have to remember whatever happens is the Lord's will."[92] Here, again, is that fluctuating rhythm between apathy or weary acceptance and sudden moments of emotional violence. The only trouble now, for Emma, is that there is a kind of sterility to the rhythm; it leads nowhere for her, except into exhaustion, emotional and physical, and, eventually, death. One reason for this, Lumpkin intimates, is that the churches of the mill towns do not even offer the chance of group emotional exorcism, ritualized catharsis that those back home in the hills afforded. The urban services are too restrained, rational, ordered; Emma can hardly share her pain and confusion with anyone else, save one or two friends. So, feelings like the ones Emma experiences have to go elsewhere for release and expression, not into religion but into politics. The church cannot give satisfaction here, Lumpkin suggests, but activism can—it can answer emotional as well as material need. And not only can but should: in making a connec-

91. Ibid., 187. See also 156, 157, 160.
92. Ibid., 227. See also 213.

tion between the emotional rhythms of the hill people as strikers and as churchgoers, Lumpkin is at once recording a fact of the time that puzzled many observers—those who wondered how mountain folk could make such alternately quiescent and rebellious workers—and registering a hope, a possibility. Properly channeled, the implication is, the impulses shaped by the emotional drama of highland religion could give birth to a new kind of activism. They were not necessarily at odds with organized union action, as both union and church leaders of the time tended to believe. On the contrary, they could enable and energize such action. The motives and drives associated with hill faith might find proper articulation in a language that was, in the last analysis, political.

This transvaluation of religious values into political ones is particularly noticeable among the younger generation in the McClure family. Bonnie McClure reveals a talent for writing and singing songs: not songs about "the blood of the Lamb," that is, but about the blood and sacrifice of the striking workers. She becomes the ballad singer for the strike, deploying skills that would have once been used to praise the Lord in celebration of the mill workers, in a language that still recalls the hymns and religious rituals of the hills. Bonnie is killed during the strike, and the speech given at her funeral offers a further telling mixture of politics and religion. As one critic, Sylvia Jenkins Cook, has observed of the speech, "the cadences of it are biblical, but the message is to remember in bitterness the evil that must be purged from the face of the earth." It is the same crossing over from one kind of faith to another, not unrelated one that is witnessed when a union colleague of Bonnie's brother, John, tells him: "We must go beyond the strike to the message . . . that we must join with all others like us and take what is ours. For it is our hands that dig the coal and keep the furnaces going; and our hands that bring in the wheat for the flour. . . . It is for us who know to make a world in which there will not be masters, and no slaves except the machines: but all will work together and will enjoy the good things of life together."[93] The

93. Ibid., 328. See also 292, 325; Cook, *From Tobacco Road to Route 66*, 115. The portrait of Bonnie McClure as ballad singer for the strike is almost certainly based on Ella May Wiggins, ballad singer for the Gastonia strike, who was killed by strikebreakers. In presenting us with a transvaluation of religious values into political ones, Lumpkin seems to be offering us a telling (if doubtless inadvertent) comment on a point made by many observers of the Gastonia strike: that it was precisely the failure of the strikers and their organizers to achieve anything like this—or, more simply, to come to terms with the conflict between their religious inheritance and their political aims—that led to their defeat. The

millennial vision, the biblical rhythms pick up on John McClure's own story, as it happens, as well as Bonnie's. John is one of the organizers of the strike, and his eventual commitment to the union and activism issues out of a memorable slippage between political and religious feeling. He is aroused by the story of Sacco and Vanzetti, and then finds something in the Bible that seems to him to endorse his growing suspicion that injustice and privilege must and will be abolished. "Go to now, ye rich," he reads, "weep and howl for your miseries that are coming upon you." In this novel, it is the inherently skeptical and irreligious among the younger generations of hill folk who are without hope of any kind. One character, for instance, alternates attacks on religious belief with a critique of the idea of progress. "There is . . . no purpose, no progress for the human race," he tells John, "history repeats itself over and over." Those with religious origins and inclinations, on the other hand, like Bonnie and John, are moving steadily and by no means slowly toward the idea of material redemption, salvation here and now in this world.

The remarkable feature of *To Make My Bread,* and in fact Grace Lumpkin's other works, is that she does not underestimate the power of residual belief, the undertow of feeling that tugs at mountain people in the towns, for ill sometimes as much as for good. The ill is certainly there. Emma McClure, for instance, is blinded by such feeling to the origins and reality of her oppression. She cannot see the factory for what it is, an engine and agent of a particular system of labor. For her, it can be understood only in terms of old hill myths and fairy tales, as a monster whose machinery is constantly murmuring, "I'll grind your bones to make my bread," and as such, invulnerable, irresistible. She is in a similar position to a black housekeeper, a "mammy" figure in another novel by Lumpkin, *A Sign for Cain* (1935), who is genuinely shocked when her activist son tells her, "My people are white people too. They are working people, white and colored." "You mean po' white people," she exclaims with a mixture of disbelief and affronted dignity, "white trash is *your* people?" In such cases, past beliefs cripple the present; and, when the experience of mountain exodus is involved, they usually involve the first

---

Gastonia strikers themselves apparently found it difficult to decide whether their battle hymn should be "Solidarity Forever" or "Praise God from Whom All Blessings Flow." And according to Liston Pope, "the antireligious tendencies of the Communists" who came to organize the strike "did more than any other single factor to divorce them from continued leadership of the workers" (*Millhands and Preachers,* 263).

generation of immigrants. The next generation, Bonnie and John Mc-
Clure and their kind, are different; so, for that matter, are many of the
younger generation of Lumpkin's black characters—like the son of that
outraged housekeeper, called Denis. They seem to be empowered by the
past, rather than disabled by it; it enables them to construct a viable
language for dealing with the present, as well as a set of practices that
open up the chance of building a more tolerable and a more decent future. "We are the new pioneers, cleaning out the world, making a new
world," declares Denis in *A Sign for Cain*, in a familiar but still very
effective harnessing of the myths of yesterday in the service of today and
tomorrow. "Because we have worked and suffered," insists a young
union member in *To Make My Bread*, "we will understand that all
should work and all should enjoy the good things of life."[94] And the
rhythms of his insistence, his idiom and cadences, recollect old pieties,
the religion of the hills, and make them the tools of social transformation.
There is no rational, dispassionate analysis of the plight of the poor in
To Make My Bread, no carefully articulated, programmatic solution:
something that incurred the displeasure of the *New Masses* reviewer
among others. What there is, however, is something subtler and, in effect,
more in touch with other writing from the South: the intimation that
the past can work in the present to alter material conditions by altering
consciousness of them—the sense that tradition can and perhaps should,
somehow, be an agent of change.

The past haunts the present in a different fashion in Harriette S. Arnow's *The Dollmaker*, a novel of mountain exodus which the author
herself described as beginning "where the graveled road led onto the
highway" and ending "in a war-time housing development in Detroit."
Again, though, the emphasis is on the experience of women. In this case,
it is the experience of one woman in particular, the protagonist Gertie
Nevels, as she struggles to come to terms with the alterations in her life.
"There is no people who can beat them," one early observer of hill folk
declared, "in endurance of strain and privation." "In so far as simplicity
means a shrewd regard for essentials, a rigid exclusion of what can be
done without," he added, "perhaps no white race is nearer a state of
nature than these highlanders of ours." Many other observers agreed—
"here," one traveler to the Southern highlands noted, ". . . one gets down

94. Lumpkin, *To Make My Bread*, 328; *A Sign for Cain* (New York, 1935), 223. See
also *To Make My Bread*, 219; *Sign for Cain*, 53.

to elemental things"—and, while doing so, often chose to place the spot-light on the trials of women and the fierce, quiet stoicism with which such trials were evidently borne. "Men and boys are frequently idle for long periods," one male commentator admitted, ". . . but there is pre-cious little leisure for the women."[95] Combining a "subordinate posi-tion" socially with the cultural role of keepers of the rites, hill women were likened to the matriarchs of legend, supplying firm moral anchorage even when their menfolk strayed. This sense of mountain character—and *female* mountain character, in particular—as a sure and elemental force, deriving its power from its capacity to simplify, to pare away all that is peripheral or ephemeral, is the heart, the driving force of Arnow's story; and it is registered right away, in the memorable opening scene. It is a cold, wet day in October 1944. Gertie Nevels, her sick child pressed tightly in her arms, forces a recalcitrant mule off the familiarity of soft mud and on to the highway. Then, forcing her legs and body to express her will, she stops the mule in the center of the road. Her aim is to stop someone and make them carry her and her son to hospital. She succeeds. An army vehicle is forced off the road; Gertie then uses her knife to help clear the underbrush surrounding it, and presses her body into service to help push the car back on the highway. Almost immediately after that, her knife is needed for an even more urgent purpose. Her child is choking to death and she has to perform an emergency tracheotomy, whittling a poplar switch into the appropriate shape for a temporary windpipe. This series of actions Gertie executes seem to have both the simplicity and the significance of primitive ritual. The woman meeting need with a passion-ate application of her craft could not be more different from the men she encounters in the army vehicle and on whom, however temporarily, she imposes herself: an ineffectual officer who faints at the sight of the opera-tion, and an indifferent driver who behaves "as if he were a part of the car to be stopped or started at the will of the other."[96] Nor could the surroundings she moves between be more different either; after all, the road on to which her mule stumbles, and along which she and her son

95. Randolph, *Ozarks*, 41. See also Kephart, *Our Southern Highlanders*, 278, 290; Morley, *Carolina Mountains*, 161. For further examples of the emphasis placed in many of these narratives on the trials of women, see, e.g., Hatcher, "Appalachian America," 390; Powell, *Who Are These Mountain People?*, 28; Thomas, *Blue Ridge Country*, 117–21. Morley, in *Carolina Mountains*, is not untypical in titling her chapter devoted to the suffer-ings and strength of mountain women (chapter 19), "Penelope and Nausicaa."

96. Arnow, *Dollmaker*, 9.

are now taken to hospital, is the one that will later carry her and her family into urban exile.

Gertie Nevels is not unaware of the significance of the road for her and her kind. When the officer asks her casually, "as if he didn't much care but wanted to make some sound above the child's breathing," "what crops do they raise in this country?," Gertie's reply is characteristically terse and telling. "Younguns fer the war," she says, "an them factories." The action of *The Dollmaker* tends to be filtered through her consciousness. That consciousness is hardly a sophisticated one; it is, though, something more interesting than that—one that is intuitively aware, sensitive almost on a prelingual level to the way things are. This comes out, for instance, when the officer's comments on her skill with the knife prompt a dismissive response. "I've allus whittled," is all she will allow herself to say at first. When the officer then presses her, by asking what she uses her knife to make, her reply is longer but still sticks to the material facts; it is as much her gaze and her gestures that disclose meaning. "She looked down at the hands that held the poplar wood," we are told, "the back brown and wrinkled . . . the palm smooth with the look of yellowed leather. It was as if the hand were a page engraved with names while, she looking now at the poplar wood, repeated: 'Hoe handles, saw handles, ax handles, corn-knife handles, broom handles, plow handles, grabben-hoe handles, churn-dasher handles, hammer handles, all kinds of handles—it takes a heap of handles.' "[97] In this plain but poetic litany, Gertie quietly, even allusively, reveals her sense of the knife as an extension of her hand, the tool that permits her to express herself through working on her environment. Her world, to borrow a phrase from Martin Heidegger, is "ready-to-hand"; she draws the world to herself, connecting with it in a way that is a matter of both instinct and craft—or, rather, of instinct realizing itself *through* her craft. This is not to say that the human and the natural are simply being equated here, as they are in some other mountain novels. Arnow is making a finer, much subtler point. Through the instruments that she uses, Arnow suggests, the skills she has learned, Gertie Nevels has established a genuinely homemade

97. Ibid., 22. See also 17. The relevance here of Martin Heidegger, and in particular *Being and Time* (translated by John Macquarrie and Edward Robinson [New York, 1962]) has been noted by Lewis A. Lawson, *Another Generation: Southern Fiction Since World War II* (Jackson, Miss., 1984), 59. I am indebted to Lawson for this point and, in general, for a very suggestive reading of *The Dollmaker*.

world, which is at once a part of nature and a part of herself. She works *with* her mountain surroundings to realize some of their possibilities and many of her own needs. The grip on the mule, her talking to animals and plants, above all her carving of the wood: all these are her language, her way of articulating her sense of being. Through the consciousness and, still more, the conduct of her heroine, Arnow in effect speaks the unspeakable: turning into the only kinds of speech a novel can accommodate a relationship with the earth that is simultaneously complex and primordial.

It is perhaps necessary to make a distinction here between Gertie Nevels and the surroundings in which we first find her. Gertie seems to have established a vital connection with her environment via her craft; her world is, quite literally, there to hand for her. The determining characteristics of the place, the rural community in which she is situated, however, are not vitality and connection but quite the opposite. Her home place has gradually been stripped of the people, the labor needed to keep the communal lifeblood flowing. The men, in particular, have gone into town to work, leaving the countryside to fall into decay and the rural community—or what remains of it—to stagnate or even wither away. "They won't be men enough left to dig the graves," Gertie caustically observes. Many of the fields are left untilled; the doctor and all the teachers have long since departed; even the keeper of the local store has gone off to seek factory work, leaving one woman to manage all by herself. "They ain't no men, nobody left in this whole country," is a constant lament as the women, left behind all week, wait impatiently for letters home from their menfolk. Even the hound dogs can only "dream of hunting," now that there are no huntsmen around to take them out. Gertie may still cherish the Jeffersonian dream of laboring in the earth for herself and her family. "We'll get us a place a our own," she insists; and she nurtures the hope of using $300 left by her brother, killed in action, to buy a neighboring plot of land, the "Tipton place"—which had once, as it happens, belonged to her family. When Gertie visits the place, though, now deserted because the Tipton family have gone to Indiana to work in a power plant, it is difficult to see it as one critic does, as "a homestead in Eden." With its air of desertion and vacancy, it seems as much a part of another age, a vanished economy and set of possibilities, as anywhere else in the hills Gertie chooses to call home: "The doors were nailed shut, like the boarded-up windows. . . . Gertie touched the Tipton dipper, rusty now, with a cobweb across it . . . the porch shelf, like the puncheon wash bench and rusty tin pan, was empty, forgotten like the ungathered walnuts that lay thick in the grass by the back porch steps."[98] Any hope of resurrecting such a decidedly dead world, in any event, vanishes when Gertie receives the call from her husband, Clovis, to join him in Detroit. In personal terms, the move is a bitterly unanticipated and unwanted one. Seen in the context of Arnow's careful depiction of rural decay, however, the evident dissolution of old habits of labor and communal leisure, it seems like a surrender to the inevitable.

What is particularly remarkable about the subsequent account of Gertie's first encounters with the city is the way it reverses her previous relationship with her immediate world. Instead of being "ready-to-hand," the subject of her patient attention and skills, her surroundings now assault her senses, exciting feelings of fear, imprisonment, and nausea. The train ride to Detroit is a nightmare. "There were bits of vomit in the air," we are told, "where the black babies and the white babies had puked. There was vomit from the red-faced, red-eyed soldiers. . . . There was a stink of cigarette smoke . . . mixed in with the smells of wet babies, of stale soda biscuit . . . fried fresh meat . . . all old and smelly now in the too hot car, but still less strong than the smell of too many bodies shut up together. No matter how much they laughed and joked and drank, there was in them all the fear sweat smell. . . . She smelled it on herself, on her oozy hands."[99] The sense that the material world is now invading her being runs all through the account of Gertie's journey to her new home in the city. In the streets, Gertie feels herself carried helplessly along by "the press of people"; the crowd seems to negate her will. Near the place where she is now to live, she is struck by how crushed and crowded out all the workers' houses look, "so little against the quivering green light" of the factories and "so low after the giant smokestacks." Meditation and the affectionate management of her environment are impossible here. As time passes, Gertie suffers only "an ever growing awareness" that her body is being attacked and overpowered. The air she breathes is "like a stinking rotten dough pushed up her nose and down her throat"; "it burned her nose," we learn, "and gave her eyes a heavy, sleepy feeling." Her language is no longer her own: "all the new Detroit words— adjustment, down-payment, and eviction . . . and communism—would get into her head and swim around for days." And she feels subject to

98. Arnow, *Dollmaker*, 44. See also 32, 61, 93, 107; Lawson, *Another Generation*, 61.
99. Arnow, *Dollmaker*, 130. See also 137, 148, 150, 163, 220, 450.

the gaze of strangers she meets on the city streets—the policemen, for example, who patrol the alleys "never speaking . . . but always watching, hunting with their hard, unsmiling eyes." What Arnow is describing here is nothing short of a loss of identity; the material world of the city has the moral and emotional effect of reducing being to nothingness; its sights, sounds, and smell invade the body of this human subject, and reduce her to anonymity and impotence. In her mountain home, Gertie could carve out a place for herself, the tools she whittled were her handle upon the world; now, by contrast, she finds herself both divided, alienated from her environment—the image of severing becomes a constant one—and subdued, overwhelmed by it. The subject/object split that was healed by her craftwork has opened up in these new surroundings; she now has a subordinated, subjected status. She is not acting, she senses, but acted upon—not a maker but a malleable instrument, to whom or to which things happen.

Gertie experiences all this, overpoweringly, as a loss of humanity and a longing for contact. The sounds of her husband leaving for work "sound for sound" mix and mingle with the sounds from other houses until "Clovis, her man, would cease to be a man and become a numbered sound, known only by number." "She thought of numbers still when Clovis was gone. Numbers instead of people," the narrator discloses: "But she wanted people. People to call her 'Gertie.' If she could have an animal to nose her hand, a red bird to watch, even a potted plant. Something alive, she had to have something alive."[100] Needing something alive through which to feel herself alive, Gertie finds it temporarily in the company of women. Arnow herself has suggested in an interview that when Gertie "reached the alley in Detroit . . . she became part of the conglomeration of people"; "she knew . . . kindness from her neighbors," the author has said, and so grew to be "part of all those strange people" and their community. Certainly, communal values are at work among the *women* of the alley. While their men are away fighting or competing for jobs, they look after each other's dependents and help each other through difficult times. Violence in this novel tends to be the prerogative of the male world. Clovis uses Gertie's knife to take revenge on someone who

---

100. Ibid., 296. See also 496; Danny Miller, "A MELUS Interview: Harriette Arnow," *MELUS*, IX (Summer 1982), 86–87. On the kind of community among women that seems to be temporarily created here, see Nina Auerbach, *Communities of Women: An Idea in Fiction* (Cambridge, Mass., 1978), 5.

has attacked him; one of Gertie's sons, in turn, tries to draw his knife on somebody making fun of his "hillbilly" crudities. The women, on the other hand, form an informal network of mutual support. When the atomic bomb falls on Nagasaki, their reaction is one of shock and genuine sympathy for a Japanese neighbor: "you still gotta say," admits even one of the more combative among them, "people is people. Why them Japs live something like this . . . all crowded up together in towns." Expressions of solidarity like this, however, scarcely alter the fact that cooperation among the women is little more than a temporary reaction to crisis; all Gertie and her friends can do is ameliorate, for a while, the effects of division and competition, they cannot even begin to change them. The women Gertie knows help one another out, but only as long as such assistance does not challenge male authority. Real power remains with male institutions; ultimate loyalty is owed to the family, with the man at its head; the determining sanctions here are still the male ones of commodification, use, and profit. So if Gertie gets a sense of being human sometimes from the company of women, it is one that is desperately provisional and partial. It offers, at best, a temporary emotional rescue, the strength and fatal weakness of which both stem from the fact that this network of female support stands well apart from the material realities of the city.

A more substantial sense of being alive comes to Gertie in another way, through a sustained pursuit of her craft. During that opening conversation with the officer, Gertie explains that, apart from whittling handles, she is working on something rather more ambitious. "I'm aimen to work up a piece of wild cherry wood I've got," she explains. "It's big enough for the head and shoulders uv a fair-sized man." That block of wood follows her by express to Detroit; and it speaks of her need to hang on to the possibility of shaping her world—to make a figure that will also be a making of her, a revelation of her being in time. Sometimes, she thinks of carving out of it the figure of Jesus, in his sacrifice; other times, Judas in his sorrow is her aim. Always, there is the suspicion that, while she has this project in hand, she has the hope of holding on to her humanity and binding her wounds—healing the gap that yawns ever wider between herself and her surroundings, as she suffers and sorrows over her move to the city. The problem here is that Gertie soon finds herself subject to a process that alienates her from most of the products of her own craft. Division in this case takes the form of a break, a fissure between her and what she makes, since what she makes turns out to be a marketable product: people begin to pay her for her carving and, gradually, Gertie starts to experience guilt whenever she is not whittling something the value of which is proved by the reward of cash. In a curious way, Gertie is still articulating her relation to the world through the activity of carving: the difference is that the relation is now one that abstracts her, and the results of her labor, from the materiality of her immediate world and makes them both subject to the market, the systems of exchange. What had once been a source and guarantor of reality for Gertie becomes a medium for immersing her ever more deeply in the unreality of the marketplace as, under the guidance of her husband, she tries to produce as many units—dolls, crucifixes, whatever will sell—in as short a time as possible—with a knife to begin with and then, later, with a jigsaw. Becoming a commodity, someone whose value is gauged precisely by the sale of her labor, she also becomes a consumer: Gertie watches both her earnings and her savings melt away because the Nevels family feels obliged to buy the things they believe they need, like a fridge, a washing machine, and a car. Strangely, Gertie feels herself melt away too. Standing by the bed of one of her sons, as her shadow is thrown on the wall by the flickering light from a nearby steel mill, "she watched herself melt," we are told, "one moment there was a thin shivering shadow, then nothing moved on the wall."[101] In this world she never made, Gertie often

---

101. Arnow, *Dollmaker*, 340. See also 23. One of the remarkable aspects of *The Doll-maker* is that, while Arnow and her heroine show themselves hostile to organized resistance to the new systems of production or indeed collective activity of most kinds, the story told here offers a striking dramatization of the processes of objectification, alienation, and reification analyzed by Karl Marx in *Economic and Philosophical Manuscripts* (1844). Capitalism, Marx argued, transforms human labor into a commodity to be bought on the market and used against the worker. "This fact," he wrote, "implies that the object produced by labour, its product, now stands opposed to it as an alien being, as a power independent of the producer." The worker is alienated from the product of his or her own labor, which becomes an alien thing; and the more he or she works the more they are dominated by the world of objects their own labor has created. "The worker puts his life into the object," as Marx expresses it, "and his life then belongs no longer to himself but to the object." Work becomes wholly instrumental, a "forced activity," an "external thing," a means simply to acquire the basic necessities and a few consumer luxuries. Since work is intrinsically unrewarding, the worker now feels free only outside work. He or she is alienated as a "species being," living entirely for the self, no longer producing for the whole of nature—an act that distinguishes human beings from animals, according to Marx—but existing as an isolated activity, a wage, a commodity. It is difficult to think of a more apt abstract analysis of what happens to Gertie Nevels in Detroit. The degree to which Arnow herself would resist an analysis such as this, however, is indicated by a letter she wrote

seems to have less presence than the products that define her life—the dolls she sells, for instance, or "Old Icy Heart," an anthropomorphic monster of a fridge she buys that seems to possess a perverse, noisy character of its own.

This harrowing analysis of Gertie's immersion in a world of commodities and consumption is not, however, presented from the standpoint of a committed radical. *The Dollmaker* is different from a book like *To Make My Bread* to the extent that its verdict on the union movement or activism of any kind is decidedly mixed. The unions that force Clovis out on strike are seen as a symptom of the disease rather than a solution to it. "A body's got a right to be free," Gertie declares. "They oughtn't to have to belong to nother, not even a union." And that view is only mildly qualified by one union member, who defends his membership as a regrettable necessity: "a man oughtn't to have to pay dues an belong to a union to get a decent wage," he says, "—but the way things are he's gotta." The emotional investment here is in another kind of legacy from the hills than the one endorsed by Lumpkin, and it is clearly recorded in the powerful closing moments of the book. With the end of the war, times are particularly hard and, to complete an order for dolls, Gertie takes her cherished block of wood to the wood lot for sawing up into manageable pieces. Before going, she makes a sacrifice by giving her share of the meager supper to the rest of her family. On the journey there, in a wagon, she seems to be performing her own imitation of the stations of the cross, as the children of the alleys watch and wonder about the embryonic figure carved in the block. At the wood lot, the owner asks her about the identity of the figure too. "Christ?," he inquires, to which Gertie's response is by turns bluntly materialist and suggestively speculative. "Cherry wood," she replies, but then, reacting to the man's observation that the unfinished figure has no face, adds, "they was so many" faces "would ha' done"—"Why, some of my neighbors down there in the alley—they would ha' done."[102] The block, it turns out, is too big for the saw in the wood lot to rip up immediately, it has first to be split with an

---

responding to an article on *The Dollmaker*. Capitalism, Arnow insisted, is not solely a product of industrial society but a development of the individualistic rural values of property ownership and productivity. "After all," she suggested, ". . . wasn't Gertie when in the hills something of a capitalist: she sold every egg she could spare, and was saving money for the purpose of buying a farm of her own" ("Letter to Barbara Rigney," *Frontiers: A Journal of Women's Studies*, I [1976], 147).

102. Arnow, *Dollmaker*, 549. See also 485–86.

axe; and, with an immense deliberation of purpose, Gertie does what she now believes is necessary. This is her final, defining action in *The Dollmaker:* in an act that is simultaneously one of destruction and creation, she wields the ax with the same craft, willpower, and passion as, once upon a time, she had handled the knife.

The extraordinary closing moments of *The Dollmaker* have been read in many ways: as an announcement of surrender to urban life, a signal of the failure to reconcile art with motherhood, a sign of commitment to a new community, an acknowledgment of the belief that it is the process of art that matters, not the product, and as a gesture of supreme self-sacrifice.[103] Without denying that the resonance of the final scene is such as to make several readings possible, it is surely simpler to see what Gertie Nevels does here as an act of continuity and change—a recollection and reinvention of her mountain heritage, and so a repetition in a different key of the novel's opening scene. Patience, the capacity to weather the trials of life with the support of courage and craft was, after all, what most commentators chose as a determining quality of the mountain community—a people for whom, as one observer put it in the 1920s, "life has been one, long, hard, cruel war." This quality, it has to be said, was not simply a passive instrument, a means of enabling hill folk to tolerate the otherwise intolerable. It was their way of meeting the world and its specifics, and coming to terms with it in a form that signified neither conquest nor submission; it was their hold on the realities of their time and place. The Kentucky writer and farmer Wendell Berry has used the term *stewardship* to describe the feelings, the relationship with things this quality was and is likely to engender. "The great study of stewardship," Berry has said, "is 'to know/ That which before us lies in daily life' and to be practiced and prepared in things that most concern.' " It is to

103. Lee Edwards, *Psyche as Hero: Female Heroism and Fictional Form* (Middletown, Conn., 1984), 229; Glenda Hobbs, "A Portrait of the Artist as Mother: Harriette Arnow and *The Dollmaker,*" *Georgia Review*, XXXIII (Winter 1979), 854–55; Charlotte Goodman, "The Multi-Ethnic Community of Women in Harriette Arnow's *The Dollmaker,*" *MELUS*, X (Winter 1983), 49–53; Harrison, *Female Pastoral*, 97–98; Dorothy Lee, "Harriette Arnow's *The Dollmaker*: A Journey to Awareness," *Critique*, XX (1978), 92–98. See also Sally L. Kitch, "Gender and Language: Dialect, Silence and the Disruption of Discourse," *Women's Studies*, XIV (1987), 67; Elizabeth Schultz, "Out of the Woods and into the World: A Study of Interracial Friendships Between Women in American Novels," in *Conjuring: Black Women, Fiction, and Literary Tradition* edited by Marjorie Pryse and Hortense J. Spillers (Bloomington, Ind., 1985), 75.

be seen, he adds, in that practice of agriculture, or indeed anything, which accepts that "the necessary thing" is "to determine what tools and methods are appropriate to specific people, places, and needs, and to apply them correctly." "Application is the crux," Berry argues, "because no two fields are alike"; discipline is a necessary accompaniment; and "the ultimate discipline here is faith: faith, if in nothing else, in the propriety of one's disciplines."[104]

Application, discipline, faith, stewardship: it is not difficult to measure just how vital all these qualities are to the behavior of Gertie Nevels, first and last. At the beginning and end of the novel (and, very often, in between as well), Gertie asks herself what "the necessary thing" is, in terms of what she has, what she wants, and what she can do, and she then acts simply and decisively to bring that necessary thing about. She focuses all her physical and mental energies on meeting two things—her needs, and the requirements of her own special time and place. This is her handle on the world in a figurative sense, just as the knife and then the ax are quite literally her handles, her tools for knowing and then dealing with what lies before her in her daily life. By the time *The Dollmaker* ends, what lies before has altered radically: but she meets it with the same patience, the same adaptive courage and imperturbable application of craft as she did before she left the hills. The breaking of the wood with the ax is neither an act of capitulation to the world of commodities and cash exchange nor a triumph of the will nor even a moment of self-sacrifice. It is something simpler, subtler, and nobler than that. It is Gertie Nevels recognizing what has to be done and, given the "specific people, places, and needs" that confront her, what she now *wants* to do—and then acting, with passionate discipline, on that recognition. The understanding that compels her issues out of her mountain heritage; it was, after all, the same fundamental knowledge of need that drove her, before she ever even imagined going to Detroit, to stop an army vehicle to save the life of her son. But that understanding now prompts a different if equally determined series of actions, because "no two fields are alike" and this is a very different field of action. Whether Gertie actually likes the difference is neither here nor there, Arnow intimates; it is *her* world, and so she has to deal with it. The room for personal maneuver, let alone sig-

104. Wendell Berry, *The Gift of Good Land: Further Essays Cultural and Agricultural* (San Francisco, 1981), 280–81; *Recollected Essays, 1965–1980* (San Francisco, 1981), 210–11. See also Kephart, *Our Southern Highlanders,* 279.

nificant social change, is minimal in *The Dollmaker.* What takes its place, though, is the sense that a lot can be made of a diminished thing—the belief that life is, in any event, a long, hard, cruel war, and so what matters is simply finding the best tools with which to continue fighting it. The triumph of the protagonist of *The Dollmaker* is coextensive with that of Arnow in writing the novel: both are built on the (probably instinctive) realization that disciplines learned in the mountains, properly applied, still have their use and integrity in the city. The book and its heroine rest their eventual certainties on the faith that, even in the abandonment of alley and factory, it is possible to realize a freedom based on service to principle. Even here, in seeing what matters most and then using the right tools to make it happen, Gertie Nevels remains her own woman; so, for that matter, does Harriette Arnow.

Born in Knoxville and growing up there and in a mountain community near Sewanee, Tennessee, James Agee could be as interested as Harriette Arnow clearly was in what a mountain woman does with her solitude. One of his most remarkable poems, for instance, "Ann Garner," describes in some detail how a woman from the hills of that name loses her child, mourns for a long time, and then finally dies on the spot where the child is buried. Like William Wordsworth's poem "Michael," or for that matter like much of the poetry of Robert Frost and Edwin Arlington Robinson, it is a tribute to rural stoicism, the toughness and quiet depth of feeling bred by the land—and, in this case, by a hard, solitary life in the highlands. Agee, however, was even more fascinated by what travelers to the Southern hill country liked to call "clan loyalty": that allegiance to blood and kin that some observers attributed to the supposed Scottish Highland heritage of the hill folk, some to the impact of social isolation, and still others to more material, economic factors. Agee himself was sometimes inclined to search out a materialist explanation for this devotion to the family, in the mountains or other, equally marginalized areas of the rural South. In *Let Us Now Praise Famous Men,* for example, he points out that the family on a tenant farm "exists for work. It is a cooperative economic unit. . . . A family is called a force, without irony."[105]

105. James Agee and Walker Evans, *Let Us Now Praise Famous Men* (1941; London, 1965 edition), 322. See also "Ann Garner," in *Permit Me Voyage* (New Haven, Conn., 1934), 24–35. Among the most useful studies of Agee's work are Alfred T. Barron, *A Way of Seeing: A Critical Study of James Agee* (Boston, 1972); Victor Kramer, *James Agee* (New York, 1975); Erling Larsen, *James Agee* (Minneapolis, Minn., 1971); *Remembering James Agee* edited by David Madden (Baton Rouge, La., 1974); Genevieve Moreau, *The Restless*

Economic or more broadly social and cultural explanations like this, however, beg the question of what happens when circumstances change. Before leaving for Harvard and later New York and Hollywood, Agee had seen for himself the changes being wrought in a thriving mountain town like Knoxville. The problem was when, if ever, material changes of the kind he had witnessed substantially altered patterns of thought and feeling: so that, for instance, it became impossible to talk about the family as a force *without* a measure of irony. This was a problem pressing upon others at the time. "Neighborhood life continues to center on the family," commented a sociologist, Marion Pearsall, after research on one small, decaying Appalachian community in the 1950s; "children spend the first six to eight years in nearly continuous contact with the family," she added, ". . . this situation is ideal for absorbing traditional behavior."[106] Nevertheless, Pearsall pointed out, the community she had observed was coming "late to a stage of disintegration passed earlier in many parts of the United States." It presented an anomaly, "the persistence of a frontier type of social organization and value system in an environment no longer suited to either"; it was considered "backward" and "primitive" even by neighboring communities in the same valley. So, with the appearance of "good roads, developing industries, and closer communication with other parts of the country," it was arguable just how long "traditional ways" could remain viable. The local culture was steadily being supplanted by "a more complex society," with "its own organizational forms outside the family"; and so the family as a significant cultural agent, and source of moral judgment, might very well not survive.

The question of the survival of the family is at the heart of Agee's novel *A Death in the Family*. It is a complex book structurally, its complexity stemming in part from the fact that it was left to editors to compile and complete it after the author's death. It is also a deeply felt, personal work: set in Knoxville in 1915, it offers a fictional version of the death of Agee's own father. Shifting backward and forward in time, and between the viewpoints of different members of the family, the basic narrative divides into three sections or movements, set before the death,

Journey of James Agee (New York, 1977); Peter H. Ohlin, *Agee* (New York, 1966); Kenneth Seib, *James Agee: Promise and Fulfillment* (Pittsburgh, 1968).

106. Marion Pearsall, *Little Smoky Ridge: The Natural History of a Southern Appalachian Neighborhood* (Birmingham, Ala., 1959), 80, 99. See also vii, 2, 42, 106, 155, 181.

during the period of waiting for news of what has happened to the father, and the funeral; and these three movements are interspersed with intensely lyrical passages drawing on memory and dream. The story is concerned, in a sense, with both an actual death and a potential one: a death *in* the family, and the possible death *of* the family as a result. The family at the center of this novel is tested in a number of ways and, above all, in the most serious way the traditional, patriarchal family structure can be tested, by the untimely death of its head or keystone. Ties of flesh and blood, living tissue, are set in opposition to the forces that would unravel those ties, leaving each member of the family lost and alone. Just how powerful those forces are is suggested by the moment when Rufus, the son, enters the room where the body of his father, Jay, has been laid out. "Dead. He's dead. That's what he is; he's dead," Rufus repeats to himself, "and the room where his father lay felt like a boundless hollowness in the house and in his own being, as if he stood near the edge of an abyss and could feel that droop of space in the darkness."[107] Vacancy, darkness, emptiness seem constantly to hover on the edges of the action and, at the moment of the death, threaten to take it over entirely. As Jay sets out on the journey from which he will never return, for instance, his wife, Mary, watches as first his figure vanishes "into the absolute darkness" and then his car seems to be swallowed up by "the enormous night." With Jay departed, "she felt as odd, alone in the bed as if a jaw-tooth had been pulled," we are told, "and the whole house seemed larger than it really was, hollow and resonant." And with Jay dead, the feeling of oddity darkens into a sense of utter abandonment; she experiences the loss at first, as her son does, as the desperate intuition that she has lost her moorings and been plunged somehow into a void.

But even at the moment when Rufus is confronted with the dead body of his father, there are feelings of warmth and intimacy playing against all this. "His mother's hand came round him," we learn, ". . . He slid his arm around her and felt her hand come alive on his shoulder." Then, standing there beside the coffin, "he felt his sister's arm" as well; "he could feel a vein beating against the bone, just below the armpit." Members of the family continually experience each other like this, in terms of touch, odor, taste, the warmth of their bodies, the beat of their pulses, the smell of their breath or skin—in short, the *feel* of their presence. Even

107. James Agee, *A Death in the Family* (1957; London, 1967 edition), 236. See also 34, 36, 41. All subsequent references are to this edition.

when Jay is gone, this is how he is remembered by, for example, his son. *"His cheeks were warm and cool at the same time,"* Rufus recalls, *"and they scratched a little . . . he smelled like dry grass, leather and tobacco. . . . His hands were so big he could cover him from the chin to his bath-thing. There were big blue strings under the skin on the backs of them."*[108] This curious "kind of warmth and impulse and . . . sweetness" that Rufus feels in the actual presence of his mother and sister, and in the recollected presence of his father, touches him, we are told, "like the beating of a heart." It grants him a fragile stay against confusion, something to wrap around and protect him against the "cold" and "dark" of coffin and corpse. Similar feelings are experienced by other members of the family. When Jay is hastily preparing for his final trip, for instance, he cannot help noticing the contrast between the darkness and chill of the early morning and the radiant warmth of his home. Getting dressed, he gazes at the bedroom window, "tenderly alight within, and the infinite dark leaking against its outer surface." Entering the sitting room for what he scarcely can suspect will be the last time, and switching on a lamp, he notices how "in the single quiet light in the enormous quietude of night, all the little objects in the room looked golden brown and curiously gentle." Home, and even more family, seem to offer a haven in this story, a refuge from the destructive element. The connotations are at once sensual and spiritual, since the family circle is inscribed as a womb and a sanctuary, a living organism and a shelter from the storm. Either way, it pulses with an energy which the reader is compelled to share; it draws us in to a source of vital contact, fleshly communion, that is bright and strong enough to survive even the most devastating loss.

The intimations of contact, one member of the family touching another and surviving through that touch, are not just literal, however. The family as a kind of communal body, in which the bodies of its members live and seem somehow to continue after life: this is rendered to us in a sensory way—in terms of flesh meeting or remembering flesh, the physical presence or recollected evidence of the loved one—but it is also tendered in a more purely emotional currency, through gestures of understanding and affection. So, when the telephone call comes in the early morning to summon Jay away from home, his wife gets up to make breakfast for him. Jay "was very faintly disappointed," the reader learns, because "he liked night lunchrooms . . . had not been in one since Rufus

108. Ibid., 78–79. See also 20, 27, 31, 232.

was born" and was vaguely hoping to eat later in one. Nevertheless, "he was warmed by the simplicity with which she got up for him, thoroughly awake." The little act of tenderness and concern from Mary prompts him to respond in kind: "He saw the rumpled bed. Well, he thought, I can do *something* for her. He put his things on the floor, smoothed the sheets, and punched the pillows. The sheets were still warm on her side. He drew the covers up to keep the warmth, then laid them open a few inches, so it would look inviting to get into. She'll be glad of that, he thought, very well pleased with the look of it."[109] When Mary returns some time later to go back to sleep, she realizes only part of her husband's intent. "She saw the freshened bed," the narrator discloses. "Why the *dear*, she thought, smiling, and got in." However, "she was never to realize his intention of holding the warmth in for her; for that had sometime since departed from the bed." This is the language of feeling, the meanings of which Agee subtly indicates can be fleeting and imperfect. Still, the tenderness of Jay's act is hardly vitiated by the fact that what he tries to do for Mary is only partially revealed to her. Arguably, its value as a symbolic gesture, brimming with feelings he cannot bring himself to speak, is only enhanced because some of its significance must remain secret. Certainly, it adds to our sense of the domestic intimacy at work here. This is a circle within which people know each other, much of the time, in terms of minute and mysterious particulars. The exchanges between them may seem commonplace on the surface, but running beneath them, granting life to those exchanges, are currents of trust and affection that they themselves can never fully understand.

There is, however, more understanding here than is measured by mere speech. The strictly verbal exchanges between wife and husband, or father and son, are laconic and frequently commonplace, sticking mostly to matters of fact and the plainest of idioms. "Well, Jay. I mustn't keep you," says Mary as Jay leaves her, for ever; "Nope," he agrees, "Time to go." Nevertheless, they are full of heart knowledge. They betray an understanding, however imperfect or occasionally blurred, of the intimate ties and histories that bind them one to another, in death as much as in life. A typically quiet illustration of this occurs at the beginning of the novel, when Jay takes his son to a picture show. After father and son have shared the enjoyment of a Charlie Chaplin movie (" 'Mad as a hornet!' . . . his father exclaimed in delight, and there was Charlie, flat on

109. Ibid., 27. See also 26, 36.

his bottom on the sidewalk"), they go first to a market bar together for a drink, where Rufus hears Jay observe to the man next to him, "That's my boy." Rufus "felt a warmth of love," we are told, and "next moment . . . felt his father's hands under his armpits" as "he was lifted, high, and seated on the bar, looking into a long row of huge bristling and bearded red faces." Very little more is said, as father and son walk back home. Without benefit of words, however, it is clear to Rufus that Jay is "just not in a hurry" to return and "liked to spend these few minutes" alone with him. Finally, man and boy sit together for a while, as is their custom on the return journey from the cinema, on a small rock in a vacant lot: where Rufus experiences what is called "a particular kind of contentment, unlike any other that he knew." "He did not know what this was in words or ideas, or what the reason was," the narrator explains, "it was simply all that he saw and felt. It was, mainly, knowing that his father, too, felt a particular kind of contentment, here, unlike any other, and their two kinds of contentment were much alike and depended on each other."[110] "There was really no division, no estrangement" at this moment, Rufus senses, "or none so strong, any how, that it could mean much, by comparison with the unity that was so firm and assured." And he senses all this without the help of language or even formulated thought or impressions. "There were no words, or even ideas" at work here, we learn, "no more in the man than in the boy child." Rufus understands, "but not, of course, in any such way as we have of suggesting . . . in words." He realizes the bond binding him closely to his father. The realization is, however, one circulating through him on a prelinguistic, subliminal level: moving "through the senses, the memory . . . the mere feeling of the place they paused at," "their feet on undomesticated clay . . . facing north . . . towards the deeply folded small mountains."

The power and privacy of this moment is temporarily disrupted by the passing of a stranger. It is then reluctantly brought to an end, when Jay decides to take his son the last quarter of a mile back to their house ("he heard a long, deep sigh break from his father, and then his father's abrupt voice: 'Well . . .' "). While it lasts, however, Rufus and his father experience a human encounter that exists outside the boundaries of their language. They instinctively *know* things, about that circuitry of power and passion we call the family, that they cannot begin to formulate to themselves, let alone *say*. What they know is hidden from strangers. The pas-

110. Ibid., 18–19. See also 14, 16, 33.

serby who momentarily intrudes on father and son merely helps, in his anonymity and obliviousness to the moment, to measure the boundaries of the kinship circle. Like others excluded from the privileged space of the family, he is a peculiar kind of "outlander," marked by his evident separation from and ignorance of blood ties. Other outsiders like this are given names. Rufus remembers, for instance, a couple called Ted and Kate who played what they believed was a harmless trick on him. Mary turned on them, he recalls, with the ferocity of a mother lion protecting her cubs. *"He's been brought up to* trust *older people when they tell him something,"* she blazes, *". . . And he trusted* you. *Because he* likes *you. . . . Doesn't that make you ashamed?"*[111] The sign of their exclusion, though, is that they show neither shame nor understanding of the trust they have broken. The family and its affections remain another country, with a language, an emotional currency unfamiliar to them.

That other country is also a literal one. As Rufus sits with Jay gazing at "the deeply folded small mountains," he realizes that his father "was a homesick man" and that "here on the rock, though he might be more homesick than ever, he was well." Jay was born and brought up in the mountains. He moved to Knoxville just eight years before the time when the novel is set. He still refers to the hills from which he came as "home." Rufus, for his part, can hardly share his father's past; he can, however, share the loyalties it enshrines, the emotions and affections it engenders. He can also begin to sense just how his father feels about his losses and gains, in passing from the hills, and why he feels this way. Rufus, we are told, "felt that although his father loved their home and loved all of them, he was more lonely than the contentment of their family love could help"; "it even increased his loneliness," Rufus senses, "or made it hard for him not to be lonely."[112] The slippage between the two meanings of "home" for Jay intimates the cause of his pain: divided loyalties, riven feelings that seem to be healed for a moment as he sits, with his son, near his present home looking back at his past one. For a while he can return, in vision and fancy, to his highland past and even permit his son to share in the return with him. For the rest, he can carry that past with him, perhaps, in his heart and memory. Out of the hills, he can nevertheless carry with him the beliefs and practices he has learned there, and then pass them on to his family. Above all, he can bring to them from there a belief in *themselves* as a nucleus, the vital center of life.

111. Ibid., 185. See also 20.
112. Ibid., 19.

Just how intensely *A Death in the Family* registers family ties as a legacy of the hills, a rooted affection that has survived transplantation to the town, is registered in a moment such as this: when father and son instinctively recognize, as the narrative puts it, "how each depended on the other, how each meant more to the other," while looking backward to that other country from which the family came. The mountains, with their deep folds and "long, narrow" valleys leading into thickly wooded centers, seem, in any event, to enjoy the same organic life, the same womblike peace and repose as the family group whose securities they foster. And the imaginative act of returning to them, revisioning them and recuperating some of the old hill life and values, is what ensures, in this narrative, that a death in the family is *not* also the death of it. An organism as deeply rooted as this can evidently survive even the wintriest of challenges. In a central, defining moment, the family return to the hills in fact as well as imagination; and, in doing so, help us to understand just how much this is a story about the past being recollected in the present through the tie of blood. In one of the episodes of memory that interrupt but also enrich the main narrative, Rufus recalls a visit that he and his parents once made to the hills, to see a great-great-grandmother who seems, his mother observes, *"as old as the country"* she inhabits. The family left the *"cold"* and *"dark"* city of Knoxville, Rufus remembers, and ventured into *"old deep"* country along *"long, slow, winding"* roads. The difficulty of the journey may suggest to us that the past—any past, including that of the hills—is not to be negotiated that easily; and, when the travelers do finally reach *"a great, square-logged gray cabin"* where the old woman lives, the problems of negotiation continue. The great-great-grandmother seems not so much old as ancient, and utterly unapproachable. *"She can't talk any more,"* Jay says, *"almost in a whisper,"* and all the visitors initially feel intimidated in her presence. *"It seemed to Rufus like a long walk over to the woman,"* we learn, *"because they were all moving so carefully and shyly."*[113] Their sense of awe and difference is such, in fact, that, as Rufus recollects, the place they were visiting *"was almost like a church"* rather than a home.

Then, however, Rufus approached the old woman, introducing himself to her; and as he did so, he remembers, a strange transformation occurred. The initial impression of remoteness vanished and, in its place, all the familiar signs, the signatures of kinship made their appearance.

113. Ibid., 178. See also 173, 175.

Rufus came into vital contact with his great-great-grandmother. He witnessed her presence with the same intimacy, the same intensity of sensory detail that he was and is accustomed to with other, nearer members of his family. *"Her smell was faint yet very powerful,"* he recalls, *"like new mushrooms and old spices and sweat like his fingernail when it was coming off. . . . Vague light sparkled in her cracked blue eye like some kind of remote ancestor's anger . . . he kissed her paper mouth, and the cold sweet breath of rotting and of spice broke from her . . . and then, as abruptly as if the two different faces had been joined without transition in a strip of moving-picture film, she was not serious any more but smiling . . . with sudden love he kissed her again."*[114] Agee takes care to skirt sentimentality here. The past comes alive for Rufus, certainly, but there is a trace of pungency as well as pathos to its forms of resurrection: the moment ends with the family noticing that *"there was water crawling along the dust"* from under the old woman's chair and Mary, *"trying not to show she was crying,"* gently drawing Rufus away from *"Granmaw."* For all that, though, the contact, the communion between yesterday and today is more deeply felt now than at any other moment in the book. Rufus and his family may have moved away from the hills, but they have managed to graft some of the old life on to the new. And what they have grafted, above all, is the sense of kinship, connection on an almost primal level of blood and body, that draws the boy to the old woman at this particular instant—and which later brings the entire family together in the companionship of grief.

So the mountain past lives in the present in a dual sense for Rufus and his relatives. A belief in kin is at once a symptom and an agent of continuity for them, drawing young and old, the living and the dead together into the body of the family. There is difference and division here, of course. The "homesick" solitude of Jay, or the subtle distinctions of grief—between, say, Rufus's regret that he has lost a protector and Mary's simple, desolate feelings of absence—are enough to make us aware of that. But there is also commonality, a sense of communion that is both sensual and spiritual, a matter of flesh as much as faith. There is no doubt that Agee sees this commonality as the most precious inheritance the family in his story have brought with them from the hills, and wants us to see that too. It is what another writer born in the Southern

114. Ibid., 179–80. See also 181.

highland, Thomas Wolfe, would call their "sign of kinship"[115] with the mountain past: a sign that they signal all the time, by the simple act of accepting kinship itself as the definitive, determining element in their lives. The protagonist in *A Death in the Family* does, certainly, enjoy a solidarity very different from the one projected in *To Make My Bread*. Still, there is the same belief here that there is in Lumpkin's novel—or, for that matter, *The Dollmaker*—that all is not lost with the exodus from the highlands: the Southern highlander, and his descendants, may carry something of their highland past with them wherever they go. This, in fact, is a measure of the success of all three novels: that they demonstrate convincingly how material change is not necessarily a cause of moral amnesia. The fabric of the present, they suggest in their different terms, is not simply built over the wreckage of the past. In each of them, the mountain woman and man express themselves in a way that is simultane-

115. Thomas Wolfe, *Look Homeward, Angel: A Story of the Buried Life* (New York, 1929), 585. The "sign of kinship" with his highland ancestors that Eugene Gant, the protagonist of Wolfe's novel, carries with him is a "small tetter of itch" on the "nape of his neck." It is the outward and visible symptom of the fact that he takes his mountain past with him wherever he goes. Another writer convinced of the connection between highland past and present was T. S. Stribling. Stribling, however, clearly viewed old hill culture with distaste and regretted the backwardness of hill people, as he saw it, even when they had moved to town. Incidents of crude violence and mob rule in *Teeftallow* and *Bright Metal* illustrate Stribling's evident belief that invasion and exodus had not brought what he defined as progress and enlightenment. "A group of hillmen were standing on a corner of the square," we are told in *Teeftallow*, "watching a man in their midst draw a figure in the dust. . . . The whole group had the gnarled, almost grotesque faces developed by generations of illiteracy; the way the man in the center stooped to the dirt . . . spoke his familiarity with it. . . . His companions were guffawing . . . in awkward hill laughter" (279). "In the meager intellectual and emotional life" of these people, according to Stribling, religious revivals in town continue to occupy "the place filled in more liberal communities by the theatre, the symphony, the lecture, the fashion show, and the church" (*Teeftallow*, 138). And, even when some of the mountain women attempt to assume a thin veneer of sophistication, Stribling insists that their crudity and moral obtuseness give them away. "All their costumes held that subtle lack of finish which stamps the home-made," we are told of the "Ladies Christian Workers Society" in *Bright Metal*, ". . . The members greeted each other with lusty country humor. . . . Any sentence that any woman said was welcomed with laughter" (90). In addition, almost every sentence spoken by these female descendants of the old hill folk betrays ignorance, bigotry, or malice. For all his liberalism on many social and racial matters, Stribling was in effect intolerant of hill traditions and hardly immune to prejudice himself—as his references to "hillbillies" (*Teeftallow*, 84 and *passim*) and "grotesque hill faces" (*Bright Metal*, 267) are, in themselves, enough to suggest.

ously strange and familiar—a response to the new conditions that involves, along the way, a recollection and reinvention of the old.

There is one fundamental difference between *A Death in the Family* on the one hand and, on the other, *To Make My Bread* and *The Dollmaker*. It is that both Lumpkin's novel and Arnow's are set in periods not long before the time of writing whereas Agee's is, of course, located many years earlier. Despite that, his book like theirs is an acknowledgment of both change and continuity. The tale all three books tell circles around a dual recognition: that the past is another country, profoundly separate from the present, and yet also connected to it in a vital way, as its precondition, its ground of being. And with Agee, this dual recognition is there in the act of narrativity, the actual telling of the tale, as well. He was, after all, reinventing a fragment of early autobiography, a past that was resolutely past by the time he came to write of it but nevertheless bound by intimate bonds of influence and affection to the present, the time of writing. The author of *A Death in the Family* was not related to the hill past in the same terms that the young Knoxville boy called James Agee was, just as Rufus is not related to it in the same way his father is, let alone his great-great-grandmother. Different though all these series of relations were and are, however, they are alike in one fundamental sense, just as they are in so many novels of mountain exodus—and, for that matter, so much of the fiction of the Southern highlands: in that they show how the hill past, while inhabiting another dimension, a decidedly lost and alien world, forms a continuity of consciousness with the present and possible futures. Behind them, circulating through them is the conviction that yesterday, today, and tomorrow, while clearly divided from one another, are all part of one uninterrupted narrative.

Another way of putting all this is to say that the beauty and power of the best mountain books, like *A Death in the Family, To Make My Bread,* and *The Dollmaker,* stem from the fact that they take cognizance of a crucial problem in the representation of history, which Fredric Jameson has called the "unacceptable option, or ideological double bind, between antiquarianism and modernizing 'relevance' or projection." If we assume the radical difference of the alien object we shall be faced with the prospect of being shut off from its otherness by all the intervening accumulations of history that have made us what we are. On the other hand, if we choose to affirm the identity of the alien object with ourselves, we shall miss "the essential *mystery* of the cultural past" and will inevitably fail to touch the strangeness of a radically different reality. Only a genuine historical understanding, Jameson argues, can give us an adequate account of an earlier culture, "which [as Jameson puts it] like Tiresias drinking the blood, is momentarily returned to life and warmth and allowed once more to speak its long-forgotten message in surroundings utterly alien to it."[116] Only a genuinely historical fiction, we could perhaps add, is capable of acknowledging that the past constitutes a foreign and vanished reality while also recognizing that there are formative links, structural connections between then and now. The different but overlapping relationships between past and present disclosed by *A Death in the Family* are really only more sophisticated examples of the relation between a rural past and an evolving urban future to be found in all the best Southern highland fiction, as it confronts the kinds of challenges Jameson outlines. The old life of the hills speaks in all these stories to a new world of 1915, 1950, or whatever in accents that are determinately different, while nevertheless speaking of earlier human struggles not unrelated to—in, fact, the grounds and preliminaries of—our own. "Our contemporary ancestors": in the finest narratives about the Southern mountains, that phrase has an additional dimension, an extra resonance that those who coined it could hardly have imagined. In these stories (and there are many of them) mountain people of the past come across to us as intimate strangers, who have helped make today different from but also a lineal descendant of yesterday; they are seen as part of a necessary, and often turbulent, prehistory of the present—a present that includes, not just Southerners and hill folk of course, but all of us whatever our contemporaries or the character and location of our ancestry.

116. Fredric Jameson, *The Political Unconscious: Narrative as a Socially Symbolic Act* (Ithaca, N.Y., 1981), 17.

6

"The world is here"

*Fiction Writing and Social Change in the
Contemporary South I*

Problems and Possibilities

Toward the end of 1994, the British magazine *The Economist*
devoted an entire section to what was described as "A Survey of the
South." The author of this survey, John Peet, began in a romantic vein
with, inevitably, a still from the film *Gone with the Wind* and the stirring
announcement, "It is the land that went to sleep." "Now all has
changed," Peet continued; "the South has, like Sleeping Beauty, awak-
ened from 100 years of slumber." Fortunately for readers of *The Economist,* who consist for the most part of businessmen and financiers, Peet
did not continue in this vein for too long. He soon jettisoned romance
and fairy tale for hard economic fact. By "the South," Peet explained, he
meant the eleven states of the former Confederacy; *this* South had recovered from the recent recession faster than California and New England
had and, in the past three years, had become "a locomotive powering the
American economy, a role previously played by California." In 1993,
readers were told, over half of America's new jobs were created in the
South ("which has only a quarter of the country's population," Peet
added); while, since 1991, eight of the top ten states in terms of growth
of manufacturing plants had been Southern. In the early 1940s, average
income per head in the region had been half that of the United States as
a whole, and Southern states "were at the bottom of league tables for
poverty, illiteracy, and education." By 1993, however, regional income

per head had risen to 90 percent of the national average. "Indeed," Peet pointed out, "allowing for lower living costs, the average Georgian or North Carolinian, say, now enjoys a higher standard of living than most Americans"; and two-thirds of the Southern states also enjoyed lower than average unemployment rates. The signs of economic transformation were almost everywhere. There was more foreign investment in the South, from Japan and Western Europe, than in any other American region. Tennessee and Georgia ranked third and fifth, respectively, among American states in car production. Texas was on its way to overtaking New York to become the country's second most populous state, while Florida was also likely to overtake New York early in the next century. In fact, if the South were to fulfill the wish of at least some Southern diehards and become a separate country, then, as Peet wryly pointed out, "it would become the world's fifth biggest economy."[1]

The evidence gathered together in *The Economist* represented a summation, and a development, of facts, figures, and arguments familiar since the invention of the term *Sunbelt*. A whole series of commentaries published in the 1970s, in particular, charted the growth of an aggressive new economy in the Southern states built on the six basic foundations of agribusiness, defense, advanced technology, oil and natural gas production, real estate and construction, and tourism and leisure. As the author of one of these commentaries, Kirkpatrick Sale, suggested, in his influential book *Power Shift*, the area stretching from North Carolina to southern California had assumed an "enormous economic importance" that was "all the more remarkable" because it had "come about only in the last thirty years, changing the pleasant little backwaters and half-grown cities into an industrial and financial colossus." "Quite simply," Sale concluded, the "balance of power in America" had "shifted . . . away from the Northeast and toward the Southern Rim."[2] And as the economy of

1. John Peet, "A Survey of the American South," *The Economist*, 10 December 1994, 1–2, 4.
2. Kirkpatrick Sale, *Power Shift: The Rise of the Southern Rim and Its Challenge to the Eastern Establishment* (New York, 1975), 6, 18–20, 55. For further discussion of the developments described here, see, e.g., *The Economics of Southern Growth* edited by E. Blair Linder and Lawrence K. Lynch (Durham, N.C., 1977); *Regional Growth and Decline in the United States: The Rise of the Southwest and the Decline of the Northeast* edited by Bernard L. Weinstein and Robert E. Firestone (New York, 1978); *From the Old South to the New: Essays on the Transitional South* edited by Walter J. Fraser Jr. and Winfred B. Moore Jr. (Westport, Conn., 1981); *Perspectives on the American South: An Annual Review of Society, Politics, and Culture*, Vols. I and II edited by Merle Black and John Shelton

the South expanded—"built upon money from Washington and a culture devoted unreservedly to growth," Sale observed—so did the population. In the 1960s, the Southern states reversed a long-established historical trend, when more people moved into the region than moved out of it. True, these immigrants moved mostly into Florida, Texas, and Virginia, while the rest of the region continued to experience a net exodus; equally true, most of them came from a fairly restricted social group, being educated, middle class, and white. By the 1970s, however, states throughout the South were witnessing a net inflow of population; and, especially significant in view of the region's past, a substantial number of these new immigrants were black. One black worker from Chicago, intent on migrating south just as his father had migrated north, summed up both the economic motives and the historical ironies at work in this reversal. "I'm moving south for the same reasons my father came here from Mississippi," he explained. "He was looking for a better job."[3]

Even in the middle of its celebration of a South "flying high," however, *The Economist* was willing to admit problems. As Peet put it, "the record is not unalloyed progress."[4] One problem was the South's dependence on incentives. Between 1956 and 1968, as the historian James Cobb has shown, Southern states were responsible for seven-eighths of all subsidized bond finance in America. And in the 1980s, as *The Economist* admitted, Tennessee, South Carolina, and Alabama offered inducements worth, respectively, $80 million, $150 million, and $250 million, to Gen-

Reed (New York, 1981–84), Vols. III and IV edited by James C. Cobb and Charles R. Wilson (New York, 1985–87); Gavin Wright, *Old South, New South: Revolutions in the Southern Economy Since the Civil War* (New York, 1986); *Developing Dixie: Modernization in a Traditional Society* edited by Winfred B. Moore Jr. et al. (Westport, Conn., 1988); Bruce J. Schulman, *From Cotton Belt to Sunbelt: Federal Policy, Economic Development, and the Transformation of the South, 1938–1980* (New York, 1991).

3. David R. Goldfield, *Promised Land: The South Since 1945* (Arlington Heights, Tex., 1987), 216. See also Earl Black and Merle Black, *Politics and Society in the South* (Cambridge, Mass., 1987), 3–49; Timothy G. O'Rourke, "The Demographic and Economic Setting of Southern Politics," in *Contemporary Southern Politics* edited by James F. Lea (Baton Rouge, La., 1988), 9–33; Randall M. Miller, "The Development of the Modern Urban South: An Historical Overview," in *Shades of the Sunbelt: Essays on Ethnicity, Race, and the Urban South* edited by Randall M. Miller and George F. Pozetta (Westport, Conn., 1988).

4. Peet, "Survey of the South," 5–6. See also James C. Cobb, *The Selling of the South: The Southern Crusade for Industrial Development, 1931–1980* (Baton Rouge, La., 1982) and *Industrialization and Southern Society, 1877–1984* (Lexington, Ky., 1984).

eral Motors, BMW, and Mercedes to persuade them to build manufacturing plants in their states. A second problem was one inherent in what *The Economist* termed "the South's low-cost labour advantage." The economic transformation that regional boosters, among others, described in terms of a transfer of power from Snowbelt to Sunbelt was, in fact, part of a deeper, structural shift from production to service—and most significantly, as economic historians have argued, to services connected with the "complex of corporate activities" supporting the great multinational companies. It was also one aspect or function of a new fluidity in working relations, the sheer speed with which capital and labor arrangements could be transferred from one place to another, in a global economy. To this extent, the transition from manufacturing products in the Snowbelt to overseeing their manufacture in the Third World and the South lay behind the economic upheavals of the 1970s and the 1980s. And the investment that could be attracted southward by what one banking analyst called "abundant, low-cost, hardworking, non-union labor; cheap and abundant land and utilities . . . low taxes" could just as easily be seduced elsewhere by even lower costs and a more compliant labor force—in Mexico, say, or Indonesia. "Most of the prime properties in town are controlled by interests elsewhere," an Atlanta journalist commented in 1981, "New York, Dallas, Boston, Toronto, Hamburg, Amsterdam, Al Kuwait." "Industrial jobs are going out the back door faster than we can get them in the front door,"[5] complained a development official in Alabama. Like that Atlanta journalist, he was, however inadvertently, signaling the fact that the celebrated "power shift" was a shift in *income* more than in real economic power. The levers controlling the movement of capital remained in the hands of those located, for the most part, elsewhere; investment, and the demand for labor, could flow into the South or any other part of the global marketplace that promised to maximize profits, and it could just as easily and quickly flow out again.

The third problem or factor complicating any account of the recent

5. James C. Cobb, "The Sunbelt South: Industrialization in Regional, National, and International Perspective," in *Searching for the Sunbelt: Historical Perspectives on a Region* edited by Raymond A. Mohl (Knoxville, Tenn., 1990), 36. See also Peet, "Survey of the South," 5; Thierry J. Noyelle and Thomas M. Starbuck Jr., *The Economic Transformation of American Cities* (New York, 1968), 18; *Atlanta Journal Constitution*, 14 February 1982; Neil Shister, "Who Owns Atlanta?" *Atlanta Magazine,* January 1981, 51.

economic transformation of the South is one of spread or distribution. Whatever material progress the region has witnessed in the past twenty years has been decidedly patchy. "The cities and suburbs have thrived," is how *The Economist* put it, "the countryside has not." It was, however, and is more complicated than that. Southern cities have grown. So have the suburban areas; and as the suburbs have expanded they have become, in the words of one historian, "increasingly self-sustaining as economic entities that are able to generate their own jobs." The result is that a typical Southern city may stand "at the greatest social and economic disadvantage in relation to its suburban ring." Richmond, Virginia, for instance, has been described by one commentator as "a city polarized between its core and its periphery, between poor and affluent, between black and white."[6] The story of the recent prospering of the South has been mostly a story of the suburbs and the metropolitan business districts. It has also been a story of certain particular Southern places: above all, what has been called "the Interstate 85 corridor" stretching from Richmond to Atlanta. Other places, notably the Deep South states of Alabama, Mississippi, Louisiana, and Arkansas, have done less well. In terms of 1993 personal income per head, for example, a figure of $19,203 in Georgia, or 92 percent of the national average, compares with $14,708, or 71 percent, in Mississippi.

And then there is, as always, the question of race: the problem of

6. Christopher Silver, *Twentieth-Century Richmond: Planning, Politics, and Race* (Knoxville, Tenn., 1984), 175. See also Peet, "Survey of the South," 6; Carl Abbott, *The New Urban America: Growth and Politics in Sunbelt Cities* (Chapel Hill, N.C., 1981), 185, 229. On Southern urban development, see, e.g., David R. Goldfield, *Cotton Fields and Skyscrapers: Southern City and Region, 1670–1980* (Baton Rouge, La., 1982) and "The Urban South: A Regional Framework," *American Historical Review*, LXXXVI (1981), 1009–34; *Sunbelt Cities: Politics and Growth Since World War II* edited by Richard M. Bernard and Bradley R. Rice (Austin, Tex., 1983); *Essays on Sunbelt Cities and Recent Urban America* edited by Raymond A. Mohl et al. (College Station, Tex., 1990). On the decline of the rural South, see, e.g., Gilbert C. Fite, *Cotton Fields No More: Southern Agriculture, 1865–1980* (Lexington, Ky., 1984); Pete Daniel, *Breaking the Land: The Transformation of Cotton, Tobacco, and Rice Culture Since 1880* (Urbana, Ill., 1985); Jack Temple Kirby, *Rural Worlds Lost: The American South, 1920–1960* (Baton Rouge, La., 1987). On the unevenness of Southern economic development and the consequent poverty in many areas, see, e.g., J. Wayne Flynt, *Dixie's Forgotten People: The South's Poor Whites* (Bloomington, Ind., 1979); *Minorities in the Sunbelt* edited by Franklin J. James et al. (New Brunswick, N.J., 1984); Jacqueline Jones, *The Dispossessed: America's Underclasses from the Civil War to the Present* (New York, 1992).

economic division, the maldistribution of wealth in the contemporary South, is even more acute when it is given a racial coloration. The lagging areas in the region tend, in fact, to be precisely those with a relatively high black population: Mississippi, Alabama, the Delta, west Texas, southern Georgia, coastal South Carolina. Certainly, there has been significant political and economic progress in certain parts of the black community. The number of elected black officials in the South increased fivefold between 1980 and 1993. Drawn by the belief that they can do better in, say, Atlanta than in a Chicago housing project, African Americans have returned in their thousands so that, once again, over half the country's African American population lives in the South. There is also a growing and increasingly affluent Southern black middle class, clustered in suburban communities such as DeKalb County near Atlanta. But the progress has been limited and reserved for the relatively privileged. The average black family in the South earns only just over a half of what the average white Southern family earns. Approximately a quarter of all black families in the region live below the poverty line; in some states, it is even higher—in Mississippi, for instance, it is more than a third. And in rural areas such as the Delta, where machines have taken over the work, four out of five children grow up in poverty. Nor has the abolition of institutionalized racial segregation meant the end of racial discrimination or the emergence of something like equal economic opportunity. On the contrary, poor blacks now tend to find themselves doubly segregated: from their white neighbors, because of race, and from the black bourgeoisie because of poverty and the simple fact that the black middle class has moved out to the suburbs.[7] Race and class are not, of course, coextensive in the contemporary South, any more than they are anywhere else. There are many poor whites, too, trapped in the public housing of

7. See, Peet, "Survey of the South," 9–11. For further discussion of the developments outlined here, see, e.g., Manning Marable, *Race, Reform, and Rebellion: The Second Reconstruction in Black America, 1945–1982* (Jackson, Miss., 1984); Steven Lawson, *In Pursuit of Power: Southern Blacks and Electoral Politics, 1965–1982* (New York, 1985); Bart Landry, *The New Black Middle Class* (Berkeley and Los Angeles, Calif., 1987); James W. Button, *Blacks and Social Change: The Impact of the Civil Rights Movement on Southern Communities* (Princeton, N.J., 1989); David R. Goldfield, *Black, White, and Southern: Race Relations and Southern Culture, 1940 to the Present* (Baton Rouge, La., 1990); Lois Benjamin, *The Black Elite: Facing the Color Line in the Twilight of the Twentieth Century* (Chicago, 1991); Andrew Hacker, *Two Nations: Black and White, Separate, Hostile, and Unequal* (New York, 1992).

the cities or living in the rural ghetto of the mobile home park ("Dixie has embraced the mobile home," one observer has commented, "trailers are becoming the most typical southern architecture.").[8] And together, at or near the bottom of the class heap, poor whites and blacks remind us that not everyone has benefited from changes in the material fabric of the region. It is tempting, but wrong, to think simply in terms of a transformation of the South into the Sunbelt or some kind of "post-Southern" economy.

Arguably, these complicating elements signal the fact that the present South is as much of a colonial economy as earlier apologists for the region—John Caldwell Calhoun, say, or James De Bow—claimed that the Old South was. Certainly, they add to our sense of the plural, layered character of economic change in the region. Any map of the present state of the Southern economy would have to take account of the vast differences between, say, Atlanta, which boasts the second busiest airport in the world (when you go to heaven, locals say, you change planes in Atlanta), and the kind of rural backwaters described in the fiction of the black writer from Louisiana Ernest Gaines and the white novelist from Georgia Harry Crews—where, as Gaines puts it, there is "nothing to do and nowhere to go." A map of this kind would also have to register the distinctions in resources and development, and the divisions of race and class, that continue to scar the region. For that matter, it would need to take account of the possibility that, thanks to the recovery of old competitors in the rest of the country and the emergence of new ones in the Third World, it is—to quote one historian—"no longer morning in the so-called Sunbelt." Nevertheless, for all the significant diversions of detail, the broader contours of such a map would surely follow the same

8. Joel Garreau, *The Nine Nations of North America* (Boston, 1981), 162–63. On poor white people in the South, see, e.g., Flynt, *Dixie's Forgotten People;* Robert Emil Bosch, *We Shall Not Overcome: Populism and Southern Blue-Collar Workers* (Chapel, N.C., 1980); *Working Lives: The "Southern Exposure" History of Labor in the South* edited by Marc Miller (New York, 1980). Also helpful here, by way of explaining differences between Southern whites, are John Shelton Reed, *Southerners: The Social Psychology of Sectionalism* (Chapel Hill, N.C., 1983) and *Southern Folk, Plain and Fancy: Native White Social Types* (Athens, Ga., 1986). And, as an aid to understanding cultural multiplicity and change in the South, an especially useful comparison could be made between James C. Cobb, *The Most Southern Place on Earth: The Mississippi Delta and the Roots of Regional Identity* (New York, 1992), and Douglas Flamming, *Creating the Modern South: Millhands and Managers in Dalton, Georgia, 1884–1984* (Chapel Hill, N.C., 1992).

outline as the one traced by that article in *The Economist*. It would still chart the same fundamental territory, telling us that in terms of its major economic imperatives—and the simple day-to-day work habits of the majority—the South has changed dramatically. For good or ill, Southerners are now exposed to the demands of the marketplace. With the collapse of the plantation system, the dispersal of the mill villages, and the breakdown of other places of settled employment, white males in particular have felt this exposure. For better and worse, though, white women and African Americans have felt it too, as they become more visible elements in the regional economy. The women's movement, together with the crumbling of traditional structures, has opened up female access to the marketplace. And the civil rights movement, together with subsequent federal legislation, has allowed blacks to become a more active and fluid, if still significantly disadvantaged, part of the labor force. The result is that the Southern workforce is now just over one-third white female, just under 10 percent black male, and just under 10 percent black female. In the words of one historian, Numan Bartley, summing up the changes of the recent past, in 1995: "A dynamic free-flowing work force unburdened by labor union membership, unity, or much in the way of state protection or social legislation complemented the drive for economic growth while it undermined family, community, and the spiritual aspects of religion."[9] Another historian, James Cobb, described this transfer to the market economy, and commodification, of most of the adult population of the South much more succinctly; the South, he said, was now "a conservative capitalist's dream come true."

9. Numan V. Bartley, *The New South, 1845–1980*, Vol. XI (1995) in *The History of the South* edited by Wendell Holmes Stephenson and E. Merton Coulter, 11 vols. (Baton Rouge, La., 1947–95), 468. See also Ernest J. Gaines, *Catherine Carmier* (1964; New York, 1993 edition), 174; David R. Goldfield, "The City as Southern History: The Past and the Promise of Tomorrow," in *The Future South: A Historical Perspective for the Twenty-First Century* edited by Joe P. Dunn and Howard L. Preston (Urbana, Ill., 1991), 34; Cobb, "Sunbelt South," 39. Along with works already cited, useful recent discussions of the development described here include Jacqueline Jones, *Labor of Love, Labor of Sorrow: Black Women, Work, and the Family from Slavery to the Present* (New York, 1985); Pete Daniel, *Standing at the Crossroads: Southern Life Since 1900* (New York, 1986); *The Evolution of Southern Culture* edited by Numan V. Bartley (Athens, Ga., 1988); *Southern Women* edited by Caroline M. Dillman (New York, 1988); Priscilla C. Little and Robert C. Vaughan, *A New Perspective: Southern Women's Cultural History from the Civil War to Civil Rights* (Charlottesville, Va., 1989); Robert Weisbrot, *Freedom Bound: A History of America's Civil Rights Movement* (New York, 1990).

Entering the global marketplace, the South has also entered the world of what has become known as "Fordism." The term is one generally applied now to a system geared to the management not only of labor, the processes of production, but also of purchase and consumption. A major point made by many recent commentators, that Southerners have significantly increased their consumption of material goods over the past ten or so years, is usefully contextualized by the equation that sums up the Fordist principle: "Pay them more. Sell them more. Prosper more." As early as the 1920s, mass manufacture of the Model T Ford introduced the risk of overproduction. By promoting higher consumption levels—standardizing distribution and marketing and, in effect, shifting the whole emphasis from production to consumption—Fordism reduced that risk. It was no accident, after all, that advertising revenues in the United States increased thirteenfold between 1900 and 1930. As the advertising journal *Printers Ink* put it, looking back in 1938: "The first advertising sold the name of the product. In the second stage, the specifications of the product were outlined. Then came the emphasis upon the uses of the product. With each step the advertisement moved farther away from the factory viewpoint and edged itself closer to the mental processes of the consumer."[10] This is a shift that has continued with the transmutation, over the past few decades, from "Fordism" into "Flexible Fordism," which, as the term suggests, involves further flexibility in the labor markets, products, and patterns of consumption. As both the pace of innovation and the growth in communications have accelerated, it has become possible to implement changes in business practice ever more rapidly and over a wider and more various territory. The net effect, in terms of labor, has been increasing job insecurity: casualization, part-time and short-term contract work, the abolition of the traditional career ladder. As for consumption, what Flexible Fordism has meant is the emergence of a culture ever more geared to the actual process, the viewpoint of exchange. What matters, seen from this viewpoint, is not the

10. Stuart Ewen, *Captains of Consciousness: The History and Development of Advertising* (New York, 1976), 80. See also Bartley, *New South*, 456. On "Fordism" and "Flexible Fordism," see, David Harvey, *The Condition of Postmodernity: An Enquiry into the Origins of Cultural Change* (Oxford, 1989). Also Michel Aglietta, *A Theory of Capitalist Regulation: The U.S. Experience* (London, 1979); Craig R. Littler, *The Development of the Labour Process in Capitalist Societies* (London, 1982); David A. Hounshell, *From the American System to Mass Production, 1800–1932* (Baltimore, Md., 1984); James O'Connor, *Accumulation Crisis* (New York, 1984).

use but the promise of a product; the purpose or function of things is subordinated to their appearance—their capacity to carry a promissory image that works by taking desires from the eyes of the viewer and bringing those desires to the surface of the commodity. This makes it much easier to sell the surfeit of goods generated by ever more sophisticated forms of production: the consumer is drawn into buying, not what he needs, but what he believes he needs according to the (potentially endless) rhythms of desire. It also locates satisfaction at the moment of buying; what happens after that—when the promise of a need fulfilled has elicited the *frisson* of purchase—must remain, inevitably, a disappointment. As a whole, the South has no more surrendered to the logic of consumerism, of course, than it has simply embraced all the other implications of the new economy. The fact that most white Southerners supported Ronald Reagan for president in 1980 and 1984 because of what one historian has called Reagan's commitment to the "broadly incompatible" ideas of "a free-market society and family values" is proof enough of that. Still, the drift is here too, toward a world of surfaces, where meaning is hooked to the point of purchase: which is surely why so many characters in recent Southern fiction, defined by what they buy more than where they are, appear to be shopping in space.

Any reference to Ronald Reagan and recent electoral trends brings into play one very clear and telling development in the contemporary South. Not so long ago, in the 1950s, the South was still, in the words of one political scientist, "the most dependably Democratic region of the country"; "to be openly Republican," she added, "was a form of deviance." Things then began to shift, so that by the 1970s and early 1980s the South had what two other political scientists christened a "one-and-a-half" party system. The Democratic Party, dominated by so-called populist moderates oriented to the needs of business (people like, say, Jimmy Carter and then later Bill Clinton), retained most of the local offices of the region. However, a Republican party dedicated to both free markets and family increasingly competed for the more prominent positions. That shift has turned out to be remorseless and, apparently, irreversible. In 1975, 92 of the 121 House seats in the South, or 76 percent, were held by Democrats. After the 1994 election, however, there were only 64 Democrats out of 137, or 47 percent. This was the first time since Reconstruction that Democrats had become the minority party in the South; and, after some party switches in 1995, Democrats went down even further, to 59 seats, or 43 percent. The pivotal years, according to surveys, were 1992 to 1994. Before the 1992 elections, Republicans held just one of Georgia's House seats, the Republican in question being Newt Gingrich. But by 1995, the Georgia delegation consisted of eight Republicans and three Democrats. Significantly, all three Democratic representatives were African Americans: the creation of "minority-majority" districts to improve the representation of blacks and Hispanics in Congress had the net effect of concentrating the African American voters, most of them Democrats, in a few districts. One congressional report on the 1994 elections prophesied on the basis of the results that "for the rest of the 1990s the 'party of Lincoln' will increasingly draw its life from the land of Jefferson Davis." And that prophecy seems to be proving to be true. In 1994, the Republicans leaped from having a majority of House seats in just one former Confederate state to majorities in five. After the 1996 elections, when the South was the only region in which Republicans gained House seats, only Virginia and Texas remained with state delegations dominated by Democrats. In the words of one observer, commenting on the 1996 results, there has been "an almost complete reversal of regional party strength." Regional distinctiveness can still be seen in American politics. But now "the backbone of the Republican Party has become the South, as well as the states of the mountain West and much of the Plains."[11]

One explanation for this reversal lies with those strange bedfellows, a free market and family values. A free market is motored by the engines of supply and demand; it is also fueled by an ideology of self-interest, and the commodification of people as paid labor and paying consumers. Family values, on the other hand, imply the subordination of self-interest to more social, consensual imperatives; for good or ill, men and women—and, in the past, women in particular—are obliged to choose

---

11. Marjorie R. Hershey, "The Congressional Elections," in *The Election of 1996: Reports and Interpretations* edited by Gerald M. Pomper (Chatham, N.J., 1997), 228–29. See also John Van Wingen and David Valentine, "Partisan Politics: A One-and-a-Half, No-Party System," in *Contemporary Southern Politics* edited by James F. Lea (Baton Rouge, La., 1988), 124–47; Bartley, *New South,* 399. On the developments outlined here, see also Numan V. Bartley and Hugh D. Graham, *Southern Politics in the Second Reconstruction* (Baltimore, Md., 1975); Jack Bass and Walter DeVreis, *The Transformation of Southern Politics: Social Change and Political Consequences Since 1945* (New York, 1976); *Southern Businessmen and Desegregation* edited by Elizabeth Jacoway and David P. Colburn (Baton Rouge, La., 1982); Black and Black, *Politics and Society in the South;* Dewey D. Grantham, *The Life and Death of the Solid South: A Political History* (Lexington, Ky., 1988).

tradition over vocation, to subject themselves not so much to the demands of the marketplace as to the prescriptions of inherited communal law. One historian has complained that, "in the name of traditional virtue," Ronald Reagan's political agenda was in fact giving a "free hand to business practices that destroy neighborhoods, separate families, promote hedonism, encourage mobility, and plan obsolescence."[12] That, perhaps, is to privilege the traditionalist side of the equation. A more neutral way of putting it might be to say that there is a latent tension in any program that aims both to deregulate the economy and to draw a protective circle, to build an insulated wall around the family. Any tensions that there might be in the Republican program have not, however, discouraged Southerners, and white Southerners especially, from voting for the Grand Old Party: quite the opposite, because the party's promise of a bright new future wedded to a golden past has hit a responsive chord with them, echoing their own vacillation between hope and memory. While the majority of black Southern voters remain loyal to the party of civil rights, the majority of white voters have shifted their allegiance to a party that embraces both productivity and primitive virtue, the pleasures of the marketplace and the pieties of blood and kin. "It is not a country at all," Karl Marx observed of the Confederacy, "but a battle slogan."[13] More than a hundred years after the Civil War ended, the nature of that slogan may have changed, but it still has currency. Despite exposure to the marketplace and material change, many Southerners continue to resist market-oriented values, and remain entrenched in difference.

The figure of entrenchment is chosen advisedly. "Southerners feel," the political scientist Charles Lerche observed in 1964, "that they are struggling against an open conspiracy and a totally hostile environment." Five years later, another observer, Sheldon Hackney, added the comment that "the Southern identity has been linked from the first to a siege mentality." And when, in 1986, John Shelton Reed came to write a concluding note to a new edition of his survey of Southern attitudes, *The Enduring South,* he found similar feelings of being marginalized and even threatened still at work among the—mostly white—Southerners surveyed. More to the point, the data accumulated for this new edition only

12. Alan Wolfe, *America's Impasse: The Rise and Fall of the Politics of Growth* (New York, 1981), 232.

13. Karl Marx and Frederick Engels, *The Civil War in the United States* (New York, 1962 edition), 72.

confirmed what he had claimed when *The Enduring South* had first appeared fourteen years earlier. "Cultural differences that were largely due to Southerners' lower incomes and educational levels," Reed declared, "to their predominantly rural and small-town residence," and "to their concentration in agricultural and low-level industrial occupations": all these, he said, "were smaller in the 1960s than they had been in the past, and they are smaller still in the 1980s." "A few" of these differences "have vanished altogether," he pointed out; and, as a result, "there are important respects in which Southerners look more like other Americans, culturally, than they have at any time for decades, if ever."[14] On the other hand, those differences that Reed labeled "quasi-ethnic," because of their putative origins in the different histories of the American regions, had, many of them, persisted. On the matters of localism, attitudes toward violence, gun ownership, and religion, white Southerners still revealed themselves to be distinctive, different.

In fact, if there appeared to be any significant change in mental maps between the 1960s and the 1980s, Reed commented, it was among non-Southerners. "Non-Southerners are becoming more like Southerners," Reed concluded, "in their tendency to find heroes and heroines in their local community, or even in the family . . . the conviction that individuals should have the right to arm themselves" and in their tendency "to have had the sort of religious experience that is theoretically central to Southern Protestantism." What has been called "the Southernization of America," by the historian John Egerton among others, suggests that one response to commodification, and the globalization of the material life, is resistance and even a kind of cultural reversion. Americans, and not just Southerners, seem to have reacted to the blanding of America, over the last two or three decades, by subscribing to cultural values that simultaneously register their anxiety about change and measure their difference from the corporate ethos. "The 'primitive' attitudes that east-coast liberals used to sneer at," the 1994 article in *The Economist* proclaimed, "are now those of America." That is surely too sweeping, but it underlines the point that surrender to the laws of the global village is not the only available option. On the contrary, Southerners have always shown

14. John Shelton Reed, *The Enduring South: Subcultural Persistence in Mass Society* (1972; Chapel Hill, N.C., 1986 edition), 91–92. See also Charles O. Lerche, *The Uncertain South: Its Changing Patterns of Politics in Foreign Policy* (Chicago, 1964), 243; Sheldon Hackney, "Southern Violence," *American Historical Review,* LXXIV (1969), 925.

how one viable response to feelings of being marginalized is to *build* on the margins, to root one's thinking precisely in the sense of being disempowered and different; and some non-Southerners, at least, appear to be imitating them. John Shelton Reed put it more wryly. "I do not want to suggest that Americans are becoming privatistic, born-again gun-slingers," he declared, "or that Southerners are." Nevertheless, he added, "perhaps there is a pattern here":[15] a pattern of convergence, that is, quite different from the one that anticipated an economically resurgent South simply becoming more like the rest of America.

Even a phrase like "the Southernization of America" is too simple, however, and, in the end, no more satisfactory than "the Americanization of the South." In its own way, it prescribes a model for understanding recent social change in the region that is just as monolithic and disablingly unitary as other terms that have become part of the currency of this debate: terms or phrases like, say, "the lasting South," "the everlasting South," "why the South will survive"—or, alternatively, "this changing South," "an epitaph for Dixie," "look away from Dixie." Non-Southerners have certainly gravitated toward Southern thinking in many respects. They range from the anonymous people surveyed in *The Enduring South* and the millions of non-Southern voters involved in what political scientists have called "an issue-driven switch" to the Republican party, to a distinguished historian from the political left, Eugene Genovese, who now appears to see the tradition of Southern conservatism as the only serious challenge—with the collapse of communism—to what he has termed "market-oriented bourgeois ideologies."[16] But several further

15. Reed, *Enduring South*, 100. See also Peet, "Survey of the South," 14. Also John Egerton, *The Americanization of Dixie: The Southernization of America* (New York, 1974).

16. Eugene D. Genovese, *The Southern Tradition: Achievement and Limitations of an American Conservatism* (Cambridge, Mass., 1994), 8. See also Hershey, "Congressional Elections," 229. Also *The Lasting South: Fourteen Southerners Look at Their Home* edited by Louis D. Rubin Jr. and James K. Kilpatrick (Chicago, 1957); Francis B. Simkins, *The Everlasting South* (Baton Rouge, La., 1963); "Fifteen Southerners," *Why the South Will Survive* (Athens, Ga., 1981); John H. Maclachlan and Joe S. Floyd Jr., *This Changing South* (Gainesville, Fla., 1956); Frank E. Smith, *Look Away from Dixie* (Baton Rouge, La., 1965); Harry S. Ashmore, *An Epitaph for Dixie* (New York, 1957). In 1983, the critic Fred Hobson observed that "if pondering and examining the mind and soul of Dixie had seemed a Southern affliction before 1945," since then it had "assumed epidemic proportions" (*Tell About the South: The Southern Rage to Explain* [Baton Rouge, La., 1983], 297); and these, among many books, appear to prove that.

twists are given to an already tangled situation by two other factors: the selling of the South, as a kind of giant theme park or American version of the heritage industry, and our growing sense of the pluralism of *any* culture including the Southern one. As for the selling of the region: in *Oral History* (1983) by Lee Smith, the old family home place still stands, but it has become an appropriately decaying part of a successful theme park called Ghostland. In the state of Mississippi, observes the central character in *Hey Jack!* (1987) by Barry Hannah, "I find there are exactly five subjects: money, Negroes, women, religion, and Elvis Presley. The rest are nothing."[17] And, as if to prove the truth of this observation, it is possible to go to Memphis, not far from where Hannah lives, and find "Negroes, women, religion, and Elvis Presley" all being turned into "money." Jostling close to each other are such signs of the times, and the new Southern tourism, as Presley's Graceland with its nine gift shops—or Beale Street reconstituted as a heritage site with the W. C. Handy statue, restaurants and shops selling African American memorabilia, and the Center for Southern Folklore.

"This is America, where money's more serious than death."[18] Harry Crews's sardonic comment alerts us to a problem here. There are no doubt noble motives at work in the construction of Southern tourist sites, among them the desire to make the past more accessible. But a tourist site is, pretty obviously, a way of making money and generating trade for the area; it belongs as much to the culture of consumerism as, say, a shopping mall. This is a very particular kind of commodification that turns the South itself—or, to be more exact, an idea or image of the South—into a product, a function of the marketplace. Like all good products, it has a clear identity. As movies such as *Driving Miss Daisy, Doc Hollywood,* and *My Cousin Vinny,* or advertisements for Jack Daniel's whiskey, tell us, the South is registered in popular perception and marketed as a desirable other, one potential, purchasable release from the pressures of living and working in a world governed by the new technologies and international capital. History is thereby displaced into aesthetic style. Via cultural work that Adorno called "receding concreteness," any possibility of a lived encounter with the past slips away, and

17. Barry Hannah, *Hey Jack!* (1987; New York, 1988 edition), 13. See also Lee Smith, *Oral History* (New York, 1983), 292.

18. Harry Crews, *Florida Frenzy* (Gainesville, Fla., 1993), 55. See also Theodor Adorno, *Minima Moralia* (London, 1974), 235.

we are left with a marketable artefact, a copy. What appears to be a process of remembering turns out, in the end, to be one of forgetting, since the realities of economic change, structural transformation are masked, for the purposes of making a sale, by an image of cultural continuity. The ironies of Southern history have always run deep, and surely one of the deepest in recent times is this curious case of change within continuity within change. Some aspects of the South retain their grip on the imagination despite the economic metamorphosis of the region, but then that drift toward the past, the undertow of resistance itself becomes a salable asset. The legends of the South are not necessarily dying, in other words, or being fiercely protected or even resurrected; in some cases, they are merely being turned into cash.

The responses of Southerners themselves to this particular irony are perhaps worth measuring. After all, they are consumers too, and can be included among those to whom the South is being sold. One measurable reaction is resistance. "I wasn't into jazz as a kid" in New Orleans, the jazz musician Wynton Marsalis told the British Broadcasting Corporation in 1993, "I thought it was just shakin' your butt for the white tourists in the French Quarter." And, given that the director of the New Orleans tourist board recently boasted, "Music is integral to our marketing plan,"[19] Marsalis's initial reluctance to become involved in a music to which he was and is so obviously suited seems understandable, if also perverse. Another reaction, its opposite, is to buy into the Southern performance of the good life. That buying ranges from the huge commercial growth of country music or what has become known as "Southern rock," in the United States generally but especially in the South, to a publishing phenomenon like *Southern Living*. Initiated as a magazine in 1966, out of a column that had run for many years in *Progressive Farmer*, *Southern Living* reinforces and defends an image of the region as a place of downhome securities, safe harbor for all those for whom, in the words of one commentator, "the South *is* distinct, *is* special, perhaps even chosen." With its articles on such traditionally Southern obsessions as hunting and fishing, entertaining and etiquette, tasteful decorating and dining, it offers a fantasy conduct manual—a guide to behaving well in a blessed, glossy landscape of gracious homes, immaculate furniture, and mani-

19. Connie Z. Atkinson, " 'Shakin' Your Butt for the Tourist:' Music's Role in the Identification and Selling of New Orleans," in *Dixie Debates: Perspectives on Southern Cultures* edited by Richard H. King and Helen Taylor (London, 1996), 154. See also 155.

cured lawns. The president of the company that began *Southern Living* said in 1985 that his company's mission was "to give people in the South a sense of pride in being Southern." This the magazine does by offering to its readers' gaze the promissory image of a place free of social anxiety or economic insecurity, in which the greatest problem becomes how to choose the right pattern for the silverware. The elusive object of desire here, to be claimed at the point of purchase, is the image of "Southern living" itself: what one analyst of the journal has called its construction of "a South without memory of pellagra or racial unrest, a South where none of the parents are divorced, where burglary and street crime are unknown, where few have Hatteras yachts but one and all play golf and tennis at the club—and in the right outfits."[20] Issues of class and race appear only in subtly coded, disguised form—in, say, articles about black college football players; the project is to reassure the mainly white, middle-class, Southern consumer by offering him (or, more often in this case, her) a familiar regional version of the culturally counterfeit—a copy of a world of easy but mannerly living for which, it turns out, there has never been an original. That project has been remarkably successful. By the middle of the 1990s, *Southern Living* could boast nearly two and a half million subscribers; of these, over 80 percent had well above average incomes and, more to the point, over 80 percent of them also lived in the South.

Another, more complicated reaction to the selling of the South is described in *The Revolution of Little Girls* (1991) by Blanche McCrary Boyd. The novel charts the growth of a young girl called Ellen Burns out of South Carolina and into womanhood, feminism, and a discovery of her own lesbianism. What is of special interest here, however, is one mo-

20. Sam G. Riley, *Magazines of the American South* (New York, 1986), 240. See also Diane Roberts, "Living Southern in *Southern Living*," in *Dixie Debates* edited by King and Taylor, 87, 90. On *Southern Living*, see also Peirce Lewis, "The Making of Vernacular Taste: The Case of *Sunset* and *Southern Living*," in *Dumbarton Oaks Colloquium on the History of Landscape Architecture: XIV* edited by John Dixon Hunt and Joachim Welsschke-Bulmahn (Washington, D.C., 1993), 107–18. On Southern "performance," see Eric Sundquist, *To Wake the Nations: Race in the Making of American Literature* (Cambridge, Mass., 1993), 273. On the popularity of country music, see Bill C. Malone, *Southern Music, American Music,* (Lexington, Ky., 1979); James C. Cobb, "From Muskogee to Luckenbach: Country Music and the 'Southernisation' of America," *Journal of Popular Culture*, XVI (1982), esp. 82, 88. On "Southern rock," see Paul Wells, "The Last Rebel: Southern Rock and Nostalgic Certainties," in *Dixie Debates* edited by King and Taylor, 115–29.

ment in her youth when, thanks to her workaholic father, the Burns family move out of a modest house on the outskirts of Charleston into "an old plantation out in the country" known as Blacklock. "I had never seen a house like the one at Blacklock, except in the movies," Ellen explains. "Each time *Gone With the Wind* was rereleased, our family, minus my father, went dutifully to see this tribute to what we had lost"—although the notion of loss is cultural rather than familial since, as Ellen points out, "my father had grown up poor." "We were minus my father," Ellen adds, "because he was tied up making money . . . so we could do things like move to Blacklock." "When 'Dixie' played," in the movie, she remembers, "I cried every time." "And when Scarlett O'Hara said, 'As God is my witness, I'll never be hungry again,' " she adds, "I'd think, *yeah, me [n]either."* Come the day the family move to Blacklock, Ellen is struck by the fact that, although "it didn't look like Tara," it has all the crucial paraphernalia of that Old South sold to an eager public in popular films and fiction, including slave cabins, huge oak trees, "a set of white columns" at the entrance to the estate, and "a white oyster-shell road that circled in front of the house on top of the hill." "I've seen this movie before," Ellen shouts out as they approach the house; and, although her father tells her to "Hush, Ellen," she cries out again, "I've seen this movie before!"[21]

Ellen Burns comes across in Boyd's novel as an edgy, sophisticated, often subversive person; and her immediate response to the plantation heritage that her family has, in effect, bought is characteristically subtle and self-conscious. With one, particularly ironic eye she can see how she and her family have been sold a product, through movies like *Gone With the Wind.* They have, she can appreciate, been taught what they have "lost," shown a gap in their lives that can supposedly be filled by the purchase of Blacklock and other gracious appendages of "Southern living." She can even perhaps perceive the irony of gazing at a relic of the past in terms of mediated images of that past, as if it were an imitation of an imitation, since in this world the authentic and the replica become interchangeable as products, transferable commodities. Nevertheless, Ellen also looks at this site of desire with genuine excitement, even elation; the fact that, as she sees it, she is moving close to a familiar movie set is an occasion for delight as well as wry humor. She is, in short, not

---

21. Blanche McCrary Boyd, *The Revolution of Little Girls* (1991; New York, 1992 edition), 77–80.

only amused but pleased. She soon comes to think of Blacklock as "cursed"[22] and is relieved when eventually, due to a downturn in the family fortunes, the estate is sold—to a group that want to replicate another image of traditional Southern living, by hunting wild duck in the rice paddies. But that is only a further element in what Fredric Jameson would call the logic of late capitalism: the climax is a matter of exchange, not of use. And it is a climax that Ellen enjoys, for all her irony: she looks at Blacklock, when she arrives there, with the gaze of the knowing consumer who desires no less because she understands the crude mechanisms of consumerism—that her desires have been generated by the marketplace. This self-aware, self-reflexive form of consumption is arguably the norm now. When we watch films like *Gone With the Wind* or, say, *Fried Green Tomatoes,* we are probably aware that we are looking at a counterfeit, a projection of our own culturally formed desires on to a particular location in Southern space and time. Still, we receive momentary satisfaction from it; we accept the counterfeit *as if* it were true currency. It is in these curiously hybrid terms that many non-Southerners currently buy the image of the South—just as Ellen Burns does when she arrives at "this movie" she has seen, she says, many times before. And that perhaps is what most contemporary Southerners do as well, including many of those subscribers to *Southern Living.*

All this, of course, begs the question of just what *kind* of South any of us may be trying to renew, transform, preserve, or purchase. Is it the South, for instance, of Wynton Marsalis or Blanche McCrary Boyd that is in the process of being sold? Or, perhaps, the South enshrined in *Southern Living?* Is it the South of those predominantly white Southerners for whom the Confederate flag is a proud emblem of regional heritage? Or of those, both black and white, for whom that same flag is a symbol of racial hatred? Questions like these have always hovered behind any attempt to chart Southern thinking, but the drawing of the mental maps of the region has become peculiarly challenging in the past few years with the growth of cultural pluralism. Makers of the South and things Southern whose work previously tended to be ignored or minimized, often for reasons of caste or gender or both, now come much more into debate

22. Boyd, *Revolution of Little Girls,* 120. See also Fredric Jameson, *Postmodernism; or, The Cultural Logic of Late Capitalism* (London, 1991), 19. In this context, Jean Baudrillard's analysis of "the liquidation of all referentials," and the process of "substituting signs of the real for the real itself," is also relevant (*Simulations* [New York, 1983], 4).

and play.[23] They range from popular novelists like Margaret Mitchell, through blues singers and jazz musicians, film directors and country songwriters, to those numerous and frequently anonymous women and men who have resurrected and reshaped the traditions of African art in the region. Just as much at issue here is our vastly expanded sense now of precisely what "making" a culture involves: the recognition that a culture identifies and in fact creates itself by a variety of means—means that include the individual book or essay, of course, but go far beyond this to incorporate the artefacts of everyday life and the potentially end-less products of mass culture, the voice heard perhaps in passing on the radio or images flickering on a screen. What emerges with particular power from all this is the possibility that even the process of commodifi-cation, the turning of an image of the South or regional icon into a mar-ketable asset, could be regarded as playing an integral part in the making of a culture. After all, whether anyone likes it or not, Southerners are "known" to themselves and others through the mass media, among many other forms of communication. And what emerges with even more power is the fact that our perception of the South must now, more than ever before, acknowledge the various and often antagonistic influences and energies that go to make it up: we are faced, not so much with Southern culture really, as with Southern *cultures.*

Even within the relatively limited playing field of the novel, the vari-ety—and, in some cases, mutual antagonism—of the influences that go to make up Southern culture(s) now is clear. "We need to talk, to tell," William Faulkner observed of Southerners once, "since oratory is our heritage." Old tales and talking have, in fact, long served as both a local art and a preservative tool—a customary, carefully cultivated skill and a vital medium for the transference of custom. Southerners talk; in doing so, they continue a tradition of storytelling and they sustain the substance of that tradition, its memories and legends—they speak, in short, both *out of* the past and *of* it. But exactly what past do they speak from and about? The answer to this, if we look for it in recent fiction, turns out to be intriguingly mixed: once, that is, we go beyond certain obvious boundaries, points staked out by the major crises in Southern history. Take two recent books that have as their narrative pivots an heroic act

23. One clear illustration of this is the range of material covered in *Encyclopedia of Southern Culture* edited by Charles R. Wilson and William Ferris (Chapel Hill, N.C., 1989).

of storytelling: *The Autobiography of Miss Jane Pittman* (1971) by Ernest Gaines and *Oldest Living Confederate Widow Tells All* (1989) by Allan Gurganus. Both revolve around an old woman recollecting and reshaping the past. Both could be described in the terms Gaines uses for his novel, as "folk autobiography" or, equally, in those Gurganus has chosen for his, as the revelation of a secret history "truer than fact." For that matter, both draw some of their energy and inspiration from the same sources—interviews conducted in the 1930s by the Federal Writers Project. The fact remains, though, that the two women have a fundamentally different story to tell. Jane Pittman, whose recollections just about begin with the whipping she received for refusing to acknowledge the name "the master and the rest of them"[24] had given her, talks of a past that is another country, not only from the present, but from the relatively, racially more privileged past of Gurganus's Lucy Marsden, the wife and then widow of a Confederate captain. Jane Pittman may see connections across the racial divide—and, in particular, the common interests poor black and poor white have in the face of "the rich people"—but connection never becomes coincidence of interest. A simple, seminal choice of pronoun says it all: her fellow blacks she includes in "we," all others are "they."

"Granny . . . would lean back in her chair and start reeling out story and memory," recalls the protagonist, Ruth Anne Boatwright (known as "Bone") of *Bastard Out of Carolina* (1992) by Dorothy Allison, "making no distinction between what she knew to be true and what she had only heard told. The tales she told me in her rough, drawling whisper were lilting songs, ballads of family, love and disappointment. Everything seemed to come back to grief and blood, and everybody seemed legendary."[25] The older generation hand down stories of the past and, in the process, hand on its burden and inspiration: that is a common motif of Southern books, including recent ones, even when there is not one domi-

24. Ernest Gaines, *The Autobiography of Miss Jane Pittman* (1971; New York, 1972 edition), 9. See also 151; William Faulkner, "An Introduction to *The Sound and the Fury*," *Mississippi Quarterly*, XXVI (1973), 412; *Conversations with Ernest Gaines* edited by John Lowe (Jackson, Miss., 1995), 61; Allan Gurganus, *Oldest Living Confederate Widow Tells All* (New York, 1989), xix.

25. Dorothy Allison, *Bastard Out of Carolina* (1992; London, 1993 edition), 26. See also 64; M. A. Harper, *For the Love of Robert E. Lee* (New York, 1992), 37; Harry Crews, *A Childhood: The Biography of a Place* (1978), in *Classic Crews: A Harry Crews Reader* (London, 1993), 21; Thulani Davis, *1959* (1992; London, 1993 edition), 35–36.

nant voice. In *For the Love of Robert E. Lee* (1992) by M. A. Harper, the heroine Garnet Laney talks of a "genetic memory" that seems somehow activated by *her* grandmother, who tells her stories of the Civil War and the Lee family; while in *A Childhood: The Biography of a Place* (1978), Harry Crews recalls his upbringing "in a society of storytelling people" where, he tells us, "nothing is allowed to die. . . . It is all . . . carted up and brought along from one generation to the next." Then there is the character called William Walker in *1959* (1992) by the African American novelist Thulani Davis who, the narrator remembers, was so old that he "had more recollections of slavery than of freedom" and would repeat stories and speeches from the old times that everyone ended up learning, "like a blues song passed down the hands on the levee." The common threads running between oral histories like these are clear but so are the differences. The past that is spoken into the present here is of a variable, plural kind. For Grant Lacey, for instance, the memories are spellbinding and romantic. They seduce her into the belief that she is actually playing a part in the Old Southern family romance, and in love with General Robert E. Lee. For Ruth Anne Boatwright, on the other hand, as for the young Harry Crews, the old tales are of dispossession, wanting and wandering, the plight of the landless and intermittently workless. There is no dear particular place as such that is recalled, only a general locality, as the Boatwrights and their kind "moved and then moved again"— "sometimes before we'd even gotten properly unpacked," Ruth Anne remembers—in search of a means to live.

"It's strange what you don't forget," begins *Machine Dreams* (1984) by Jayne Anne Phillips before moving into an account of the indelible nature of memory, and how memory charges that elaborate network of feeling and faith we call the family. Similarly, early on in *The Annunciation* (1983) by Ellen Gilchrist, we learn of the memories the young central character "must carry with her always" because they are her "cargo," as she sees it, part of her that she carries *inside* her. This is a past of the bloodstream, kin, and instinct rather more than storytelling, but it carries with it the same burden of communality and difference—the same feeling that now, more than ever, the South needs to be read in plural terms. Most obviously, there are differences of racial memory. Jane Pittman tells of another country from the one mapped out by Lucy Marsden, peopled by what Gaines himself has called the "Black 'peasantry,' " "the blacks of the fields" whom "white writers" can only present as "caricatures." William Walker, in *1959*, tells stories of how he and his family were quite literally bought and sold, their bodies along with their labor made the subject of exchange. "He went to the white man's court to get his wife and children out after buying their freedom," Walker tells the several generations of his audience, "and the white man told him point-blank, 'You may say they are wife and children to you, but they are property still. Possession is nine-tenths of the law.' "[26] These are recollections inscribed in race, whose main cultural work is to identify what it means to be a *black* Southerner. As such, they are determinately other, outside and apart from the remembrances of whites—even the white dispossessed. And, in the same way, the instinctual past, the secret memories of African Americans tend toward difference. Even a relatively privileged African American character, like the main character of *Meridian* (1976) by Alice Walker, is haunted by ghostly voices and presences that mark her off from the young white female protagonists of *Machine Dreams* and *The Annunciation*. "But what none of them seemed to understand," Walker says of her character, "was that she felt herself to be, not holding something from the past, but *held* by something in the past: by the memory of old black men in the South who, caught by surprise in the eye of the camera, never shifted their position but looked directly back, by the sight of young girls singing in a country choir, their hair shining with brushings and grease, their voices the voices of angels."[27] Walker, like Gaines or Davis, is speaking of the South, certainly, but of a South that has disentangled itself from many of the threads of white culture(s). It has its own projects and pieties, issuing from its own store of memories. So, much of the time, it writes its own separate history.

A separate history—one that connects up with other, mainly white stories of the past but never becomes submerged in them—is also what is at stake in the work of Ishmael Reed. There is a case, certainly, for saying that books like *Mumbo Jumbo* (1972) and *Flight to Canada* (1976) are just as concerned with resurrection and revival as any number of books by white Southerners, among them recent ones such as *Blue Rise* (1983) by Rebecca Hill, *In Country* (1985) by Bobbie Ann Mason, and *A Summons to Memphis* (1986) by Peter Taylor. What is resurrected, though, how, and for what purpose are all entirely different. Take, by way of

26. Davis, *1959*, 35. See also Jayne Anne Phillips, *Machine Dreams* (London, 1984), 3; Ellen Gilchrist, *The Annunciation* (1983; London, 1984 edition), 15; *Conversations with Gaines* edited by Lowe, 7, 17.

27. Alice Walker, *Meridian* (1976; London, 1983 edition), 14.

contrast, a book like *In Country,* which relocates a familiar narrative of the "Southern renascence" in a freshly seen, fundamentally altered landscape. Set in what is called, at one point in the story, "contemporary, state-of-the-art U.S.A.," Mason's novel introduces us to a world that is notable, above all, for its motion and surfaces, and its exclusion of everything but the present. Three characters are on the road, among them Samantha Hughes, who likes to be called Sam: an eighteen-year-old girl whose father died in the Vietnam War. "Everything in America is going on here, on the road," Sam tells herself. And the places that slip by her are defined by the pure products of America, media-generated icons, while the language that describes them for us crackles with the urgency, the immediacy, and the depthlessness of an on-the-spot news report. This is how *In Country* begins: watching America at the vanishing point—a culture of "surface intensity and pure meaninglessness," in the words of Baudrillard, existing "in a perpetual present of signs"—as Sam and her companions drive steadily toward the Vietnam War Memorial in Washington. It ends, however, in another territory altogether. Arrived in Washington, Sam touches the name of her father on the stone walls of the Memorial, and then her own name—which is, of course, the name of a namesake—nearby. "Sam touches her own name. How odd it feels, as though all the names in America have been used to decorate this wall."[28] Through this strange, startling experience, Sam "is just beginning to understand," we are told: that is, she is just on the threshold of knowing the past—and starting, quietly, to accept her part in it and its part in her. Following a path beaten out by many earlier Southern heroes (Jack Burden in *All the King's Men,* say, or Lucius Cree in *The Velvet Horn*), Sam has come to feel the immanence of the present in the past, by meeting her own name inscribed in history. In the process, *In Country* has also followed a classic regional route, moving out of the traditions of the past

28. Bobbie Ann Mason, *In Country* (1985; London, 1987 edition), 244–45. See also 17, 240; Jean Baudrillard, *America* translated by Chris Turner (London, 1988), 28, 63, 76. Useful discussions of *In Country* include Robert H. Brinkmeyer Jr., "Finding One's History: Bobbie Ann Mason and Contemporary Southern Literature," *Southern Literary Journal,* XIX (1987), 20–33; Katherine Kinney, " 'Humping the Boonies': Sex, Combat, and the Female in Bobbie Ann Mason's *In Country,*" in *Fourteen Landing Zones: Approaches to Vietnam War Literature* edited by Philip K. Jason (Iowa City, 1991), 38–48; Owen H. Gilman Jr., *Vietnam and the Southern Imagination* (Jackson, Miss., 1992), 47–60. Rebecca Hill, *Blue Rise* (1983; London, 1984 edition); Peter Taylor, *A Summons to Memphis* (1986; London, 1987 edition).

and then back into them again—as its words, like those Sam encounters on the wall, set up a channel, a current of sympathy, between the dead and the living.

Ishmael Reed has said that he too is interested in the connection between the dead and the living. In fact, he has described his narrative project in exactly these terms. "Necromancers used to lie in the guts of the dead or in tombs to receive visions of the future," he observed in an interview; "that is prophecy." And, he added, "the black writer lies in the guts of old America, making readings about the future." With Reed, however, what he resurrects goes back to what he has called "the genius of Afro satire": this he excavates, and then exploits in his fiction, so as to catch a sense of reality that is protean, extemporaneous, intuitive, frequently combative—and at odds with any definition of culture in singular terms. "Nowhere is there an account or portrait of Christ laughing," we are told in *Mumbo Jumbo*. "Like the Marxists who secularized his doctrine, he is always stern, serious and as gloomy as a prison guard." In order to restore the laughter, and with it a sense of risk, the tricky, tricksy complexity of things, Reed has elaborated what he describes as his "Voodoo aesthetic," the determining feature of which is its roots in plurality, a mutually reflective, uncoercive "crisscross" of cultural forms. Monoculturalism, or what Reed has termed "Atonism," lies at the heart of Western thought: politically, people may be "left," "right," or "middle" but, he argues, "they are all together on the sacredness of Western civilization and its mission." His task, simply and radically, is to "humble Judaeo-Christian culture," with its presumptions to a monopoly on the truth, and to affirm instead, not African American culture (that would simply mean substituting one monolith with another), but the multiplicity of cultures: to replace the cultural subordination of "Western civilization" or "the melting pot" with the idea of a "multiculture." "Voodoo is the perfect metaphor for the multiculture," Reed has suggested. "Voodoo comes out of the fact that all these different tribes and cultures were brought from Africa to Haiti. . . . It's an amalgamation like this country." And unearthing the Voodoo past for use in the present is, as he sees it, a vital act of continuance and renewal. "I began to realize," he has confessed, "that. . . . We had to become multicultural, and I think this will be a major factor in determining who finally survives in this country. It's like evolution—if you have a limited viewpoint you are at a disadvantage. Those who have incorporated other perspectives and allowed their vision to embrace other ways of looking at the world have a better chance of surviving."[29]

What all this means for Reed's creative practice is serious fun and a teasing, passionate waywardness. Voodoo, Reed has said, "teaches that past is present"; and each of his fictions offers the same lesson in a sly, subversive, jokily disjunctive way. The resistance here is to the narrow fictional forms favored by what one of Reed's characters dismisses as the "neo-social realist gang"—and, more particularly, to any traditional kind of African American narrative that (as Reed puts it) "limits and enslaves us" by confining black experience to a singular, linear model. The writer metamorphoses into the voodoo-man or magician, the trickster god weaving backward and forward in time and between different levels of narration. And the writing turns on a syncretic, densely textured, and multilayered vision of reality—with the familiar Southern theme of the presence of the past suddenly given a multicultural, multiethnic twist. In *Flight to Canada*, for instance, Reed picks up the old African American form of the slave narrative and then, through a transformation of style, changes a remembrance of servitude into an act of liberation. A flight from slavery is enacted twice in the book: the first time in a poem called "Flight to Canada" written by a character called Quicksill, and the second time in Quicksill's escape to Canada. But a flight from slavery also *is* the book. "For him, freedom was his writing,"[30] it is said of Quicksill;

29. Interview with Ishmael Reed, in *Afro-American Writing Today,* An Anniversary Issue of the *Southern Review* (Baton Rouge, La., 1989), 207. See also Interview with Ishmael Reed, in *The New Fiction: Interviews with Innovative American Writers* edited by Joe D. Bellamy (Urbana, Ill., 1974), 133; *Mumbo Jumbo* (New York, 1972), 50, 97, 136; *Shrovetide in Old New Orleans* (Garden City, N.Y., 1978), 133, 232–33. Useful discussions of Reed include Robert E. Fox, *The Black Postmodernist Fiction of LeRoi Jones (Amiri Baraka), Ishmael Reed, and Samuel Delany* (New York, 1987); Reginald Martin, *Ishmael Reed and the New Black Aesthetic Critics* (New York, 1988); Jan Boyer, *Ishmael Reed* (New York, 1993). Also useful are Robert E. Fox, "Blacking the Zero: Towards a Semiotics of Neo-Hoodoo," *Black American Literary Forum,* XVIII (1984); A. Robert Lee, "Afro-America, the Before Columbus Foundation and the Literary Multiculturalization of America," *Journal of American Studies,* XXVIII (1994), 433–50.

30. Ishmael Reed, *Flight to Canada* (New York, 1976), 88–89. See also 19, 28; *Shrovetide in Old New Orleans,* 233; *Yellow Back Radio Broke-Down* (1969; New York, 1988 edition), 36; Interview with Ishmael Reed, in *Interviews with Black Writers* edited by John O'Brien (New York, 1973), 174; "America: The Multinational Society," in *Writin' Is Fightin': Thirty-Seven Years of Boxing on Paper* (New York, 1988); Henry Louis Gates, Review of *Flight to Canada, Journal of Negro History,* LXIII (1978), 78. Reed has said that the novel *Flight to Canada* actually evolved out of the poem "Flight to Canada" (Inter-

and freedom is the writing of *Flight to Canada* the novel as well as "Flight to Canada" the poem, as Reed deploys self-reflexiveness, parody, deliberate anachronism, and constant crisscrossing between different histories and cultures to maneuver himself out of the straitjacket of social realism. The traditional slave narrative was constrained by its moral earnestness, its patient accumulation of detail. It was a clear illustration, according to Henry Louis Gates, of "the political uses to which the abolitionists put black literacy": with a prescriptive and "painstaking verisimilitude" denying blacks the possession of their own story, or the possibility of breaking out of monocultural forms. *Flight to Canada,* on the other hand, with its punning title, its mixing of an antebellum setting with casual references to the *dreck* of contemporary culture, and its irreverent humor ("Go to the theatre," a slave owner advises Abraham Lincoln. "Get some culture.") slips off all these shackles. The Civil War is spliced with the civil rights wars of the 1960s (with the image of Lincoln's assassination, for example, being constantly replayed in slow motion on the late night news); Edgar Allan Poe, the Marquis de Sade, and Captain Kidd mingle with such props of modern times as satellite television, jumbo jets, and *Time* magazine; a slave owner declares himself doubly outraged at his runaway slaves because, as he puts it, "they furtively pilfered themselves." Through meaningful mischief such as this (slaves are property but also, for the purposes of moral censure, people), through shrewd mixing and the sudden splicing of stories, Reed slips the reader the message that freedom springs from confluence not control, an easygoing commerce between cultures. Reed refuses to be slave to his narrative; in the process, he resites the act of connection between living and dead in an altered demography—an America that he once called "the Multinational Society."

"The world is here," Reed ends one of his essays—the one, in fact, actually titled "America: The Multinational Society." That remark brings us right back to the problem, and the promise, of cultural pluralism. Even talking about the past, that old Southern pastime, suddenly becomes tricky when that talking takes place as Reed's does, in the mobile marketplace of modern culture, with its mix and occasional collisions of race and class. And gender: the shifting patterns of work practice among Southern females are clear. By 1970, women made up 39 percent of the

---

view, *Iowa Review,* XIII [1982], 129). A particularly useful analysis of this novel is, Richard Walsh, " 'A Man's Story Is His Gris-Gris': Cultural Slavery, Literary Emancipation and Ishmael Reed's *Flight to Canada," Journal of American Studies,* XXVII (1993), 56–71.

workforce in the South, and by 1980 it was 43 percent. Affirmative action increased work opportunities, particularly for educated women, to the extent that one historian, writing at the end of the 1980s, could describe the change in the work and family patterns of Southern women as "a revolution." "The economic, demographic, and social changes that have occurred since World War II," she declared, "have diminished the differences between women in the urban South and women in other American cities."[31] Or, as one of Bobbie Ann Mason's characters snappily puts it, "Times are different now, Papa. We're just as good as the men." Not all women live in the urban South, however, even now. And even those that do find, like many of their country counterparts, that changes in labor practice do not necessarily equal changes in belief and behavior. "Men could do anything," the narrator of *Bastard Out of Carolina* recalls of her upbringing, well after World War II, "and everything they did, no matter how violent or mistaken, was viewed with humor and understanding." "What men did was just what men did," she adds. "Some days I would grind my teeth, wishing I had been a boy." The same wish, to become a member of an exclusive club of male privilege, prompts the more middle-class heroine of *The Revolution of Little Girls* to insist on playing the boy's parts in all her childhood games. "After the Tarzan serial at the movies every Saturday afternoon," she remembers, she insisted on playing Tarzan because "Tarzan had more fun." Unfortunately for her, though, "the real world was suspicious of girls who did not want to play Jane."[32]

And in the real world of the South many women continue to "play Jane." They remain wedded to a particular regional mystique, roles that slyly or more obviously are forms of subjection. "The past—not the one validated in schoolbooks but another kind, unanalyzed and undefined—hangs upon Southern women as if they were dispossessed royalty," Shirley Abbott has observed in *Womenfolks: Growing Up Down South*. "I never learned," she adds ruefully, "to construe the female sex as downtrodden and disadvantaged."[33] Abbott is talking, in particular,

31. Julie K. Blackwelder, "Race, Ethnicity and Women's Lives in the Urban South," in *Shades of the Sunbelt* edited by Miller and Pozetta, 78, 88. See also Reed, "America: The Multinational Society."

32. Boyd, *Revolution of Little Girls*, 3. See also Bobbie Ann Mason, *Shiloh and Other Stories* (1982; London, 1988 edition), 110; Allison, *Bastard Out of Carolina*, 23.

33. Shirley Abbott, *Womenfolks: Growing Up Down South* (New Haven, Conn., 1983), 31. For accounts of themselves by Southern women, see also *Speaking for Ourselves: Women of the South* edited by Maxine Alexander (New York, 1977).

of her own conflicted role as an educated Southern white woman. The situation is all the trickier, however, and the conflicts even more conflicted, because many of the old divisions between women of different classes, and in particular between black and white women, remain. A measure of the grip traditional female roles still have on the Southern imagination is that ten of the fifteen states that never ratified the Equal Rights Amendment in the 1970s were in the South. And a measure, in turn, of the degree of tension *between* and *within* Southern women is that many of those Southerners opposed to the amendment—maybe seeing it, as one of them put it, as a piece of "country club feminism"—were female. "Most working-class women . . . will never fall prey to the media-created fads which advertise themselves as 'women's liberation,' " a female labor activist from the South declared shortly after the Stop ERA campaign began in 1972. "Middle-class women's lib is a trend," a working woman in the region commented during the same period, "working women's liberation is a necessity." An African American woman put it even more baldly and, besides, registered some of the resentment that strict demarcation between traditional white and traditional black female roles in the South has tended to produce. The women's movement, she insisted, "is just a bunch of bored white women with nothing to do—they're just trying to attract attention away from the black liberation movement."[34]

"It is going to take time," one social observer of Southern white women has argued, "for them to catch up to women in other parts of the country": catch up, that is, in terms of customary assumptions and social roles. Even professional women in the region, the evidence suggests, are less directed toward personal achievement and career goals than they are elsewhere in the United States; and for many other Southern women the pull toward the past is doubly powerful because there has been less of a significant *economic* advance. "I was raised in southern Georgia where any female past puberty was referred to as a lady," Harry Crews confesses in one of his essays. "You may by now have recognized in what I've written thus far," he goes on, "that I've referred to the other half of

34. Helen H. King, "Black Women and Women's Lib," *Ebony*, March 1971, 70. See also Donald G. Mathews and Jane Sherron De Hart, *Sex, Gender, and the Politics of ERA: A State and the Nation* (New York, 1990), 145; *Hillbilly Women* edited by Kathy Kahn (New York, 1973), 19, 183; Dolores Janiewski, *Sisterhood Denied: Race, Gender and Class in a New South Community* (Philadelphia, Pa., 1985), 152–78.

the human race alternately as woman, lady, and girl. There is great confusion on the part of some men—and certainly I am one of them—about just what the hell we should call females."[35] The confusion that Crews admits to, about the right names and roles for women, is something shared by many other Southerners, male *and* female. And it can be crippling. It has led some critics to suggest, for instance, that Crews himself is incapable of creating plausible women characters in his fiction. It can also be frustrating, especially for those many women in the South who experience division actively within them, in their understanding of themselves as well as in everyday social exchange. But sometimes it can be useful, even fruitful, provoking imaginative analysis of just what has caused the confusion; it may encourage those caught in the slippage between old beliefs and new behavior to think carefully about their plight.

As far as the possibly fruitful nature of confusion is concerned, something that Lucien Goldmann says is worth mentioning here. "All forms of consciousness," Goldmann argues, "express a provisional and mobile balance between the individual and his social environment; when this balance can be fairly easily established and is relatively stable . . . men tend not to think about the problems raised by their relationship to the external world. On the social as well as on the individual plane, it is the sick organ which creates awareness, and it is in periods of social and political crisis that men are most aware of the enigma of their presence in the world."[36] A moment of special crisis, when the terms of our relations to things—which include, most crucially, our language—are brought into question, can force anyone to think more critically, argue more provocatively, and write with more imaginative force and daring than those living in more comfortable times. If the recent past has been a

---

35. Crews, *Florida Frenzy,* 33–34. See also Caroline M. Dillman, "Southern Women: In Continuity or Change?," in *Women in the South: An Anthropological Perspective* edited by Holly F. Mathews (Athens, Ga., 1989), 17. On the problem of the relationship between material change and changes in perception, see also Susan Middleton-Deirn and Jackie Howsden-Eller, "Reconstructing Femininity: The Woman Professional in the South," in *Women in the South* edited by Mathews, 59–70. On the particular problems faced by black women, see Jones, *Labor of Love, Labor of Sorrow.* For a critique of Harry Crews's fictional representations of women, see Patricia V. Beatty, "Crews's Women," in *A Grit's Triumph: Essays on the Work of Harry Crews* edited by David K. Jeffrey (Port Washington, N.Y., 1983), 112–23.

36. Lucien Goldmann, *The Hidden God* translated by Philip Thody (London, 1956), 49.

period of such crisis for Southerners, it has been acutely so for females—as the conflicting demands of "woman, lady, and girl" are pressed into debate. So it is, perhaps, no surprise that many of the best books coming out of the South in the past few years have been by women, as they struggle with the enigma of their presence in their own particular corner of the world.

What all this comes down to, really, is that Southerners are living *between* cultures. Some are living there more openly than others, and with more sensitivity to the problems that come with the territory; among these are Southern writers. All of them are living there, too, in a double sense. In local terms, Southerners are caught between the conflicting interests and voices that constitute the region and the regional debate. Similarly, on the national and even international stage, they betray intense uncertainty about whether to assimilate or to resist. Southern books, in particular, very often become a site of struggle between, on the one hand, the culture(s) of the South and, on the other, the culture of the global marketplace. As a matter of general practice, or even regional history, this is not quite as unusual, as extraordinary as it may sound. The South as a term of self-identification was, after all, born out of crisis; and the area known as Southern has remained almost continually in a critical state. All that has happened recently is that change—and, especially, the information and consumer revolutions of the past few decades—has made things even more acutely critical than usual; there is a difference of degree, fundamentally, rather than of kind. Besides, no society anywhere is immune from crisis or exempt from the conflicting practices and interests that promote it. The South now is not a monolith but, then, no historical epoch is. On the contrary, as Fredric Jameson has argued, *any* social formation is a complex overlay of different methods of production which serve as the bases of different social groups and, consequently, of their worldviews. And in any given epoch a variety of kinds of antagonism can be discerned, conflict between different groups and interests. One culture may well be dominant: but there will also be—to borrow Raymond Williams's useful terms—a residual culture, formed in the past but still active in the cultural process, and an emergent culture, prescribing new meanings and practices. Southerners, in effect, like any other members of a society, are not the victims of some totalizing structure, since—to quote Williams—"no dominant culture ever in reality includes all human practice, human energy and human intention." Nor are Southern writers: they have the chance, maybe even the obligation, to insert themselves in the space between conflicting interests and practices and then dramatize the contradictions the conflict engenders. Through their work, by means of a mixture of voices, a free play of languages and even genres, they can represent the reality of their culture as multiple, complex, and internally antagonistic. They can achieve a realization of both synchrony and diachrony: a demonstration, on the one hand, of structural continuities between past and present and, on the other, of the processes by which those continuities are challenged, dissolved, and reconstituted. So they have a better opportunity than many other members of their society have of realizing what Hayden White has called "the human capacity to endow lived contradictions with intimations of their possible transcendence."[37] They have the chance, in short, of getting "into" history, to participate in its processes, and, in a perspectival sense at least, getting "out" of it too—and so enable us, the readers, to begin to understand just how those processes work.

About midway through *Edisto* (1983) by Padgett Powell, the narrator of the novel, Simons Everson Manigault, describes how his mother, known locally as the Duchess, refuses to have a faulty air conditioning unit in their rundown "Southern barony" replaced. "Honey, when I was little, we didn't have all this," she tells her son. "Just consider we're going back through Margaret Mitchell's wind." The men who remove the unit refuse at first to believe that she will not order a new one. "They didn't know she was one of those readers of Southern literature who talk about progressive light changes at dusk," says Simons by way of explanation, "and how the air in the country is different than in the city, and how country crickets sing a different, more authentic tune than city crickets." The sort of "Southern literature" the Duchess favors is clearly not the sort in which she appears. *Edisto* begins on an old estate, "reduced . . . to a track of clay roads cut in a feathery herbaceous jungle of deerfly for stock and scrub oak for crop." And it ends in the suburbs, with Simons and his "vestigial baroness" of a mother moving into a place where, he says, "the oaks are all pruned . . . so they look like perfect trees in cement zoo cages." "It's somehow pleasant enough here," Simons comments, ". . . Condominia are all over, roads deliberately curve everywhere when

---

37. Hayden White, "Getting Out of History," in *Tropics of Discourse: Essays in Cultural Criticism* (Baltimore, Md., 1978), 17. See also Raymond Williams, *Marxism and Literature* (New York, 1977), 120. Also Fredric Jameson, *The Political Unconscious: Narrative as a Socially Symbolic Act* (Ithaca, N.Y., 1981).

they could go straight, the tinkling postcard marina, lobbies, lounges, links, limousines." "All the Negroes are in green landscape clothes," he observes, "or white service jackets, or Volvos with their kids in tennis togs." "It's the modern world," he concludes, "I have to accept it."[38] It is this kind of registering of pluralism and alteration in the contemporary South—"new Negroes in Volvos," others less privileged in mass-produced service outfits—that marks out much of the best recent Southern writing. And, in distinct contrast to Simons Everson Manigault, acceptance is not the right word for what writers like Padgett Powell do. They do not "accept" the contemporary South; they take the measure of it by being a part of it and apart from it, and working at the consequent tensions. Writing both in and about their culture(s) and the changes, people like the author of *Edisto*—and there are many of them—dramatize what it means to be a Southerner now. In the process, they tell us what it means to live in history, Southern or otherwise, and potentially out of it; they offer the possibility of experience with understanding.

Of course, there is no single model of Southern writing now, any more than there is a singular frame for present or recent Southern culture(s). There are any number of strategies for dramatizing the slippage between old and new and the edgy, protean character of the contemporary South. Notably in fiction, where even traditional themes and familiar writing practices are given fresh and often unexpected twists. The small town social comedy that was a particular skill of earlier novelists like Ellen Glasgow, for instance, is still alive—in books like *Raney* (1985), *Walking Across Egypt* (1987), and *Killer Diller* (1991) by Clyde Edgerton; *A Short History of a Small Place* (1985), *The Last of How It Was* (1987), and *Call and Response* (1989) by T. R. Pearson; *North Gladiola* (1985) and *Modern Baptists* (1989) by James Wilcox; and even *Family Linen* (1985) by Lee Smith and *July 7th* (1992) by Jill McCorkle. Only now the small town is a place like Listre, North Carolina, in Edgerton's fiction, Neely, North Carolina, in Pearson's work, or the eponymous North Gladiola, Louisiana: a place, not too far from the interstate highway, "jacketed with golf links and shopping centers,"[39] where the young eat

38. Padgett Powell, *Edisto* (1983; New York, 1985 edition), 182. See also 9–10, 104–5, 177–78.

39. Fred Chappell, *The Gaudy Place* (1979: Baton Rouge, La., 1994 edition), 6. Clyde Edgerton, *Raney* (Chapel Hill, N.C., 1985), *Walking Across Egypt* (Chapel Hill, N.C., 1987), and *Killer Diller* (Chapel Hill, N.C., 1991); T. R. Pearson, *A Short History of a Small Place* (New York, 1985), *The Last of How It Was* (New York, 1987), and *Call and*

Big Macs crouched in front of the television, while the well-heeled older folk are rich enough, not only to join the country club, but to travel regularly to Europe. Sometimes, every other Southern novelist seems to be commemorating another regional fictional tradition—that of, say, Thomas Wolfe—by producing something that might be subtitled "growing up in the provincial South." Examples here, among many, are *Ride with the Horseman* (1982) by Ferrol Sams; *The Cheer Leader* (1984) by Jill McCorkle; *Edisto* by Padgett Powell; *A World Made of Fire* (1985) by Mark Childress; *Ellen Foster* (1987) by Kaye Gibbons; and *1959* by Thulani Davis. To mention *Edisto* and *1959* together, however, is to measure the difference between these novels: one the story of an exceptionally sophisticated, fatherless white son of a college professor, the other the tale of a motherless young African American woman, growing up in a place where "there really wasn't anyplace a boy could take a girl"[40]— that is, if the boy and girl in question are black.

"When I was little I would think of ways to kill my daddy," Ellen Foster begins *her* story of growing up in the South. "I would figure out this or that way and run it through my head until it got easy." A battered child, whose mother dies while she is still young and whose father consistently abuses her, Ellen eventually finds refuge with a new family and a "new mama," signaling her entry into a new life by adopting a new name. It is as a "Foster" child, she recognizes, that she is now offered a real chance to grow up. Her story of gradual entry into maturity is different, in turn, from the tale Jill McCorkle tells, of a young girl who slowly, painfully grows into a woman by learning to dissociate herself from the traditional female support role of "cheer leader"—there simply to confirm masculine competitiveness, and to celebrate the centrality of male power. These fictions of growing up in the South measure the pluralism of Southern life, not only via their differences from each other, but through the changing, conflicted, contingent worlds that each narrative separately represents and explores. "Starletta and her mama both eat dirt," Ellen Foster observes of her black friend and her family. Ellen plays

---

Response (New York, 1989); James Wilcox, *North Gladiola* (New York, 1985) and *Modern Baptists* (New York, 1989); Lee Smith, *Family Linen* (New York, 1985); Jill McCorkle, *July 7th* (Chapel Hill, N.C., 1992).

40. Davis, *1959*, 17. Ferrol Sams, *Run with the Horseman* (1982; New York, 1984 edition); Jill McCorkle, *The Cheer Leader* (Chapel Hill, N.C., 1984); Powell, *Edisto;* Mark Childress, *A World Made of Fire* (London, 1985); Kaye Gibbons, *Ellen Foster* (Chapel Hill, N.C., 1987).

with Starletta and visits her family but, she admits, "as fond as I am of all three of them I do not think I could drink after them." "I try to see what Starletta leaves on the lip of a bottle," she adds, "but I have never seen anything with the naked eye. If something is that small it is bound to get into your system and do some damage."[41] Small, nuanced moments like this help to gauge the intimacies and the distances that characterize Southern life now: in this case, the intimacies that neighborhood and a new social fluidity create, and the distances that remain thanks to extreme poverty and, still more, to lingering prejudice. On a larger scale, a similar sense of a shifting, kaleidoscopic culture is registered even in the title of *1959*, set at the dawn of the civil rights era, or *The Cheer Leader*, with its wry, casual allusion to what many men, especially but not only in the South, seem to want of women.

"The day of regional Southern writing is all gone," a writer of an earlier generation, Walker Percy, claimed in 1971. "I think that people who try to write in that style are usually repeating a phased-out genre or doing Faulkner badly."[42] That claim, however, rests on a familiar and surely tendentious argument. The South is perceived as a cultural monolith; the Southern writer, if he or she exists, is defined as someone writing from within that monolithic structure; if nobody exists like that, then there can be no such thing any more as Southern writing. But the culture that, as a matter of self-identification, has defined itself as regional and Southern has always been more mixed and fluid than this argument allows. The South represented itself historically as aberrant; and it is marked, for good or ill, by its own aberrations. Southern writing, in particular, has consistently been produced by writers who resisted the monolith—not least because they worked from both inside and outside of their culture. That situation, of historical contingency and writerly resistance, has been exacerbated by the mix of recent social changes, but it has always been there. To assume otherwise is simply to accept a reading of Southern literature that equates it, more or less, with the Agrarian project. What we have now, in short, is an extension of what we have always

41. Gibbons, *Ellen Foster,* 20, 29–30. See also 1, 5. A remarkable novel that explores racial connections and differences from a comparable but resolutely black perspective is Dori Sanders, *Clover* (Chapel Hill, N.C., 1991). Clover, a ten-year-old black girl, tells the story here of her relationship with her white stepmother after her father dies.

42. Interview with Walker Percy, in *Conversations with Walker Percy* edited by Lewis A. Lawson and Victor A. Kramer (Jackson, Miss., 1985), 69.

had: different, developing social formations that those writers who are experiencing them choose to identify in regional terms—or, at least, choose to mark out using "South" and "region" as part of their fictional vocabulary. Even within the relative confines of prose fiction, there is no simple way of summing these writers up; certainly, terms like "South" and "Southern" offer only the broadest of brush strokes. Still, some idea of just how, and how much, storytellers are working both in and out of present Southern culture(s) may be suggested by pointing toward five different kinds of writerly practice—which, for the sake of clarity and economy, I will identify with five different characters or possible personae. Those five characters are housekeepers and household chroniclers; mavericks and rebels; taletellers and talkers; expatriates and exiles; and returners and revivalists. Needless to say, this does not exhaust the different strategies employed by, or available to, Southern prose writers; and the best of contemporary Southern fiction (of which there is a good deal) generally offers a mix, a plurality of approaches. There are many ways to dramatize the different cultures at work in the South now. Most good texts use several; these five personae merely suggest some of them.

HOMEKEEPERS AND HOUSEHOLD CHRONICLERS

The writing practice of those I have labeled homekeepers and household chroniclers is more adventurous and tentative than perhaps that label suggests—at least, to those familiar with the family chronicle in earlier Southern writing. What is at issue here is no simple allegiance to domesticity, or nostalgic drift, but a dramatically fluid exchange between the different dimensions of Southern culture. Writers such as these react to the pluralism of their found world by attempting a strategy of salvage and restoration; they pursue a searching—sometimes skeptical, at other times hopeful—examination of the degree to which moral continuity is possible in a materially changed world. This examination can take a number of forms. Establishing a connection between an atomistic present and a familial past in a very singular way is, for example, the subject not only of Bobbie Ann Mason's *In Country* but of two recent novels by Reynolds Price: *Kate Vaiden* (1986), in which the protagonist Kate has to decide whether or not to make the acquaintance of the son she abandoned when she was only seventeen, and *Blue Calhoun* (1992), where a sixty-five-year-old man attempts to win the affection of his granddaughter by narrating the story of his life. More obviously, there are those novels that trace the story of a family through several generations and, in doing so, balance the certainty of economic and social change against the possibility of cultural and emotional retrenchment. Among these are single texts dealing with several generations, such as *Oral History* and *Family Linen* by Lee Smith and *The Sixkiller Chronicles* (1985) by Paul Hemphill; series or sequences that carry the narrative of several generations through time, like *The Surface of Earth* (1975) and *The Source of Light* (1981) by Reynolds Price and the Beulah Quintet, ending with *The Killing Ground* (1982) by Mary Lee Settle; and texts that, while focusing on one generation, circle back to resurrect earlier family memories, such as *A Mother and Two Daughters* (1982) and *A Southern Family* (1987) by Gail Godwin and *Feather Crowns* (1992) by Bobbie Ann Mason.[43]

"Life has come down to a few little things," concludes the central character of *Feather Crowns,* Christianna Wheeler; and those things circulate around the memories initially generated and transmitted by the family. So far, the story is a traditional one. What makes it new here is novelists like Mason's recognition of the social forces that tend to disrupt and commodify the family unit. A keynote of *A Mother and Two Daughters,* for instance, is divorce; while the narrative of *Feather Crowns* is set in motion by a family occasion (the birth of quins) that quickly becomes a media event. Even memory is materially altered in many of these stories. The protagonist of *The Killing Ground* is the putative author of the first four novels in the Beulah Quintet: which is not so much a postmodernist conceit, surely, as a measure of the degree to which remembering is now an act of the written rather than of the spoken word. The title of *Oral History,* in turn, plays slyly on another instance of the difference between now and then: the youngest member of the clan whose story forms the substance of the novel returns to the home place to tape the old tales and talking of her forebears, and so turn oral history into an oral history project. Theodor Adorno on the character of memory in the modern world may be relevant here. "The pronouncement . . . that memories are the only possessions which no-one can take from us, belongs,"

43. Mary Lee Settle, *O Beulah Land* (New York, 1956), *Know Nothing* (New York, 1960), *Prisons* (New York, 1973), *The Scapegoat* (New York, 1980), and *The Killing Ground* (New York, 1982); Reynolds Price, *The Surface of Earth* (New York, 1975), *The Source of Light* (New York, 1981), *Kate Vaiden* (New York, 1986), and *Blue Calhoun* (New York, 1992); Gail Godwin, *A Mother and Two Daughters* (London, 1982) and *A Southern Family* (London, 1987); Smith, *Oral History* and *Family Linen;* Bobbie Ann Mason, *In Country* and *Feather Crowns* (New York, 1992); Paul Hemphill, *The Sixkiller Chronicles* (New York, 1985).

Adorno argues, "in the storehouse of impotently sentimental consolations that the subject, resignedly withdrawing into inwardness, would like to believe the very fulfillment he has given up." "In the process of setting up his own archives," he goes on, "the subject sizes his own stock of experiences as property so making it something wholly external to himself."[44] None of these novelists would go as far as that. Nevertheless, there is the quiet intimation in books like *Oral History* and *The Killing Ground* that memory itself is under threat of being commodified—a manufactured and negotiable product, and so part of the systems of exchange.

What is remarkable despite such imaginings of disaster, though, is the resilience or recuperative power of the family in most of these stories. The family unit is threatened in them or subverted and then, like some primitive, adaptive form of life, it is restored—altered, but usually the stronger for the crisis. This pattern of resistance, coupled with accommodation to necessity, runs through *Dale Loves Sophie to Death* (1981) and *Fortunate Lives* (1992) by Robb Forman Dew, two books about one couple learning the lesson of marital continuance in the face of crises; *The Accidental Tourist* (1985) by Anne Tyler, which tells the twinned stories of loss and rediscovery of domesticity; and *Spence and Lilla* (1989) by Bobbie Ann Mason, which celebrates the survival of domestic love despite age, the assault of suffering, and social change. More remarkable still, perhaps, are those narratives in which domestic feeling is refracted, redirected into other social forms. The family, with its assumptions of rooted allegiance and affection, an understanding issuing out of a shared archive of experiences, is dissolved and then reconstituted; it metamorphoses into related kinds of mutual recognition and intimacy. Pseudo-familial groups of this type include the university classmates in *Superior Women* (1984) by Alice Adams; some uneducated, unmarried women working in a small-town beauty parlor in *It's a Little Too Late for a Love Song* (1984) by J. K. Klavans; a left-wing baseball team harassed by right-wing evangelicals in *The Dixie Association* (1984) by Donald Hays; and two women, one white and one black, who have worked together in the white woman's kitchen for fifteen years in *Can't Quit You Baby* (1988) by Ellen Douglas.[45] In all such cases, while the

44. Adorno, *Minima Moralia*, 166. See also Mason, *Feather Crowns*, 454.

45. Robb Foreman Dew, *Dale Loves Sophie to Death* (New York, 1981) and *Fortunate Lives* (New York, 1992); Alice Adams, *Superior Women* (New York, 1984); Donald Hays, *The Dixie Association* (New York, 1984); J. K. Klavans, *It's a Little Too Late for a Love Song* (New York, 1984) (also published under the title *God, He Was Good* [London,

term *family* is in literal terms inaccurate it still seems somehow appropriate because it expresses a deeper, emotional truth. These are groups of people who feel connected, tied irrevocably together by past forces and present feelings; to that extent, they are families in all but name.

"Our family is not what it was," observes the seventeen-year-old narrator, Lucille Odom, of *Rich in Love* (1987) by Josephine Humphreys, after she has described how the marriage of her parents broke up. "But," she adds, "we are all gravitating back into family lives of one sort or another; it is a drift that people cannot seem to help, in spite of lessons learned the hard way. . . . I think often of the ancient times, long before Latin, when words stood for single things. 'Family' meant people in a house together. But that was in a language so far back that all its words are gone, a language we can only imagine."[46] For the homekeepers and household chroniclers, this redefinition of the language of family lies at the heart of the narrative. What they attempt to observe, and imagine, is a process during which, it seems, the vocabulary of domestic feeling acquires new dimensions of meaning and that fundamental fact of Southern life, the family group, is reshaped to accommodate it to radically changed circumstances. The old cultures, these writers admit, may have expressed themselves in "a language we can only imagine": but they and the words they formulated are still there, running like a hidden stream beneath the new regional cultures. Those words connect up inexorably to the past even while they acquire a different edge; in short, they are the coinage—which is to say, the active medium and expression—of both past and present, continuity and change. "I've never seen a normal family," one of Josephine Humphreys's characters confesses; and the work of Humphreys, in particular, offers a convenient and beautiful paradigm of how, in many recent books, the sanctions and sanctities traditionally identified with the "normal family" are to be found now in the most apparently

---

1985]); Anne Tyler, *The Accidental Tourist* (New York, 1985); Ellen Douglas, *Can't Quit You Baby* (New York, 1988); Bobbie Ann Mason, *Spence and Lilla* (New York, 1989).

46. Josephine Humphreys, *Rich in Love* (1987; London, 1988 edition), 260. See also *The Fireman's Fair* (1991; London, 1992 edition), 149. Humphreys has not so far received the critical attention she deserves. The critical work I have found most useful in my own approach to Humphreys's work and, in particular, in framing the larger conceptual issues outlined here, are Elizabeth Stone, *Black Sheep and Kissing Cousins: How Our Family Stories Shape Us* (New York, 1988); Fred Hobson, *The Southern Writer in the Postmodern World* (Athens, Ga., 1991); Robert O. Stephens, *The Family Saga in the South: Generations and Destinies* (Baton Rouge, La., 1995).

abnormal of places. That discovery fires all of her work into life—and, not least, her third and arguably most accomplished novel, *The Fireman's Fair,* published in 1991.

The Fireman's Fair is set in familiar terrain for Humphreys, in and around contemporary Charleston, South Carolina. For white, middle-class folks, this is a small world where "people continually run into each other in spite of rifts and irreconcilable differences." "Divorced partners find themselves in the same grocery aisle twice a week," we are told, "men who have cheated each other in business drink together at cocktail parties." Families from this section of society are constantly on the move. "The old Charleston families had been gradually disappearing into the suburbs," the reader learns; while the steadily growing army of the single, separated, and divorced live in apartment complexes, some of them blessed with names like "Fort Sumter House" or "the Old South Apartments" and all of them furnished according to "a decorator's idea of southern comfort." The old live apart from all this, in sheltered housing—if they are rich and lucky enough, in "another scaled-down plantation replica" with all the appropriate Old South appurtenances, including "veranda, white with a blue ceiling and rocking chairs." The poor, in turn, are sectioned off in public housing projects and trailer parks; and the black, nearly all of them, are still further segregated, living in a separate part of town from the white. "What will happen to these black people, now the movement is dead, their heroes tucked away in public offices?" a character in Humphreys's 1984 novel, *Dreams of Sleep,* asks herself, as she walks nervously through a housing project. "Was the whole civil rights movement nothing but a minor disturbance . . . ? White people have started telling jokes again. Black and white live farther apart than ever." "Blacks stayed uptown," the reader is reminded in *The Fireman's Fair,* ". . . if they came downtown, if they *congregated,* the white people got nervous." This is a landscape of economic change, certainly, but change for the better is reserved for only a part of the population, and that mostly white. As Lucille Odom in *Rich in Love* explains, there is plenty of "new money" in and around Charleston, from "German pharmaceuticals, French tires, Belgian chemicals," and "tourists (millions every year)," and "every third car was a German luxury sedan." But those cars are not signs of widespread "prosperity in the land—only of money in certain hands."[47]

47. Humphreys, *Rich in Love,* 177. See also *Fireman's Fair,* 30, 52–53, 151, 211; *Dreams of Sleep* (1984; London, 1992 edition), 134–35, 159.

Like all of Humphreys's protagonists, the central character of *The Fireman's Fair,* Rob Wyatt, is not one of those "mysteriously rich people" who drive a luxury car, but neither is he poor or black. He comes from the materially comfortable, unremarkably suburban world of the white majority: people, as he admits to himself, "marooned in places unsuitable to their souls" and filling in time with golf at the country club, work and cocktail parties, watching television and having affairs. Rob is a sadly contracted hero, who usually cannot find "the right words" for what he has to say—and a man who, unlike the prototypical Southerner of fiction, finds the past not so much a burden as an irritation. "He didn't mind history if it was recent and relevant," we are told. "What he disliked was pluperfect history, a double shift into the past, into the dead and gone. The world would be better off if history were limited to the range of memory alone, and better still if the range of memory were fairly short."[48] It is characteristic of Rob that, although he has eaten at a local café run by a Vietnamese immigrant for years, knows the café owner, Huong, well, and is aware he is a Vietnam War veteran, he does not know on which side Huong fought. He is too polite and reserved, and too indifferent to "the dead and gone," ever to ask. Two events in Rob's life, one large and one relatively small, suggest the strategies Humphreys deploys to search beneath the bland surfaces of her protagonist's life—to use him as the center of narrative consciousness (he is, after all, the only character whose unspoken thought we have access to), but never to allow her and our perception of things simply to be his. The small event is a kind of epiphany: the moment when Rob, lying on his front in the grass, sees an ant colony, and notes to himself that "acute and close observation of anything will reveal worlds you did not suspect were there." In an analogous way, by attending closely to the minutiae of Rob's social world, and the ironies, the ebb and flow of his thought processes, Humphreys exposes other, unsuspected worlds. "Acute and careful observation" of her often unreliable hero allows her to discover possibility, muddle, and even mystery, amid the unpromising details of contemporary, bourgeois Southern life.

The large event is a hurricane. Humphreys is fond of the sudden, arbitrary event that gives a sense (as Rob Wyatt puts it to himself) of "life gone strange"—and that compels us, perhaps, to reappraise the terms on which we have lived life and seen things up until then. "On an afternoon

48. Humphreys, *Fireman's Fair,* 151–52. See also 13, 44, 138; *Rich in Love,* 177.

two years ago my life veered from its day-in day-out course," Lucille Odom tells us at the beginning of *Rich in Love,* "and became for a short while the kind of life that can be told as a story—that is, one in which events appear to have a meaning." And one day in the thirty-second year of his life, things swing similarly away from the mundane for Rob Wyatt: when he finds "the general ruin" of a hurricane sweeping through Charleston has coincided with personal crisis, "the specific ruin of himself." Everything has changed. Or, as Rob feels and expresses it, "a veil was lifting" so that, all of a sudden, "he saw things anew." There are "possibilities afoot, even in the midst of ruin," he believes. He has quit his job as a lawyer and moved out of a luxury apartment, renting a house in the Isle of Palms in an area scheduled for redevelopment. However, even though these changes make him see himself sometimes as "a free man," he is still not sure he has done the right thing. And as he pursues "the old southern method of sitting, mulling one's fate, watching things that don't move much" in the acres of time now available to him, he finds himself meditating on the lives of "his four people," the "mainstays" of his existence. They are not a conventional family as such but a quartet of misfits, "someone else's wife, a reclusive black man, and his own two parents." "Without them," he acknowledges, "he would be lost."[49] His mother, Maude, is an eccentric, someone who has "thrived on thrill," Rob observes; "that was why she had once loved acting." Many years ago, Rob and his father, Jack, had collaborated in committing Maude to a mental institution in the belief that she was "crazy." Jack has felt guilty about this, and his occasional philanderings with other women, ever since. He, now, is as depressed and disconcerted by the hurricanes that have swept through his son's life and the locality as Maude is exhilarated by them. The "reclusive black man," Albert, is someone Rob got to know while Maude was committed. Albert is a character as different from the black choric figure of traditional Southern fiction as it is possible to imagine. Rob is drawn to him, in fact, by feelings of kinship rather than of difference, otherness; as he sees it, Albert "seemed to know sorrow" and is an outsider, an observer much like himself. The woman who is "someone else's wife," Louise Camden, is also a person Rob has known for years. They had a "mock-romance" once upon a time but somehow, Rob recalls, he had never "gotten around" to marrying her. In the event, Lou-

49. Humphreys, *Fireman's Fair,* 5. See also 1, 14, 15, 17, 47, 55, 59, 60, 68; *Rich in Love,* 1.

ise went off and married Rob's sometime business partner, Hank Camden, a man whom Rob thinks of, half in amusement and half in envy, as "the last of the Southern gentlemen." Now Rob conducts a relationship with Louise that is as uncertain as nearly all of his liaisons: hovering somewhere between irony and genuine feeling, companionship, and—on Rob's part, at least—adoration.

The delicacy with which Humphreys probes her main character's romantic longings and casual evasions suggests an imaginative kinship with Walker Percy or earlier Southern novelists such as Ellen Glasgow and James Branch Cabell. Like Percy's Binx Bolling in *The Moviegoer* (1962), say, Rob is a waiter and a dreamer. When Louise accuses him of being a dallier, for example, Rob's defense is that he is going to "wait and see." What he is waiting for is not entirely clear. Perhaps it is a woman. Certainly, Rob admits to himself that he seems to be seeking "something *via* women." Attracted to what is just beyond his reach, he is a Southern romantic reborn in suburbia. Distance, for him, lends enchantment; the elusive object of desire is desired precisely because it is elusive; consummation is inevitably accompanied, as it was for Poe's heroes, by a sense of loss. "This was what he wanted," he reflects at moments of contentment or joy, "but it wasn't enough." "His one talent," he admits bitterly at other moments, is "imagining women" rather than making any real connection with them: something that could be said, with equal acerbity and pity, about all those other regional Galahads from Roderick Usher through Judge Galamiel Bland to Quentin Compson. What is his problem, he asks himself, and answers, *"my head spins when I see a flock of birds. My heart breaks when I see a bare-armed girl."* The two fugitive objects of his passion, his dreaming imagination, birds and women, are linked for him. He is drawn to both, watches them both for what he believes is their mystery, the magical beauty they manifest just at the moment of vanishing. He loves birds, he explains, because "you cannot make them love you." "Culmination, the longed-for moment when a wild bird would eat from his hand or perch on his shoulder never occurred," he admits, but "it hardly mattered." "Desire and imagination and observation were nearly enough"[50] for him, he feels: he is talking of birds to himself here but, as usual, he is also thinking of women.

A twist in the narrative occurs at a party, as it does so often in these novels: for the contemporary household chronicler, cocktail and dinner

---

50. Humphreys, *Fireman's Fair*, 25. See also 30, 69, 80, 91, 107, 116.

parties, neighborhood barbecues, and visits to restaurants have taken over from family reunions as the major occasions of social exchange and crisis. Rob glimpses a girl across the room, "la femme déjà vu" as he describes her to himself. She seems at once fresh and familiar, a "discovery" who might open up "a whole possible life." Her name is Billie Poe— "like Edgar Allan," Rob later comments, alerting us to the nostalgic yearnings and the intertextual reference at work here. She is only nineteen, and she seems as marginal a figure as Rob himself as well as even more vulnerable. "I have a feeling I've seen you before," Billie tells Rob when they are introduced. She seems as drawn to him as he is to her; and, since she is drifting, homeless, she becomes a lodger in Rob's home—an arrangement that turns out to be a dangerously ideal one. "The fact was," Rob reflects after Billie has moved in, "living with Billie was like going back into childhood, into a good childhood."[51] In their world elsewhere they regress; or, as Rob perceives it, "he, in her presence, regressed to that innocent stage in which she still existed." Rob may have no interest in the historical past, but the mythic past clearly lures and captivates him; and, with Bobbie, he begins to feel thankfully as if he were "Adam readmitted after the eviction." His new life corresponds to those dreams of refuge, simply drifting that he shares with so many of Poe's and Mark Twain's heroes: dreams captured early on in the story when he thinks, with the fascination of longing, of houses uprooted by the hurricane and "bobbing away" to sea. And Bobbie adds to the sense of voyage and escape, the feeling that they have become moral vagabonds, in the arrangements she makes for her new dwelling and its surrounds. The garden she turns into a "bower," a "hideaway" with vines and ferns stolen from the forest; while the chimes and other adornments she adds to the house make it look, Rob feels, like "Gypsy headquarters."

"The rest of the world simply hadn't occurred to him," Rob realizes after a while with Billie. There is no need for him to "create an image . . . mocking [his] own mediocre self" because there is nobody to witness that image; the two of them seem to be fulfilling a familiar dream of irresponsibility and intimacy, by living apart from social obligation and yet together. Like Roderick and Madeline Usher, Rob and Billie enjoy a "shared loneliness." For a time, the suburban romantic so often "drawn as if to his sister self" and the girl-child with the strangely androgynous name simply float, wander through life. Humphreys walks a fine tight-

51. Ibid., 128. See also 26, 34, 35, 50, 131, 134, 153, 160.

rope here, balancing a sense of the magic of this apartness with premonitions of danger—and all the while reminding us that the place her two "misfits" share is a small rented house not a mansion, let alone the castle of Usher. And things change, disaster threatens as it does so often in the more traditional Southern family romance, when the rumors of "incest"—which is to say, crossing the line from domesticity to fulfilled desire—become actual. Rob sleeps with Billie, the woman he had previously thought of as a housemate, a surrogate daughter or sister, and then, reluctantly, admits what has happened to Louise. Billie can no longer be simply a part of some shared dream of innocence. Even in an earlier stage of their relationship, Rob had caught glimpses of Billie, unawares, which made it difficult to "think of her as a child." Now, he finds it impossible. Rob and Billie cannot remain "cooped up," as Billie now puts it—not least, because Louise is jolted into action by what she learns. "You've been lying to me for years," Louise tells Rob, and she herself has been "nothing for five years," "ruined" by Rob's adoration of her and reluctance to do anything about it. Rob is still reluctant, although the reluctance has to be more direct; the "habit of irony" is not available to him any more, as an emotional defense in his constantly deferred, insistently unconsummated relationship with Louise. "Is this *normal?*" Louise asks him, after, at her insistence, they have tried to unmake their love by making love, destroy desire by realizing it. "Do all people suffer this much in their ordinary, normal lives?" The burden of this story is that they do, that "normal" is a shifty, tricky term even in the suburbs. Rob's reply, though, is characteristically noncommittal: "Some do, I guess."[52]

The major moment of crisis in *The Fireman's Fair* is the fair of the title: a suburban carnival where, as in all carnivals, "rules were relaxed." Humphreys has used various quiet strategies up until this event to expose the unreliability and the moral myopia of her central character: irony, the comments of other characters like Louise, Rob's own vacillating and conflicted thought processes. Now Rob himself is coming to know how little he knows. His friend Albert has already pointed out to him, angrily, how little he understands about the two groups of people he had thought of as his natural allies, because of their similarly marginal status. "You don't know how to treat women right," Albert tells him, "like to pretend you got a nigger friend." As a telling instance of Rob's willful ignorance here, Albert reminds him that he has never asked about his black friend's

---

52. Ibid., 223. See also 14, 86, 129, 146, 148, 203, 221, 222.

family. Rob's response, when he suddenly learns that Albert's father is an imprisoned murderer and his mother committed to a mental institution, is a plaintive "I had no idea." As it turns out, he has almost "no idea" about anything that matters. For the first time, at the fair, when he sees his parents talking and confessing their feelings for each other, he realizes the strength of the bond between them despite all their differences. "His mother loved his father," he now acknowledges; it is this that has kept them together rather than what he has always supposed, "the net of habit and children and intricate history of wrongs harbored and half-forgiven."[53] Even closer to the emotional bone, Rob is forced to confront his own duplicity in his dealings with women. Louise and Billie have the chance to talk at the fair; and Louise admits not what Rob fears, the fact that he and Louise have slept together, but something far more serious as far as Billie is concerned: that she was and still is in love with him. *"Not that many people have been good to me,"* Billie once confessed to Rob. Louise has, and Billie believes she cannot pay her back by wounding her: which is what she would be doing, she suspects, if she stayed. Billie leaves; and Rob, just when he is beginning to feel that he is finally "caught up in the celebration" of the Fireman's Fair, and life, is left alone—reflecting mournfully that he has not so much *"acted"* as "fallen, without plotting, into a tangle of troubles rising to meet him."

"Life gone strange" generates the narrative and the culminating moment of crisis in *The Fireman's Fair*: the meteorological strangeness of the hurricane, the social strangeness of carnival. With the fair over, and the streets cleared of the more obvious wreckage caused by the hurricane, the denouement returns us to the "ordinary," the appearance of normalcy. Rob assumes his customary routines. He even becomes "a lawyer again," although taking only cases in which he is interested: not, as before, handling divorce cases but, for example, an appeal on behalf of Albert's father (which fails) and the case for releasing Albert's mother from the sanitarium (which shows signs of possible success). The routines are a mask, however, for a sense of failure, even despair. Humphreys is now remorseless in her dissection of her hero. She is tougher, in fact, on the "failed dreams and petty pleasures and lack of action" of her Southern romantic than even Glasgow or Cabell were on theirs. "Time seemed stuck," "the worst that can happen has happened," "some days . . . there was nothing . . . to do": like a series of melancholy refrains, phrases

53. Ibid., 243. See also 226, 227, 228, 238, 240, 255.

like this recollect and rephrase Rob's own fundamental sense that his misrecognitions, of his family, friends, and lovers, have finally turned his life into ruin. "He expected nothing," we are told, "he was thinking of nothing."[54] Far from the dreams of voyaging or just drifting he had once upon a time, he seems now hopelessly marooned.

Humphreys is clearly a moralist to the extent that she blames Rob Wyatt for his misrecognitions and forces him into a corrosive self-analysis. In fact she is much more fiercely and openly the moralist here than Poe or, for that matter, William Faulkner. The mournful refrain, "nevermore," may well suit the narrator of "The Raven" or Quentin Compson in *Absalom, Absalom!*, as they contemplate ruin and succumb to the luxury of melancholy, but it is hardly appropriate or adequate for Humphreys's failed romantic, as he surveys the wreckage of his life—and is forced to acknowledge that the principal architect of ruin is himself. If anything, the relevant comparison here is with those writers from England or New England—Jane Austen, say, George Eliot, or Henry James—for whom an ethical language defines the master narrative, rather than with those, like Poe or Faulkner, who tend to interrogate questions of personal morality by placing them in other frames—by seeing ethics as necessary but also as a function of history. Equally clearly, though, and consistently, along with being a fierce moralist, Humphreys makes a distinction between judgment and justice; questions of right and wrong tend to be hived off, in her novels, from notions of reward or punishment. Her characters get what life happens to give them, not what they deserve or work for. Things happen throughout her stories in odd, unexpected, often arbitrary ways that have very little to do with motive or morality. The broken family in *Rich in Love* come together suddenly in the penultimate chapter "as if nothing had happened," as Lucille Odom wryly puts it—"as if these last six months were like a television serial that had gotten so complicated the plot could only be resolved by calling itself a dream, backing up, and starting over again." Then, in the final chapter, just as quickly and surprisingly, it splits apart again into other, little "family lives of one sort or another." Similarly, ruin is followed by restoration for Rob Wyatt, right at the end of *The Fireman's Fair*, just when he least expects or deserves it; and in this instance—no thanks or credit to him—the resolution sticks, there is no further twist. Billie returns to him—found and brought by Louise, who has now made her own

54. Ibid., 261. See also 16, 257, 258, 259.

separate peace with her husband. The elusive object of desire comes back, not as a reward but a "pure gift," to save him from either simply drifting or being marooned, emotional aimlessness or paralysis, and offer him something like safe harbor. Rob has learned something, of course. He has moved beyond his habits of irony and imagination, using distance or dream to disengage himself from other people; he is also beginning to see those who matter to him, like his parents, his friend Albert, and Billie, in all their simplicity and strangeness. But he is not transfigured or redeemed. Above all, as Humphreys quietly intimates, he does not get what he merits: it is quite clear he merits very little. Rob is simply presented with something "no more meant for him," he recognizes, "than the marsh or the birds lifting from it and stretching to a line in the sky":[55] the chance of some passing happiness with a strange family household made up of a "trio of misfits"—himself, an odd, stray girl little more than half of his age, and his "nigger dog," Speedo—all living in a rented house scheduled for demolition.

Early on in *The Fireman's Fair*, the reader learns that Rob's father, Jack, is "at the point in his life (the winding down of it) when a man can see the drama of himself, and is hoping for a denouement, an outcome that will cast light on all that's gone before." What he is after, we are led to understand, is "a reward, preferably; lacking that, a penalty—as in a play, when the last events reveal a secret justice: the marriage of the lonely king, the blinding of the unseeing son." There is no such reward or retribution in Humphreys's own work; things, as she describes them, are much trickier and close in a far more muted way. There is no major climax, or closure, just a momentary stay against confusion. Characters like Rob and Jack Wyatt drift or struggle along, sometimes dazed by the changes taking place around them, more often insulated by habit and (relative) privilege; and they achieve, if they are lucky, no more than a chance to salvage something from lives of general routine, occasional risk. As they drift or struggle, however, Humphreys slips beneath the surface of each life, to catch and disclose its hidden mystery and magic: everything that makes it, in its own way, aberrant, abnormal, extraordinary. Like other homekeepers and household chroniclers, too, she taps the vein of feeling running between the Southern past and present—a

55. Ibid., 263. See also 93, 164; *Rich in Love*, 250, 260. "Nevermore" occurs, of course, as a refrain in Poe's "The Raven"; it is also a word that haunts Quentin Compson, defining his sense of loss, in *Absalom, Absalom!* (New York, 1936), 373.

connection that exists despite the fact that, as one of her characters in *Dreams of Sleep* puts it, "growing up in a city, you learn history's one true lesson: history fades." It is this connection, after all, this vein of feeling that makes Rob Wyatt, for all his suburban surroundings, a Southern dreamer, his story a sentimental education in the tradition of Southern romance, and the household with which he ends up his own personal kind of Southern family. "I liked history," Lucille Odom declares at one point in *Rich in Love*. "I also felt that history was a category comprising not only famous men of bygone eras, but *me, yesterday.* Wasn't I as mysterious as John C. Calhoun, and my own history worth investigating?"[56] If history does not fade entirely for Humphreys, it is precisely because she finds it there, active and still worth investigating in people like Lucille Odom and Rob Wyatt. She, and writers like her, delve into the secret history of the normal, the ordinary, and find it, after its own fashion, typically Southern and wonderfully strange.

MAVERICKS AND REBELS

A different kind of relationship to the histories of the region, and by extension to its residual culture, is suggested by those writers I have referred to as mavericks and rebels. Here, the sense of distancing, loosening ties with the past is unmistakable, even if a total break turns out in the end to be impossible and maybe undesirable. "Meg is puzzled and troubled by my obsession with the past," Ellen Burns in *The Revolution of Little Girls* observes of her lesbian partner. "You haven't lived in South Carolina for twenty years," Ellen reports Meg as saying, "but it's always on your mind."[57] Like a lot of protagonists in recent books by female mavericks, Ellen finds that what is on her mind specifically is the South's habit of marginalizing white women by translating them into myth. As ladies, guardians of hearth and home, they can be idolized and, whenever necessary, ignored: that is the discovery in many novels of the rebellious

56. Humphreys, *Rich in Love*, 46–47. See also *Fireman's Fair*, 8; *Dreams of Sleep*, 112.

57. Boyd, *Revolution of Little Girls*, 183; Beverly Lowry, *Daddy's Gift* (New York, 1981) and *The Perfect Sonya* (New York, 1987); Sylvia Wilkinson, *Bone of My Bones* (New York, 1982); Joan Williams, *Country Woman* (New York, 1982) and *Pay the Piper* (New York, 1988); Rita Mae Brown, *Sudden Death* (New York, 1983), *High Hearts* (New York, 1986), and *Bingo* (New York, 1988); Allison, *Bastard Out of Carolina;* Harper, *For the Love of Robert E. Lee.*

"new woman" in the South. Along with Boyd's account of Ellen Burns and her growing up into an understanding of her own sexuality, these books include *Daddy's Girl* (1981) and *The Perfect Sonya* (1987) by Beverly Lowry; *Bone of My Bones* (1982) by Sylvia Wilkinson; *Sudden Death* (1983), *High Hearts* (1986), and *Bingo* (1988) by Rita Mae Brown, *Bastard Out of Carolina* by Dorothy Allison, and *For the Love of Robert E. Lee* by M. A. Harper. For that matter, they also include some of the more recent fiction by older Southern women writers like Joan Williams, the former protégé and lover of William Faulkner, whose *Country Woman* (1982) and *Pay the Piper* (1988) both show a female protagonist discovering herself—in the one case, a young woman coming to maturity during the civil rights movement and, in the other, a character forced to reassess her traditional values when she finds herself suddenly single again in middle age.

Some of these books by female mavericks adopt an openly lesbian posture. *The Revolution of Little Girls* does so, of course. So does *Sudden Death* by Rita Mae Brown, in which the author uses her own relationship with the tennis player Martina Navratilova as the basis of her fiction. Less overtly, a book like *Bastard Out of Carolina* juxtaposes male violence and arrogance with the comforts to be found in the company of women. "I liked being one of the women with my aunts," Ruth Anne Boatwright recalls, "liked feeling a part of something nasty and strong and separate from my big rough boy-cousins and the whole world of spitting, growling, overbearing males." There is, however, tension within that company in many of these novels and, in particular, between generations—as the daughter struggles against the model of appropriate female behavior offered by her mother. In *Bone of My Bones,* for instance, the protagonist Ella Ruth Higgins addresses her mother in her journal in order to tell her that she does not want to be like her, a childbearer and a homekeeper. "Any girl can have a baby Mama," Ella Ruth writes. "I have all the things inside me to make one and they probably would work if I used them." "But," she adds, "I have to make my life into something it wasn't going to be naturally." That "something" turns out to be authorship. In a quiet way, Wilkinson uses the forms and procedures of feminist fiction—which include, among other things, the notion that the book is about a woman preparing to liberate herself by writing a book; and, by the end of the novel, Ella Ruth has both chosen her vocation and given the reasons for her choice. "That's the way things come to me," she declares. "They go into words so I can deal with them. And I feel better. But I know it's more than this . . . it's something I want to share."[58] Rejecting the conventional female role, Ella Ruth takes a path familiar to readers of contemporary women's writing, toward the freedom offered by the written word. Like her own creator, she resists identification in traditional Southern terms and forges a new identity for herself, devises a model of reality using a language that is at least partly of her own invention.

A similar resistance to the figure of the mother, and translation of a biological imperative into writerly terms, is at work in *The Revolution of Little Girls*. "You are severed from your mother now," Ellen Burns is assured at the end of her story. A successful writer in a stable relationship with another woman, she is no longer haunted by the need to imitate the woman who bore her by giving birth herself. And the "imaginary children" who inhabited her dreams, reproaching her for her own failure to reproduce, have disappeared. "I knew," Ellen concludes, "I would not see them again. *Unless you call us,* a voice whispered inside my head."[59] The struggle with the mother is, at heart, a loving one; and it provides an appropriate trope, in these books, for the mix of resistance and remembrance that defines the relationship of the female maverick with the South. Characters like Ella Ruth Higgins and Ellen Burns may see themselves as different from their mothers, and determinately so. Nevertheless, they are drawn into intimate conversation and communion with them. "I would always want my mother's approval," Ellen admits; she and Ella Ruth still seek to explain themselves to the women who bore and raised them and, to this extent at least, they continue some kind of rapport with the past. In turn, authors like Sylvia Wilkinson and Blanche McCrary Boyd may tell tales of rebellion. But they do so in narratives that are like a palimpsest, where one may encounter traces of earlier Southern fictions: about growing up in the South, carrying it "always in your mind" wherever you go (as, we may recall, Ellen Burns's lover tells her she does)—and hearing voices out of other times whispering that they are still there, waiting to be called.

The claim to authority that the past makes to the present was described by Mikhail Bakhtin as "the word of the fathers": as a system of language, that is, which dictates the terms in which we speak the world,

---

58. Wilkinson, *Bone of My Bones*, 255. See also 256; Allison, *Bastard Out of Carolina*, 91.
59. Boyd, *Revolution of Little Girls*, 204. See also 193, 203.

including ourselves, into life. In these novels by female mavericks, "the word of the mothers" seems a more accurate description; and the way the best of them respond to that word is to redefine and rehabilitate it. The daughter rebels against the mother, perhaps; she certainly defines herself as different, inhabiting a strange, newly mobile world and using a brave, freshly coined language. Still, she sees and speaks of herself as connected. Separated from her mother conclusively at the end of *Bastard Out of Carolina,* Ruth Anne Boatwright nevertheless feels herself emotionally close to her; "I was who I was going to be," she confesses, "someone like her, like Mama, a Boatwright woman." Garnet, the heroine in *For the Love of Robert E. Lee,* puts it in another way. "I suddenly envisioned that unbroken chain, that great dance of life engraved on the heart," she says. "Mildred Moser was passing the dance on to me," she observes of her grandmother, "expecting me . . . to find my place in the unimaginable long procession of family"—and so, in her own, utterly personal way, to "join in."[60] There is no escape from the fact that these novels of the "new woman" breach familiar boundaries. This goes not only for their portraits of female characters crossing traditional lines, challenging established sanctions, but also for their violation of familiar narrative habits: both *The Revolution of Little Girls* and *For the Love of Robert E. Lee,* for instance, play fast and loose with time—with Boyd's book quickstepping through many years in a couple of paragraphs and Harper's skipping between centuries at a pace that sometimes approaches the bewildering. But neither is there any escaping the fact that to be a maverick can itself be a sly way of admitting regional allegiance. These books about daughters finding themselves apart from and yet a part of their mothers help to remind us that to be a rebel and to be Southern can often be one and the same thing.

"All the generations of wonderful dead guys behind us," observes the narrator of *Boomerang* (1989) by Barry Hannah. "All the Confederate dead. . . . All of Faulkner the great. Christ, there's barely room for the living down here." "Down here" is Mississippi; and that remark suggests just how stifled many of Hannah's characters are by the burden of Southern history—and just how much male mavericks and rebels in general, like their female counterparts, feel inclined to shuffle off that burden. The

60. Harper, *For the Love of Robert E. Lee,* 78. See also Mikhail Bakhtin, *The Dialogic Imagination* translated by Caryl Emerson and Michael Holquist (Austin, Tex., 1981), 342; Allison, *Bastard Out of Carolina,* 309.

burden is one of language, as much as anything. After a particularly long peroration in *Boomerang,* for instance, the narrator asks plaintively, "where the shit is the end of this sentence, Faulkner?" Overwhelmed by the canonical figures of Southern writing—and, in particular, by the man whom Flannery O'Connor famously referred to as "the Dixie Limited"—as well as by the great, iconic moments in Southern history, writers like Hannah have tried, as it were, to end the sentence: to mark their rebellion against regional institutions, and make room for their living, by devoting themselves to the aberrant and the arbitrary. Formally, structurally, this leads to a denial of structure or even the idea of it. Hannah's narrators tend to skip backward and forward in time, just like so many of the female mavericks. "I live in so many centuries," says the narrator and title character of *Ray* (1980). "Everybody's still alive." "I don't care about plot that much," Hannah has admitted; and in all his novels he is inclined to jettison anything like linear development or a consecutive narrative in favor of the random and disjunctive. Books like *The Tennis Handsome* (1983) or *Hey Jack!* or *Boomerang* are cut up into small lumps, segments, some of which may be only a few sentences long. One segment in *Hey Jack!,* for instance, reads simply: "I couldn't get over the quietness there." "Nothing is ever as you have explained it," observes the narrator of *Boomerang.* Everything in a Hannah novel is strange, dissonant, denying explanation. Even personality is destabilized. At the opening of *Ray,* for instance, Ray announces himself in terms that deny the possibility of coherent selfhood, by shifting with disconcerting speed from the third person to the first person and then to the second:

> Ray is thirty-three and he was born of decent religious parents, I say. . . .
> Ray, you are a doctor and you're in a hospital in Mobile . . . but you're still me. Say what? You say you know who I am?[61]

61. Barry Hannah, *Ray* (1980; New York, 1981 edition), 3. See also 41; *Boomerang* (1989; Jackson, Miss., 1993 edition), 94, 100, 137–38; *Hey Jack!,* 96; "The Spirits Will Win Through: An Interview with Barry Hannah," *Southern Review,* XIX (1983), 322, 326, 328; Flannery O'Connor, "Some Aspects of the Grotesque in Southern Fiction," in *Mystery and Manners* edited by S. and R. Fitzgerald (New York, 1972), 45. Hannah's characters are usually as familiar with the media-generated imagery and movements of postmodern life as the narratives are. "Sixty per cent of what Daryl knew about America," we are told of a character in *The Tennis Handsome* (1983; New York, 1987 edition), "he had read off liner notes on the albums in the record departments, and the rest he had seen in pictures and drive-in movies" (97). In turn, the passage quoted here from the beginning of *Ray*

"Who I am" here or elsewhere in Hannah's work is never really established, since the constant in all this is not the personality, the character of the narrator, any more than it is plot. It is, on the contrary, the process, the rhythm of the narrative voice as it responds to the rapid, discontinuous movements of postmodern life. It is a rhythm that Hannah says he has learned from jazz and rock music; rather than telling "some cranked up southern story again," as Hannah himself has put it, *his* Southern rebels indulge in a "new logic" of existential freedom, achieved through "skipping, illogical skipping."

"What do we know?" asks Homer, the narrator of *Hey Jack!* "What do we mere earthlings, unpublished and heaving out farts like wonderful puzzled sighs, know, but what is in our blood?" And, just in case we do not get the iconoclastic point, Homer supplies his own bodily illustration; "I gave out this private marvelous fart," he says, "that was equal to a paragraph of Henry James." Inhabiting the margins of society and glorying in the marginal, the hidden places of the body, Hannah's characters aim their sights at anyone claiming significance or authenticity. "Nothing is sacred, I tell everything," declares Homer. In this shifting, mobile landscape, there is no fixed axis or circumference, the center does not hold. What is needed, then, is what we learn in *Ray* to call "a healthy sense of confusion." "And yet without a healthy sense of confusion," Ray explains, "Ray might grow smug." "It's true, isn't it?" he adds, "I might join the gruesome tribe of the smug. I think it's better with me all messed up."[62] Ray speaks here only for himself, of course. But that originating sense of things in flux, a world slipping toward vanishing point and maybe enjoying itself along the way, is something Ray shares with many of Hannah's other characters. For that matter, it stings the characters of many other mavericks into action. A powerful motor driving books like *A Confederacy of Dunces* (1980) by John Kennedy Toole, *Handling Sin* (1986) by Michael Malone, *Dirty Work* (1989) by Larry Brown, *Redeye*

---

offers a fascinating contrast with the final section devoted to Darl Bundren in William Faulkner, *As I Lay Dying* (1930; London, 1963 edition), 202–3. Darl similarly fluctuates between first, second, and third person singular. For Faulkner, however, this is evidently a sign of Darl's mental disintegration, whereas Hannah uses exactly the same verbal device to signal Ray's existential freedom, his immersion in process. This in itself suggests something of the connection and of the difference between a postmodern writer from the South like Hannah and the most famous of Southern modernists.

62. Hannah, *Ray*, 103. See also *Hey Jack!*, 60, 64.

(1995) by Clyde Edgerton,[63] and the fiction of Harry Crews is the imagination, not so much of disaster, as of absurd mess: a depthless muddle that has effectively abolished the distinction between the serious and the trivial, the central and the eccentric, beliefs and jokes.

"I am at the moment writing a lengthy indictment against our century," explains Ignatius Reilly, the protagonist in *A Confederacy of Dunces*. "When my brain begins to reel from my literary labors," he goes on without skipping a beat, "I make an occasional cheese dip." The lives and language of characters like Reilly are not so much deviant as belonging to a world, a cultural landscape where there is no norm from which to deviate. Set apart from what Homer in *Hey Jack!* calls "functioning, money-making reality," denying its claims to a monopoly hold on the real, these are people for whom nothing seems impossible or impermissible. The appropriate intertextual reference here is not to social realism but to the tall tale, fairy tale, or fantasy. Characters are as odd as creatures in a dream; their words and actions can be as surprising—but, in their own terms, remorselessly logical—as those of figures in a movie cartoon. Raleigh Hayes in *Handling Sin*, for example, makes his Ford Fiesta car sashay down the street "like a square dancer's skirt." A character in *Never Die* (1993) by Barry Hannah is said to be "so sad he was turning androgynous"; "the bitterness is . . . making my eyes wilt," he laments. And Ignatius Reilly enters *A Confederacy of Dances* like some strange cross between Oliver Hardy and the hunter in a Bugs Bunny cartoon: "A green hunting cap squeezed the top of the fleshy balloon of a head. The green earflaps, full of large ears and uncut hair and fine bristles that grew in the ears themselves, stuck out on either side like twin signals indicating two directions at once. Full, pursed lips protruded beneath the bushy black moustache and, at their corners, sank into little folds filled with disapproval and potato chip crumbs."[64] In *Dirty Work*, an African American with no arms or legs dreams of being an African king so fiercely that at times the dreams seem to take over from waking reality. "Boy, go down the river," he tells his imaginary son. "Take you a spear

63. John Kennedy Toole, *A Confederacy of Dunces* (Baton Rouge, La., 1980); Michael Malone, *Handling Sin* (1986; London, 1988 edition); Larry Brown, *Dirty Work* (1988; New York, 1989 edition); Clyde Edgerton, *Redeye* (Chapel Hill, N.C., 1995).

64. Toole, *Confederacy of Dunces*, 1. See also 6; Hannah, *Hey Jack!*, 64; *Never Die* (1991; Jackson, Miss., 1993 edition), 7; Malone, *Handling Sin*, 14. In his Foreword to *Confederacy of Dunces*, Walker Percy calls Ignatius Reilly "a mad Oliver Hardy, a fat Don Qixote, a perverse Thomas Aquinas rolled into one" (vi).

and . . . some impala jerky. . . . Them lions eating too much of my meat. . . . Got to teach them a lesson." In *Redeye,* a dog talks. "My job grab front the head taste lock into it. shake it," explains the bounty hunter's catch dog, Redeye, ". . . i sit. i sit. i sit. i sit. i wait. i sit. . . . i race forward with all my might. i jump. i clasp. i am partly in the bones of the point it comes off i clasp shake. i will hold on forever. it is down. it tastes good."[65] The only strangeness to such things is that they do not seem strange at all. After all, as Barry Hannah's Ray observes, "If I could happen, anything could."

But Ray says something else that is equally telling about his state of exile from the norm: "I am losing myself in two centuries and two wars." The two wars are the one in Vietnam, in which he fought as a pilot, and the Civil War, which haunts his imagination. These rebels are more Southern in temper than they might at first appear to be. Ignatius Reilly's absurd project, for example, what preoccupies him between the occasional cheese dip, is an account of "the breakdown of the Medieval system" that transforms the Agrarian reading of history into freakish caricature. "After a period in which the western world had enjoyed order, tranquility, unity, and oneness with its True God and Trinity," Ignatius scribbles away in one of his Big Chief writing tablets, "there appeared winds of change which spelled evil days ahead." "Having once been so high, humanity fell so low," he goes on, beginning to sound like Allen Tate on speed.

> What had once been dedicated to the soul was now dedicated to the sale. . . .
> Merchants and charlatans gained control of Europe, calling their insidious gospel "The Enlightenment." . . . The gyre had widened; The Great Chain of Being had snapped like so many paper clips strung together by a drooling idiot; death, destruction, anarchy, progress, ambition, and self-improvement were to be Piers' new fate."[66]

Ignatius Reilly and others: these are rebels with an old cause at the back of them, haunting them with visions of apocalypse and anchoring their anarchy in things determinately regional. "It is terribly, excruciatingly difficult to be at peace," Ray's friend Charlie De Soto tells him, "when

---

65. Edgerton, *Redeye,* 235. See also Brown, *Dirty Work,* 1–2; Hannah, *Ray,* 97.
66. Toole, *Confederacy of Dunces,* 25–26. See also Hannah, *Ray,* 16, 45.

all our history is war." And "our history" here is at once American and Southern. Ray's dreams of violence, it turns out, have their source in one of the defining moments in Southern history and myth, just as Ignatius's mad ruminations spring from some classic Southern origins. The new, rebellious logic of these stories has an older, Rebel logic working within it.

"There is a day for everybody who ever practiced cruelty," the narrator of *Boomerang* insists, and then explains what he means by explaining the book's title. "The boomerang, if you throw it well . . . almost comes back into the palm," he says. "Every good deed and every good word sails out into the hedges and over the grass and comes to sit in your front yard." The boomerang: it is an image that neatly captures both the errant mobility and the sense of a specific history, revolt, and return, at work in these novels. There is anarchy here, a leaning toward anger and absurdity, but there is also plenty of feeling for the past. That feeling can be open. In *Hey Jack!*, for instance, Hannah has his narrator make a visit to the Civil War battlefields in Shiloh, where he admits to hearing "the deafening silent volleys in the orchard" and seeing, in his mind's eye, "the rushing loud old ghosts." More interestingly, it can be implicit in what Hannah himself has called the "open field" of these novels. The ease with which so many of these maverick characters cross the centuries could be seen, after all, as something both radical and traditional, an act of narrative disruption and another sign of the region's old belief in the presentness of the past. "God has cursed me with a memory that holds everything in my brain," Ray confesses at one point. "There is no forgetting with me. Every name, every foot, every disease, every piece of jewelry hanging from an ear. Nothing is hazy."[67] The details may be different from those that haunt, say, Poe's Roderick Usher, Wolfe's Eugene Gant, or Faulkner's Quentin Compson. But the sense of being called back constantly from out of the past, of being possessed in a way, is very much the same. Like those figures from other, earlier Southern literatures, Ray and his kind cannot go home again, it seems, but they cannot really leave it and enter into complete exile either.

A similarly powerful mix of the radical and the traditionally regional is to be found in the work of one of the most interesting of the maverick

---

67. Hannah, *Ray*, 51. See also *Boomerang*, 34; *Hey Jack!*, 102; "Interview with Hannah," 328.

writers, Harry Crews. "I don't think of myself as a Southern novelist," Crews has insisted, adding that he would prefer to have no "adjective put in front of the word 'novelist.' " But that disclaimer cuts two ways, since—as several critics have pointed out—denying regional affiliation is in itself a venerable Southern tradition. "The woods are full of regional writers," Flannery O'Connor once observed, "and it is the great horror of every serious Southern writer that he will become one of them." More to the point, Crews has admitted more than once that "you write out of the manners of your people and the customs of your people, and that is all you've got." "Whatever I am," Crews declares in *A Childhood: The Biography of a Place,* "has its source back there in Bacon County [Georgia] from which [*sic*] I left when I was seventeen years old . . . and to which I never returned to live." And at the heart of whatever he is or has done is voice, storytelling—that capacity for weaving a world out of words that Faulkner perceived as inherently Southern, and that Crews himself has acknowledged as his birthright, what he has learned from his own little postage stamp of native soil. Sometimes, Crews's acknowledgment of the presence of a dear, particular place and past in his writing can be wary, reluctant. "It's true that I come out of the South," he said cautiously during one interview, "and because of that, *maybe,* I have some sense of place—of a *certain, particular* place." On other occasions, he seems positively keen to admit the undertow of memory in his work. "I come from a people who believe the home place is as vital and necessary as the breathing of your heart," he asserts proudly in *A Childhood* (a book that, after all, links biography and place quite explicitly). "It is your anchor in the world, that memory of your kinsmen at the long supper table every night and the knowledge that it would always exist, if nowhere but in memory."[68] Whatever the tone, though, the degree of

68. Crews, *Childhood,* 31. See also 22; "Harry Crews: An Interview," *Fiction International,* 617 (1976), 84; "Arguments Over an Open Wound: An Interview with Harry Crews," *Prairie Schooner,* LVIII (1974), 64; "Harry Crews: An Interview," in *Grit's Triumph* edited by Jeffrey, 146; William M. Moss, "Postmodern Georgia Scenes: Harry Crews and the Southern Tradition in Fiction," ibid., 33. Apart from the essay by Moss, other accounts of Crews that usefully examine the Southern dimensions of his work include John Seelye, "Georgia Boys: The Redclay Satyrs of Erskine Caldwell and Harry Crews," *Virginia Quarterly Review,* LVI (1980), 612–26; Donald R. Noble, "Harry Crews Introduces Himself," in *Grit's Triumph* edited by Jeffrey, 7–20; Jack Moore, "The Land and the Ethnics in Crews's Work," ibid., 46–66; Ruth L. Brittin, "Harry Crews and the Southern Protestant Church," ibid., 76–99; Michael Pearson, "Rude Beginnings of the Comic Tradition in Georgia Literature," *Journal of American Culture,* II (1988), 51–54; Frank W. Shelton,

enthusiasm (or otherwise) with which Crews pays tribute to his place and past, his recognition of the part they have played in helping him make up stories in which voice is a dominant remains constant and clear-sighted. He is a Southern writer, perhaps above all, because he is a storyteller whose stories hinge on speech—that concern for saying things right, hitting the right rhythm and pitch, that is the seminal skill in any oral culture.

"Since where we lived and how we lived was almost hermetically sealed from everything and everybody else," Crews has said of his childhood home in backwoods Georgia, "fabrication became a way of life. Making up stories, it seems to me now, was not only a way for us to understand the way we lived but also a defense against it." Tale-telling became a tool for coping with the mysteries of the world—"not so that we could understand them," Crews suggests, "but so we could live with them." It also spoke the tale-teller, and those he told of, into being; it gave them a voice, an articulate identity. That voice assumes many accents in Crews's work. There is, for instance, the down-home rural speech of characters like Willalee Bookatee Hull in *The Gospel Singer* (1968): "Everybody knows you power and you glory," Willalee tells the Gospel Singer, "white folks know it, colut folks know it. You the way and the salvation." There are also the deadpan, citified rhythms of, say, Marvin Molar, the narrator of *The Gypsy's Curse* (1974), who begins his story with a hard-boiled variation on the opening of *Moby-Dick:* "For the record, call me Marvin Molar." Common to many of these voices, though, are forms of deference that can also be strategies of aggression: as one observer of the region and of Crews has said, Southerners can be polite to the point of blood. And resonating at the back of most of them is that peculiar, harsh music that Pete Butcher, the protagonist of *Scar Lover* (1992) hears when he first meets the woman he falls in love with. "He recognized her voice as the voice of his people, flat, nasal, with hard *r*'s," we are told, "a voice that had drifted down into Jacksonville, Florida, out of the pine flats of Georgia."[69] It is the voice of social transit,

---

"The Poor-Whites' Perspective: Harry Crews Among Georgia Writers," ibid., 47–50; R. C. Covel, "The Violent Bear It as Best They Can: Cultural Conflict in the Novels of Harry Crews," *Studies in the Literary Imagination,* XXVII (1994), 75–86.

69. Harry Crews, *Scar Lover* (New York, 1992), 14. See also *Childhood,* 67; *The Gospel Singer* (1968; London, 1995 edition), 152; *The Gypsy's Curse* (1974), in *Classic Crews,* 185. Also Barbara Johnstone, "Violence and Civility in Discourse: Uses of Mitigation by Rural Southern White Men," *SECOL [Southeastern Conference on Linguistics] Review,* XVI (1992), 1–19.

transients following the path Crews himself took from an "almost her-metically sealed" past to a restless, rootless present—out of a world of custom and constraint and into one of commodities.

Early on in *A Childhood,* Crews describes his book as an account of "a way of life gone forever out of the world." Now, he admits, "there is nowhere I can think of as the home place": a sentiment that is echoed by one of the characters in *The Gospel Singer,* who announces, "You can't go home! Nobody can go home!" Crews tells tales of drifters, struggling for the means to gain some control over their lives but discovering in the process that they hardly have the means to survive. Even those who stay behind in the backwoods, in Crews's fiction, are fundamentally adrift, believers with just about nothing to believe in beyond the possibility of going somewhere themselves. "Leave Enigma! Escape! Escape the heat, the drought," dreams a character called Gerd in *The Gospel Singer.* "Get to a place where men didn't sweat . . . where the streets were cool as wind and happy as rain, where the streams lay on the honeyed land like milk." And their dreams of leaving signal their emotional and imagina-tive possession by the culture of the global marketplace: for Gerd, the place "where money rang and children laughed," we learn, is a "Holly-wood heaven where Rock Hudson and Doris Day, sweatless, bloodless, hurtless, sat on either side of God."[70] Those of Crews's characters who do leave (and they are the majority) find, not escape, the cash paradise that Gerd yearns for, but the bitter fact of their own instrumentality; they are, they soon learn, not the chosen people of God but functions of the marketplace and the machine. Discovering that "his body was the only thing he had to sell," Eugene Talmadge Biggs in *The Knockout Artist* (1988) attempts, with conspicuous lack of success, to become a profes-sional boxer. A character called Dorothy Turnipseed in *Body* (1990) takes the same discovery even more literally: she becomes Shereel Du-pont, a professional bodybuilder and for a while one of the elite whose "skins circumscribed their worlds"—as both subjects of worship and di-rect source of income. In a more bizarre fashion, Herman Mack in *Car* (1979) takes the logic of consumption and his own need for control as a

70. Crews, *Gospel Singer,* 28. See also 42; *Childhood,* 22. On issues of place and place-lessness, and the possibly seminal influence on Crews of the environment described in *Childhood,* see, e.g., Frank Shelton, "A Way of Life and Place," *Southern Literary Journal,* XI (1979), 97–102; Victor Kramer, "Patterns of Adaptation: Place and Placelessness in Contemporary Southern Fiction," *Studies in the Literary Imagination,* XXVII (1994), 1–7.

kind of challenge: he determines to become the first American to eat an American car and so, in effect, make the machine, the motor of American capitalism, and his own body one and the same. He fails, inevitably, as all Crews's characters do. But, in his own strange way, he illustrates the concern all these novels have with what their author has called "men doing the best they can with what they've got to do it with":[71] searching for material survival and moral belief in a brutally competitive environment and finding little beyond their own bone, muscle, and blood.

"I like to start with something that is obviously a world that nobody can quarrel with," Crews has said, ". . . Then in a very slow kind of left-handed way . . . it slides off the edge of the real world into a thing that can't possibly be true. Except it is true; at least, I think it is."[72] Like other Southern writers from the Southwestern humorists to Flannery O'Connor, Crews deploys freaks to defamiliarize, to expose what may be concealed by the tyranny of habit and so make us see how remarkable, how truly strange, the supposedly normal can be. "If you're going to be anything or know anything, you've got to be abnormal," one character tells another in *The Hawk Is Dying* (1973). "Whatever's normal is a loss. Normal is for shit." And, as Crews's protagonists seek the impossible of something to believe in other than the brute necessity of their own labor, they are forced into aberrations that invite, not so much our empathy, as our cool, clear recognition that this truly is the way things are in a world governed by the laws of the market. Marvin Molar in *The Gypsy's Curse* is deaf and dumb, has useless, tiny legs, and walks on his hands. For entertainment and money, he stands on his fingers, progressively fewer of them, until by way of a finale he is standing on "one incredible finger" then "turning round and round on it slow and steady as a clock ticking."

71. "Crews: An Interview," *Fiction International*, 84. See also *The Knockout Artist* (1988; New York, 1989 edition), 18; *Body* (1990; New York, 1992 edition), 17. Also *Car* (1979), in *Classic Crews*. The epigraph to *Childhood* is "Survival is triumph enough." On Crews's examination of class and the "illusion" of upward mobility, see, e.g., Larry W. Debord and Gary L. Long, "Harry Crews on the American Dream," *Southern Quarterly*, XX (1982), 35–53, and "Literary Criticism and the Fate of Ideas: The Case of Harry Crews," in *Texas Review*, IV (1983), 69–91. On Crews's fascination with the automobile as a sign and symptom of American consumerism, see, e.g, Jennifer Randis, "The Scene of the Crime: The Automobile in the Fiction of Harry Crews," *Southern Studies*, XXV (1986), 213–19.

72. "Crews: An Interview," *Fiction International*, 92–93. See also *The Hawk Is Dying* (New York, 1973), 79; *Gypsy's Curse*, 198. On Crews's exploration of the freakish, see, e.g., David K. Jeffrey, "Crews's Freaks," in *Grit's Triumph* edited by Jeffrey, 67–78.

It is his way of putting his body out for hire; and, according to the freakish logic of his story, it is not fundamentally different from any other form of labor—any other terms by which the human body may be commodified, made the subject of commercial exchange.

Molar is not what he himself dismissively refers to as "a normal" (a term that neatly reduces normality to a category, no more privileged than any other). Joe Lon Mackey in *A Feast of Snakes* (1976) is, in physical terms at least; he was, in fact, once a football hero. But his apparent normality conceals its own kind of freakishness, a taste for violence that erupts at the end of the novel into random killing. "Christ, it was good to be in control again," he tells himself as he unloads a twelve-gauge gun into a crowd. That remark can be taken, and has been, as a reminder of the killer inside us all. It is that, certainly; the origins of that killer, though, are carefully particularized. "These were not violent men, but their lives were full of violence," Crews has said of the poor folk, his relatives and the male friends of his youth; "it was a hard time . . . and a lot of men did things for which they were ashamed and suffered for the rest of their lives."[73] Hard times have, if anything, grown harder in Crews's perception, as an economy in which considerations of custom and skill complicated the profit motive is replaced by one based, with very little complication, on exchange, the manipulation of the body for money. Mackey is not excused for what he has done. Crews is no sentimentalist, intent on personal extenuation of a particular offense; still, he exposes the freakish emotional logic that drives Mackey, like so many of his characters, to violence. It is to assert his power in a world that would deny him any; Mackey reacts to the denial of himself—a denial he internalizes as a form of self-hatred ("Jesus, he wished he wasn't such a sonofabitch")—by using violence to make the crowd pay attention. The crowd does so for a moment and then, inevitably, overwhelms and kills him. Mackey responds to legitimated force by deploying force of his own; all he succeeds in doing finally, though, is satisfying his own self-hatred by (in effect) inviting immolation. His act is one of both homicide and suicide that masks a confirmation of his own impotence as an attempt

73. Crews, *Childhood,* 57. See also 24; *Gypsy's Curse,* 201; *A Feast of Snakes* (New York, 1976), 176. On the uses of violence in Crews's fiction, see, e.g., David K. Jeffrey, "Murder and Mayhem in Crews's *A Feast of Snakes,*" *Critique: Studies in Modern Fiction,* XXVIII (1986), 45–54; Gary L. Long, "Naked Americans: Violence in the Work of Harry Crews," *Southern Quarterly,* XXXII (1994), 117–30.

at denial, evidence that he is "in control again." What Mackey does is grotesque. But it shows what Crews can do by sliding "off the edge of the real world." "To the hard of hearing you shout," Flannery O'Connor argued, "and for the almost blind you draw large and startling figures." Unlike O'Connor, Crews is no believer in the traditional sense ("What does a believer do," asks one of his characters, "when there is nothing to believe?"). But he too uses extremism, degenerate characters, and deviant behavior, to map the brute facts lurking at the heart of the normal. What he locates through the absurd, obscene actions of someone like Mackey is the motor, the will to power driving society; Crews strips away public narrative, social image, deference—all that protects "the disguised human being"—to lay bare "the lust for blood and money" that identifies what he calls "the *naked* American."[74]

A Feast of Snakes is set in a small town, Mystic, Georgia, where nothing much happens apart from the annual "rattlesnake roundup." The setting for the earlier The Gospel Singer is similar. "Enigma, Georgia, was a dead end," the novel begins, before introducing us to a brooding, melancholy, stealthily disturbing place that might have been relocated from Yoknapatawpha, Mississippi—or, for that matter, from the imaginative territory of Southern writers from Mark Twain to Carson McCullers—were it not for the fact that the people of Enigma watch television, drive trucks, and eat at hamburger joints. In his more recent work, Crews tends to leave places like Mystic and Enigma for the city and the urban hinterland: a wasteland of wrecking yards, unchecked development, and instant obsolescence where (as the narrator puts it in Scar Lover) even the river "smelled of garbage, gasoline, and raw human waste." Wherever he sets his work, though, Crews's imaginative practice is marked, in particular, by two things: an iconoclastic approach to the local gods of Southern literature and a nicely turned ability, nevertheless, to play familiar Southern tunes in a different key. The iconoclasm is conspicuous in a book like Karate Is a Thing of the Spirit (1971), where Crews even goes so far as to use William Faulkner as a running joke: a way of poking fun at, among

<hr>

74. Crews, Florida Frenzy, 57. See also Feast of Snakes, 12; Karate Is a Thing of the Spirit (New York, 1971), 208; "Crews: An Interview," in Grit's Triumph, 145; O'Connor, "The Fiction Writer and His Country," in Mystery and Manners edited by S. Fitzgerald and R. Fitzgerald, 34. On desire and the search for belief in Crews's work, see, e.g., W. J. Schafer, "Partial People: The Novels of Harry Crews," Mississippi Quarterly, XLI (1988), 69–88.

other things, professional Southerners, the institutionalization of Southern literature, and the welcoming of some Southern writers into the canon, the literary pantheon of the good and the great. The central character, another of Crews's drifters called John Kaimon, always wears a jersey with Faulkner's face embroidered on it. When asked why he does so, he simply replies, "I come from Oxford, Mississippi, so I keep the face of Faulkner around." "If I was a Catholic, I'd wear a Saint Christopher medal," he explains. "But . . . I'm not a Catholic. I'm from Oxford, Mississippi." Of course, Kaimon has never read any of Faulkner's books. His girlfriend, though, Gaye Nell Odell, vaguely remembers that she had a "whole month of Faulkner" at high school, on a book she never got around to reading called, she thinks, "the fury of sound." "They say Faulkner wrote over twenty books!" Kaimon tells his girlfriend in "a savage whisper." "That's *twenty*. Have you ever actually *looked* in a book?" he asks her. "I mean really looked? All them little words there. All them letters. Did you ever think what that might take out of a man? Have you ever thought about sitting down with a pencil and copying a book? Just word for word, writing it down on another piece of paper?"[75] Kaimon has, he reveals. "I copied the first twenty pages of a book called *The Sound and the Fury*," he declares, "and saw that it was impossible. It was there in front of me so it was true, a fact, but impossible."

"Do you read Faulkner much?" Crews was, perhaps inevitably, asked once in an interview, to which the reply was, "I've read him all, but I never read him when I'm writing." That fits in with the spirit of comedy that created John Kaimon: Faulkner may be someone all of whose work is worth reading, but reading him when writing clearly involves, for Crews, the danger of "copying"—and that is not only "impossible," to use Kaimon's term, but also manifestly absurd. There is no sense in writing about the South by rewriting Faulkner; there is, however, sense in reading him thoroughly, knowing him well, since he is by now one of the means by which we know the South. The region is mediated for all of us, including current writers like Crews, through seminal works of regional fiction such as *The Sound and the Fury* (even if we know of them only at second or third hand, through imitation, allusion, commercial use, or whatever). And they are as much a subject of knowledge as a means of knowing: they are, by now, part of what we know and how we know it

---

75. Crews, *Karate Is a Thing of the Spirit*, 141. See also 79–80; *Feast of Snakes*, 17; *Gospel Singer*, 7; *Scar Lover*, 19.

when we try to "tell about the South." Crews makes Kaimon put this in his own, inimitable way during a conversation with another character, called Belt: Faulkner, they agree, is one of the things Mississippi is "famous for," along with "starving dogs and sick niggers" and "beauty queens." Kaimon says something else about Faulkner, just after this, that is also useful for measuring Crews's relationship to the traditional practices and pieties of Southern writing. Faulkner, Kaimon recalls, was condemned by "an editor from one of the best newspapers in the state of Mississippi" for belonging to "the privy school of literature." "You don't expect to find honey in a privy," Kaimon observes sagely. "And besides, all his stuff is full of freaks."[76]

The persona Crews favors is a rude, raunchy one, playing on what he calls "the Grit I am"; "I am the kind of guy," he boasts, "who if he can't have too much of a thing doesn't want any at all." He has also, many times, declared an interest in a sort of rough innocence. "It has almost become a crime in this country to be vulnerable," he has said, "and that's what I want to be. I want to be naked."[77] Innocence, however, is not ignorance. Crews may be a "naked" writer, but he is also a very knowing one; and he knows, in particular, that his work is no more "full of freaks," nor more liable to provoke disgust among some sections of the public ("the privy school of literature"), than the by now canonical works of William Faulkner are. He is, and recognizes that he is, pursuing a familiar path in Southern writing, in search of the raw and marginal, disrupted lives presented in a deliberately disruptive way. Like, say, Erskine Caldwell's Jeeter Lester and Ty Ty Walden, Crews's people inhabit an environment defined by the material processes of the body and the abstract processes of the market and money. "Your shit don't smell no worst than mine," observes one character in a curious moment of male bonding; "whores have to sell whatever there's a market for," says another by way of explaining some of her more bizarre business practices. Like many of the poor folk in Southern fiction from *Georgia Scenes*

76. Crews, *Karate Is a Thing of the Spirit*, 142. See also 138–39; "Crews: An Interview," in *Grit's Triumph*, 142.

77. Noble, "Crews Introduces Himself," 7. See also *Blood and Grits* (New York, 1979), 99, 145; *The Mulching of America* (New York, 1995), 202; *Car*, 427. The characters mentioned here appear respectively in *Gospel Singer, Feast of Snakes, Knockout Artist*, and *Body*. Several of Crews's characters reappear in different books: Willalee Bookatee, for instance, is a remembered friend in *Childhood*, while Gaye Nell Odell appears in both *Karate Is a Thing of the Spirit* and *The Mulching of America*.

through *The Adventures of Huckleberry Finn* to *As I Lay Dying* and *Tobacco Road* and then on to *A Good Man Is Hard to Find,* such characters as Willalee Bookatee Hull, Joe Lon Mackey, Eugene Talmadge Biggs, and Dorothy Turnipseed fight, trade, and, when necessary, cheat, constantly aware of the debt and death that threatens their frail envelopes of flesh. They are bodies put out for hire for a while before dying.

Then again, like George Washington Harris's Sut Lovingood or Faulkner's Jewel Bundren or O'Connor's Haze Motes, Crews's characters are creatures of obsession. They seek redemption, or relief, in some compulsive physical activity such as karate, boxing, bodybuilding, weightlifting, the training of hawks, or snake hunting, or in the worship of some utterly inappropriate object—a car, perhaps, or a gospel singer glimpsed on television. They are grotesque people seen in a grotesque way, one that uses deliberate bad taste, and a narrative that careers as dangerously as a race track, to surprise and subdue readers—to make us feel that we have suddenly met some strange, twisted kin. Arguably, all Southern writing is aberrant. But some, from *Sut Lovingood's Yarns* through the work of Twain to that of Faulkner, Caldwell, and then O'Connor, has had aberrance as its fundamental subject and strategy; what it describes and how it describes it are both determinately deformed, maladjusted. "I ain't so sho that ere a man has the right to say what is crazy and what ain't," says a character, Cash Bundren, in one triumphant example of such writing, *As I Lay Dying:* "It's like there was a fellow in every man that's done a-past the sanity or the insanity, that watches the sane and insane doings of that man with the same horror and the same astonishment."[78] That sums up the form and feeling of this particular, maverick breed of Southern literature, as well as anything can; and it is to this breed, as he senses, that Crews clearly belongs.

This ability to dissect "the sane and insane doings" of humankind—and, in particular, Southern varieties of humankind—with a coldly comic scalpel is evident in Crews's novel published in 1995, *The Mulching of America.* Beginning, as so many novels of the region do, in the dog days of August, the book introduces us to a door-to-door salesman, Hickum Looney, who has worked for the same company, Soaps for Life, for twenty-five years. "The air was a shimmering of heat," the reader is told,

78. Faulkner, *As I Lay Dying,* 189. The obsessive activities or forms of worship mentioned here are dramatized in, respectively, *Karate Is a Thing of the Spirit, Knockout Artist, Body, Gypsy's Curse, Hawk Is Dying, Feast of Snakes, Car,* and *Gospel Singer.*

"and it felt to Hickum Looney as though with every step he took the weight of the sun on the top of his balding head and his thin shoulders became heavier." This may be "just another ordinary August day in Miami," but it offers a familiar comic portrait redrawn: the traveling salesman as freak, a recurrent figure in Southern humor from, say, the itinerant horse traders in *Georgia Scenes* to the Bible salesman in Flannery O'Connor's story "Good Country People" or R. J. Bowman, the lost feverish shoe salesman in Eudora Welty's "Death of a Traveling Salesman." Relocated in the city, Looney still fondly recalls old times "back home" in rural Tennessee, before, like so many characters in Crews's fiction, he was drawn into the city to find a way of selling himself. Now the city, like the heat, presses down on him, traps him in a world of surfaces—signs that signify no more than the compulsion he is under, every day, to make a trade in order to survive. A description of Looney, a little later on in the narrative, shows the peculiar blend of the colloquial and the oracular, clichés borrowed from the mass media and remnants of biblical rhetoric, that Crews deploys to map the strange landscape his characters inhabit. It also unveils something of the way Crews uses odd, quirky behavior and random, frequently violent action to snap us into awareness of the sheer strangeness of our modern world. What the novelist John Hawkes once said of Flannery O'Connor is true for Crews as well—he is intent on realizing "the truth of the fractured picture":

> It had been a good day, an unprecedented day, for Hickum Looney. As he eased his dirty yellow dented Dodge through bumper-to-bumper traffic, he whistled a gay little tune, his favorite. It had been a Coca-Cola kind of day and he was whistling a Coca-Cola commercial from a good while back. . . . And he loved it so much, he invariably saved it for those days when sickness, suffering, death, and the rankest kind of blasphemy . . . opened every door he knocked upon. . . .
>
> Without quite being able to help it, he suddenly pushed back his seat, stretched his neck, and sang: "Co-o-oke is the *re-al* thing." He pounded the steering wheel . . . and sang at the top of his voice, "And so is Hickum Looney!"[79]

79. Crews, *Mulching of America,* 22. See also 9, 64; Tony Tanner, *City of Words: American Fiction, 1950–1970* (London, 1971), 204. Also Augustus Baldwin Longstreet, "The Horse-Swap," in *Georgia Scenes: Characters, Incidents etc. in the First Half-Century*

What turns out to be at stake in a passage like this, and in *The Mulching of America* as a whole, is just what "the real thing" is. By most standards, Hickum Looney hardly seems "real." As a character, he is a freak whose freakishness is constantly foregrounded—and the lineaments of whose existence seem to have been drawn by some mad cartoonist or conjuror of dreams. So, for that matter, are the other, variously weird figures in this book: among them, Ida Mae, a rambunctious old lady who helps Hickum sell his soap, Gaye Nell Odell, the sassy, sexually confident young woman who took on John Kaimon in *Karate Is a Thing of the Spirit* and now hitches up with Looney, and "the Boss" of Soaps for Life, a man of enormous, unmentionable influence with a hare lip that distorts just about everything he says. Like Hickum Looney himself, all these characters are taken from the cabinet of the Southern grotesque. Ida Mae, for instance, has her prototypes in the fiction of Flannery O'Connor, while Gaye Nell Odell recalls many of Erskine Caldwell's earthier young women. The extremism of Crews's art pushes things a little further, however. So, the Boss demonstrates his power by systematically beating up the male help and insisting that all his female assistants look the same, right down to the color of their hair. The violence is as commonplace, instantaneous, and bizarre as in any Tom and Jerry feature: not once but twice an injured body is hurled from a passing car at the entrance of the Accident and Emergency Ward ("Nobody but [a] handcuffed Cuban looked their way," we are told the first time, "as Hickum put the old Dodge in gear and moved away. 'God, I love Miami,' said Gaye Nell Odell."). And when Hickum and Gaye Nell start to make love, Gaye Nell's dog Bubba, catching "the fragrance of her arousal . . . or her drippings or both," tries to join in by clamping "Gaye Nell's knee with his forelegs and giving it a vicious non-fuck." The characters are depthless, dysfunctional, the action aggressively random, inconsequential; it is as if we were being asked to inspect a world in fragments. What we learn about the people we look at here has a lot to do with body parts and functions. "The good Lord didn't make one single, solitary human being on the whole face of the earth that doesn't shit,"[80] Gaye Nell observes; and, as if to prove the point, Crews's characters do it all the time.

---

of the Republic (1835; New York, 1848 edition); Flannery O'Connor, "Good Country People," in *The Complete Stories* (New York, 1971); Eudora Welty, "Death of a Traveling Salesman," in *Complete Stories* (London, 1981).

80. Crews, *Mulching of America*, 63. See also 118, 225. For a useful summary of initial responses to this book, see Matthew Teague, "How Do You Like Your Blue-Eyed Boy Now?," *Oxford American*, December 1995, 69–71.

The distance that Crews's radical techniques establishes between characters and reader is one thing, the distance between what they do and what they say another one, not unrelated. A character like Hickum Looney functions much of the time as a ventriloquist's dummy, since a lot of what he says is dictated by something called "the Soaps for Life manual." "You don't sell soap," Gaye Nell tells him. "You sell the Soaps for Life manual." As a matter of fact, he has never seen the soap he sells, all he carries with him is his wax samples. The motor driving him is not to sell something, but simply to sell; and, in order to do that, he has simply to believe in the power of selling ("believing was the first condition of employment") and follow his "Bible," the company manual. The manual supplies him with everything to say, along with appropriate performative gestures such as "the Hearty Company Laugh." It even makes room for the occasional deliberate mistake: "the Company threw in error," we are told, ". . . to make the salesmen seem more human." "A good salesman could play a customer like a banjo," Hickum has been told, and learned; and so he does not so much use language as he is used by it, to close the deal and sell something the consumer believes he needs—"something," as another salesman admits, "that we're not even sure is soap." "You and the soap are the same thing," Ida Mae suggests to Hickum Looney. He is, because he is simply what he sells. The irony, the further twist of the knife is that, as the Boss intimates, there is "no soap thing"; what Hickum is selling is "a belief, a force." It is spelled out in the meaningless palindrome formed by the wax replicas Hickum carries in his sample case, each sample soap bearing one letter: "S-A-I-P-P-U-A-K-I-V-I-K-A-U-P-P-I-A-S." "A palindrome ends where it begins," declares Ida Mae "in a dry whisper," as she gazes at the letters, "and lives inside itself, a self-contained, self-justifying madness."[81] Hickum Looney is not so much "the real thing" as "the same thing" as the soap, but there is "no soap thing." If he is defined by what he sells, then he is defined by nothing but a promissory image playing across the surface of a product that may not even exist. He lives and works within the "self-contained, self-justifying madness" of a culture of consumption—a world of depthless images promising a satisfaction that is constantly deferred—to which he is rather less important, in the end, than a popular brand of soft drink.

"Everything's about fucking money," one of the Boss's employees says, by way of explaining why he allows the Boss to beat him. "Can you

81. Crews, *Mulching of America*, 32–33. See also 17, 19, 26, 27, 135, 231, 246.

understand that?" And it is the "madness of money" that everything in *The Mulching of America* is about: a system of exchange that commodifies everything and everyone, denying any substance or satisfaction outside the moment of purchase. Within this system, people are like products: what matters about them is surface, appearance, what can be deployed to make a sale. They circulate in a landscape of replicas, copies with no trace of an original; and they are expendable, they are as much a part of an economy of planned obsolescence as the things they are persuaded to consume. "Everybody fails sooner or later," Hickum Looney is told near the end of the narrative; there is no such thing as success, really, only what Crews calls "belief," the dream of success driving people on to sell and to buy. As if to prove the point, both Hickum and the Boss finally find themselves obsolescent. When the novel closes, both are about to be mulched by the company that no longer has any use for them; they are to become literally what, in another sense, they have always been, more or less useful raw material. The mulching of the Boss, now simply called "Roy," is particularly significant because it indicates that this is not about personal success or individual achievement. Gliding through the city in a chauffeur-driven Rolls Royce, the Boss might well seem "one of the chosen." The power he enjoys for a while, however, is what the narrative describes as a "collective belief" in the power of his money. "The rumor that everyone had somehow heard," the reader is told, ". . . was that there was no problem in the whole world that the Boss could not solve by simply throwing money . . . at it."[82] The real power lies not with him—he is, after all, as much of a depthless image, a focal point for the needs and desires of others, as the wax replicas his salesmen sell. It lies with a system that crushes and chews up everyone who serves it. Ida Mae, renamed "Ms. I. M. Milk," replaces the Boss but, as she admits, she will follow her predecessor to the mulcher in the long run; "the world grinds on," as she tells Hickey, and only "the company controls everything."

Hickum Looney is summoned to the mulcher after a telephone call made by another salesman called Bickle. Yet another freak, a huge "slab of fat" of a man with a "head . . . so tiny that it seemed hardly larger than a cue ball," Bickle is confined to a wheelchair after being shot in both feet by Gaye Nell Odell. It is one of the novel's many moments of sudden violence. One more such moment occurs when Bickle himself

82. Ibid., 71. See also 80, 125, 183, 267, 268.

shoots and kills the man who has been helping him sell "day in and day out" and whom he knows as Slimy. It is after murdering Slimy, in fact, that Bickle makes two calls to the mulcher, one to get rid of his victim, the other to do the same for Looney. There is no evident reason for the second call; the idea of making it comes to him out of the blue, as what is called "a totally improbable course of action." In this nightmarish world, "nothing is written" as Ida Mae puts it. There is no absolute explanation, no master narrative operating outside the "self-contained, self-justifying madness" of the cycle of consumerism. "Things did happen, though," is all that Hickum Looney could come up with earlier, when he tried to explain life to himself; "They did happen, things did." And now things happen, not only without but against explanation, to propel Hickum toward death. Bickle's second call is without reason; it is as arbitrary, as dreamlike and depthless as anything else that occurs in the novel. And both phone calls are without rational context, in the sense that Bickle has no idea how he came to know the mulcher's telephone number in the first place. "He assumed sometime, a long time ago," we are told, "he had been issued that number by personnel,"[83] but he cannot be sure.

Rumor is at work here, as amorphous and unassailable as belief: "rumor assured every head and heart," including Bickle's, "that every single employee of Soaps for Life had such a card," with the phone number on it, "to be used when necessary." Nobody admits to knowing the number, let alone knowing how they have it; "rumor said that to do so would show disloyalty to the firm and distrust to its officers." "Rumor spread the same kind of appeals for the same kind of trust during the Vietnam War," the narrator adds. "It was quintessential rumor work."[84] This is one of the few directly historical allusions in a book that generally tends to make its historical points in a jokey, offbeat way. The point is clear enough, perhaps, without it. In a society dedicated to the commodification of desire and the consumption of dreams, the public narrative is inevitably a lie. Its cultural work, as the Boss declares, is simply "to make a piece of shit and sell it." What people know in this situation, or admit to knowing, is at best irrelevant; all that matters is that they should behave according to the script. Things happen without motive or meaning in the novel, often to the bewilderment of the people who do them, not because Crews eschews explanation, but because he is trying to explain

83. Ibid., 253. See also 29, 46–47, 193, 253, 255.
84. Ibid., 253. See also 103.

a world in which the actual will to explain becomes subversive—in which to see something outside the terms of the public narrative, be it a war or "a piece of shit," is to jeopardize the deal.

"The Boss himself emphasized that it did not matter what the salesman said or promised," Hickum Looney reflects, "as long as he sold the product. He was only trying to sell, sell as much as he could. That was the way it had always been. That and nothing else." Like most of Crews's characters, Hickum is grounded in a material reality that he can barely see or acknowledge because he is enmeshed in the public narrative. More specifically in his case, language and action are shaped by the Sales Manual while what passes for thought is mostly defined by "belief," that commitment to a repetitive cycle of trading which is the prior condition of his employment. Even when a character is permitted a glimpse of the plain facts that determine his or her life, they can make little of it. As Bickle makes his first call to the mulcher, for instance, he catches sight through the window of "a shapeless mound of fat" of a woman, "heedlessly making a replica of herself" by feeding her small child "unlimited quantities of ice cream." The woman, Bickle notices, continues to feed the girl after the body of Slimy has been collected by the mulcher and the room where he was shot thoroughly cleaned. So, as he swivels himself round in a circle in his wheelchair, he sees in quick succession "the wall where Slimy had been shot" now "faultlessly repaired" and "the heavy woman in the sweat-stained mummu" offering her daughter "yet another cup of ice cream." "He kept turning," the reader learns, "and gradually it seemed to him that the large woman busily making a replica of herself by keeping ice cream in the hand of the child and the spot across the room where Slimy died were at different ends of the spectrum. But he did not know the nature of the spectrum or why he should think they were at opposite ends of it."[85] Bickle does not understand, but Crews does and thanks to him the reader does too. The consuming child turning into the consuming adult and then into the consumed body is the fundamental rhythm of the narrative. Obeying this rhythm, beating out their lives in

85. Ibid., 254–55. See also 30, 252; Peet, "Survey of the South," 6. It is probably unnecessary to point out that the timing of this sequence does not "work" in any conventionally "realistic" sense. Like many other maverick writers, Crews skips through time or stretches it out at will—or, as in this case, makes two temporally quite different sequences of action (the child eating the ice cream/the call to the mulcher, the collecting of Slimy's body, the cleaning of the room) coextensive. The result is that his books can take on the often dizzying temporality of a dream or a cartoon.

time to it, the characters in *The Mulching of America* allow themselves to be mass-produced. They become what that survey in *The Economist*, with no apparent trace of irony, called "Confederate consumers," subjected to a process of endless replication in which (un)fulfillment, (dis)satisfaction is located at the moment of buying. As a result, they are trapped in the desires manufactured by their culture; "the Company" requires them to eat and never be full, until they in turn are eaten.

"We all live in dreams," Gaye Nell Odell tells Hickum Looney. "Well, bless your sweet little heart," Hickum replies, recognizing the source of the remark. "You've been studying the Sales Manual, haven't you?" Gaye Nell is not alone. Nearly everyone in the novel seems to have studied the Sales Manual—or, if not that, then some other fragment of the cultural text—with the result that their words have a counterfeit quality. Their dialogue is manufactured, a marketable commodity; so, for that matter, are their lives and dreams. Nearly everything they dream, do, and say, too, becomes transferable into everything else, since what matters here is not identity but exchange value. All the world, for these characters, is, not a stage, but a volatile marketplace, where there are no stable exchange rates and the worth of something is simply what anyone at any particular time is willing to pay for it. Apparent opposites consequently collapse into one another: "soap" and "shit," for example. "Soap? Bullshit," observes the unfortunate Slimy, shortly before he is killed. "The soap we know about," agrees Slimy's killer, Bickle, *is* indistinguishable from "horseshit"; it is, in the end, only the particular "piece of shit" that the Soaps for Life Company has been set up to make and sell. "Soap," or "shit," is defined by the deal, as everything else is. All meanings boil down to power; as the Boss persists in saying, the thing that matters is not "what might or might not be true" but what is needed "to win the point at issue."[86] In drawing us a map of this unstable world, like all the best maverick writers, Crews uses the instruments of other, relatively stabler times—but to new effect; *The Mulching of America* speaks with a Southern accent, but in a language that is also radically contemporary. The trickster, after all, is a stock figure in regional humor; Faulkner even used *his* main trickster, Flem Snopes, as Crews does, to explore the comedy of capitalism. It is left to Crews, however, to draw us the portrait of a confidence game in which "everybody fails" because success—or, rather, the dream of it—is simply part of the trick, designed to keep the

86. Crews, *Mulching of America*, 29. See also, 224, 244.

system grinding on. Similarly, it is left to Crews to take, say, the surreal, sexually inflected social comment of a writer like Caldwell, or Flannery O'Connor's coolly comic interrogations of secular belief, and give them a further, manic spin. *His* South is one from which the possibility of social reform or spiritual redemption has vanished; there is no way out here, because all human motive and action is driven back, and then back again, to the moment of purchase. The only exit, as Hickum Looney learns, is to the mulcher. As Looney takes that exit, too, on the last page of the novel, he catches sight of something that suggests just how much his life is defined by imposture as well as closure: the fire he has been standing by, he notices "to no point whatsoever," is, "in fact, a fake, not fire at all, only colored light."[87] It is an instant of typically random revelation. "The real thing" eludes him, as it does consistently all Crew's characters, because they are the victims of a freakish logic that turns their lives into shadow-play. Others might call it the logic of late capitalism. True to his true grit *persona,* though, and the rough magic of his craft, Crews calls it by a simpler name: "bullshit."

87. Ibid., 268. I have attempted to discuss Flem Snopes in terms of the comedy of capitalism in *The Life of William Faulkner: A Critical Biography* (Oxford, 1994), 253–70. As far as the connection with O'Connor is concerned, useful comparisons could be made between, say, Crews's representation of the Soaps for Life Company and its system of "belief" and O'Connor's account of the preaching of "the Church of Christ Without Christ" in *Wise Blood* (1949; New York, 1962 edition), 60.

7

"The world is here"

Fiction Writing and Social Change in the Contemporary South II

TALE-TELLERS AND TALKERS

In an early interview, published in 1931, William Faulkner suggested that *The Brothers Karamazov* would have been a much better book if, as he put it, Dostoevsky "had . . . let the characters tell their own stories instead of filling page after page with exposition." He was joking, of course, in his own typically deadpan way, but the joke contained a serious point—and one taken up, more recently, by the writers I have referred to as tale-tellers and talkers. It is the same point a Mississippi writer of another generation, Eudora Welty, was making when she explained that what she was trying to do in *Losing Battles,* arguably her finest novel, was to concentrate on voice. "I wanted," she said, "to see if I could do something that was new for me: translating every thought and feeling into speech." "Tell it!" one character instructs another in *Losing Battles;* and that injunction has been at work in Southern writing for many years. Growing up in a traditionally oral culture, writers from the South of earlier generations—among them, Faulkner, Welty, and, before them, Mark Twain—have seen the need to talk as not just a moral imperative but an existential one. For them, in other words, it was not just something that human beings should do but something they had to do if they were fully to function as human. In *Their Eyes Were Watching God,* for example, Zora Neale Hurston creates what Alice Walker has called "a sense of Black people as complete, complex, *undiminished* human beings" by allowing her characters to talk themselves into life. "When the people sat around on the porch and passed around the pictures of their thoughts for others to look at and see, it was nice," the heroine Janie Crawford Killicks Starks reflects. "The fact that the thought pictures were always crayon enlargements of life made it even nicer to listen to." "Yo' wife is uh born orator,"[1] one of Janie's neighbors tells her husband; and, in this neighborhood, that is the highest compliment one person can pay another. The people of Hurston's South, like those in the South of Twain or Faulkner or Welty, become flesh through their own conversations. They speak themselves into being, not only as individuals, but as a community.

Traces of an oral culture survive still, in parts of the South; and the point was made earlier that, in contemporary Southern fiction, tale-telling and talking remain a vital medium for transferring different versions of the past to the present. What is notable about this more recent fiction, however, is just how foregrounded the notion of struggle is: history is defined, in many books from the South now, in terms of voices frantically striving to make themselves heard—fighting to resurrect the past and register presence in a culture more mobile and plural, even more on edge than ever before. "I can't reconstruct things," says Jean Mitchell to her daughter Danner in Jayne Anne Phillips's *Machine Dreams*. (1984). "I try to remember. A few days isolated from each other by months or years, swim up. Then I have to think hard to know what years those were. . . . You know, I don't remember my own face then."[2] "Then" is the 1940s, recollected with effort some thirty years later. "Life wasn't like it is now," Jean tells Danner. "Look at you—born here and think you have to get to California, go so far, do so much so fast. Crazy situations, strange people—all this about drugs." Voices like Jean's try to speak of a past that is only erratically recalled, and a present so restless and changeable that it seems to defy articulation. In times of accelerated change, constant and exacerbated social transformation, it appears even more difficult than ever to tame and subdue things by naming them.

1. Zora Neale Hurston, *Their Eyes Were Watching God* (1937; London, 1986 edition), 92. See also 80; *Lion in the Garden: Interviews with William Faulkner* edited by James B. Meriwether and Michael Millgate (New York, 1968), 18; Linda Kuehl, "The Art of Fiction: Eudora Welty," *Paris Review,* LV (1972), 77; Eudora Welty, *Losing Battles* (1970; New York, 1978 edition), 236; Alice Walker, "Dedication," *I Love Myself When I Am Laughing: A Zora Neale Hurston Reader* (New York, 1979), 4.

2. Jayne Anne Phillips, *Machine Dreams* (London, 1984), 159. See also 13–14.

As the title of Welty's own 1970 novel indicates, of course, this idea of life as a difficult, potentially desperate warring of voices is not a new one in the South. A key text here, apart from *Losing Battles,* is *Absalom, Absalom!;* and a key passage is the one where Faulkner has a character, Judith Sutpen, volunteer the image of struggle. "You are born with a lot of other people," Judith famously declares, "all mixed up with them . . . all trying to make a rug on the same loom, only each one wants to weave his own pattern into the rug and it cant matter . . . or the Ones that set up the loom would have arranged things a little better, and yet it must matter because you keep on trying or having to keep on trying."[3] Human experience is clearly figured at this moment as a complex web of voices into which each individual tries feverishly to weave his own pattern. This is the figure at work shaping the multiple narrative planes of *Absalom, Absalom!,* along with so much of Faulkner's other fiction; and it is rendered all the more complex by the suggestion that the terms in which anyone speaks are mediated by others. The voice that fights for a private identity—Quentin Compson's, say, or that of Joe Christmas—is an irretrievably public one; it is not only surrounded by other voices talking before and after, it is also—as Faulkner was not alone among earlier Southern writers in saying—shaped and inhabited by them. Recent Southern writers have not invented this figure of the web, the collision of voices all inextricably bound up with one another. They have only taken it up and made it more disturbing—but significantly so. History, in some current Southern stories, has accelerated. In others, it has simply stopped: "they say the world ends in fire and ice," declares a character in *Black Tickets* (1980) by Jayne Anne Phillips, "I say it's already over." Either way, the individual voice fighting to make itself heard, saying "it cant matter . . . and yet it must matter," finds itself more than usually challenged. The task of weaving the right pattern, making a way through history and telling a coherent, convincing tale of its changes, becomes all the more of a problem.

"At night I listened to music and wondered if Mama was listening to the same songs," says Violet, one of the narrators in *Crazy Ladies* (1990) by Michael Lee West. It is the 1960s and Violet's "Mama" Clancy has left Tennessee for "a hog farm in New Mexico . . . she called The Garden." "I propped the portable radio next to my ear," Violet goes on,

---

3. William Faulkner, *Absalom, Absalom!* (New York, 1936), 43. See also Jayne Anne Phillips, *Black Tickets* (1980; London, 1993 edition), 91.

and it was almost like the songs were being whispered. The lyrics spoke of California and wild hippie nights. Mama had started out being a simple song, like "Doo Wah Diddy Diddy." I didn't know for sure, but I suspected she'd gotten real complex, like the song "Light My Fire." Then it came to me that our lives didn't resemble music; it was more like math, an algebra equation:

$$Y \text{ (Hart)} + X \text{ (Clancy)} = Z \text{ (me)}.$$

Z could have been anyone.[4]

The lives of characters like Violet are measured out in hit tunes, messages from the mass media. Popular songs, the public soundtrack of everyday life, become not just a means of locating identity ("Where was I when I first heard that?") but a tool for defining it ("I am the person in that song, or someone I know intimately is."). The personal voice of Violet traces the personality of her mother on the shifting surfaces of mass culture, in the music she hears on the radio. These are her emotional language; and, when that language fails her, she falls back, not on some more individualized vocabulary, but on mathematical abstractions, equations that anonymize her—as Violet puts it, "Z could have been anyone."

People like Violet—and there are many of them in contemporary Southern fiction—have the tricky task of maneuvering their way through a public space saturated by rock music, soap operas, advertisements, and so on because that, by now, is the place they live most of the time. They have to deal in the idiom of a kind of virtual reality—the real as defined by, say, the voices that whisper on the radio—for the simple reason that this is the medium their own immediate reality inhabits; even in "The Garden," there is no escaping it. Not everyone in these narratives of taletelling and talking is as openly confronted with this task as Violet is, of course. There are books that incorporate the voices of different people and generations, like *Machine Dreams* by Jayne Anne Phillips, *The Floatplane Notebooks* (1988) by Clyde Edgerton, *The Picture Makers* (1990) by Emily Ellison and *Crazy Ladies* by Michael Lee West. There are also those that trace the accents of a single and singular voice, such as *The Autobiography of Miss Jane Pittman* (1971) by Ernest Gaines, *A Lifetime Burning* (1982) by Ellen Douglas, *Almost Innocent* (1984) by Sheila Bosworth, *Edisto* by Padgett Powell, *Oldest Living Confederate Widow Tells All* (1989) by Allan Gurganus, and *A Tidewater Morning* (1993) by Wil-

4. Michael Lee West, *Crazy Ladies* (1990; New York, 1991 edition), 90–91.

liam Styron. Each one, in turn, registers in a different key just how Southerners now speak their past into the present. In all of them, though, there
is a feeling for what the narrator of *A Tidewater Morning* calls "the
power of history to utterly victimize humanity, composed of forgettable
ciphers like myself":[5] a power made all the more powerful by the emergence of global communication. In every one, in short, the individual
voice fights to be heard—not simply to become a victim of the vocabulary
of mass culture but to appropriate it, genuinely to use it.

"Can't conversation ever cease?" asks a character in *Losing Battles*. For
Jayne Anne Phillips, in particular, the answer appears to be "no." Voices
within, and voices without: the entire process of life assumes for her, as
it does for so many Southern writers, the character of an uninterrupted
flow of speech. To this extent, Phillips's entire work so far seems to find
an epigraph in a remark made by Eudora Welty when she was trying to
explain her own fiction in her memoir of her life and craft, *One Writer's
Beginnings*. "The mystery lies," Welty said, "in the use of language to
express human life." Phillips's first collection of stories, *Black Tickets,* is
full of people trying to make sense of their aimless lives, their world of
broken families, truck stops, strip joints, people on the move by talking
about them, to themselves or others. "My cousins and uncles was all

5. William Styron, *A Tidewater Morning* (1993; London, 1994 edition), 37. Ernest
Gaines, *The Autobiography of Miss Jane Pittman* (1971; New York, 1972 edition); Ellen
Douglas, *A Lifetime Burning* (New York, 1982); Sheila Bosworth, *Almost Innocent* (1984;
Baton Rouge, La., 1996 edition); Padgett Powell, *Edisto* (1983; New York, 1985 edition);
Phillips, *Machine Dreams;* Clyde Edgerton, *The Floatplane Notebooks* (Chapel Hill, N.C.,
1988); Allan Gurganus, *Oldest Living Confederate Widow Tells All* (New York, 1989);
Emily Ellison, *The Picture Makers* (New York, 1990); West, *Crazy Ladies.* The locus classi-
cus in discussions of the Southern fondness for talk is W. J. Cash, *The Mind of the South*
(New York, 1941): see, e.g., chapter 1, section ii. Very useful, for the point I am trying to
make here about how Southerners struggle even now to establish a sense of community
through talk, is Fred Hobson, *Tell About the South: The Southern Rage to Explain* (Baton
Rouge, La., 1983), and, on a more general, theoretical level, the arguments of Mikhail
Bakhtin concerning the fundamentally social origins of language. Bakhtin argues, for instance, that language "does not belong to the individual but to his *social group* (his social
environment)" (*Freudianism: A Marxist Critique* translated by I. R. Titunik [New York,
1976], 128), and that "no member of a verbal community can ever find words . . . that are
neutral . . . uninhabited by the other's voice" (*Problems of Dostoevsky's Poetics* translated
by W. W. Russel [Ann Arbor, Mich., 1973], 131). It is precisely this, the socially mediated
character of language, that I think now makes the construction of a Southern "verbal
community" such a complicated and risky enterprise.

lobstermen ever since I can remember," a character called simply "The Blond" recalls. "My dad too, but he died when I was so young all he is to me is a furred chest and a smell of oiled rope." "I split way south with a rich dude. Red birds and black-eyed men," she adds later. "Been some time since then. I'm doing O.K. I got it made, and the cold don't come so much now."[6] More ambitiously, Phillips's first novel, *Machine Dreams,* uses voices talking to one another (particularly mother to daughter), talking to themselves (particularly in dream or memory), and talking through letters, to tell the story of an entire family from the Depression to 1972 and their presence in a series of verbal communities, the local, the regional, the national, and international—all of which, while experiencing critical change, are trying somehow to forge some link between yesterday and today.

Machine Dreams begins with Jean Danner Hampson reminiscing to her daughter Danner about the hard times her family endured before World War II. It ends with Danner's "machine dream" of her brother Billy, missing in action during another war, in Vietnam: a brother she recalls making "airplane sounds," "war-movie sounds" as they walked, many years earlier, in the growing dusk through the woods—"sounds like a song," she recollects, "and the song goes on softly as the plane falls, year after year, to earth."[7] In between, Phillips weaves together the oppositions caught in the apparently oxymoronic title of her book. People rise and fall through time in *Machine Dreams,* their lives compounded equally of tangible history and intangible memory. Their desires and their despair circulate around the substantial presences that constitute their experience: the cars in which intimacies are shared, the buses, trains, boats, and planes that promise a world elsewhere, the radios that

6. Phillips, *Black Tickets,* 89–91. See also Welty, *Losing Battles,* 372; *One Writer's Beginnings* (Cambridge, Mass., 1984), 10.

7. Phillips, *Machine Dreams,* 331. See also 132, 160, 184, 239. A useful discussion of *Machine Dreams* is to be found in Owen Gilman, *Vietnam and the Southern Imagination* (Jackson, Miss., 1992), 47–69. On "magic realism" in contemporary Southern fiction such as Phillips's see, e.g., Philip D. Beidler, "Re-Writing America: Literature as Cultural Revision in the New Vietnam Fiction," in *America Rediscovered* edited by Owen Gilman and Lorrin Smith (New York, 1990), 3–9; Julius Raper, "Inventing Modern Southern Fiction: A Postmodern View," *Southern Literary Journal,* XXII (1990), 3–18. On the imaginative use of the machinery of the Vietnam War, see, e.g., Philip D. Beidler, *American Literature and the Experience of Vietnam* (Athens, Ga., 1982); *The Legacy: The Vietnam War in the American Imagination* edited by Michael D. Shafer (Boston, Mass., 1990).

offer "words drifting off like air," "notes . . . shaped like words"—"a sound coming back and coming back" to give articulate shape to need. Just as in James Agee's *A Death in the Family*, the house at night, with its intimate but strange noises, supplies a recurring image for the magically realistic element the characters inhabit. The voices of her parents and the other night sounds Danner hears as she "lies drifting" in her childhood bed (before sinking into "a dream she will know all her life") tell of a world of tangible mystery. This is a world in which "machines" both issue out of "dreams" and generate them: where the plane or helicopter falling to earth or the house in darkness—creaking, settling, alive with half-heard voices or "the breathing of sleepers"—inhabits a neutral territory, somewhere between everyday experience and reverie, the palpable and the chimerical. What the sounds, songs, and speech of *Machine Dreams* disclose to us is that, for good *and* ill, our mental and emotional lives are married to the materials of our existence. Much the same disclosure lies at the back of Phillips's second and even finer, still more haunting novel, *Shelter*, published in 1994.

Like *Machine Dreams*, *Shelter* invites us in to a world on the edge of revelation. *"Concede the heat of noon on summer camps,"* the book begins, *"The quarters wavering in bottled heat, cots lined up in the big dark rooms that are pitch black if you walk in out of the sun. Black, quiet, empty, and the screen door banging shut three times behind you. Allowed in alone only if you are faint. Perhaps the heat has come over you. . . . The cots are precisely mute, you see the bodies there, each in its own future. You are frightened because it is you here with the future."*[8] It is late July 1963 at Camp Shelter in Shelter County, West Virginia, a summer camp for girls. The summer heat, the sense of loneliness, absence, the darkness, the silence punctuated by the banging of a screen door or *"occasional cries no louder than the sounds of invisible birds"* outside: all these add to the sense of expectation, and slight menace, that is aroused by the laconic yet mysterious terms of address (Who, exactly, is *"you"?*), a descriptive idiom that is at once exact and evasive (Just how mute is *"precisely mute"?*), and a vocabulary that draws on everyday speech (*"pitch black"*) and something more strangely, dreamily melodic (*"Concede the heat"*). This is Phillips's neutral territory again, where familiar material objects seem to float in time, "oceans of it." "Camp was

8. Jayne Anne Phillips, *Shelter* (1994; London, 1995 edition), 3. See also 7, 8, 79, 162, 170, 215, 264.

like being asleep, like a long, long dream," one of the characters is to reflect. Another, lying on her cot, feels that "she nearly slept but didn't sleep, and floated." Floating, "slowly spinning" in an element that, especially in the shimmering of midsummer heat, seems to mingle earth and water, the people in *Shelter* are familiar with both the mundane and the mysterious. This is a place where more than one character may appear like "a ghost," "a dream," a "devil," or an "angel" to another, but where there is room too for the homely and the historical—gossip in the local beauty shop, popular heroes of the day like Troy Donahue and the Beach Boys, talk about John and Jackie Kennedy, Khrushchev and the fears aroused by the Cuban missile crisis.

The fluid element that is Camp Shelter and its surrounds is perhaps best measured by the shifting, metamorphic nature of its inhabitants. At one point in the story, for instance, a character dreams of a snake only to awaken and find one coiling its way into his shack. Seeing it as a "probe of God," he "makes a basket of arms for the snake to fill and it does."[9] He then carries it through the woods, appearing to those he meets like someone out of *their* dreams in turn. So, one young girl he encounters is enchanted by "the spell" he seems to cast, as the thing in his arms turns from a "vine" into a "snake" and then a "vine" again—"shining," as she perceives it, "moving over him." Drifting through all these sea changes, "the shapely dark" of night or "the amoebic mist" of day, the characters often behave like sleepwalkers, absorbed in memory or desire or both. So many of the adolescent girls at Camp Shelter are caught up in remembering and longing. They recollect voices—their parents, say, arguing or making love in a nearby room—and, haunted by such recollections, they find themselves consumed with what is called at one point "sick wanting"—dim intimations of a need that they are only just beginning to name and understand.

There are four characters through whose presence and perception the story of *Shelter* is told. They are two sisters, Lenny and Alma Swenson, who are spending the summer at Camp Shelter with their friends Cap Brierley and Delia Campbell, Buddy Carmody, whose mother, Hilda, is the camp cook, and Parson, who is working with a crew laying pipes along the nearby Mud River. Dividing the forty-two sections of the novel between them, these four, Lenny and Alma, Buddy and Parson, are revealed to us through their dialogues with others, their dreams, the wan-

9. Ibid., 118–19. See also 13, 123, 137–38.

derings of each consciousness, and their more instinctual moments. Although the story is written in the third person, the reader has the sense
of being immersed in an individual voice and vision all the time: each of
the four has a personal tale to tell, and in each case Phillips plays a particular variation on her general strategy of dipping down from conversation
to lower levels of feeling and then surfacing into conversation again. The
strategy is one that Faulkner used, of course, consistently and obsessively.
"I listen to the voices," Faulkner said once, "and when I put down what
the voices say, it's right." And listening to the "voices" of her characters
in the full sense—that is, the voices inside as well as around them—
Phillips seems to be following, and playing on, Faulkner's example here.
Not only that, the shadowy figure of the "Sole Owner & Proprietor" of
Yoknapatawpha County seems to hover over the small town of Shelter
("wasn't a town," we learn, "just a dirt road and a few hicks"), some of
those living nearby for a while, and even seminal moments of action.
Even the title of Phillips's novel carries a sly, intertextual allusion to the
decaying rural environs of Frenchman's Bend and Faulkner's most notorious novel. And the allusion is underlined when Parson comes across a
clearing in the woods, "a squat of spoiled land" where "tree stumps
stood up in burnt configuration, silent amongst the shapes of discarded
furniture, torn motorcycles, piles of tires." In this setting, at once depress-
ingly naturalistic and gothic (the discarded tires, the "silent" trees), Parson finds "damaged bounty," we are told, and draws "sustenance" there,
"like a creature at a water hole." At the moment in question, his bounty
is a "piece of knife the size of his palm, just right for his hand." As he
bent "to retrieve the metal shard," the narrator goes on, "there was a
silence as he knelt down, a kind of sanctuary."[10]

Parson himself recollects, not so much a figure out of *Sanctuary,* as
the character of Joe Christmas in *Light in August.* An "orphan kid,"
taunted as a "dark kid, *guinea kid*" at school, he is known as "the
stranger" to those who know him at all, his name given to him by "the
Preacher," a wild, charismatic figure who took over Parson's life for a
while and left him with an indelible sense of evil. "He knew he was born
dark,"[11] we are told. That is about all Parson knows for sure. He can

10. Ibid., 175–76. See also 43. On voice in Faulkner, see, e.g., Richard Gray, *The Life
of William Faulkner: A Critical Biography* (Oxford, 1994), 6–12. On Faulkner as "Sole
Owner & Proprietor," see, e.g., Philip Weinstein, *Faulkner's Subject: A Cosmos No One
Owns* (Cambridge, 1990).
11. Phillips, *Shelter,* 9. See also 14, 46, 150, 203.

only answer the question that haunts him, *"where you from?,"* by recalling the "long road" he has traveled without finding a home, a road that includes prison, reform school, work camp, and abusive foster parents. Like Joe Christmas, Parson hears and is driven by voices from out of his past, and above all the voice of "the Preacher." These are his familiars, or, as he calls them, "his legion." Apart from that, he has no real company; he is friendless as well as homeless, the "dark inside him" helping to make him a mystery both to himself and to others. If the older male protagonist in *Shelter* carries the traces of one inhabitant of Yoknapatawpha with him, then the younger, Buddy Carmody, bears the dim signature of another, Benjy Compson in *The Sound and the Fury.* Buddy is "an enchanted creature," a "wood elf" who is at home only in the forest and claims to have "nobody" as his father. Certainly, he is not the child of the man, called simply Carmody, from whom he takes his surname, and who believes it a paternal right to abuse him. "You know 'honeysuckle' was one of your first words?" his doting mother asks him. "Nearly three before you talked, and you come out with a big word like that. I figured you was going to be a late-blooming genius."[12] Buddy is no genius but, as his mother insists, he is "someone who's different from other folks." Unlike Benjy Compson, he can talk when he chooses to. Like Benjy, however, he seems to know "more, out of nowhere" even though he "might only know about a certain thing"; and he tends to exist outside language. Silent most of the time, straying through the woods alone—"his kingdom," as he sees it—he understands things through the senses. Words, especially written ones, matter to him little. What enchants him is "the white space between the letters," the vacancies where his dreaming imagination "can put any good thing." "He could fall into that space," we are told; there, he and his "Mam" can be alone together, just as Benjy Compson dreams of being with his sister, and mother surrogate, Caddy. "Here," in the woods or in the vacancy between words, "is always a white space he can make"; this is his sanctuary, his shelter.

What rescues *Shelter* from being just a rehearsal of familiar Faulknerian obsessions is really a matter of place and voice. For all the connections with the broken world of *Sanctuary,* the place called Shelter is different not least because it mixes visions of angels and devils with the material signs and cultural symbols of the early 1960s. It is also of the South, in particular, in an historically specific as well as a more romanti-

12. Ibid., 20. See also 124, 146, 291, 295.

cally allusive way. There is "kudzu and honeysuckle" in these woods: both the regional emblem of desire, sexuality, and fleshly hunger (Quentin Compson, most famously, is haunted by the odor of honeysuckle in *The Sound and the Fury*) and the far more mundane plant, imported from Japan not long ago, that now threatens to take over large areas of the Southern countryside. As for voice: that is partly a matter of the fluent magic of Phillips's craft. This means, for instance, that the voices inside Buddy Carmody's head echo a book like *The Robber Bridegroom* by Eudora Welty as much as they do *The Sound and the Fury*, to the extent that they play off fairytale, enchantment against the everyday. And it is also, even more, a matter of bias, inclination: Phillips places far greater emphasis on the voice and vision of her female characters, above all Lenny and Alma. The lineaments of desire are traced out here from the perspective of girls growing into women. A notable instance of this occurs when Lenny experiences an erotic awakening. Naked, she encounters Frank, a camp employee, in the waters of a local fishing spot known as Turtle Hole. Her friend Cap Brierley participates in this strange, nighttime moment of initiation by helping to buoy Lenny up in the water while Frank holds her in his arms and touches her. Parson, meanwhile, watching all this unobserved from the woods, finds this vision of what he sees as "the girl who was a fish"[13] mingling with an earlier vision of a similar kind: the memory of a girl "like a fish with thin human arms outspread" whom he once ran over while driving a truck.

Nobody coming across this moment of revelation, and familiar with the work of Faulkner, can surely fail to catch the echoes. A woman like a wood spirit or twilight dream, a woman proffering promises of love and death, a woman associated with the primal element of water—a woman, too, to whom the man who pursues her reaches out like the lover on Keats's Urn and who may, or may not, be touched for a moment: no reader of Faulkner needs to be reminded just how much the fabric of his fiction is woven out of these ideas and associations, with their deployment of the male as the poet, lover, maker of words and the female as the beloved, tantalizingly ungovernable object. They are there in his work as early as 1925, in a story called "Nympholepsy," and they are there, of course, in the conception of his own "heart's darling," Caddy Compson in *The Sound and the Fury*. What is striking about this primeval encoun-

13. Ibid., 42. See also 47, 50. Compare, e.g., the description of "the old Natchez Trace" in *The Robber Bridegroom* (1942; London, 1982 edition), 104.

ter, as it is replayed in *Shelter,* is that now it is the woman—mostly Lenny, but also Cap—whose dreamlike desires shape our experience of it. It is a moment of initiation into the mysteries of the body, and the unappeasable nature of both romantic hunger and sexual need, that is determinately female. The man here is the elusive object of desire. "Now he was close, his face, his eyes," Lenny observes of Frank. "He was unbearably fragrant, like flowers and dust, and his thick dry hair was warm." "Lenny felt a core of blurry fear," we are told: "His mouth was on hers but she pulled away, gasping; she had to cry out, then she couldn't stop her voice. Shattering, she heard a coarse, continuous moaning as she turned, over and over, tumbling through space. She felt a hot rush and knew she was urinating. . . . She let the warmth happen and the turning eased. . . . Lenny remembered the water again as an element separate from herself."[14] It is surely no coincidence that the adoption of the womanly view is accompanied by powerful feelings of immersion in the fluid element and a more palpable sense of the body. Lenny's desire, and her possible, quicksilver moment of gratification, is expressed here, not just by her voice, but by a magical process whereby she briefly forgets that the water is something "separate from herself," becoming one with its tumbling and turning—and by a "hot rush," a physical release that she cannot, perhaps does not want to, stop. This is an erotic meeting at once more enchanted and much earthier than anything Faulkner ever permitted himself. Parson is there, of course, to interpret it later in his own male language ("the girl who was a fish"). But, in the end, this serves only to emphasize the primacy of the female vision. It is the experience of Lenny that takes us to the heart of things here; Parson remains just the observer of a moment that belongs, first and last, to a woman.

Turtle Hole, where Lenny encounters Frank, is also the site for the dramatic climax of the novel. In another, far more violent moment of revelation, Lenny, Cap, Alma, and Delia meet Buddy there, accompanied by the man who calls himself Buddy's father. Carmody, who knows only the language of force and brutality, attacks Lenny. Parson, who has already rescued Buddy from a beating at Carmody's hands, appears as if by magic out of the woods and attempts to intervene. This time, he fails

14. Phillips, *Shelter,* 41–42. See also *Faulkner in the University: Class Conferences at the University of Virginia, 1957–1958* edited by Frederick L. Gwynn and Joseph L. Blotner (Charlottesville, Va., 1959), 6. Also "Nympholepsy," in *Uncollected Stories of William Faulkner* edited by Joseph Blotner (London, 1980), 331–37.

and is knocked down, but Buddy, who now sees Parson as his guardian "angel," knocks Carmody to the ground with a stone. All four girls then follow Buddy by pelting Carmody with stones until he is dead. After a brief moment of communion between Parson and Buddy, in which the man carries the boy into the water in a strange, surreal act of baptism, "the stranger"—as the five young people have come to know him— disappears back into the woods. "There is an absence, a blank around his body," Parson observes of Carmody, before he disappears, "and the absence is empty: everything has gone away."[15] The senses, the vital spark of the man have been snuffed out, and with them too his mystery, and in this case menace; like the words used once to describe him, he is no-thing. Nothing has to be hidden, however. So Buddy and the four girls conceal the body in a cave and swear each other to secrecy. They must never tell anyone else what has happened, they believe, or they will have to "tell it and tell it" and "it'll never be over." Their voices as well as their bodies have joined together to meet the crisis—this entire episode is an act of collaboration in terms, not only of what is done, but how it is told: the narrative switches quickly back and forth between Lenny, Buddy, and Parson. Now, though, is a time for silence, a mute acknowledgment that some things are impossible to tell.

It is left to Lenny to muse over the meanings of these summer encounters with love and death at Turtle Hole. They have, she senses, discovered "a world inside them all." Carmody "took them in and showed them" the darkness of things. Buddy had "saved" them and then, by joining in the stoning, they had in turn "saved" him. Through such things as this, and her encounter with Frank, she and the other young people have been initiated, she knows, learned about the "concentration of evil and grace" sheltering within each one of them. And all this Lenny knows she knows without being able or even wanting to say it, to speak the knowledge. "She understands now that she doesn't believe in words at all," we learn. "None of it translates."[16] Like Addie Bundren in Faulkner's *As I Lay Dying*, she is now convinced that (as Addie puts it) "words are no good," even though she has to use words to express that conviction, and so signal at once the impossibility and the necessity of language. The truth of things lies for her, not in signs and inscriptions, but in the sensuous mate-

15. Phillips, *Shelter*, 261. See also 260, 266.

16. Ibid., 278. See also 46, 282–83; William Faulkner, *As I Lay Dying* (1930; London, 1963 edition), 136.

rial and the spiritual mystery of experience. What matters to her, in the end, is not so much language—which, like the corpse of Carmody, simply registers "an absence, a blank" around the body of life—as what can be communicated by touch, taste, smell, hearing, and gaze, or happened upon in visions and in dream.

It is left to Buddy, in turn, to inherit the site, and announce further the significance, of all these events. The girls leave at the end of the summer. Parson is never heard of again; Buddy imagines him continuing his life of wandering across America, to the oceans he has heard of somewhere to the east or west. Buddy roams freely through the woods, Turtle Hole and its surrounds: all of it, that is, except for "a certain spot . . . not a part of his kingdom" where the killing took place. In "his kingdom," "sometimes he can feel the angel pass by," the figure of "the stranger" Parson whom Buddy witnessed saving him, offering him shelter from Carmody, and trying similarly to shelter Lenny at Turtle Hole. "Buddy had been praying all his life," Lenny reflects before she leaves Camp Shelter. Throughout the moments of crisis, everything Buddy has done has borne testimony to the apocalyptic meanings inhabiting the ordinary—a testimony all the more telling for not being in the form of words. And as he dances on a high rock in his woods, just above Turtle Hole, after the girls have gone, he feels "beneath his stomping feet . . . the world within the rock and the world beneath that world, the black world, escaped, vast and deep and no bigger than his mind."[17] What he sees and senses is like that rock, and his own mind intimately aligned with it: at once a hard fact and a vast mystery, something he understands "because it's the truth, not because it's real." The "truth" he knows exceeds the "real"; it is a nature, not a physics, and exists apart from articulation. *Shelter* ends on this note, using a characteristically metamorphic image to suggest the direction of Buddy's discoveries—which, of course, are also those of the narrative. Buddy has a "God's eye Mam made for him . . . from white yarn" hanging above his bed, we learn. And "God's eye never closes," Mam explains to him. "It doesn't think, it only sees and knows." Now, in the final pages of the book, coming down from the rock where he has been dancing, Buddy comes across a young rabbit; "he knows it by the nearly perceptible trembling of animal breath, a slow flutter in the weeds and plants." "Rabbits got nothing but knowing," he observes. Closing the distance between the young rabbit and him, he deftly picks it up and

17. Phillips, *Shelter*, 298. See also 209, 266, 279, 292.

holds it near to him, eye to eye—only to see that "its left eye is limned with a milky glaze." The rabbit is one-eyed. "There's no wound he can see. The eye holds still, smooth with a skin like an egg."[18]

From God's eye through Buddy's eye to the rabbit's eye: the common thread running through all these variations on seeing is that seeing and knowing are matters of instinct and intuition. Both the plain facts and the persuasive magic of life can be understood only through a gaze that recognizes how intimately tied the material is to the mysterious, how our world is one of "machine dreams." That gaze may be achieved through language of a special kind: a form of storytelling that acknowledges just how necessary and impossible words are—how we may need to talk in order to know, but in talking we also need to note the silences and exclusions, what exists apart from anything we may manage to say. The storytelling in *Shelter* is of this kind. Accepting the dangers and the deviousness of speech, Phillips then deploys different voices and different *levels* of voice to approach the kind of knowing that Lenny comes to cherish and that Buddy apparently possesses. She works with and beyond the ordinary ranges of discourse, so as to search out both the hard surfaces of things and their subterranean channels. This makes her a poet in the very specific sense meant by Sigurd Burckhardt, in his essay "The Poet as Fool and Priest." "Where the philosopher seeks certitude in the sign—" Burckhardt argued, "the 'p' of the propositional calculus—and the mystic in the ineffable—the 'OM' of the Hindoos—the poet takes upon himself the paradox of the human word, which is both and neither and which he creatively transforms in his 'powerful rhyme.' This rhyme is his deed; it dissociates, dissolves the word into its components—mark and bark—but simultaneously fuses it into a new and sacramental union."[19] What Burckhardt is trying to locate here, concerning the truth of poetry, is also what Octavio Paz was gesturing toward when he said that poetry characteristically moves between two poles, the "revolutionary" and the "magical." The "revolutionary" aim Paz explained, is a "conquest of the historical world and nature"; the "magical," on the

18. Ibid., 298. See also 209, 266, 279, 292.
19. Sigurd Burckhardt, "The Poet as Fool and Priest," *ELH: A Journal of English Literary History*, XXV (1956), 298. See also Octavio Paz, *L'Arc et la lyre* (Paris, 1965), 40–41, 46. "What characterises a poem," Paz also explains here, "is its necessary dependence on words as much as its struggle to transcend them" (246). This is another useful way of locating Phillips's ways with words in *Shelter*.

other hand, consists in an impulse to return to nature by dissolving the self-consciousness that separates us from it, "to lose oneself . . . in animal innocence, or liberate oneself from history"; both are ways of healing the same divisions and distances—and reconciling the "alienated consciousness" to the places it inhabits. These two approaches to the problems of absence and exile endemic in experience, and inscribed in language, are comparable to the strategies defined by Burckhardt. They are also, surely, at the heart of Phillips's fascination with "machine dreams." She takes on "the paradox of the human word" in her stories, and struggles to transform it into an appropriate instrument of understanding and being in the world. Dissolving that word, and her world of West Virginia, into their component elements, giving voice to the different possibilities of the sign—the polarities of "revolutionary" insistence on "certitude" and "magical" pursuit of the "ineffable"—she then welds them into a new knowledge of reality. In the process, she invents a fictional language that acknowledges, and articulates, both the material and mystery so as to bridge the gap between ourselves and our surroundings; and she turns tale-telling and talking into something very like poetry, a spellbinding revelation of "the truth."

EXPATRIATES AND EXILES

The writing practice of at least some of the expatriates and exiles is implicit in their change of locality. Richard Ford and Madison Smartt Bell have moved in and out of the South; James Wilcox has gone to New York; and, having been born in Tennessee, Ishmael Reed was brought up in Buffalo then later moved to San Francisco. With such changes, very often, have come an alteration in the fictional landscape and a shift in perspective (very often but, of course, by no means always—there is no simple causative pattern at work here). After earlier novels in the vein of Ellen Glasgow, provincial comedies of manners like *Modern Baptists* and *North Gladiola*, James Wilcox, for instance, has graduated to cross-cultural humor. In Wilcox's *Sort of Rich* (1989), a New Yorker finds herself marooned in Louisiana, baffled by what she perceives as its insularity. In his *Polite Sex* (1991), in turn, Louisianians displaced in New York experience both condescension and change. "It was almost as if," one character in *Polite Sex* reflects, "being from Louisiana, she was considered backward, a little slow." Still, we learn of another exiled Louisianian a little later on in the novel, "although she had only lived in New York a few months, Clara thought of herself as an entirely different person from the naïve smalltown girl who had said hello to strangers on the street. She had matured incredibly fast and no longer saw life in her mother's narrow-minded way."[20] While Wilcox pokes gentle, evenhanded fun at two cultures—small town narrowness of mind and big town arrogance— Ishmael Reed has placed multiculturalism at the heart of his imaginative project: his South, it was noted earlier, forms just one element in "the Multinational Society." Arguably, Reed is a writer for whom the term coined by Lewis P. Simpson, "postsouthern," might also be appropriate. So, for that matter, are Richard Ford and Madison Smartt Bell. Ford and Bell, in particular, have produced fiction that could be subtitled, "notes for a novel about the end of the South," since it seems designed for a world in which a sense of place has been supplanted by drifting, a sense of the past by aimlessness and process. Their characters drift in an any-place, anytime the determining feature of which is its subjection to the anonymizing processes of the market, and the dominant feelings are ones generated by that subjection—a vague anxiety and an even vaguer sense of dissatisfaction, yearning.

The central characters in both Bell's *Straight Cut* (1986) and Ford's *The Sportswriter* (1986) are, in fact, dangling men. Tracy, in *Straight Cut*, is a maverick film director with a taste for Kierkegaard and bourbon. Frank Bascombe, in Ford's book, is someone who has given up a promising literary career ("there were some good notices," he confides) to become a sportswriter. Wryly ill at ease, at odds with themselves and the world, the two of them recall many of the figures in Walker Percy's fiction, men and women whose desperation is, inevitably, quiet and who live in what Percy once called "the sphere of the possible." Unrealized in

20. James Wilcox, *Polite Sex* (New York, 1991), 93. See also 30; Lewis P. Simpson, *The Brazen Face of History: Studies in the Literary Consciousness in America* (Baton Rouge, La., 1980), 255. Also James Wilcox, *Sort of Rich* (1989; New York, 1990 edition); see, e.g., 23. The fact that the relationship between a change of locality and a shift in writing practice is not a simple causative one is illustrated by the careers of Ernest Gaines and Alice Walker—as we shall see in the next section. Although Gaines moved to northern California while still quite young, the trope of return is still a crucial, determining factor in his work. That trope is also important to the first few novels of Alice Walker, although the later work does begin to register in other ways, more reminiscent of the strategy of the exiles and expatriates, her earlier move to the West Coast. On yearning as a characteristic response to the condition of postmodernity, see, bell hooks, *Yearning: Race, Gender, and Cultural Politics* (Boston, Mass., 1991).

action, these "postsouthern" people live not so much in the stream of history as on its margins from where, like compulsive voyeurs, they watch everything that passes with a glazed sense of uninvolvement. Their problem, really, is not like that of their predecessors, an excess of narrative (an excess flowing from the conviction that the past is never dead), but rather its absence, the suspicion that no stories or ceremonies apply, that there are no more tales worth telling or parts worth playing. So they spend their time spying on life, playing the games of their culture, entering its movie, when they are required to, and waiting for something to happen—in the belief that, as Frank Bascombe puts it in *The Sportswriter,* "in these literal and anonymous cities of the nation . . . even your New Jerseys, something hopeful and unexpected can take place." For them, the great narratives have been written out; what remains is a life of petty compromises and little victories, unease punctuated by the chance of an occasional, fleeting emotional connection. "I was born into an ordinary modern existence in 1945," Bascombe tells us, "an only child to decent parents of no irregular point of view, no particular sense of their *place* in history's continuum, just two people afloat on the world and expectant like most others in time, without a daunting conviction about their own consequence."[21] That "daunting conviction" does not possess him either. "I suppose our life was a generic one," he remarks casually of his failed marriage, "X was a housewife and had babies, read books, played golf and had friends, while I wrote about sports and went here and there collecting my stories, coming home to write them up, mooning around the house for days in old clothes, taking the train to New York and back now and then."[22] This takes the measure of what Bascombe sees as his own deep inconsequence. So does the flat, lambent style Ford uses to record the passage of his works and days. Like Walker Percy's characters—and, in particular, his protagonists—Bascombe oscillates between a tacit acceptance of the banality of contemporary life, and the absurdly delimited sense of identity it prescribes, and what is almost

---

21. Richard Ford, *The Sportswriter* (London, 1986), 30. See also 9, 13; Walker Percy, *The Second Coming* (1980; London, 1981 edition), 146. Also Madison Smartt Bell, *Straight Cut* (1986; London, 1987 edition): see, e.g., 9–10.

22. Ford, *Sportswriter,* 15. Compare, e.g., Binx Bolling's dryly ironic recording of his own inconsequentiality in Walker Percy's *The Moviegoer* (1961; London, 1966 edition): "My wallet is full of identity cards, library cards, credit cards. It is a pleasure to carry out the duties of a citizen and to receive in return . . . a neat styrene card with one's name on it certifying, so to speak, one's right to exist" (11).

a dream state—in which he does not seem to be attached to anything or anyone—and least of all to himself.

"Whose history can ever reveal very much?" Bascombe dryly inquires in *The Sportswriter*. "I know I'm always heartsick in novels . . . when the novelist makes his clanking, obligatory trip into the Davy Jones locker of the past." "Most pasts," he adds, "let's face it, aren't very dramatic subjects"; "my own I think of as a postcard with changing scenes on one side but no particular or memorable messages on the back." For Bascombe the past is neither in the present nor explains it; so what he has to narrate dwells in the now, and casually circumvents narrative shape or the sense of an ending. "Life will always be without a natural, convincing closure," he points out. "Except one." That "one" form of closure, dictated by biology, is something that he is closer to, certainly, in *Independence Day* (1995), the novel that traces his metamorphosis from sportswriter into estate agent. He is still no closer, however, to an ending that makes sense for him of either his life or himself, or to anything that makes him believe that he is not ground in the mill of the conventional. "To anyone reasonable," Bascombe admits in *Independence Day,* "my life will seem more or less normal-under-the-microscope, full of contingencies and incongruities none of us escapes and which do little harm in an existence that otherwise goes unnoticed."[23] If anything, Bascombe's sense of his own contingency is aggravated, in the second book devoted to him, by the simple passing of time, an accumulation of insignificance. It is, he observes, "a natural part of the aging process" to "find yourself with less to do and more opportunities to eat your guts out regretting everything you *have* done"; and he seems more convinced now than ever before that all the great stories, Southern or otherwise, have been told. What we dread, Bascombe suggests at one point in Ford's 1995 novel, is "the cold, unwelcome, built-in-America realization that we're just like the other schmo, wishing his wishes, lusting his lusts, quaking over his idiot frights and fantasies, all of us popped out from the same unchinkable mold."[24] That dread seems to have been realized here. The sense of

23. Richard Ford, *Independence Day* (1995; New York, 1996 edition), 7. See also *Sportswriter*, 30, 372.

24. Ford, *Independence Day,* 57. See also 54. Compare Binx Bolling's account of "everydayness" in *Moviegoer*, 17, or the total, blank immersion in the present that characterizes other narrators in postmodernist fiction (e.g., Maria Wyeth in Joan Didion, *Play It as It Lays* [New York, 1970]).

being "tucked even more deeply," as Bascombe puts it, "more anony-mously, into the weave of culture" is one of the narrative premises of *Independence Day,* prescribing its tone, dictating its rhythms. And the culture into which Frank Bascombe is tucked is itself anonymous. It could be anywhere; it might be in the suburbs to the south or north of the Mason and Dixon line; it is, above all, not just ordinary but blank.

Not all expatriates and exiles have literally transplanted themselves, though; nor have all of them turned from the South to quite such a termi-nal vision of the ordinary. On the contrary, one remarkable feature of some recent work by writers from the region is a sense of the American West as a place of redemption: in imagination, and sometimes in fact, they have traveled westward and found there the chance of shaking off the mundane and the moribund. This is most obvious in the work of Rick Bass, who now lives on a remote ranch in northern Montana. In *Platte River* (1994), for example, a collection of three stories, Bass de-scribes people who live apart from the ordinary; in a landscape that re-calls earlier American pastoral from Thoreau to Hemingway, they strenuously pursue regeneration through an active encounter with the elements. Harley, the central figure in the title story, lives in an aban-doned hunting lodge that is "separate from the real world." Going fishing with friends, "he feels like a sea creature returning to the ocean, some evolutionary throwback trying to reverse history." Pursuing the woman who lives with him, called Shaw, through the woods—after a falling-out that is, characteristically, almost wordless—he is "like a hound after a fox, like a wolf chasing a deer." And, when he catches her, "he doesn't try to calm her with words," we learn, "with promises or apologies, or ask for forgiveness." Instead, he relies on touch, gesture, ritual. Picking her up, he carries her back "to what used to be their cabin—theirs, not simply hers nor his—and to what Harley hopes will be theirs once again";[25] laying her down in front of the fireplace, he then wraps her tenderly in a blanket.

What gives an edge to the lyricism of moments like these in Bass's stories is, not just the author's sharp sense of sexual politics (Shaw, it emerges, is not calmed at all; she only hates Harley the more "for trying to control her"), but also his understanding of the cultural forms that

25. Rick Bass, *Platte River* (New York, 1994), 103. See also 100, 125. I am grateful to Robert H. Brinkmeyer Jr. for first drawing my attention to this tendency among some contemporary writers from the South to find imaginative sustenance in the West.

threaten to swamp this world elsewhere. Harley himself is an aging foot-ball star, Shaw used to be a model; both are wounded creatures, seeking relief in the wilderness from their wounds and from the society that in-flicted them. Still, despite such encroachment, that wilderness remains more or less intact in Bass's work as a source of being and knowing. The epigraph to "Platte River" is from Thoreau, and it alerts us to this. "The man must not drink of the running streams, the living waters," it reads, "who is not prepared to have all nature reborn in him—to suckle mon-sters." The violence ("a wolf chasing a deer"), it turns out, the delibera-tion or effort of will ("trying to reverse history"), is part of the recuperative process, just as vital to the project of healing as in earlier American versions of the pastoral. An interesting comparison could be made here with another Southern disciple of Thoreau, who has chosen to stay, farm, and write in his native Kentucky, Wendell Berry. Berry gives a different twist to the idea of redemption through nature—and one that is more traditionally Southern; the mere presence of the terms *cultural* and *agricultural* in the title of one of his books, *The Gift of Good Land: Further Essays Cultural and Agricultural* (1981), helps measure the dif-ference. Doing what the Nashville Agrarians preached rather than what, on the whole, they practiced, Berry has stayed in the region, and stayed close to what he has called "the great study of stewardship"—a study that has required sustained cultivation of the land. Bass, on the other hand, is happier thinking in terms of regeneration beyond the pale, out-side and even in opposition to the terms dictated by *any* culture—which may well be one reason why he has moved westward. The determining act for him is not cultivation of the land but simply being there on it, going gently over its surfaces—by being continuous with it, rather than its guardian or steward. As Harley's friend says of him with awe and affection—trying to sum him up "as if . . . Harley were only a poem"— *"He just walks in the woods."*[26] For Bass, as for some of his characters, it is evidently still possible to front only the essential facts of life, to sim-plify and so be reborn—by becoming the nomad rather than the cultiva-tor, wandering in the wilder parts of the American continent, if not in the South.

Another, no less redemptive version of experience in the West is to be found in two remarkable novels by writers who have remained stead-

26. Ibid., 138. See also 98, 103; Wendell Berry, *The Gift of Good Land: Further Essays Cultural and Agricultural* (San Francisco, 1981), 281.

fastly in the South—working, in fact, at Southern universities—*Heading West* (1981) by Doris Betts and *Painted Desert* (1995) by Frederick Barthelme. Betts had produced six works of fiction before *Heading West.* Before *Painted Desert,* Barthelme had established a reputation as a chronicler of what one of his characters calls the "domestic-unit-of-the-eighties" in books like *Second Marriage* (1984), *Two Against One* (1988), and *Natural Selection* (1990).[27] With their books of the West, however, both moved into an altered imaginative as well as geographical terrain, using the trope of the journey to open up the possibility of a new life. In *Heading West,* the journey begins as an involuntary one. The central character, Nancy Finch, a woman stuck in the small town Southern roles of "Big Sister, Elder Daughter," local librarian and member of the Presbyterian choir, is seized by a gunman who calls himself Dwight Anderson (which is not, she learns eventually, his real name), and carried off in a car from North Carolina westward. Fear is accompanied by a strange sense of exhilaration, escape from a life that "Nancy decided . . . could be summarized in two words: Unsatisfactory Conditions." "I've never been anywhere," Nancy reflects. Now, despite the violence of her abduction and the strength of her resistance to it, she does not reveal who she is to two suspicious patrolmen who stop the car to interrogate its occupants. "She had made the trip hers," she tells herself, as they then cross a bridge over the Mississippi; "she . . . would have her chance to see muted reds and blending golds in the layered cliffs." Joined by a third traveler, a disgraced judge who comes under the sway of Dwight, they move on into New Mexico and beyond. "I'm seeing the west at last," Nancy thinks with growing excitement. The judge, however, is much less enthusiastic: " 'west' did not mean romantic frontier" to him, we are told, "but hinted at perishing, pointed to sunsets and evening stars. Thanatopsis."[28] His recently dead wife, he suspects, "had gone alone to the Ultimate West." In effect, Betts aligns the judge with a more traditionally Southern notion of the West—to be found in the work of writers of the Southern renaissance like John Peale Bishop, Andrew Nelson Lytle, and Robert Penn Warren and, before them, the poems and stories of

27. Frederick Barthelme, *Second Marriage* (1984; New York, 1995 edition), 47. Also *Two Against One* (1988; New York, 1989 edition); *Natural Selection* (1990; New York, 1991 edition).

28. Doris Betts, *Heading West* (1981; New York, 1995 edition), 109. See also 22, 30, 35, 73.

Edgar Allan Poe—which identifies the frontier experience with anarchy, chaos, and waste. "The long man strode apart," writes Bishop in his poem, "Experience in the West,"

> In green no soul was found,
> In that green savage clime
> Such ignorance of time.[29]

For Bishop, as for the judge, the Western "wilderness oblivion" offers man only "a will / To his own destruction." For Poe and Warren, in turn, journeying westward is inevitably accompanied by intimations of escape, sleep, and death. The West in Poe's poem "Eldorado," for instance, lies beyond "the Valley of the Shadow"; while Jack Burden, the protagonist and narrator of Warren's *All the King's Men,* goes West to escape some unpleasant facts about the woman he loves—and there, "at the end of History, the Last Man on that Last Coast," simply lets go, allowing himself to "drown" (as he puts it) in sleep and dream. For Nancy Finch, however, as for Rick Bass's characters, experience in the West could not be more different. Or, rather, the terms of judgment are simply reversed; the death of the old self announces the birth of the new, the end of history becomes something devoutly to be wished.

The emotional climax to Nancy Finch's Western experience comes in the Grand Canyon. Having escaped from Dwight, Nancy treks alone through the canyon, going "steadily down through the record of the earth's biography" and discovering places where " 'old' and 'deep' fade . . . into 'ancient' and 'endless.' " Her descent "through eras and strata . . . to the spot where perhaps the world's first virus had not yet twitched"

29. John Peale Bishop, "Green Centuries," poem II in "Experience in the West," in *Selected Poems* (New York, 1963), 68, lines 3–5. See also "The Burning Wheel," poem III, 67, line 24; "Loss in the West," poem III, 69, lines 20–21; Edgar Allan Poe, "Eldorado," line 21, in *Complete Poems* (London, 1993), 87; Robert Penn Warren, *All the King's Men* (1946; New York, 1959 edition), 311. See also Poe's unfinished story "The Journal of Julius Rodman," in *The Complete Works of Edgar Allan Poe* edited by James A. Harrison (1902; New York, 1965 edition), vol. IV, and Warren's account of the journey west taken by Jeremiah Beaumont, in *World Enough and Time* (New York, 1950)—in search of an illusory "innocence," only to find what one critic has called "a kind of upside-down Eden . . . a frightening parody of the related notions of the noble savage, human perfectibility, and the Golden Age" (Robert Berner, "The Required Past: *World Enough and Time*," in *Robert Penn Warren: A Collection of Critical Essays* edited by Richard Gray [Englewood Cliffs, N.J., 1980], 70). For Andrew Nelson Lytle's response to the frontier, see chapter 3 of this book.

completes a transformation that began when she was snatched up out of the ordinary and everyday. "Out West," Nancy observes later, she had "looked far back at rumors of spring and winter that had left signatures on rock every million years"—and "none of those seasons had been tamed to human need; none of those cycles was the size to domesticate." Some of what she has experienced she is able to communicate to a man whom she has met in Arizona and now resolves to marry, Hunt Thatcher, a horse breeder who also raises wolves as a hobby. "I'm talking about being free of choices," she tells Hunt. After a flood once, she recollects, a few of the people who went missing for a while "just walked away. They just broke off one life and walked away into a new one." A similar release, she explains, has been triggered in her; she too has found a new life by walking away and down into the Grand Canyon. Returning to North Carolina briefly to visit her family, Nancy measures the change in her as a failure in language. "Oh, I'll never explain!" she declares hopelessly, after trying to tell her mother what has happened to her; the Western experience does not translate into any Southern terms that she knows. Only her brother begins to understand, and shows he does by giving her as a parting gift—before she goes back to Arizona—a book called *Canyons of Colorado* by a J. W. Powell. "The book sprang open to a much-thumbed chapter some earlier owner had marked and underlined," we learn, as Nancy takes it from her brother. " 'We are now ready to start on our way down the Great Unknown' was the line from Powell's journey that had first been underscored."[30] That catches the resonance of Nancy's own wayward exploration: like Powell, she has gone from the known to the unknown, from closure to freedom—or, in her own terms, from South to West—and witnessed, as a result, the death of her old, imprisoned self. "I've been sensible all my life," Nancy had said to herself when she first surrendered to the journey westward and downward. Now, thanks to that surrender, she has found something more real, more elemental in herself and her surroundings—a more authentic base on which to build the remains of her days.

The vision of Western experience that unrolls in *Heading West* owes more to Western myth than it does to any Southern one. "There's rural life, and it's human, human," Nancy tries to explain to her mother. "And then there's countryside that's inhuman. I may go live there." The liberatory effects of the journey to and into the Grand Canyon, the superiority

30. Betts, *Heading West*, 350. See also 193, 198–99, 297, 359.

of the "inhuman" to the "human" and of archaeology to history, the elemental authenticity of rocks and rivers: all this recalls writers like, say, Robinson Jeffers or Gary Snyder more than it does most Southern fictionalists of country life—farm or plantation. To this extent, Betts is an imaginative expatriate, turning her book into a border territory, a point of crossing between different cultural perceptions. And so is Barthelme in *Painted Desert*—a novel that, if anything, paints an even more emancipatory picture of life in the West. *Painted Desert* begins in a media-cool world, an anywhere in America which just happens to be the South. "We started carrying a TV in the car because Jen liked tiny TVs," are the very first words of the novel, ". . . liked the idea of never being out of touch with things, liked being able to swoop in on stuff electronically from beach, mall, restaurant, movie theater." "I love a crisis on TV," the narrator Del adds, before launching into an excited account of the day police chased O. J. Simpson along the Los Angeles freeways. And when there is no crisis to entertain him, Del is a channel surfer, most of whose recollected experience involves what he glimpses as he hits the button on his remote control. His girlfriend Jen, at times when she is not watching TV, is, for her part, a cybermuckraker, constantly plugged into the Internet—and obsessed, in particular, with the Rodney King case and the riots in Los Angeles that followed the acquittal of those policemen who beat King up. Medium is message here. The pacy, repetitive prose, the accumulation of meaningless detail, the devotion to surface and the instant: all these, in *Painted Desert,* are signs of a culture where identity is coextensive with image—or, as Del puts it, where "we all want to be on TV." Aggravated by the spectacle, though, Jen insists "we've got to do something," to act rather than watch. They need, she says, to step out of virtual reality for a while and head for "ground zero," Los Angeles. What precisely they are going to do there remains unclear to them, beyond a vague sense that they ought to enact vigilante justice on wrongdoers. And they are haunted by the suspicion that, as Del says, "we're probably not going to make much difference in the world." "I'm not sure anybody makes much difference," he adds hopelessly; "even the people who seem to be making a difference in the world aren't really making a difference."[31] He then presses his point home inadvertently, by choosing as his examples of "people who seem to be making a difference" a movie

31. Frederick Barthelme, *Painted Desert* (1995; New York, 1997 edition), 77. See also 1–2, 42, 47, 65; Betts, *Heading West,* 259–60.

actor and a director, Kevin Costner and Francis Ford Coppola. At this stage, it seems, he is unable to think, let alone live, outside the parameters of a media-made world.

On the road, the sense of being trapped in this world hardly abates. Every interstate they drive along is just "an odd bit of space, a narrow slot fenced by high trees." "It was a strange kind of moving city out there," Del observes, "sometimes people would wave or laugh or salute with a Coke from McDonald's or Burger King." "Everyone looked at everyone else," he adds, "nonchalantly as cars passed one another"; people are not living, still, just looking. Unable to find freedom on the road, Del and Jen also fail to find meaning in the past. They visit Dealey Plaza in Dallas, Texas, where President Kennedy was killed. But all Del can say, mournfully, is "it didn't look like history to me." "I'm supposed to feel the weight of history here," Jen comments to Del. "Great events on which our future turned." "It's not exactly working for me," she confesses. "How about you?" "Nope," Del replies. "You have to believe in history . . . I don't, so it doesn't do much for me."[32] For both of them, the past has become just another commodity, a media-generated image. "Thirty years later the public version has *become* the truth, the history," Jen reflects some time after they have left Dealey Plaza. "Nobody remembers or cares what it was actually like." The past is no longer a resource here; ambushed in the "public-consumption version" of what went on once, Jen and Del feel closer to the familiar imagery glimpsed on the TV screen than they do to the inert mass of buildings they stare at in Dallas. For them, virtual reality has become the touchstone of the real; what is more, as knowing consumers, they know this—but that knowledge, far from being a source of power, is only another sign of their impotence.

Things change for both characters, though, as they did for Nancy Finch, when they travel further west to the Grand Canyon. "The canyon was nice to look at," Del records in a suddenly downbeat way. "Reduced a little by its flamboyant press, but more lovely than almost anything we see in ordinary life. It was big and colorful, with a graceful apple-green river winding through its floors."[33] Unlike Nancy, Del and Jen do not descend into the canyon. Still, they encounter there, and elsewhere in the Far West, what Del now accepts as "the truth." "Once you're here," Jen tells him, "all the easy ways you use to understand the world no longer

32. Ibid., 97. See also 80, 81, 95, 204.
33. Ibid., 232. See also 224, 226.

work; and you're left with a mountain or a sea or a river or a canyon." As the two of them come closer to true experience in the West, the prose becomes stripped, leaner: like Ernest Hemingway, say, or William Carlos Williams, Barthelme is evidently trying to make words cleave to natural objects—to measure the miracle of things by calling them by their right names. Jen and Del decide now not to continue their journey to Los Angeles. Jen explains why, although Del knows why already. "The reason," she says, "is that putting one foot in the Painted Desert is more satisfying, more rich and human and decent, than all the vengeance in the world." Their half-formed dreams of avenging some of the crimes they have seen on TV dissolve before the spectacle of the real; they are still looking, but now they are looking at what Jen calls "first order experience" rather than the mediated kind. The closing moments of *Painted Desert* register the sense of liberation, escape up and out of the prison house of culture, that Nancy Finch felt in her own way after *her* journey from South to West. "For a minute all I could think of was what we must look like from the sky," Del confides, "the two splintered headlights shooting out into nothing, the two taillights glowing red tracers behind us, the big flat space everywhere and all this dust swelling around us like a land-speed-record attempt. We rocketed across the desert sand."[34] Like so many American heroes before them, they have lit out ahead of the rest; heading westward, they have floated free of historical contingency and media imagery, to realize a direct contact with the world. "All around us," that eminent New Englander Ralph Waldo Emerson once declared, "what powers are wrapped under the coarse mattings of custom." "Make the aged eye sun-clear," Emerson pleaded elsewhere, in a poem. It is difficult to see how, by this stage, Del or Jen—or, for that matter, Frederick Barthelme—could disagree with Emerson's plea for what he once described as "the power to fix the momentary eminency of an object." After all, what *Painted Desert* pleads for is much the same: the power to look at the unmediated real—to gaze at things, not in terms of their "public-consumption version," but with what Del comes to call "natural wonder."

Nothing could be further from all this than the world of Cormac McCarthy. One of the finest of the expatriates and exiles, McCarthy has marked all of his work with an indelible sense, not so much of evil (although that

---

34. Ibid., 243. See also Ralph Waldo Emerson, *Complete Works* (Boston and New York, 1903), vol. IX, 181, and vol. III, 285.

is certainly there) as of homelessness. One critic has referred to "that elemental and highly ambiguous activity of human 'settlement' which is essentially the subject of all McCarthy's fiction." Another, perhaps more accurately, has called McCarthy's novels a series of meditations on the unhomelike nature of our environment, the "scary disconnection of the human from the not-human that both Freud and Heidegger called the *unheimlich*." Whether McCarthy can, in any event, be described as a Southern writer has vexed these and many other commentators. Some insist on the presence in his work of traditionally regionalist themes, such as the calamitous breakdown of "inherited embodiments of value— religion, community relationships, agrarian connections with the earth." Others have made the wry suggestion that McCarthy is Southern if only because he participates "in the South's second-oldest intellectual tradition, that of anti-pastoral."[35] Still others have argued that, on the contrary, quite different allegiances are at work in McCarthy's writing: the ancient traditions of Gnostic thought or moral parable, the narratives of Xenophon of Ephesus, major figures of the American Renaissance (notably, Herman Melville), or writers of the American West. These are not all mutually exclusive, of course; and perhaps the most useful way of looking at McCarthy's developing career is precisely in terms of their confluence—and in the context of his own preoccupation with homelessness, orphanhood, and wandering. McCarthy is a "literary hybrid," one critic has suggested. Reading any of his books is "like strolling through a museum of English prose styles," while the most recent novels appear to have been written "by the illegitimate offspring of Zane Grey and Flannery O'Connor."[36]

---

35. John M. Grammer, "A Thing Against Which Time Will Not Prevail: Pastoral and History in Cormac McCarthy's South," in *Perspectives on Cormac McCarthy* edited by Edwin T. Arnold and Dianne C. Luce (Jackson, Miss., 1993), 29. See also Thomas D. Young Jr., "The Imprisonment of Sensibility: *Suttree*," ibid., 95; Vereen Bell, *The Achievement of Cormac McCarthy* (Baton Rouge, La., 1988), 33; Paul Ragan, "Values and Structure in *The Orchard Keeper*," in *Perspectives on McCarthy* edited by Arnold and Luce, 15. For the possible literary allegiances mentioned here, see, respectively, Leo Daugherty, "Gravers False and True: *Blood Meridian* and Gnostic Tragedy," in *Perspectives on McCarthy* edited by Arnold and Luce, 157–72; Margaret Ann Doody, "Where a Man Can Be a Man," *London Review of Books*, XXV (1993), 20–22; Steven Shaviro, " 'The Very Life of Darkness': A Reading of *Blood Meridian*," in *Perspectives on McCarthy* edited by Arnold and Luce, 143–56; Terri Witok, "Reeds and Hides: Cormac McCarthy's Domestic Space," *Southern Review*, XXX (1994), 136–42.

36. Tom Pilkington, "Fate and Free Will on the American Frontier: Cormac McCarthy's Western Fiction," *Western American Fiction*, XXVII (1993), 312, 318.

Strongly put, this nevertheless contains a kernel of truth. McCarthy *is* a "hybrid." And, if he is so, it is surely because he senses, more acutely than most of his contemporaries, the mixed, plural medium that all of us inhabit now, and perhaps always have: the border territory that is our place of being in the world, made only the more starkly remarkable to us all (including Southerners) by the collapse of those cultural barriers that used to give us shelter—the illusion of belonging to one stable community and set of traditions. The landscape of all McCarthy's novels is a liminal, constantly changing one, on which different human cultures encounter one another's otherness, and appropriate it through language. His characters cross and recross that landscape, dissolving and reconfiguring what might have once seemed a series of static oppositions: civilized and savage, past and present, South and West, town and wilderness and, more recently, the United States and Mexico. What is at stake here is at once metaphysical—or, more precisely, an argument against metaphysics—and social. McCarthy is intent on melting down the structures of perception, to reveal to us what one of his characters calls "a world . . . without measure or bound."[37] He is also clearly fired into imaginative life by his own experience and knowledge of the fluid social geography of the contemporary: his recognition that, as another character of his comments, "lots of people on the road these days." Homelessness is the source as well as the subject of McCarthy's work, because at the heart of it lies an uncanny understanding of the "dark parody of progress" (as one novel calls it) that *is* our lives, now more than ever: the restless wandering, the displacements cultural and topographical, that turn every day into a crossing of borders.

The literal geography of McCarthy's first four novels is, though, scrupulously confined: all four are set within a one-hundred-mile radius of Maryville, Tennessee. His first book, *The Orchard Keeper* (1965), maps that geography. It also sets in motion many of McCarthy's characteristic preoccupations, formal and thematic. "By Jamesian standards," as one critic has observed, "*The Orchard Keeper* is a shambles." The narrative shifts, without evident reason, between different points of view and perspectives. The story lines are linked only tenuously to one another. There are three major characters—a fatherless boy John Wesley Rattner, Marion Sylder who has killed John's father, and John's "Uncle Ather," Ar-

---

37. Cormac McCarthy, *Blood Meridian* (1985; London, 1990 edition), 138. See also *Outer Dark* (1968; London, 1994 edition), 240, 241.

thur Ownby—but they form a ghost community rather than an actual one, since they never meet as a group. Plots stir occasionally, only to die away: John Rattner's mother, for instance, tells him to avenge his father's death ("Goin to find the man that took away your daddy. . . . You *swear* it, boy.") but, after being sworn to vengeance, the boy soon loses interest. There are even long, densely descriptive passages where plot and identifiable point of view are put in abeyance; the narrative comes to a halt, as it were, and the prose takes on a fluid life of its own—moving frequently, and without warning, from the comic and laconic to the gravely metaphorical. What *The Orchard Keeper* resists, in short, is control, closure, assimilation. "Cats is smart," observes Arthur Ownby, ". . . they won't learn nothin. They too smart;" and it is this kind of smartness the book attempts to instill, the knowledge that to know properly is to know "nothin." Wandering is both the narrative rhythm and the narrative subject here. "They are gone now," *The Orchard Keeper* concludes, bidding farewell to all of its characters: "Fled, banished in death or exile, lost, undone. Over the land sun and wind still move to burn and sway the trees, the grasses. No avatar, no scion, no vestige of that people remains. On the lips of the strange race that now dwells there their names are myth, legend, dust."[38] The curious archaisms and inversions of phrase here compel our attention by slowing us down. The repetitions of word and phrase imitate that pattern of gathering replication which is perhaps the only guiding principle of the narrative as a whole. The end of the fictional journey is, as it is in all McCarthy's novels, a dead end: we are brought up, abruptly, to that one word, "dust." Like the story that precedes it, this is a valediction forbidding mourning because, as a character in one of McCarthy's other books puts it, "nothing ever stops moving." "They are gone now" but another, equally "strange race" continues their restless straying through a world that resists any attempt to domesticate or know it—to make a home in it, or give it a name.

Wandering, straying is, if anything, even more the compelling rhythm of McCarthy's next two books, *Outer Dark* (1968) and *Child of God* (1973). In *Outer Dark,* that wandering is utterly literal. The two central

38. Cormac McCarthy, *The Orchard Keeper* (1965; London, 1994 edition), 246. See also 66–67, 227; *Suttree* (1979; London, 1994 edition), 461; Bell, *Achievement of McCarthy*, 11. Another critic has suggested that McCarthy's erratic plot lines chart "the disconnectedness of actual experience" (Mark Royden Winchell, "Inner Dark: or, The Place of Cormac McCarthy," *Southern Review*, XXVI [1990], 296).

characters, Culla Holme and his sister Rinthy, stray through a dreamlike landscape of woods, swamps, and gorges as if they were in a maze: Rinthy, in search of the child Culla has fathered on her, and then taken from her at birth. The Faulknerian echoes are obvious. Rinthy, for example, recalls Lena Grove in *Light in August*. More remarkable, however, is how McCarthy subdues the Faulknerian elements in his story to the characteristic narrative pressures, his obsession with living as departure and loss. So, at the close of the novel, Culla meets a blind man on the road, "ragged and serene," who comments on their common lot. "People goin up and down in the world like dogs," he observes, "as if they wasn't a home nowheres." To Culla's proffered sympathy—"I believe you'd like to see your way"—he responds with scorn. "What needs a man to see his way," he replies, "when he's sent there anyhow?" The road is there, the journey "from nowhere, nowhere bound" is inevitable, whether it is seen or not. Culla then wanders on until "the road brought him to a swamp. And that was all." "He wondered," we are told, "why a road should come to such a place." Going back the way he came, he encounters the blind man again. And wonders again. "He wondered," we are now told, "where the blind man was going and did he know the road ended. Someone should tell a blind man before setting him out that way."[39] The road, like every other signifier in McCarthy's novels, leads nowhere, into the metaphorical "nothin" of the swamp. And then it leads back again, compelling a potentially endless cycle of crossings and circlings—or, as a later book puts it, "inversions without end upon other men's journeys." Nobody can see the way. As another blind man in another of McCarthy's stories has it: "Origins and destinations become but rumors. To move is to abut against the world." To this extent, we are all not only homeless, but sightless.

And fatherless—without a father in heaven, or anywhere else, to guide us: killed in *The Orchard Keeper,* simply absent in *Outer Dark* (if we discount, that is, Culla's active betrayal of his own fatherhood), the father kills himself in *Child of God,* leaving the central character, Lester Ballard, utterly without family. His mother gone, his father dead, the

---

39. McCarthy, *Outer Dark,* 242. See also 233, 239–41; *Blood Meridian,* 121; *The Crossing* (London, 1994), 291. For a more positive view of the narrative burden of *Outer Dark,* see Edwin T. Arnold, "Naming, Knowing and Nothingness: McCarthy's Moral Parables," in *Perspectives on McCarthy* edited by Arnold and Luce, 43–67, where Arnold refers to "McCarthy's highly moralistic world" (52).

Ballard house and farm taken from him and put up for auction, Lester has to make his own way in the world. That way is typically wayward. Lester is introduced to us as "small, unclean, unshaven . . . with a constrained truculence. Saxon and Celtic blood. A child of God much like yourself perhaps." And the last phrase, connecting character to reader, resonates with irony, since in the course of the action Lester becomes a voyeur, a murderer, and a necrophiliac. There is, as usual, a high degree of narrative "wandering"—we are nearly halfway through *Child of God* before its main preoccupation, Lester's necrophilia, is properly under way—but what we descend into eventually here is a search for home and family gone horribly wrong. Moving to levels of existence that are ever more elemental, Lester retreats in the end into a cave with a cathedral-like ceiling where he places the bodies of his victims—as the narrator puts it—"on stone ledges in attitudes of repose." There is a peculiarly suggestive mixture of animalistic and theological references in these later pages. "Here" in the cave, we are told, "the walls with their softlooking convolutions, slavered over as they were with wet and bloodred mud, had an organic look to them, like the innards of some great beast. Here in the bowels of the mountain Ballard turned his light on ledges or pallets of stone where dead people lay like saints."[40] The mixture of idioms is reminiscent of Flannery O'Connor. So, for that matter, is the locating of incidents of violence and perversion in settings of unnerving peace, disturbing quietude. What marks McCarthy out from O'Connor, though, is what measures his distance from Faulkner in *Outer Dark*. This is a bleak parody of home and family and church. Responding to his own abandonment, and his dim feeling that living is loss, Lester has set himself up with the most primal of homes and with companions who can never refuse or leave him. That way, he has found shelter against a strange, stormy world and the "fell dark," the inhospitable vastness of space. "Lying awake in . . . the cave," we are told, Lester thinks he hears his father whistling as he used to "on the road coming home" in the evening. It is, however, only "the stream where it ran down through the cavern to empty it may be in unknown seas at the centre of the earth." Lester Ballard is a homeless creature dreaming of home—although, like so many

---

40. Cormac McCarthy, *Child of God* (1973; London, 1989 edition), 135. See also 4, 170, 195, 197. On the emphasis on seeing in this book, see Andrew Bartlett, "From Voyeurism to Archaeology: Cormac McCarthy's *Child of God*," *Southern Literary Journal*, XXIV (1991), 3–15.

of McCarthy's characters, he neither understands nor can articulate his agony. In this, he offers the reader his or her own image seen through a glass darkly; in short, he is much like ourselves, perhaps.

"I was huntin my father," says the protagonist in McCarthy's first screenplay, *The Gardener's Son,* shown on television in 1977. The eponymous central character in McCarthy's fourth novel, *Suttree* (1979), is, however, not so much hunter as hunted. The "huntsman" who pursues Cornelius Suttree—whose "hounds tire not . . . slaverous and wild and their eyes crazed with ravening for souls"—is death: the consciousness, that is, rather than the condition of death, our ultimate reminder that the world is not our home, nowhere is. "How surely are the dead beyond death," Suttree reflects. "Death is what the living carry with them. A state of dread, like some uncanny foretaste of a bitter memory."[41] Written on and off over twenty years, *Suttree* seems at first different from McCarthy's other novels. It has an unusually self-conscious protagonist; it is set in the city (Knoxville, Tennessee); and in it both author and character appear to be seeking affirmation. "A man is all men," Suttree eventually tells himself. "I know all souls are one soul and all souls lonely." And in that idea of a shared loneliness, a community of the dying, he is inclined to find, if not salvation, then at least some solace. But difference, distinction is not really what any of McCarthy's work is about. "All tales are one," someone in a later novel, *The Crossing* (1994), insists. "Rightly heard all tales are one." "Always the teller," he goes on, "must be at pains to devise against his listener's claim . . . that he has heard the tale before"; "all is telling," because "things separate from their stories have no meaning." This is not an argument for simple repetition, of course, but for that rhythm of deepening replication that plays through *all* McCarthy's novels: that coming back, and then coming back again, in a narrative motion that is also an existential one.

So, Knoxville in *Suttree* offers a landscape as dreamlike and amorphous as the Southern countryside of McCarthy's earlier novels, and as disturbing. It is, the narrator points out, *"constructed on no known paradigm, a mongrel architecture reading back through the works of man in*

41. McCarthy, *Suttree,* 153. See also 422, 459, 471; *Crossing,* 143, 155; Dianne C. Luce, "Cormac McCarthy's First Screenplay: 'The Gardener's Son,' " in *Perspectives on McCarthy* edited by Arnold and Luce, 81. One critic, describing McCarthy's style, talks about "a hypnosis of detail" in books like *Suttree* (Anatole Bruyard, "Where All Tales Are Tall," *New York Times,* 20 January 1979, 19).

a brief delineation of the aberrant disordered and mad."[42] Suttree, in turn, haunted by the knowledge that he had an identical twin brother who died at birth, his "dead self," is as much of a lonely, dispossessed wayfarer as Culla Holme, say, or even Lester Ballard. And his own aberrant wayfaring is replicated by a narrative that is as apparently random and directionless, bulging with unassimilated material, as all McCarthy's other work is. The tale *Suttree* tells, tells us that—to quote that figure in *The Crossing* again—"the tale has no abode or place of being except in the telling only . . . and therefore we can never be done with the telling." In this sense, McCarthy's stories are as "homeless" as his characters are because they have no fixed coordinates beyond those supplied by a potentially endless circling. Suttree's journey has no real end, no significant beginning, crisis, or conclusion; neither does the narrative journey that is *Suttree*. For both, existence not only stands before but also supplants essence. Both journeys are predicated, not on notions of linear progress or organicist principles of growth and decay—but, rather, on the idea of an open topography, deep space without boundaries "that no man's mind can compass, that mind being but a fact among others."

That last remark comes, not from *Suttree*, but from *Blood Meridian*. Published in 1985, and subtitled *The Evening Redness in the West, Blood Meridian* is commonly regarded as the book that marks the beginning of McCarthy's departure from the South to the West. That may be so. To claim this, however, is to ignore the fact that McCarthy's fiction has been a plural medium from the beginning, using Southern tropes among many others to explore the fluid contingencies of experience. Quite apart from that, the story begins in Tennessee, even though it soon moves westward; and, as one critic has pointed out, it draws heavily on the history and legends of that state. Whatever the rights and wrongs here, *Blood Meridian* does clearly offer us yet another of McCarthy's orphans, an unnamed "kid" whose "origins," we are told right at the start of the story, "are become as remote as his destiny" once he runs away from home. "It is the death of the father," another major character called Judge Holden tells the kid, "to which the son is entitled and to which he is heir." And, once his father is "dead" to him, the kid takes up a life of nomadic wandering that *is* his earthly inheritance—and, besides, measures whatever boundaries the novel has: *Blood Meridian* does no more than carry the kid through life, from his birth in 1833 to his death in 1878, and then

42. McCarthy, *Suttree*, 3. See also 14; *Crossing*, 143; *Blood Meridian*, 245.

simply ends. The kid, and those he meets, travel through what is called "the silence of the world," revealing the plain truth that their condition is not so much one of exile—since there is nothing for them to be exiled *from*—as of primordial absence, noninhabitance. "We live in a place / That is not our own," Wallace Stevens observed, "and, much more, not ourselves"; and *Blood Meridian* responds to a similar understanding, as it records a journey that seems limitless. "In the affairs of men," the Judge suggests, incidentally explaining the title of the book, "there is no waning and the noon of his expression signals the onset of night." Zenith and horizon change places; a person's "meridian is at once his darkening and the evening of his day";[43] and so, in the measureless distances of this world, there are no true boundaries or definitions—traveling, and telling, never really come to an end.

McCarthy's version of the West is, in effect, the reverse of the one to be found in traditional Western fiction—or the Western books of writers like Barthelme, Bass, and Betts. The endless, unobstructed extension of Western space triggers here, not a sense of freedom, but the feeling of empty immensity. "In the neuter austerity of that terrain," the narrator informs us,

> all phenomena were bequeathed a strange equality and no one thing nor spider nor stone nor blade of grass could put forth a claim to precedence. The very clarity of those articles belied their familiarity, for the eye predicates the whole on some feature or part and here was nothing more luminous than another and nothing more enshadowed and in the optical democracy of such landscapes all preference is made whimsical and a man and a rock become endowed with unguessed kinships.[44]

---

43. McCarthy, *Blood Meridian*, 146–47. See also 3, 4, 14, 313; Wallace Stevens, "Notes Toward a Supreme Fiction: It Must Be Abstract," poem IV, lines 13–14, in *Collected Poems* (London, 1954), 383. Also John Emil Sepech, "What Kind of Indians Was Them?: Some Historical Sources in Cormac McCarthy's *Blood Meridian*," in *Perspectives on McCarthy* edited by Arnold and Luce, 136. One critic has complained that *Blood Meridian* is "repetitious" to the point that the reader is numbed and the violence evokes "boredom" (Winchell, "Inner Dark," 308): but in portraying a world that is a void deprived of "men's judgments" (*Blood Meridian*, 106) that, however perversely, may be part of McCarthy's point. On the connection between McCarthy's South and West, see also the third volume in the border trilogy, *Cities of the Plain* (London, 1998), 185.

44. McCarthy, *Blood Meridian*, 247. See also 116, 121, 245, 252, 345.

This is a landscape that denies definition, distinction. And, beyond the indeterminate, ineluctable flatness of the open plain, there is only more vacancy—more empty space, and the equally overwhelming infinitude of the ocean "out there past men's knowing." The "truth" about this world, Judge Holden suggests, ". . . is that anything is possible," nothing is excluded. "Books lie," the Judge insists, but "stones and trees, the bones of things" do not; they tell us of a material existence without origin or end, "the mystery . . . that there is no mystery." If "books lie," then of course there is a real problem for McCarthy—which he tries to meet via a passionate, stylistic devotion to "optical democracy." More even than in his earlier novels, he pursues an open verbal topography here, in which any kind of language can be accommodated, and a narrative of crossing and recrossing, abrupt encounters and "inversions without end." Everything can be drawn into this open verbal landscape; nothing, no word or moment is seen as "more luminous" than any other. And, to this extent, the book imitates the world where it is set; it is a life of elemental repetition and undifferentiation translated into language.

Which is to say that *Blood Meridian* is another "literary hybrid," a fluid border territory where different voices and human agents can encounter each other without warning. Into this territory, in particular, are drawn two characters who seem to invite comparison, not so much with Southern tropes or Western ones, as with another mythology entirely: an Ishmael-like kid and a judge who tends, very often, to echo Herman Melville's Ahab. "Whatever in creation exists without my knowledge exists without my consent," Judge Holden insists. For him, the bleak, limitless horizons of the desert offer the chance to assert the supremacy of the will. Power precedes and predicates being, since there is nothing else; or, as he puts it, "the man who sets himself the task of singling out the thread of order from the tapestry will by the decision alone have taken charge of the world." Despite what some critics have suggested, the Judge does not speak for McCarthy, any more than Ahab's similarly defiant expression of the will to power, and the pioneering impulse, speaks for Melville in *Moby-Dick*. Nevertheless, in his recognition that "moral law is an invention of mankind" and that "there is no mystery" to life, the Judge is close to the articulable perceptions of the book, just as the kid is closer to its inarticulable rhythms. The kid simply circles and drifts, his experiences folding in on themselves. He is not innocent but simply passive, resigned to his fate, unwilling or unable to act even when he is advised to kill the Judge in order to save himself. Clearly enough, his drifting and

passivity do not enable him to survive, any more than the Judge's assertion of himself enables him to control the terms of his own life. At the
end of *Blood Meridian,* in an ironic inversion of the story Melville tells,
it is its Ishmael, the kid, who dies, killed by its Ahab, a man still laboring
under the delusion that "he will never die" because his will is always the
stronger. Long before that, just after Judge Holden and the kid first meet,
the narrator, as if measuring the distance between the two characters,
talks of "something beyond will or fate" suggested by the "void" of the
open plains and the "vortex" of winds that sweep across them, "some
third and other destiny."[45] Just what that something, that destiny might
be—lying beyond the Judge's willfulness and the kid's surrender to fate-
fulness—is never put into words. But it is, surely, there in the actual experience, the reading of *Blood Meridian,* with its daunting openness, its
fluent and often turbulent exchanges of speech and story. What is presented here is by no means a salvation narrative, still less (as some have
suggested) a portrait of regeneration through violence. It is, though, an
account of how we live, and have to live, as expatriates—in a place that
is stubbornly not our own.

"This is still good country," a character in *All the Pretty Horses*
(1992) tells the protagonist, John Grady Cole. John's reply is terse.
"Yeah. I know it is," he says. "But it aint my country." "Where is your
country?" he is then asked; and his response might have been spoken by
almost any of McCarthy's characters. "I don't know," he confesses, "I
don't know where it is." As McCarthy has shifted to the Southwest and
the Mexican border, and made that rather than Tennessee the site of his
fiction, there has been a tendency to see this as a further shift in allegiances. Even more than *Blood Meridian, All the Pretty Horses* and then
later *The Crossing* are said to mark an imaginative departure as well as
a literal one. Things are still not as simple as that, however. As John's
remarks about "country" make clear, he is another homeless nomad, circling back along tracks he has usually covered before. And the terrain he
passes over—for that matter, the land that all the characters in all three

45. Ibid., 96. See also 198, 199, 250, 252, 335. Two critics whose otherwise very fine
accounts of *Blood Meridian* seem to me to tend toward seeing the Judge as a spokesman
for the author are Bell, *Achievement of McCarthy,* and Shaviro, "Very Life of Darkness."
Shaviro also makes the connection with Melville (151). Michael Herr is quoted on the
dustjacket of the London, 1990, edition of *Blood Meridian* as saying that the book is "a
classic American novel of regeneration through violence."

volumes of McCarthy's "border trilogy" travel over—is as dreamlike, diverse, and yet dauntingly material as ever—as this passage, taken from near the beginning of *All the Pretty Horses,* suggests:

> In the evening he saddled his horse and rode out west from the house. The wind was much abated and it was very cold and the sun sat blood red and elliptic under the reefs of bloodred clouds before him. . . . At the hour he'd always choose when the shadows were long and the ancient road was shaped before him . . . like a dream of the past where the painted ponies of that lost nation came down out of the north. . . . When the wind was in the north you could hear them . . . nation and ghost of a nation passing in a soft chorale across the mineral waste to darkness bearing lost to all history and all their remembrance like a grail the sum of their secular and transitory and violent lives.[46]

Reading this, we are likely to remember the description of McCarthy's prose as a museum of styles. It begins by imitating Hemingway's gift for simple words and connectives, but then modulates into a recollection of the old, ineradicable rhythms of Faulknerian speech. As it does so, it rewrites the Western myth of the lone rider heading out toward the horizon, and conflates that with a sense of the immanence of the past in the present that is perhaps the signature, the distinguishing mark of Southern texts. Haunting almost every word, too, is a characteristic feeling of lostness, displacement: generations of "transitory and violent" wanderers making their way across a bleak, cold territory, their only destination the "blood red" setting of their lives. Elsewhere in the border novels, it is true, a fresh, unfamiliar mix of anglicisms and the hispanic adds a new touch, a further dimension to this particular border area; this landscape of exile and expatriation is still more a site of encounter, a crossroads, than even the ones mapped out in McCarthy's earlier fiction. It reminds us, perhaps, of those postcolonial writers who have transplanted diverse

---

46. Cormac McCarthy, *All the Pretty Horses* (1992; New York, 1993 edition), 5. See also 299. Despite the narrative repetitions, Madison Smartt Bell argued in his review of the novel that *All the Pretty Horses* was "quite conventionally plotted" by comparison with its predecessors ("The Man Who Understood Horses," *New York Times Book Review,* 17 May 1992, section 7, 9). Another critic has argued that it is "a coming of age story" (Gail M. Morrison, "*All the Pretty Horses*: John Grady Cole's Expulsion from Paradise," in *Perspectives on McCarthy* edited by Arnold and Luce, 176). For a similar moment and landscape in *Cities of the Plain* (London, 1998), the third volume of the trilogy, see 233.

styles, including the Faulknerian, in order to pursue their interest in historical intersection, conflict, and exchange—among them, the Colombian novelist Gabriel Garcia Marquez and the Australian writer Tim Winton. To that extent, there is change here, a difference of imaginative register and attention. But there is also continuity. Like one of his own characters, McCarthy is still circling back over old paths, retracing his tracks or taking new routes over old terrain. Nothing illustrates this better than his 1994 novel, and maybe his best so far, which even in its title, *The Crossing*, suggests that for McCarthy at least "all tales are one."

At the heart of *The Crossing* are some of the elemental plots of Western fiction: stories of quest and revenge, pursuit and discovery, men in the company of other men, wolves and Indians, the search for horse thieves and killers. Even more than is the case in *All the Pretty Horses,* though, those plots are refracted and aborted. McCarthy refuses to use the generic conventions of the Western in anything like a conventional way. Typically for him, two stories precede and delay the "main" story. In the first, the brothers Billy and Boyd Parham meet a trespassing Indian, whom they feed for a while and who then vanishes. In the second, after capturing a she-wolf who has crossed the border, Billy returns her to Mexico where she is seized as contraband. Both are stories of wandering, homelessness, journeys that fail to reach a satisfactory destination. "Where are you from?" Billy asks the surly Indian trespasser. "From all over," he responds. "Where you headed?" he then asks and, this time, receives no reply. "Where do you reckon he come from?" Boyd inquires of his older brother later, after the Indian has vanished. "I don't know," Billy admits, ". . . He's just a drifter." Eventually, the "main" plot does get under way, when Billy returns from his time in the company of wolves to find his parents murdered and the house empty—and then, together with Boyd, begins a long, rambling trip evidently in pursuit of the murderers and the horses they have stolen. If there is a revenge plot, however, it is never announced as such. At first, no reason is given for the return journey to Mexico; later, when it is, that reason hinges on the stolen horses. Billy and Boyd drift. So does the plot: it is full of accidental meetings, chance events, the eruption of the arbitrary. On the road south, Billy and Boyd happen to meet a girl who becomes Boyd's lover, soul mate, and "twin." Further along the journey, Boyd is suddenly shot by men who might or might not be the murderers of their parents. Nursed back to health, Boyd then disappears with the girl and is never seen by Billy again. Crossing back to the United States for a while, to discover the country is at war, Billy makes three frustrated attempts to enlist in the army. Crossing over a third time into Mexico in search of his brother, Billy hears songs about a "young man come down from the north" who might be Boyd; discovers Boyd has been killed by those who might also have murdered his father and mother; and exhumes Boyd's remains from a grave that carries "no name." Traveling back, retracing a by now familiar route northward, Billy encounters bandoleros, one of whom knifes and nearly kills his horse "for no good reason"; buries his brother near what used to be the family home; then returns to a life of aboriginal, terminal exile. Horses are recovered, then lost; the killers of Billy's parents may be glimpsed but are never brought to account. There is no retribution here, nor does Billy grow into maturity through his journey: like so many of McCarthy's characters, he is and remains both grounded and unearthly—simply, almost silently, living through his life. "He did not know what the end of his journey would look like," he tells a Mexican woman he happens to meet, "or whether he would know it when he got there."[47] Certainly, he has not "got there" by the conclusion of *The Crossing;* and no doubt he never will, while he remains alive.

Just how much *The Crossing* frustrates our readerly expectations of the Western can be measured by the difference between its opening and closing moments. "When they came south out of Grant County," the novel begins, "Boyd was not much more than a baby and the newly formed county they'd named Hidalgo was itself little older than the child." "The new country was rich and wild," we are told; "the bones of a sister and . . . maternal grandmother" had been left behind, buried "in the country they'd quit." This, it seems, is a land for men promising liberation in the wilderness. What companionship there is here comes from the call of the male and the call of the wild: at night, we learn, Billy "would lie awake . . . and listen to his brother's breathing"—and "on a winter's night in that first year he woke to hear wolves in the hills to the west." But no companionship is truly necessary, it seems, in this place of freedom that also opens up the possibility of limitless power. "You could ride clear to Mexico and not strike a crossfence," the narrator tells us; Billy "carried Boyd before him in the bow of the saddle" as he rode around, "and named to him features of the landscape and birds and animals in both spanish and english." Naming his surroundings, experiencing strange, silent encounters with wolves about which "he never told

47. McCarthy, *Crossing*, 354. See also 10, 14, 323, 375, 389, 397.

anybody," Billy seems for a moment like another American Adam; and his story promises a retelling of the Western myth of masculine crisis and redemption, a violent entry into manhood in the mountains and woods. If anything, style compounds promise here. The stark language, the muscular, rhythmic syntax, the refusal to explain (the narrative begins in media res, and we do not learn at first that "he" is Billy Parham), the figurative references to the vastness of space and creatures who seem like "phantoms in the snow . . . and cold moonlight . . . of another world entire":[48] all this adds to our sense that we are about to embark on a distinct and determinately male ritual that leaves hard facts, and even harder actions, heavy with implication.

The promise is never kept, however. By the end of *The Crossing*, Billy is not so much an Adam as a Job whom God has permanently forsaken. Sitting down on the road, "he took off his hat," we are told, "and placed it on the tarmac before him and he bowed his head and held his face and wept." The world about him is an "alien dark," and "inexplicable darkness" at first. Then, "after a while the east did gray and after a while the right and godmade sun did rise, once again, for all and without distinction."[49] There has been no crossing into the power and presence of manhood here. On the contrary, Billy seems more dispossessed and distracted than ever before; after numerous crossings that have left him with nothing, he appears lost not only to the world but to himself. There is a resonance to the language now, a bleak, overbearing majesty like that of the landscape it describes, which dwarfs the human form. Overpowered, the lone hero promised in the opening pages of the story has shrunk into a lonely child: a pathetic figure but also, we are obliged to feel, a pointless one—which is to say, just one element in a world "without distinction," where man is simply a fact among many others. It is possible to make a connection with the new Western historians here since, like them, Mc-

48. Ibid., 3–5.
49. Ibid., 425–26. For the new Western history, see, e.g., *Trails: Towards a New Western History* edited by Patricia M. Limerick et al. (Lawrence, Kan., 1991); *Under an Open Sky: Rethinking America's Western Past* edited by William Cronon et al. (New York, 1992); *The Oxford History of the American West* edited by Clyde A Milner II et al. (New York, 1996). Another interesting connection is with the recent argument that critics and literary historians need to revise their concept of the frontier, replacing it with the term *border* so as to suggest a more fluid, open, and less conflictual sense of cultural geography: see Annette Kolodny, "Letting Go Our Grand Obsessions: Notes Toward a New Literary History of the American Frontier," *American Literature*, LXIV (1992), 1–18.

Carthy adopts an interrogative approach to the West and the writing of it. He probes those narrative acts that have turned experience in the West into a national rite of initiation; he exposes the myth of the frontier as just that, a myth. But the connection, while useful for tracing the general route McCarthy's imagination follows in his Western fiction is one of coincidence not calculation. It follows from McCarthy's impulse, right from the beginning, to see crossing as confluence not confrontation, to think in terms of a fluid border country rather than the fixed oppositions of the frontier. McCarthy is weaving his own story of the West, first and last, not unraveling old ones.

That story is one of dismay: the series of episodes McCarthy stitches together in *The Crossing* shows frustration and disappointment deflating or dissolving generic Western tropes. The communion with a Native American that has been a defining fragment of Western myth at least since the novels of James Fenimore Cooper—when Natty Bumppo found companionship and counsel about the wilderness from Chingachook—is promised only to be withheld. All Billy sees in the trespassing Indian's eyes is a reflection of his own "miswandered" self, "as if it were some cognate child to him that had been lost who now stood windowed away in another world where the red sun sank eternally." All the Indian wants from him is food and things to sell. To Billy, he remains unnamed as well as unknown; he offers nothing in return for the gifts, not even thanks, and then he is gone—leaving a camp fire that is "cold and bleak," as a kind of token of the cold comfort he has bestowed on the two Parham boys. In turn, the story of Billy and the she-wolf works subtly against the mythic construction of that animal as an emblem of primitive integrity, the incarnation of all the untamed and instinctual energies to be found in the wilderness. Billy may have brief fantasies of a wild, animal plenitude that would not be out of place in, say, the Kevin Costner film *Dances with Wolves* or Robert Bly's meditations on new age masculinity—or, for that matter, in *Platte River* or *Heading West*: as he lies awake listening to their cries, sees them running in the moonlight over the snows, or gazes into the eyes of the she-wolf he rescues from the trap. But, as an old man he meets on his first journey south tells him, "no man knew what the wolf knew." "The wolf is made the way the world is made," the old man warns. "You cannot touch the world."[50] The attempt to

50. McCarthy, *Crossing*, 46. See also 6, 13, 45. In Bass's *Platte River*, we may recall, Harley is compared to "a wolf chasing a deer" (103) when he pursues Shaw. And in Betts's

return the she-wolf to the Mexican mountains is aborted; Billy not only loses it to the local authorities, he is forced to witness its humiliation and mutilation in a series of dogfights, and to shoot it to save it from further pain. And communion, connection with her remains blocked. The violence of the slow, bloody destruction of the she-wolf is bleached of all heroic resonance; Billy's fantasies of wilderness rescue and redemption are projected against a reality where bleak, meaningless assaults on the wild seem to be the norm. He cannot "touch" the wolf, or the world, in any true sense, it remains impervious to him. Unlike the mythic Western hero, in short, Billy cannot take possession of the new land.

Taking up most of the book, Billy's subsequent journeys into Mexico after the death of his parents promise another classic story of the West. But the straight line of vengeance is diverted into the random wanderings and aberrations that characterize all McCarthy's work. And there is no crossing the frontier from childhood into adulthood, only a series of crossings without end in an amorphous no-man's-land—one that seems, not so much new, as inexorably old. True, there are masculine rituals and exchanges toward the beginning of this story, and the previous ones, that appear to outline a way of being in the world. Preparing a wolf trap, for example, Billy and his father Will enjoy the silent solidarity of their craft; and Will, as he concentrates on making the trap just right, looks to his son "like a man bent on fixing himself someway in the world. Bent on trying . . . the space between his being and the world that was."[51] But the sense of making the world "ready-to-hand," to use the Heidegerrian term, is never sustained. Neither Billy nor anyone else in *The Crossing* can find the right tool or ceremony for making a genuinely homemade world, at once a part of nature and a part of their selves. Nor can they find the means to change things. The world Billy inhabits may be a resolutely masculine one; "you're Will Parham's boy," a neighbor observes, and that seems right—the mother seems oddly superfluous, we never even know her name until almost the end of the novel. There is no sense of masculine effort and achievement here, however, no suggestion of getting

---

Heading West, the man from the West whom Nancy Finch eventually plans to marry, the appropriately named Hunt Thatcher, raises wolves as a hobby because, as he puts it, "raising wolves will reconcile you to your own species" (287). Both these books, in short, enthusiastically accept and use the mythic construction of the wolf familiar from more traditional Western narratives—as a sign of human connection to the wild.

51. McCarthy, *Crossing,* 22. See also 65, 141, 176. For Heidegger's idea of a world made "ready-to-hand," see the discussion of Harriette S. Arnow in chapter 5 of this book.

things done through strenuous acts of mind or muscle. By the end, Billy is still just drifting—or, as he admits, merely "passin through"—along a track and tale that appear to be without clear demarcation.

That lack of demarcation is in itself a bold rewriting of familiar Western tropes. In the narrative construction of the West, geography and plot are symbiotically connected. The Western hero, the critic Leo Marx has observed, traditionally follows a route of self-discovery or growth, his journey from town into wilderness powering his development; while the Western story, another critic, Stephen Fender, has pointed out, sets a strong linear narrative against the unstructured landscape—the more putatively empty and wild the land, the more directed the plot. *The Crossing* certainly acknowledges the symbiotic link between land and story, traveling and telling. At one moment, for instance, we are told that Billy's "own journeying began to take upon itself the shape of a tale"; at another, places where a "wretched" track diverges are described as "separate schools of thought." But the link here hinges, as it always does in McCarthy's fiction, on the shape of shapelessness, divergence—the aberrant, literally pointless nature of journeying and storytelling. All the "world wanderers" Billy meets on his travels—Gypsies, Indians, traveling players—live by making trips and telling tales that have no real origin or end. "The world was made new each day," some Gypsies tell Billy (whom they call "un hombre de camino"); it has no significant history, no narrative sequence or logic. "All is telling," "the road has its own reasons"; and, as Billy tells himself once when he is returning from Mexico, "whether a man's life was writ in a book someplace or whether it took its form day by day was one and the same for it had one reality and that was the living of it."[52] Tale, trail, life: there is no linearity here, no purpose or fit, just simple process. All that is required, then, in telling, traveling, living is what Billy sees in the eyes of some Indians he meets: "a state of improvident and hopeless vigilance. Like men committed upon uncertain ice." Inhabiting what is called "that ocular ground in which the country appeared out of nothing and vanished again into nothing," *The Crossing* jettisons directed narrative, since the arbitrary "nothing"

52. Ibid., 380. See also 155, 188, 230, 278, 331, 409, 411. Also Leo Marx, *The Machine in the Garden: Technology and the Pastoral Idea in America* (Oxford, 1964); Stephen Fender, *Plotting the Golden West: American Literature and the Rhetoric of the California Trail* (Berkeley and Los Angeles, 1982). I am indebted to Guy Reynolds for first drawing my attention to this comparison and other significant aspects of *The Crossing*.

of the West, or anywhere, cannot be measured or plotted. Nor can it be mapped: asking for directions one time in Mexico, Billy provokes a debate about maps among idle bystanders. "One needed to know the country itself and not merely the landmarks therein," they conclude; so maps can be useless, even dangerously misleading. "In any event," they add, "graves make no claim outside of their own simple coordinates and no advice as to how to arrive there but only the assurance that arrive we shall."[53] In "a world provisional, contingent, deeply suspect," there is no place for the mirage of clear boundaries and denouements; the only simple, certain coordinates are those that lead us to death. No mapping, or storytelling, can afford to avoid the primal facts of traveling and living—which are drift and loss, the waste, sad times of "outcasts in an alien land."

Inseparable from this absence of plot, narrative construction in the conventional terms of the Western tale, is an absence of that sense of historical enterprise and crisis that usually informs stories of the West. It is surely not accidental, for instance, that *The Crossing* is not set at a conventionally key moment in the history of the American West (such as the late nineteenth century) or Mexico (the early twentieth century), but at a time when that history had turned definitively into a commodity, along with the Dodge cars and hillbilly music that partially populate *this* landscape: which is to say, the 1940s. When crises of the past are recalled, they are uncoiled to us as if wrapped in deep layers of old tales and telling. So, when the girl who becomes Boyd's "twin" tells the story of how the Mexican revolution affected her family, that story is reported to the reader in one immensely long sentence—which seems to seal it off, both syntactically and temporally, from the surrounding narrative. And, when Billy meets a man who has participated directly in the revolution, that man is symbolically sightless. More to the point, his story is told not by him but by his wife, and the nub of what he has to tell, involving the cruel casualties of war, is told at no less than four removes: the wife tells how her husband told her how a girl told him how a gravedigger told her that her father and brothers had all been killed. History as event and crisis exists on the margins here, and not only history in the past but also history in the narrative present. When Billy returns from his second journey to Mexico, he does not know that the United States has entered the Second World War. "You don't know what's happened?" asks an

53. McCarthy, *Crossing*, 185–86. See also 193, 231.

incredulous border guard. "Hell fire, boy. This country's at war."[54] Having learned about the war, that is the end of it for him; he is prevented by a heart murmur from joining in. Either after or apart from defining moments, Billy seems like some characters out of the legends, not of the West, but of the South: one of those many sad young men in the novels of Faulkner, say, who manage to miss out on any war. Like Quentin Compson of *The Sound and the Fury* and *Absalom, Absalom!* or Horace Benbow in *Sanctuary,* he lives in a strange afterward, where history only appears as a vanishing, a trace.

Discussing Mircea Eliade's theory of time, Frank Kermode remarked that, according to Eliade, "myths take place in a quite different order of time—*in illo tempore.*" "Then occurred the events decisive as to the way things are," Kermode goes on, "and the only way to get at *illud tempus* is by ritual re-enactment." It is not difficult to see how, in this way, Southern thinking traditionally leans away from the historical and toward the mythical. *Then,* so the regional story goes, in some mythicized version of the past, occurred the events decisive as to the way things are. And the only way to recover their precious essence is by invocation and imitation: the kinds of repetition and reenactment that so many different Southerners have engaged in over the past few hundred years. What may be more difficult to grasp, though, is how this thinking fits into McCarthy's story of the West. "Doomed enterprises divide lives forever into the then and now,"[55] *The Crossing* tells us just as the second story, Billy's journey in the company of a she-wolf, is about to end. This is a fiction that seizes and pictures things at the point of vanishing; the characters are haunted by a "then" that never was, dreams of truly being in the world, and a "now" that is defined as unbeing—homeless, purposeless, lost. McCarthy's prose is crucial here. The slow-motion, obsessively accretive attentiveness of much of the language slows us down and translates behavior into mannerism. Who else, apart perhaps from Faulkner, would say that workers tending the fields were "like soiled inmates wandered from some ultimate Bedlam to stand at last hacking in slow and mindless rage at the earth itself"? We are witnessing a world become ossified, petrified, as the cowboy and the myth he enshrines are caught at the moment of their disappearance; just as, in earlier, Southern writing, a South that never existed except in terms of some mythic *illud tempus*

54. Ibid., 333.
55. Ibid., 129. See also 235; Frank Kermode, *Continuities* (London, 1968), 333.

was caught at the moment of *its* vanishing, gone with the wind, only to be recollected and reenacted. McCarthy is not subscribing to the heroic myth of the Old West, of course, any more than the finest Southern writers have uncritically embraced the legend of the Old South. He is simply, like them, registering the myth as a trace, a significant absence. For him, in particular, it underwrites that pervasive existential sense of loss that is coextensive with the condition of living. The division between "then and now," in short, is a tool to help him take the measure of the cold, dark world through which Billy journeys; and, to this extent, at least, his is a story of the South craftily secreted in a story of the West.

Mixed with Faulknerian cadences, here in *The Crossing* as in *All the Pretty Horses,* is a biblical resonance that similarly prescribes absence: religion, too, functions only as a memory, a verbal residue. If Billy is Adam, and later Job, then he is so without benefit of God. It is a remarkable fact of the story that most of the churches Billy comes across in his journeys are ruined, the priests former priests; and, when the sun also rises for him at the end, it does so without any intimation of spiritual requital or special reward. This is a book of wandering up and down the earth which, unlike the Old Testament—the language of which it frequently imitates—resists even the possibility of divine intervention. The museum of styles in *The Crossing,* in effect, often serves to remind us of what is missing. Echoes of Hemingway tell us, eventually, that this is *not* a tale of male bonding and liberation. Echoes of the Western remind us that this is *not* about regeneration through violence. Echoes of Faulkner, in another way, underline the fact that a redemptive "then" does *not* course through the veins of "now." And echoes of the Bible toll for a divine presence and purpose that is determinately *not* there either, for the absence of any substantial grounds for belief. They are the verbal equivalents of that episode in the novel when a former priest, searching for evidence of God in the remains of an earthquake, "something in the rubble" as proof of His anger, finds "Nothing. A doll. A dish. A bone"[56]—no trace, that is, except the urgency of his own need. The Spanish that laces the narrative, in turn—usually untranslated and sometimes dominating whole conversations—serves a different but distinctly related purpose. After all, the traditional Western tale domesticates the West; it subdues it to a prototypically Anglo-Saxon and Protestant narrative, in which a civilized elect confirm their election, their role as conquerors of

56. McCarthy, *Crossing,* 142.

the wilderness and tamers of the unregenerate alien. *The Crossing*, on the other hand, does not so much domesticate as defamiliarize. Among other things, it uses a foreign language to announce the West as untranslatable, untamable—in other words, disconcertingly other. There is no divinely favored language here, just as there is no divinely appointed destiny. The familiar and the foreign, the "normal" and the "exotic" are all folded into one another. McCarthy denies a monopoly of naming for a world that fundamentally can have no name, any more than it can be marked off by any other barriers or boundaries—and where the suffering of one man is continuous with that of all others.

"The world has no name": that is said to Billy by the man, Quijida, who tells him that his brother is dead. "It was because the world was lost to us already," Quijida adds, "that we have made those names. The world cannot be lost. We are the ones. And it is because those names and those coordinates are our own naming that they cannot save us. They cannot find for us the way again."[57] This is the pivot on which *The Crossing*, and all McCarthy's novels, turn. Words are one more sign the world is lost to us or, rather, that we are lost to the world. No naming, traveling, telling can "find for us the way again" because we are homeless nomads like Billy; like him, we would have finally to admit, "I don't have any place to go." That is the pathos of McCarthy's work. Its power stems, not just from his recognition of the impulse to name, travel, and tell tales that survives despite that (and to which he gives substantial shape in so many of his characters), but from his own urgent attempts to name the unnameable. If there is sometimes a sense of strain in his prose, it is surely because he knows what he is trying to do is impossible: to translate into words a world that is brutally material and bafflingly mysterious—one that, like the world experienced by his blind men, is abruptly at hand but unseen. And if there is always a sense of other voices, other visions in his books ("Should a novel be quite so reminiscent of other novels as this one is?" one exasperated critic asked of *All the Pretty Horses*), then that, in turn, is because his imaginative geography charts a proliferating chain of borders rather than a single frontier. For him, the condition of confluence, a mix of cultures, springs inevitably from the experience of exile we are all obliged to share. "Men wish to be serious," an old Mexican observes in *The Crossing* "but they do not know how to be so." "They see the acts of their own hands," he explains, "or see that which they name

57. Ibid., 387. See also 46, 341; Doody, "Where a Man Can Be a Man," 20.

and call out to one another but the world is invisible to them." McCarthy cannot, by his own reckoning, bridge that gap between the world and human acts and ceremonies. He can, however, and does make us terribly aware that it is there. He cannot make a gift to us of being in the world, and truly seeing it: but he can, and does, make us feel what it is to be stray and sightless—to live in the absence of what we need fully to be and know.

REVIVALISTS AND RETURNERS

If expatriatism and exile are now part of the verbal currency among writers from the South, then the language of return, possibly accompanied by revival, has always been there. The return may be, and usually is, one in time as well as space: turning back to his Southern home place, the Southerner may well be addressing the old coercions of his heritage as he visits the place where he was born, his family and neighborhood, the people he knew. That returning back is there, for example, in two seminal poems of the Southern renaissance, "Ode to the Confederate Dead" by Allen Tate and "The Ballad of Billie Potts" by Robert Penn Warren. "Turn your eyes to the immoderate past," declares the narrator in Tate's poem, as he struggles to situate a heroic image in place and time, among the graves of the Confederate soldiers to which he has returned. "Turn to the inscrutable infantry rising / Demons out of the earth—they will not last." "The salmon heaves at the fall," observes the storyteller in "The Ballad of Billie Potts,"

> and, wanderer, you
> Heave at the great fall of Time, and, gorgeous, gleam
> In the powerful arc, and anger and outrage like dew,
> In your plunge, fling, and plunge to the thunderous stream:
> Back to the silence, back to the pool, back
> To the high pool, motionless, and the unmurmuring dream.[58]

Responding to "the long compulsion and the circuit hope / Back," Billie Potts, like so many Southern protagonists, returns to the place where "the father waits for the son" and, in doing so, comes to terms with his

---

58. Robert Penn Warren, "The Ballad of Billie Potts," in *Selected Poems: 1923–1975* (New York, 1976), 283. See also 284; *All the King's Men*, 429; Allen Tate, "Ode to the Confederate Dead," in *Poems* (Denver, Colo., 1961), 21, lines 44–46.

own inheritance and humanity. He sees his connection with his place and past by returning to his childhood home, and so achieves, not only reconciliation with his historical and emotional roots but a secular form of redemption—or, as one of Warren's other characters, Jack Burden in *All the King's Men,* memorably puts it, he takes on "knowledge . . . paid for by blood."

Except that, in recent stories by writers from the South, the place of return is not always one where the father waits for the son. More often than not, it is where the mother or mother country waits for the daughter. The return of the son is still there, of course, in some of these books: in the deeply autobiographical *I Am One of You Forever* (1985) by Fred Chappell, for instance, or in *The Prince of Tides* (1986) by Pat Conroy, which begins simply with the confession, "My wound is geography. It is also my anchorage, my port of call." More remarkably, the return of the son to the father lies at the heart of *A Summons to Memphis* (1987) by Peter Taylor: a novel that is not so much about one return visit as a cycle of returning, the narrative circling around the subject—in a manner familiar from Taylor's short stories—before alighting on its inner core of meaning. The occasion of return is simple, but urgent: the central character, Phillip Carver, is summoned back to Memphis by his sisters to help prevent their aged father from remarrying. Phillip has taken refuge for many years in the anonymity of New York City and what he admits is a "systematic, well-ordered life."[59] Now he is drawn out of that refuge, and his "middle-aged doldrums," and into family intrigues. In particular, he is awkwardly reminded of how, forty years ago, his family was forced to move from Nashville to Memphis following the treachery of his father's best friend, Lewis Shackleford ("a disaster for everyone except Father," Phillip observes of the move). And he is forced to recall how he and his two sisters were prevented from marrying those whom they loved when their father interfered, using his own force of will and their equivocal devotion to him to get his way.

"Certain events of the past will have to be dredged up," Phillip explains to the reader, "if present events are to be fully comprehended." This is Taylor's characteristically knowing way of alerting us to the narrative direction of *A Summons to Memphis,* and the moral work it is

59. Peter Taylor, *A Summons to Memphis* (London, 1987), 9. See also 16; Pat Conroy, *The Prince of Tides* (1986; New York, 1987 edition), 1. Also Fred Chappell, *I Am One of You Forever* (Chapel Hill, N.C., 1985).

about to do. On his first visit home, Phillip finds his old feelings of resentment against his father being "dredged up," as he recalls how the old man put an end to his romance with "my wonderful Clara Price," the woman he intended to marry. On the other hand, an emotional connection is tentatively made: talking to his father, seeing him again, he discovers that he is now, as he puts it, "able to imagine more about Father's life than I had in the past ever had any conception of." And this process of painful resurrection and revision of old feelings continues when Phillip makes his second return trip. Happening on Clara Price herself this time, a mature woman now and a mother of five, Phillip realizes to his consternation that all he cares about is, not Clara herself, but "how I had been treated by family in the long-ago affair" with her. "It was a painful . . . realization," Phillip confesses, "for it caused a deep hurt to know that about myself."[60] The hurt, and surprise, grow when Phillip and his father together chance to meet another "ghost" out of the past, Lewis Shackleford, and Lewis and his father then proceed to embrace. Up until now, Phillip has paid homage to what he terms "my doctrine of forgetting," he has simply tried to run away from the rawer areas of his life. What he sees and learns from his father is quite different: the doctrine, not of forgetting, but of forgiveness. And that doctrine is at least hesitantly embraced when, on his third return trip, Phillip begins to learn how to commiserate with his father, and to see him as a friend.

Taylor is careful to avoid any neat resolutions. So, for that matter, is his protagonist. Eschewing what he calls "inconclusive nonsense about the reconciliation of fathers and children," Phillip even admits that, by preventing his father's remarriage, he has enjoyed some belated revenge. Still, thanks to a series of return trips to Memphis, father and son have revived old affections—and realized a kind of understanding, along perhaps with respect. The long talks that follow over the telephone (in which, Phillip says, "we were able to speak of things we had never been able to talk about face to face") end suddenly when Phillip's father dies. But, by then, return has brought its due reward in feelings of rapport; the two men have learned how to forgive, and begin to accept, each other. Back in New York City with Holly Kaplan, the woman he has lived with off and on for about a dozen years, Phillip is returned to his retreat and old routines. "And so Holly and I are still here," Phillip admits; "there is nothing in the world that can interfere with the peace and quiet of life." Eventu-

60. Taylor, *Summons to Memphis*, 192. See also 15, 83, 159, 181, 189.

ally, he speculates, they will not so much die as fade away, their "serenity . . . translated into a serenity in another realm of things." "How else," Phillip asks wryly, "can one think of an end to such serenely free spirits as Holly Kaplan and I?"[61] It is an appropriately muted denouement: Phillip has not changed his life substantially, it has simply acquired another shading, a richer nuance. He and his father have come to a rapprochement rather than a reconciliation; and, rather than knowing himself now, he has come to some not entirely amorphous notion of who he might be and what probably made him that way. Dredging up the past has allowed Phillip, if not full comprehension of the present, then at least the quiet chance of insight—and the opportunity of coming to terms with mistakes made by both his father and himself. At one point a little earlier on in the story, Phillip makes the discovery that his partner Holly must have had "a male equivalent of Clara Price," someone she thinks of as the grand, failed passion, the lost love of her youth. "I was happy to realize that *I* didn't mind about that," Phillip discloses. And that lesson of learning not to mind, through strength of affection rather than lack of it, is what Phillip Carver returns to in the end. The summons to Memphis has inspired, not revelation, but the recognition that pardon for the past is the least we can offer to others—and the most we can expect for ourselves.

"I have come home to this little agrarian capital to forgive and be forgiven," writes Anna Hand in the novel named after her, *The Anna Papers* (1988) by Ellen Gilchrist. "To kiss my father's cheek and listen to his advice," she goes on. "To be my mother's friend, to stop being jealous of my brothers and sisters. To count my blessings and bestow kindness on my kin." "Coming home" is, in fact, the choice taken not only by Anna Hand but also by a number of heroines in recent novels: among them, Crystal Spangler in *Black Mountain Breakdown* (1980) by Lee Smith, Hannah McKarkle in *The Killing Ground* by Mary Lee Settle, and Jeannine Lewis in *Blue Rise* by Rebecca Hill. The daughter returns to the mother, or the mother land, in these novels; and, in a different way, she does so too in *Meridian* (1976) by Alice Walker. That return has very mixed results. "I have failed," admits Anna Hand. "All I can do is count the waste and make mental lists of changes all the way back to 1961." Failure for Anna, however, turns out to be restoration for someone else. After her death by suicide, her sister and co-executor Helen Abadie goes through her papers and discovers there reasons to believe in a bolder,

61. Ibid., 208–9. See also 206, 207.

more adventurous response to life. "I am a normal, well-meaning woman with five spoiled-rotten children," Helen confesses, "grieving, mad as hell" at her sister's death. "No one ever knew Anna," Helen tells us. "She never stayed long enough in one place."[62] But now, after reading the Anna papers, Helen feels that she knows her sister and has been liberated by that knowledge. In an emotional, imaginative sense, at least, Anna has returned to her and Helen has been restored to herself.

A return home has similarly emancipatory results in *Blue Rise* and *The Killing Ground*; and here, in both cases, it is the woman returning who is eventually emancipated. In *Blue Rise,* Jeannine Lewis returns to her home in Mississippi, and her mother, and learns how to break free of both—and, not only that, to break free of "believing," as she puts it, "that there is salvation by relationship." "You can't help me," Jeannine tells her mother just before she leaves to go back to New York. "And I can't help you. I have to live my own life and you have to live yours." Her homecoming has enabled her to measure her difference. "My mother and I," she confesses, "are descended from a long line of . . . women who take as their motto and creed *I suffer, therefore I am*." Now she has learned not to adjust, not to be frightened of being called selfish (among her kin, "selfish is the worst thing a woman can be called," Jeannine tells us), but to "open my hand to grasp something new." "I am finished trying to earn my mother's approval or her permission to live my life," she declares at the end of her trip home. "I am finished with the kind of dependency that I have carried through my life like a touchstone." Resolved to go her own way and live her own life ("That's all you can do," she decides. "Live your own life."), Jeannine flies back north resolved to break with her husband now, as well as her mother. "Mississippi is disappearing below," she says as she looks out of the plane window. "I want to hold this in my mind, have it be a place apart, a place I know." But "it all looks like that from up here," she reflects. "This could be Tennessee, for all I know."[63] For her, the journey back has ended as a journey away, a dissolution of place as a motivating element in her life and an absolution, a shaking off of other people and her past.

Return leads to a revival that is a liberation from place in *Blue Rise*.

62. Ellen Gilchrist, *The Anna Papers* (New York, 1988), 232, 236. See also 242; Lee Smith, *Black Mountain Breakdown* (1980; New York, 1982 edition), 236. Also Walker, *Meridian* (1976; London, 1983 edition); Settle, *Killing Ground*; Hill, *Blue Rise*.
63. Hill, *Blue Rise*, 295–96. See also 13, 138, 288, 293.

In *The Killing Ground,* on the other hand, the liberation the protagonist experiences comes precisely from her return *into* place and its true meanings. By journeying home to West Virginia, Hannah McKarkle comes to realize that, as she sees it, she has "joined the wanderers" who constitute the true part of her heritage. "I have come to this place, on this day for a reason," she tells the reader as she looks out over her home place. And that reason turns out to be "a thing deeper than the land," although it is the land that gives it. It is a memory embedded in the land—or, as Hannah puts it, "stratum on stratum of connection" with the people there, many of whom are still there buried in "the killing ground." With their help, she realizes a personal emancipation that is also a social one, since by the end of her journey home—after she has searched out the past of herself, her family, and community—she has made, as she has it, "the choice to choose, to be singular, burn bridges, begin again in a new country or a new way of seeing"—a choice "as ancient as wandering itself."[64] The "price of freedom," she has learned from her mother land, is that "itch, a discontent, an unfulfilled promise, perpetually demanding that it be kept" that drove the best of her own people (those who resisted "the way things are")—and that has prompted her to return and, in the end, leave again. Personal and social, the emancipation Settle's heroine experiences is also aesthetic. Hannah, it was observed much earlier on in this book, is the putative author of the Beulah quintet—a family chronicle, when taken as a sequence, of which this novel of return and revival is the fifth and final installment. Here in *The Killing Ground,* she tells us, she is "building that house" where her ancestors lived "from other people's memories, a house of words." And it is this "house of words," "her" book of homecoming, that enables her to salvage what is meaningful and motivating out of the past and then use it as a beacon for the future. It is an act of narrativity, really, as much as an act of journey that allows her to excavate "a thing deeper than the land"; to that extent, it is not return but the *writing* of it which leads eventually to her revival.

Neither return nor the imagining of it can save Crystal Spangler in *Black Mountain Breakdown,* however. In her story of Crystal, Lee Smith begins by tracing a familiar route. A cheerleader and a beauty queen in her early years, a "beatnik" for a while later on in college, Crystal ends up as what seems like an immaculate success. Certainly, to her hometown friends she seems so, as they gaze at photographs of Crystal; as the wife

---

64. Settle, *Killing Ground,* 384. See also pp. 4, 7.

of a wealthy businessman and potentially powerful politician, she is "all over" the newspapers, "smiling out of the society pages every Sunday." Crystal herself, though, feels more and more inauthentic, "like a person in a play"; and, in the middle of her husband's campaign for political office, she suddenly breaks down. "I need to go home," is just about all she can say. Returning home to Black Mountain, North Carolina, "she isn't even listening" to what others say to her, we learn. Instead, she is "thinking back to the way the river was when she was little and the way it was even before she was born, the way her daddy said it was."[65] And, returned there to her mother who now takes care of her, she sinks into mental and physical torpor. "She just stops moving," the narrator discloses. "She stops talking, stops doing everything." Restored to "her old room" from childhood, "she just lies up there . . . every day. She won't lift a finger. She just lies there." Earlier on, when she was younger, Crystal had sought to find "what she ha[d] been looking for" in an old journal discovered in the old family home, "something to establish the past, continuity." She failed then, so the reader understands; and she fails now. Unwilling to live in a present that has become pure performance, and unable to make any vital contact with memories, she has become a dangling woman, connecting nothing with nothing. For her, return brings only retreat, a spiraling down to the minimal case; there is no revival here, just paralysis.

As a process of constant renewal, returning has been central to the fiction of Alice Walker. That returning always brings with it, though, a sense of determination and of difference. Walker's characters are enabled to renew themselves by revisiting their roots and discovering what helped make them the way they are: but they are also made sharply aware of inevitable, and necessary, change—the fact that they cannot, even if they wanted to, step back into the stream of time past. This is surely why Walker is interested in revisiting and revising myths of origin. "Did I mention my first sight of the African coast?" asks Nettie, in one of her letters home to her sister, Celie, in *The Color Purple* (1982): "Something struck in me, in my soul, Celie, like a large bell, and I just vibrated. Corrine and Samuel felt the same. And we kneeled down right on deck and gave thanks to God for letting us see the land for which our mothers and fathers cried—and lived and died—to see again."[66] This, among

---

65. Smith, *Black Mountain Breakdown*, 235. See also 202, 214, 221, 234, 237, 238.

66. Alice Walker, *The Color Purple* (1982; London, 1983 edition), 120–21. See also 137, 143, 231; Gloria Steinem, "Alice Walker: Do You Know This Woman: She Knows You," in *Outrageous Acts and Everyday Rebellions* (New York, 1983), 273; "If the Present

many other things, represents a radical revision of the standard American myth of origin, according to which the first white settlers encountered the fresh, green breast of a New World that was also an old one—a place of hope that was also a site of lost possibility. The experience of Nettie invites us to consider an alternative myth. "They say everybody before Adam was black," Celie says, as she retells the story told to Nettie by Africans, ". . . Adam wasn't the first white man. He was just the first one the people didn't kill." And it also alerts us to the danger of paying uncritical devotion even to that alternative mythology. As Nettie observes the insularity of the Africans she lives with ("I think Africans are very much like white people back home," she says, "in that they think they are the center of the universe"), and the way African men refuse to see African women as anything other than an inferior species ("reminds me too much of Pa," she observes caustically), she seems to be performing the task Walker set herself when she declared, "We're going to have to debunk the myth that Africa is a heaven for black people—especially black women." The trick is not simply to return but to renew: to search out origins and then use the results of that search to figure new and better reasons to believe. One of Walker's essays is titled "If the Present Looks Like the Past, What Does the Future Look Like?" That question, with its assumptions of connection but necessary incongruence (likeness is not, after all, sameness), lurks at the back of many of Walker's stories. It is there, for example, in her attempt to rewrite the white, Western version of human origins in *The Temple of My Familiar* (1989). More modestly, and perhaps successfully, it is there too in *Meridian.*

One critic has commented that, for Walker, "the South provides a spiritual balance and an ideological base from which to construct her characters." That is certainly true for the story of Meridian Hill. Meridian, we are told, is *"held* by something in the past": a "something" that includes, above all, her mother and a church that is both her mother's church and—whether she likes it or not—her mother church. "Her mother's life was sacrifice," we learn, "a blind, enduring, stumbling—though with dignity—through life. She did not appear to understand much be-

Looks Like the Past, What Does the Future Look Like?" in *In Search of Our Mother's Gardens* (New York, 1983). *The Temple of My Familiar* was published in New York, 1989. For useful accounts of the rewriting of the past and the process of recovery in *The Color Purple,* see, e.g., Frank W. Shelton, "Alienation and Integration in Alice Walker's *The Color Purple," College Language Association Journal,* XXVIII (1985), 382–92; Lindsay Tucker, "Alice Walker's *The Color Purple:* Emergent Woman, Emergent Text," *Black American Literature Forum,* XXII (1988), 81–95.

yond what happened in her own family, neighborhood and in her church." For Meridian, her mother is "a giant," "Black Motherhood personified." And her main feeling, when she thinks about her, is guilt: guilt over being born and so "stealing her mother's serenity," guilt over abandoning her own child and so betraying "maternal history," and guilt over involving herself in politics. "You've wasted a year of your life," Meridian's mother tells her when she learns that her daughter has been involved in the civil rights movement. "It never bothered *me* to sit in the back of the bus, you get just as good a view." Meridian never comes to personal terms with her mother but, by returning to her mother's history and ancestry, she does experience a symbolic rapprochement. In a delirium, Meridian rehearses the story of her female ancestors, from the great-great-grandmother who had been a slave; it is, in a way, a history in miniature of African American women. At the close of the rehearsal, she dreams she is on a voyage with her mother, who is "holding her over the railing" of the ship "about to drop her into the sea"; there is "danger all around" and her mother refuses to let her go. "Mama, I *love* you. Let me go," Meridian whispers. And the reply comes, not from her mother, but from the old black woman nursing her. "I forgive you," the older woman answers, "as if Meridian were her own child."[67] It is not her mother but, thanks to Meridian's dreaming return to her mother's past, it is symbolically and emotionally enough. Meridian has made her peace, and can now move on.

The return to the mother is a purely imagined one in *Meridian,* although it supplies the basis for real emotional renewal; the return to mother church is rather more literal. Coming back South, and "moving from one small town to another," Meridian starts to visit churches like the one she was taken to in her childhood by her mother. "The people looked exactly as they had ever since she had known black churchgoing

---

67. Walker, *Meridian,* 121–23. See also 14, 41, 71, 81, 87, 93; Bettye J. Parker-Smith, "Alice Walker's Women: In Search of Some Peace of Mind," in *Black Women Writers (1950–1980): A Critical Evaluation* edited by Mari Evans (Garden City, N.Y., 1984), 478. Hazel V. Carby argues that black women writers have "addressed, used, transformed and on occasion subverted the dominant ideological codes" (*Reconstructing Womanhood: The Emergence of the Afro-American Woman Novelist* [New York, 1987], 21): a suggestion I have tried to develop here. On redefinition and transformation in Walker's work, see also Melvin Dixon, *Ride Out the Wilderness: Geography and Identity in Afro-American Literature* (Urbana, Ill., 1987); Molly Hite, "Writing—and Reading—the Body: Female Sexuality and Recent Feminist Fiction," *Feminist Studies,* XIV (1988), 121–42.

people," Meridian observes while visiting "a large white church, Baptist," "but they had changed the music! She was shocked." This is not the church music she remembers from her youth, when, despite her mother's pleas, "she had sat mute" and refused to say that she was saved; it has a "triumphal forcefulness" and is "quite martial." This, in short, is the late 1960s, and this is the church militant. The minister speaks, "in a voice so dramatically like that of Martin Luther King's," of active resistance—to racial oppression, the war in Vietnam, and the system that appears to sustain both. And, as a climax to the service, an old man testifies at the altar, talking not of God but of his own son "destroyed by clubs" in an act of racial violence. As the congregation responds to the old man's testimony, "there was a breaking in Meridian's chest," we learn, "as if a tight string binding her lungs had given way, allowing her to breathe freely." It is a kind of rebirth. Meridian understands, "finally, that the respect she owed to her life was . . . to live it, and not to give up any particle of it without a fight to the death, preferably *not* her own." Leaving the church, she makes a silent promise to the old man at the altar. "Yes indeed she *would* kill," she tells herself, "before she allowed anyone to murder his son again."[68]

The point and power of this moment, which occurs almost at the end of the novel, is that, previously, Meridian has been unable to make such a commitment. Much earlier on in the story, for example, Meridian is lost in a daydream about her mother, her mother church, and the conditions both made for love ("conditions Meridian was never able to meet") when she is jolted awake by someone asking, "fallen asleep, have you?" "It was a voice from the revolutionary group" she now belongs to, we are told, "calling her from a decidedly unrevolutionary past." As for the group, "love was not what they wanted. It was not what they needed"; on the contrary, "they needed her to kill. To say she would kill." But Meridian cannot say this, any more than she could say to her mother once that she had been saved. She cannot utter the words that would bind her to either her revolutionary present or her "unrevolutionary" past. What her return to the South in later life enables, though, and her return to the "large white church," is something that ties her to both: a new language, expressing a new form of personal *and sociopolitical* salvation. A church transformed by the civil rights revolution allows Meridian to be transformed too, using words that speak of both loving and

68. Walker, *Meridian*, 198–200, 203–4. See also 18–19.

killing to become "resolute and relatively fearless." Meridian has learned a new song, she tells herself as she leaves the church. "It is the song of the people, transformed by the experience of each generation, that holds them together";[69] and, thanks to it, she knows now how to connect her past to her present. Her return to origins here has initiated change, but change that is continuous with the earlier experiences of her community; in that way, she has come back to her own history only to transcend it. The act of reversion to yesterday—in this case, the yesterdays of her churchgoing youth—empowers a promise to today and tomorrow—a promise, that is, both to herself and to her people.

"I go to San Francisco but I cannot stay away from here." The words are those of Ernest Gaines; and "here" is Louisiana, where Gaines spent his childhood and most of his youth. Born to a black sharecropping family in Point Coupee parish, Gaines was working in the fields by the time he was nine and, after his parents separated and his father disappeared, he was brought up by a crippled but indomitable great aunt, Miss Augusteen Jefferson who, Gaines was to say later, "did not walk a day in her life but who taught me the importance of standing." Then, in his fifteenth year, he joined his mother and her new husband in northern California, which has been his main place of residence ever since. He returns regularly to Louisiana, however. More to the point, his collection of stories, *Bloodline* (1968), and all of his novels so far are set in the fictional parish of St. Raphael, based on the parish in which he was born. San Francisco, where he has settled, appears as a setting in none of them—although it is, for instance, the city from which Jackson Bradley, the protagonist in Gaines's first novel, *Catherine Carmier* (1964), returns to his Louisianian home place, and the place where the secret family of the Reverend Phillip Martin, the main character of *In My Father's House* (1978), live after he has denied them. "I've tried to write about San Francisco," Gaines has explained. ". . . But everything comes back to Louisiana. . . . It is *that* place I cannot escape; I must keep returning to that place." "I'm always in Louisiana even though I'm not living there,"[70] he has said elsewhere. In the imaginative topography of Gaines's fiction, the West is a place of flight and exile, secrecy and anonymity; the South—and, more specifi-

---

69. Ibid., 205–6. See also 17.
70. *Conversations with Ernest Gaines* edited by John Lowe (Jackson, Miss., 1995), 152. See also 275, 298; Dedication to *Jane Pittman*. Also *Bloodlines* (New York, 1968).

cally, the plantation land of southern Louisiana—is where the act of return brings with it the possibility of revival—a reconnection of past with present that restores the returner to his or her full humanity.

What kind of South, exactly, do Gaines's fictions return to? Gaines has called himself "a Southern writer" and spoken of "the Southern thing in me": but, despite a Faulknerian obsession with the past and a small postage stamp of native soil, *his* South represents a significant departure from the one to be found in most earlier, mainstream Southern writing. "When I first started reading I wanted to read about my people in the South," Gaines has recalled, "and the white writers whom I had read did not put my people into books the way that I knew them." "Much of our history has not been told," Gaines has suggested, "our problems have been told, as if we have no history." And most other black writers have been as responsible for this erasure of the African American past in the South, Gaines has argued, as the white writers have: "so much of our literature deals with the big-city ghettos," he points out, "and we existed long before we came to the big city." Gaines is intent on resurrecting what he sees as a missing history, returning to a Southern past that has either been ignored or actively suppressed. The point is made neatly, and in human terms, by the fictive historian who introduces *The Autobiography of Miss Jane Pittman*. Asked why he wants to record the recollections of Jane Pittman, he explains that he teaches history and he is sure that, as he puts it, "her life's story can help me explain things to my students." To the further question, "What's wrong with them books you already got?" his response is even simpler. "Miss Jane is not in them,"[71] he says.

Jane Pittman, of course, tells her own past; the act of return is, primarily, one of voice. "I come from a long line of storytellers," Gaines has

71. Gaines, *Jane Pittman*, v–vi. See also *Conversations with Gaines* edited by Lowe, 28, 74, 110. Elizabeth Jane Harrison has suggested that the reason why it has taken African American writers so long to rewrite and revise Southern pastoral (apart from a few notable exceptions such as Zora Neale Hurston) is that "a prevailing literary model in African-American fiction is based upon the slave narrative rather than the plantation romance so that escape from the rural homeland, the South, became a necessary component in character growth" (*Female Pastoral: Women Writers Re-Visioning the American South* [Knoxville, Tenn., 1991, 102]). Robert Stepto, in *From Behind the Veil: A Study of Afro-American Narrative* (Urbana, Ill., 1975), and Bernard Bell, in *The Afro-American Novel and Its Tradition* (Amherst, Mass., 1987), also hold that view. For a contrary viewpoint, particularly in relation to writing by African American women, see, e.g., Carby, *Reconstructing Womanhood*.

explained. Folk memory and folk tale, the talk of his family and community have ensured that, as Gaines himself has put it, "dialogue is the meat of my writing." As he acknowledges, his fictions work best when he "can git into the persona of some other character and let him carry the story." African American music is vital here too. "What I'd like to see in our writing," he has said—the "our" referring here, of course, to writers who share his Southern black heritage—"is the presence of music;" and what Gaines has clearly aimed for in his prose style is the rhythmic recurrence of the spoken or sung—the kind of "repeating and repeating to get the point over" (to use his own words) to be found in the music of "great blues signers [*sic*] like Bessie Smith, Josh White, Leadbelly" or the more complex, syncopated rhythms of a musician like Lester Young. Speech and song, old tales and talking are, in fact, as central here in Gaines's fiction as they are in the work of two Southern writers to whom he has acknowledged a debt, William Faulkner and Zora Neale Hurston. "I could no more agree with his philosophy . . . than I could agree with Wallace's," Gaines has declared of Faulkner. "But this man taught me how to listen to dialogue." In Gaines's work, as in that of Faulkner and Hurston, place and past are spoken into being; the community locates and perpetuates itself through talk; and individual characters certify their existence, and their independence, through speech. "I think Faulkner once said the characters take over on page 114 unless the book ends on page 113," Gaines has observed, adding, "I do think they take over."[72] Like Faulkner, Gaines carries this belief in the independence of the individual character to an extreme, often talking about them in interviews as if they enjoyed free will and privacy of motive ("I really don't know," he admitted, for instance, when asked about what drives one character in *Of Love and Dust* [1967]). Their voices guarantee that freedom and privacy, their presence in what Mikhail Bakhtin would call "a world of autonomous subjects, not objects." Gaines's is, in effect, a fundamentally democratic idea of community in which each individual member has the right to be heard, the chance to tell his or her own history.

One critic has commented that the history Gaines's fiction as a whole has to tell "covers a span of time from the Civil War to the present," a period that "witnessed the decline of the old plantation economy, the rise

72. *Conversations with Gaines* edited by Lowe, 156. See also 19, 34, 58, 94, 143, 209, 243; Mikhail Bakhtin, *Problems of Dostoevsky's Poetics* edited and translated by Caryl Emerson (Manchester, 1984), 7.

of the Cajun class to a position of control," and the gradual "displacement of black labor by machinery with a corresponding challenge to the integrity of black communities."[73] This is broadly true. It is worth adding, however, that most of Gaines's stories return to the more recent past. Apart from *The Autobiography of Miss Jane Pittman* (in which, as Gaines explained, he "wanted to go further and further back" to the 1860s), his novels are set, as he puts it, "between the thirties and the late seventies." *Catherine Carmier* is set at the time of the Freedom Riders, both *Of Love and Dust* (1967) and *A Lesson Before Dying* (1993) in the late 1960s, *In My Father's House* two years after the death of Martin Luther King, and *A Gathering of Old Men* (1983) not long after that in the 1970s. Each of these novels offers a reprise and revision of certain themes—manhood, and in particular what Phillip Martin in *In My Father's House* calls "the gap" between black fathers and their sons; womanhood as the arbiter of value and guarantor of continuity in the Southern black community; the moment of trial, testing, when a person has the "chance to stand" (to borrow a phrase from *A Gathering of Old Men*) and so assert his courage and define himself. These themes clearly grow out of Gaines's own past, but just as clearly they are part of the missing history of his people. As both he and several of his black characters observe, it is ultimately the economic dispossession of the black male in America that has denied him an adequate role in the community, encouraged him to run—to absent himself, just as Gaines's own father did—rather than stand, and obliged black women to take a disproportionate share of the moral and social burden. Gaines focuses, for the most part, on the last few decades when the transformation of the Southern economy and agricultural practices has further destabilized the black community and challenged personal standing by denying the opportunity for *any* kind of labor—even those few, poor ones offered by the tenant and sharecropping systems. As a character in *A Gathering of Old Men* says, "that tractor . . . getting rid of all proof that black people ever

73. J. A. Bryant Jr., *Twentieth-Century Southern Literature* (Lexington, Ky., 1997), 161. See also *Conversations with Gaines* edited by Lowe, 189, 259; *In My Father's House* (1978; New York, 1992 edition), 165; *A Gathering of Old Men* (1983; New York, 1992 edition), 18. Other useful discussions of Gaines include Valerie Babb, *Ernest Gaines* (Boston, 1991); Anne K. Simpson, *A Gathering of Gaines: The Man and the Writer* (New York, 1991); David C. Estes, *Critical Reflections on the Fiction of Ernest J. Gaines* (New York, 1994); Herman Beavers, *Wrestling Angels into Song: The Fiction of Ernest J. Gaines and Alan McPherson* (New York, 1995).

farmed this land with plows and mules—like if they had nothing from the starten but motor machines."[74] While focusing on those more recent years, though, Gaines is determined to show how they are part of an older story (even if, apart from *The Autobiography of Miss Jane Pittman,* he does not tell that story directly). Society, and the machinery at its service, may be geared to the erasure of black history and identity, but Gaines is passionately interested in restoring that "proof" his character speaks of. The act of return is at the heart of his narratives precisely because he wants to leave no doubt in his readers' minds that the personal *is* the political and, related to this, that the present is caused by the past—even though, in the last analysis, it is not controlled by it.

The forms of returning in Gaines's stories are, unsurprisingly, as various as the stories themselves. Sometimes, as in *Catherine Carmier,* the return is literal. Jackson Bradley, a young plantation black educated like Gaines in California, goes back to Louisiana only to be reminded that, as he puts it to himself, "he had to get away. He would either go mad or get into trouble if he did not get away." His problems are aggravated by his falling in love with the woman who gives the novel its title, a Creole deeply attached to her father who "cannot leave," as she sees it, any more than he can stay. He, and she, are the victims of caste and history, a complex social system in which everyone is judged in terms, not just of color, but of subtle shadings. Catherine's father, Raoul, for instance, despises anyone darker than himself, while Jackson's great-aunt Charlotte believes that Creoles are, as she says, "just's bad's white." It is a system designed to separate and subjugate, so that nearly everyone and not just the interloper Jackson seems to live apart and alone. It is also a system subject to such drastic transformation that nearly everything Jackson encounters appears to him "familiar" yet somehow "strange." As Aunt Charlotte tells him, "Cajuns cropping all the land now"; black farmers and farm laborers have been excluded. Houses have been torn down to extend cultivation so that, as another local points out, "you might have a tractor running up to your fence any time." And people of working age either hang around with "nothing to do" or else, as Jackson did, head for the city. "There was no returning home," Jackson reflects, not least because home has altered almost as much as he has. But there is no escaping it either. The same "wall" of inherited racial prejudice, "that had gotten so high by now that he had to stand on tiptoe to look over it,"

74. Gaines, *Gathering of Old Men,* 92.

surrounds and confines Jackson whether he is in the South or the North. So Jackson ends as he began: "like a leaf . . . that's broken away from the tree," as he figures himself—rootless, drifting, while searching for something that may be found, "some of it in California . . . some of it here" in Louisiana, "but not all of it . . . in any one place."[75] Return here, as in *Black Mountain Breakdown,* leads to a kind of paralysis; the protagonist is disabled rather than revived. Appropriately, in the final moments of the novel, Jackson stands still outside the Carmier home, "hoping that Catherine would come back outside" and join him in departure—unable to stay but not quite ready yet, either, to leave.

"I feel trapped in the omniscient," Gaines has said; and, if there is any problem with his first novel, it is that it is told in the third person. None of the characters, not even Jackson, is permitted to carry the story, which to that extent is told from the outside. This is not a merely formalistic point, as Gaines's next two novels indicate. The power of both *Of Love and Dust* and *The Autobiography of Miss Jane Pittman* springs from the fact that, in both cases, characters return to the past by telling us about it. Memories haunt them; they tell us their memories; in the process, their past, and their part in black history, become available to us. The storyteller of *Of Love and Dust* is Jim Kelly, a black tractor driver on a Louisiana plantation. He recalls how Marcus Payne, a rebellious "city boy" bonded out to the plantation for a term of five years continued his rebellion and, by refusing either to run or surrender, brought about his own death. The rebellion included seduction of the wife of the Cajun overseer, Sidney Bonbon; it is Bonbon, in fact, who eventually kills Payne, using a scythe. The story charts the transformation of Payne from a simple rebel and lawbreaker into a subtle and sympathetic outsider. It also traces Kelly's growing understanding of Payne (he "liked" and "admired him" "at the last," Kelly reveals), whose fate he comes to see as symptomatic of the problems facing black people—and his feeling even for Bonbon, whom he recognizes as just another of the "little people," one more social victim "brought up in a brute-taught world and in brute-taught times."[76] Modeled in part on Nick Carraway in *The Great Gatsby,* Kelly is, as Gaines has put it, "a guy who could communicate with different sides.

75. Ernest Gaines, *Catherine Carmier* (1964; New York, 1993 edition), 79–80. See also 24, 26, 29, 77, 93, 119, 167, 174.

76. Ernest Gaines, *Of Love and Dust* (1967; New York, 1994 edition), 67. See also 34, 79, 258, 270, 280; *Conversations with Gaines* edited by Lowe, 107, 243.

. . . And through this . . . learn to love, to . . . understand." He is also (and, again, like Carraway) talking about the past in order to come to terms with it. Gaines deploys a characteristically rhythmic, repetitive style here, as Kelly tells us he "thought back" to the heat and dust of endless days with Payne and Bonbon working in the fields. Although Kelly is the one talking to us throughout the novel, he also reports the observations and commentary of others. The moment when Bonbon killed Payne, for instance, is recalled by local witnesses, five in all and all of them black; they have told Kelly what they saw and heard, their voices are now filtered through his voice. In this way, *Of Love and Dust* shows memory becoming history in both personal and collective terms. Kelly excavates his past, and turns it into an enabling force by making some sense of it, but so do the local people around him. Through an act of narration, imaginative return, the individual can learn from what has happened and so can the community; both can then grow, change, and go on.

In both *Of Love and Dust* and *The Autobiography of Miss Jane Pittman,* a character returns to the past and is revived by the experience. A missing history is found and made available as a resource to both them and us. In the tale of Jane Pittman, a return of a sort is also made by the author. As Gaines himself has pointed out, her story is at least four stories about four men. Each of those men, in turn, is associated with a particular moment in Jane Pittman's life and a particular period in African American history—"the War Years," "the Reconstruction Period," "the plantation" in the early twentieth century, and "the civil rights years." And, in writing about each of these moments, Gaines is returning to familiar narrative tropes and reshaping them. In the first story, for instance, centering on the flight of Jane through the swamps with the young boy, Ned, for whom she has assumed responsibility, Gaines is rewriting what he has called "Huck and Jim on the boat." A classic mainstream American narrative is imaginatively restored, rewritten in terms closer and truer to what Gaines sees as a largely untold history of black dispossession and exodus. This is a darker, wearier, and far more desperate flight than was ever imagined, even in *The Adventures of Huckleberry Finn.* Ned becomes Jane Pittman's charge, for example, after his mother and baby sister are slaughtered in a wholesale massacre of fugitive black people by "the patrollers." "We walked, we walked, we walked" is the refrain throughout this episode; there is none of Huck and Jim's idyllic "lazying" as they float downstream on the Mississippi; this is a journey measured in blood, sweat, and tears. It is also, however, much more of a *communal* experience than Huck and Jim ever knew. Other people are not "spirits"—distant, dimly seen figures on the river shore—or unwelcome interlopers on a shared idyll but fellow victims, companions in suffering with Jane, or, or if not that, then their common oppressors—either "us" or "them." Jane is an orphan. "My mother was killed when I was young," she tells us, "and I never did know my daddy. He belong to another plantation. I never did know his name." Nevertheless, she has her own "family" in flight: not only Ned, but the other black refugees and exiles she meets and links up with on her journey. The moments just before the massacre are particularly to the point here—when Jane and other blacks in flight, gathered "in a thicket of sycamore trees," begin to adopt or exchange new names. "We must have been two dozens of us there," Jane recollects, "and now everybody started changing names like you change hats. Nobody was keeping the same name Old Master had given them. This one would say, 'My new name Cam Lincoln.' That one would say, 'My new name Freeman.' . . . Another one would say, 'My new name Job.' 'Job what?' 'Just Job.' 'Nigger, this ain't slavery no more. You got to have two names.' 'Job Lincoln, then.' "[77] Jane already has her "new name." "My name ain't Ticey no more," she had told her "mistress," before she left the old plantation, "it's Miss Jane Brown"; and, despite a whipping from her "mistress" would not go back to her "slave name" any more ("Every time she hit me she asked me what I said my name was. I said Jane Brown."). Here and now, her renaming becomes a shared experience, her voice is echoed by the voices of others. Just as Gaines revises an old story of rebellion and exodus—of lighting out for freedom ahead of the rest—so Jane and her companions in flight revise their own histories, old stories of oppression, by speaking themselves into other identities, fresh lives. Author and character both "return" here, as it

77. Gaines, *Jane Pittman,* 17. See also 8, 9, 14, 21, 39; *Conversations with Gaines* edited by Lowe, 303. On "lazying" as a positive activity in *The Adventures of Huckleberry Finn,* see, e.g., Tony Tanner, *The Reign of Wonder: Naivety and Reality in American Literature* (Cambridge, 1965), 161. Huck Finn tells us that while he and Jim would "kind of lazy along, and by-and-by lazy off to sleep" on their raft, the sounds of people on the distant shores of the Mississippi would make them seem "like spirits." (Mark Twain, *The Adventures of Huckleberry Finn* [London, 1884, New York, 1885], chapter XIX). This measures in one way their shared distance from others—just as the tendency of characters like the Duke and Dauphin, or even Tom Sawyer, to assume the status of interlopers, intruders on the idyll, does in another way.

were, and, in returning, find "new names," another, more accurate vocabulary—new and better, much more inclusive ways of telling about the
missing history of the South.

In *In My Father's House* and *A Gathering of Old Men*, on the other
hand, people do not return to the past, it returns to them. They are forced
to confront memories, a history that seems not just secret but suppressed.
In My Father's House deals with what Gaines has called his "pet theme"
of the historical division between fathers and sons among African Americans. Phillip Martin, a respected minister and civil rights leader in a small
rural black community, is faced with the inescapable presence of his past
life in the shape of an illegitimate son. Another outsider from the city
appears in Gaines's fiction, this time to make the protagonist recall the
family he has abandoned and review his own past self, his former life of
drinking, gambling, and casual sex. The book encourages us to see the
rupture between Martin and his son in general terms, as a historical failure as well as a personal one. And, as Martin makes a return to his past
haunts in downtown Baton Rouge that is also a journey into memory,
the stories of lost boys multiply: a black youth killed by the police, an
unidentified corpse floating in the Mississippi River, an embittered Vietnam veteran advocating guerrilla war against whites, black boys sent to
the electric chair who call out as they die for anyone but their fathers.
Martin and his son never achieve a resolution of their differences, or heal
their rupture. Unable to kill his father, as he had intended when he returned to the community, the son kills himself; unable to acknowledge
his son until it is too late, the father loses local respect. But Martin at
least feels changed by his eventual recognition and acknowledgment of
his lost son and so able, as he puts it, to "start again" and "work toward
the future."[78] To that extent, recollection of lost history—a reconnection
of father with son that is also a communion between past and present—is
seen, not only as a need, but also as a possibility. The chance is there, the
intimation is, for the whole black community, and not just individual
African Americans, to understand what they are by knowing truly what
they were.

That chance is seized with a vengeance in *A Gathering of Old Men*, in
which the old men of the title overcome their lifelong surrender to the
white social system and stand together—protecting one of their number

---

78. Gaines, *In My Father's House*, 213. See also *Conversations with Gaines* edited by
Lowe, 87.

by all claiming responsibility for the killing of a Cajun farmer called Fix Boutan. "There's not a black family in this parish Fix hasn't hurt sometime or other," one sympathetic white character comments, adding of the old men, "Now is their chance to stand."[79] The murder confronts the old men with their own past failures of will or nerve; and now, as Gaines himself has commented, "they're trying to make up" for what they were never willing or able to do before. Each of the old men, in turn, claims the killing for himself and, in rehearsing his supposed motives, outlines the humiliations visited on him, his family, and community that now demand recognition and recompense. They are made to admit the return of a past of inequality and injustice; they then bear witness to their willingness at last to "stand up for something" (as one of them has it) and so perform an act of redemption. It is an act that represents a gathering together of a people in a revision of its history, something that another black novelist, Toni Morrison, might call a moment of "rememory." It is also a collective gesture that is the sum, and more, of individual ones; the voice of a people sounds here so powerfully because it is a medley, a chorus of voices. There are fifteen narrators in the novel, eleven of them black. Most of the old men get a chance to speak, to tell a personal story. As a result, the narrative rhythm is richly accumulative; the fictive and vocal planes are layered, accretive; the voices tell and retell their overlapping stories so that meanings insinuate themselves, the message of the book (and it clearly has one) slowly seeps into the reader's ears and mind. Gaines has said that an influence here was the method of multiple narration used by Faulkner: but closer to home, perhaps, is that practice of testifying to past sins and present salvation so characteristic of black religious services. This is a book of testifying. The old men are saved, not in a religious sense of course but in a personal and political way, by acknowledging their own past weakness and announcing their newly found courage. Theirs is a return to, and renewal of, an earlier, fallen

---

79. Gaines, *Gathering of Old Men*, 18. See also 36; *Conversations with Gaines* edited by Lowe, 250. One interviewer pointed out to Gaines that "none of the 'main,' the most involved characters," black and white, "do any of the narration." Gaines agreed. "I just felt those people, as observers, could do much better [at narrating] than the people involved" (*Conversations with Gaines* edited by Lowe, 167). The net effect of this is to reinforce the sense of the action as *communal*. Action and narration are evenly divided, as it were; there is no single, heroic protagonist placed in a determining, dominant position by his or her actions or voice.

self—a state of abjection changed into one of purely social resurrection—that is at once experienced and declared, felt and told.

Witnessing and testifying also occur in Gaines's sixth and surely most powerful novel so far, *A Lesson Before Dying,* in which he again explores the chances for a personal and social transformation based on place and voice—a return to origins that allows a new self to be spoken into life. Two men are at the center of the action. They are the narrator, Grant Wiggins, a college graduate returned to the plantation school who longs to leave again, and the protagonist, a young man called Jefferson, who is awaiting execution in the local jail. Wiggins reluctantly bows to the request of the condemned man's godmother to visit Jefferson and prepare him to die with dignity. At the trial, the public defender had presented his client as "a cornered animal" rather than a man. "Why, I would just as soon put a hog in the electric chair as this,"[80] he declares, pointing at Jefferson. Now it is Wiggins's task, imposed on him by an old lady, to convince the condemned man that he *is* a man—not "a thing that acts on command," as the lawyer has it, but someone who matters. Gaines is revisiting some familiar preoccupations of his here: the nature of manhood, womanhood as the guide and arbiter (it is an old woman, after all, aided and abetted by his own aunt, who assigns Grant his task and keeps him to it), the question of whether to run or to stand (Grant believes, at first, that black men in America have only three choices: to die violently, to be "brought down to the level of beasts," or "to run and run"), change in the community and the violent disruptions of race. He is also rewriting certain tropes and situations that have become almost obsessions with him. Grant, for instance, is drawn toward staying in the local community

80. Ernest Gaines, *A Lesson Before Dying* (1993; New York, 1994 edition), 8. See also 7, 62. On the relationship between *A Lesson Before Dying* and *Catherine Carmier,* see *Conversations with Gaines* edited by Lowe, 302. I describe Jefferson as the protagonist here because he occupies the center of the narrative space in the same way that, for example, Jackson Bradley does in *Of Love and Dust*—or, for that matter, Kurtz in Joseph Conrad's *Heart of Darkness,* Jay Gatsby in *The Great Gatsby,* and Thomas Sutpen in *Absalom, Absalom!* In some cases—for example, *Absalom, Absalom!* and the novel now under discussion—the narrator is also an initiator of action, but, in all cases, it is the person I have referred to as the protagonist whose disruption of the normal generates the narrative—or, to use a more down-to-earth phrase, gets things going—and whose behavior and development remain the ultimate focus of attention. A more accurate term might be *victim-hero* or *narrative focal point;* however, these terms seem clumsy and distract attention from my main concern here, which is to distinguish between, but also relate, the different "voices" of Gaines, Grant, and Jefferson.

because of his relationship with another schoolteacher, Vivian Baptiste, who cannot leave even if she wanted to because of family complications: her husband will give her a divorce only if she will stay and allow him access to their children. It is not hard to see this as a replay of the relationship between Jackson Bradley and Catherine Carmier; Gaines has, in fact, admitted as much. Once again, the suggestion is that to be restored to the community is to be restored to a woman. And this time, in the end, the man decides to stay.

He decides to stay because of another developing situation that recalls some of Gaines's earlier work. What happens between Grant Wiggins and Jefferson echoes what happens, in *Of Love and Dust,* between Jim Kelly and Marcus Payne. The narrator, someone who is drifting, tells us the story of his encounter with a strange, aberrant, and violent younger man: how that man suddenly intruded on his life, how an odd friendship grew between them and how both were transformed by the experience. If there is repetition here, however, it is (as in all Gaines's best work) with a difference. And some of that difference can be measured by the novelist's own comments on *A Lesson Before Dying* when it was an untitled work in progress. "I'm having to deal with a character in this book I'm working on now," he explained to an interviewer in 1988,

> He's too damned close to me, and I'm having all kinds of problems.
> . . . He's too much like me. He's cynical at times. . . . He's the
> narrator. . . . It's the voice, not the person himself. . . . He speaks
> too much like me. . . . The teacher is sort of like I am. . . . I've
> reached the point now . . . that he's deciding whether or not he will
> go in to visit this guy. . . . I can create the jail. That's easy for me to
> do. But to get that character to tell the damned story in a way that
> makes it flow smoothly . . . I don't know what the teacher wants.[81]

Later on in the same interview, when Gaines was talking about how he planned to show Grant enabling Jefferson to see and speak of his own manhood, he defined what he was after in terms of some famous analogies. "It's a pygmalion type thing," he explained, "the Elephant Man type thing. . . . The Helen Keller thing, you know." All this adds a fresh dimension to Gaines's concern with getting the voice right so the character can know and announce his own subjectivity, since the relationship between Grant and Jefferson clearly replicates what Gaines saw as his

81. *Conversations with Gaines* edited by Lowe, 235–38. See also 239.

own relationship with Grant—although (as usual with this author) the replicating also allows for difference. Grant helps Jefferson to gain access to his own identity—his own manhood, to use one of Gaines's favorite terms—by helping him toward a voice; in the process, Grant returns on himself and experiences his own transformation, to which *he* gives voice in telling us the story. In turn, by finding a voice for Grant after what was clearly a struggle, Gaines was returning on *himself,* his own ways of speaking and being ("He speaks too much like me. . . . The teacher is sort of like I am."). Admittedly, the return comes from another angle: the key with Grant and Jefferson is a closure of distance, whereas with Gaines and his narrator Grant it is the opening up of sufficient space, separation that allows autonomy of speech. Nevertheless, in both cases, it is a matter of one man empowering another with language and, in the course of this, empowering himself: this is, after all, the novel in which Gaines retraces old themes and concerns with a new conviction and energy. *A Lesson Before Dying* is the most convincingly positive, most powerful, of Gaines's novels so far because the voices of author, narrator, and protagonist reinforce and grow alongside each other, acquiring strength of speech by giving it. It is, to adopt Gaines's own tendency to compare writing and sports, a singular illustration of working skillfully, independently, but also as a team.

Listen, for example, to the voice of Grant Wiggins right at the beginning of the book: "I was there, yet I was not there. No, I did not go to the trial. I did not hear the verdict, because I knew all the time what it would be. Still, I was there. I was there as much as anyone else was there. Either I sat behind my aunt and his godmother or I sat beside them . . . his godmother became as immobile as a great stone or as one of our oak or cypress stumps . . . staring at the boy's close-cropped head."[82] As in so many of Gaines's novels, there is a sense of doom there from the outset. This is mainly due to the temporal framing. In terms of the action recollected, the trial has ended, the man has been condemned, death is waiting for him. And in terms of narration, the act of recollection, things have moved even further on in time: like Jim Kelly, Grant is looking back at a life that is already over, trying to make sense of it both for the man who lived it and himself. The style—as usual, direct, intimate, repetitive—carries us back, to the trial, then to the murder being tried, before

---

82. Gaines, *Lesson Before Dying,* 3. See also 255, 256; William Faulkner, *The Sound and the Fury* (1929; London, 1964 edition), 261.

carrying us forward, not to the present time of the narrator but to his more recent past. As it does so, it reveals to us a superfluous, aimless man, who describes himself in terms of ambiguities ("there . . . not there") and absence ("I did not go to the trial") and whose words are evasions. The society he inhabits, where secrets and lies infect the verbal community, must take some of the blame for this: the simple absence of a "sir" or "Mister," for instance, when a black man addresses or refers to a white man, can cause outrage, even violence. Grant's own failure of commitment, however, his moral indifference at this stage must take most. What he has to learn, and does eventually, is to speak in other terms. Not least, what he learns is the eloquence of feeling—the language of emotion and the capacity to talk in something more than the first person singular. "School is just about ready to end, huh?," he is asked at the end of the book. "Yes," he replies. "We get out two months earlier than the whites do." "What are you going to do when school is over?," comes the further question: to which his reply is simply, "It depends on Vivian. Whatever she wants." He then returns to the classroom to find a way of reporting the death of Jefferson to his pupils. "I was crying," are his last words and the last words in the book. These are small verbal gestures, certainly, but even by themselves they help to measure the length of his journey. He has gone from a language that is the coinage of moral failure to something like a true verbal currency: which in some cases, as in this final one, requires the eloquence of silence or simple inarticulacy—what Faulkner would have called "measures beyond the need for words."

Men act, women observe and commemorate: this tends to be the social geography of Gaines's novels, founded on his belief that these are the roles forced on African Americans by material conditions that require the men to be slaves, exiles, or dead and the women to weave the threads of moral continuity. "I suppose that the idea that man is determined by society runs through most of my work," he has said; and that is evident, perhaps, even in such little touches as the women sitting "immobile" at the trial while the men go about their business of arguing and killing. Argument and death are not the real measure of manhood, though; the voice that Gaines gives to Jefferson tells us that. "Tell Nannan I walked," Jefferson can say at the end. He learns an alternative to flight or slavery or dying like an animal. It is the substance of what Grant also learns, to meet his life with courage, to walk unflinchingly toward it, and the needs of others (like "Nannan," Jefferson's godmother) with genuine concern.

How Jefferson voices this lesson, however, is not so much through speech (which, Gaines has said, he thought would be "phoney") as through some faltering attempts at writing. He gets the chance to speak of himself in a diary Grant gives him. "I just thought it would be an elevation to himself," Gaines has explained of the diary, ". . . its aim was to show that he had been trying to say something, that he had accepted his position, not being able to express his humanity, and now he was called upon to do so."[83] Like Grant's crying, the diary of Jefferson allows a character to articulate the otherwise inarticulable, to voice the depths of his being, his recognition of self and connection with others. And even more than with Grant, Gaines clearly sees this as a political gesture. Jefferson has never been in touch with or able to talk about his own humanity because his society has never allowed him to do so; the chance to know and name himself has been systematically denied him. Now he has that chance and, with the help of Grant, seizes it, in an act of resistance to both the laws and the language of white supremacism.

"i dont kno what to rite," Jefferson begins his diary, "i aint never rote a letter in all my life . . . i cant think of too much to say but maybe nex time." Next time, and the times after that, he does find something to say, about love, work, and courage. "i kno i care for nanan," he confides: "but i dont kno if love is care cause cuttin wood and haulin water and things like that i dont know if thats love or jus work to do an you say thats love but you say you kno i got mo an jus that to say an when i lay ther at nite and cant sleep i try an think what you mean i got mo cause i aint done this much thinkin and this much writin in all my life befor"[84] Any love he has felt up until now has had to be expressed in terms of labor and duty, and he has never been able to acknowledge this to himself as love; he has never, in short, been able to see, let alone state, his own humanity. Now he is able. "i hope i can see her one more time on this earth fore i go," he writes of his godmother; "is that love mr wigin," he then asks both Grant and himself. Before he dies, he knows the answer. "when they brot me in the room," he records in the diary, not long before he is executed,"an i seen nanan at the table i seen how ole she look an how tied she look an i tol her i love her an i tol her i was strong an she jus look ole and tied an pull me to her an kiss me an it was the firs time she never done that an it felt good an i let her hol me long is she want cause you say it was good for her an i tol her i was strong an she didn need to come back no mo cause i was strong."[85] Knowing he can love and stand, Jefferson knows himself as a human being. "goodbye mr wigin," he ends his diary, "tell them im strong tell them im a man . . . sincely jefferson." He is given the means and the material, and he gains the will and the opportunity for words, to transform himself from "a hog" into "a man." In an act of self-fashioning and self-recognition that has been denied to him up until now—and to which Grant opens the door—he is returned to his own humanity, and can say so.

Returning of a kind, and finding the right voice to announce it, is also what Gaines himself does in *A Lesson Before Dying*. The point has been made already that the book revisits the concerns of earlier novels and replicates the character of the novelist and *his* relationship with his narrator. Gaines is turning back and turning in, in order to explore his place and self in probably more depth than ever before. It goes further. Asked why he chose 1948 as the year in which to set the novel, his answer was simple. "That's the year I left,"[86] he said—left Louisiana, that is, for California. It is perhaps superfluous to dwell on the fact that Grant Wiggins chooses in the end not to leave, unlike Gaines himself or earlier characters caught in a similar dilemma such as Jackson Bradley and Jim Kelly. This is an act of imaginative reinvestment in the place that has nurtured all Gaines's fiction, a journey back to and settlement in his material roots and moral origins. "That's the school I went to," Gaines has admitted of the plantation school where Grant teaches, "and my folks went there too." "This happened to me," he has said of other events in the book. There is a sense of recurrence—inevitably, with a difference—throughout *A Lesson Before Dying*, a coiling back on earlier fiction and facts, the work and life of its author; and it is this that helps make the book such a powerful example of a writer achieving his own voice. That voice has been heard before, of course, but it has never been quite so assured or suggestive. The story of Grant and Jefferson is embedded in preoccupations that Gaines has made peculiarly his. More to the point, it is measured in verbal rhythms, accents that compel us to historicize and generalize: to see the connection, in other words, between, on the one hand, the developing relationship of the two men and, on the other,

85. Ibid., 231. See also 229, 234.
86. *Conversations with Gaines* edited by Lowe, 307. See also 309, 310.

both black history and the history of the reader—even if he or she is not an African American.

These verbal rhythms in *A Lesson Before Dying* are at once social and seasonal. The social ones are marked by Gaines's acute understanding of the maneuverings of a particular society at a particular moment in time, and its changes. Grant Wiggins, the narrative discloses, is allowed to visit Jefferson regularly because Jefferson's godmother gets permission. She gets it because of the moral debt owed her by white people, owners of the local plantation, whom she has served faithfully for years. That debt, however, does not require the kind of courtesy that whites believe they owe only to each other. When the godmother goes to the "large white and gray antebellum house" of the plantation owner, she is received in the kitchen; she is never asked if she wants to sit down, although she is patently exhausted; and, having heard her out, by no means with patience, the white men simply go back to the drawing room, drinks in hand, leaving the godmother to make her own way out. When Grant in turn goes to the big house, to be told he has permission to visit, he is made to wait for two and a half hours. He declines an offer of food from the cook because his pride will not let him eat where he knows, as a black man in the big house, he would have to eat, at the kitchen table. And the whole conversation between him and the white men, when they deign eventually to spare time to see him, is conducted in a kind of code, with Grant walking a tightrope—between retaining his self-respect by talking in his customary, educated manner, and avoiding angering the whites by appearing too clever and articulate for a person of his color. "To show too much intelligence would have been an insult to them," is how Grant himself puts it. "To show a lack of intelligence would have been a greater insult to me." Even to use "doesn't" instead of "don't" turns out to be risky; every interchange here is mined with danger because it depends on an elaborate language of deference, designed to keep "the nigger" in his place. Gaines, even more than Grant, knows that language well and uses it to explore the intricacies of a society founded on separation and supremacism. "You're smart," one of the white men says to Grant. "Maybe just a little too smart for your own good."[87] This is the voice of white culture, announcing its own superiority and addressing blacks as unhuman, outside the moral and social order.

"All ideology," the critic and theorist Louis Althusser has argued,

87. Gaines, *Lesson Before Dying*, 49. See also 17, 47, 48.

"represents in its necessarily imaginary distortion not the existing rela- tions of production . . . but above all the (imaginary) relationship of individuals to the relations of production and the relations that derive from them. What is represented in ideology is therefore not a system of real relations which govern the existence of individuals but the imaginary relation of those individuals to the real relations in which they live."[88] In terms of this formula, ideology is not simply a matter of conscious beliefs, nor is it a matter of "false consciousness"—sets of false ideas imposed on individuals to persuade them there is no real conflict of class or caste interests in their society. It is, rather, a matter of imaginary versions of the real social relations that people live: imaginary versions that impose themselves not merely through consciousness nor through disembodied ideas but through systems and structures. Ideology is inscribed, Althusser insists, in the representations, the signs and practices or rituals of every- day life. And its end result is an act of subjection, whereby "concrete individuals" are "hailed" or addressed as "concrete subjects": persuaded to see, or rather "(mis)recognize," themselves according to the terms dic- tated by the culture. This process of "(mis)recognition" has been at work in the family romance of the South. And clearly the most radical example of this process has been offered by the representation of black people as beneficiaries of the system, living in familial contact with authority— rather, that is, than what they *have* been: victims of a fundamentally repressive and divisive social apparatus, a system designed to keep them down and apart. Conversations like the one that takes place in the kitchen of the big house between Grant and the white men are based, finally, on Gaines's acute, intuitive understanding of precisely this: the fact that the ideology that would deny full humanity to African Ameri- cans is inscribed in the everyday speech acts of the whites. They do not have to insist on their sense of their own superiority, Grant's inferiority, or the attitude of grateful, childlike dependence Grant should assume. They simply, and without really thinking about it, "hail" or address Grant, to use Grant's own words, not "like the teacher I was" but "like the nigger I was supposed to be." Their language is an ideological weapon, an "imaginary distortion" of Grant and all the other African Americans they meet: an act of naming that is effectively an act of subjec-

88. Louis Althusser, "Ideology and the State," in *Lenin and Philosophy, and Other Essays* translated by Ben Brewster (London, 1977), 154. See also Gaines, *Lesson Before Dying*, 47.

tion. "Been waiting long?" one white asks Grant when they first come into the kitchen. "About two and a half hours, sir," Grant replies, knowing that even the "sir" will not soften the blow. "I was supposed to say, 'Not long,' " Grant points out, "and I was supposed to grin; but I didn't do either." Inscribed in everything Gaines's white characters say here, and elsewhere, is the message that Grant, Jefferson, and indeed all black people have a particular, fixed identification, a definite subject(ed) status. Grant reads this throughout his conversation in the big house, and comments later on what, according to the rules of the verbal game, he was "supposed to" do. To read it, however, is not enough, either for him or for Gaines—any more than it was for Miss Jane Pittman and her fellow refugees when each sought out and announced a "new name." To fight it is also necessary: which is why Grant comes across to his white interlocutors as "too smart" for his own good; in its own modest way, his language here is an act of resistance.

Resistance, of course, brings change. Change is, in any event, inevitable; Gaines's quiet observation of the alterations taking place in farming practices, or the emergence of educated, potentially middle-class blacks like Grant Wiggins and Vivian Baptiste, makes that clear. But what the commitments made by the two main male characters promise is change of a special kind, for the better—an "elevation" of humanity, to use Gaines's own term. Black humanity may be elevated, the intimation is, in the way that both Jefferson and Grant manage it: with voice and human dignity restored to them, both are returned to the community before either death or departure makes it too late. And white humanity may be elevated too, as it is in the case of one of the jailers, called Paul Bonin, who befriends both Jefferson and Grant. That is suggested, among other things, by the simple exchange that takes place between condemned man and jailer not long before the execution. "Paul? You go'n be there, Paul?" Jefferson asks, "there" being the place where the electric chair has been set up. "Yes, Jefferson," Paul replies; "I'll be there." The simplicity of this is a far cry from the edgy evasions, the verbal fencing that characterizes most other conversations between blacks and whites in the novel. A plain request is met with a plain and positive answer. The two men address each other as friends and equals, without the crippling disability of terms like "boy" or "Mister" or "sir." The same occurs later, in the talk between Paul and Grant after Jefferson has been executed. "Well, I better go into the children," Grant concludes their talk, outside his school, after they have discussed "the transformation" that took place in Jefferson. "Paul stuck out his hand," Grant remembers:

> "Allow me to be your friend, Grant Wiggins. I don't ever want to forget this day. I don't ever want to forget him." I took his hand. He held mine with both of his. "I don't know what you're going to say when you go back in there. But tell them he was the bravest man in that room today. I'm a witness, Grant Wiggins. Tell them so." "Maybe one day you will come back and tell them so." "It would be an honor."[89]

There is a transparency of feeling in such interchanges, need candidly expressed and met, respect and affection openly admitted, that opens up the chance of a new social order built on a just relationship between the races. Even Paul's repetition of "Grant Wiggins," although it might seem a little heavy-handed on first reading, has its point and justification; the use of the full name is part of a new habit of address that admits the full humanity of the person being addressed, his status as a "concrete individual." This is the voice of another, possible culture, in which, African Americans announce their new names and some whites, at least, hail them as such—so that conflict is replaced by community.

The exploration of actual and possible communities is, inevitably, set in a specific history; the voices we hear there belong to a very particularized place and time. Still, Gaines encourages us to extrapolate from this: while honoring the peculiarities of his own postage stamp of native soil in 1948, he invites us to make connections between his and our separate moments in history—to see how the narrative illuminates what is actual and potential in our own lives. This invitation comes in a number of ways. The sheer intimacy of Grant's voice, for example, invites us to share in his experience and make it a part of our own. And the rhythms of fieldwork and the farming year that sound, like a subdued bass note, through the novel link what is happening to the old, ineluctable movement of the seasons and the compulsions that we are all subject to, in our own works and lives. Even Gaines's use of religious references plays a part here. "Me to take the cross?" Jefferson asks his teacher, after he is told that the next day is Good Friday, that he will be executed in about two weeks and that, in the meantime, he should try to "walk like a man" and "do something to please" his godmother. "Your cross, nannan's

---

89. Gaines, *Lesson Before Dying*, 255–56. See also 245.

cross, my own cross. Me, Mr Wiggins. This old stumbling nigger. Y'all axe a lot, Mr Wiggins." There are dangers here, of course, as there are in any use of religious references—particularly those that invite us, as these ones do, to make a connection between a fictional character and the story of Christ. The connection may seem strained; it may lead to attenuation and abstraction (as it does in William Faulkner's *A Fable*); it may, as in any number of Hollywood movies, seem simply bogus—a stock, stereotypical way of imposing an illusion of significance. Those dangers are neatly evaded here, though, because Gaines effectively *historicizes* his use of myth. He shows how such references grow out of the communal experience: the Christian story is something that even an agnostic like Grant Wiggins cannot ignore, because it is part of his inheritance and idiom as an African American living in the South. It is also a story, Gaines reveals, that impinges on and influences the political life of the locality. "I would learn later . . . that the governor had originally signed an execution order to be carried out two weeks before Ash Wednesday," Grant explains. But then it was shifted. "Another execution was scheduled during that time," he tells us; "and because of the state's heavily Catholic population, it might not go too well to have two executions before the beginning of Lent." "What make people kill, Mr. Wiggins?" Jefferson plaintively asks. "They killed His son, Jefferson," Grant offers by way of explanation: to which Jefferson's caustic response is, "And He never said a mumbling word."[90] If the network of allusions to the suffering, death, and resurrection of Christ invite us to generalize—to link Jefferson's fate to the idea of revival, a broader possibility of moral regeneration—then commentary like this keeps us tied down, at the same time, to the realities of a particular character and the politics of a specific society. Jefferson's reminders of difference—he is, after all, "an old stumbling nigger" who *does* manage to say "a mumbling word"—are just one sign of an attempt, on Gaines's part, to be true to both myth and history. The myth is there, certainly, associating Jefferson with Jesus; the generalizing tendency is inescapable. But it is there in terms of a series of material conditions that are carefully defined and convincingly dramatized—the muddy facts of an ultimately unrepeatable moment.

90. Ibid., 223. See also 156, 222, 224. For comments on the abstract quality of William Faulkner's *A Fable* (New York, 1954), see, e.g., Cleanth Brooks, *William Faulkner: Toward Yoknapatawpha and Beyond* (New Haven, Conn., 1978), 230; David Minter, *William Faulkner: His Life and Work* (Baltimore, Md., 1980), 206; Gary Harrington, *Faulkner's Fable's of Creativity: The Non-Yoknapatawpha Novels* (London, 1990), 97.

"I like listening": that simple remark of Gaines's is the key, if anything is, to the success of *A Lesson Before Dying*. It is through such listening that he has been able to find a voice for Grant and Jefferson, and a voice for the book—which is also his own narrative voice—charting social realities and potential, crises that are personal and historically situated but also connected to the critical moments of others, including ourselves. Each of those voices speaks of a return, to earlier times, other places, and the secret depths of the self, that leads in turn to the promise of revival. And in Gaines's case, at least, the voice speaks of a place to which he seems compelled to go back again and again. Gaines may have left the South, but he still evidently carries it with him, engraved on his memory and imagination; and he still comes back to it as if it were somehow a lifeline, a means of access to the real. There is a pungent irony at work here. One of the writers who speaks most powerfully now of a possible return to, and redemption in, the South comes from a race that, traditionally, has been denied a proper place in Southern culture—at best marginalized and, at worst, marked out as less than human. The chance of taking a stand for humanity and community in the region is ventured here in terms that the Nashville Agrarians might have found not totally unfamiliar. It is, though, ventured by a writer who knows and says just how much the stand taken by the Agrarians and their like depended on reducing a people to disposable property and dispensable labor. Gaines's project of restoration and revival is precisely *not* the same as that of the Agrarians because it does not shift the African American to the margins; it does *not* reduce him or her to "a thing that acts on command," to quote that lawyer in *A Lesson Before Dying* again, "a thing to hold the handle of a plow, a thing to load your bales of cotton, a thing to dig your ditches, to chop your wood, to pull your corn."[91]

Just how far Gaines's imaginative project differs from that of the Agrarians, despite some superficial similarities, is measured by a telling moment in *A Gathering of Old Men*. It occurs toward the end of the novel. The African American, called Mathu, whom everyone believes responsible for the killing of Fix Boutan (believes wrongly, as it turns out)

---

91. Gaines, *Lesson Before Dying*, 7–8. See also *Conversations with Gaines* edited by Lowe, 245. A memorable sentence in Toni Morrison's novel *Beloved* (London, 1987) is perhaps relevant here: "He wants to put his story next to hers" (287). In a sense, what Gaines is doing in *A Lesson Before Dying* is putting his story next to those of Grant Wiggins and Jefferson in order to explore the common (his)story of their—and, ultimately, our—race.

offers to give himself up. His offer is strenuously resisted by a white woman, Candy Marshall, whose family own the plantation where Mathu lives—and whom, after the death of her parents, he has helped to raise. "This is not Marshall, without you," she explains, referring to the plantation. "You knew . . . the first Marshall," she reminds him. "You knew them all. Grew up with my grandpa. Raised my daddy. Raised me. I want you to help me with my own child one day." The point she is trying to make may sound a paternalistic and sentimental one at first, associating Mathu with the stereotypical figure of the "Uncle," blessed black surrogate father and sentinel, protector of plantation hearth and home. But it is not; it is more, and other, than that; Candy, and Gaines through her, make that clear. "I want you to hold his hand," Candy goes on, speaking of the child she has not yet had. "Tell him about the field. Tell him how the river looked before the cabins and wharves. No one else to tell him about these things but you." "You'll die if they put you in jail," she warns Mathu. "And this place'll die too. There's no reason for this place to be if you're not here. My daddy, he said, you, you, you." "My daddy, all of them, said it was you, you, you," she repeats as if it were a prayer, an act of invocation. "They said it was Mathu. . . . They said you were. They said it was you." "They said," she ends desperately (almost as if she were trying to woo him into agreement), "if you went, it went, because we could not—it could not—not without you, Mathu."[92] Mathu is not, after all, a minor figure here but a major one, the keystone. Without him, Candy warns, the home place has no reason to exist and cannot even survive as a resource, a memory. The African American, evidently, is the one person who can return to whatever was valuable in the past and lead others there, then make that act as a driving force—an inspiration in the struggle to create something rooted in the familiar, a dear particular place, but also better and new. It is not difficult to see how this applies to people other than Mathu, Candy, and the Marshall family. Gaines's entire work teaches this lesson before dying, in fact, that only those originally dispossessed and oppressed by the South are able and have the right to repossess it, recover and reshape it according to the demands of justice and present need. Nor is it hard to see how radical and ironic all this is. Not for the first time, maybe, but certainly with fresh edge and urgency, aberration is being defined as the only viable way of sustaining a tradition. The supposedly marginal figure, it turns out, is the seminal one—and the closest thing the South has to a center, or is ever likely to have.

92. Gaines, *Gathering of Old Men*, 176–77.

"Porch Talk" and Making a Difference

A Concluding Note on Southern Regionalism

In 1932, a young woman who had managed to complete her first novel wrote to a friend about what she called her "family curse." "I remember so well, saying when I was twenty that God being willing, the curse . . . would never fall on me," she recalled. She then tried to explain the nature of that curse and relate it to the book she had written: "The curse I refer to is loving land enough to give everything you've got to get it. Never would I own a foot of it, city or country land. If I had spare money it would stay in the bank or the stock market but never in red clay. Then about two years ago when I set out to write the great American novel I was confronted by the fact that whether I liked it or not, it was a story of the land and a woman who was determined not to part with it."[1] The woman was Margaret Mitchell and the book was, of course, *Gone With the Wind*. As far as dates are concerned, Mitchell was telling something other than the truth. As her biographer points out, "she had not begun to write in 1930; on the contrary, she had by then effectively completed her fiction." The emotional truth of what she said, however, is utterly convincing. It is also utterly Southern: in the sense that attachment to the Southern land—or, as William Faulkner would have it, loving and hating that land—is a determining feature of what it means

1. Darden Asbury Pyron, *Southern Daughter: The Life of Margaret Mitchell* (Oxford, 1991), 290. To Harvey Smith, 14 July 1932. See also 291. William Faulkner expands on the theme of loving and hating the South in "Mississippi," in *Essays, Speeches and Public Letters* edited by James B. Meriwether (London, 1967), 11–43.

to be Southern. And attachment to it, however it is defined. It has never really been possible to talk about the South in the singular, that would be feasible only for a culture frozen in time—and that the South decidedly never was. It has grown ever more impossible, as the pace of change has accelerated and cultural pluralism (and, not least, our perception of that pluralism) has steadily grown. So the slippage of meaning at work in regional self-identification has become inescapable. To be Southern could always mean many things, despite the attempts of those like the Nashville Agrarians, who tried to align it with relatively specific notions of human culture and the body politic ("relatively" because, of course, the Agrarians differed among themselves). And those many things have now become more.

Writing about the South some fifty years after Margaret Mitchell completed *Gone With the Wind*, another, very different Southern writer, Alice Walker, said this: "No one could wish for a more advantageous heritage than that bequeathed to the black writer in the South: a compassion for the earth, a trust in humanity beyond our knowledge of evil, and an abiding sense of justice. We inherit great responsibility as well, for we must give voice to centuries not only of silent bitterness and hate but also neighborly kindness and sustaining love."[2] A very different writer and a very different experience and idea of the South. In their confessional moments and in their work, Mitchell and Walker may both give voice to the sense of being rooted in a dear, particular place and, with that, a feeling for the past that is part of their earth and therefore a part of them. Where exactly that place may be, however, how that past is constituted, and what place and past may signify are hardly identical; whatever the correspondences or points of congruence between these two ideas of a region, they are in no sense one and the same. Walker's description of the inheritance of the black writer in the South echoes the suggestion sounded in the work of Ernest Gaines, that, if any writer now has a seminal role to play in the rewriting of the South, it is the African American. And, set beside Mitchell's disclosure of her "family curse," it brings us right back to the vital point that those who call themselves Southern have this in common, whatever else they may have—much or little: that their Southernness is defined against a national "other." There is a familiar series of oppositions at work here: "Southern" versus "American" / "Northern"

---

2. Alice Walker, "The Black Writer and the Southern Experience," in *In Search of Our Mothers' Gardens* (New York, 1983), 21.

(the slippage between these two terms is, in itself, a measure of the Southern sense of aberrance) = place versus placelessness = past versus pastlessness = realism versus idealism = community versus isolation. As an act of self-definition, the oppositions are usually and defiantly weighted in the way I have just suggested. Admittedly, not everyone has been willing to go quite so far, or argue in quite so morally loaded a way as William Lowndes Yancey, the antebellum politician and orator from South Carolina, did, when he declared:

> The Creator has beautified the face of this Union with sectional features. Absorbing all minor sub-divisions, He has made the North and the South; the one the region of frost, ribbed in with ice and granite; the other baring its generous bosom to the sun and ever smiling under its influence. The climate, soil, and productions of these two grand divisions of the land, have made the character of their inhabitants. Those who occupy the one are cool, calculating, enterprising, selfish, and grasping; the inhabitants of the other are ardent, brave and magnanimous, more disposed to give than to accumulate, to enjoy ease rather than to labor.[3]

Nevertheless, this primary act of setting "the one" against "the other" was and still is a commonplace in Southern self-fashioning. So is the sense of arguing against an "other" that is too commonly taken as the norm. "The world will not hear our story," a young Georgia girl wrote in her diary just after Lee surrendered to Grant at Appomattox, "and we must figure just as our enemies choose to paint us." Stripped of the bitterness provoked by war and its aftermath, and the anger ("I hate the Yankees more and more," the Georgia girl added, "every time I . . . read the lies they tell about us"), that feeling of being sidelined is commonly there. The other is not named as the enemy, certainly—but it is, more often than not, seen as more successful in getting its story told. The South, in short, *any* South, tends to be named and identified *against* the historical tide.

This, I should perhaps emphasize, is the first of the three points I have been trying to make in this book. The South has customarily defined itself against a kind of photographic negative, a reverse image of itself—with

3. John W. Du Bose, *The Life and Times of William Lowndes Yancey,* 2 vols. (New York, 1942), I, 301. See also Eliza Frances Andrews, *The War-Time Journal of a Georgia Girl, 1864–1865* (New York, 1938), 371. Entry for 18 August 1865.

which it has existed in a mutually determining, reciprocally defining relationship. The South *is* what the North *is not,* just as the *North* is what the *South* is not. It may be that all cultures do this. The difference with the Southern strategy is that it usually begins from a consciousness of its own marginality, its position on the edge of the narrative. The constitutive otherness of the North or the American nation is considered central; the South, in whatever terms it is understood, is placed on the boundary, posed as an (albeit probably preferable) aberration. This is a piquant reversal of customary cultural self-positioning. It would never have occurred to those who constructed the idea of the Orient, for example, to see their object of study as anything other than inferior to the enlightened West and on the dangerous borders of Western culture. The lesser breed was, famously, without the law. The idea of Southernness may—or may not—carry a moral burden; it may project on to the typology of itself, and its opposite, a sense of its own superiority and a claim to historical centrality (of the kind Allen Tate was thinking of when he said, "The South was the last stronghold of European civilization in the western hemisphere"[4]). Nevertheless, the claim cannot be made effortlessly, without a powerful sense of past exclusion, present discontent, and future peril. Southerners start seeing others with a more than usually astringent sense of how others see them; their arguments begin, as it were, *within* an argument already made that has shifted them on to the edge.

A word of caution is necessary here, which will also bring me to the second point that lies at the heart of this book. These acts of regional self-definition are not, of course, simply fake. It is not that the South and the North or the American nation—even in the crudely simplistic terms imagined by a William Lowndes Yancey—are merely falsehoods, fables—no more in touch with historical contingencies than, say, stories of the lost city of Atlantis. They are, however, *fictive*—and in a double sense. They are fictive, first, because they involve a reading of existence as essence. What Anwar Abdul Malek has to say about Orientalism is relevant here. Orientalists, he points out, "adopt an essentialist conception of the countries, nations and peoples of the Orient under study, a conception which expresses itself through a characterized ethnist typology."[5] In short, they form a notion of a cultural "type" based on a real specificity but divorced from history. Similarly, the cultural work that has

---

4. Allen Tate, *Jefferson Davis: His Rise and Fall* (New York, 1929), 301.
5. Anwar Abdel Manwak, "Orientalism in Crisis," *Diogenes,* XLIV (1963), 107–8.

evolved ideas of the South and Southerners, and their opposites, occurs in history, and is a result of the forces working in the field of historical evolution. But its end result is to transfix the beings, the objects of study, and leave them stamped with an inalienable, nonevolutive character—to sever them from the living tissue of their moment in time. These constructions of regional types are fictive also in the sense that perhaps Yancey had at the back of his mind when he conveniently skipped over what he called "all minor sub-divisions." The South—and this is the second, basic point I have been working with in this book—has never *not* been made up of a number of castes, classes, and smaller communities that at best live in uneasy coexistence with each other and at worst are in active conflict—and some of which, at least, choose to claim that *their* South is *the* South, their story the master narrative. Readings of the South are just that, readings—of its past, present, and possible futures, the plurality of its cultures; for better or worse, they involve selection and abstraction; they involve a figuring, and, in the purest sense of that word, a *simplifying* of history.

In trying to get at what goes on in this reading and figuring of Southern history, one of the more common critical practices of recent years has been to see a link between Southern self-fashioning and nationalism. So Michael O'Brien, writing in 1979, discerns a connection between Southern sectionalism and the tendency of Romanticism to locate "the wellspring of man's being in national groups"; and John Shelton Reed, writing three years later, finds in some arguments for the South, at least, what he calls "more than glimmerings of the typical nationalist responses: cultural defense, economic autarchy, even political self-determination."[6] The nationalist analogy is an interesting, potentially productive one. As both O'Brien and Reed indicate, though, it begs the question, what is a nation? What compels a series of discrete individuals and interest groups, despite all their differences, to admit, not necessarily a communality of purpose but a certain common cultural ground? The answer seems to come back to figuring. "Nationalism is not the awakening of nations to self-consciousness," argues Ernest Gellner, "it invents nations where they do not exist." " 'Nationalism,' " declares Tom Nairn in his

6. John Shelton Reed, "For Dixieland: The Sectionalism of *I'll Take My Stand*," in *A Band of Prophets: The Vanderbilt Agrarians After Fifty Years* edited by Louis D. Rubin (Baton Rouge, La., 1982), 51. See also Michael O'Brien, *The Idea of the American South, 1920–1941* (Baltimore, Md., 1977), 7.

book on British nationalism, "is the pathology of modern developmental history, as inescapable as 'neurosis' in the individual, with much the same essential ambiguity"; while Hugh Seton-Watson in his *Nations and States* sadly admits, "I am driven to the conclusion that no 'scientific definition' of the nation can be devised"—and yet, he adds, "the phenomenon has existed and still exists." The shared perception here—whatever the differences of judgment—is that the nation is a cultural artefact. "All I can find to say," says Seton-Watson, "is that a nation exists when a significant number of people in a community consider themselves to form a nation, or behave as if they formed one." A nation is, in this sense, what Benedict Anderson has christened an "imagined community." No community larger than what Anderson terms a "primordial village" is "real" in the sense that everyone in it knows everyone else. No community is one based on the denial of difference and conflict. To call myself English, for instance, is not to say that I am either the same or have precisely the same origins, aims, or interests as anyone else who describes themselves as English; the term allows for multiple signification—even more so, if I substitute "British" for "English." Similarly, Margaret Mitchell and Alice Walker may both call themselves Southern, but that permits difference; their common term is also a fluid one—a distillation of a complex crossing of discrete historical forces. "Communities are to be distinguished," Anderson has argued, "not by their falsity/genuineness, but by the style in which they are imagined."[7] And it is "style" that distinguishes that strange resistance to the American "norm"—itself made up of a whole series of internal resistances—known as the South.

This "style," the terms in which the South has been imagined, depends on many things. The book is only one of them. Communities are constructed, changed, defended, and resisted by language (spoken as much as, or perhaps—as I have already intimated—even more than written), by monuments (to the Confederate soldier, to Martin Luther King), by maps and museums—and, more recently, by a mass technology that enables difference up to a point to both consumer and producer. Difference to the consumer comes from the media making of the South; Southerners

7. Benedict Anderson, *Imagined Communities: Reflections on the Origin and Spread of Nationalism* (1983; London, 1991 revised edition), 6. See also Ernest Gellner, *Thought and Change* (London, 1964), 169; Tom Nairn, *The Break-Up of Britain* (London, 1977), 359; Hugh Seton-Watson, *Nations and States: An Enquiry into the Origins of Nations and the Politics of Nationalism* (Boulder, Colo., 1977), 5.

can see themselves in terms of the many Souths imagined on film, television, and other electronic/mass media. Difference to the producer comes from the chance that the newer information technology gives for cultural diversity; it is, quite simply, easier, thanks to the multiple opportunities now for "publication"—which is to say, communication beyond the immediate, face-to-face community—for any group to make its voice heard. The mistake made by some commentators is to see these newer forms as invention in the sense of *fabrication* and *falsity* (just as the mistake made by some observers of nationalist movements and ideology is to assume that, if nations are invented, then nationalism is fake and irrelevant). They are not *necessarily* that; as I intimated earlier, they are simply some of the terms in which Southerners now come to think of themselves, and the South. They are no more false, inevitably, than were, say, the old tales and telling that generations of earlier Southerners used to make up and transmit *their* identity. They simply offer new ways of working at the interface between consciousness and history; their potential is as new tools for old habits.

This is the third point I have been working with at times in this book: the potential for Southern self-definition offered by recent social and economic change. The potential and also the peril: to say that there are new tools for old tendencies made available by the developing technologies is not to ignore the other possibility—that the net effect of mass culture may be to homogenize and commodify. Either the flattening out of cultural diversity that the logic of the global marketplace dictates, or the devotion to surface image demanded by the logic of late capitalism could wipe out all the benefits to cultural diversity promised by the exponential increase in forms of communication. To put it simply, Southerners may be too busy being "Confederate consumers"[8] to continue imagining *any* kind of community and/or they may buy, rather than invent, themselves. The evidence here is certainly mixed. But if any generalization is to be ventured at all, it is, surely, that change has brought an even more acute self-consciousness and an even greater pluralism than ever before. The South is still a concept active in the everyday lives and exchanges of communities; it is still there as a determining part of their mental maps and speech acts. The difference now is that inventing or imagining—or simply *assuming the existence of*—the South occurs within an environment where the sheer diversity of information available, and the multiplicity

---

8. John Peet, "A Survey of the South," *The Economist,* 10 December 1994, 6.

of systems supplying that information, make cultural insularity close to impossible. More than ever before (and with more deliberation than ever before), acts of regional self-identification have to be made against the grain. Rapid change, increasing social mobility, and the accelerating exchange between cultures all mean that any reading of the South now requires a peculiarly intense and focused gaze.

So why does it still happen? Why does Southern self-fashioning continue? The answer, or the closest thing to an answer, has surely not altered since the invention of the South. It is a matter of *language* and *communal ritual:* the human habit of positioning the self with the help of the word and others—giving a local habitation and a name to things to secure their and our identity, and establishing a connection or kinship with other people that is also an anchorage, a validation of oneself. There are many possible ways of illustrating this; as usual, the poets and storytellers have put it better than probably anyone, and certainly I, can. As for language and its compulsions, few Southern writers have expressed the matter more memorably than Eudora Welty. A remark of hers quoted earlier on in this book is well worth repeating: "the mystery," Welty has said, "lies in the use of language to express human life." To this extent, we can infer, inventing the South is a product of an aboriginal impulse we all share—to render life comprehensible through the use of the spoken and written word. Welty describes her own discovery of that impulse in her account of what she terms her "sensory education"; in the process, she cannily measures both its strength and the drastic limitations of its reach. "At around six, perhaps," she recalls,

> I was standing by myself in our front yard waiting for supper, just at that hour on a late summer day when the sun is already below the horizon and the risen full moon in the visible sky stops being chalky and begins to take on light. There comes a moment, and I saw it then, when the moon goes from flat to round. For the first time it met my eyes as a globe. The word "moon" came into my mouth as though fed to me out of a silver spoon. Held in my mouth the moon became a word. It had the roundness of a Concord grape Grandpa took off his vine and gave me to suck out of its skin and swallow whole, in Ohio.[9]

9. Eudora Welty, *One Writer's Beginnings* (Cambridge, Mass., 1984), 10. See also Linda Kuehl, "The Art of Fiction: Eudora Welty," *Paris Review,* LV (1972), 77.

The beauty of a passage like this is that Welty manages to convince us simultaneously that words are everything *and* nothing. They are everything because they constitute all the world we make for ourselves. Issuing out of a fundamental, definitively human rage for order—not only to see, but to know—they are as vital to us as breath. They register for us the irresistible otherness of things in terms that are, at their best, vivid and sensory. Another writer, William Carlos Williams, suggested that a thing known passes from the outer world to the inner, from the air around us into the muscles within us. And the word *moon* seems to achieve the same vital transit: as Welty remembers it, *moon* is not just an abstract, arbitrary sign, it has the "roundness" of a sensory object—it generates the sense that contact between the namer and named has taken place. This is the gift, given with "a silver spoon," that we are all offered. And it can fill us with a sense of presence, as it does the six-year-old girl recollected here: we, like her, can feel that we know and can participate in the world through the word. It is everything, then. It is, however, quite literally nothing. The word *moon,* despite the way it assumes shape and fullness in the mouth, is "no thing": it is, at best, a powerful, sense-laden sign for the mysterious, distant object that shimmers in the evening sky. There is probably no need to labor the point that, in the talk and writing of generations of Southerners, the word *South* and its variants has assumed the same power and pathos as the word that came into Welty's mouth at a seminal moment in her sensory education. It has become a vital instrument of knowledge, linked to the broader human project of trying to spin a sense of reality out of language. It is also a palpable sign of ignorance to the extent that the histories it maps must remain irreducibly other, constantly altering and apart. One of the determining concepts of American history, it is a measure of how much and how little that history can be known—or, for that matter, of the scope that any of us have for making sense of our own, individual and collective lives.

As for communal ritual, that is linked to language even though it is not confined to it. We know who we are and where we belong, after all, because we engage in social exchanges that substantiate and complicate our sense of belonging. And those exchanges are, many of them, vocal; talk, speech is our link between external and internal worlds. Verbal exchanges embody and then reembody the changing relations between classes, sexes, and races, help to shape beliefs and behavior—and, in general, exist in a genuinely dialectical relationship with the developing rituals of a group. "As a social animal, man is a ritual animal," the anthropologist Mary Douglas has observed, "ritual focusses attention, by framing; it enlivens the memory and links the present with the past. In all this, it adds perception because it changes the selective principles. . . . It does not merely externalise experience . . . it modifies experience in so expressing it."[10] "Ritual and beliefs change," Douglas insists, "they are extremely plastic"; and their plasticity, as she sees it, derives above all from their being used, spoken, and energetically debated. They can be engaged in and argued over in what Fredric Jameson has termed "the privileged meeting places of collective life," which in the South include the bar and restaurant, the dinner table and shopping mall, and the courthouse square. They can be engaged in and argued over inside the head. Either way—or, rather, both ways, since the two are inseparable—rituals become a site of struggle, as different groups, classes, and individuals seek to appropriate and use them. And inventing the South, in turn, an idea of being and belonging *somewhere,* becomes a field of ideological contention, in which those same groups, classes, and individuals seek to control the sign "South" and imbue it with their own meanings.

In *Their Eyes Were Watching God* (1937), one privileged meeting place, a main site of communal ritual, is the front porch. Whenever she manages to, the heroine of the novel, Janie Crawford Killicks Starks, joins her neighbors on the porch for a "lyin' " session that helps to bring them together as a group. As we know, Zora Neale Hurston drew on her own experience of an incorporated town entirely inhabited by blacks in rural south Florida—Eatonville, where she was born and lived until she was nine—to draw her portrait of a black community. And what is remarkable about that drawing is how it shows us the *making* of a Southern community—*a* South, not *the* South—and just how vividly it shows that making as a matter of energetic ritual and debate. On the front porch, "the people sat around . . . and passed around pictures of their thoughts," we are told, projections of their inner world into the outer one that "were always crayon enlargements of life." "Take for instance the case of Matt Bonner's yellow mule," the narrator suggests. "Sam and Lige and Walter were the ring-leaders of the mule-talkers"; "all they needed," evidently, "was to see Matt's long spare shape coming down

10. Mary Douglas, *Purity and Danger: An Analysis of the Concepts of Pollution and Taboo* (1966; London, 1984 edition), 64. See also 62 and "Couvade and Menstruation," in *Implicit Meanings* (London, 1975), 61; Fredric Jameson, "Metacommentary," *PMLA,* LXXXVI (1971), 15.

the street and by the time he got to the porch they were ready for him."[11]
Hurston describes a communal legend in the making: a man so mean that
he keeps his mule starved and a mule so skinny that, as Sam puts it, "de
women is usin' his rib bones fuh uh rub-board, and hangin' things out
on his hock-bones tuh dry." There are stories about "how poor the brute
was; his age; his evil disposition and his latest caper." There are tall tales,
jokes and anecdotes, exchanges of wonder and humor. "Everybody in-
dulged in mule talk," we learn. "He was next to the Mayor in promi-
nence, and made better talking." Where Hurston's interest lies here is
clearly in the process by which different people come together to turn
strange fact into startling fiction—and, in doing so, accommodate it to
themselves, make it a part of the story of *their* lives. It also lies, and more
remarkably, in the way conflicts are assimilated or placed in abeyance by
the simple activity of verbal exchange. Janie's oppressive husband,
Mayor Joe Starks, for instance, claims that the porch talkers are "trashy
people." Nevertheless, Janie observes, "while he didn't talk the mule
himself, he sat and laughed at it." And while he tries to stop Janie, as he
has it, "treasurin' all dat gum-grease from folks dat don't even own de
house dey sleep in," she does manage to join in "and sometimes she
thought up good stories on the mule." Storytelling is a ritual here that
helps authenticate the lives of those who tell and listen; it enlivens memory and familiarizes by linking the extraordinary with the ordinary, the
present with the relevant past. The strange mule of Matt Bonner is absorbed into the fabric of the works and days of the community (the
fieldwork of the men, the washdays of the women) in a way that allows
that strangeness to be both acknowledged and made acceptable, explicable, turned into a recognizable comic character; difference—inside and
outside the group of "mule-talkers"—is faced but also placed in a manageable frame.

To "talk the mule," however, is not simply to subdue it to the familiar;

11. Zora Neale Hurston, *Their Eyes Were Watching God* (1937; London, 1986 edition), 81. See also 83, 85. Material for the episode concerning Matt Bonner and his mule
was borrowed by Hurston from *Mule Bone,* the opera she had written in collaboration
with Langston Hughes. For the autobiographical sources of Hurston's portrait of the black
township and other background information, see Robert E. Hemenway, *Zora Neale Hurston: A Literary Biography* (Urbana, Ill., 1977). Hurston's own sometimes evasive autobiography, *Dust Tracks on the Road* (1942; Philadelphia, 1971 edition) is also helpful for an
understanding of what she called the "pure Negro town—charter, mayor, council, town
marshal and all" (3) in which she was born and began to grow up.

mule-talking also becomes a measure of how rituals and beliefs can change—and articulate the *need* for change. "Honey, de white man is de ruler of everything as fur as Ah been able tuh find out," Janie's grandmother, Nanny, tells her; "de white man throw down de load and tell de nigger man tuh pick it up." "He pick it up because he have to, but he don't tote it," Nanny adds. "He hand it to his womenfolks. De nigger woman is de mule uh de world so fur as Ah can see." The stories of Matt Bonner and his mule surely have to be read in terms of this notion of the black man as the mule of the white man, and the black woman as the mule of the world. There is mockery of the skinny mule, even teasing and harassing of him: "They oughta be shamed uh theyselves!" Janie mutters to herself, watching the men "goosing him in the sides and making him show his temper," "teasin' dat poor brute beast lak they is! Done been worked tuh death." But the mule also mimics their own feelings of misery, work without end, and that fires their sympathetic interest; it even explains why, at times, the "mule-talkers" are so cruel—because they are hitting back, as it were, at this strange, crayon enlargement of their own plight. Seeing in the mule a comic reflection of themselves, their mockery is at once a way of acknowledging and coming to terms with pain. And that acknowledgment, the circuitous facing up to their pitifulness as "mules," is taken a stage further when Janie's husband buys the yellow mule, explaining, "Didn't buy 'im fuh no work. I god, Ah bought dat varmint tuh let 'im rest." This magnanimous announcement is met with "a respectful silence." "The town talked it for three days," we learn, "and said that's just what they would have done if they had been rich men like Joe Starks." A "free mule" is "something new in the town"; and, rituals and beliefs being "extremely plastic" as Mary Douglas observes, a new ritual is evolved to take account of the change. Nearly everyone in the town begins to take a hand in feeding the mule, so that "he almost got fat and they took a great pride in him. New lies sprung up about his free-mule doings."[12] If the earlier mockery of the skinny working mule had been a rite for alleviating pain by ruefully acknowledging it, then these new exchanges offer a handy means of transcendence. The people of the community come together now, not so much to make sly fun of the mule, as to chuckle and marvel over its newfound liberty—and to trace, in their doings and sayings, the shadowy chance of their own release from working and toting someone else's burden. The

12. Hurston, *Their Eyes Were Watching God,* 92. See also 29, 89, 91.

rituals of the "free mule"—talking about it, caring for it—celebrate possibility, in short, the hidden promise of their lives.

The final act in this drama—the mythologizing of a "poor brute beast" that is also the ritualistic making, and sustaining, of a community—comes when the mule dies. "When the news got around, it was like the end of a war or something like that," the narrator tells us. "Everybody that could knocked off from work to stand around and talk." In the end, "there was nothing to do but drag him out like all other dead brutes"; the harsh fact of death has to be accepted and dealt with. But not just accepted: like the mule's life, the death is ceremonialized, transformed by communal ritual. The carcass is dragged out of town to a nearby swamp, and there everybody "made great ceremony over the mule. They mocked everything human in death." Joe Starks leads off with a "great eulogy on our departed citizen, our most distinguished citizen and the grief he left behind him, and the people loved the speech." His place "on the distended belly of the mule for a platform" is then taken by Sam, one of those "ringleaders of the mule-talkers," who expands in imitation of the local preacher on "the joys of mule-heaven to which the dear brother had departed this valley of sorrow." "*No Matt Bonner*" there, Sam explains, "with plow lines and halters to come in and corrupt"; and his hymn to a blessed afterworld with "miles of green corn and cool pasture" and "mule-angels flying around" is received with a wry rapture by the attendant mourners. Listening to him, "the sisters got mock-happy and shouted and had to be held up by the menfolks," we learn. "Everybody enjoyed themselves to the highest and then finally the mule was left to the already impatient buzzards."[13] The serious foolery of this ceremony absorbs an even greater conflict than the ones between rich folk and poor, men and women, white and black: the conflict between life and death that everyone, not just the mule, is destined to lose. The ritual does not ignore or even mitigate the brute fact of death, nothing can; the buzzards are waiting there impatiently, waiting to take over. But it does make it tolerable; it faces death by making it part of the style, the continuing story of the community. It places this, along with everything else to do with one more poor, pitiful creature, within a framework—the narrative of a South to which all the members of this strange congregation belong.

After the story of the funeral ceremony, Hurston goes on to turn the

13. Ibid., 96. See also 95.

dismemberment of the carcass into another story. It is a story addressed more directly to the reader, by the narrator, now that the earlier interlocutors—the orators, the sisters and their menfolk—and, indeed, all the human characters have gone back to town. The buzzards are figured by the narrator as waiting for their "white-headed leader," nicknamed "the Parson," to light down beside the corpse, inspect it, and confirm that it is dead. That being accomplished, a new, even stranger ritual is imagined taking place: an exchange between the Parson and the other buzzards as a kind of induction, a preparation for their ghastly meal. "What killed this man?" the Parson asks. His congregation answers, "Bare, bare fat." This call and response is made three times. "Who'll stand his funeral?" the Parson then demands to know. "We!!!!" is the ecstatic reply. "Well, all right now," the old, "white-headed leader" finally concedes, picking out the eyes of the mule "in the ceremonial way." The feasting then begins and, following that, "the yaller mule was gone from the town except for the porch talk, and for the children visiting his bleaching bones now and then in the spirit of adventure."[14] In this way, the narrative *in* the book modulates into the narrative *of* the book. The transformation of the necessarily stark experiences of living and dying turns from the act of a fictive community into an act of communion between narrator and reader; we, the readers, are being invited to share, as the narrator addresses us, in the metamorphosis of mundane fact into mock rites and magical story. Hurston not only shows us how a small group of people ground themselves, begin to make sense of their trials and changes through the maneuverings of "porch talk" and ceremony. She opens up the chance of grounding to us as well, by inviting us into the process of debate. She describes *a* South caught in the act of making and remaking itself; and she links that to the endless, restless human activity of trying to make the world around us (even its buzzards) "talk" to us, announce itself and belong to us—while we, in turn, "talk" to each other (even anonymous narrator to reader) and so confirm our shared existence, our feeling of being there for a moment and nowhere else.

   Zora Neale Hurston's account of the "mule-talkers" in a small black township tells us more about communal ritual than any abstract analysis can; in doing so, it hints at why Southerners feel compelled to invent themselves. Not everyone has experienced the cultural insularity of Janie and Joe Starks and their neighbors; it is difficult, in fact, to believe that

14. Ibid., 97. See also 96.

any group in the South could live quite so apart from other cultures now. Not everyone, for that matter, has suffered the same oppression, a similarly harsh division between the facts and promises of their lives. Nor has every Southern community been so local and intimate: this, after all, *is* a group that thrives on face-to-face contact, and to that extent its sense of mutuality, contiguous relations, and common ground, is more than simply imagined. In a way, though, this helps make the point. The South is an imagined community made up of a multiplicity of communities, similarly imagined. Some of those communities are more imagined than others (where, say, there is little or no immediate contact). Some individual Southerners, perhaps most, belong to several communities (think, for instance of all the writers who write in one Southern place about another). Some are more active and aware in their imagining. Still, what all these communities have in common *is* the act of imagination. And what all members of all those communities share, in turn, is what links them to the young girl Eudora Welty remembers and the young woman Zora Neale Hurston describes: the need to make a place in the world with the aid of talk and ceremony, language and communal ritual. This, both Welty and Hurston intimate, is a determinately human need since we are, by definition, verbal and social creatures. It is also a need that issues out of the aboriginal process of self-awareness and self-recognition ("Who am I"): a process that involves the discovery of both resemblance ("I am like this") and difference ("I am not like that"). Less abstractly, it is something that drives Southerners to position themselves *with* others in their locality, communality of interest or area, and *against* or *apart from* others elsewhere. It is also something, a need, a compulsion that, in satisfying, enables them to make some sense of their lives and histories. This is why Southern self-fashioning has played such a decisive part in the making of America, and why, surely, Southerners will go on doing what they do: insisting on their vital connection with some, many, or all other Southerners in their *difference*—on their being alike in their aberrations.

INDEX